Equality for Same-Sex Couples

The Legal Recognition
of Gay Partnerships
in Europe and the United States

Yuval Merin

The University of Chicago Press
Chicago and London

YUVAL MERIN is law lecturer at the College of Management School of Law in Tel Aviv.

The University of Chicago Press, Chicago 60637
The University of Chicago Press, Ltd., London
© 2002 by The University of Chicago
All rights reserved. Published 2002
Printed in the United States of America

11 10 09 08 07 06 05 04 03 02   1 2 3 4 5

ISBN: 0-226-52031-5 (cloth)
ISBN: 0-226-52032-3 (paper)

Library of Congress Cataloging-in-Publication Data

Merin, Yuval.
    Equality for same-sex couples : the legal recognition of gay partnerships in Europe and the United States / Yuval Merin.
        p. cm.
    Includes bibliographical references and index.
    ISBN 0-226-52031-5 (cloth : alk. paper) — ISBN 0-226-52032-3 (paper : alk. paper)
        1. Same-sex marriage—Law and legislation—Europe.   2. Gay couples—Legal status, laws, etc.—Europe.   3. Same-sex marriage—Law and legislation—United States.   4. Gay couples—Legal status, laws, etc.—United States.   I. Title.

    K699 .M37 2002
    346.401′6—dc21

                                                                            2002018968

♾ The paper used in this publication meets the minimum requirements of the American National Standard for Information Sciences—Permanence of Paper for Printed Library Materials, ANSI Z39.48-1992.

To my parents and my sisters

There is always need of persons not only to discover new truths, and point out when what were once truths are true no longer, but also to commence new practices, and set the example of more enlightened conduct.

—John Stuart Mill, *On Liberty*

The past provides many instances where the law refused to see a human being when it should have. . . . The challenge for future generations will be to define what is most essentially human. The extension of the Common Benefits Clause to acknowledge [same-sex couples] as Vermonters who seek nothing more, nor less, than legal protection and security for their avowed commitment to an intimate and lasting human relationship is simply, when all is said and done, a recognition of our common humanity.

—Justice Jeffrey L. Amestoy, *Baker v. State of Vermont*

Contents

Tables

Acknowledgments

This book began as a doctoral dissertation at the New York University School of Law. The dissertation was completed in May 2000, following three years of extensive research into the legal status of same-sex couples worldwide and a comparative study of their positions in different countries and regions. Thereafter, I revised the thesis, continued updating it, and turned it into a book. Many people have aided work on the dissertation and on the book, and I am indebted to all of them.

First and foremost, I thank my thesis adviser, my teacher and mentor Prof. David A. J. Richards, for his superb, illuminating, and persistent guidance during the countless hours he spent with me, in addition to reading and commenting on the many drafts of this work for a period of more than three years. He has always been accessible and supportive and has continually deepened my comprehension of crucial issues pertaining to this work. I am equally grateful for his constant support, invaluable advice, and immense efforts and encouragement, without which this work would not have seen print. I also thank the members of my thesis committee, Prof. Burt Neuborne and Prof. Sylvia Law of the New York University School of Law, for their insightful comments and helpful advice.

I extend my deepest gratitude to Douglas Mitchell, senior editor at the University of Chicago Press, for his dedication and advice, his kindheartedness, and his enthusiastic support. I also thank Robert Devens, Christine Schwab, Liz Cosgrove, Joan Davies, and Mark Heineke of the Press for their excellent work on the book. I am particularly grateful for the superb copyediting work of Lois Crum, who did an extraordinary job.

Revision of the book was aided by helpful and illuminating comments from the two readers of the manuscript for the University of Chicago Press, Prof. Robert Wintemute and an anonymous reader. I am grateful to both of them, but especially to Robert Wintemute, whose critical and insightful comments were invaluable to me. I also thank my assistant, Yonit W. Peleg, and my friends Boaz Dalit and Lynn Gilbert for their assistance and support.

Above all, I am grateful for the love, encouragement, and unfaltering support of my parents, Lea and Gideon Merin, and my sisters, Tamar Friedman-Merin and Michal Alfon, who have also provided me with exceptionally valuable comments, assistance, and advice. I dedicate this book to them, with love.

Chapter 1

Introduction

During the past three decades, nations all over the world have been considering and debating whether same-sex couples should be accorded the right to enter the institution of marriage or granted various rights that are associated with marriage. The idea of providing rights to same-sex couples in general, and the prospect of opening up the institution of marriage to gay men and lesbians in particular, have instigated an extremely heated public debate in many Western countries. National courts and legislatures, as well as some international organizations, have been faced with the demands of gays for equality in terms of the rights, benefits, and protections that flow from marriage. The current progress in these directions is among the most interesting and significant legal developments in recent times. Beyond that, this process has highly significant implications for social change: it raises issues of equality between the sexes and reflects on common conceptions of gender roles. Conversely, it is the way the institution of marriage has been transformed throughout the past two centuries and its current new forms, characteristics, and objectives that allow its application to same-sex couples to be considered (see chap. 2).

Not until the late 1980s did a few countries begin to regulate the status of same-sex partners by providing them with comprehensive legal protections. Much progress has been made since then, and various models for the recognition and regulation of same-sex partnerships have been developed and implemented in different countries. This book introduces four principal models for the recognition and regulation of same-sex partnerships worldwide: same-sex marriage, registered partnership, domestic partnership, and cohabitation. The latter three are to be considered as alternatives to civil marriage for same-sex couples (see chap. 2).

Same-sex marriage is currently a key term in the fight of gay men and lesbians for equality in the Western world. Not only is the issue of same-sex marriage at the heart of the current debate in the field of gay rights, but it is also a part of the larger civil rights movement. And today, at the beginning of the new millennium, the gay rights movement is at the forefront of the campaign for civil rights, which began with the pursuit of equality by racial minorities and women (see chap. 2).

Both among the general public and in academic circles, misconceptions abound as to the scope of recognition that same-sex couples in the United States and abroad are entitled to. Many believe that gay couples are already able to marry, if not in the United States, then in one of the Scandinavian countries. However, except for the Netherlands, which has opened civil marriage to same-sex couples, *nowhere* in the world today do same-sex couples have the same right to marriage as do opposite-sex couples. Other than the Netherlands, the five Nordic countries—Denmark, Norway, Sweden, Iceland, and Finland—are to date the only countries that have enacted legislation at the national level that purports to regulate the legal status of same-sex partnerships in a comprehensive manner akin to marriage (see chaps. 3 and 4). Albeit to a lesser extent, Hungary, France, Germany, Portugal, Belgium, Canada, and New Zealand have also enacted legislation recognizing the status of same-sex partnerships (see chaps. 5 and 6).

The recognition of same-sex couples that has been legislated in the Nordic countries is termed *registered partnership* (see chap. 3). The Netherlands opened its institution of civil marriage to same-sex couples in April 2001 and retained its Registered Partnership Act of 1998, which was based on the Nordic model (see chap. 4). Hungary has amended its Common Law Marriage Act to provide similar recognition, and Portugal has also given same-sex couples common law marriage rights (see chap. 5), whereas the French Pacte Civil de Solidarité (PaCS) and similar acts in Germany and Belgium regulate, inter alia, some aspects of cohabitation in same-sex partnerships (see chap. 5).

With a few exceptions, the northern European[1] registered partnership

1. I use the phrase *northern European countries* throughout this book to refer to the six countries in which comprehensive registered partnership acts have been adopted thus far, i.e., the five Nordic countries (Denmark, Norway, Sweden, Iceland, and Finland) and the Netherlands.

acts attempt to place same-sex couples on an equal footing with opposite-sex married couples. The United States, in contrast, is far from granting to same-sex unions legal recognition approximating that reserved for marriage, at either the national or the state level (see chap. 7). Only the state of Vermont's civil union act, which is an exception within the United States, has come close to equalizing the status of same-sex couples with that of married ones.[2] The act is a significant breakthrough and is one of the most important recent developments in the status of same-sex partnerships worldwide. However, the new status is limited to the state of Vermont; the act does not and cannot confer rights that flow from marriage at the federal level and has not thus far been recognized by any other state. Owing to the Defense of Marriage Act (DOMA) at the federal level and similar legislation in more than half the states, even if one or more states decided to make marriage available to same-sex couples, such legislation would likely remain limited in its scope and applicability and would probably not be given recognition in other states. The various defense of marriage acts, whose constitutionality is questionable, represent the reluctance of the United States to place same-sex couples on an equal footing with opposite-sex married couples.

Other countries are progressing toward the recognition of same-sex partnerships (see chaps. 5 and 6). Some have accorded protection to same-sex couples at the local or regional level (e.g., Spain), whereas others are considering national legislation modeled after the Danish Registered Partnership Act (e.g., Switzerland).

The first part of the book, chapters 2 through 7, begins with a historical overview of how the institution of marriage has changed through the ages and how it currently applies to same-sex couples. Following is an extensive account and analysis of the legal developments toward the recognition of same-sex partnerships worldwide. This section also provides an overview of such partnerships' current legal status, with emphasis on the rights of the partners to a same-sex relationship in the field of family law, and a discussion of the vast differences between various regions in terms of parental rights of gays and lesbians.

The first portion of the book thus examines the various models of recognition and their unique application in specific countries around the world, especially the Nordic countries, the Netherlands, and the United States. It further analyzes the unique status of same-sex partnerships in Hungary, France, Germany, Belgium, and Portugal (countries

---

2. *See* An Act Relating to Civil Unions, 2000 Vt. Acts & Resolves 91 (codified at Vt. Stat. Ann. tit. 15, §§ 1201–7 [Supp. 2000]).

that have adopted a "light" version of registered partnership) and summarizes the status of same-sex partnership in countries that are in the process of implementing the cohabitation model (Canada, Australia, and New Zealand) and countries that are considering the adoption of a registered partnership act (Italy, Spain, Switzerland, and the Czech Republic). Since the book's main concern is with countries that have adopted comprehensive models for the recognition of same-sex partnerships or that are progressing toward such broad-based recognition in family law, it does not address developments in countries that provide only a few rights to same-sex couples for a specific purpose in one or more limited fields, such as the United Kingdom, Israel, South Africa, and Brazil (see appendix B).

In the second part of the book (chaps. 8–11), I compare the status of same-sex couples in northern Europe with their status in the United States and study the underlying rationales for the differences (in Europe, expansive institutional regulations recognizing the partners' relationship, with the exclusion of most parental rights; in the United States, little such regulation of the partnership, with, however, legal recognition of extensive parental rights for same-sex couples). This part contrasts three models: same-sex marriage, registered partnership, and domestic partnership. The comparative discussion does not include the fourth model, the cohabitation model, since the focus of the book is a comparison of Europe and the United States and since that model is dependent upon the existence of extensive legal regulation of heterosexual nonmarital cohabitation (which is akin to marriage). The cohabitation model is not applicable to countries that do not already provide such regulation. The second part of the book also evaluates, from a normative point of view, the different models of recognition that have been implemented or proposed and their desirability in comparison to marriage for same-sex couples. Building on the doctrine of "separate but equal" of *Plessy v. Ferguson*[3] and its repeal in *Brown v. Board of Education*,[4] I argue that models other than marriage for the regulation of same-sex partnerships, models that are both separate from and unequal to opposite-sex marriage, are objectionable (see chap. 10). I thus reject alternatives to marriage such as domestic or registered partnerships and argue that the only remedy for the existing discrimination against same-sex couples is their inclusion in the institution of marriage, which "is at once the most socially productive and individually fulfilling

3. 163 U.S. 537 (1896).
4. 347 U.S. 483 (1954).

relationship that one can enjoy in the course of a lifetime."[5] Finally, I suggest utilizing an existing and necessary socio-legal process for comprehensive recognition of same-sex partnerships that is common and applicable to most countries. Accordingly, I assess the feasibility of opening up marriage to same-sex couples both in Europe and in the United States (see chap. 11).

A comparative examination of the different models for the recognition of same-sex partnerships has not been conducted to date. This book thus sheds new light on the current same-sex-marriage debate in the United States and Europe.

One of the leading scholars in the field of comparative family law has suggested that the United States can only benefit from greater awareness of the ways in which other nations have approached problems with which it is currently struggling and from learning the benefits and disadvantages of alternative solutions to such problems.[6] This study attempts to offer a deeper understanding of and a wider perspective on American law, in order to provide such enhanced awareness.

5. Elden v. Sheldon, 46 Cal.3d 267, 274–75 (Cal. Supreme Ct., 1988).

6. Mary Ann Glendon, The Transformation of Family Law: State, Law, and Family in the United States and Western Europe 4 (1989).

Chapter 2

The Changing Institution
of Marriage and the Exclusion
# of Same-Sex Couples

2.1 A Few Words about the Idiosyncrasies of the Institution
of Marriage and Its Ends from Ancient Greece to the Present

Throughout history, there has been dissension over the definition of marriage and over the exclusion or inclusion of particular groups within the institution. Marriage is and has always been subject to change. From antiquity up to the present day, the institution of marriage has displayed wide geographical and historical variety. There have been radical changes in the concept of marriage, the way marriages are arranged (who has the power to make decisions about marriage), the motives behind marriage, and the degree of equality between the spouses. Current justifications for marriage and the perceived goals of the institution are based primarily on the assumption of mutual love between two people who come together on equal terms. Most discussions regarding same-sex marriage fail to take into account that throughout most of history, the affinity between love and marriage was not viewed in causal terms; it is only relatively recently that love has become the commonly assumed basis for marriage and its primary justification. Thus, a discussion of the connections and tensions between love and marriage and a historical overview of the nature of heterosexual marriage, however brief, are imperative for an understanding of the current debate over same-sex marriage.

Until the twentieth century, procreation and the creation of bonds between families, clans, countries, and various other social groups—in order to consolidate land, money, power, or politics—were the main goals of marriage, and marriage did not call for passionate sexual attraction. Emotional, loving relationships often existed outside the institution of marriage as much as within its confines.[1] Whereas the common concept of modern Western marriage is of a secular, state-sanctioned, legally recognized, permanent, and exclusive union between two equal individuals who love each other, marriage in the Roman period and throughout the Middle Ages was largely a private institution with legal consequences and was usually characterized as a property arrangement between two families. Status and economic circumstances were the most important considerations in selecting a potential spouse. Even among people lacking property and the poor, who probably had much more leeway, the choice of partner was not based solely, perhaps not even primarily, on love; rather, a spouse was often chosen for her (or, somewhat more rarely, his) qualities as a workmate, since husband and wife were an economic unit as much as a social one. Boswell suggests the composite nature of the institution with a schematic chronology: "In premodern Europe marriage usually began as a property arrangement, was in its middle mostly about raising children, and ended about love. Few couples married in fact 'for love,' but many grew to love each other in time as they jointly managed their household, reared their offspring, and shared life's experiences."[2]

Of course, generalizations about interpersonal relationships are as hazardous as they are tempting. Moreover, insofar as marriage was an arrangement, and later an institution, that was not primarily predicated on law, we have little access to its original meaning and conception in historical periods when fewer records were kept than in our own time— let alone in antiquity. However, it seems relatively safe to assume that the "invention of love" during the romantic period,[3] which continues to wield its influence over our present-day popular culture, has left an indelible mark on the modern concept of marriage (or the ideal thereof) and that this view of the married state is not necessarily inherent in the institution of marriage itself. Boswell would suggest, to radically simplify and compress a complex argument, that Greco-Roman marriage did not involve erotic satisfaction, sexual fidelity, or romantic fulfillment. The approach of medieval Christianity, which was largely retained by the

---

1. Boswell defines modern marriage not only as a permanent and exclusive union but also as one "which would produce legitimate children if [the partners] choose to have children." John Boswell, Same-Sex Unions in Premodern Europe 10 (1995). However, although marriage is frequently accompanied by offspring, marriage no longer constitutes a prerequisite for the legitimacy of children; furthermore, it is inaccurate to define modern marriage as an institution whose main goal is procreation. The connection between modern marriage and procreation is further discussed in later chapters.

2. *Id.* at xxi.

3. *See* 2 Irving Singer, The Nature of Love: Courtly and Romantic 1–2 (1984).

Protestant Reformation, insisted upon the goodness of married love but considered it a nonpassionate partnership. This understanding largely ignored sexual and passionate love between the spouses. Paradoxically, in periods that saw the greatest idealization of love, such as the late Renaissance and the romantic period, it became ever more difficult to reconcile the fact of marriage with the transcendental aspirations that attached themselves to sexual love, so that for considerable stretches of history, the two remained culturally, if not actually, separate.[4]

Needless to say, cultural and religious attitudes toward sexuality, which directly influence the perception of marriage, have themselves fluctuated on the wide scale between tolerance and "liberalism" on the one hand and repression and intolerance on the other. We cannot simply assume some ongoing steady movement toward openness regarding sexuality within and outside marriage. For example, what some may regard today as promiscuous sexual relations seem to have been commonplace in certain parts of ancient Greece; and whereas the sixteenth century in Europe may be characterized by "moderate toleration" of sexuality, we find attitudes of repression in the seventeenth century, a move back to "permissiveness" in the eighteenth century, a repeat of sexual repression—especially of women's sexuality—in the nineteenth century, and a return to sexual permissiveness in the twentieth century.[5] Similarly, there has not been steady ongoing progress toward equality between men and women, either in general or in marriage; we find, for example, that the woman of the sixteenth century was in many respects more equal to her husband than the nineteenth-century woman and that "[a] woman of 1200, even if she was unmarried or widowed, would have had no cause to envy a woman of 1700, and even less one of 1900."[6] In the same way, attitudes toward homosexuality and same-sex unions have undergone dramatic shifts, from complete acceptance of such relationships between older men and younger, less powerful men in ancient Greece to full condemnation and repression during the Middle Ages. Likewise, the current concept of the "traditional family" is as contingent and mutable as views of the family in history, and it is inevitable that our ideas of family will further change and develop in the future. Historian Lawrence Stone has aptly made this point:

---

4. *Id.* at 12, 13, 47–48.

5. *See* Lawrence Stone, The Family, Sex, and Marriage in England 1500–1800, at 545 (1977).

6. *See* E. J. Graff, What Is Marriage For? 217 (1999), quoting from 2 A History of the Family 426 (André Burguière et al. eds., Sarah Hanbury Tenison et al. trans., 1996).

It is wholly false to assume that there could have been any such thing as straightforward linear development. There is no reason to assume that the end-product of the affective individualism, namely the intensely self-centered, inwardly turned, emotionally bonded, sexually liberated, child-oriented family type of the third quarter of the twentieth century is any more permanent an institution than were the many family types which preceded it. This is strongly suggested by the fact that the cause of change lies in an unending dialectic of competing interests and ideas; by the historical record showing the highly erratic course of this evolution; by its very variable impact on different classes; by the strains to which it is currently being subjected; and by its very restricted geographical spread around the world.[7]

In much the same way that marriage and the family have been subject to various degrees of oscillation, we find varying views on the essential qualities of marriage, its nature, and its importance for the individual and society. Goethe argued that marriage is the greatest achievement of European culture and the solid foundation of any private life.[8] Others, such as Benedetto Croce, viewed marriage as "the grave of savage love" and the grave of sentimentality.[9] Similarly, there is little unanimity about what constitutes or constituted marriage in both modern and pre-modern societies.[10] To quote a stance from the Greco-Roman period, "This is what it means to be married: to have sons one can introduce to the family and the neighbors, and to have daughters of one's own to give to husbands. For we have courtesans for pleasure, concubines to attend to our daily bodily needs, and wives to bear children legitimately and to be faithful wards of our homes."[11] Undoubtedly, such an instrumental definition is not the one that springs to mind in the modern Western world. Not only the purpose and function of marriage, but also its very meaning—be it religious, social, or legal—vary from society to society and have altered over time. Such transitions have been conditioned, as we shall see, by politics, culture, and religion.

2.1.1 From Custom to Law
There has been a tension throughout history between two interlocking aspects of marriage: marriage as a publicly policed institution and

---

7. Stone, note 5 above, at 682–83.

8. Denis De Rougemont, Love in the Western World 287–88 (Montgomery Belgion trans., rev. ed., 1983).

9. Benedetto Croce, Etica e politica, aggiuntovi il "Contributo alla critica di me stesso" (1931), quoted in De Rougemont, note 8 above, at 288.

10. Boswell, note 1 above, at 9.

11. Demosthenes, Against Neaera 122, quoted in Boswell, note 1 above, at 28.

marriage as an individual experience. In different periods the emphasis has shifted from a definition of marriage as a private matter to a concept of it as a publicly bestowed institution and vice versa. However, as the discussion below shows, we can detect a gradual historical shift from the private to the public sphere, "from custom to law,"[12] and "from sacrament to contract."[13] According to both Roman and Jewish law, marriage was a private act. During the Roman period, the state could police only the consequences of marriage, not its formation—the judge investigated only whether the couple lived together with *affectio maritalis*, "the intention of being married," as evidenced by their behavior and words.[14] Until the end of the Roman period, the law had little direct involvement with the social institution of marriage. The origins of the earliest legal characteristics of marriage were dowry, the agreement to support the wife and pay her compensation upon abandonment, and the support of children; but when property was not involved, the relationship was dissolved simply by desertion or separation. Marriage, throughout much of the Middle Ages, was controlled by economic, political, and largely impersonal considerations. When no exchange of property was involved, marriage was simply a private decision of the partners to live together. It was sufficient that they regarded themselves as husband and wife and represented themselves to the community as such; no formal religious or civil ceremony or registration was required.

Thus, in Western Europe before the Reformation, there was no de jure secular state-sanctioned marriage; marriage was a private matter regulated and governed only by custom or religious norms. Two people were held to be married not because they had gone through any particular ceremony but because they in fact lived together as man and wife; that is, people could form marriages simply by exchanging consents and cohabiting.[15] During the late Middle Ages, the church developed a system of courts and procedures and a body of legal rules regarding marriage. In the thirteenth century, with the decree that marriage was a sacrament,

12. *See* Mary Ann Glendon, The Transformation of Family Law: State, Law, and Family in the United States and Western Europe (1989).

13. John Witte Jr., From Sacrament to Contract: Marriage, Religion, and Law in the Western Tradition (1997).

14. *See* Graff, note 6 above, at 194–95.

15. *See* Glendon, note 12 above, at 7, 15, 17, 19–21. The act or ceremony by which the marriage union was created has differed widely at different times and among different peoples. One of the earliest and most frequent customs associated with entrance into marriage was the capture of the woman by her intended husband, which later gave way to wife purchase. Various other ceremonial forms have accompanied or constituted the entrance upon the marriage relation, the most common of which was some kind of feast; yet among many peoples, marriage took place without any formal ceremony. *See* John A. Ryan, *History of Marriage, in* The Catholic Encyclopedia, vol. 9 (Robert Appleton, 1910).

Roman Catholic canon law fully transformed marriage into a formal in-stitution, indissoluble and subject to far-reaching official regulation, with a system of ecclesiastical courts to enforce the rules.[16] Once the rule of indissolubility was instituted—by establishing a procedure for judicial separation and providing causes of annulment—marriage was defined with more precision, and the canon law system of marriage impedi-ments and prohibitions emerged.[17]

By the early sixteenth century, the church's canon law was the pre-dominant law governing marriage in the West; it was the Council of Trent that in 1563 formalized and systematized the canon law, declaring contraception and abortion violations of the predominant goal of mar-riage: propagation and child rearing.[18] The formal public ceremony in the presence of a priest, later required by nearly all Western legal systems as a condition for the validity of marriage, was not made mandatory until the late sixteenth century, and in England the church continued to recognize informal marriages as valid until the middle of the eighteenth century.[19] Although Luther declared, during the first half of the sixteenth century, that marriage was not a sacrament but a "worldly thing" and an independent social institution subject to the state, Protestants preserved the religious aspects of marriage (for example, the requirement of the pres-ence of a clergyman) and retained the view that procreation was its main goal.[20] It was at the same time that Calvin introduced the concept of mar-riage as a covenant entered into by the entire community, otherwise con-firming most of the Lutheran theological and legal reforms.[21]

The idea that regulation of marriage or adjudication of disputes concerning marriage could or should be conducted by the secular politi-cal community was not seriously considered before the sixteenth cen-tury and the Protestant Reformation.[22] Owing to the influence of the Lutheran view and later that of the French Revolution, mandatory civil

16. *See* Glendon, note 12 above, at 23; Graff, note 6 above, at 195–96. This was termed by John Witte "the Catholic Sacramental model" of marriage, symbolizing the eternal union between Christ and his Church and bringing sanctifying grace. *See* Witte, note 13 above, at 16–41.

17. *See* Glendon, note 12 above, at 26–27.

18. *See* Witte, note 13 above, at 4, 16–41.

19. *See* Glendon, note 12 above, at 28–30.

20. *See* Ryan, note 15 above; Witte, note 13 above, at 42–73.

21. *See* Witte, note 13 above, at 74–129. It is noteworthy in this respect that although Calvin emphasized the subordination of women with striking misogyny, even by sixteenth-century standards, he also articulated the mutual love and support of hus-band and wife as an important element of marriage, while viewing procreation as its main goal. *Id.* at 96–97, 105.

22. *See* Glendon, note 12 above, at 26.

marriage and registration were gradually instituted in almost all countries of Europe and North America; this was the official replacement of marriage as a private matter by marriage as a state-regulated institution. As industrial capitalism and urbanization emerged, people ceased marrying without official recognition, and the state gained control of the institution. By the mid-eighteenth century, the definition of marriage was transformed in England as in the rest of Europe from a private sacrament to a secular and publicly authorized contract regulated by the state,[23] but not until the nineteenth century did marriage come to be fully and extensively regulated by the law. By the middle of the nineteenth century, with the secularization of marriage jurisdiction and of the content of marriage law, countries all over the world had already created public registration and provided the option of a civil marriage ceremony. Yet some countries, such as the United States, continued to recognize informal marriages as an established legal institution (that recognition is still in effect as common law marriage in several states).[24] Thus, marriage in America during that period could be made by the two partners themselves and only afterward recognized by law. This could be viewed as preservation of marriage as a private institution (a return to the privatization of marriage), but the recognition of common law marriages became very limited, and marriage in the United States had also been transformed into a public, state-regulated institution.[25] We can safely say, then, that throughout the ages marriage has become more state regulated and less private and has thus been transformed from custom to law. Another change has taken place independently: romantic love has become *the* acceptable justification for getting or staying married. This is not to say that previous justifications, such as finance and procreation, are no longer justifications for marriage, but it is love—as the primary goal of marriage—that has become the ideal.

2.1.2 Conceptions of Love and Marriage from Plato to the Troubadours
Much of Western thinking about sexual love and romantic love is rooted in Plato's philosophy. One expression of this can be found in a speech delivered by Oscar Wilde at his first trial in 1895:

> The "love" that dare not speak its name in this century is such a great affection of an older for a younger man as there was between David and Jonathan, such as Plato made the very base of his philosophy and such as you find in the sonnets of Michelangelo and Shakespeare—

23. *See* Graff, note 6 above, at 202–3.
24. *See* Glendon, note 12 above, at 19, 33, 34.
25. *See* Graff, note 6 above, at 203–5.

a deep spiritual affection that is as pure as it is perfect and dictates great works of art like those of Shakespeare and Michelangelo. . . . It is beautiful; it is fine; it is the noblest form of affection. It is intellectual, and it repeatedly exists between an elder and a younger man, when the elder man has intellect, and the younger man has all the joy, hope and glamour of life. That it should be so the world does not understand. It mocks at it and sometimes puts one into the pillory for it.[26]

Plato says little about the connection between love and marriage. In fact, he seems to assume no connection between the two. In the *Republic,* Plato expresses opposition to the institution of marriage, calls for its abolition, and proposes that "women shall be wives in common to all the men, and not one of them shall live privately with any man; the children too should be held in common so that no parent shall know which is his own offspring, and no child shall know his parent."[27] However, viewed as part of Plato's concept of a collective republic, this account is not necessarily an attack on marriage per se. Moreover, Plato does not address in the *Republic* his concept of love between individuals; that concept is explicated in the *Symposium* and the *Phaedrus* and is sharply distinguished from the institution of marriage.

Plato's *Symposium*—the dialogues between Socrates and others in the praise of love, written in the fourth century B.C.—is the earliest treatise on companionate male same-sex relationships; it portrays homosexual passionate love as the ideal.[28] In the *Symposium* no women are present, and it seems that for Plato, true love cannot be experienced by women

26. Frank Harris, Oscar Wilde 175–76 (1960).

27. Last sentence of book 5, Plato's Republic 11 (G. M. A. Grube trans., 1974).

28. Plato, Symposium, reprinted in On Homosexuality: Lysis, Phaedrus, and Symposium 103 (Benjamin Jowett trans., with selected retranslation, notes, and introduction by Eugene O'Connor, 1991). It should be noted, however, that in *The Laws,* Plato's view of homosexual acts seems to have changed: he condemns male homosexuality as unnatural and departs from his praise of homosexual love in the *Symposium* and the *Phaedrus.* *See generally* Gregory Vlastos, *The Individual as Object of Love in Plato,* in Platonic Studies 3–34 (1981). *See also* William N. Eskridge Jr., The Case for Same-Sex Marriage: From Sexual Liberty to Civilized Commitment 221 n. 12 (1996) [hereinafter Case for Same-Sex Marriage], referring to Eva Cantarella, Bisexuality in the Ancient World 61–63 (Cormac Ó Cuilleanáin trans., 1992). Litigation in the lower courts in the matter of Romer v. Evans instigated a scholarly dispute as to whether *The Laws* is indeed a clear condemnation of male homosexuality. *See* Evans v. Romer, 63 Empl. Prac. Dec. (CCH) P 42, 719 (Colo. D. Ct. 1993); John Finnis, *"Shameless Acts" in Colorado: Abuse of Scholarship in Constitutional Cases,* Acad. Questions 10 (fall 1994); and Martha Nussbaum's response: *Platonic Love and Colorado Law: The Relevance of Ancient Greek Norms to Modern Sexual Controversies,* 80 Va. L. Rev. 1515 (1994). For criticism of the interpretive accounts of both Finnis and Nussbaum, *see* Randall Baldwin Clark, *Platonic Love in a Colorado Courtroom: Martha Nussbaum, John Finnis, and Plato's Laws in Evans v. Romer,* 12 Yale J.L. & Human. 1 (2000).

or really directed toward them; heterosexual desire has no place within the hierarchy that leads to ideal love.[29] In one of the dialogues, Aristophanes describes companionate love as a yearning for the other half from whom one has been separated: "[W]hen one of [those boys who have reached manhood] finds his other half, whether he be a lover of youth or a lover of another sort, the pair are lost in an amazement of love and friendship and intimacy, and one will not be out of the other's sight, as I may say, even for a moment: these are they who pass their lives with one another." And Pausanias similarly states, "I am convinced that a man who falls in love with a younger man of this age is generally prepared to share everything with the one he loves—he is eager, in fact, to spend the rest of his own life with him."[30] Phaedrus, in his speech in praise of love, also found in the *Symposium,* cites as the ultimate in love and commitment the maxim that "love will make men dare to die for their beloved" and provides as one example Achilles' willingness to die for his lover Patroclus.[31] These statements and Socrates' final speech in the *Symposium* serve as the basis for subsequent idealistic thinkers' works about love.[32] The love depicted by Plato in the *Symposium* and in the *Phaedrus* is thus sexual affectionate love between two men, separate and distinct from the institution of marriage. It has been asserted that the homosexual Greek relationships as described by Plato were often more akin to modern companionate marriages than to the Greeks' own institution of marriage, in which the husband and wife had little emotional affinity and the husband had great freedom to engage in outside sexual liaisons.[33]

Christianity departed from the Platonic view, and God became the object of love. For a long time, religious love was defined as a search for union with God. In the Middle Ages attempts were made to humanize the love that Christianity reserved for man in relation to God,[34] but throughout the Middle Ages, Europe was dominated by the religious concept that the love of God was above all other kinds of love.

The French troubadours of the twelfth century were the first (since Plato) to speak of an ideal love between human beings rather than between man and God, and their poetry is thus the starting point of most studies of love and marriage. The troubadour poetry was the first expres-

29. *See* 1 Irving Singer, The Nature of Love: Plato to Luther 76 (2d ed., 1984).

30. Symposium, note 28 above, at 124 (lines 191d–192c), 103 (line 181d).

31. *Id.* at 111–12; William N. Eskridge Jr., *A History of Same-Sex Marriage,* 79 Va. L. Rev. 1419, 1442 (1993) [hereinafter *History of Same-Sex Marriage*].

32. Singer, note 3 above, at 8–9.

33. *See* David M. Halperin, One Hundred Years of Homosexuality and Other Essays on Greek Love 85–87 (1990).

34. *See* Singer, note 3 above, at 9–10.

sion of a new ideal, the concept of "courtly love," which was to permeate the secular literature written in Europe between the twelfth and the fifteenth centuries.[35] Troubadour poetry spoke of this idealized and largely unconsummated love as being noble and ennobling, superior to and even irreconcilable with marriage, "for marriage implies no more than a physical union, but 'Amor'—the supreme Eros—is the transport of the soul upwards to ultimate union with light, something far beyond any love attainable in this life."[36] Whereas the Swiss philosopher Denis De Rougemont depicts a continuing conflict in the Western world between passion and orthodoxy, and thus between love on the one hand and marriage and established religion on the other,[37] the historian Irving Singer argues that different conceptions of love were established at different periods of time and that these conceptions of love do not necessitate a conflict between passion and marriage.[38] De Rougemont goes so far as to say that in the West "it was marriage which in the twelfth century became an object of contempt, and passion that was glorified precisely because it is preposterous, inflicts suffering upon its victims, and wreaks havoc alike in the world and in the self."[39] As we shall see, these are both rather extreme views; the disagreement between the scholars seems to lie in their different opinions as to whether the conflict could and should be resolved, rather than in the question of whether the conflict has in fact been resolved.

The new and ideal concept of heterosexual courtly love in the twelfth century, which detailed a new courtly ethos—a set of rules of conduct as well as of chivalric values—was largely about unattainable love, about love as a quest, and thus it was sharply distinguished from the institution of marriage. Both as a cultural construct and as a real possibility, it was always illicit, often adulterous, and definitely outside marriage—limited to extramarital or premarital relationships—and was conceived of as inherently incompatible with marriage.[40] Courtly love established a fealty that had nothing to do with the sphere of legal marriage and much to do with feudal relationships and a world in which the majority of young knights indeed could not hope to marry at all.[41] This concept

35. *Id.* at 19.

36. De Rougemont, note 8 above, at 75–76.

37. *See id.*

38. Singer, note 3 above, at x–xi.

39. De Rougemont, note 8 above, at 71–72.

40. Singer, note 3 above, at 23, 29. For example, Chretien de Troyes, who in the twelfth century recounted the adventures of Lancelot and Guinever in his romance "Le chevalier de la charrette" (The knight of the cart), describes adultery against a background of a feudal society that held that nothing can justify a violation of the marital vow. *See id.* at 20.

41. *See* De Rougemont, note 8 above, at 33.

is exemplified by the twelfth-century French poet Andreas Capellanus, who offers his vision of courtly love as an alternative to marriage: "We declare and hold as firmly established that *love cannot exert its powers between two people who are married to each other*. For lovers give each other everything freely, under no compulsion or necessity, but married people are in duty bound to give in to each other's desires and deny themselves to each other in nothing."[42] Andreas denies that love can exist within a marriage; indeed, he seems to echo the sad moral (if moral it be) of the earlier medieval legend of Tristan, in which love and marriage conflict dramatically when Tristan's beloved Isolde is withheld from him and he refuses to sleep with his own wife.[43]

Likewise, in the famous correspondence of Abélard and Heloïse from the twelfth century, Heloïse opposes Abélard's marriage proposal, implicitly reasoning that marriage and love are incompatible; eventually the two did marry, and as a consequence, Abélard was castrated by Heloïse's uncle and Heloïse became a nun.[44] Heloïse saw marriage as an impediment to love, stating in one of her letters, "I preferred love to wedlock, freedom to a bond." Abélard explains this assertion, stating, "How much dearer it would be to her, and more honorable to me, to be called mistress than wife, that affection alone might hold me, not any force of the nuptial bond fasten me to her." For Heloïse, and her followers in succeeding generations, love was a "transcendent consummation," a "sacred friendship through sexuality that matrimony alone could not create."[45]

Mainstream medieval society, being inherently Christian, took a different view of marriage: it condemned adultery as a crime, took marriage for granted, and later made it into a sacrament. The opposing view was a product of "heretical courtesy": it condemned Catholic marriage and upheld adultery as a virtue, thereby promoting a set of values according to which marriage was a mistake.[46] In literature, at least (and one could

42. Andreas Cappellanus, The Art of Courtly Love 10 (John Jay Parry trans., 1969), my emphasis. Singer disagrees with Denis de Rougemont's understanding of this passage as an attack on marriage, yet he agrees that it reinforces the view that courtly love competes with married love by offering emotional possibilities that marriage itself may not offer. *See* Singer, note 3 above, at 80. It is noteworthy, however, that in his *Tractatus*, Cappellanus renounces all sexual love and, in apparent contradiction to the above passage from *The Art of Courtly Love*, seems to defend marriage as the only sacred bond. *See id.* at 85.

43. Singer, note 3 above, at 81–82.

44. *See* The Letters of Abélard and Heloïse (C. K. Scott-Moncrieff trans., 1925). *See also* Etienne Gilson, Heloïse and Abélard (1960); Singer, note 3 above, at 880.

45. Quoted in Singer, note 3 above, at 100.

46. *See* De Rougemont, note 8 above, at 275.

argue that literature was indeed the main realm in which courtly love existed to begin with), the courtly impulse would come to be integrated to a certain degree into the religious impulse, and the knightly quest would become the quest for the Holy Grail. Be that as it may, courtly love, or passion, was incompatible with marriage in the flesh, especially with marriage understood as not being based on passion,[47] and traditionally manifested itself in adultery. In reaction, the church condemned the concept of courtly love as heresy; and throughout most of the Middle Ages, the idea that the love of God was above all predominated: "Marriage was holy, but only as a means of reproducing the species. It could not serve as the basis for an ideal love. That is why St. Paul says that it is better to marry than to burn, but that chastity is best of all. According to St. Jerome, 'an ardent lover of his wife is an adulterer.'" However, as a reaction to the narrowness of medieval religious idealizations, the love of God became increasingly anthropocentric,[48] beginning with Dante and extending into the philosophy of thinkers like Ficino, and there was a gradual movement to conceptualize love in a manner akin to that of Plato and the troubadours.

2.1.3 Love and Marriage in Milton's Divorce Tracts

Marriage in sixteenth-century England was still primarily a contract between two families for the exchange of concrete benefits; the choice of spouse was made by parents, kin, and influential patrons and was primarily based on economic, social, or political considerations; the future spouses had little say in the matter, and prior affection was not an important consideration.[49] In the late sixteenth and early seventeenth centuries, with the rise in the power of the state and the spread of Protestantism, there was a decline in the importance of kinship; loyalty for one's lineage or patron was replaced by loyalty to the state or sect. This was true throughout Europe. The household became the center and the symbol of the whole social system, and the family began to be characterized by passive obedience to the husband and father in the home. Power relations within the family became ever more authoritarian and patriarchal under the strong encouragement of both church and state. The state emphasized the subordination of the wife to the head of the household as a main guarantee of law and order in the body politic.[50] The subordi-

47. *Id.* at 276–77.

48. Singer, note 29 above, at 365.

49. *See* Stone, note 5 above, at 271. *See also* Lawrence Stone & Jeanne C. Flawtier Stone, An Open Elite? England 1540–1880, at 12 (1984) [hereinafter Stone & Stone].

50. *See* Stone, note 5 above, at 653–54, 202.

nation of wives to husbands was less evident among the lower classes in preindustrial society, because husband, wife, and children tended to form a single economic unit in which the wife had a critical role: managing the domestic economy. But women's economic participation did not accord the wife greater power, authority, or higher status.[51] Lawrence Stone represents England as a country where interpersonal relations between husbands and wives were usually remote, with little or no emotional bond or friendship, because of cultural patterns that dictated the arranged—rather than consensual—marriage and because of the subordination of women.[52] Likewise, in seventeenth-century France and Germany, forms of physical affection pertaining to the erotic were apparently rare among married couples, and passionate characteristics continued to be manifested mostly in extramarital affairs. Even among aristocratic women who had some sexual freedom and pursued their independent sexual pleasure, that pursuit was usually not connected with marriage.[53] Stone claims that in France there was no trace of affection in the marital relationship, and it was said that all over France, "if the horse and the wife fall sick at the same time, the . . . peasant rushes to the blacksmith to care for the animal, and leaves the task of healing his wife to nature";[54] this statement could well be an articulation of popular humor, but it seems, nevertheless, to have had some truth.

The prevailing view among seventeenth-century philosophers, such as Montaigne and Descartes, was that there was an inevitable conflict between sexual love and marriage, implying that the spouses may have had to seek the goodness of sexual love outside marriage.[55] In *The Princess of Clèves,* Madame de La Fayette critiques the ideal of married love, as did other writers among her contemporaries.[56] Her protagonist, the Princesse de Clèves, has every reason to marry Monsieur de Nemours, whom she views as her only hope for happiness. Nevertheless, the princess decides not to marry him, because she becomes convinced that marriage and passionate love are by their very nature irreconcilable. She fears that if they get married, they will lose interest in each other and their passionate love will disappear. Therefore, she is certain that she can be happy only by *not* marrying Monsieur de Nemours. In *Zaïde,* Ma-

---

51. *Id.* at 199–201.

52. *See id.* at 102.

53. *See* Anthony Giddens, The Transformation of Intimacy: Sexuality, Love, and Eroticism in Modern Societies 38–39 (1992).

54. Stone, note 5 above, at 103.

55. *See id.* at 257–58.

56. *See* Madame de La Fayette, The Princess of Clèves (Walter J. Cobb trans., 1961).

dame de La Fayette explains that permanent relationships such as marriage destroy passionate love through the mere passage of time. One is obliged to choose between marriage and sexual love.[57]

It is against this background that the integration of love and marriage in the works of John Milton, written in the middle of the seventeenth century, should be regarded as extremely innovative. The significance of Milton's work in this context is his unique perception of love as the essence of marriage. He was much ahead of his time in defining such a connection. Since concepts of divorce and its justifications are closely related to concepts of marriage, we find a unique approach in Milton's divorce tracts—*The Doctrine and Discipline of Divorce* (1643) and *Tetrachordon* (1643)[58]—expressing views that were not accepted until two centuries later.[59]

In *The Doctrine and Discipline of Divorce,* Milton asserts that "the chief and noblest purpose of marriage" is the "cheerful conversation of man with woman," using the word "conversation" to mean companionship, mutual concern, and the friendly communication of feelings and ideas.[60] In *Paradise Lost,* where he exposes, among other things, the story of the first marriage—that of Adam and Eve—Milton depicts love as the key to harmonious marriage and the lack thereof as the cause of marital failure. The aspects of Adam's "conversation" with Eve that most delight him are

> Those graceful acts,
> Those thousand decencies that daily flow
> From all her words and actions, mixt with Love
> And sweet compliance, which declare unfeign'd
> Union of mind, or in us both one Soul;
> Harmony to behold in wedded pair
> More grateful than harmonious sound to the ear.[61]

57. For discussion of the works of Madame de La Fayette, see Singer, note 3 above, at 273–76. Similar pessimism as to the possibility of reconciling love and marriage can be found, for example, in Molière's *Misanthrope,* where Alceste cannot harmonize his feelings for Célimène with married love. *See* Singer, note 3 above, at 279–80.

58. Both John Milton's *The Doctrine and Discipline of Divorce* (1643) and his *Tetrachordon* (1643) are reprinted in 2 Complete Prose Works of John Milton (Ernest Sirluck ed., 1959) [hereinafter Prose of Milton].

59. Further elaboration on Milton's philosophy on matrimony can be found in two of his great works—*Paradise Lost* and *Samson Agonistes.* For additional works by John Milton addressing divorce, see "The Judgment of Martine Bucer concerning Divorce" (1644) and "Colasterion: A Reply to a Nameless Answer against the Doctrine and Discipline of Divorce" (1645). Written between 1656 and 1660, "De Doctrina Christiana" is another work that embodies some of Milton's views on marriage and divorce.

60. Milton, The Doctrine and Discipline of Divorce, in Prose of Milton, note 58 above, at 235–36. For interpretation see Singer, note 3 above, at 25.

61. John Milton, Paradise Lost, at book 8, lines 600–606.

Elsewhere, Milton defines marriage as inherently connected to love and argues that all marriages lacking love and affection are invalid: "The form of marriage consists in the mutual exercise of benevolence, love, help, and solace between the espoused parties, as the institution itself, or its definition, indicates." This concept led Milton to argue in favor of divorce, on the basis of his belief that marriage should not and could not exist if and when love ceases to exist between husband and wife: "[W]here love cannot be, there can be left of wedlock nothing, but the empty husk of an outward matrimony; as undelightful and unpleasing as any kind of hypocrisy."[62] Milton argued that divorce should be granted on the grounds that it is unnatural to force two people who are incompatible and who no longer love one another to remain married; otherwise, it is "forced cohabitation and a sinful act."[63] Milton's suggestion of divorce on grounds of spiritual incompatibility was unique and unpopular at the time, because the traditional view during the sixteenth and seventeenth centuries in England was clearly against divorce. It was seen as a necessary evil, acceptable only on the grounds of adultery or fornication, nonconsummation, or desertion.[64]

It is noteworthy that in other respects Milton's views were not groundbreaking and did conform with prevailing beliefs of his time, especially his understanding of the role of women in marriage and his additional justifications of divorce on religious grounds: Milton regarded the duty to love God as above all things, including matrimony; in his writings, the love of God is more important than any kind of human love.[65] However, in order to fully love God, one needs to be

---

62. Milton, The Doctrine and Discipline of Divorce, in Prose of Milton, note 58 above, at 155, 256. Another thinker of the same era whose view of marriage was close to that of Milton was William Gouge. He believed that mutual love must exist between husband and wife: "Love is the fulfilling of the law, that is, the very life of all those duties which the law requireth. It is the bond of perfection, which bindeth together all those duties that passe betwixt partie and partie. Where love aboundeth, there all duties will readily and cheerfully be performed." William Gouge, Of Domestical Duties (London, 1622), quoted in Gladys J. Willis, The Penalty of Eve: John Milton and Divorce 41 (1984).

63. Milton, The Doctrine and Discipline of Divorce, in Prose of Milton, note 58 above, at 320.

64. *See* Willis, note 62 above, at 31–32.

65. Milton seems to be more concerned with the love of God than with the mutual love between the spouses, although he makes a connection between the two. In Milton's view, a man's love for his wife above God is detrimental to his spiritual welfare, and this is presented as another reason to justify divorce: divorce is justified because without love there can be no spiritual communion in marriage and the man is bound to defy God. In his divorce tracts, rather as in traditional Jewish interpretations of the Law, Milton defines marriage as a spiritual institution wherein spiritual happiness is greatly dependent upon the mental fitness of the wife; the wife finds salvation through her husband and is used

happily married, and one can be happily married only if, and as long as, love exists between the couple. Moreover, unlike his contemporaries, Milton denied children, parents, commonwealth, and church an essential role in the marital relationship, considering procreation to be only a secondary end of marriage.[66] Milton stresses that love is the most important end of marriage:

> It is universally admitted that marriage may lawfully be dissolved, if the prime end and form of the institution be violated; which is generally alleged as the reason why Christ allowed divorce in cases of adultery only. But the prime end and form of marriage, as almost all acknowledge, is not the nuptial bed, but *conjugal love,* and mutual assistance through life; for that must be regarded as the prime end and form of a rite, which is alone specified in the original institution. Mention is there made of the pleasures of society, which are incompatible with the isolation consequent upon aversion, and conjugal assistance, which is afforded by love alone, not of the nuptial bed, or of the production of offspring, which may take place even without love: from whence it is evident that conjugal affection is of more importance and higher excellence than the nuptial bed itself, and more worthy to be considered as the prime end and form of the institution.[67]

Notwithstanding Milton's views, the predominant concept of marriage and its ends had not greatly changed since the fourth century, when Augustine came up with three justifications for marriage in the following order: first, *proles* (procreation); second, *fides* (fidelity, or avoiding fornication); and third, *sacramentum* (a permanent bond).[68]

---

by her husband in his quest for complete union with God. According to Milton's "rule of charity," divorce is morally good if the wife hinders her husband's spiritual life; an "unfit" wife may destroy her husband's domestic peace, the peace that leads him to love the Lord with all his heart. *See id.* at 30–31, 40–44.

66. *See* John Halkett, Milton and the Idea of Matrimony: A Study of the Divorce Tracts and Paradise Lost 13, 28 (1970).

67. Milton, The Doctrine and Discipline of Divorce, in Prose of Milton, note 58 above, at 176. Milton expresses similar ideas in Tetrachordon, in Prose of Milton, note 58 above, at 599, 623. Moreover, Milton's *Samson Agonistes* represents a husband's progression toward spiritual accomplishment after he has justifiably divorced his spiritually incompatible wife. In this poetic drama, Milton portrays Delilah as the faithless wife of Samson and describes their marriage as a bondage that should be ended out of respect for the holiness of married love itself. For analysis of this work, see Willis, note 62 above, at 77–84, 101–28; Singer, note 3 above, at 243–44, 253.

68. *See* Witte, note 13 above, at 21; Graff, note 6 above, at 59–60.

This perspective continued throughout the Middle Ages; both Christians and Jews considered any sex outside marriage a capital offense and sex inside marriage an obligation.[69] When Milton wrote his divorce tracts, this was still most other scholars' concept of marriage. It was exemplified by Henry Smith in his "Preparative to Marriage," where he asserted, in a manner reminiscent of Augustine, that there were three ends of marriage: first and foremost, the procreation of children; afterward, the avoidance of fornication; and only then, the avoidance of loneliness.[70] Milton's views on marriage and divorce were largely ignored or rejected in his day; later English reformers looked back to Milton as a brilliant thinker who anticipated many of the divorce reforms of the nineteenth and twentieth centuries.[71]

2.1.4 The Transformations of Marriage from the Enlightenment to the Nineteenth Century

By the middle of the eighteenth century, there had been a shift to official legal regulation of marriage, because gradually, from the sixteenth century to the eighteenth century, the Catholic Church lost its jurisdiction over marriage in the greater part of western Europe; in Protestant regions, the same shift occurred as a consequence of the Reformation. As the church lost its monopoly on the regulation of marriage, the newly emerging states acquired jurisdiction, and the secular governments simply incorporated many of the canon law rules. Not until the rise of the secular state and the emergence of the Enlightenment's humanism and individualism did a true antithesis to traditional Christian attitudes toward marriage begin to appear; marriage law then began to be affected by trends of the times. Marriage came to be seen as a civil contract, and the state began to regulate not only the formation and dissolution of marriage but also its very contents and some of its most intimate aspects.[72]

It was in the eighteenth century that a new family type emerged, based on what Lawrence Stone terms the principle of "Affective Individualism": the rise of individualism in relation to society and of affection between husband and wife.[73] Some historians base their explanations for this change in the concept of the family on the theory of modernization,

69. *See* Willis, note 62 above, at 67–68.

70. Henry Smith, *Preparative to Marriage, in* The Sermons of Maister Henre Smith (1657). Discussed in Willis, note 62 above, at 33–34.

71. *See* Witte, note 13 above, at 186.

72. *See* Glendon, note 12 above, at 30–32.

73. *See* Stone, note 5 above, at 222, 655. For a discussion of the economic, social, and political factors that led to the rise in individualism, see id. at 258–62.

manifested by the move toward urbanization, secularization, and personal autonomy.[74] However, it is not certain that there is a clear causal link between modernization, industrial capitalism, and individualism on the one hand and the evolution of the modern nuclear family on the other.[75] Whether or not the transformation of the family can be directly linked or attributed to other social and political changes (a matter for historical interpretation), for present purposes it will suffice to point out that the changes in the family and the major sociopolitical transformations took place at the same time.

During the eighteenth century, the nuclear family had become relatively independent of kin, and there was a new recognition of the need for personal autonomy and a new respect for the individual pursuit of happiness. Consequently, the authority to select spouses was largely transferred from the extended family to the future spouses themselves; their parents retained only a right of veto over socially or economically unsuitable candidates.[76] The companionate marriage had emerged, and for the first time, the choice of mate was mainly made on the basis of mutual affection—the concept of "holy matrimony"—instead of economic and social considerations. This in turn involved a fundamental change in power relations within the family. According to Stone, until the eighteenth century the roles of wife and mistress were separated— the wife was to run the house and provide a male heir, and the mistress was to provide companionship and sexual pleasure. In the eighteenth century the symbolic roles of wife and mistress were united, and the ideals of affectionate marriage and sex within marriage were adopted. Moreover, there were beginnings of a shift away from domestic patriarchy: women had greater autonomy, and there was a move toward greater legal and educational equality between the sexes in general and between the spouses in particular; women were granted increased status and decision-making power within the family. However, these phenomena were still largely limited to upper-class circles. Among the rest of society, the subordination of women to men was preserved.[77]

74. *Id.* at 658–66.

75. Engels, for one, argued that it was industrialization that brought the practice of marriage based on love to the working classes, as the free-contract system of labor relations, on which industrial society in the West was based, presupposed a free-contract system of marital relations. Lawrence Stone disputes this evaluation, arguing that most of the features of the modern family emerged before the rise of industrialization, but concedes that industrialization had some effect upon family structure. *See id.* at 661–65.

76. *Id.* at 272–74, 325. *See also* Stone & Stone, note 49 above, at 122.

77. *See* Stone, note 5 above, at 273, 328; however, Stone holds that for those without property, affective and companionate marital relations did not develop before the nineteenth century. *Id.* at 333, 389, 542, 656, 657.

Anticipating these social developments, John Locke articulated in his *Two Treatises on Government* the principle of men and women as free and equal persons and the principle of equality between husband and wife, arguing that Adam and Eve were created equal before God in terms of their mutual rights and duties. Based on his concept of marriage as a voluntary contract between free and equal persons, Locke rejected the idea of the wife's subjection to her husband, while still viewing the man as the abler and the stronger.[78] Locke paved the way for many of the reforms in Anglo-American marriage law that took place in the next centuries, for example, the departure of marriage law from established theological doctrines. His views on marriage, like Milton's, proved prescient without having any immediate legal impact.[79] The legal establishment resisted the calls for reform until well into the nineteenth century. It was in 1765 that Lord Blackstone articulated the famous common law concept of coverture: "By marriage, the husband and wife are one person in law: that is, the very being or legal existence of the woman is suspended during marriage, or at least is incorporated and consolidated into that of the husband under whose wing, protection and cover she performs everything . . . and her condition during her marriage is called her coverture. Upon this principle, of a union of person in husband and wife, depend almost all the legal rights, duties and disabilities, that either of them acquires by marriage."[80] Accordingly, in common law countries, the husband overtook the wife's legal identity, and the wife could own no personal property, make no personal contracts, and bring no lawsuits.[81] As Daniel Defoe observed, "the very nature of the marriage contract was, in short, nothing but giving up liberty, estate, authority and everything to the man, and the woman was indeed a mere woman ever after—that is to say a slave."[82]

We thus find that during the second half of the eighteenth century,

---

78. *See* John Locke, Two Treatises on Government (1698) (Peter Laslett ed., 1960). For analysis see Witte, note 13 above, at 186–93. However, in his theological writings, Locke retreated to a literal biblical understanding of marriage without the qualifications he had defended in his *Two Treatises*. Moreover, feminist theorists have argued that underlying Locke's account there is actually a sexist and patriarchal view. *See, e.g.,* Carol Pateman, The Sexual Contract 52–55 (1988).

79. *See* Witte, note 13 above, at 191–93.

80. 1 William Blackstone, Commentaries on the Laws of England 44 (1832), cited in Glendon, note 12 above, at 94 n. 29.

81. *See* Graff, note 6 above, at 27–28. However, this was not the status of women all over Europe: some European laws—Dutch, French, and Spanish—adapted the Roman system that allowed a married woman a separate legal personality, enabling women to contract, sue, buy, sell, and inherit. *Id.* at 256.

82. Daniel Defoe, Roxana 148 (J. Jack ed., 1964), quoted in Stone, note 5 above, at 195, 332.

there was a new wave of moral reform and sexual repression—especially of women's sexuality—in addition to a reassertion of patriarchal authority and an increase in the subordination of women. As late as 1869, John Stuart Mill described the legal position of most women in England as one of total dependence on their husbands.[83] Mill asserted that "the legal subordination of one sex to the other is wrong and ought to be replaced by a principle of perfect equality with no favor or privilege on the one side nor disability on the other" and that if marriage were an equal contract, it could be a true institution of liberty and affection.[84] Mill called for complete equality between husband and wife, men and women, in all aspects of private and public life, including an equal right of husband and wife to sue for divorce and remarriage, not only in cases of adultery but also, quoting Milton, at any time when the couple "becomes conscious that affection never has existed, or has ceased to exist between them."[85] The legal status of women in England did not improve dramatically until the second half of the nineteenth century: the Matrimonial Causes Act of 1857 was not only the first divorce legislation; it also transferred marriage and divorce jurisdiction from the church courts to the common law courts and reversed the traditional presumption that child custody belonged to the father, allowing the wife to claim custody.[86] Deserted wives were granted control of their own property in the same year; the two Married Women's Property Acts of 1870 and 1882 gave wives some control over their own estates and the ability to enter contracts and sue in court with respect to their property.[87] Legal reforms regarding contraception and abortion were also of great significance to the equality of women and to the new concept of marriage.[88] Similar changes in the status of women, implicating not only the relations between husband and wife but also the concept of romantic love within marriage, took place at the same time in North America and in other Western countries.

Love and marriage became gradually more and more intertwined and were eventually reconciled. I would ascribe this shift to three interrelated factors: first, the decline in the view of marriage as a property

83. Stone, note 5 above, at 331, 545, 666–67.

84. Witte, note 13 above, at 200–201, quoting from 21 Collected Works of John Stuart Mill (John M. Robson ed., 1984), at 261.

85. Witte, note 13 above, at 201, quoting from 23 Collected Works of John Stuart Mill (John M. Robson ed., 1984), at 677–80.

86. Witte, note 13 above, at 204–5.

87. See Stone, note 5 above, at 668–69.

88. See Carl E. Schneider, Moral Discourse and the Transformation of American Family Law, 83 Mich. L. Rev. 1803, 1805 (1985).

arrangement and as an institution whose main goal—and even obligation—was procreation;[89] second, the gradual attainment of equality between men and women, as discussed above,[90] accompanied by the decrease in the intervention of the family in the selection of spouse and
the disappearance of forced marriages; and third, the introduction of
the concept of romantic love.[91]

Before the nineteenth century, for a long time, "if love was spoken
about at all in relation to marriage, it was as companionate love, linked
to the mutual responsibilities of husbands and wives for running the
household or farm."[92] At the turn of the nineteenth century, the idea
of love underwent a dramatic new development, and the concept of
romantic love replaced the idea of courtly love. Nineteenth-century
concepts of romantic love arose as a response to the thinking of
seventeenth- and eighteenth-century rationalists who asserted that passionate love was incompatible with marriage. The romantics of the nineteenth century were the first who began systematically idealizing married love.[93] They inherited from Plato the idea that true love is an ideal
relationship that rarely appears in the empirical world, and true to their
wider precept of unification and persistent efforts to overcome dualism,
they made an effort to unify the separate concepts of love and marriage
in the context of a world no longer supporting matrimony as a feudal
institution.[94] However, the connection between love and marriage was
still not fully established. The tenet of courtly love regarding marriage,
namely, that love was not necessarily related to the institution of marriage, persisted. Thus, for example, Mary Wollstonecraft argued that "in
the choice of a husband, [women] should not be led astray by the qualities of a lover, for a lover the husband . . . cannot long remain" and that

89. For discussion of this development, see above, sec. 2.1 of this chapter.

90. It is generally agreed that the beginnings of romantic theory can be traced to mid-
eighteenth-century England. Singer links its emergence to the fact that at this time and
place, more than anywhere else, women were able to choose their husbands and determine the nature of the married life. *See* 2 Singer, note 3 above, at 302.

91. In this respect Lawrence Stone has an interesting theory. He maintains that "the
growth of marriage for love in the eighteenth century was caused by the growing con-
sumption of novels" in which romantic love was the principal theme; after 1780, according to Stone, romantic love and the romantic novel grew together, and for the first
time in history, romantic love became a respectable motive for marriage. *See* Stone, note
5 above, at 283–84.

92. Giddens, note 53 above, at 43.

93. *See* 3 Irving Singer, The Modern World 31 (1984). However, critics of romantic
love, such as de Rougemont, insist that the romantic attitude toward passionate love is
a rejection of marital fidelity and an attempt to ascribe superior value to adultery or extramarital fantasies.

94. *See* 2 Singer, note 3 above, at 283–85.

women should "be contented to love but once in their lives; and after marriage, calmly let passion subside into friendship."[95]

On the whole, the romantics were convinced that for sexual love to succeed, there must be equality at a high cultural level between men and women, and thus they wanted to provide women maximum opportunities of intellectual and personal development.[96] Being a devotee of "free love," Shelley criticized conventional marriage as he knew it and argued that love must not be impeded by the prohibition of extramarital experimentation.[97] Even Rousseau, who is widely considered one of the precursors of romanticism, did not always equate passionate romantic love with marriage; in some of his writings, he viewed them as distinct, although he clearly saw the unification of love and marriage as the ideal to be aspired to.[98]

Kant's ideas about sexual love and marriage are closer to current conceptions of the ideal marriage: despite his view of sexuality as inherently immoral, Kant concludes that love and sex can be compatible and harmonized only in a monogamous legal marriage; his concept of marriage is of "an agreement between two persons by which they grant each other equal reciprocal rights, each of them undertaking to surrender the whole of their person to the other with a complete right of disposal over it."[99] Kant's account of sexuality represents, albeit implicitly, the beginning of the new concept of marriage as inherently connected with and dependent upon love. In a similar manner, Hegel, in his *Phenomenology of Mind*, conceptualizes the marital union as the ethical goal of romantic love. For Hegel, married love includes (and also transcends) sexual love.[100]

As Anthony Giddens maintains, for the first time, owing to the concept of romantic love, love was associated with freedom and self-realization. In his view, "romantic love detaches individuals from wider social circumstances [and] it creates a 'shared history' that helps separate out the marital relationship from other aspects of family organization and give it a special primacy."[101]

95. Mary Wollstonecraft, A Vindication of the Rights of Women (1792) (London: Everyman ed., 1970), quoted in Stone, note 5 above, at 284.

96. *See* Singer, note 3 above, at 300.

97. *Id.* at 420–21.

98. *See, e.g.,* Jean-Jacques Rousseau, Emile (Barbara Foxley trans., 1974).

99. Immanuel Kant, Lectures on Ethics 167 (Louis Infield trans., 1963), discussed in 2 Singer, note 3 above, at 377–81.

100. For discussion see 2 Singer, note 3 above, at 406–8.

101. Giddens, note 53 above, at 39–40, 44–45.

2.1.5 Harmonization of Love and Marriage in the Twentieth Century

Even in the twentieth century, when most people assert a connection between love and marriage, there are thinkers who still view love and marriage as antithetical. Proust, for one, finds marriage inimical to passionate love, stating that "one only loves that which is not totally possessed."[102] Thus, from Plato to Proust, we find descriptions of love and marriage as irreconcilable. That statement should be qualified, however: the skepticism of some romantics and modern thinkers as to the connection between love and marriage does not necessarily stem from a concept of the institution of marriage as separate from love per se but rather from a belief that any long-lasting love is an unattainable ideal. Furthermore, most of the Western world today, especially American culture, is characterized by an attempt to harmonize love and marriage. In the twentieth century love has become the most important if not the only rationale and objective of marriage. The clear dichotomy between love and marriage that existed for so many centuries has finally vanished.

The return toward sexual permissiveness that began at the end of the nineteenth century slowly spread among different social groups in the 1960s and 1970s. The sexual revolution led to the loss of the shame with which for two thousand years Christian morality surrounded the sexual drive.[103] Moreover, the women's liberation movement, which rejected male superiority, led to much erosion in patriarchy and to women's formal equality with men before the law. It should be noted that my concern here is with the *ideology* that developed during the twentieth century regarding the relationship between love and marriage and between the sexes. We should keep in mind, however, that full formal equality has been achieved only at the theoretical level. In terms of actual equality between the sexes (in general and in marriage law), we still have a long way to go; contemporary gender relations in modern American and European marriage are in fact still far from the goal of full substantive equality and the ideal of mutual love; in this respect, ideology and reality may still be very much in tension.

Other developments include the legalization and availability of contraception and abortion, which isolated sexual pleasure from procreation and enabled marriage to become a union "for the close companionship and sexual pleasure of the pair,"[104] rather than a means for

102. 3 Marcel Proust, A la recherche du temps perdu 106 (1954) (the quoted sentence was translated by Irving Singer; 3 Singer, note 93 above, at 190); similar ideas are expressed in De Rougemont, note 8 above, at 292.

103. *See* Stone, note 5 above, at 680–81.

104. Graff, note 6 above, at 84.

procreation. The direct influence of parents in the determination of the marriage choices of their children is today no longer taken for granted. As an acknowledged social (rather than psychological) factor, it is mostly limited to minority groups and isolated segments of society. Love, more than other rationales, has become the widely respected and generally admitted motive for mate selection, and potential spouses have come to expect emotional and sexual fulfillment through marriage.[105]

The demands of the "free love" movement of the nineteenth century have been absorbed into current Western codes of sexuality and marriage. This is evidenced by current marriage rules, such as no-fault divorce and the definition of marriage in the U.S. Uniform Marriage and Divorce Act simply as "a personal relationship between a man and a woman arising out of a civil contract to which the consent of the parties is essential."[106] Marriage has thus become "a terminal sexual contract designed for the gratification of the individual parties."[107] Freedom of contract and sexual privacy have become the most prominent characteristics of the current laws of marriage and divorce. Heterosexual "traditional" marriage now only superficially appears to retain its central position in the social order: in reality, its position is being gradually undermined, and the institution seems on its way to becoming just one lifestyle among others.[108]

Until the 1970s, marriage was an institution that, as defined by the state, gave men and women very different roles (there was a support-service dichotomy). During the period when marriage defined very different rights for men and women (the latter being regarded as the serving partner and the former the supporting partner), it was difficult to think how gay marriage could fit the model. Since the 1970s that gender-differentiated concept of marriage has been repudiated, both constitutionally and culturally. The demise of the support-service dichotomy that existed from the 1600s through the 1970s is one of the main factors in making gay marriage a viable concept. Since marriage in the traditional sense is disappearing, that is, the so-called traditional gender roles in marriage have eroded, "it is the gays who are pioneers in this respect—the prime everyday experimenters. They have for some while experienced what is becoming more and more commonplace for heterosexual couples."[109] In the context of the foregoing transformations in

105. *See* Stone, note 5 above, at 680.

106. Sec. 201 of the Uniform Marriage and Divorce Act, cited in Witte, note 13 above, at 209.

107. Witte, note 13 above, at 209.

108. *See* Giddens, note 53 above, at 154.

109. *Id.* at 135.

the concept and the nature of the institution of marriage, it is not surprising that gay men and lesbians argue today that they fully fit within current conceptions of sex, love, and gender roles within marriage.[110] The same-sex marriage movement that began in the late twentieth century, discussed in detail in later chapters, could thus be viewed as a natural development, as part of the transformation in Western conceptions of love and marriage—namely, the shift in the concept of marriage from a patriarchal property arrangement for the purpose of procreation, with specific gender roles for each partner, to a relationship based on equality, affection, and the love of two people for each other.

2.2 Current Concepts and Characteristics of Marriage Law and Cohabitation in Northern Europe and the United States

We have seen in the previous section that there has never been one universally accepted concept of marriage and that the institution has been in constant fluctuation, as both the definition of marriage and its ends have been dramatically transformed over the ages. Social change preceded legal change, new legislation merely reflecting trends that were similar in most western European and North American countries.[111] One of the major changes has been the shift from an understanding of marriage as a predominantly procreative institution to the current concept of marriage as mainly a relational, unitive, and companionate institution. This is a relatively recent shift, which began in the late nineteenth century and was not articulated by the courts until the past few decades. For example, in the United States, the Supreme Court still emphasized the procreative goal of marriage associated with religious and natural law traditions as recently as the late 1960s.[112] It is only from the late 1980s that we find a clear articulation of the dominant goal of marriage as the creation of a unitive and equal companionship, based on love and commitment: in the case of *Turner v. Safley,* in which the issue was whether the state could limit marriages of prison inmates, the court did not even once mention childbearing as a necessary basis for marriage;

---

110. *See* Graff, note 6 above, at 87.

111. Glendon, note 12 above, at 2.

112. *See, e.g.,* Loving v. Virginia, 388 U.S. 1 (1967). In *Loving,* the Supreme Court struck down Virginia's antimiscegenation statute. The reasoning of the state of Virginia had to do with the implications of interracial marriages on the children of mixed-race couples. The state did not view the couple itself as a separate unit from their (potential) children; rather, the state's argument was based on the premise that the major purpose of marriage was procreation. In rejecting the state's argument, the Supreme Court did not depart from the concept of marriage as a child-oriented institution; the decision reflects an implicit presumption about the goals of marriage at the time.

rather, the court stated, "[M]any important attributes of marriage remain, however, after taking into account the limitations imposed by prison life," including "expressions of emotional support and public commitment," "spiritual significance," sexual consummation, government benefits (e.g., Social Security benefits), property rights (e.g., tenancy by the entirety and inheritance rights), and other, less tangible benefits (e.g., legitimation of children born out of wedlock).[113] Moreover, modern family law does not link marriage and procreation in that it does not require a married couple to live together, have sex, or procreate; many couples who marry do not intend to have children or cannot have children, and the state still encourages them to get married; contraception is legal and available all over the Western world, and couples have a constitutional right to engage in sexual relations when procreation is not the objective.[114] I find the most cogent articulation of the shift in the concept of the connection between marriage and procreation in a decision of the South African Constitutional Court:

> From a legal and constitutional point of view procreative potential is [no longer] a defining characteristic of conjugal relationships. Such a view would be deeply demeaning to couples (whether married or not) who, for whatever reason, are incapable of procreating when they commence such relationship or become so at any time thereafter. It is likewise demeaning to couples who commence such a relationship at an age when they no longer have the desire for sexual relations. It is demeaning to adoptive parents to suggest that their family is any less a family and any less entitled to respect and concern than a family with procreated children. I would even hold it to be demeaning of a couple who voluntarily decide not to have children or sexual relations with one another; this being a decision entirely within their protected sphere of freedom and privacy.[115]

113. *See* Turner v. Safley, 482 U.S. 78, 95 (1987); William N. Eskridge Jr., Gaylaw: Challenging the Apartheid of the Closet 275 (1999) [hereinafter Gaylaw]; *see also* Eskridge, Case for Same-Sex Marriage, note 28 above, at 129–30.

114. For an elaborate discussion of the connection between marriage and procreation, see David A. J. Richards, Women, Gays, and the Constitution: The Grounds for Feminism and Gay Rights in Culture and Law 444 (1998) [hereinafter Women, Gays, and the Constitution]; David A. J. Richards, Identity and the Case for Gay Rights: Race, Gender, Religion as Analogies 160 (1999) [hereinafter Identity and the Case for Gay Rights]; Eskridge, Case for Same-Sex Marriage, note 28 above, at 96–98; see also Michael S. Wald, Same-Sex Couples: Marriage, Families, and Children: An Analysis of Proposition 22—the Knight Initiative 13 (1999) [hereinafter The Knight Initiative Report]. *See also* the previous section regarding the historical development of the de-linking of marriage from procreation.

115. National Coalition for Gay and Lesbian Equality v. Minister of Home Affairs, Case CCT 10/99, issued December 2, 1999 (holding that the Aliens Control Act had to be changed in order to recognize same-sex couples as having essentially the same immigra-

Beginning in the 1960s, the same basic changes in marriage law took place in both the western European countries and the United States, and despite contrasts in the legal and political contexts of law reform, the national differences among Western family law systems have diminished steadily over the past few decades. Independently but at the same time, similar legal developments have taken place in countries otherwise diverse. The changes that have taken place during these years are characterized by a move toward privatization and deregulation of family law, that is, by "a progressive withdrawal of official regulation of marriage formation, dissolution, and the conduct of family life on the one hand, and by increased regulation of the economic and child-related consequences of formal or informal cohabitation on the other."[116] The changes in family law in general and in marriage law in particular stem from various social and political developments, such as the declining influence of formal religion, transformations in the economic and social roles of women, the emphasis on family members' being individuals with their own rights and freedoms, the increasing varieties of family forms and types, the growing separation between marriage and procreation, and the improved control over the reproductive process (via women's right and access to abortion and contraception). Individualistic, egalitarian, and secularizing trends have become the chief characteristics of marriage law.[117] In both the United States and the northern European countries, family law today focuses primarily on individuals, rather than on family units or households, and treats members of the family as separate and independent. Yet, to this day, family law remains marriage-centered in many aspects. In the Nordic countries, which are advanced welfare states, family law is becoming less and less regulated by private law; it consists mostly of public laws and programs that affect the family. In the United States, public law tends to be more significant for poor families, whereas traditional family law is more prominent in the middle class. Deregulation of marriage law can be regarded as an indication of the declining importance of marriage as a determinant of social standing and economic security in modern societies.[118]

---

tion rights as legal spouses), available at http://www.law.wits.ac.za/judgements/1999/natcoalsum.html.

116. Glendon, note 12 above, at 1, 2, quotation at 2. There is correlation between the extension of rights to unmarried cohabitants and the deregulation of marriage: the move toward unmarried cohabitation as a widespread and an acceptable norm (even if regulated) stems from the declining importance of marriage and may be attributed to the tendency toward deregulation of the institution, which is exemplified by, inter alia, the relaxation of the grounds for divorce.

117. *See id.* at 292.

118. *Id.* at 35, 293–95.

Thus, at the turn of the twenty-first century, marriage is viewed "as a private bilateral contract to be formed, maintained, and dissolved as the couple sees fit."[119] In most Western countries, marriage is currently understood as a legal, secular, contractual, and unitive institution open to most people on an equal basis. The features of marriage and its consequences are quite similar in most Western countries today.[120] The tendency in marriage law is to refrain from trying to articulate a common morality; instead, "it confines itself merely to defining the current outer limits of permissible diversity in family matters . . . while leaving maximum room for choice and avoiding value judgments other than those favoring individual liberty."[121] These relatively new characteristics of marriage have made same-sex marriage a viable possibility.

Modern Western marriage laws confer upon married couples unique legal rights and obligations. In the United States, for example, in addition to the several hundred rights and benefits that each state provides, there are 1,049 rights and benefits at the federal level that are contingent upon marriage.[122] Most modern Western marriage codes provide rights, benefits, and obligations similar to those provided in the United States. Michael S. Wald makes a distinction among three basic categories of legal regulation of marriage, each with rules designed to further one or more of the reasons the state has for supporting marriage.[123]

First, the state has an interest in *furthering the affective or emotional bonds associated with marriage*. Examples of regulations that recognize emotional attachments and needs are the power to make medical decisions with respect to a person's spouse in case the latter becomes incompetent to make such decisions, a spouse's priority in being appointed guardian of an incapacitated individual, and the right to take family care and medical leave from work in order to care for one's spouse and

119. Witte, note 13 above, at 195.

120. Indeed, from a social, personal, and cultural point of view, marriage has not become disassociated with religion and religious beliefs, and many people in the United States seem to think that even civil marriage cannot be separated from its religious origins. However, in both northern Europe and the United States, the rules of civil marriage, as a state-regulated legal institution, have become independent from the religious rules governing marriage. Since marriage is legally defined as a secular contractual institution that is not regulated by religion, countries like Germany, France, and the Netherlands recognize only civil marriage, and a church wedding has no legal effect; even in the Nordic countries, which have a state church and recognize both a church ceremony and a civil ceremony, the church ceremony does not alter the legal nature of the marriage as a secular civil contract.

121. Glendon, note 12 above, at 14.

122. *See* U.S. General Accounting Office, a list of the 1,049 rights afforded by marriage and denied to gay couples, available at http://www.marriageequality.com.

123. *See* Wald, The Knight Initiative Report, note 114 above, at 7.

children.[124] Also in this category are regulations and laws pertaining to hospital and prison visitation rights; all rights relating to the involuntary hospitalization of the spouse, including the right of petition, the right to be notified, and the right to initiate proceedings leading to release; the right to bring a lawsuit for the wrongful death of the spouse and for the intentional infliction of emotional distress through harm to one's spouse; and immigration rights for the noncitizen partner. Further examples for this rationale are the right to claim an evidentiary privilege for marital communications and the right not to testify against one's spouse in a court of law.[125]

Second, the state *facilitates economic sharing* so as to enable the couple to organize their lives in ways that maximize their joint well-being. Examples of regulations to encourage and reflect economic sharing are the employment of marital property principles in the laws of most U.S. states (although only nine states are "community property states" per se); the partners' obligation to provide mutual support during the marriage and, in the event of separation or divorce, alimony and an equitable division of property; the automatic qualification of married partners as dependents for purposes of medical or other forms of insurance; the priority given to the surviving spouse to inherit the couple's assets when the other spouse dies intestate; and restrictions on the ability of one spouse to disinherit the other. In case of divorce, not only are the rules intended to discourage couples from breaking up too easily; they are also designed to protect the economically weaker party.[126] Marriage entails other economic rights and benefits, such as the right to receive additional Social Security benefits based on the spouse's contribution, the right to file joint tax returns and to qualify for gift tax exemptions and deductions, and the right to marital deduction from estate tax.

Third, the state *supports parents in the raising of children.* In addition to the right to joint custody of children, one of the most important areas of parenting regulation has to do with the adoption of children by stepparents. Those rules, for married couples, virtually automatically enable the establishment of legal parenthood by the partner not biologically related to the child (provided that the noncustodial biological parent is dead, has abandoned the child, or does not object to the adoption).

---

124. *Id.*

125. In the United States this is evidenced by the right of a non-American spouse to qualify as an "immediate relative" given preferential immigration treatment (8 U.S.C. ¶ 1151[b][2][A][i]) and become an American citizen under federal law (*id.* ¶ 1430[a], [b], [d]). *See* William N. Eskridge Jr. and Nan D. Hunter, Sexuality, Gender, and the Law 793 (1997).

126. *See* Wald, The Knight Initiative Report, note 114 above, at 7–8.

"Second-parent adoption," which is the only option for establishing a legal connection in the case of unmarried couples, including same-sex couples, is a much more difficult, lengthy, and costly process than step-parent adoption, and it is not available in many U.S. jurisdictions or in most European states.[127] Moreover, in most European countries, access to artificial conception is limited to married couples (see chaps. 3 and 4 below). In addition to these three categories, there are a number of rules that regulate how third parties, businesses, and the government deal with the marital unit.[128]

The statutes and case law of most countries do not provide the above-mentioned rights, benefits, and mutual obligations to unmarried couples.[129] Some of the rights and benefits associated with marriage can be created by the partners by means of various contractual devices, wills, living testaments, joint checking accounts, the purchase of property in joint tenancy, and the like.[130] However, these methods of securing some of the benefits of marriage require more planning and money than most couples are able and prepared to invest. There are other benefits that cannot be secured privately between the parties because they depend largely on third parties and the state. Some advantages—such as spousal immunity and tort rights—are provided as a matter of law only to married couples.[131]

In addition to the aforementioned consequences and general characteristics of modern Western marriage law, the emergence of no-fault divorce, the large number of divorces and remarriages, and the increase in cohabitation with the accompanying decrease in marriage rates have also contributed to the new structure and concept of the family. These changes, too, have direct implications for the status of same-sex partnerships in Europe and the United States.

As explained in the previous section, concepts of divorce are closely connected to the concept of marriage, since there is an interplay between the exit and the entrance rules of marriage.[132] The Nordic

---

127. *Id.* at 8.

128. *See* Wald, The Knight Initiative Report, note 114 above, at 8. Eskridge classifies the goals of the legal regulation of marriage as follows: providing economic rights and benefits for the couple; enabling the partners to be with one another, physically and sexually; providing the couple with social insurance against bad times, financially and emotionally; and protecting the couple from outside interference. *See* Eskridge, Case for Same-Sex Marriage, note 28 above, at 66–70.

129. *See generally* Eskridge, Case for Same-Sex Marriage, note 28 above, at 66–70.

130. *Id.* at 68–69.

131. *See id.*

132. *See above*, discussion of Milton's divorce tracts.

countries were the first in the Western world to introduce the idea of no-fault divorce. In both law and practice, no-fault divorce was readily available in the Nordic countries from the early twentieth century. In 1915 the Swedish legislature introduced no-fault grounds for divorce—in addition to the existing fault-based grounds—including mutual consent with legal separation for one year as a basis for divorce; unilateral divorce was also obtainable with little difficulty. The Swedish example was followed by Norway in 1918 and by Denmark, Finland, and Iceland in the 1920s.[133] During the 1970s Sweden went one step further than the other Nordic countries in liberalizing its divorce grounds, based on the principles that "not only entry into marriage but also its continued existence, should be based on the free will of the spouses [and that] the wish of one of the spouses to dissolve the marriage should always be respected." The 1973 law reform in Sweden eliminated all fault grounds and made unilateral divorce an unqualified legal right; further, there was no need to provide reasons for the divorce, requirements of the old law that efforts be made to bring the spouses to a mediator were eliminated, and, in most cases, divorce became available without any waiting period.[134] The other Nordic countries have adopted similar approaches; for example, the Finnish divorce law of 1988 resembles the Swedish model. It is therefore to be concluded that "divorce, as such, is almost a dead subject in the Nordic countries." Most other European countries chose not to repeal their fault grounds and instead modernized their laws simply by adding no-fault grounds to the traditional ones.[135]

In contrast, for most of the twentieth century and in the majority of the states in the United States, divorce was based on fault. In 1969 California became the first American state to enact a divorce law from which fault grounds were completely absent and according to which unilateral termination by one spouse was possible. Many jurisdictions have followed California's lead, whereas other states simply added no-fault to their fault grounds providing for unilateral termination or required that both spouses consent to the no-fault divorce.[136] By 1985 every American state allowed divorce on no-fault grounds, in addition to or without fault grounds.[137] Thus, in most American jurisdictions, one spouse could terminate a marriage without the other's fault or consent and without

133. *See* Glendon, note 12 above, at 184–85.

134. *Id.* at 185, 186–87, quotation at 185.

135. *Id.* at 187–88, 192, quotation at 187–88.

136. *See id.* at 188–89.

137. *See* Mark Ellman, *The Place of Fault in a Modern Divorce Law,* 28 Ariz. St. L.J. 773, 782 (1996).

much delay. Nonetheless, American states are more involved in marriage termination than the Nordic countries, since in the United States a reason—the breakdown of the marriage—must be given, and the court must certify that the reason exists.[138] Furthermore, as an attempt to lower divorce rates, a few U.S. jurisdictions have recently attempted to amend their statutes and shift away from the exclusive use of no-fault divorce to a new, more binding form of marriage contract—covenant marriage—with stringent divorce requirements.[139] There is a clear correlation between relaxing the grounds for divorce and relaxing the impediments to entrance into the institution of marriage; "[t]he same liberal shift that brought [the country] no-fault divorce and high rates of marital breakups now brings gay people to the altar."[140] In other words, developments such as no-fault divorce serve to pave the way for future recognition of same-sex marriage, since both stem from the same kind of socio-legal processes, namely gender equality; I argue that the extent to which such changes have occurred serves as an indicator for the degree of equality that can be achieved by same-sex couples.

In addition to no-fault divorce, one of the most striking characteristics of the changing family in all Western countries during the past few decades is the shift away from formal unions, which is reflected in declining marriage rates and the increase in cohabitation as an alternative to marriage.[141] In this context I use *cohabitation* to refer to a de facto heterosexual marriage, that is, an intended long-term relationship in which the partners attest to the relevant social environment (relatives, community, and the like) that they regard themselves as belonging together and are accepted as such, without compliance with the procedures established by the state for formation of a legal marriage.[142]

Opposite-sex cohabitation has been and still is more widespread in

---

138. Glendon, note 12 above, at 189, 190. Note, however, that in practice, in states that allow divorce for irretrievable breakdown, courts almost never examine whether this claim is true.

139. Louisiana became the first state to make this shift, in June 1997. *See* Nicole D. Lindsey, Note, *Marriage and Divorce: Degrees of "I Do," an Analysis of the Ever-Changing Paradigm of Divorce*, 9 J.L. & Pub. Pol'y 271 (1998). It should be noted that people who choose covenant marriage can still get divorce on demand, although they must live apart for a period of time.

140. Eskridge, Gaylaw, note 113 above, at 280.

141. The shift in the past few decades toward unmarried cohabitation is relatively recent. However, unmarried cohabitation is not a modern phenomenon: according to various records, up to one-half of European adults in the sixteenth century were officially unmarried; many of them were cohabitants who believed that they, not the Church, made their companionship into a marriage. *See* Graff, note 6 above, at 199.

142. *See* Glendon, note 12 above, at 11.

the northern European countries than in the United States. The legal regulation of unmarried cohabitation in the United States is very limited, and the number of cohabiting couples is proportionately much lower than in the Nordic countries. The Scandinavian states have, and have had historically, the highest rates of cohabitation in the developed world.[143] The popularity of nonmarital cohabitation in the Nordic countries and its legal regulation also account for the more advanced status of same-sex couples in these countries: there is more acceptance of alternative family types and living arrangements, less significance is attached to the institution of marriage, and most importantly—owing to the high percentage of nonmarital opposite-sex cohabitation in the Nordic countries as compared to the United States—the lifestyle of many opposite-sex couples in those countries is much closer to that of same-sex couples. The difference in percentages between the regions and the differences in the degree of legal regulation and social acceptance of nonmarital cohabitation also account for the higher degree of social acceptance of gay couples in these states and the more comprehensive legal recognition of their partnerships.

As late as the 1960s, informal cohabitation was not considered a legal subject, and couples who had not entered into formal marriage were ignored by the law and were regarded as legal strangers to each other, with no claims at all rising from their relationship; it was only in the 1970s, and most extensively in the Nordic countries, that explicit law dealing with the relationships among de facto family members developed and various countries began using a variety of techniques to regulate some aspects of cohabitation.[144]

Sweden was the first country to legally regulate the status of opposite-sex cohabitants. Compared with other countries in the Western world, it is still the one in which informal marriages are the most widespread and the most socially accepted and legally approved. The legal reaction to the spreading phenomenon of cohabitation in Sweden has been to increase the legal effects of cohabitation and to eliminate many of the features that distinguished legal marriage from cohabitation.[145] This has been a consequence of the unique Swedish ideology not to favor the institution of marriage in any way as compared with other forms of cohabitation. In 1969 the Swedish minister of justice advised that future

143. Graff, note 6 above, at 99. About 20% of all couples in Sweden at the end of the 1980s were unmarried cohabitants. *See* Glendon, note 12 above, at 273.

144. *See* David Bradley, *The Development of a Legal Status for Unmarried Cohabitation in Sweden,* 18 Anglo-American L. Rev. 322 (1989); Glendon, note 12 above, at 252–53.

145. *See* Glendon, note 12 above, at 274.

family law legislation should be drafted so as not to impose "unnecessary hardship or inconveniences on those who have children and build families without marrying"[146] and that the law should not "give a privileged status to one form of cohabitation over another [and] as far as possible be *neutral as regards different forms of cohabitation and different moral ideas.*"[147] Consequently, most differences between marriage and cohabitation were removed in the 1973 Swedish law reform, and further elimination occurred with the enactment of the Cohabitees (Joint Homes) Act of 1987. That act provides that, unless otherwise contracted by the parties, upon separation of a couple that has lived in a "marriage-like" relationship, their dwelling and household goods, if acquired for their joint use, shall be divided equally with the court's discretion to accord to the partner with the greater need the right to *occupy* the home, regardless of title. These features are similar to the property division rules of married couples.[148]

Nonmarital cohabitation has become more popular during the past few decades in the United States as well, but the practice is far less common and less encouraged than in the Nordic countries, and its legal regulation is minimal. The United States has eliminated only a few of the differences between marriage and other forms of cohabitation and still holds marriage to be the predominant legal institution for couples sharing their lives. Other forms of cohabitation are somewhat discouraged and largely not recognized or regulated by law. Case law in state courts accords cohabitants a few of the rights associated with marriage, mainly in the field of property division upon the separation of opposite-sex couples.[149] Some localities have enacted domestic partnership ordinances according cohabiting couples some work-related benefits equivalent to those of married couples.[150] Although cohabiting unmarried couples are

146. *Id.,* quoting from Jacob Sundberg, *Recent Changes in Swedish Family Law: Experiment Repeated,* 23 Am. J. Comp. L. 34, 48 (1975).

147. Glendon, note 12 above, at 274, quoting from Note, *Family Law—Sweden,* 22 Int'l & Comp. L.Q. 182 (1973), my emphasis; and Note, *Current Legal Developments, Sweden,* 19 Int'l & Comp. L.Q. 164 (1970).

148. *See* Glendon, note 12 above, at 275–77. Sweden has also been the first country to statutorily regulate the status of same-sex couples: in 1987 it extended the application of the Cohabitees (Joint Homes) Act to homosexual cohabiting couples. For further discussion of these acts and their application to same-sex couples, see chap. 3 of this volume, sec. 3.3.2.

149. *E.g.,* Marvin v. Marvin, 557 P.2d 106 (Cal. 1976) (holding that a couple's agreement could be implied from their conduct during the period they lived together). The case was not followed by many other jurisdictions. For discussion of the case, its implications, and other decisions pertaining to nonmarital cohabitation see chap. 7 below.

150. For a detailed discussion of the regulation of cohabitation in the United States and a thorough analysis of domestic partner ordinances and policies, see chap. 7, secs. 7.2, 7.4.

closer to married couples than they once were in the eyes of the law, the American solution for nonmarital cohabitation is very limited and is far from satisfactory, as most of the rights associated with marriage are not attainable by cohabitants (see chap. 7, sec. 7.2). Moreover, state laws prohibiting discrimination on the basis of marital status have proved not to place cohabiting couples in a better position, closer to that of married couples.

The way in which a particular legal system approaches the various issues generated by informal family behavior—that is, the legal status of cohabitants—is closely related to the place of legal marriage within that system.[151] Sweden's unique concept and regulation of informal cohabitation are unlike those of the other Nordic and West European countries and the United States. In Western countries other than Sweden, there is no such comprehensive regulation of nonmarital cohabitation, and there is clear legislative and judicial intent to preserve, "protect," and promote marriage as the superior and the predominant form of cohabitation. However, since cohabitants must prove that their situation is similar to that of a married couple in order to obtain the consequences that follow automatically from legal marriage, which is often an expensive and difficult process, it seems that to different degrees in both the United States and northern Europe—including Sweden—marriage retains its privileged status. Married couples in all these countries are in a better position as far as property division is concerned, and economic rights derived from marriage continue to play an important role. Thus, although cohabitation has increasing legal effects, a distinction between marriage and cohabitation is maintained everywhere, with marriage being accorded a central position in family law.[152]

2.3 Equality in Marriage: Race, Sex, and Sexual Orientation

The increasing freedom to exit marriage and the increasing withdrawal of state regulation of marriage discussed in the previous section are connected to the increasing freedom to enter the institution of marriage; these trends react upon and reinforce each other. The common themes in family law development in both the United States and the northern European countries during the twentieth century have been the progressive liberation of individuals from constraints on their freedom to marry and women's participation in marriage on equal terms. What is unique to the developments of the past few decades in marriage law, compared

151. *See* Glendon, note 12 above, at 284.
152. *Id.* at 287–90.

to prior changes in the institution during the course of history, is the rapidity with which the roles of the sexes have been changing. The implementation of equal rights for women, I would surmise, being *the* most important recent transformation in family law, has been the catalyst for the movement toward same-sex marriage.

It should be noted in this connection that family behavior in fact, in most Western societies, never corresponds to the set of official judicial and legislative norms. Social behavior is usually one step ahead of the courts and the legislatures in the field of family law. There is a changing relationship between the set of laws affecting families "and the patterns of behavior that constitute the social institution of the family."[153] Thus, the family law reforms that began in the 1960s—including, inter alia, a move toward equality in marriage for women and racial minorities—largely reflected social phenomena that were already in progress. The same is to be expected in regard to equality in marriage for same-sex couples, who already operate as family units in many parts of the Western world.

In the 1960s, courts at the highest levels in both Europe and the United States, dealing with the few remaining restrictions on an individual's freedom to marry or to choose a spouse, began to articulate the issues as involving a basic right, and the "freedom to marry" came to be legally recognized as a basic human right.[154] Recognition in the United States of the freedom to marry came in 1967 in the case of *Loving v. Virginia,* in which the Supreme Court struck down antimiscegenation laws, thus holding unconstitutional a color bar as a condition of marriage. The Court stated that "the freedom to marry has long been recognized as one of the vital personal rights essential to the orderly pursuit of happiness by free men."[155] Presently, in the United States and northern Europe, the only restrictions that are framed as absolute prohibitions are those based on kinship (marriage between close relatives, i.e., incest) or currently existing marriage (simultaneous marriages, i.e., bigamy and polygamy) and marriage of same-sex couples (because of implicit or explicit statutory definitions of marriage as the legal union of a man and a woman). Until recently, same-sex marriage was not even conceptualized as the subject of a marriage prohibition: same-sex relationships were regarded as outside the scope of marriage altogether.[156] Thus, constraints

153. *Id.* at 5. There is thus a difference between what a particular legal system may classify as families or marriages and the conduct that an anthropologist or sociologist is likely to describe as family or marriage behavior. *Id.*

154. *Id.* at 35, 76.

155. Loving v. Virginia, 388 U.S. 1, 12 (1967).

156. *See* Glendon, note 12 above, at 49. At the time Glendon's book was written, 1989, same-sex marriage was indeed outside the scope of marriage in most Western countries

on who may marry and on who may marry whom have gradually been relaxed,[157] especially in the case of restrictions based on race, and state involvement in these questions has been generally diminishing, opening up the institution of marriage to more and more people and emphasizing the individual's basic right to marry. To date, however, and except for the Netherlands, such relaxation has not included same-sex couples.

The current debate over same-sex couples' inclusion in or exclusion from the institution of marriage is thus part of a larger movement, a movement that began in the 1960s in the direction of reducing impediments and formalities regarding marriage, making the entry into the institution easier and opening it up to more people.[158] These changes were the consequence of the antiracist and antisexist movements. African Americans in the United States were excluded from full participation in marriage; and for centuries, in both Europe and the United States, women had been excluded from participating in marriage on equal terms.[159] Until the 1960s, nearly every legislative attempt to regulate the family decision-making process gave the husband and father the dominant role. Beginning in the 1970s, not only the Nordic countries, France, Germany, and the Netherlands but also Italy, Portugal, and Spain—countries in which the political influence of Roman Catholicism has been strong—all revised their civil code provisions on marriage in light of the principle of gender equality.[160] Similar developments took place during the same period in the United States. What is significant is not only the achievement of equality in marriage between the sexes per se but also the fact that "the law has abandoned its former express or implicit stereotyping of sex roles within marriage and has moved toward a new model in which there is no fixed pattern of role distribution."[161]

---

and was not even regarded as a marriage prohibition. However, during the last decade it has definitely become a marriage prohibition: the possibility of opening up marriage to same-sex couples and subsequent legislation in the United States to prohibit such unions are evidence of the move from viewing same-sex marriage as outside the scope of marriage to viewing it as a marriage prohibition. Nonetheless, opponents of same-sex marriage still argue that it is by definition excluded from the scope of marriage altogether.

157. This process began with the repeal, at the turn of the twentieth century, of statutes prohibiting the marriage of persons with health-related problems, such as epilepsy, tuberculosis, and alcoholism. Individuals were thus gradually freed from most constraints on their ability to marry or on their choice of marriage partner. *See id.* at 35–36.

158. *Id.* at 83.

159. For a brief historical overview of the subordination of women in marriage throughout the ages, see sec. 2.1 of this chapter.

160. *See* Glendon, note 12 above, at 3.

161. *Id.* at 102. One example of the move toward equality between the sexes in marriage is the regulation of marital property more equally between the sexes, either through comanagement of community property in the United States or the deferred community property regime in the Nordic countries. According to the latter system, so long as the

In *Identity and the Case for Gay Rights,* David Richards analogizes between race, gender, and sexual orientation.[162] He provides an account of the similarities in the struggles of the three groups—racial minorities, women, and homosexuals—for equality. This account is applicable to the fight for equality in the specific context of marriage. Thus, a careful examination of the roots of discrimination against blacks and women reveals some of the rationales for the current exclusion of same-sex couples from marriage. Likewise, the advances made by these groups toward equality in marriage serve as an indicator for the feasibility of similar progress toward equality for same-sex couples. Not only are the civil rights movement and the women's liberation movement analogous to the gay rights movement in that race, sex, and sexual orientation are comparable bases of discrimination, but also the movements have been influenced by one another. The civil rights and women's liberation movements have paved the way for the possibility of opening up marriage to same-sex couples. In other words, without the shift in social conceptions regarding race and gender and the consequent legal reforms that were brought about by the struggles of racial minorities and women for equality, even discussing same-sex marriage today would not be possible. The achievement of equality in marriage by women and racial minorities has thus opened the door for same-sex marriage: "Once the theory of white supremacy had been toppled, interracial marriage could no longer be barred. In just the same way, once the theory of male supremacy and female inferiority was dismantled—the theory that man must rule and woman must serve—there is no longer any justification for barring marriage between two women or two men."[163] Therefore, gender equality serves as an indicator of the degree of equality that may be achieved by gays and lesbians in any given country; where a higher degree of such equality has been achieved, there is much more probability of broad recognition of same-sex partnerships, including same-sex marriage. In this respect we should draw a distinction between the two regions: since sexist views and sex stereotyping are less prevalent in the northern European countries as compared to the United States, and as evidenced by the Dutch act making marriage available to same-sex couples, the probability of same-sex marriage in those countries is much higher than in the United States, and it is to be expected that the Nordic

---

marriage lasts, each spouse independently manages all the assets he or she brings in, but when the marriage comes to an end, the funds that remain are shared equally as if there had been a community scheme all along. *Id.* at 118.

162. Note 114 above. For discussion of these analogies, see also Richards, Women, Gays, and the Constitution, note 114 above.

163. Graff, note 6 above, at 223.

states will follow the Netherlands' lead much sooner than any state within the United States.

The American movement for gay rights emerged in the wake of the successes of the antiracist and antisexist civil rights movements.[164] Despite extensive recent immigration to various European countries (e.g., immigration from foreign colonies to France and the Netherlands and the acceptance of a large number of refugees from outside Europe by Denmark and Sweden), the European countries addressed in this book are still more homogeneous than the United States and do not have a history of racial segregation and discrimination in marriage. Nonetheless, I regard the analogy to race as also valuable and instructive in the European countries.[165] In both regions there has been an interplay between the feminist movement and the gay rights movement. Since these two movements have sometimes led to different consequences in Europe and in the United States, the analogy between them is extremely helpful to an understanding of the developments that have led to the different status of same-sex couples in the United States and Europe.

According to Richards, what the evils of sexism, racism, and homophobia have in common is that all three are forms of "moral slavery," since racial minorities, women, and gays have all been excluded from unjust hierarchical structures of power: "Homophobic prejudice, like racism and sexism, unjustly distorts the idea of human rights applicable to both public and private life. Like the other main forms of moral slavery (racism and sexism), such prejudice, remitting homosexuals to a degraded private sphere, injures their basic human rights to both a public and private life."[166] Both Sylvia Law and Andrew Koppelman have argued that homophobia historically depended upon and contributed to sexism, including the maintenance of the sex hierarchy in which men dominate women.[167] Similarly, Richards contends that homophobia reflects a tradition of moral slavery similar to the tradition of sexism: "[T]he root of homophobia is, like sexism, a rigid conception of gender roles and spheres, only here focusing specifically on gender roles in

---

164. *See* Richards, Women, Gays, and the Constitution, note 114 above, at 288–89.

165. For an extensive discussion and analysis of the analogy between race and homophobia, see Richards, Identity and the Case for Gay Rights, note 114 above, at 6–38; for a discussion of the analogy between race and gender, see id., at 41–64. For the application of the analogy between racial segregation and the exclusion of same-sex couples from marriage, see chap. 10 below.

166. Richards, Women, Gays, and the Constitution, note 114 above, at 367.

167. *See* Andrew Koppelman, *Why Discrimination against Lesbians and Gay Men Is Sex Discrimination,* 69 N.Y.U. L. Rev. 197, 255–57 (1994); Sylvia A. Law, *Homosexuality and the Social Meaning of Gender,* 1988 Wis. L. Rev. 187; *see also* Suzanne Pharr, Homophobia: A Weapon of Sexism (1988); Eskridge, Gaylaw, note 113 above, at 221.

intimate sexual and emotional life." Using the racial analogy, Richards maintains that a culture of pervasive degradation of homosexuals legitimates "the uncritically irrationalist outrage at the very idea of gay and lesbian marriage, which unjustly constructs the inhumanity of homosexual identity on the basis of exactly the same kind of vicious circle of cultural degradation unjustly imposed on African Americans through antimiscegenation laws."[168]

The rights-based identity-focused struggle for gay and lesbian persons should be viewed as part of the larger rights-based feminist struggle.[169] In light of women's subordination and male supremacy, Adrienne Rich, a rights-based feminist, argues that much of the sectarian orthodoxy of gender roles rests on what she terms "compulsory heterosexuality"—the idea that sexuality must consist of a man having sex with a woman— which is viewed as the exclusive normative model for moral relationships. She further argues that the enforcement of a sectarian theory of normative gender roles is illegitimate.[170] As Richards asserts, being gay or lesbian is a way of life that is critical of mandatory gender roles and compulsory heterosexuality. Thus, the mere existence of gays and lesbians challenges and calls for a reevaluation of traditional conceptions of gender roles and gender hierarchy: "Such relationships embody a normative model for intimate life that apparently more fully develops features of egalitarian sharing in intimate life that are more often the theory than the practice of heterosexual relationships." Because homosexuals violate traditional gender roles, they are viewed as unworthy of being accorded respect for their basic human right to intimate life, which includes the fundamental right to marriage,[171] a right that thus far has not been extended by any court or legislature, except for the Dutch legislature, to apply to same-sex couples. As to the connection between compulsory heterosexuality and compulsory gender binarism, Eskridge notes that "[e]mpirical studies have found correlations between antigay feelings and 'a belief in the traditional family ideology, i.e., dominant father, submissive mother, and obedient children,' as well as 'traditional beliefs about women.' A few studies claim a causal link: 'a major determinant of negative attitudes toward homosexuality is the need to keep

168. Richards, Women, Gays, and the Constitution, note 114 above, at 346, 348.

169. *Id.* at 229, 308.

170. Adrienne Rich, *Compulsory Heterosexuality and Lesbian Existence, reprinted in* The Lesbian and Gay Studies Reader 227 (Henry Abelove et al. eds., 1993); *see also* Richards, Women, Gays, and the Constitution, note 114 above, at 344–46.

171. Richards, Women, Gays, and the Constitution, note 114 above, at 246–47, 440–41, quotation at 345. *See also* Richards, Identity and the Case for Gay Rights, note 114 above, at 155–56.

males masculine and females feminine, that is, to avoid sex-role confusion.'"[172] Compulsory heterosexuality is the main ground for the discrimination against gay men and lesbians and thus against same-sex couples. Building on Richards's account of women's inequality, it seems that full recognition of homosexuals' human right to intimate life will not be possible as long as mandatory gender roles are the measure of such rights.[173] Homosexuals are the scapegoats for the backlash against feminism because "they, unlike women, remain a largely marginalized and despised minority."[174] Here, too, we should emphasize the differences between northern Europe and the United States: the facts that concepts of gender roles are less rigid and that "compulsory heterosexuality" is less prevalent in the former than in the latter. These differences have led to different solutions for the discrimination against same-sex couples in the two regions.

Thus, I suggest that the degree of equality achieved by other historically disadvantaged groups, especially women, serves as a measure of the degree of equality that can be gained by gay men and lesbians, in particular the possibility of gays' gaining access to the institution of marriage. Compared to women in the United States, women in northern Europe enjoy substantial benefits (state-sponsored child-care services, generous family-leave policies, legal guarantees protecting participation in the labor market and treatment on the job) and a higher degree of equality.[175] Gender equality in Scandinavia is largely due to the extensive welfare system and the social democratic ideology, in which equality is the major policy goal.[176] The higher degree of gender equality in the northern European countries is also due to the fact that these are centralized states with strong labor movements, whereas the United States is decentralized and fragmented and has a weak labor movement.[177]

172. Eskridge, Gaylaw, note 113 above, at 224.

173. *See* Richards, Identity and the Case for Gay Rights, note 114 above, at 158.

174. *Id.* at 165.

175. *See* Christine Ingebristen, The Nordic States and European Unity 56 (1998).

176. *See* Sophie Watson, *Unpacking "the State": Reflections on Australian, British, and Scandinavian Feminist Interventions, in* Going Public: National Histories of Women's Enfranchisement and Women's Participation within State Institutions 111, 131, 134 (Mary F. Katzenstein & Hege Skjeie eds., 1990). This is not to say that gender inequalities do not exist within the Scandinavian states; the powerful corporate organizations are still dominated by men, and corporate decision making takes place with little input from women. *Id.* at 131. *See also* H. Hernes, Welfare State and Women Power 151 (1987).

177. *See* Mary Fainsod Katzenstein, *Comparing the Feminist Movements of the United States and Western Europe: An Overview, in* The Women's Movements of the United States and Western Europe: Consciousness, Political Opportunity, and Public Policy 3, 6–7 (Mary Fainsod Katzenstein & Carol McClurg Mueller eds., 1987). Katzenstein makes the interesting observation that in the Scandinavian countries, where the state has an explicit commitment to gender equality, policy success is won at the price of feminist organiza-

Sweden in particular is unparalleled in its advances toward gender equality.[178] Thus, in terms of formal equality, the status of women in the Nordic states and the Netherlands is more advanced than anywhere else in the world in both the private and the public spheres. That is to say, in those areas there is greater equality in family matters (marriage and divorce, provision of child care, division of labor in the household, maternity/parental leave, and reproductive rights) and in women's economic participation, political representation, and representation in the professorate.[179]

Equality between men and women seems to have become much more a reality in the northern European countries than in the United States. The gap between the formal equal status of women and their status in fact is wider in the United States than in the northern European countries. The regime of spousal support obligations following divorce in the Nordic states further demonstrates how these countries, more than the United States, have internalized the concept of full equality between

---

tional weakness, whereas debate and consciousness-raising in the United States are sometimes pursued at the expense of policy success. *Id.* at 16.

178. Equality has in fact been achieved in both private and public spheres in Sweden. *See* David Bradley, *Sexual Equality and Maintenance Allowances in Sweden,* 9 Oxford J. Legal Stud. 403 (1989); David Bradley, *Perspectives on Sexual Equality in Sweden,* 53 Mod. L. Rev. 283 (1990); Birgitta Silén, *Women and Power,* 76 Scandinavian Rev. 91–101 (1987–88). Moreover, unlike the United States, Sweden provides generous, paid, gender-neutral parental leave. *See* Linda Haas, *Nurturing Fathers and Working Mothers: Changing Gender Roles in Sweden, in* Men, Work & Family 258 (Jane C. Hood ed., 1993); Nancy E. Dowd, *Maternity Leave: Taking Sex Differences into Account,* 54 Fordham L. Rev. 699 (1986). It is interesting to note, however, that despite the fact that the Swedish government has evinced a higher level of commitment to gender equality than have most states in western Europe or North America, the feminist movement in Sweden is considerably less of a presence than in the United States, where state policy lags way behind. *See* Mary Fainsod Katzenstein, *Comparing the Feminist Movements of the United States and Western Europe: An Overview, in* Katzenstein and Mueller, note 177 above, at 3, 5.

179. Thus, for example, whereas the five Nordic states and the Netherlands rank at the top of the list of "Women in National Parliaments" worldwide (having the highest percentage of women in parliament in the world, ranging between 43% in Sweden [first place] and 35% in Iceland [sixth place]), the United States ranks fiftieth, because its House of Representatives has only 13% women and its Senate has only 9%, which is also below the world average of 14%. *See* The Inter-Parliamentary Union: Women in Parliaments: World and Regional Averages, at http://www.ipu.org/wmn-e/world.htm; and Women in Parliaments: World Classification at http://www.ipu.org/wmn-e/classif.htm (both last updated on May 25, 2000). On the representation of women in politics, see also Women in Nordic Politics: Closing the Gap (Lauri Karvonen & Per Selle eds., 1995). Moreover, the Nordic states have the highest level of female participation in the labor force in the world. *See* Ingebristen, note 175 above, at 56. The equal status of women in the Nordic states is protected and provided for by national legislation: Denmark has several laws on equal opportunities, and Finland, Iceland, Norway, and Sweden also have legislation mandating equality between women and men in various fields (*see, e.g.,* Sweden's Equal Opportunities Act of 1992). *See* Nordic Council of Ministers, Women and Men in the Nordic Countries: Facts and Figures 17 (1994).

the spouses: postdivorce spousal support in these countries is legally available only in exceptional cases and is rare in practice. This is due to women's economic equality with men and their self-sufficiency, which stems from the fact that most women in the Nordic states work outside the home and earn as much as men do, as well as the fact that the Nordic states, as welfare states, absorb much of the cost of divorce through programs of public benefits for one-parent families. Therefore, there is less need for spousal support in the Nordic countries.

In the United States, despite recent statutes that treat spousal support as a temporary and exceptional consequence of divorce, the courts in a majority of jurisdictions have broad powers to award spousal support as they deem equitable under the circumstances. The need to award such support is an indication of the degree to which women's economic status is inferior. As compared to the Nordic countries, fewer women in the United States work outside the home, and those who do generally earn less than men do. Thus, there is greater economic equality between the spouses in the Nordic countries than in the United States. Furthermore, although the American states endorse a Nordic degree of commitment to spousal independence and self-sufficiency, they do so only at the theoretical level; they fail to establish the conditions necessary to realize this ideal in practice, since unlike the Nordic states, the United States does not provide general public benefits and services for one-parent families.[180] This, among other things, accounts for the fuller equality in fact provided to women in fields other than family law in the Nordic countries as compared to the United States.

There seems to be a correlation between the degree of both formal and substantive equality of women in the northern European countries and the United States on the one hand and the status of same-sex couples in these countries on the other. As Eskridge maintains, the acceptance of equal rights for women contributed to equality of homosexuals as well, and cities and states with populations favoring equality for women have not been only more likely to decriminalize same-sex intimacy but have also been much more likely to adopt laws prohibiting sexual-orientation discrimination.[181]

The attitude toward sexuality in general and the concept of gender roles in particular are somewhat different in northern Europe than in the United States. In both regions there has been an increase in official tolerance of nonmarital sexual relations exemplified by the decriminal-

180. *See* Glendon, note 12 above, at 224, 229, 236–37, 249.
181. *See* Eskridge, Gaylaw, note 113 above, at 226, referring to James W. Button et al., Private Lives, Public Conflicts: Battles over Gay Rights in American Communities 76–86 (1997).

ization of adultery and the ongoing movement toward the elimination of adultery as a separate ground for divorce (although some U.S. states still preserve adultery as a fault ground for divorce) or as the basis for legal action against a third party who disturbs the marital relationship.[182] However, there is more tolerance of nonmarital sexual relations, as well as more tolerance of diverse sexual practices in general, in the northern European countries than in the United States. Whereas "Americans have strong feelings and beliefs about sexual morality," and the United States "is still a sex-ambivalent society, alternately fascinated and repelled by sexuality," with "public suppression of the lesbian or gay person's sexuality,"[183] the Nordic countries show a more free and open attitude toward homosexuality and sexuality in general and a more liberal and less rigid concept of gender roles in both social and cultural life. As exemplified in the history of its statutory regulation of sexuality, northern Europe scrutinizes to a lesser extent the morality of sex outside marriage.[184] Even where same-sex couples are tolerated in middle-class small-town America, they are expected not to flaunt their sexuality. The "double standard" regarding sex and gender in the United States stands in the way of sexual minorities' and women's demands for formal equality.[185] The northern European countries show more openness toward alternative sexual expressions and a distinct move toward the degendering of marriage. For these reasons, and as shown by the Dutch recognition of same-sex marriage, the attitude toward and the legal recognition of same-sex partnerships is more advanced in the northern European countries than in the United States.[186]

In the United States, compulsory heterosexuality stems from the double standard according to which "the same sexual conduct that is socially permissible and legally protected for different-sex couples is socially questionable and sometimes legally prohibited for same-sex couples."[187] No such double standard exists in the northern European countries, where there is also much less covert and overt discrimination

182. *See* Glendon, note 12 above, at 286.

183. Eskridge, Case for Same-Sex Marriage, note 28 above, at 183–84, 186.

184. For example, adultery was decriminalized in Sweden as early as 1937. *See* Glendon, note 12 above, at 274. Moreover, whereas thirteen states still criminalize sodomy in the United States, no northern European country does so.

185. Eskridge, Case for Same-Sex Marriage, note 28 above, at 184, 188–89.

186. *See* chap. 7, sec. 7.3, for a discussion of the status of same-sex couples in the European countries as compared to their status in the United States.

187. Eskridge, Case for Same-Sex Marriage, note 28 above, at 186. The majority in Bowers v. Hardwick, 478 U.S. 186 (1986) apparently would have regarded opposite-sex sodomy as constitutionally protected; this further supports the argument that a double standard exists in the United States.

against homosexuals (see chap. 11 below). Thus, compulsory heterosexuality in those countries is no longer an accepted model, and the northern Europeans' treatment of same-sex partnerships is evidence of that.

Every "marriage war"—for instance, the fight of women and racial minorities for equality in marriage—and any fundamental change in the concept of the family or the status of its members throughout history has encountered more or less the same kind of opposition, stemming from the same kind of fears. In that respect, the current fight for same-sex marriage is no different. Furthermore, the arguments for barring outsiders from marriage have remained similar regardless of which group of outsiders was being targeted. Thus, for example, proponents of antimiscegenation laws argued that mixed-race marriage and sexual relations between the races were bestial and disgraceful.[188] Similarly, by the end of the nineteenth century, when women struggled to own property, or when twentieth-century feminists fought to legalize birth control and abortion, conservatives reacted with the same fears and predicted that changing the law so that women would become equal and contraception and abortion legal would lead to incest, polygamy, adultery, and violation of the institution of marriage and would threaten children, the family, and society at large. Similar language has been used by conservatives against any proposed change in the marriage rules, whether granting married women the right to own property, legalizing contraception, or allowing interracial marriage.[189] The current opposition to same-sex marriage draws on the same arguments, and it is important to note that such outcries are always a backlash against social and economic changes that have already taken place, the dire predictions have always proved to be wrong, and the objections have always been defeated.[190]

2.4 Marriage for Same-Sex Couples and Alternative Models for the Recognition of Same-Sex Partnerships

2.4.1 Is There a History of Same-Sex Marriage?
Now that the inequalities *within* the institution of marriage have been addressed and largely resolved, human-rights advocates have begun to address inequalities between marriage and other forms of cohabitation. In previous sections I discuss these inequalities and the analogies and similarities in the status of women, racial minorities, and gays as three disadvantaged groups that have been discriminated against in the field

188. *See* Graff, note 6 above, at 157.
189. *Id.* at 86–87, 220–22, 239.
190. *See id.* at 87.

of marriage law. The subject of this section is the unique characteristics of the struggle of gays to be accorded the right to marriage.[191]

Unlike women, who suffered inequality in marriage, African Americans were completely banned from marriage under American slavery.[192] Later, antimiscegenation laws in the United States perpetuated discrimination by limiting interracial couples' marriage choices. Despite the ethnic dehumanization and extreme discriminatory impact of antimiscegenation laws, however, African Americans were no longer excluded from marriage per se; in many cases, they could marry the object of their love. Thus, in the twentieth century, racial minorities (as well as women) fought for participation in marriage on equal terms, but unlike same-sex couples, they were not fully excluded from the institution. In contrast, the unions of homosexuals have not yet been socially acknowledged in most Western countries, let alone legally recognized.

It is not only that the unions of same-sex couples have never been recognized as marriage; such unions, which have always existed, have never fitted within *any* definition of marriage. Contrary to other historical interpretive accounts, I maintain that throughout history, same-sex unions have never been characterized as (opposite-sex) marriage or viewed by society as akin to marital relationships. Furthermore, the insistence that there is a history of same-sex marriage does not strengthen the argument for same-sex marriage in the context of the current debate.

191. It should be noted that although my main concern here is with the opening of marriage to same-sex couples, same-sex marriage should not necessarily be viewed as an end in itself but also as part of a larger social change in the conceptions of sexuality and gender; it could be regarded as only an interim step in the struggle of gays for equality, a struggle that is connected to a much broader change in the long run of social views in general: the "normalization" of homosexuality, changes regarding sexual autonomy, and changes in gender expectations. On these matters, see Nancy J. Knauer, *Domestic Partnership and Same-Sex Relationships: A Marketplace Innovation and a Less Than Perfect Institutional Choice*, 7 Temple Pol. & Civ. Rts. L. Rev. 337 (1998); Urvashi Vaid, Virtual Equality 174–306 (1995).

192. In this respect, it should be noted that although the unions of other slaves, such as those in Rome and Greece, were also not recognized by law as marriage, their exclusion from marriage is not comparable to that of African American slaves in the United States. The exclusion of the latter was based on cultural racism—the view of blacks as ethnically inferior and subhuman, whereas the exclusion of the former was not coded in terms of ethnic dehumanization; slaves in the ancient world were not viewed as ethnically inferior. On these points see generally Classical Slavery (M. I. Finley ed., 1987); and M. I. Finley, Ancient Slavery and Modern Ideology (1983). Thus, the exclusion of slaves from marriage becomes relevant to our discussion only when it is associated, as it is in the modern period, with enforcing patterns of ethnic dehumanization on the basis of the racialized pedestal. Only then does such exclusion become comparable to that of same-sex couples, since they too are considered second-class citizens, and their exclusion from marriage is based on comparable grounds—homophobia and sexism. *See* Richards, Women, Gays, and the Constitution, note 114 above, at 244–49; Richards, Identity and the Case for Gay Rights, note 114 above, at 75–78.

Eskridge provides a thorough overview of what he terms the "history of same-sex marriage."[193] It is not coincidental that historian John Boswell called same-sex relationships in premodern Europe "same-sex unions," rather than marriages.[194] Both scholars point out various similarities between the relationships of same-sex couples throughout history and the relationships of heterosexual married couples. Eskridge, however, insists on equating the two, stating that "same-sex marriages are a commonplace in human history." He claims that various relationships of same-sex couples in premodern Western and non-Western cultures were "the same as different-sex marriages."[195] Thus, for instance, Eskridge argues that the Achilles-Patroclus and other homosexual relationships depicted in Plato's *Symposium* and in the *Phaedrus*—which are assumed to have reflected same-sex relationships as they existed in some of the Greek city-states—were "the functional equivalents of legalized marriage" of that era[196] and were "treated . . . similarly to marriages involving different-sex partners."[197] As noted in the first section of this chapter, the homosexual relationships in Plato's works were separate and different in nature from the concept of marriage at the time, which was viewed as procreative, nonaffectionate, distinct from love, and characterized by the husband's freedom to engage in extramarital sexual affairs.[198] Are we to conclude, as Eskridge suggests, that because a tomb of a pharaoh (Akhenaton) contains a somewhat intimate portrayal of the pharaoh and his male consort, same-sex unions were accepted in ancient Egypt as "functionally similar to marriages"? I find it difficult to comprehend how the fact that some women were able to legally marry other women by passing as men supports a "history of same-sex marriage" or the argument for social, legal, or other recognition of same-sex marriage.[199] The same-sex relationships mentioned in Eskridge's account that seem to have been in fact the closest to what was socially and legally regarded as marriage were those with *berdaches*—persons who took on the gender role of the opposite sex—especially among Native Americans.[200]

193. Eskridge, *History of Same-Sex Marriage,* note 31 above; *see also* Eskridge, Case for Same-Sex Marriage, note 28 above, at 15–50.

194. *See* Boswell, note 1 above.

195. Eskridge, Case for Same-Sex Marriage, note 28 above, at 16, 17.

196. Eskridge, *History of Same-Sex Marriage,* note 31 above, at 1442–44.

197. Eskridge, Case for Same-Sex Marriage, note 28 above, at 18.

198. *See* discussion above of David M. Halperin's interpretation of Greek same-sex relationships as compared to marriage.

199. Eskridge, Case for Same-Sex Marriage, note 28 above, at 18–19, 38–39, quotation at 18–19.

200. For an overview of these relationships, see id. at 27–30.

However, except for berdache marriages and a few other isolated instances in which same-sex unions were recognized as marriage, the predominant attitude toward same-sex intimacy throughout the ages has been characterized by hostility rather than recognition and acceptance, to say nothing of recognition as marriage, and most same-sex relationships have in fact been distinct from any concept of marriage.

Marriage in the ancient world was legally regulated only as far as property was concerned; it was the family's and the community's recognition of the union that made it a reality, not the law.[201] Thus, when assessing whether there is a "history of same-sex marriage," the issue to be addressed is whether same-sex unions were *recognized as marriage by society*. Their mere existence or the degree of their "functional equivalency" to marriage does not support or attest to their characterization as marriage. Moreover, since marriage became the subject of legal state regulation and came to be defined as *whatever the law regarded as marriage*, there definitely has not been recognition of same-sex partnerships as marriage.

Despite evidence of loving homosexual relationships throughout history, there is no proof that same-sex relationships were equivalent to (opposite-sex) marriage nor that they were regarded by society, law, or religion as such. There is a distinction that Eskridge fails to make between *tolerating* same-sex partnerships, as was the case in ancient Greece, and affirmatively recognizing these unions socially or legally as marriages, for which no clear evidence exists. Eskridge's suggestion that same-sex marriage existed at certain periods in various places serves as the basis for his assertion that same-sex marriage is not a new phenomenon and that therefore it should not be viewed as "unnatural" or against "tradition." Eskridge relies on his historical interpretation to argue that marriage should not necessarily be conceptualized and defined as traditionally limited to a union of a man and a woman. However, this account is factually wrong, since marriage has been historically limited to opposite-sex couples and is indeed by definition a union of one man and one woman. In this respect, U.S. courts faced with the issue of same-sex marriage were correct in stating, as their starting point, that the definition of marriage is and has traditionally been a union between a man and a woman.[202] They were not correct, however, as is explained in chapter 7, section 7.6, in finding that the exclusion of same-sex

201. Boswell, note 1 above, at 46.
202. *See, e.g.,* Singer v. Hara, 522 P.2d 1187 (Wash. Ct. App. 1974), review denied, 84 Wn.2d 1008 (1974); Baker v. Nelson, 191 N.W.2d 185 (Minn. 1971), appeal dismissed 409 U.S. 810 (1972); Jones v. Hallahan, 501 S.W.2d 58 (1973).

couples from marriage was constitutional based solely on the definitional argument.

Thus, the opening up of the institution of marriage to same-sex couples is an innovation: it is a new concept of marriage that does not rest
on tradition and does not find its roots in history. The historical distinction between homosexual relationships and marriage does not weaken
the argument for same-sex marriage, however; on the contrary, as discussed in the first section of this chapter, since throughout history same-
sex relationships have been based on love and affection, and since love
and affection have become important justifications for marriage today,
there is no logical reason to continue the exclusion of same-sex couples
from the modern institution of marriage.[203] This is so *not* because a homosexual relationship today is similar to a heterosexual one but rather
because *the institution of marriage* has changed—from procreative to unitive—so that now it could encompass same-sex couples, notwithstanding and independent from any differences that may exist between same-
sex relationships and those of opposite-sex partners, differences that are
irrelevant as far as the institution of marriage is concerned.[204] For the
same reasons that homosexual acts should not be subjected to criminal
sanctions only because the acts were illegal and viewed as immoral at
different periods in history,[205] same-sex marriage should not be barred
simply because the right asserted is a new one. Hence, the lack of historical evidence of same-sex marriage does not weaken the case for its recognition. Eskridge's alternative argument in this respect—that even without a tradition of same-sex marriage, it should not be disallowed—is
much more appealing: "That the thing to be changed has existed for a
long rather than a short time ought not to be decisive. Should its longev-

203. This is not to say that love and affection are the *only* remaining justifications for
marriage today: the ideal emphasizes love and affection, but the reality is more complex,
and there is a variety of reasons for getting and staying married, such as raising children,
promoting social stability, fulfilling religious duties, creating a mutually beneficial financial relationship, and the like—all of which do not support precluding same-sex marriage
and some of which would apply similarly to same-sex couples who wish to marry, for
example, in the Netherlands. My emphasis is on the shift from procreation as the chief
justification for marriage to the current concept, according to which procreation is no
longer the sole reason for getting married. It is love and affection that have become major
goals of marriage during the past few decades. See also sec. 2.1 above, on the transformations in the nature of love and marriage.

204. On this point, i.e., the question whether the differences between same- and
opposite-sex partnerships are relevant for the purposes of the institution of marriage,
see chap. 10, sec. 10.5, discussing the intracommunity debate as to whether same-sex
couples should be recognized within or outside the institution of marriage.

205. See Bowers v. Hardwick, 478 U.S. 186 (1986), in which the court made a selective
as well as a misleading use of history as a justification to uphold homosexual sodomy
laws as constitutional.

ity have entrenched slavery in the United States? For most of American history different-race marriages were not acceptable, but that was no argument to perpetuate this discrimination once our society rejected the racist assumptions of that exclusion."[206] Similarly, despite the fact that for centuries women were not accorded property rights and the legal identity of a woman was *defined* as part of her husband's identity, at the end of the nineteenth century the law was amended to accord women property rights and a separate legal identity (and later, during the twentieth century, full equal rights). These changes have taken place *in spite of* the traditional concept and definition of the legal status of women. In much the same way, we should accept the fact that the definition of marriage was traditionally limited to a man and a woman and still maintain that the lack of any (legal) tradition of same-sex marriage does not weaken the current argument for the recognition of same-sex marriage. Based on principles of constitutional law, and *notwithstanding* the absence of a tradition or custom of gay marriage, there is no public-policy reason to continue the exclusion of gays from marriage.

2.4.2 Existing Models for the Recognition and Regulation of Same-Sex Partnerships

During the past two decades, different countries have adopted various models in order to provide same-sex couples with some or most of the rights associated with marriage. Those different models of recognition of same-sex partnerships have developed as most Western countries have come to recognize the inequality—or the second-class-citizen status—of same-sex couples as compared to opposite-sex married couples. Consequently, since the beginning of the 1970s, countries in western Europe and North America have been debating and considering various ways to place same-sex couples on an equal footing with married couples.

I find it useful to divide the models for the legal recognition and regulation of same-sex partnerships that have been adopted by different countries around the world into four principal categories:[207] same-sex marriage, registered partnership, domestic partnership, and cohabitation.

1. *Civil marriage for same-sex couples.* The institution of marriage is the most expansive model for the recognition of a couple's partnership,

206. Eskridge, Case for Same-Sex Marriage, note 28 above, at 91.

207. *See also* Yuval Merin, *Models for the Legal Recognition and Regulation of Same-Sex Partnerships—A Comparative Overview,* 26:1 N.Y.U. Rev. L. & Soc. Change 169, 191 (2001); Yuval Merin, *Same-Sex Marriage and the Failure of the Alternatives for the Legal Regulation of Gay Partnerships,* 7 Hamishpat, College of Management L. Rev. (2001) (in Hebrew).

both in the degree of state regulation and in terms of the rights and benefits it accords. Until recently, nowhere in the world did same-sex couples have the right to marry as opposite-sex couples do. The Netherlands is thus far the only country to recognize same-sex marriage; it opened up the institution of marriage to same-sex couples in April 2001.[208] Other countries may follow suit in the future.[209]

2. *The registered partnership model.* The most comprehensive and the broadest legal recognition of same-sex partnerships that exists today— other than the Dutch expansion of the definition of marriage to include same-sex couples—is the model of registered partnership, a legislation at the national level that was adopted by the five Nordic countries— Denmark (1989), Norway (1993), Sweden (1995), Iceland (1996), and Finland (2002)—and by the Netherlands (1998).[210] Bills on registered partnerships are pending and being debated in various other countries, such as Switzerland (see chap. 6). The Nordic countries limit the applicability of their acts to same-sex couples, whereas the Dutch registered partnership act applies also to opposite-sex couples. The Dutch act on same-sex marriage of 2001 did not repeal the institution of registered partnership; according to the act, registered partnership in the Netherlands will continue to exist for at least five more years alongside marriage, and conversion of a registered partnership into marriage and vice versa is possible.

This model is based on the marriage model. Registered partnership acts refer to and incorporate existing marriage legislation, offering same-sex couples the rights, benefits, and responsibilities associated with marriage, with a few exceptions. They thus come close to placing same-sex couples on an equal footing with different-sex married couples. The northern European acts substitute the words *registered partnership* for *marriage.* This terminology is somewhat misleading, since marriage also requires registration and is in fact a statutory regulated form of cohabitation for two people. However, the distinction between marriage and registered partnerships is not merely a semantic one. There are substantive differences in terms of the different duties, rights, and benefits accorded by the two institutions. The registered partnership model provides the closest alternative to marriage available, but, for example, it contains

208. For a detailed discussion of same-sex marriage in the Netherlands, see chap. 4.

209. There is some probability that in the future the Nordic countries, Belgium, or one or more states in the United States will also open up marriage to same-sex couples. For these possibilities, see chap. 3; chap. 5, sec. 5.2; and chap. 7, pertaining to same-sex couples in the Nordic countries and the United States, respectively.

210. For a discussion of the Dutch and Nordic registered partnership acts, see chaps. 3 and 4.

citizenship and residency requirements that do not exist for marriage in those countries, and it excludes same-sex partners from various parental rights and from the right to officially sanctify their union through religious ceremonies in the state churches. Moreover, because most other countries refuse to recognize registered partnerships, the legal effects of these acts are largely limited to the country in which the partnership is registered. Registered partnerships are mutually recognized only among the Nordic countries. Other countries do not recognize registered partnerships, and same-sex registered partners are considered legal strangers outside northern Europe.

3. *The domestic partnership model.* This model is not based on the marriage model, since it accords only a few of the rights that flow from marriage (e.g., work-related benefits, hospital and prison visitation rights, etc.). It is also difficult to categorize it as one standard model, because, unlike marriage, which carries standard protections, each domestic partnership ordinance, act, or plan is different and unique in its definition of domestic partnership, scope, applicability, and availability. This model reflects only partial recognition: it is quite limited in its scope and applicability and is usually much less comprehensive than the other models. Domestic partnership has thus far been implemented by local and state or provincial jurisdictions or by nongovernmental entities, including private businesses and corporations, but—unlike the registered partnership model—not at the national level.[211] I therefore define domestic partnerships in terms of their scope and their geographical application, that is, as local or state ordinances or acts that accord same-sex couples a limited set of enumerated rights, as opposed to legislation at the national or federal level that is based on the marriage model, such as registered partnership.

Most domestic partnership schemes are in fact more limited in their scope than either the registered partnership or the marriage model; there is thus usually a correlation between the scope of domestic partnerships and their applicability.[212] This model entails very few rights—mostly work-related benefits—and provides a limited set of legal consequences in a few specific areas. The partnership is usually defined in gender-

211. *See Registered Partnership, Domestic Partnership, and Marriage: A Worldwide Summary,* ILGA Fact Sheet, November 3, 1998, available at http://www.iglhrc.org/news/faqs/marriage_981103.html.

212. For example, the European registered partnership acts are not only national but also broader in their scope than any existing domestic partner plan or act, with the exception of Vermont's civil union act. Accordingly, and although the latter is more akin in its scope to both the marriage model and the European registered partnership model than to other domestic partner schemes in the United States, I categorize Vermont's civil unions as a version of domestic partnership because it is limited to the state of Vermont.

neutral language and is applicable to both same- and opposite-sex couples (in the past, most domestic partner plans were limited to same-sex
couples, but this has changed in recent years). There are two kinds of
domestic partnerships: one is provided by private-sector employers' benefit plans, and the other pertains to state and municipal statutory regulation of same-sex partnerships. Domestic partnership ordinances (as distinguished from private employers' domestic partner plans)[213] usually
provide for the registration of the partnership and require a minimum
duration of the relationship and proof of cohabitation and of other factors pertaining to the relationship. The degree of recognition at this level
differs from one country to another and from one region to another in
the same country.

Domestic partnership is thus far the predominant model of regulation of the status of same-sex couples in the United States.[214] With the
exception of the states of Connecticut, Hawaii, New York, Massachusetts, California, and Oregon, which provide domestic partner benefits
to their public employees,[215] and Vermont's civil union act (which is an
exception within the United States; it more closely resembles the northern European model than other domestic partner schemes in the United
States)[216]—all of which are not recognized by other states within the
United States—domestic partnership in the United States is limited to
various cities, counties, and private employers and provides very few of
the rights associated with marriage.

Unlike registered partnership and marriage, the domestic partnership model provides no rights vis-à-vis third parties or the state, and the

213. For a detailed analysis of the characteristics of the domestic partnership model
and the differences between private employers and public-sector domestic partner
schemes, including a list of domestic partner plans that are restricted to same-sex couples,
see chaps. 8 and 9 and table 2 (in chap. 8). My discussion here is limited to public sector ordinances, since my main concern here and throughout the book is with state-
sanctioned regulations of same-sex partnerships.

214. For discussion of domestic partnerships in the United States, see chap. 7.

215. *See* Kim I. Mills & Daryl Herrschaft, The State of the Workplace for Lesbian, Gay,
Bisexual, and Transgendered Americans 16 (Washington, D.C.: Human Rights Campaign,
1999). For further discussion see chap. 7, sec. 7.4.

216. Following the groundbreaking decision of the Supreme Court of Vermont in
Baker v. State of Vermont, 744 A.2d 864, Vt. Sup. Ct., 1999, the state legislature enacted
the civil union act, which extends to same-sex couples the benefits and protections associated with marriage. The act provides the broadest protection of domestic partnerships in
the United States and is akin to the European registered partnership model rather than
to any existing American domestic partner scheme. *See* An Act Relating to Civil Unions,
2000 Vt. Acts & Resolves 91 (codified at Vt. Stat. Ann. tit. 15, §§ 1201–7 [Supp. 2000]).
Civil unions, however, are limited to the state of Vermont and to the rights and benefits
that are within the state's power, with none of the rights and benefits that flow from
marriage at the federal level, and presumably would not be recognized by most other
states. For a detailed discussion of Vermont's act, see chap. 7, sec. 7.5.

partners have no obligations toward each other. However, irrespective of domestic partner schemes, many U.S. state courts recognize same-sex couples as parents and provide for second-parent adoption, joint custody, and full access to artificial conception. (This is in contrast to the status of same-sex parental rights in the European countries.) Other regions where a variation of the domestic partnership model has been adopted include Catalonia and Aragon in Spain.[217]

4. *The cohabitation model.* Like domestic partnership, this model has been implemented only at the state or provincial level (as opposed to the national or federal level), depending on the country. This model purports to equate the status of same-sex couples with that of opposite-sex cohabiting couples or with that of opposite-sex de facto relationships. Its scope is dependent upon the degree of regulation of the status of heterosexual cohabitants in the relevant country, and thus it is most effective in countries that have extensive regulation of heterosexual nonmarital cohabitation or recognition of de facto family relationships, such as Australia, Canada, and New Zealand.[218] These countries have been considering extending the rights and responsibilities that legally flow from that status to same-sex couples. Accordingly, same-sex couples have been accorded some of the rights associated with marriage by equating their status to that of opposite-sex cohabitants in various Canadian provinces (including Quebec, Ontario, and British Columbia) and in a few Australian states (including New South Wales and the Capital Territory). Moreover, bills to that effect have been presented in New Zealand and at the federal level in Canada. The latter countries are similar to the United states in that they tend to accord most parental rights to same-sex couples.

France, Germany, Belgium, Hungary, and Portugal have adopted models for the recognition of same-sex partnerships at the national level that differ, to a certain extent, from the four principal models discussed just above;[219] whereas the acts recognizing the status of same-sex couples in France, Germany, and Belgium could be regarded as a "light" version of the registered partnership model, legislation in Hungary and Portugal resembles more the cohabitation model.

The French Pacte Civil de Solidarité of 1999 (PaCS) provides fewer

217. The Spanish acts, like those in the United States, are limited to a few rights between the partners without any application to third parties or to the State. *See* chap. 6.

218. For discussion of same-sex partnership in Canada, Australia, and New Zealand, see chap. 6.

219. For a detailed discussion of same-sex partnerships in France, Germany, Belgium, and Hungary, see chap. 5.

rights and benefits than either the registered partnership model or the Hungarian common law marriage model (see below), but it is more expansive than most American domestic partner schemes. It confers a limited set of rights at the national level upon same-sex as well as opposite-sex couples.

In November 2000, the lower house of the German parliament passed a version of a registered partnership act that recognizes same-sex couples as next of kin and accords them a few enumerated rights in a manner similar to that of the French PaCS. The second part of the bill, which would have accorded gay couples various economic benefits, was defeated in the German upper house in December of the same year.

In 1998 the Federal Parliament of Belgium enacted a law creating a new institution—"statutory cohabitation"—intended to regulate the cohabitation of *any* two adults, including opposite- and same-sex couples. The law took effect in January 2000.

Hungary's Common Law Marriage Act of 1996 applies to both same-sex and different-sex couples, so that same-sex partnerships are included in the definition of common law marriages and are accorded the same rights as common law opposite-sex married couples. This act confers comprehensive recognition at the national level and is akin to the registered partnership model in terms of its scope and applicability.

In March 2001 Portugal enacted a new bill on de facto unions for both heterosexual and homosexual couples. However, the Portuguese act does not provide nearly as many rights and protections as the aforementioned legislation in France, Germany, Belgium, and Hungary.

Like the Nordic states, these five countries limit their regulations to the relationship between the partners themselves and exclude same-sex couples from most rights pertaining to parenthood.

Finally, various private contractual devices may be used to secure some of the rights and benefits associated with marriage. I do not regard non-state-sanctioned private contractual devices as an additional or an alternative model, since my focus is on recognition and regulation of same-sex partnerships by state law. Furthermore, contracting is not an adequate substitute for marriage law. It does not automatically confer on the partners hundreds of rights free of charge. Private contracting is costly, financially and emotionally, and enforcing contracts requires long court procedures, the outcome of which may be uncertain. In addition, there are significant rights, benefits, and obligations associated with marriage that cannot be obtained or altered by contract.[220]

220. *See* Wald, The Knight Initiative Report, note 114 above.

Chapter 3

Registered Partnerships in the Nordic Countries

The five Nordic countries, Denmark, Norway, Sweden, Iceland, and Finland, have registered partnership acts in place. In this chapter I provide an overview of the history and the reform processes that led to the enactment of these laws, address the legislatures' objectives in enacting them, and analyze the acts in terms of their limitations, impediments, and requirements for registration; the legal consequences and effects of registration; and the acts' provisions for dissolution of a registered partnership. I also discuss the degree of involvement of the gay movement in these reforms and the arguments made by proponents of and opponents to the legislation, and I give a detailed account of the rights that are excluded from these acts as compared to the rights associated with marriage.

3.1 The First Registered Partnership Act—Denmark

3.1.1 Background—The Reform Process
In Denmark, the first country in the world to provide comprehensive legal recognition of same-sex partnerships, the issue of legal arrangements for same-sex couples had been debated since the late sixties. Various forms of legislation on registered partnership were discussed and proposed by some of the same parties and the national gay organization over a twenty-year period before the Registered Partnership Act was eventually passed into law by Parliament in 1989.

In 1968 the Danish Socialist People's Party (SF) presented a bill to revise the Marriage Act in order to provide legal status for new forms of cohabitation that had emerged in the 1960s and that were far removed from the traditional pattern of the nuclear family, including same-sex partnerships.[1] The bill was not adopted, but a committee was appointed to look into the broader consequences of and the ideas behind the SF proposal. In 1973 the committee debated and rejected the idea of marriage for gay men and lesbians, because it would have meant a breach with the traditional view of marriage and might have had an unfortunate effect on other countries' evaluations of the validity of Danish marriages. The committee's report, "Cohabitation without Marriage," published in 1980, stated that the committee did not wish to create a framework for registration of cohabiting same-sex couples but rather was interested in solving isolated legal problems concerning cohabitation.[2]

At the same time, Denmark's National Organization for Gay Men and Lesbians (LBL) pushed for legislation recognizing same-sex couples and played a major part in the developments that led to the adoption of the Registered Partnership Act. As an interest organization, LBL had to call upon a broad range of decision makers and put pressure on them through a public discussion about discrimination and equality in order to have its opinions justified and acted upon. Since it is a Danish custom to include the interest organizations in the political process, it was natural that the LBL be included in the consideration of partnership legislation.

During the 1970s LBL began developing three potential strategies to approach the authorities: request equality with heterosexuals (either marriage or the complete abolition of marriage); create a special framework for the cohabitation of same-sex couples, providing the same legal rights as heterosexuals had; or apply certain of the legal effects of marriage to the cohabitation of same-sex couples. The latter option involved the application of a somewhat random list of demands concerning the legal effects of marriage.[3] In 1975 the LBL concluded that the gay and lesbian community was no longer interested in a heterosexual-type marriage. It seems that the reason for LBL's "opposition" to same-sex marriage was not an ideological one but rather was based on its under-

1. Bent Hansen & Henning Jørgensen, *The Danish Partnership Law: Political Decision Making in Denmark and the National Danish Organization for Gays and Lesbians, in* The Third Pink Book: A Global View of Lesbian and Gay Liberation and Oppression 86, 89 (Aart Hendriks et al. eds., 1993).

2. Leslie Goransson, *International Trends in Same-Sex Marriage, in* On the Road to Same-Sex Marriage 165, 169 (Robert P. Cabaj & David W. Purcell eds., 1998).

3. Hansen & Jørgensen, note 1 above.

standing that both the public and Parliament would reject such a revolutionary solution and that a political compromise was thus inevitable if the organization was to present a proposal that would have a realistic chance of being adopted. Therefore, LBL focused on the third strategy.

In 1978 LBL introduced the concept of partnership, having certain legal effects and involving "public registration of lasting cohabitation" as a parallel to marriage. LBL prepared a detailed proposal that included very thorough research into the effect registered partnership might have on existing marriage laws. During its preparation of the proposal, LBL realized that marriage in Denmark had an effect on more than one hundred different laws. The proposal, which was adopted by the appropriate bodies in LBL in 1981, attempted to explain and address as fully as possible both the legal and the economic problems that arose for same-sex couples and present models for their solution. On most points, the proposal incorporated the same legal effects as did heterosexual marriage, addressing such issues as housing, pension, inheritance, death, and divorce. In spite of criticism of certain aspects of the legal effects of marriage, LBL considered these effects overall to be so sensible that they should be included in its own proposal for partnership. With respect to some of the legal effects of marriage, LBL adopted its own special position. The purpose of this was to make clear that it was not marriage that was being demanded, the committee on marriage having made it clear in 1980 that it would not accept a "second-class marriage" or a relationship that resembled marriage. At the same time, LBL could calm the fears of the Christians, who thought of marriage exclusively as a relationship between a man and a woman. No one doubted, however, that if and when the proposal became a reality, LBL would have to accept some compromises. Thus, the proposal did not grant the right to adopt children—neither a partner's children nor unrelated children.[4]

The Danish gay community itself was not unanimous on the issue of registered partnership. A minority in the gay and lesbian community opposed the proposed legislation, claiming mainly that partnerships should not be modeled after heterosexual marriage. They argued that marriage denied individuality, repressed conflict, and created economic dependence, social isolation, emotional stagnation, and physical violence. Further, by suggesting a common model of marriage, the proposal discouraged acceptance of alternative lifestyles and traditions.[5] The

---

4. *Id.* at 92; Goransson, note 2 above, at 170.

5. Martin D. Dupuis, *The Impact of Culture, Society, and History on the Legal Process: An Analysis of the Legal Status of Same-Sex Relationships in the United States and Denmark,* 9 Int'l J.L. & Fam. 86, 106 (1995).

opponents within the gay community called for equality through individualized contracts not tied to love, religion, or tradition.[6] Since this position was held by a small number of people, it did not receive much attention in the public debate. The arguments of the proponents of registered partnership, the majority of the gay and lesbian community, were centered on principles of equality, justice, and freedom, and it was suggested that bringing about these principles had a value in its own right. The principle of equality had been the main argument and justification: when two adult members of a society wish to marry, they should be given this opportunity, whatever their sex is.[7] Homosexuals deserve a freedom of choice equal to that of heterosexuals, in relation to privileges and obligations of couple building.[8] Legal equality implied an official, societal acknowledgment of the equal value of homosexual and heterosexual relationships; in Danish, equal value (*ligevaerd*) is a matter of human worth and dignity, and equality (*lighed*) refers to social and legal rights and opportunities.[9] It was also suggested that legal recognition of homosexual relationships would increase the positive image of the homosexual community within itself and would positively influence the attitudes of others external to the community. Proponents also used Denmark's status in the world as an argument. They claimed that Denmark had a reputation for tolerance and equal rights that put the country in the forefront of civilization and that thus it had an obligation to set an example and lead the way for other countries in this field.[10]

The debate outside the gay community over the proposed legislation contained many of the familiar arguments over homosexuality. The opponents of the act were mainly Christian and conservative groups. The major argument against the act expressed by these groups was that homosexuality was in conflict with the Bible or with nature.[11] Opponents argued that homosexuality was sinful and perverse and thus should not be officially recognized by society.[12] Another opposition theme that carried a lot of weight had to do with concerns regarding the dissolution

6. Goransson, note 2 above, at 172.

7. Hansen & Jørgensen, note 1 above, at 95.

8. Henning Bech, *Report from a Rotten State: Marriage and Homosexuality in Denmark, in* Modern Homosexualities: Fragments of Lesbian and Gay Experience 134, 136 (Ken Plummer ed., 1992).

9. Dupuis, note 5 above, at 106, referring to Bech, note 8 above, at 145. However, Bech contends that the proponents of the act merely thought homosexuals should be treated *as if* of equal value, precisely because they did not consider them to be so. *Id*. at 142.

10. Dupuis, note 5 above, at 106.

11. Bech, note 8 above, at 135.

12. Dupuis, note 5 above, at 105.

of marriage and the family. The fear was that marriage would be devalued and ridiculed; families would be broken; children would be harmed; homosexuality would spread, as would crime, drugs, and disease in its wake; and the gates would be open for further decay. These arguments, especially those stressing marriage and the family, were presented by respectable and influential conservatives not tied with religious fundamentalism, such as newspaper editors and members of Parliament.[13] A third type of argument focused on juridical-administrative problems, asserting that there was no need for the legislation or that no one would use it. Hundreds of related laws would have to be changed. Moreover, a new influx of immigrants could be created by expanding access to Danish citizenship, and Denmark could become the object of ridicule and lose standing in the world community.[14] Some of these arguments were merely pretext for the notion that homosexual relationships in themselves were of less value than heterosexual relationships. The opponents were mainly Christian groups that arranged meetings and wrote petitions to Parliament and the press. The small Christian party made it a primary theme of their campaign.[15] Thus, the debate consisted in the assertion of two fundamentally opposed sets of principles and values: "traditionalist" ones relating to God, nature, and the family, and "modern" ones relating to liberty, equality, and justice.[16]

The arguments in favor of the bill were espoused by politicians from left and center parties, and opinion polls in 1988 and 1989 reported that the majority of Danes supported legal recognition of same-sex relationships. The majority "thought homosexuals should be given more of the same rights that heterosexuals had."[17] This was the central argument of the proponents and was what the majority endorsed in their answers to opinion polls.[18]

The proposal was an expression of a pragmatic balancing act between friends and enemies, internal and external. Principally because of this, it was possible for it to become the object of serious discussion with the political decision makers. This proposal determined the form of the

---

13. Bech, note 8 above, at 135.

14. Dupuis, note 5 above, at 105.

15. They made the withdrawal of the legislation a condition of their participation in government after the 1988 election and threatened to organize a referendum if the bill passed. However, the party, which received only 2% of the vote in 1988 and was not included in the government, was not able to gather support in Parliament to call a referendum after the bill was passed. *Id.* at 106–7.

16. Bech, note 8 above, at 137.

17. *Id.* at 138, 141, quotation at 141.

18. Dupuis, note 5 above, at 107.

debate on cohabitation for gays and lesbians in the years ahead, both among politicians and in the press. Despite the varying views in the gay community, the achievements of the Danish gay community should serve as proof of the importance of a well-organized gay and lesbian activist group and, moreover, of the group's ability to reach compromise within itself.[19]

There were several more years of pressure, lobbying, and public meetings before the LBL succeeded in persuading the Danish parliament to set up a "Commission to Elucidate the Social Circumstances of Homosexuals" in Denmark. The commission's purpose was to investigate, inter alia, the legal, social, and cultural position of homosexuals and to make proposals for removing current discrimination and improving the overall situation of homosexuals in Denmark. The proposal to set up the commission was prepared by LBL in collaboration with representatives of the political parties that had a majority in Parliament.[20] The proposal was approved by Parliament in 1984, and during the same year, the minister of justice appointed the commission, which included two representatives of LBL. Parliament worded the commission's mandate as follows:

> Recognizing that homosexuals ought to have the possibility of living in accordance with their identity and of arranging their lives in society thereafter, and recognizing that adequate possibilities of doing this are not present, the commission shall collect and present available scientific documentation on homosexuality and the homosexual way of life, as well as institute investigations to elucidate the legal, social, and cultural circumstances of homosexuals.
>
> In this connection, the commission shall propose measures aimed at removing the existing discrimination within all sectors of society and at improving the situation of homosexuals, including proposals making provision for permanent forms of cohabitation.[21]

Through its interim juridical reports, the commission had direct influence on some legislative initiatives, such as the extension of the anti-discrimination legislation to include a prohibition against discrimination on the basis of sexual orientation as well as on the bases of sex,

19. Goransson, note 2 above, at 186.

20. When an agreement is reached between a majority in Parliament and LBL, it amounts to a guarantee that LBL will support the question among its own members and in homosexual circles, so that the majority does not have difficulties later. The whole system is dependent upon LBL's appearing as a reliable negotiating partner that has its membership behind it. Only then does the organization become a valuable ally for the Danish authorities. Hansen & Jørgensen, note 1 above, at 96.

21. *Id.* at 92–93.

race, and religion. Furthermore, in 1986 the commission published a provisional report regarding homosexuals and inheritance taxation, which created the basis for the adoption of an amendment to the Inheritance and Gifts (Taxation) Act. Persons of the same sex sharing a home were placed on an equal footing with married couples as far as the paying of inheritance tax was concerned.[22]

More importantly, the commission considered the LBL registered partnership proposal. As a result of LBL's successful lobbying in Parliament,[23] and although the proposal for registered partnership was introduced before Parliament in January 1988 by only a minority in the commission,[24] a majority of Parliament members supported the measure.[25] Hence, on June 1, 1989, the Folketing (the Danish parliament) passed the Registered Partnership Act by an overwhelming vote of 71 to 47 (with 5 abstentions).[26] The act came into force on October 1, 1989. The legislation is short and essentially incorporates the existing marriage law by reference and extends it to same-sex couples, with a few exceptions.[27] The partnership act was extended to Greenland seven years later,[28] and

22. Michael Elmer & Marianne Lund Larsen, *Explanatory Article on the Consequences etc., of the Danish Law on Registered Partnership* 1 (1990). The English translation of this article is available from Landsforeningen for Bosser øg Lesbiske Forbundet af 1948 (National Danish Organization for Gays and Lesbians), Copenhagen.

23. LBL pushed for the law on registered partnerships for gays and lesbians by making use of the parliamentary rules, by lobbying members of Parliament, by a conscious press strategy that provided backing in the media, by a clear formulation of the proposal, by a strong membership backing, and by its cogent argument for equality. *See* Hansen & Jørgensen, note 1 above, at 98.

24. Some members of the commission who initially opposed the partnership act have changed their minds since and today declare that their reservation was wrong. It *seems* that their fear was due to declarations by other Scandinavian countries that they would not follow Denmark's lead. Because the other Scandinavian countries since then did follow in Denmark's footsteps, some opposing members of the commission later realized they had nothing to worry about and today view the statute as a "positive thing." *See* Deb Price, *Roads to Equality: Gay Rights in Europe: Danes Pave the Way for Partnerships: Copenhagen's Gay and Lesbian Couples Enjoy Rights That Remain a Distant Dream for American Same-Sex Couples,* Detroit News, October 29, 1997, at E1:4.

25. Hansen & Jørgensen, note 1 above, at 94–95.

26. Sheila Rule, *Rights for Gay Couples in Denmark,* New York Times, October 2, 1989, at A8.

27. Danish Act no. 372, June 7, 1989 (Registered Partnership Act); Danish Act no. 373, June 7, 1989 (amending the Danish marriage, inheritance, penal, and tax laws to conform to the Registered Partnership Act) [hereinafter the Act]. For the English translation of the act, see appendix A, sec. A.1.1.

28. Greenland and the Faroe Islands (north of the Shetland Islands, near Norway) are self-governing external territories of Denmark. As such, Greenland voted in 1994 to ask the Folketing to extend the 1989 law to Greenlanders, and on April 26, 1996, Greenland adopted the Danish Registered Partnership Act. *See* Goransson, note 2 above, at 173; http://users.cybercity.dk/~dko12530/greenlan.htm (last visited July 7, 1999). However, the partnership law is not valid in the Faroe Islands. *See* Elmer & Lund Larsen, note 22 above, at 5.

on June 2, 1999, ten years after the act was first passed, the Danish parliament made an important amendment to the act, which was effective July 1, 1999.[29] The first registrations took place at the town hall in Copenhagen on the same day the act took effect. Eleven gay male couples registered on that day under Denmark's partnership law.[30] During the first seven years of registered partnerships for Danish lesbian and gay male couples, 2,083 unions took place, 70 percent of them between men. Of these unions, a total of 17 percent have divorced—14 percent of gay couples compared to 23 percent of lesbian couples. The rates of divorce for gays and lesbians who register are lower than those of heterosexual couples.[31] Over 10 percent of the partnerships (219) in total, practically all of them between men, ended with the death of one spouse.[32]

Three major steps in the reform process in Denmark could be identified. First, the government decided that the status of gay and lesbian couples was an issue deserving further investigation. Second, the question was delegated to a commission with specific guidelines, which reflected the underlying philosophy of the government, that is, the Danish government's wish to keep marriage separate and distinct from cohabitation. Consequently, the commission recommended certain reforms and not others. The commission identified discrimination against homosexual couples and recommended strategies for its elimination in the form of legislation. Third, the government implemented the recommendations of the commission by enacting a statute to protect same-sex couples.[33]

29. For the English translation of the amendment, see appendix A, sec. A.1.2.

30. L. Hosek, *Denmark: Special Report on Same-Sex Marriage,* Honolulu Star Bulletin, January 22, 1997, at 16–18. At the center of the festivities was seventy-four-year-old Axel Axgil and his sixty-seven-year-old partner of forty years, Eigil Axgil. Axel founded the Danish gay rights movement by coming out of the closet in 1948. *See* Rex Wockner, Danes Make History: Gays Legally Marry, available at http://users.cybercity.dk/~dko12530/internet.html.

31. According to statistics for the period October 1989 through January 1, 1996, 10% of gay men had divorced, compared to 14% of heterosexual married men; and 15% of lesbians had divorced, compared to 19% of married women. *See* Hosek, note 30 above. Thus, despite stereotypes regarding gay relationships as short-lived, especially between men, the statistics show that the divorce rate among Danish homosexuals is lower than that for heterosexuals. *See* Marian M. Jones, *Lessons from Gay Marriages,* Psychology Today, May–June 1997, at 22.

32. Goransson, note 2 above, at 171. As is evident from these figures, the law was less popular among lesbians during the first few years after it came into force. However, more recent figures show that during the period 1994 to 1997, the interest shown by gay men fell to the same level as that of lesbians, and in 1997 the interest of gay men was lower than that of lesbians: they have entered into 81 partnerships, and lesbians have entered into 159 partnerships. *See* Danish Partnership Statistics October 1989–December 1997, available at http://www.lbl.dk/partstat.htm (last visited 1/14/99).

33. *See* Deborah Henson, *A Comparative Analysis of Same Sex Partnership Protections: Recommendations for American Reform,* 7 Int'l J.L. & Fam. 282, 296–97 (1993).

3.1.2 The Objectives of the Registered Partnership Act

The main purpose of the legislation was to equalize the social and legal status of homosexuals with that of heterosexual married couples. The assumptions underlying the reform, according to the explanatory part of the bill on registered partnership, were as follows:

> The social acceptance of a relationship between two persons of the same sex manifested in specific legislation will give the parties to such a relationship the same rights and duties as married couples.

> The creation of a legal institution for homosexual partners will improve their opportunities for regulating their lives in accordance with their own wishes and choices. This is of particular importance for young people, for whom it may be a difficult and long process to make a choice that reflects their feelings and needs if they are forced to take the reactions of society into account.

> Formal recognition through express legislation will improve the chances of long-lasting and steady relationships developing between persons of the same sex. A hostile social response may impede such a development.

> A legal institution for two persons of the same sex who live in a permanent partnership is the precondition for securing the same legal rights as married couples, rights regarding such matters as housing, pensions, immigration, and entitlement to work.

> The device of registration gives the partners the right to choose between formalization and nonformalization. Thus they will have the same choice as heterosexual partners.

> A more positive attitude toward long-lasting partnerships between homosexuals may reduce the number of short-term relationships and thus contribute to reducing the risks of AIDS.[34]

3.1.3 Registration and Its Legal Consequences

The act provides same-sex couples inside Denmark with almost all the rights and obligations of married heterosexual couples. Along with the legislation of registered partnership, Parliament passed amendments to the Marriage Act, the Inheritance Act, the Civil Penal Code, and the Inheritance and Gifts (Taxation) Act, so that these statutes would also

---

34. Linda Nielsen, *Family Rights and the "Registered Partnership" in Denmark,* 4 Int'l J.L. & Fam. 297, 298 (1990). It was emphasized, however, that this latter argument was of minor significance compared to the others.

cover registered partners. The act applies only to same-sex couples (sec. 1). Cohabitants of the opposite sex cannot register. The reasoning behind this was and still is the general policy of maintaining "the primacy of marriage." The Danish government wanted to keep the institution of marriage separate and distinct from the institution of cohabitation and to encourage opposite-sex couples to get married.[35] For the first ten years of the legislation, the act required that at least one partner be a permanent resident of Denmark and a Danish citizen. The amendment of June 2, 1999, repealed this requirement; since then, it has been sufficient for both partners to have been permanent residents of Denmark for the two years preceding registration. In order for the partners to obtain the benefits provided by the act, they must register according to rules laid down by the minister of justice.[36] The partnership is registered by the municipal authorities at the town hall with a ceremony similar to a civil wedding for heterosexuals.[37] The registration equivalent of a marriage license is called a partnership certificate.[38] In order to register, as in marriage, the parties need not intend to live together or have sexual relations. According to section 2(1) of the Registered Partnership Act, the Danish Marriage (Formation and Dissolution) Act applies to the registration of partnerships, and it is a prerequisite that the conditions for marriage in part one of the Marriage Act be met; that is, a person wishing to enter into a registered partnership shall have reached the age of eighteen; registered partnerships may not be entered into between persons related to each other in lineal ascent or descent, or between siblings. Likewise, a former marriage or registered partnership must have been dissolved before a registered partnership can be entered into.

35. *See* Henson, note 33 above, at 286, 296. Because Danish law is concerned with encouraging different-sex partners to marry, there has been no legislation covering cohabitation; therefore, no special advantage can be gained by partners who choose to live together instead of getting married. Since same-sex couples could not "marry" and had no legal rights through cohabitation, permanent same-sex relationships were denied legal benefits and recognition. The objective of the Registered Partnership Act was to remedy this situation by equalizing the social status of same-sex and different-sex relationships. Thus, different-sex and same-sex partners can obtain legal recognition and its accompanying rights and duties, through marriage for the former and registration for the latter. Cohabitants of either type are not covered by any specific legislation. *See* Nielsen, note 34 above, at 298–300, 305.

36. Sec. 2(3) of the act. Such regulations were issued by the minister of justice: Order no. 626 of September 1989, according to which the registration must take place in the presence of at least two witnesses and the partners shall declare, when asked by the person responsible for carrying out the registration, that they are willing to enter into a registered partnership with each other. *See* Elmer & Lund Larsen, note 22 above.

37. Hansen & Jørgensen, note 1 above, at 95.

38. Marianne H. Pedersen, *Denmark: Homosexual Marriages and New Rules Regarding Separation and Divorce*, 30 J. Fam. L. 289, 290 (1992).

The registration of a partnership has the same legal effects as the contracting of marriage, except where otherwise provided by legislation. Thus, most sections of Danish law pertaining to marriage and married partners apply similarly to registered partnership and registered partners (secs. 3[1] and 3[2] of the act). In other words, the legal consequences of marriage were transferred to registered partnership. As the act makes a general reference to existing marriage law, it is not possible to infer directly from the act which rules are applicable to registered partnership; one must look for other legislation to find the rules that deal with marriage and married partners and then apply these rules similarly to registered partnership and registered partners. References to "marriage" or "spouse" in Danish law automatically include registered partnerships and registered partners. The effects of registered partnership that benefit the partners over cohabitation and that are identical to those of marriage include these, for example:

Mutual liability for maintenance during the partnership. The contribution of each partner can be made either through pecuniary assistance or through work in the home, according to the ability of each partner. There is also a possibility of a reduction of the social security benefits received by one partner from the state because of the level of income or property of the other partner.

A choice between common and separate property. If the partners opt for a separate-property system, a settlement must be executed and registered in a public registry. Otherwise, the regime is that of community of property, which is comprised of assets acquired during the partnership, including gifts and inheritance, and assets brought into the partnership by each partner. The main consequence of community of property is not activated until the partnership comes to an end by dissolution or by death. During the partnership, each partner may dispose of property brought into the partnership or acquired during the partnership but may not misuse this right to the detriment of the other party; mutual consent is required to alienate, lease, or mortgage the joint home and furnishings therein.

Joint income tax assessment.

The right to a residence permit for the foreign partner.[39]

39. Kees Waaldijk, Tip of an Iceberg: Anti-Lesbian and Anti-Gay Discrimination in Europe 1980–1990, at 31 (International Lesbian and Gay Association 1991); Nielsen, note 34 above, at 301–2.

3.1.4 The Dissolution of a Registered Partnership

The act simply refers to and applies the sections dealing with divorce and separation in the Danish Marriage Act (secs. 2[1] and 5[1] of the act). Thus, the dissolution of a registered partnership can be effected by immediate divorce (the grounds for which should be met, such as adultery) or by divorce after a period of at least six months of separation, at the request of one of the partners. Separation and divorce may be granted either by the court or administratively, by the county governor, if there is a joint application with a mutual agreement as to the matter of maintenance. If granted by the court, the judgment includes a decision on the question of maintenance between the partners. Maintenance between registered partners, as in the case opposite-sex spouses, is limited in time and confined to situations in which one of the partners has been working in the home and the partnership was long-standing.[40] The procedure for dissolution of a registered partnership is the same as that for the dissolution of a marriage. In the case of death of one of the partners, the surviving partner has the same legal rights and benefits as a surviving spouse in a marriage under the Law of Succession. That is to say, there is an automatic right of inheritance, including the right to retain the undivided possession of the estate, and the lowest inheritance tax applies. Pension rights that are provided or guaranteed by law attach to registered partners as well.[41] However, a registered couple has no claim to a mediation performed by the clergy prior to separation or divorce.[42] It should be noted that the legal status of cohabitants of the same sex in Denmark is similar to that of opposite-sex cohabitants. Regarding the problem of property relations upon dissolution of the cohabitation of a couple who had not registered their partnership, the Danish courts have introduced a model based on an "enrichment principle": Upon termination of the relationship, the financially weaker party is awarded a modest compensation by the party who is better off if the latter has achieved an "unjust" enrichment at the expense of the other party.[43] A cohabitant has no legal right to take over a residential property or household goods that belong to the other party; however, if the cohabitants

40. Nielsen, note 34 above, at 303.

41. For a more detailed discussion of the application of the Danish Law of Succession and provisions relating to pensions and insurance on registered partnerships, see id. at 303–4.

42. Pedersen, note 38 above, at 290.

43. Ingrid Lund-Andersen, *Cohabitation and Registered Partnership in Scandinavia: The Legal Position of Homosexuals, in* The Changing Family: International Perspectives on the Family and Family Law 402 (John Eekelaar & Thandabantu Nhlapo eds., 1998). *See also* Ingrid Lund-Andersen, *Moving Towards an Individual Principle in Danish Law,* 4 Int'l J. L. & Fam. 338–39 (1990).

have maintained a joint household for at least two years and live in a rented apartment, the cohabitant who did not rent the apartment may be entitled to take it over when special reasons so indicate.[44]

3.1.5 Rights Excluded from the Act

According to section 4 of the act, there are four exceptions to the general reference to opposite-sex marriage:[45] Subsection 4(1) exempts the provisions of the Danish Adoption Act from applying to registered partners. Consequently, registered partners were unable to adopt jointly, and one partner could not adopt the other's child. The 1999 amendment to the act partially lifted the ban on same-sex adoptions.[46] Subsection 4(2) exempts the regulations of the Danish child custody law from applying to registered partners. Therefore, the partners cannot have joint custody of each other's children. In addition, according to legislation regulating artificial procreation, lesbian couples are completely denied such services. Subsection 4(3) exempts section 11 of the Marriage (Legal Effects) Act—requiring a husband to be responsible for "his wife's ordinary contracts entered into in satisfaction of her own special needs"—from applying to registered partnerships. Subsection 4(4) exempts the partnership act from international treaties unless the contracting parties agree otherwise.

Furthermore, unlike opposite-sex couples who wish to get married, same-sex couples who wish to register their partnership are not permitted to have church weddings. And provisions in Danish legislation that use the terms *husband* and *wife* or rules that define the spouse by sex do not apply to registered partnership.[47] In these respects, homosexuals have not yet obtained complete formal equality with heterosexuals.

The main legal rights that are excluded from the act are those pertaining to parenthood: the right to jointly adopt unrelated children, the right to jointly have custody of a child, and the right to use artificial

44. Lund-Andersen, note 43 above, at 402. Norway and Sweden both accord more protections to the financially weaker party than the judicially constructed Danish model does. *Id.* at 403. *See also* the sections below that discuss the status of same-sex partnerships in Norway and Sweden.

45. *See also* Jorge Martin, Note, *English Polygamy Law and the Danish Registered Partnership Act: A Case for the Consistent Treatment of Foreign Polygamous Marriages and Danish Same-Sex Marriages in England,* 27 Cornell Int'l L.J. 419, 432 (1994).

46. For a detailed discussion of the ban on adoption and the 1999 amendment, see below.

47. Danish Law in a European Perspective 184 (Børge Dahl et al. eds., 1996). Thus, for example, provisions in Danish law that for biological reasons could not apply to homosexuals, such as secs. 2 and 3 of the law on children, which assume that a husband is regarded as the father of the child born in wedlock, do not apply in determining the fatherhood of a child born in a registered partnership. *Id.*

insemination services. According to the old version of section 4(1) of the act, homosexual couples were not permitted to adopt children, neither a partner's children nor unrelated children, and thus they did not enjoy the rights of adoption that heterosexual married couples did. In 1989 LBL began working to change the law so that gay men and lesbians living in a registered partnership would be able to adopt children, at least the children of their partner.[48] Consequently, the act was amended in 1999 to allow homosexuals to adopt their partner's child, unless the child had originally been adopted from another country; and as of July 1, 1999, a child can legally have two fathers or two mothers.

The ban on adoption that existed until 1999 was based on the legislature's assumption that registered partners could have children separately but not together because it is best for a child to have both a "father" and a "mother."[49] The main reason for the 1999 reform was a new understanding of the phrase *the child's best interests*. First, it has been suggested that since many children in registered partnerships between two women were in fact raised by only one biological parent—because the other parent was deceased or because the mother had refused to reveal the identity of the father to the authorities—the child had an inferior legal status compared to that of children in marriage regarding inheritance rights and in cases in which the partnership is dissolved. Second, the authorities became aware that in practice, the nonbiological parent cared and provided for the child as a natural parent. Moreover, when a biological parent entered a partnership, all social benefits that she was entitled to as a single parent ceased despite the fact that the other partner was not recognized as a parent and had no rights or obligations vis-à-vis the child. It was thus inconsistent for the parent to be no longer considered a single parent and at the same time for the other partner to be unable to obtain legal rights and take on legal obligations with respect to her stepchild.[50] A majority in Parliament thus concluded that adoption of the other partner's children was not an issue of favoring the adopting partner but rather of safeguarding the child's best interests.[51] A further reason for denying joint adoption for registered partners was the fear

48. *See* ILGA-Europe, Equality for Lesbians and Gay Men: A Relevant Issue in the Civil and Social Dialogue 38 (Brussels 1998) [hereinafter Equality].

49. Nielsen, note 34 above, at 305.

50. *See* Ingrid Lund-Andersen, The Danish Registered Partnership Act, 1989—Has the Act Meant a Change in Attitudes? A paper presented at the conference Legal Recognition of Same-Sex Partnerships, King's College, University of London, July 1–3, 1999.

51. The minority in Parliament—the Conservative Party, the Christian Party, and a small right-wing party—still emphasized the child's right to have both a father and a mother. *See id.*

that it might deter Third World countries from sending children to Denmark for adoption.[52] This reasoning is still being applied, since same-sex couples are still prohibited from jointly adopting an unrelated child either from within Denmark or from abroad and since the 1999 amendment specifically exempts adoptions by registered partners if the child was originally adopted from a country other than Denmark.

According to section 4(2) of the act, the regulations contained in section 13, clause 3, and section 15, subsection 3, of the law on child custody that apply to married couples are not applicable to registered partnerships. This means that a registered couple has no possibility of obtaining custody of each other's children.[53] Additionally, the Registered Partnership Act did not grant lesbian couples access to artificial insemination. In fact, no legislation existed in Denmark governing artificial procreation until 1997. In practice, only opposite-sex spouses could obtain artificial insemination in Danish hospitals, and women in a lesbian relationship were denied these services. In 1990 an Ethical Advisory Committee proposed that lesbians should be allowed to obtain artificial insemination, in vitro fertilization, and egg donation. The issue of egg donation became regulated by a law enacted in 1992, again leaving artificial insemination unregulated.[54] In June 1997 the Danish parliament passed a bill that banned assisted insemination for unmarried women, including lesbians. The bill was originally proposed in a form that carried no constraints regarding who could be treated. During the bill's second reading in Parliament, a change requiring marriage or opposite-sex cohabitation in order to obtain assisted insemination was passed. The majority of Parliament concluded that for lesbians, childlessness is a result of choice by way of lifestyle and that a child has a right to have both a father and a mother; thus, access to insemination for lesbians would not be in the best interests of the child and would only accommodate the wishes of lesbians.[55] The LBL mounted a huge lobbying campaign in Parliament to remove the article introduced, but its proposal was rejected. According to the statute, assisted insemination in a medical environment is no longer available to single women or lesbians, neither in public hospitals nor in private clinics. The law does not, however, regulate nonclinical treatment. Thus, artificial insemination in

52. Nielsen, note 34 above, at 305.

53. However, there is nothing to stop one of the registered partners from obtaining sole custody of a child in accordance with the regulations that apply to other persons, whether married or single. Elmer & Lund Larsen, note 22 above, at 3.

54. Nielsen, note 34 above, at 305, 316.

55. Lund-Andersen, note 50 above.

private was not criminalized.[56] The issue was debated again, and in June 1998 Parliament voted against lifting the nation's ban on artificial insemination of single women. Proponents of the ban argued that lesbian motherhood is unnatural and that children were harmed by not knowing their fathers.[57] The 1997 act banning assisted insemination for lesbians (and single women) marked the first time since 1961 that the Danish parliament had voted against the interests of lesbians and gay men.[58]

The Registered Partnership Act further distinguishes homosexuals from heterosexuals by not requiring the state Lutheran Church to offer marriage ceremonies for gays and lesbians. Thus, partnerships cannot be registered in churches, and same-sex couples cannot have church wedding ceremonies. Partners who wish to register, unlike married couples, have no freedom to choose between a civil ceremony and a church wedding. Marianne Hojgaard Pederson of the Danish Ministry of Justice stated that this lack of freedom was due to the wording of the legislation, which specifies that the registration can be performed only by public authorities.[59] Moreover, a month after the law had come into force, and following complaints from various Christian groups, a unanimous Parliament amended the Registered Partnership Act by voting that, in case of impending divorce, same-sex partners in registered partnerships, unlike married couples, had no right to obtain conciliatory counseling by a vicar. The reason adduced for this provision was the regard for the conflicts of conscience to which vicars might be exposed.[60] In order to decide whether the state church should introduce a new blessing for registered partners, a committee was set up by twelve bishops of the Danish State Lutheran Church. The committee released its report in June of 1997, recommending that gay and lesbian partners should be able to obtain some kind of church blessing.[61] It proposed three different

56. ILGA-Europe Euroletter no. 51, July 1997 (Steffen Jensen et al. eds.) at http://www.qrd.org/qrd/www/orgs/ILGA/euroletter.

57. ILGA-Europe Euroletter, note 56 above, no. 61, July 1998.

58. ILGA Europe, Equality, note 48 above, at 38.

59. Pedersen, note 38 above, at 290. However, as Sloane argues, this justification is highly questionable since it does not answer the threshold question of why a registration may be performed only by public authorities to begin with. A more plausible rationale for the exclusion was that the Danish parliament did not want to impose same-sex marriage on the Danish Lutheran Church because the church and its teachings were opposed to these unions. *See* Craig A. Sloane, *A Rose by Any Other Name: Marriage and the Danish Registered Partnership Act*, 5 Cardozo J. Int'l & Comp. L. 189, 207 (1997).

60. Bech, note 8 above, at 145 n. 1.

61. For a translation of the committee's report, see Registered Partnership, Common Life, and Blessing (Gunnar Martin Nielsen trans.) at http://www.folkekirken.dk/udvalg/partnerskab/ENGLISH.htm (last visited February 25, 1999).

options: a blessing similar to that given to heterosexual partners who want their civil marriage blessed, another kind of blessing taking into account that the couple is gay or lesbian, and an intercessory prayer for the couple. The bishops' reaction to the report was not, as had been expected, to opt for the introduction of some kind of blessing for gay and lesbian couples, and in October 1997 they voted unanimously not to perform gay weddings, for the sake of church unity, ignoring the recommendations of their own committee. Instead, the bishops adopted a policy that enables priests to offer an intercessory prayer for the couple—the format of which is subject to approval by the bishop in each case.[62] Thus, priests do have the church's permission to bless an otherwise civilly registered partnership, but this blessing is not state sanctioned.

Some Danish vicars in fact perform religious blessings in the home for same-sex couples, and some bishops allow these actions. For example, Denmark's senior bishop, Ole Bertelsen of Copenhagen, expressed his desire that the Danish church would soon bless same-sex marriages; he stated, "I hope that time is not far off."[63] Thus, symbolic religious ceremonies are already being performed for same-sex couples by many of the Danish clergy. It seems likely that Denmark, being the first country in the world to accord same-sex couples many of the rights of marriage, will also be the first to create possibilities for official church blessing. However, it would be untenable for the Danish Parliament to require the church to conduct a marriage ceremony for same-sex couples identical to the one for opposite-sex couples. The Danish parliament should, however, amend the Registered Partnership Act to *permit* religious officials to conduct same-sex marriage ceremonies in church and perform mediation outside the church.[64]

Another exception is the failure to extend pension rights to registered partners under certain pension plans. Although, as indicated above, pension rights that are provided or guaranteed by law attach to registered partners, many of the pension plans in Denmark are regulated by private contracts. Most of these private-contract pension plans extend benefits only to spouses, so registered partners are not covered.[65]

Finally, the law on partnership is primarily a law for Danes. First, although two different-sex foreigners who are in the country for only a short period of time can enter into a marriage, the act requires that in

62. ILGA Europe, Equality, note 48 above, at 38.
63. Sloane, note 59 above, at 207; Dupuis, note 5 above, at 104.
64. *See* Sloane, note 59 above, at 207.
65. Nielsen, note 34 above, at 304.

order to obtain a partnership registration, at least one of the partners must be a Danish citizen and a resident in Denmark or—according to the 1999 amendment—that both partners must have resided in Denmark for the preceding two years. Second, partnerships can be entered into only in Denmark and have legal effect only while the partners are in Denmark. The Danish parliament thought it undesirable that aliens without any special ties to Denmark should be able to enter into a registered partnership that would be without legal effect in their home country.[66] Furthermore, Danish partnerships are not recognized by other countries except for Iceland, Norway, and Sweden; and when in other countries, the partners are regarded as legal strangers.[67] Another exception relating to international law is that, according to the act, provisions in international treaties that refer to marriage do not extend to registered partnerships, unless the other contracting parties agree to such application.[68] Since September 1995, a common Nordic commission on marriage has debated the question of mutual recognition of registered partnerships between Denmark, Norway, Sweden, and later Iceland. The commission concluded that partnerships from one of the countries should be recognized in the other countries as well.[69] Thus, there exists an agreement among those countries to recognize one another's partnerships, so that a registered partnership contracted in one of the four countries has full legal consequences in any of the other countries.[70] As far as Denmark is concerned, this agreement was incorporated into its domestic legislation, and the 1999 amendment provides that similar partnerships in Norway, Sweden, and Iceland will automatically be registered and recognized in Denmark. The amendment further provides that the minister of justice is authorized to give citizens of countries other than Norway, Sweden, and Iceland, which have or will have a law on registered partnership equivalent to the Danish one, the same rights.[71] However, with regard to most countries, which will refuse to recognize Danish registered partnerships, problems of private international law remain, such as in the case of inheritance and the settling of estates.[72]

66. Elmer & Lund Larsen, note 22 above, at 2.

67. Hansen & Jørgensen, note 1 above, at 95.

68. Nielsen, note 34 above, at 299.

69. ILGA-Europe Euroletter, note 56 above, no. 35, September 1995.

70. *See* Lund-Andersen, note 43 above, at 400.

71. *See* new section 2(2) of the Act (appendix A, sec. A.1.2). The first country to be considered is the Netherlands. *See* Lund-Andersen, note 50 above.

72. *See* Elmer & Lund Larsen, note 22 above, at 5–6. For further discussion of private international-law problems pertaining to registered partnerships, see chap. 9, sec. 9.1, below.

In sum, because of the aforementioned exceptions made by the Registered Partnership Act, the act can be criticized as constituting second-class marriage for homosexual couples.[73] However, despite the act's exclusions, it is a tremendous accomplishment by and for homosexuals in Denmark. Most politicians and government officials today consider the partnership law a success, believing it enhances the country's reputation and gives committed same-sex couples improved protection and legal status. Ingrid Lund-Andersen argues that the main purpose of the legislation was political, since the only way toward full social acceptance was to give homosexual couples almost the same legal framework as married couples; the legislation was used as an instrument to change social attitudes toward homosexuals in Denmark, which indeed it has done.[74] The adoption of Denmark's registered partnership law has resulted in much greater visibility and acceptance for gay men and lesbians, both in Denmark and abroad. For example, all Danish government forms now must include questions about partnership as well as marital status.[75] Internationally, the Danish partnership law affected and inspired similar legislation in other countries, especially in northern Europe. The 1999 amendment of the Danish act, which now provides partners the option to adopt each other's children, will most probably lead to the reopening of the debate regarding assisted insemination for lesbians and the right of same-sex couples to joint custody over each other's children. Whereas adoption grants the nonbiological parent full legal parental rights vis-à-vis the child (e.g., the right of the child to inherit from that partner), joint custody only provides that both partners share responsibility and authority with respect to the child (e.g., making decisions pertaining to the child's life or the provision of maintenance to the child). There is thus no reason why same-sex couples should not be granted automatic joint custody prior to the adoption of a partner's child or in cases in which such adoptions are impossible.

There is no doubt that there is a move in Denmark from insistence on a traditional type of family to acceptance of a more functional definition of the family. In recent years there has been a debate to repeal the exceptions from the act, which led to a legislative reform. The 1999 reform is a further step toward according gays and lesbians in Denmark equality with opposite-sex married couples. It seems that the process is

73. Some commentators have harshly criticized the Danish parliament for not according homosexuals total equality with heterosexual married couples. *See, e.g.,* Sloane, note 59 above; Bech, note 8 above. For the argument that the act indeed serves as second-class marriage and is thus objectionable, see chap. 9, sec. 9.1, below.

74. Lund-Andersen, note 43 above, at 397.

75. Goransson, note 2 above, at 172.

one that will lead eventually to the repeal of all the exceptions the act makes and thus to formal equality for same-sex couples.

3.2 Registered Partnership in Norway

3.2.1 Background—The Reform Process

Norway was the second country to enact a statute on registered partnership for homosexuals. Its act became effective in August 1993. For several years a committee representing gay organizations had lobbied Parliament for such legislation. Ultimately, in 1990, five members of Parliament from three different parties introduced the act as a private initiative based on the Danish precedent. After passage of the bill in the Odelstinget chamber of the Norwegian parliament by a vote of 58 to 40, the private initiative was passed on to the Ministry of Children and Family Affairs, which, as is customary in Norwegian legislation, called for the opinions of public institutions and interest organizations.[76] The ministry consulted with various institutions and organizations and then prepared a lengthy proposal and a draft bill, similar to the Danish act, which included an explanation of the objectives of the act, the reactions of different organizations to the proposal, and the ministry's own stand on the debate with its rationales for its final proposals.[77] In July 1992 the Ministry of Children and Family Affairs circulated its draft proposal of the act to a large number of organizations and institutions, including religious organizations, various legal groups, official authorities, gay organizations, and the like. More than seventy organizations responded, only twenty of which opposed the bill, the majority of them religious groups. The rest either positively supported the proposal or were neutral as to the question of same-sex partnerships; among the supporters were a few religious organizations.[78]

The Ministry of Children and Family Affairs considered four alternative solutions for the legal regulation of same-sex partnerships and proposed the first one.[79] The first legal solution was *statutory regulation based on an analogy with marriage.* According to this alternative, all provisions that apply to married couples would also apply to registered partnerships, with the exception of adoption of children and marriage as such. It was the view of the government that same-sex couples should have

76. Rune Halvorsen, *The Ambiguity of Lesbian and Gay Marriages, Change and Continuity in the Symbolic Order,* 34 J. Homosexuality 207, 208, 207–31 (1998).

77. *See* Ministry of Children and Family Affairs, The Norwegian Act on Registered Partnerships for Homosexual Couples (Oslo, 1993) [hereinafter The Proposed Bill].

78. *Id.* at 41, 7.

79. *See id.* at 19–30.

approximately the same rights and obligations as married couples, based on the Danish model. The government reasoned that in most legal and economic contexts, the situation of a homosexual couple living together in a committed relationship is similar to that of a married couple, except that "a homosexual couple cannot have children together." The government's view was that the legal matters relating to spouses were separate from any matters concerning children and that the statutory regulation of economic and legal rights and obligations between the partners, on the one hand, and their obligations and rights toward society, on the other hand, had nothing to do with regulating relationships between parents and children.[80] The government opposed opening up marriage to same-sex couples, since "marriage is the fundamental social institution and the natural environment for upbringing of children" and is "a relationship between a man and a woman." Moreover, "a homosexual relationship . . . can never be the same as marriage, neither socially nor from a religious point of view. It does not replace or compete with heterosexual marriage."[81]

The second alternative was *an act restricted to certain economic dispositions.* This alternative would offer more limited legal consequences than the marriage model and would be confined to some central economic rights in the private sphere, such as inheritance rights, statutory regulation of property ownership between partners, a duty to support one another, social security, old-age pensions, and income tax. The ministry opposed this alternative because it would exclude many provisions that are just as relevant for homosexual partners as for married couples who share a long-lasting emotional relationship with interwoven joint economic interests. Moreover, it would be practically impossible to decide on the principles for selecting some provisions rather than others.[82]

The third solution was *an amendment to the Joint Household Act of 1991,* extending the Joint Household Act[83] to cover the needs of same-sex couples. That act regulates the disposition of the joint residence and household goods for anyone who has shared a household with others for more than two years, including relatives, friends, cohabiting couples, and homosexual partners. The government opposed this alternative, stating that the Joint Household Act could not be expanded; it has a very limited scope and is applicable to all persons sharing a household, other than married couples and nuclear families, and most of those covered by the

80. *Id.* at 19, 20, quotation at 20.
81. *Id.* at 12.
82. *Id.* at 23–24.
83. Act no. 45 of July 4, 1991.

act retain separate economies with limited commitment to the common arrangement. The situation of homosexual couples is similar to that of a nuclear family and married couples, and expanding the Joint Household Act would meet neither the needs of the homosexual partner nor those of society. The purpose of the act was to limit its consequences to areas of joint residence and household goods. The act is thus not applicable to an emotional committed relationship akin to marriage. Expanding the act to meet the needs of same-sex couples would necessitate an expansion of the rights provided by the act and inclusion of corresponding mutual obligations of the parties; such expansions could not be made applicable to friends, siblings, and others to whom the act applies.[84]

The fourth and final alternative proposed by the ministry was *an act for both heterosexual and homosexual cohabitants.* The ministry opposed this solution because of the fundamental difference between heterosexual cohabitants and homosexual couples; the former may marry if they wish but have chosen not to do so, whereas the latter do not have the same option. Moreover, the Norwegian government opposed regulating opposite-sex partners' cohabitation, since these couples would benefit from the advantages of marriage without being subject to the whole body of marriage law, including most of its duties; such legislation might be exploited by many who may choose what is best for their own financial situation at any given time. The government opposed an act that would provide rights with no corresponding duties and obligations. It seems, however, that this objection stemmed from the Norwegian view of marriage as the predominant social institution and from the fear of undermining the status of marriage.[85]

In reaction to the alternatives proposed by the government and its endorsement of the Danish model, a debate regarding the proposed legislation took place both within and outside the gay community, as well as among religious authorities and organizations. Most lesbians and gays who participated in the public debate supported the act, including the representatives of the National Association for Lesbian and Gay Liberation (Landsforeningen for lesbisk og homofil frigjøring [LLH]). The lesbians and gays who publicly supported the act formed an alliance with the members of Parliament who favored the act.[86] The Joint Council of Gay and Lesbian Organizations in Norway did not demand access to marriage but called for economic and legislative equality between gay

84. The Proposed Bill, note 77 above, at 25, 27.
85. *Id.* at 27, 28, 30.
86. *See* Halvorsen, note 76 above, at 208, 211.

and heterosexual partnerships. It stated that its aim was not to equate the two but to give them equal worth and provide equal opportunities to all; it said only a partnership act similar to the Danish one would meet these requirements. A few gay organizations expressed the opinion that the bill did not go far enough, since it excluded the right of homosexual partners to adopt children.[87] Rune Halvorsen suggests that it is not the legal and economic advantages associated with the Act on Registered Partnerships that have been the most important to the gay and lesbian supporters of the bill but rather the questions of equality of life, self-development, equal participation, and human rights. The lesbians and gays in favor of the bill appealed to the values of individual freedom and justice, such as the right to choose. Moreover, they regarded it as an official acknowledgment of their existence and their relationships.[88]

An almost invisible minority within the gay and lesbian community opposed the act, viewing it as a new form of normalization, as disciplining of the lifestyles of lesbians and gays, and as a pressure on gays and lesbians to conform to one "legitimate" style of life. One of these opponents, Dag Strand Nielsen, stated publicly that "the point of living homosexually was to destabilize, to challenge, to rebel. . . . Personally I prefer . . . to live in the periphery and perversion, and to choose to fight to position myself in the margin, in contamination, in lack, in the thought of the end."[89] It appears that the arguments of the lesbian and gay opponents of the bill were dependent on their experience of themselves as different and their perception that these differences would not be maintained by an act built on the model of heterosexual marriage.

Outside the gay community, although supporters of the bill claimed that registered partnerships were not "gay marriages," conservative opponents to the bill insisted that they were. These opponents claimed that institutionalization of a relationship between two men or two women would decrease the social and symbolic significance of the institution of marriage. The supporters of the act tended, to some degree, to see the question of partnership as a strictly legal-economic question, whereas the opponents regarded the proposal as a value issue.[90] At the same time, the supporters of the bill invoked the similarities in the emotional, social, and legal needs of heterosexuals and homosexuals; the alleged innate differences between heterosexuals and homosexuals were

87. The Proposed Bill, note 77 above, at 26–27, 45.
88. Halvorsen, note 76 above, at 212, 226.
89. *Id.* at 211, 220–21, quotation at 220–21.
90. *Id.* at 214.

presupposed and taken for granted. Equal rights were thus claimed on the basis of differences.[91]

The Norwegian Lutheran State Church was the most outspoken representative of traditional values and the sharpest opponent of the lesbian and gay movement and of the proposed act.[92] Some bishops appreciated the government's wish to regulate the legal status of same-sex couples, but they felt that this should be achieved through amendments to existing legislation. In particular, they favored the alternative that would extend the Joint Household Act.[93] Accordingly, they stated that there was a need to regulate fundamental private economic and legal rights and obligations between homosexual cohabitants, but they were against providing homosexual partnerships a legal form that would place them in the same position as marriage would. This relatively liberal view of the church could be attributed to changes in its attitudes toward homosexuals during the 1970s and the 1980s. These changes were manifested by the church's acceptance, at the beginning of the 1990s, of the idea that homosexuality represented a largely predetermined identity or disposition, which must be recognized as such.[94] The church, however, made a clear distinction between homosexual identity and homosexual acts, refusing to accept the latter. Thus, only a small minority of homosexuals within the Norwegian church have dared to live openly.[95] As in Denmark, the Church of Norway initiated a committee in 1987, the Hygen Committee, to study the status of homosexuality and to determine whether the church should change its attitudes toward gays and lesbians. The committee's report presented a thorough study of biblical and historical material and evaluated its relevance to modern conditions,

91. This presumption may also serve to explain why opening up the institution of marriage to homosexuals was never suggested, and a different institution for gays was proposed. *See id.* at 226–27. Halvorsen interprets what he labels the "moral entrepreneurship" of those who supported the bill as a form of double discipline or twofold control through segregation and normalization: lesbians and gays were encouraged to come out and register their partnerships. According to Halvorsen's argument, by identifying themselves as lesbians and gays, people also define themselves as different, producing a difference, a distance, and a cultural asymmetry between "us" and "them," between heterosexuals and homosexuals. However, as Halvorsen himself notes, such an interpretation of the introduction of the Registered Partnership Act might miss particular forms of cooperation and alliance-building between heterosexuals and homosexuals. *Id.* at 223.

92. *See id.* at 211.

93. This was the view of the National Council of the Church of Norway. *See* The Proposed Bill, note 77 above, at 7, 26.

94. *Id.* at 26, 37.

95. *Id.* at 38. However, in 1989 a large group of clergymen and church workers supported a gay clergyman who lived with his love openly and brought a suit against the National Council of the Church of Norway on his right to hold a position in the church. *See id.* at 39.

concluding that "not all homosexual relationships are in opposition to the Bible's general ethical norms. On the other hand, there is no indication in the Bible of a positive acceptance of homosexual relations on a level with marriage between a man and a woman."[96]

As in Denmark, the bishops were more restrictive in their reaction to the report; they stated that "the Church can neither maintain the traditional unequivocal condemnation nor give the approval and blessing of the Church to homosexual relationships."[97] Thus, the majority in the Norwegian church opposed the registered partnership bill, although certain Christians in influential positions supported it, as did a number of authoritative bodies, such as the Faculty of Theology at the University of Oslo and the Student Christian Movement. The bishops and the National Council of the Church of Norway felt that the proposal went too far in the direction of creating equality between homosexual partnerships and marriage. They opposed giving homosexual couples "special rights" compared to other forms of joint households. Emphasizing the fundamental status of marriage, they considered that the proposed legislation would weaken the institution of marriage, its prevalence, and its traditionally central role and would lead to the dissolution of family ties and traditions. They expressed the view that society ought to continue to signal, including through its laws, its support for marriage between a man and a woman as the primary form of cohabitation.[98] The significant point, however, is that both the Church of Norway and that of Denmark did not condemn homosexuality outright and did not view homosexuals as having less worth or as being undeserving of rights and protections; on the contrary, the church agreed that some sort of state-legal regulation of homosexual partnerships should be undertaken. In comparison with the attitudes of some church authorities within the United States, this is a very progressive view for a religious institution.

The members of Parliament who supported the bill advocated justice in distribution of rights and duties and the freedom of all citizens to choose their own lifestyle. They also emphasized the welfare of individuals and couples and the need to improve the position of lesbians and gays in a

96. *Id.* at 38.

97. *Id.* at 39. The contrast between the views of the Norwegian and the Danish committees, on the one hand, and those of the bishops of both countries, on the other hand, reflects a common situation in churches: special committees and groups of experts often turn out to be less opposed to changing long-established views than the highest church authorities. This contrast is mainly due to differences in the interpretation of biblical materials. *See id.*

98. *Id.* at 40, 41, 42.

welfare society. Furthermore, the supporters said they wanted to encourage the visibility of lesbians and gays through the new legislation. Those who opposed the bill considered traditional values, such as protecting and maintaining the marital institution, as being of primary importance. The politicians who were against the proposed act tended to support the alternative proposal by the government that would have regulated the relationship of same-sex couples on equal terms with other forms of cohabitation, which would have aggregated lesbian and gay couples with siblings and friends who live together.[99] The Act on Registered Partnerships was eventually proposed by the Labor Government and was finally passed by the Lagtinget chamber of Parliament by a close vote of 18 to 16 on April 1, 1993. It became effective on August 1 of the same year.[100]

Relatively few Norwegian same-sex couples have chosen to register their relationship. Between August 1993 and May 2000, only 759 couples did so. Sixty-five percent of the partnerships are between men.[101]

3.2.2 The Objectives of the Act on Registered Partnerships

According to the government's proposal, the legislation had four objectives.[102] First was the need to regulate the financial and legal rights and obligations between the partners themselves on the one hand and the couple and society on the other. In this context, the government emphasized that regardless of the significance of the institution of marriage and its origins, marriage was *also* a legal contract that regulated the financial situation of two people who lived in a close union and became dependent on each other and that there was an increasing number of gay couples who formed permanent relationships with close ties and an interwoven economy. The economic conditions under which gay couples lived were of the same nature as those for married couples, apart from the ones that concerned responsibility for children. Moreover, "gay and lesbian couples [had] the same emotional and practical reasons for

99. Halvorsen, note 76 above, at 212, 210, 211.

100. Goransson, note 2 above, at 173 [hereinafter the Act]. *See* Act no. 40 of April 30, 1993. For the English translation of the act, see appendix A, sec. A.2.

101. Rex Wockner, *Norway Counts 759 Gay Marriages,* Wockner International News no. 322, June 26, 2000, available at http://www.queer.org.au/QRD/news/world/1996/wockner-111.html. Halvorsen claims that the small number of partnerships is evidence that few lesbians and gay men have actually supported the act. This claim is based on the assumption that choosing to make use or not to make use of the right to register a partnership is a form of approval or disapproval, respectively. Halvorsen, note 76 above, at 208.

102. For a brief summary of the reasons for the legislation, see Peter Lødrup, *Registered Partnership in Norway,* 1994 Int'l Surv. Fam. L. 387, 388–92.

desiring reciprocal rights and obligations, and there [was] the same need to protect the weaker party." The option of achieving some of the rights of marriage by private contracts was viewed by the government not only as insufficient but also as an inappropriate solution owing to the limitations of private contracts regarding various family law matters.[103]

Second, the changes in legislation governing homosexuality during the 1970s and the 1980s in other fields, such as the repeal of the Norwegian sodomy law and the enactment of antidiscrimination statutes, coupled with the general changes in society's view of homosexuality, justified progress toward recognition and regulation of same-sex partnerships. In this context, the government expressed its view of the interplay between changes in legislation and societal tolerance toward gays and lesbians, stating that "the authorities have a responsibility in influencing public opinion . . . [homosexuals] are surrounded by prejudice and misunderstanding [and] are still in a difficult situation. A Partnership Act will in itself help to increase understanding of their needs. The Act will mean a public acceptance of homosexual relationships. The Act will therefore encourage more gays and lesbians to come out, and thus reduce the problems created by their need to hide their own nature and live in isolation."[104]

The third stated goal of the act was the stabilization of homosexual relationships. The government's view was that most homosexual relationships were stigmatized and thus kept secret from family and friends and lacking any kind of support. Homosexuals had the same need for security and growth within a lifelong relationship as did heterosexuals. Thus, they deserved the same support in establishing such relationships. Moreover, a formal registered partnership would be a signal from gay couples to their families, friends, and society that they wished to enter into a committed and lasting relationship. Registered partnerships would imply openness and a departure from the traditional invisibility of gay and lesbian couples and would provide many homosexuals with positive role models. Finally, the government concluded that like heterosexual couples, gay and lesbian couples aspired to a lifelong close and stable relationship with another person that involved strong feelings, closeness, mutual respect, care, and support. They too wished to give their relationships an institutional binding framework in order to

103. *Id.* at 9. Moreover, the government explained that experience showed that, like cohabiting heterosexual couples, very few homosexual partners make use of the opportunity to enter into such agreements, partly because they do not foresee the need for them in case of crisis, such as the death of one of the partners or the termination of the relationship in other ways. *Id.*

104. *Id.* at 10.

demonstrate to society their mutual commitment, and the registered partnership act was intended to enable them to achieve this. The lack of an accepted social framework for gay and lesbian relationships made such relationships vulnerable, made it more difficult to establish permanent and mutual commitments, and placed these couples on a par with any two people who share a home, such as siblings or friends.[105] The right to legal and publicly recognized partnerships would help to reinforce the values of permanent, mutually committed emotional relationships and would confer greater equality between gay couples and married couples in terms of rights, obligations, and responsibilities, which would encourage permanence and stability of the relationships.[106] In addition, more positive attitudes on the part of the public toward homosexual relationships and homosexuals' own increased self-acceptance would probably result in an increasing number of gay and lesbian couples, and their lives would have become easier.

As is evident from the proposed bill, one of the reasons for introducing the act was to fight against alleged sexual excess and to compensate for the alleged lack of stability among same-sex couples. All through its proposal, the government emphasized the similarities between gay and heterosexual relationships and the heterosexual marriage model as the model that gay couples do or should aspire to. The government stated time and again that gays and lesbians had the same desires and expectations in their relationships as heterosexuals; the fact that many homosexual couples still lived separately was attributed not only to the couple's own fear of negative attitudes from the social environment but also to society's view of gay relationships as being unstable and involving weaker ties—especially between men—more akin to friendship than to a committed loving relationship.[107] It seems that the main purpose of the legislation, in the eyes of its drafters, was to encourage permanent and committed relationships between homosexuals and to further society's acceptance of such relationships. Other lifestyles than monogamy were depicted as unstable by both supporters and opponents of the bill. However, the wording of the explanatory part of the bill suggests that same-sex couples were viewed as defective compared to heterosexual couples, who were viewed as developed and mature. Heterosexuality was applied as the model for preferable conduct for homosexuals. These underlying presumptions constituted the basis for the intentions to im-

105. *Id.* at 11, 12, 37.
106. *See id.* at 13, 37.
107. *Id.* at 37, 36.

prove the living conditions of lesbians and gays.[108] Yet these presumptions may also account for the insistence on a separate institution for same-sex couples rather than their inclusion in marriage.

3.2.3 Registration and Its Legal Consequences

The Norwegian Act on Registered Partnerships, quite similar to Denmark's Registered Partnership Act, is also limited to same-sex couples. Originally, section 2(3) of the act required that at least one of the partners be a citizen of Norway, domiciled there. In order to register their partnership, a same-sex couple must satisfy the same requisites as heterosexual couples. They must be over eighteen years old and may not be closely related to each other (sec. 2 of the act, which refers to the Marriage Act). According to the first chapter of the Regulations Relating to the Partnership Act on the Verification of Compliance with the Conditions and the Procedures for the Registration of Partnerships, compliance with the foregoing conditions must be verified before registration can take place.[109] The registration procedure is somewhat similar to a nonchurch wedding ceremony for opposite-sex couples. The registration is performed by a public notary (city recorder, district judge, etc.), who declares the parties registered partners upon their request. As in the Marriage Act, there is no requirement that the couple live together or have sexual relations. In addition to the nationality requirement, homosexual couples are excluded from adoption of children, artificial insemination, and a church ceremony (see below).

As in Denmark, registration of a homosexual partnership in Norway has the same legal consequences as marriage for heterosexuals (sec. 3 of the act), with exceptions (listed in sec. 4). The act simply makes a generic reference to all the legislation and jurisprudence that already concerns heterosexual spouses. The whole body of rules, with the exception of those relating to marriage as such and parental rights, is applicable to homosexuals as well. Thus, even in addition to the Marriage Act itself, all laws and regulations that apply to married couples and spouses also apply to registered partners, with the same exceptions as those made by the Danish act. Accordingly, the legislation provides for social security benefits (which include, inter alia, provider's supplements in old age, disability pensions, and rehabilitation allowances).[110] The act applies tax

108. Halvorsen, note 76 above, at 217.

109. Marianne Roth, *The Norwegian Act on Registered Partnership for Homosexual Couples,* 35 U. of Louisville J. Fam. L. 467, 468 (1996–97).

110. *See* The Proposed Bill, note 77 above, at 21. Note that persons receiving benefits as a single provider, such as supplementary child benefit, transitional pensions, etc., will lose these benefits if they enter into a partnership. *Id.* at 51.

provisions for spouses to partners in a registered partnership (affecting both the level of income tax deductions and property taxes) and mandates the responsibility of couples to support each other financially. The parties must contribute as far as they are able toward their joint maintenance, and the couple is jointly responsible for the work and expenses of maintaining a joint household.[111] Property acquired by both partners is community property, and, with some exceptions, each party is liable for the debts the other has incurred.[112] Furthermore, pensions or life insurance provisions benefiting the surviving spouse, which are provided for by law, apply to registered partnerships.[113] In all, about eight hundred rules, distributed among approximately 120 different laws from a wide variety of areas that apply to married couples, apply also to registered partners.[114] The few legal acts or provisions that apply only to a spouse of a defined sex do not apply to registered partners, including section 9 of the Children's Act, which provides for artificial insemination.[115]

3.2.4 The Dissolution of a Registered Partnership

The rules governing divorce of married couples apply similarly to the dissolution of a registered partnership while both parties are living (sec. 3 of the act). Thus, the partnership may be dissolved by means of immediate divorce or divorce following separation pursuant to the provisions in chapter 4 of the Marriage Act.[116] The court has the power to divide the partners' property in accordance with the rules of divorce, and one partner may be obliged to pay maintenance to the other. If the partnership is dissolved by the death of one of the partners, the legal consequences of marriage law apply, so that the surviving partner has the same right of inheritance as a widow or widower and is exempt from

111. *See id.* at 20.

112. *Id.* at 21.

113. Other pension and insurance agreements need to be adapted to take into account the partnership act and to give equality to registered partners as compared to married couples. Roth, note 109 above, at 469.

114. For example, provider's supplement for those serving in the armed forces or working abroad for the Ministry of Foreign Affairs. *See* The Proposed Bill, note 77 above, at 21–22.

115. *Id.* at 52. Another example is sec. 4 of the Children's Act, which provides that the father of the child is the man to whom the mother is married at the time of the child's birth. *Id.*

116. *Id.* at 53. A registered partnership may also be dissolved pursuant to sec. 24 of the Marriage Act, for example, on the grounds of bigamy. *Id.* According to sec. 5 of the Act on Registered Partnerships, if a couple enters into a registered partnership in Norway and then moves to another country, and one or both of the parties wish to dissolve the partnership, it is possible for them to do so in Norway, even if the plaintiff is not a Norwegian national.

inheritance tax. The survivor may retain an undivided estate, and if the surviving partner was dependent for support on the deceased, he or she will receive a survivor's pension from the National Insurance Office.[117] In Norway, though not in Denmark, the status of both same-sex couples who have not registered their partnership and opposite-sex cohabitants is similar to that of spouses, as far as division of property is concerned.[118] Under Norwegian law, work in the home is considered a contribution to co-ownership of the assets, and a system of joint ownership has been established. When partners have lived together for at least two years, the division of their property is regulated by the Joint Household Act of 1991.[119] Accordingly, in some instances, there is a right to take over a residential property or part of a residential property that belongs to the other party and a right to take over or acquire a portion of ordinary household goods.[120] Thus, the financially weaker party has more protection under Norwegian law than under the Danish regime.

3.2.5 Rights Excluded from the Act

Unlike heterosexual couples, same-sex couples are not given the opportunity to choose a church wedding instead of a civil ceremony; they are limited to the latter. The reason offered by the government for the exclusion of gay couples from church weddings was that this was an internal matter for the church to decide and Parliament did not want to force the state church to bless homosexual couples.[121] The ceremony that is used when contracting a registered partnership differs from the one used in a civil wedding for heterosexuals. The liturgy for the registered partnership ceremony has a technical terminology: it is merely stated that the partnership has been legally contracted; the liturgy is relatively short compared to the civil wedding liturgy of heterosexuals, and it does not state that the couple is, and should be, an important and positive contribution to the integration of society; furthermore, the partners do not promise each other eternal fidelity.[122]

Another difference from marriage is that at least one of the parties to a registered partnership must be a citizen and a resident of Norway. It was felt that foreign citizens without special connections to Norway would not have an interest in registering their partnership in Norway

---

117. *Id.* at 21.

118. Lund-Andersen, note 43 above, at 402.

119. *See above* for discussion of the act.

120. Lund-Andersen, note 43 above, at 402.

121. *See* The Proposed Bill, note 77 above, at 47; Halvorsen, note 76 above, at 209, 228 n. 7.

122. Halvorsen, note 76 above, at 216.

because, in general, their home countries would not recognize Norwegian registration.[123] The nationality requirement was opposed by many gay organizations, including the Norwegian Gay and Lesbian Association. They claimed that all groups had the same need for security and a framework around their partnership as long as they resided in Norway. It was unreasonable, they said, that foreigners who were permanent residents of Norway but had retained their original citizenship should be forced to give up that citizenship in order to enter into a registered partnership. The Ministry of Children and Family Affairs indicated that the question might be reconsidered if other countries subsequently enacted similar legislation,[124] and it is thus probable that Norway will follow Denmark's footsteps and amend its act so that permanent residents will also be allowed to register their partnerships in Norway.

Same-sex registered partners are also excluded from the right to adopt each other's children, to jointly adopt an unrelated child, or to have joint custody of a child.[125] Lesbian couples are not allowed to use methods of assisted procreation such as artificial insemination or in vitro fertilization. The Ministry of Children and Family Affairs reasoned that adoptive parents are chosen with the child's best interests in mind and that adoption must benefit the child; since "little is known about the effects of growing up in a family setting of two adults of the same sex . . . the question of adoption must be considered independently of the right to a registered partnership."[126] Thus, the supporters of the bill did not favor the inclusion of a right to adopt for same-sex couples. They made a distinction between establishing a gay or lesbian relationship and having children, arguing that there is no necessary connection between the two. In Norway, as in the other Nordic countries, there is an act for the regulation of the relationships between children and parents,[127] which is separate from marriage legislation.

Legislation regulating marriage in Norway increasingly suggests that marriage is a private matter, whereas the relationship between children and parents is considered a matter in which society at large has a responsibility and a right to intervene. The relationship between parents and children and the relationship between the partners themselves are seen more and more as two different social phenomena that are independent from each other. The supporters of the act thus emphasized that

123. Roth, note 109 above, at 468.
124. The Proposed Bill, note 77 above, at 48, 49.
125. *See* sec. 4 of the act.
126. *Id.* at 13.
127. The Act on Children and Parents. *See* Halvorsen, note 76 above, at 225.

marriage was not mainly about children but mainly about those who have married. This was used, on the one hand, to legitimate the use of the institution of marriage as a model for homosexual partnerships. On the other hand, the distinction between the parent-child relationship and the relationship between spouses was also used as an argument to exclude gays and lesbians from adopting children. The supporters considered children to be irrelevant to the issue of same-sex partnerships and avoided mentioning them. The Minister of Children and Family Affairs simply stated, "[L]esbians and gays cannot have children together." The reality that in fact many lesbians and gays do have children and do raise them with a partner of the same sex was completely ignored. The opponents of the act argued that the right of gay and lesbian couples to adopt children would soon be the next step; they also claimed that a main purpose of marriage is to protect children, as marriage gives them a stable frame and environment. Consequently, the right to reproduce or otherwise to be legal parents together became the major difference between heterosexuals and homosexuals in the eyes of both the supporters of the bill and its opponents.[128] The gay organizations were in favor of allowing the adoption of children, and they considered it to be particularly relevant when one of the partners brought a child into a partnership; they stated that the act should reflect social reality and thus provide for adoption of homosexual cohabitants' children.[129]

Finally, it is interesting to note that according to opinion polls taken in Norway prior to the adoption of the act, there was never a clear majority in the population that was in favor of the bill, not even among the people who voted for the Labor Party, which proposed the bill; these polls suggest that if there had been a referendum on the Act on Registered Partnerships in Norway, the act would not have been approved.[130] Therefore, Halvorsen contends that the enactment of the Act on Registered Partnerships does not reflect a general change in Norwegians' attitudes toward gays and lesbians but rather the opinions of the social strata from which the decision makers are recruited. Members of Parliament themselves who were in favor of the act did not necessarily assert that they had support from a majority of the population at the time when the act was passed, but they wanted to obtain this in the future. Notwithstand-

128. Halvorsen, note 76 above, at 226, 218, quotation at 218.

129. The Proposed Bill, note 77 above, at 52–53.

130. Halvorsen, note 76 above, at 213. However, the percentage of those in favor of the act increased: in 1983 only 16% of the population would "accept marriages for gays," whereas in 1988, 22% agreed that "gays should be able to marry," and in 1992, 26% "totally agreed . . . with the introduction of a partnership act." *Id.*

ing Halvorsen's account and the accuracy of the empirical data on which he bases his arguments, it is clear that the process of enacting registered partnership did not necessarily reflect the majority view in society but rather served as a tool for changing people's attitudes toward homosexuality. Such a purpose can be seen in the words of member of Parliament Lesbeth Holand, of the Socialist Left Party: "I would say that the rights for minorities, which this is all about, probably is the kind of case where we can trust the least in public opinion and opinion polls, and this is an area where we, as politicians, have a responsibility to take the lead and establish the norms of society."[131]

3.3 Registered Partnership and Cohabitation in Sweden

Sweden accorded limited recognition to same-sex cohabiting couples in its family law legislation as early as 1987, being one of the first countries in the world to offer protection to homosexual couples.[132] Almost a decade later (in 1995), Sweden expanded its recognition by adopting the Danish model of registered partnership.

3.3.1 The Homosexual Cohabitants Act of 1987

During the late 1960s, when the need for a new marriage code and the regulation of heterosexual cohabitation were first discussed, the issue of homosexual cohabiting couples was not on the agenda.[133] By the early 1970s, however, as an official statement from the Parliamentary Standing Committee on Laws indicated, cohabitation by two partners of the same sex had become fully acceptable from a societal standpoint.[134] On January 17, 1978, after the Swedish parliament had discussed the status of homosexuals on several occasions with the intention to find a solution, the Swedish minister of social affairs called upon a parliamentary commission of experts to investigate the situation of homosexuals in Swedish society. The purpose of the commission was to conduct an overall investigation of the status of gays and lesbians and to determine what measures should be taken to eliminate remaining discrimination against

131. *Id.* As Halvorsen explains, the decision makers are influenced by values that are ranked high by those with the highest economic and educational capital; thus, the act seems to be a product of changes in the values of the dominating strata of the population. *Id.*

132. *See* the Homosexual Cohabitants Act of 1987, SFS 1987:813. For discussion of this act, see below.

133. Anita Dahlberg & Nadine Taub, *Notions of the Family in Recent Swedish Law, in* Family Law and Gender Bias: Comparative Perspectives 133, 142 (Barbara Stark ed., 1992).

134. *See id.*

them. The commission was to carry out a comprehensive survey of all available scientific materials and study the history of homosexuality in various parts of the world.[135]

In 1984 the commission submitted its final report, entitled "Homosexuals and Society."[136] It found that there were two decisive factors regarding the social situation of homosexuals. The first was that there was complete silence surrounding homosexuals and homosexuality: that is, that homosexuality was not a "natural" part of society and thus was not present as a social and cultural institution. The second factor was that there existed a social prohibition on homosexuality, which was reinforced by the view of homosexuality purely as an act of sexuality. The commission concluded that although there was need for some legislation, the law alone could not solve the problem of discrimination; society must be able to recognize homosexuality as a fact of life. Only when it was admitted that homosexuality existed as a social and cultural institution within society would it be possible to conclude that all discrimination against homosexuals had ceased.[137] The commission also decided that there was no need for legislation pertaining to the relationship between homosexuals and children and that adoption of children by homosexuals should not be allowed, reasoning that too little was known about the impact on children of growing up in a homosexual family.[138]

Nonetheless, the commission proposed certain legislative measures, one of which led to an amendment prohibiting discrimination against homosexuals in the workplace, in public places, and the like. The commission also recommended that homosexual cohabitants be granted the same status as unmarried heterosexual cohabitants, and it proposed to amend several laws so that they would apply to homosexuals living together: these included the Cohabitees (Joint Homes) Act, tax laws, real property laws, and other relevant acts. A minority within the commission was of the opinion that homosexuals should be able to enter into a legal marriage and be entitled to adopt children. However, the commission decided against recommending such measures to Parliament based on its views that at the time, value judgments with regard to marriage were so firmly rooted that it was impossible to speak of same-sex

135. F. Nozari, *The 1987 Swedish Family Law Reform*, 17:3 Int'l J. Legal Info. 219, 230 (1989).

136. Report of a Commission on Homosexuality and Society 63 (SOU 1984). *See* Ake Saldeen, *Sweden: More Rights for Children and Homosexuals*, 27 J. Fam. L. 295, 296 (1988–89) [hereinafter *More Rights*].

137. Nozari, note 135 above, at 230.

138. Saldeen, *More Rights*, note 136 above, at 296.

marriage[139] and that according same-sex couples the right to marry "would run counter to public opinion on a central area of life."[140]

In 1987, seven years before the Registered Partnership Act was adopted, Sweden implemented a major family law reform, which included the enactment of a new marriage code. Following the commission's recommendations, part of the reform was to greatly expand an existing law, the Cohabitees (Joint Homes) Act, that affected property rights between unmarried cohabitants, thereby narrowing the gap between married and unmarried couples.[141] The expanded law provides unmarried cohabitants limited rights in property acquired by either party for mutual use during the time they cohabited, such as the home and its furnishings.[142] The Cohabitees (Joint Homes) Act applies only to unmarried heterosexuals living together in a "marriage-like" relationship.

During the same session, and based on the commission's report, the government proposed another law, the Homosexual Cohabitants Act, which was subsequently adopted by Parliament and became effective on January 1, 1988, extending the Cohabitees (Joint Homes) Act to homosexual couples.[143] The commission held the view that since the parties in many homosexual cohabiting relationships, like the parties in many heterosexual cohabiting relationships, developed an interconnected economy, the same needs existed for homosexual cohabiting couples when it came to legal regulation of the dissolution of the relationship.[144] Sweden was thus the first country in the world to include homosexual couples under the protective provisions of family law.[145]

The Homosexual Cohabitants Act not only expressly applies the Cohabitees (Joint Homes) Act to homosexual couples; it also applies a number of other statutes—such as the Civil Procedure Code, the Housing

---

139. Nozari, note 135 above, at 231.

140. Saldeen, *More Rights,* note 136 above, at 296.

141. SFS 1987:232 as amended by SFS 1987:814. *See* Matthew Fawcett, *Taking the Middle Path: Recent Swedish Legislation Grants Minimal Property Rights to Unmarried Cohabitants,* 24 Fam. L.Q. 179, 179 (1990); Henson, note 33 above, at 287. The original law was enacted in 1973 and was entitled the Unmarried Cohabitants Joint Home Act. It contained provisions concerning the tenant rights upon dissolution of a cohabitation similar to marriage. According to this law, upon dissolution, the party who did not have the right to the joint residence but was most in need of it had a right to take over the lease rights from the other party. The law applied only to opposite-sex partners who had children together. This law was a provisional one and was replaced in 1987 by the Cohabitees (Joint Homes) Act, according to which having children together was no longer a principal condition for the legal recognition of cohabitation. *See* Nozari, note 135 above, at 227–30.

142. Fawcett, note 141 above.

143. Nozari, note 135 above, at 231; *see also* Henson, note 33 above, at 287.

144. *See* Saldeen, *More Rights,* note 136 above, at 296–97.

145. Dahlberg & Taub, note 133 above, at 142.

Law, the Inheritance Code, and the Tax Code—to cases in which "two persons are living together in a homosexual relationship."[146] The act provides that when the cohabiting relationship is terminated, the joint home and household goods are to be divided equally between the parties, after debts have been deducted, if one of the parties so wishes. Upon the death of one cohabitant, the surviving cohabitant has the right, pursuant to the General Insurance Act, after division of their home and household goods, to receive as his or her share of the property remaining after deductions of debts, to the extent it suffices, an amount corresponding to twice the "base amount" at the time of the cohabitant's death.[147] The parties may opt out of the provisions of the act by entering into a written contract stipulating that the rules of division of property provided by the act shall not apply in their case.[148]

However, the act is more limited than the one that applies to opposite-sex cohabitants, since the right to assume possession of the dwelling and household goods is very much influenced by the presence of joint children. Thus, in practice, homosexual couples who do not have children together do not benefit from the provision to the same extent as heterosexual couples do; nor do homosexual couples have the option of automatically regulating their relationship.[149] The legislation itself does not prescribe the elements of a qualifying relationship; the relationship must be judged as a whole, based on various factors, such as the parties' own concept and understanding of their cohabitation, rental contracts, welfare applications, registration with the public insurance authority, and the like.[150] The length of the cohabitation is also a very important element: there is a five-year minimum.[151] Another essential element is shared housing and housekeeping, as the law requires that

146. David Bradley, *The Development of a Legal Status for Unmarried Cohabitation in Sweden*, 18 Anglo-American L. Rev. 322, 327 (1989). *See also* Fawcett, note 141 above, at 185; Michael L. Closen & Carol R. Heise, *HIV-AIDS and the Non-Traditional Family: The Argument for State and Federal Judicial Recognition of Danish Same-Sex Marriages*, 16 Nova L. Rev. 809, 812 (1992). The application of the Inheritance Code is limited: it provides that a surviving homosexual cohabitant may be counted as part owner of an estate, but no right of inheritance exists between homosexual cohabitants. *See* Saldeen, *More Rights*, note 136 above, at 297.

147. One "base amount" was 25,800 crowns in 1988. *See* Saldeen, *More Rights*, note 136 above, at 297.

148. *See id. See also* Mary Ann Glendon, The Transformation of Family Law 276 (1989); Michael Bogdan & Eva Ryrstedt, *Marriage in Swedish Family Law and Swedish Conflicts of Law*, 29 Fam. L.Q. 675, 677 (1995).

149. Dahlberg & Taub, note 133 above, at 142.

150. Fawcett, note 141 above, at 185.

151. The cohabitation begins when the cohabitees move into a joint residence. *See* Bogdan & Ryrstedt, note 148 above, at 677.

the parties live together and that their shared life consist of more than just shared quarters; in addition, a normal sex life is important.[152]

The reform process that led Sweden to adopt the Homosexual Cohabitant Act was very similar to that in Denmark.[153] First, the government decided that the status of homosexuals warranted study and investigation. Second, a commission was set up to study the issue and present its recommendations to Parliament with specific guidelines as to the underlying philosophy. The underlying philosophies in Denmark and Sweden differed, as did the final recommendations of the two commissions. Whereas the Danish government wanted to keep the institution of marriage separate and distinct from the institution of cohabitation, Sweden seemingly wanted to remove some economic disadvantages by enacting the property and inheritance regimes for both heterosexual and homosexual cohabitants.[154]

3.3.2 The Swedish Registered Partnership Act

In 1991 a Partnership Commission, consisting of representatives from various political parties, was formed by the government to study the possibility of Swedish legislation modeled after the Danish Registered Partnership Act for same-sex couples.[155] In 1993 the commission presented its report[156] recommending the adoption of a partnership act. The ideological foundation for the Partnership Commission's proposal was equality under the law in general, with an acknowledgment that homosexuality was equal in value to heterosexuality. Thus, the commission's view was that society should enable people to live in accordance with their own preferences and personalities, so long as that did not harm others. The commission found that the desire of homosexual couples to regulate their relationships and their need for economic and legal security in their relationships should be accommodated. The objective of the proposal, according to the commission, was to create greater awareness, openness, and acceptance of homosexuals, which could only be achieved by establishing legal parity between the relationships of homosexuals and heterosexuals.[157] Despite mixed reactions from the bodies

---

152. The reason for the requirement for a sex life is to rebut any inference of mere cohabitation without other intent. *See* Fawcett, note 141 above, at 186.

153. See the section above regarding Denmark.

154. Henson, note 33 above, at 296, 297.

155. Ake Saldeen, *Sweden: Family Counseling, the Tortious Liability of Parents and Homosexual Partnership*, 33 U. Louisville J. Fam. L. 513, 519, 521 (1995) [hereinafter *Family Counseling*].

156. SOU 1993:98.

157. *See* Saldeen, *Family Counseling*, note 155 above, at 519, 520.

that were consulted for opinions during the process of preparing the bill, and based on the commission's recommendations, the Swedish parliament passed the Registered Partnership Act on June 7, 1994, by a vote of 171 to 141, with 5 abstentions and 32 absences. The act came into effect on January 1, 1995.[158]

Registration and Its Legal Consequences

As in Denmark and Norway, the Swedish Registered Partnership Act grants same-sex partners all the rights of marriage except access to adoption, joint custody, artificial insemination, in vitro fertilization,[159] and church weddings.[160] As far as adoption is concerned, the Swedish government is examining the option of allowing same-sex couples living in registered partnerships to adopt children; it has appointed a parliamen-

158. Goransson, note 2 above, at 174 [hereinafter the Act]. *See* Act no. 1117 of June 23, 1994. For the English translation of the act, see appendix A, sec. A.3.

159. *See* chap. 3, sec. 2, of the Act. According to the Commentary on the Act, the exclusions from adoption, custody, and artificial insemination were made in response to public concern about children raised in a homosexual environment; it is stated in the commentary that this does not constitute discrimination since Swedish law does not recognize a "right to have a child." *See* Peter Nygh, *Homosexual Partnerships in Sweden,* 11 Australian J. Fam. L. 11, 12 (1997). As in Denmark, and according to the Insemination Act (Act no. 1140 of 1984) and the Fertilization Outside the Body Act (Act no. 711 of 1988), which apply to registered partners, insemination and other forms of artificial fertilization are allowed in Sweden only if the woman is married or is cohabiting with a man; single women or women living in a lesbian relationship are explicitly excluded from the right to artificial fertilization in a state health-service institution. However, the law does not interfere with private insemination. *See* Björn Skolander, *in* ILGA Europe, Equality, note 48 above, at 92.

160. As the Commentary to the Act explains, the legislature did not wish to impose any obligations on the Lutheran State Church. *See* Nygh, note 159 above, at 11. Two Swedish church-appointed working groups have produced reports on homosexuality and the church (one in 1974 and the other in 1988). The reports propose that the church support stable, long-term relationships between homosexuals and an institutional framework for them. *See* The Proposed Bill, note 77 above, at 40. The 1988 committee, which was also to draw up a liturgy for the blessing of gay couples, chose to use the word *intercession* instead of *blessing,* so that it would be more acceptable to Swedish Christians. The committee did not draw up a complete liturgy but only recommended a prayer and suggested that the parish priests would be free to work out their own version of the intercession. It did restrict the priests from designing an intercession that might be confused with a marriage service (thus not including in the proposed prayer any reference to children or child-rearing) or one that would express the idea that homosexual life together is an equal alternative to heterosexual marriage; it also emphasized that the basis for its report was the scientific evidence that homosexuality is immutable; the committee stated that its proposal was not applicable to "self-chosen" homosexuality. Furthermore, it viewed its proposed intercession as applicable to both registered and unregistered same-sex partnerships, since it did not consider the intercession as equivalent to the church's blessing of couples married in a civil ceremony. However, to date, the Swedish church has not expressed its view on these matters in an official decision or declaration. *See* Gert Nilsson, *Intercession or Blessing? Theological Reflections on a Swedish Liturgy for Homosexual Couples,* 50 Ecumenical Rev. 64 (1998).

tary commission to study this matter. In January 2001 the commission recommended that registered same-sex couples be permitted to adopt children, including children from foreign countries.[161] It is not yet clear whether this recommendation will result in an amendment to the Swedish Registered Partnership Act. The proposal will likely be debated in Parliament in 2002.

Moreover, the provisions concerning husband and wife that are dependent on the spouses being of opposite sex do not apply to registered partners.[162] And the capacity to enter into a registered partnership, unlike marriage, is always governed by Swedish law, even if the person in question is a foreign national domiciled abroad.[163] The act is restricted to same-sex couples,[164] although it does not require a particular sexual orientation;[165] and like marriage, it does not require shared sexual life or a common household.[166] One partner must be a Swedish citizen domiciled in Sweden.[167] The connection with Sweden was required based on the same rationale as in Denmark and Norway, namely, the assumption that no other state would recognize Swedish partnerships; this assumption was recently put to the test in a challenge brought before the European Court of Justice and proved to be correct.[168] In July 2000 the Swedish act was amended by removing the requirement for citizenship, so that foreigners could also register their partnership if both had been residents of Sweden for at least two years prior to registration.[169] Moreover,

---

161. *See* ILGA-Europe Euroletter, note 56 above, no. 86, February 2001.

162. *See* chap. 3, sec. 3 of the Act. This primarily concerns rules that accord special economic benefits to married women and widows. *See* Saldeen, *Family Counseling,* note 155 above, at 520.

163. *See* sec. 3 of the Act. *See also* Bogdan & Ryrstedt, note 148 above, at 678.

164. *See* sec. 1 of the Act.

165. *See* Nygh, note 159 above, at 11.

166. *See* Saldeen, *Family Counseling,* note 155 above, at 520.

167. Sec. 2 of the Act.

168. D, a Swedish gay man, moved from Sweden with his registered same-sex partner to work for the European Council in Brussels. The partner was not recognized by the council as a spouse according to the "Staff Regulations of Officials of the European Communities" and therefore could not benefit from the household allowances provided for married officials. The Court of Justice (case [C-122/99 P and C 125/99 P]) upheld the interpretation of the terms *marriage* and *spouse* according to their traditional meanings and stated that even in member states that allow arrangements for registering relationships, such registrations are being distinguished from marriage. The Court's narrow interpretation therefore sets a problematic precedent for same-sex registered partners who want to move freely within the European Union without losing the legal rights and protections they enjoy in their home country. *See On the Judgment of the European Court of Justice in Case D. and Sweden v. Council,* ILGA-Europe Euroletter, note 56 above, no. 89, June 7, 2001.

169. *See* http://www.riksdagen.se/bik/beslut.asp?ptnr=1233.

the act includes a specific clause providing that similar partnerships founded in other countries are automatically recognized in Sweden.[170]

According to section 3 of the act, the applicable preconditions for marriage—that the parties be of marriageable age (eighteen) and that they not be closely related to each other or already married—apply to partnerships, and an existing partnership precludes either another partnership or marriage.[171] Before registration takes place, an inquiry based on the Marriage Code procedure is made as to whether one or more of the foregoing impediments to registration exist.[172]

Since there is no option of a church wedding, the registration ceremony is a purely civil one. Some individual clergymen and priests offer blessings to registered partners, but no general religious ceremony for registered partners has yet been agreed upon.[173] The civil ceremony rules require the presence of witnesses and of both parties seeking the registration. Each of the two must give separate consent to the registration in answer to a question by the authorized person conducting the registration; that person must then declare them to be registered partners.[174] The registration is void if this procedure is not followed or if the person conducting the registration was not authorized.[175] A district court judge or a person appointed by the county administration is qualified to be a registrar.[176] The ceremony is similar to a civil marriage, and the partners can choose between a long and a short version.[177] Following the ceremony, the registrar gives the couple a registration certificate and enters the partnership in the official registry of marriages and registered partnerships.[178]

---

170. *See* the conclusion of sec. 9 of the Act. Since most registered partnership acts require citizenship and residence of one of the partners, some rather odd situations may occur. For instance, there is a case of two Swedish gay men, who have been living together in Norway for twenty-five years and cannot register their partnership either in Norway (because neither is a Norwegian citizen) or in Sweden (because both are not domiciled in Sweden). *See* Steffen Jensen, Recognition of Sexual Orientation: The Scandinavian Model, available from Landsforeningen for Bosser øg Lesbiske Forbundet af 1948 (National Danish Organization for Gays and Lesbians), Copenhagen, at 6.

171. *See also* Saldeen, *Family Counseling,* note 155 above, at 520–21.

172. Secs. 4 and 5 of the Act.

173. Skolander, note 159 above, at 90.

174. *See* secs. 6 and 7 of the Act.

175. Sec. 7 of the Act.

176. Sec. 8 of the Act.

177. Skolander, note 159 above, at 91. The abbreviated version of the solemnization of a partnership before a registrar is as follows: "You have decided that you wish to enter a partnership through registration. Do you N. N. take this woman/man to be your partner? (response: 'I do'), do you N. N. take this woman/man to be your partner? (response: 'I do'); I now pronounce you registered partners." *See* "Solemnization of Partnership before a Registrar," available from the Swedish Justice Department (copy on file with Merin).

178. *See* Skolander, note 159 above, at 91.

Once a partnership has been registered, the relationship has all the legal consequences of a heterosexual marriage, subject to the above-mentioned exceptions.[179] Thus, registered partners have the same responsibilities and benefits as married couples, including the mutual duties of maintenance, property rights and property division upon separation, inheritance upon the death of one of the partners, and rights regarding family name, pensions, and the like.[180] They are treated as a couple for tax purposes and national insurance. Although a partner cannot adopt the other partner's child, a child of one of the registered partners is considered a stepchild of the other partner. Thus, any child-related benefits, such as parental leave until the child is eighteen months old and subsidies for a parent who needs time off from work to take care of a sick child, can be claimed by the stepparent instead of the biological parent.[181]

The Dissolution of a Registered Partnership

A registered partnership is dissolved by the death of one of the partners or by a court decision.[182] If the partnership is dissolved by the death of a partner, the surviving partner has not only the right of inheritance but also a right to receive a pension for a year following the death, and if the death was caused by an accident at the partner's workplace, the surviving partner is entitled to a life annuity.[183] The partnership can also be dissolved by judicial decree, the process for which is similar to that for the dissolution of a marriage.[184] An application for dissolution must be handled by a lawyer and may be filed by one or both of the parties; it is submitted to the local district court, which decides whether to grant the dissolution immediately or after a six-month separation period. The grounds for dissolution are the same as for marriage.[185] In most cases in which the partners agree and no children below the age of sixteen are involved, the partners are granted immediate dissolution of the partnership.[186]

Since 1995 cohabitation of gay men and lesbians in Sweden has been eligible for regulation either by the Homosexual Cohabitants Act or by

179. *See* chap. 3 of the Act.
180. *See* Saldeen, *Family Counseling,* note 155 above, at 520.
181. Skolander, note 159 above, at 90, 92.
182. Chap. 2, sec. 1, of the Act.
183. Skolander, note 159 above, at 91.
184. *See* chap. 2, secs. 2–3, of the Act.
185. *See* Nygh, note 159 above, at 11.
186. Skolander, note 159 above, at 91.

the Registered Partnership Act, though the Cohabitants Act provides less legal protection than the Registered Partnership Act does; for example, a cohabitant does not automatically inherit a deceased partner's assets, as a registered partner does.[187] Moreover, for a cohabitation to be established, as opposed to a registered partnership, a couple simply has to have cohabited for a long enough period and to regard themselves as a couple, whereas partnership requires affirmative action by the couple— a special registration and a ceremony. Furthermore, the Cohabitants Act applies only to joint home and household goods and furnishings that were acquired for joint use; cohabitants must jointly consent to the alienation, lease, sale, and mortgage of the property, or, if they cannot agree, they must obtain court approval; inheritance provisions consist only of mandating that the surviving cohabitant, upon the other's death, receive a forced portion of the joint assets of the relationship.[188] The Cohabitants Act does not include the right to take each other's name and does not provide for automatic inheritance, joint taxation, or maintenance obligations.[189] Although the Swedish Homosexual Cohabitants Act grants many property benefits to lesbian and gay couples, the objective of the legislation was to equalize the status of gay couples with that of cohabiting heterosexual couples rather than with married couples.[190]

Before the adoption of the Registered Partnership Act, there was a clear hierarchy between the three kinds of couple formation in Sweden. Marriage was regulated to the greatest degree and had the most developed system of protection for the economically weaker party; the law provided far less protection for the economically weaker party in heterosexual cohabitation, and homosexual cohabitation ranked even lower because homosexual partners did not even have the possibility of getting married.[191] The fourth kind of couple formation, registered partnership, should be ranked after marriage, since it lacks some of the rights afforded to opposite-sex couples by marriage, and higher than the two types of cohabitation regulation, since it provides more protection for the economically weaker party.

3.4 Iceland's Registered Partnership Act

Following in the footsteps of its Scandinavian neighbors, the Icelandic parliament, the Althingi, passed a Registered Partnership Act on June 4,

187. *See* Goransson, note 2 above, at 175.
188. Henson, note 33 above, at 296.
189. Skolander, note 159 above, at 90.
190. Henson, note 33 above, at 296.
191. Dahlberg & Taub, note 133 above, at 143.

1996, with one opposing vote and one abstention. The law, which is based on the Danish precedent, came into effect on June 27, International Gay Pride Day.[192] The new act enjoyed the support of all political parties represented in Parliament, some of which spoke eagerly about enacting an even more progressive law that completely equates homosexual partners and married couples.[193] Public opposition to the act was minimal.[194]

For a long time, Iceland was the least progressive Nordic country with regard to lesbian and gay rights; this led many homosexuals to emigrate to Sweden, Norway, and Denmark.[195] However, during the 1980s attitudes began to change. A parliamentary motion protesting discrimination against homosexuals in Iceland was first brought before the Althingi in 1985 on behalf of the National Icelandic Organization for Lesbians and Gay Men—Samtoekin '78. The motion did not pass, and the organization put in seven more years of struggle and hard work before Parliament agreed to address the issue again. In 1992 the Icelandic parliament passed a resolution creating a parliamentary commission to examine the legal, cultural, and social condition of homosexuals in Iceland and to propose legislative measures to abolish discrimination. The first legislative change effected by the commission was the repeal of Iceland's sodomy law in 1992; at the same time, a common age of consent was established for homosexuals and heterosexuals.[196] In 1994 the commission recommended that Iceland legalize gay and lesbian marriage, criminalize discrimination against homosexuality, and substantially increase education about homosexuals in schools. The majority of the commission recommended adopting laws similar to those in Denmark, Norway, and Sweden. The commission minority, comprising members from Samtoekin '78, urged the adoption of more expansive laws that would completely equate heterosexual and homosexual relationships.[197]

At the beginning of 1995, the minister of justice and church asked the bishop of Iceland to issue an opinion of the Icelandic National Church on whether the representatives of the church could carry out recognition of a partnership. The church was also asked whether it felt

192. Goransson, note 2 above, at 175 [hereinafter the Act]. *See* Act no. 87 of June 4, 1996. For the English translation of the act, see appendix A, sec. A.4.

193. *See* ILGA-Europe Euroletter, note 56 above, no. 43, August 1996.

194. *See* Wockner International News no. 111, June 12, 1996, at http://www.queer.org.au/QRD/news/world/1996/wockner-111.html.

195. *See* Peter Tatchell, Europe in the Pink: Lesbian and Gay Equality in the New Europe 117 (1992).

196. *See* ILGA-Europe Euroletter, note 56 above, no. 43, August 1996.

197. Goransson, note 2 above, at 175.

it should have the right to marry persons of the same sex and, further, whether it should be obliged to marry persons of the same sex even if doing so was against the convictions of individual priests. It was also suggested that the issue should be clarified by both the Church Assembly and the National Church Board. Shortly afterward, the bishop established a working group to deliberate these issues and asked it to present its findings to the Church Assembly by fall 1995. The group could not complete its mission by the time set; instead, the National Church Board formulated the opinion of the church on the matter. The reply letter of the bishop of Iceland of November 21, 1995 presents the church's position: "The church well understands that the priests do not only serve religious people but they have also functions of authorities. The law of the state applies to them, too. The church does not, however, wish that a possibility for church wedding for persons of the same sex be incorporated in the legislation. It is obvious that the priests and other servants of the church pray for those who are in the need thereof but this is only the question of need and the status of the person in need is not questioned."[198]

The passage of the Registered Partnership Act in 1996 was based both on the commission's recommendations and on the reaction of the Church of Iceland.[199] Before that legislation was enacted, Iceland did not regulate same-sex partnerships, and none of the existing family law provisions were applicable to same-sex partners. Furthermore, like Denmark, Iceland has no rules regarding the cohabitation of either heterosexual or homosexual couples.[200]

Iceland's registered partnership legislation is similar to that of Norway, Sweden, and Denmark, both in the process of registration and in its legal consequences.[201] Thus, most of the rules regarding marriage,

198. Remarks on the Icelandic Registered Partnership Bill, at http://www.casti.com/FQRD/texts/partnership/is/iceland-remarks.html.

199. *See* Goransson, note 2 above, at 175. On the day the act took effect, Samtoekin '78 organized a reception at the City Theatre, inviting all members of Samtoekin '78 and their friends and families, all members of Parliament, the mayor of Reykjavik and the City Council, human rights activists, the press, and others. The guests of honor were the nation's first "married" gay couples and the president of Iceland, Vigdis Finnbogadottir. *Id.*

200. David Thór Björgvinsson, *Iceland: General Principles and Recent Developments in Icelandic Family Law, in* The International Survey of Family Law 215, 225, 226 (Andrew Bainham ed., 1995). However, there are a few Icelandic court decisions holding that "joint property" has been acquired by opposite-sex cohabitants. Moreover, with respect to opposite-sex cohabitants who have a child and have lived together for at least two years, there has been a certain tendency to equalize their rights and obligations with those of married people in relation to rights under the Child Act and under the social security system. *Id.*

201. *See* discussion above of the Danish Registered Partnership Act.

based on the Icelandic Marriage Act,[202] are also applicable to registered partnerships, including the prerequisites for marriage and the legal rights and obligations associated with marriage.[203] Section 1 of the act explicitly limits the applicability of the act to same-sex couples, but like the Swedish act and unlike the Norwegian act, it does not stipulate that the partners must be homosexuals.[204] The Icelandic act is similar to those of the other Nordic countries also in the exceptions it makes: it does not allow joint adoption of unrelated children, and until recently, it did not allow the partners to adopt each other's children. In 1998 five members of the Icelandic parliament presented a bill that allows registered partners to adopt a stepchild,[205] and in May 2000 the bill amending the 1996 registered partnership act took effect, so that now gay registered partners are permitted to adopt each other's children (but they are still excluded from joint adoption of an unrelated child).[206] This amendment is similar to the one passed by the Danish parliament in 1999; Iceland thus became the second country in the world, after Denmark, to allow stepparent adoption by same-sex registered partners. Like the other Nordic countries' legislation, Iceland's act does not extend artificial insemination rights or the option of church weddings to same-sex couples.[207] The act also requires that at least one of the partners be a citizen and a resident of Iceland or that both partners have been resident in Iceland for at least two years prior to registration.[208] The dissolution of a registered partnership is also similar to divorce of opposite-sex couples. However, in cases of separation, the head of the police district or a judge is to seek conciliation, since the priests are not required to participate in conciliation; according to the Marriage

202. Act no. 31 of 1993.

203. *See* secs. 2–5, 8, of the Act. Among other rights and obligations, the act applies to the registered partners the rights of inheritance, the tax laws, and insurance and social welfare just as they are applied to married individuals. *See* Remarks on the Icelandic Registered Partnership Bill at http://www.casti.com/FQRD/texts/partnership/is/iceland-remarks.html. *See also* Thór Björgvinsson, note 200 above, at 217, 225.

204. *See* Remarks on the Icelandic Registered Partnership Bill, note 203 above.

205. *See* The Changing Family: International Perspectives on the Family and Family Law 401 (John Eekelaar & Thandabantu Nhlapo eds., 1998).

206. *See* Rex Wockner, *Iceland Expands Gay Rights*, Int'l News, no. 321, June 19, 2000, available at http://www.qrd.org/qrd/world/wockner/news.briefs/111-06.12.96.

207. Sec. 4 of the Act provides that partnerships are to be officiated by heads of police districts in order to make it clear that only civil weddings are possible. *See* Remarks on the Icelandic Registered Partnership Bill, note 203 above.

208. The rationale given here is similar to the rationale for this requirement in the other Nordic states, i.e., that the connection with Iceland is justified by the fact that such partnerships would not be recognized outside the Nordic countries. *See* Remarks on the Icelandic Registered Partnership Bill, note 203 above.

Act, conciliation involving a priest is the norm in cases of heterosexual divorce.[209]

Although Icelandic registered partners are still not allowed to adopt each other's children or an unrelated child, Iceland allows registered partners to have joint guardianship and custody of biological children brought into the relationship if the biological parent had sole custody at the time of registration.[210] This provision is different from the registered partnership laws in the other Nordic countries. Consequently, the act applies the rules of the Marriage Act concerning common custody and support of children in cases in which one or both parties have children when registration takes place.[211] Thus, during the partnership and following a divorce, the stepparent is required to support his or her stepchild collectively and individually with the biological parent, as if such children were his or her own.[212] From this perspective, the Icelandic legislation has been until recently the most progressive and expansive, compared to that of other Nordic countries.[213]

3.5 Finland's Registered Partnership Act

Finland was the last Nordic country to adopt a registered partnership act; its legislation is similar to that of the other Nordic countries. In Finland, as in Norway, Denmark, and Iceland, there is no legislation regarding the cohabitation of either opposite- or same-sex couples.[214] Lesbian and gay partnerships were recognized only in the limited field of social welfare benefits.[215] A proposal for registered partnership legislation for

209. *See* sec. 8 of the Act; *see also* http://www.casti.com/FQRD/texts/partnership/is/ iceland-chng.html.

210. The Changing Family, note 205 above, at 400; Goransson, note 2 above, at 176.

211. *See* Thór Björgvinsson, note 200 above, at 225.

212. *Id.* at 229–30. Joint custody over each other's children is accorded in Iceland to any couple living together; this stems from the general principle in Icelandic law of equality between the parents (including stepparents and cohabiting partners) vis-à-vis their children regardless of their marital status. *Id.* Upon dissolution of the partnership, each partner has an equal opportunity to show that he or she should be awarded custody, but in reality custody is accorded to the biological parent. *Id.* at 234. However, when the partnership is dissolved by the death of the biological parent of the child, the surviving partner can retain custody, unless that is considered not to be in the best interests of the child. *See* Remarks on the Icelandic Registered Partnership Bill, note 203 above.

213. Now that the amendments to the Registered Partnership Act in Denmark allow same-sex couples to adopt each other's children, the Danish act is the most progressive one of its kind in the Nordic countries. *See* discussion of the Danish act, above.

214. Rainer Hiltunen, oral presentation at the conference Legal Recognition of Same-Sex Partnerships, King's College, University of London, July 1–3, 1999 [hereinafter London Presentation].

215. Tatchell, note 195 above, at 109. Same-sex couples have been treated as common law spouses in a few other instances when the wording of the law allowed it; for example,

same-sex couples was first introduced in Finland in 1993, and different versions of that bill were reintroduced in May 1996 and June 1999. In November 2000 the Finnish government approved the proposal, and finally, following a heated and passionate debate, on September 28, 2001, the Finnish Parliament passed the 1999 version of the bill by 99 votes to 84 with a few minor revisions.[216] The act took effect in March 2002.

In 1992 a Committee on Family Issues was established by the Ministry of Justice. In its report of spring 1992, it advised the Finnish government to draft a legislative proposal enabling same-sex couples to register their partnerships in order to provide equality before the law with opposite-sex married couples. The committee held the opinion that, like marriage, a registered partnership should be understood as a juridical relationship, since legal regulation of marriage no longer aims at supporting certain ethical or religious convictions but rather focuses on solving practical questions that arise in the course of the relationship. The committee thus saw no ethical or religious obstacles to regulating a partnership of persons of the same sex in a manner similar to marriage.[217] The committee's findings and its ideology served as a basis for the subsequent bills on registered partnership. However, no government action followed the committee's report. In 1993 eleven Parliament members presented a private member's bill according to which two persons of the same sex would be entitled to register their partnership with legal effects similar to those of marriage, including the right to adopt each other's children. But the bill eventually expired because of the 1995 parliamentary elections.[218] The newly elected government was divided on the issue, and during the years 1995–96, no preparatory work for legislation was introduced.[219] In May 1996 a new private member's bill was presented to Parliament.[220] The proposed bill was similar to the registered partnership acts of Denmark, Norway, and Sweden both in its scope and in its limitations and exceptions.[221] Following a debate in Parliament in June 1996, the bill was signed by 58 members of Parliament, includ-

---

residence permits have been granted to a homosexual partner of a Finnish citizen if they had lived together for at least one year. *See* Rainer Hiltunen, *Report on Finland,* in ILGA Europe, Equality, note 48 above, at 42–43.

216. *See* Anna Peltola, *Finland Approves Gay Couples Law,* Reuters, September 28, 2001. For the English summary translation of the bill, see appendix A, sec. A.5.

217. KM 1992:12, Families and the Law. *See* the Explanatory Part of the 1996 Bill at http://www.casti.com/FQRD/texts/partnership/fi/finland-expl.html.

218. Hiltunen, London Presentation, note 214 above. *See also* Hannelee Lehtikuusi, *Finland Update, in* ILGA-Europe Euroletter, note 56 above, no. 39, February 1996.

219. Hiltunen, London Presentation, note 214 above.

220. For the English translation of the bill, see http://www.casti.com/FQRD/texts/partnership/is/iceland-bill.html and http://www.casti.com/FQRD/texts/partnership/is/iceland-chng.html.

221. For detailed discussion of these acts, see previous sections of this chapter.

ing the prime minister and eight other ministers in their capacity as members of Parliament.[222] A parliamentary committee was established and began studying the proposed bill. According to the committee's recommendation, Parliament decided in September 1997 not to approve the bill. Instead, it accepted the committee's proposal that the government prepare legislation that would eliminate the existing inequality concerning same-sex couples.[223] In December 1997 the Ministry of Justice appointed a committee to study the issue and to draft legislation on the matter. That committee consisted of representatives of three ministries, the National Research Institute of Legal Policy, and the National Gay and Lesbian Finnish Organization (SETA).[224]

The committee presented its conclusions on June 1, 1999, and proposed a registered partnership act.[225] This proposal was similar to the 1996 Finnish bill on registered partnership, which was based on the Danish model. However, Finland's registered partnership act and other existing law and practices in Finland regarding the rights of same-sex couples are more advanced than existing partnership legislation in some of the other Nordic countries. Finland has no law concerning artificial insemination, and lesbian couples have been able to use nongovernmental artificial insemination services.[226] The initial bill on registered partnership denied the right of single women and lesbian couples to receive artificial insemination services.[227] This proposal met with considerable opposition, and thus, in the final version of the bill, the ban on artificial insemination was dropped and the existing status of artificial insemination was retained. The upshot is that since there have been no regulations and no limitations regarding access to assisted reproduction, lesbian couples will continue to have access to alternative insemination techniques. Moreover, the registered partnership act does not alter current legislation that was interpreted by the Ministry of Justice to enable same-sex couples to gain joint custody over each other's children. The Finnish Act on Child Custody allows the custody of a child to be given

222. Hiltunen, London Presentation, note 214 above. The bill also had wide support of the Finnish public: in a poll conducted at the time the bill was presented, 67% of Finns supported it, and 44% of that group approved of opening up marriage to same-sex couples; only 33% opposed any kind of gay unions. *See* Wockner International News no. 111, June 12, 1996, at http://www.qrd.org/qrd/world/wockner/news.briefs/111-06.12.96.

223. *See* Hannele Lehtikuusi, *The Finnish Partnership Legislation,* in ILGA-Europe Euroletter, note 56 above, no. 51, July 1997; Hiltunen, London Presentation, note 214 above.

224. Hiltunen, London Presentation, note 214 above.

225. The committee's report and proposals in Finnish with a summary in Swedish can be found on the Finnish Ministry of Justice Web page, http://www.om.fi/uploads/cqei3ir/RTF.

226. *See* Hiltunen, Report on Finland, note 215 above, at 42.

227. *See* Lehtikuusi, note 223 above.

to persons other than the biological parents, and Finnish courts have on numerous occasions granted joint custody of a child to same-sex couples. Furthermore, in October 2001, Finland's Supreme Court made a landmark ruling to award custody of two children to their deceased mother's female partner instead of their natural father.[228]

The citizenship and residency requirements are similar to those in the newly amended Danish act: under the 2002 Finnish registered partnership act, it is sufficient for both partners to have been residents of Finland for the two years prior to registration; and the requirement that at least one of them be a Finnish resident and citizen is only an alternative to permanent residency of both partners. The 2002 act goes further than the amended Danish act insofar as it recognizes partnerships entered into outside of Finland from *any* country in which the registration is valid, and citizenship in *any* country where registered partnership is provided can be designated as qualifying nationality for the purposes of registering a partnership in Finland. The act, which is restricted to same-sex couples and at the same time expressly provides that there is no requirement that the couple be of a particular sexual orientation, enables two persons of the same sex to register their partnership by the same authority as for civil marriage. The legal consequences of the partnership are the same as those of marriage, with a few exceptions: there is no right to adopt children, either each other's children or unrelated children, and no possibility to have a church wedding. Both the impediments to registration and the dissolution of a partnership are according to the provisions of the Marriage Act.[229]

228. *See* Reuters, *Landmark Custody Case Decided in Finland,* October 23, 2001.
229. Hiltunen, London Presentation, note 214 above.

Chapter 4

Same-Sex Partnerships in the Netherlands

The Netherlands, which is the first and thus far the only country in the world to recognize same-sex marriage, has been concurrently considering and implementing three different models of recognition of same-sex partnerships: First, the Netherlands has equalized the status of same-sex cohabitants with that of opposite-sex cohabitants and accorded to both many of the rights that flow from marriage. Second, following the example of its Scandinavian neighbors, the Netherlands has adopted a Registered Partnership Act based on the Nordic model. It took effect January 1, 1998.[1] Third, a proposal to extend Dutch marriage law to include same-sex couples and a bill on adoption by persons of the same sex have been debated in the Netherlands since 1996; they have finally become law, effective April 1, 2001. With the adoption of the two bills, Netherlands became the only country to accord same-sex couples full equality with opposite-sex married couples. Chapter 4 addresses these four matters: cohabitation, registered partnership, adoption by same-sex couples, and the opening up of marriage to same-sex couples.

---

1. *See* Brochure on Registered Partnership 1, Dutch Ministry of Justice, December 1997, available at http://www.xs4all.nl/~nvihcoc/regpartner.htm [hereinafter Registered Partnership Brochure].

4.1 Cohabitation of Same-Sex Couples

Cohabitation of both same- and opposite-sex couples has been a frequent and accepted phenomenon in the Netherlands for the last thirty years.[2] Since the 1970s, both heterosexual and homosexual Dutch cohabiting couples have been increasingly given legal rights and duties similar to those of married couples in a variety of fields, such as rent law, social security and income tax, state pensions, and death duties. In none of these areas has a distinction been made between same-sex and opposite-sex cohabitation.[3] The level of benefits is normally not influenced by whether the recipients are married or living together with a partner.[4] With respect to inheritance tax, the provisions relating to married couples apply fully to cohabiting partners after five years of cohabitation.[5] The Dutch Nationality Act of 1984 provides that a foreigner who has been living in the Netherlands in a permanent nonmarital relationship with a Dutch national for at least three years can acquire Dutch citizenship.[6] A residence permit can also be obtained on the basis of a nonmarital relationship, including a same-sex one, provided the partners live together and can demonstrate some permanency—a six-month relationship is usually considered sufficient—and provided the Dutch citizen has adequate income and housing to maintain the foreign partner.[7]

---

2. Family Law in Europe 323 (C. Hamilton et al. eds., 1995). *See also* A. M. van de Wiel, *Cohabitation outside Marriage in Dutch Law, in* Marriage and Cohabitation in Contemporary Societies: Areas of Legal, Social, and Ethical Change: An International and Interdisciplinary Study 212 (John M. Eekelaar & Sanford N. Katz eds., 1980).

3. *See* Kees Waaldijk, *Small Change: How the Road to Same-Sex Marriage Got Paved in the Netherlands* [hereinafter *Small Change*], *in* Legal Recognition of Same-Sex Partnerships: A Study of National, European, and International Law 437 (Robert Wintemute & Mads Andenas eds., 2001). *See also* Homosexuality: A European Community Issue 94 (Kees Waaldijk & Andrew Clapham eds., 1993).

4. *See* Kees Waaldijk, Towards Full Equality in Dutch Law for Same-Sex Partners and their Children, Dutch Association for the Integration of Homosexuality COC, Information Brochure no. 6, July 1998 [hereinafter Towards Full Equality].

5. *See* Yvonne Scherf, Registered Partnership in the Netherlands: A Quick Scan 9 (1999) [hereinafter Quick Scan].

6. The Third Pink Book: A Global View of Lesbian and Gay Liberation and Oppression 308 (Aart Hendriks et al. eds., 1993).

7. The required income is slightly higher for unmarried than for married partners. In a court case from 1995, a Dutch court found this distinction to be discriminatory in certain circumstances when applied to same-sex couples and equated their status to that of a married couple for the purposes of immigration law. *See* Kees Waaldijk, *Free Movement of Same-Sex Partners*, 3 Maastricht J. European & Comp. L. 271, 275 (1996). *See also* Waaldijk, Towards Full Equality, note 4 above; Aelens Brauckman, Information concerning Relationships between Dutch Citizens and Foreigners and the Residential Permit (obtained from the Dutch Association for the Integration of Homosexuality COC in Amsterdam).

Dutch homosexuals in some professions, including civil service, health care, and education, as well as employees of some major companies and industries, receive spousal employment benefits.[8] During this period "cohabitation contracts" drawn up by a notary became common and were fully recognized by the courts.[9] These developments led to the enactment of the General Equal Treatment Act of 1994, which made it illegal for any employer or provider of goods and services to discriminate on the basis of sexual orientation or to distinguish between married and unmarried couples.[10] However, there remain differences between married couples and cohabiting ones. Cohabiting partners are required to prove that they have been living together for a certain period, and some private pension funds are still in the process of adjusting their rules to cover unmarried surviving partners. In the fields of tax, property, inheritance, and death duties, cohabiting partners can obtain by way of contract only some of the advantages provided automatically to married couples.[11]

Beginning in 1991, Dutch cities and towns (eventually more than one hundred of them) started offering semiofficial registration for lesbian and gay partners. Such registration was not based on any kind of legislation, it had no legal implications, and no rights were granted by the process. The registries thus had only political and symbolic significance.[12]

8. Leslie Goransson, *International Trends in Same-Sex Marriage, in* On the Road to Same-Sex Marriage 165, 181 (Robert P. Cabaj & David W. Purcell eds., 1998).

9. Such a contract has no effect on third parties, although some employers, including the state, do award spousal benefits to those who have entered into a cohabitation contract. *Id.* By formalizing a written cohabitation agreement, the parties can make mutual arrangements regarding many of the rights enjoyed by married couples, including the division of joint property, maintenance obligations upon separation, pensions, and next-of-kin visiting rights in hospitals and prisons. If the couple wish to make provisions for each other with respect to inheritance, they need to draw up wills. *See* Martin Moerings, *The Netherlands, in* Sociolegal Control of Homosexuality: A Multi-Nation Comparison 309 (Donald J. West & Richard Green eds., 1997). *See also* Peter Tatchell, Europe in the Pink: Lesbian and Gay Equality in the New Europe 122 (1992); Quick Scan, note 5 above, at 9.

10. This made the Netherlands the only country where such discrimination on the basis of civil status, not merely on the basis of sexual orientation, has been forbidden, since registered partners are now considered to have a new type of civil status. *See* Waaldijk, Towards Full Equality, note 4 above.

11. *See* Waaldijk, *Small Change,* note 3 above. For the previous regime regarding statutory pensions, see Moerings, note 9 above, at 308.

12. Waaldijk, Towards Full Equality, note 4 above. *See also* Madzy Rood-de-Boer, *The Netherlands: New Legal Facts,* 31 J. Fam. L. 389, 394–95 (1992–93); Rex Wockner, *Netherlands to Legalize Gay Marriage,* ILGA-Europe Euroletter no. 34, July 1995 (Steffen Jensen et al. eds.) at http://www.qrd.org/qrd/www/orgs/ILGA/euroletter.

4.2 The Dutch Registered Partnership Act

4.2.1 Background

In 1990 the major gay organization in the Netherlands, the Dutch Association for the Integration of Homosexuality COC, organized a conference that challenged existing marriage laws and proposed new legislation to make marriage available to same-sex partners. Since then the Dutch gay organization has been fighting for legislation equalizing same-sex partnerships with marriage and allowing homosexual couples to adopt children;[13] both goals have finally been achieved by the passage in April 2001 of the bills allowing adoption and marriage to same-sex couples.

In 1992 a Dutch Government Advisory Commission for Legislation produced a report recommending the introduction of registered partnership in the Netherlands along the lines of the Danish model.[14] A bill on registered partnership was first introduced before the Dutch parliament in June 1994. It included almost all the legal consequences of marriage but excluded any form of parental rights and duties.[15] The government strongly opposed the bill, and it was not until four years later, after being heavily amended, that the bill was reintroduced before Parliament and legislation took place. The act on registered partnership, which came into effect on January 1, 1998, is a complex of several laws amending the Civil Code and more than one hundred other statutes.[16] The act introduces to book 1 of the Dutch Civil Code, which deals with the law of persons and family law, the possibility of concluding a registered partnership. The text of the act is closely interrelated with articles of book 1 of the Civil Code by the many references it makes; it is not an independent statute.[17] Unlike the Nordic model, registered partnership in the Netherlands is open to both same- and opposite-sex couples. The Dutch legislation was intended both for couples who could not marry because

---

13. *See* Han van Delden et al., Fifty-One Years of the COC, Dutch Association for the Integration of Homosexuality COC, Information Brochure no. 5, July 1998.

14. Waaldijk, Towards Full Equality, note 4 above.

15. *See* Kees Waaldijk, Dutch Parliament Demands Legislation to Open Up Marriage and Adoption for Same-Sex Couples, April 17, 1996, at http://www.coc.nl/index.htm/?file=marriage (last visited August 18, 1999) [hereinafter Dutch Parliament Demands].

16. Act of July 5, 1997, Netherlands Law Gazette 324; and Act of December 17, 1997, Netherlands Law Gazette 660. *See* Kees Waaldijk, Dutch Government Decides against Same-Sex Marriage, but in Favor of Adoption by Same-Sex Couples, February 8, 1998, at http://www.coc.nl/index.htm/?file=marriage (last visited August 18, 1999) [hereinafter Dutch Government Decides].

17. *See* Quick Scan, note 5 above, at 7. For this reason, the text of the legislation is not included in this book.

they were of the same sex and for heterosexual couples who did not wish to marry but still wanted to regulate their relationship.[18] With the passage of the Registered Partnership Act, same-sex couples could choose between a registered partnership and a cohabitation contract.[19] Following the opening up of marriage to same-sex couples in April 2001 (three years after the adoption of the Registered Partnership Act), registering a partnership remains an option for those couples (either homosexual or heterosexual) who simply do not wish to marry but still want to have legal recognition and regulation of their relationship. During the period January 1998 through the end of 2000, 10,804 couples—4,433 different-sex couples, 3,398 male couples, and 2,973 female couples—contracted registered partnerships.[20] Thus, compared to other countries with registered partnerships, the interest in registered partnership in the Netherlands is relatively high. Another striking point is the unexpectedly large number of opposite-sex couples who utilized the option of registering a partnership.[21]

4.2.2 Registration and Its Legal Consequences

The Dutch registered partnership is similar to marriage, and its consequences are virtually identical, with only a few exceptions.[22] The prerequisites for marriage apply similarly to registered partnerships: a person wishing to enter a registered partnership must be at least eighteen years old, must not be closely related to the other person, and must not be married or be involved in another registered partnership.[23]

In order to register their partnership, the couple has to declare their intention to the registrar of births, marriages, and deaths in the place of residence of one of the two partners and prove that they meet the conditions for registration. A deed of declaration is then drawn up, and the couple is allowed to register after a waiting period, which also applies

18. Registered Partnership Brochure, note 1 above, at 1.

19. A cohabitation contract regulates only what the two parties agree upon between themselves; they do not acquire rights and are not subject to obligations prescribed by law; in addition, the consequences of the contract are limited to the relationship between the partners and do not apply to third parties. *Id.* at 3.

20. *See* Kees Waaldijk, Partnership Registration of Two Men or Two Women (Or between a Man and a Woman), available at http://ruljis.leidenuniv.nl/user/cwaaldij/www/NHR/news.htm (last updated March 30, 2001).

21. Quick Scan, note 5 above, at 13. However, the vast majority of opposite-sex couples still seem to prefer marriage. *See* Gregor Van Der Burght, Registered Partnership in the Netherlands, draft of June 11, 1999 (copy on file with Merin).

22. The Registered Partnership Act was amended soon after its enactment, and the discussion of the act below reflects and incorporates these amendments. For an overview of the amendments, see Waaldijk, Dutch Government Decides, note 16 above.

23. Registered Partnership Brochure, note 1 above, at 4–5.

to marriage, of two weeks. Registration requires the presence of both parties and at least two witnesses. The ceremony is different from a marriage ceremony in that the partners do not make an oath to each other; they simply express their consent to the registration and sign the deed in the presence of the registrar.[24]

Registered partners have most of the same rights and obligation as married couples do, including a mutual obligation of maintenance during the course of the partnership; they are obliged to support each other financially as far as they are able and to share the costs of the household.[25] The property regime is one of full community: all possessions and ordinary debts are joint, including all property that was owned by each partner separately before the partnership. The parties may choose a different property regime by way of an explicit written and notarized agreement between them.[26] In the fields of taxation, social security, property, inheritance, and death duties, the same rules that apply to married couples apply to registered partners.[27] Registered partners may also take each other's surname.[28]

Parenthood was the most striking exception in the Registered Partnership Act; the act entailed no parental rights or obligations for the partner of the parent, nor did it provide the partners with the possibility of adopting each other's children or jointly adopting unrelated children.[29] However, subsequent legislation has provided same-sex couples with most parental rights that are granted to heterosexual married couples. In April 2001 a separate act recognizing the rights of same-sex couples to adopt (both each other's children and unrelated children from within the Netherlands) came into force.[30]

24. *Id.* at 3–6.

25. *Id.* at 3, 6.

26. Van Der Burght, note 21 above. Certain contracts require the permission of the other partner and are otherwise voidable, such as contracts to sell the joint home or the household goods. *Id.*

27. Registered Partnership Brochure, note 1 above, at 7.

28. *When My Old Dutch Is a Man,* Economist, January 24, 1998, at 52. However, the partner's pension for a surviving registered partner may sometimes be lower than for a surviving spouse. *See* Quick Scan, note 5 above, at 8.

29. *See* Astrid Mattigssen & Mirjam Turksma, *Report on the Netherlands, in* ILGA-Europe, Equality for Lesbians and Gay Men: A Relevant Issue in the Civil and Social Dialogue 80 (Brussels 1998). Waaldijk argues, however, that the former ban on adoption by same-sex partners should not be viewed as an exception to the Registered Partnership Act, since the right to adopt is not a legal consequence of marriage in the Netherlands. *See* Waaldijk, *Small Change,* note 3 above. For a more detailed discussion of adoption rights in the Netherlands, see below.

30. For discussion of the act opening up adoption to same-sex couples, see sec. 4.3 below, regarding adoption by Dutch gay men and lesbians.

Moreover, same-sex registered partners can obtain joint custody over each other's children. In May 1994 a bill on joint custody pertaining to same-sex couples and also to different-sex couples who are not both the legal parents of the children they are bringing up was first introduced before Parliament.[31] On January 1, 1998, legislation introducing joint custody for nonparents took effect.[32] Thus, in addition to the right to adopt, a parent and his or her partner—both same-sex couples and heterosexual couples—can apply for and subsequently obtain a court order giving them joint custody over the child of the parent.[33] Joint custody places support and maintenance obligations upon the partner of the parent with respect to the child, and the child is regarded as her or his own for the purposes of reduced inheritance tax in case the child benefits from the will of the nonparent.[34] However, joint custody is not automatically assumed, as it is for a child born to a heterosexual couple; and if not adopted, the child cannot automatically inherit from the co-parent.[35] Furthermore, under this legislation, if the partners did not adopt each other's children or seek and obtain a joint custody court order, the existence of a registered partnership did not affect the position of the children of either partner, and the partner had no rights or obligations toward the child.[36] According to the new act opening up marriage to same-sex couples, a stepparent in a registered partnership is now obliged to financially support his or her registered partner's children under the age of twenty-one.[37] In addition, no exceptions

31. Waaldijk, Dutch Parliament Demands, note 15 above. For a detailed discussion of the 1994 proposal, see Caroline Forder, *Re-Thinking Marriage, Parenthood, and Adoption, in* The International Survey of Family Law 1995 (A. Bainham ed., 1997), at 367–70.

32. Act of October 30, 1997, Netherlands Law Gazette 506. *See* Waaldijk, Towards Full Equality, note 4 above.

33. Waaldijk, Dutch Government Decides, note 16 above.

34. The child can also acquire the surname of the parent's partner. *See* Registered Partnership Brochure, note 1 above, at 7. *See also* Waaldijk, Dutch Government Decides, note 16 above.

35. *See* Nancy Maxwell et al., *Legal Protection for All the Children: Dutch-American Comparison of Lesbian and Gay Parent Adoptions,* 3.1 Electronic J. Comp. L. 11 (1999) at http://law.kub.nl/ejcl/31/art31-2.htm.

36. Waaldijk, Dutch Government Decides, note 16 above. However, if the Bill on Opening Up of Marriage becomes law (see discussion of the bill below), during the marriage or the registered partnership, a stepparent would be obliged to provide financial support for the minor children of his spouse or registered partner. *See* Text of Dutch Bill and Explanatory Memorandum on the Opening up of Marriage for Same-Sex Partners, summary, translation, and comments by Kees Waaldijk (draft version, July 15, 1999), *in* ILGA-Europe Euroletter, note 12 above, no. 72, August 1999 [hereinafter Text of Dutch Bill].

37. *See* sec. 4.4, "The Dutch Act on Same-Sex Marriage," below, regarding the opening up of marriage to same-sex couples.

have been made regarding artificial procreation, for which marriage is not a condition.[38] In February 2000, after four out of the nation's thirteen in vitro fertilization clinics were found to have discriminated against lesbians, the Dutch Committee for Equal Treatment announced that such clinics must serve lesbian couples;[39] Dutch lesbians thus enjoy affirmative protection from discrimination in access to artificial conception services.

The Registered Partnership Act initially provided that a foreigner without a valid residence entitlement could not register a partnership in the Netherlands—either with a Dutch citizen or with another foreigner.[40] The law required that both partners have either Dutch citizenship or a valid residence entitlement.[41] A bill amending the Registered Partnership Act (bill 26862), which allows partnership registration when only one of the partners has Dutch citizenship or residency (the same requirements that pertain to marriage in the Netherlands), was signed into law in December 2000.[42] However, most rules of private international law, and rules based on international or European law that apply to marriage, have not been declared applicable to registered partnership.[43] Finally, the act, unlike registered partnership acts in the Nordic countries, makes no exceptions regarding church weddings, simply because the Netherlands does not have a state church, church weddings have no legal effect in Dutch law, and the marriage ceremony is civil and secular and can be legally performed only by a registrar.[44]

38. *See* Waaldijk, Dutch Government Decides, note 16 above. The number of lesbians having children has increased enormously during the past few years as artificial insemination has become more popular. Despite legal prohibitions, there are still some hospitals that deny lesbians or single women artificial insemination, but most hospitals do offer these services. *See* Mattigssen & Turksma, note 29 above, at 79.

39. *See International Couples Brief: Netherlands IVF for Lesbians*, PlanetOut News & Politics, February 15, 2000, at http://www.planetout.com/news/article.html?2000/02/15/2.

40. Waaldijk, Dutch Government Decides, note 16 above. It is not clear in Dutch law exactly what amounts to residence entitlement, and a residence permit for less than one year, which is routinely given to European Union citizens looking for work in the Netherlands, may not be enough. *See id.*

41. *See* Kees Waaldijk, Dutch Law Reform in Progress (Adoption & Marriage, Foreign Partners), January 1, 1999, at http://www.coc.nl/index.htm/?file=marriage (last visited August 18, 1999) [hereinafter Dutch Law Reform in Progress].

42. *See* Kees Waaldijk at http://ruljis.leidenuniv.nl/user/cwaaldij/www/ (last visited January 14, 2001).

43. Waaldijk, Dutch Government Decides, note 16 above.

44. *Id.* A church wedding ceremony following the civil one has become less and less common owing to the secularization of the Netherlands. *See* Paul Vlaardingerbroek, *Marriage, Divorce, and Living Arrangements in the Netherlands*, 29 Fam. L.Q. 635, 636 (1995). The situation is different in the Nordic countries, where there are state churches and opposite-sex couples can choose between a civil ceremony and a church wedding, both having the same legal effect. In this context it should be noted that in November 1994

4.2.3 The Dissolution of a Registered Partnership

A partnership can be dissolved by divorce proceedings in court similar to the dissolution of a marriage upon unilateral request; in cases of mutual consent, the partners may end the partnership without court intervention by an agreement, stating that there is an irreparable breakdown of the partnership. The latter option is unique to registered partnerships; it is not available to married couples who wish to terminate their marriage.[45] The dissolution agreement has to include the division of property between the partners, alimony, accommodations, and the settlement of pension rights. In such cases, the partnership ends when the termination agreement between the parties has been recorded by the registrar of births, marriages and deaths. In the absence of mutual consent, either partner can apply to the court for a divorce similar to the divorce of married couples. Upon termination of the partnership, the partner with the greater financial resources has a duty to pay alimony to the other partner, and pension rights are equalized in accordance with the Dutch Pension Rights (Equalization on Separation) Act.[46]

In case the partnership is dissolved by the death of one of the partners, the entire estate can accrue to the other partner provided, as in marriage, that there is a will to that effect. Moreover, the rules of inheritance tax for married couples apply similarly to registered partners, and the surviving dependent's pension goes to the longer-surviving partner.[47]

4.3 Adoption by Same-Sex Couples

As in the case of marriage for same-sex couples, the Netherlands is the first and thus far the only country to have enacted legislation allowing

---

the Dutch Reformed Church stated that it would allow congregations to turn away gays; in May 1995 it reversed its prior decision and mandated that local parishes may not refuse communion to gays and must fully accept gay relationships. *See* Rex Wockner, *Dutch Church Embraces Gays,* ILGA-Europe Euroletter, note 12 above, no. 33, May 1995. In November 1995, a synod of the twenty-thousand-member Dutch Lutheran Church declared its support of church blessings of gay unions, stating that "there are no theological arguments against blessing two people who are strongly committed to one another, faithful and dedicated. . . . The blessing of a commitment for life between two women or two men can give extra meaning to a relationship." The synod also called for reconsideration of the theological notions of "wedding vows," "fidelity," and "blessing." *See* Rex Wockner International News no. 83, November 30, 1995, at http://www.qrd.org/qrd/world/wockner/news.briefs/083-11.30.95. Thus, despite the lack of any legal consequences, some Dutch churches even perform a "marriage ceremony" for same-sex registered partners. *See* Mattigssen & Turksma, note 29 above, at 80.

45. *See* Mattigssen & Turksma, note 29 above, at 80.

46. Registered Partnership Brochure, note 1 above, at 8, 9.

47. *Id.* at 7, 6.

adoption by same-sex couples (to be distinguished from second-parent adoptions in the United States; see chap. 7, sec. 7.1). Until 1998 adoption in the Netherlands was possible only for married couples and married stepparents, and until April 2001 same-sex couples were excluded from the right to adopt. The Dutch adoption laws were amended in April 1998 so that marriage was no longer a requirement for adoption: heterosexual cohabiting partners, as well as individuals—even if an individual was living with a partner of the same sex—could also adopt a child.[48] The criteria for joint adoption required the couple to have cohabited for three continuous years before the adoption request and to have cared for the child in their home for at least one year; a single person had to have cared for the child in his or her home for three continuous years before she or he could adopt.[49] However, the 1998 legislation did not accord gay and lesbian couples the right to jointly adopt children.[50] In April 1996 the lower chamber of the Dutch parliament passed a resolution by a vote of 83 to 58 demanding that the government prepare a bill to allow same-sex couples to adopt.[51] Consequently, an advisory committee of legal experts, known as the Kortmann Committee, was appointed in June 1996 to study, among other things, the desirability of allowing same-sex couples to adopt.[52] Meanwhile, in September 1997 the Hoge Raad (the Dutch Supreme Court) refused to allow a lesbian couple to adopt each other's children, who were conceived via artificial insemination from the same donor, the donor having waived all rights regarding the children.[53] The couple argued violation of the nondiscrim-

48. *See* Waaldijk, *Small Change,* note 3 above. *See* also Maxwell et al., note 35 above, at 2. As early as May 1995, a court in Amsterdam ruled that unmarried couples and single people should be allowed to adopt. However, this ruling was limited to juridical adoption by a single parent who had already been taking care of the child, and thus it did not effect a change in the law. *See* ILGA-Europe Euroletter, note 12 above, no. 33, May 1995.

49. *See* Maxwell et al., note 35 above, at 24 n. 11. According to Dutch law, prospective adopters of a child first care for the child as foster parents, and only then, if all goes well and all conditions are fulfilled, the adoption proceedings begin; hence the requirement of caring for the child prior to any adoption proceedings. Personal E-mail from Kees Waaldijk of August 24, 1999.

50. Waaldijk, Dutch Government Decides, note 16 above.

51. *See* Waaldijk, Dutch Parliament Demands, note 15 above. Parliament's resolutions are nonbinding on the government. *Id.* For the text of the resolution, see appendix A, sec. A.6.1.

52. *See* Janet McBride, Dutch in Favor of Gay Marriage, Adoption, Reuters, Amsterdam, October 28, 1997, at http://www.coc.nl/index.htm/?file=marriage (last visited August 18, 1999). For an extensive discussion of the committee's establishment and its tasks, see the discussion below regarding the opening up of marriage to same-sex couples in the Netherlands.

53. Hoge Raad, September 5, 1997, *NJ* 1998, 686, rek. nr. 8940. For a detailed analysis of the case, see Maxwell et al., note 35 above, at 9–10, 30 n. 66.

ination clause (art. 14) of the European Convention on Human Rights, based on the Dutch law's distinction between same-sex couples, who were not allowed to adopt, and married heterosexual couples, who could adopt in the same circumstances. The Hoge Raad did not debate the merits of the case, reasoning that it was a political decision for the legislative branch to consider. However, the Court stated that adoptions by same-sex couples would require a more elaborate legal recognition than the law provided at the time.[54]

The Kortmann Committee submitted its report in October 1997, recommending unanimously to allow the gay partner of a child's parent or two people of the same sex to adopt.[55] In February 1998 the Dutch government stated that it had decided to act on the committee's recommendations and to amend the law on paternity and adoption. Despite its statement, and as mentioned above, the government presented a narrower bill to revise the laws on paternity and adoption, which became effective in April 1998, allowing adoption by an unmarried opposite-sex couple or by an individual person.[56] The government took no further action on adoption by same-sex couples. In April 1998 the lower chamber of the Dutch parliament therefore repeated its call for same-sex adoption and, for the second time, passed a resolution, this time by a vote of 95 to 42—a considerable increase compared to the adoption resolution of 1996—demanding legislation to that effect and implementation of the government's decision of February 1998.[57] In August 1998 the newly elected government stated that it would introduce a bill for adoption of Dutch children by same-sex couples,[58] and in November of the same year, the Dutch government approved a bill to allow such adoption, the text of which was sent to the Council of State for advice.[59]

On July 8, 1999, the bill was introduced before Parliament.[60] The explanatory memorandum to the bill stated that "[a] child being cared for

54. Maxwell et al., note 35 above, at 9. However, the Hoge Raad did not refrain from deciding the merits of similar cases involving the protection of children within a heterosexual relationship; for example, it extended joint parental authority to unmarried and divorced heterosexual couples. These rulings were treated as advisory to the legislature, which amended the law accordingly. *Id.*

55. *See* McBride, note 52 above.

56. Waaldijk, Dutch Government Decides, note 16 above.

57. *See* Kees Waaldijk, Dutch Parliament Repeats Calls for Same-Sex Marriage and Adoption—but Still No Legislation, April 19, 1998, at http://www.coc.nl/index.htm/?file =marriage (last visited August 18, 1999) [hereinafter Dutch Parliament Repeats Calls].

58. *See* Kees Waaldijk, New Dutch Government Committed to Opening Up Marriage and Adoption to Same-Sex Couples, August 11, 1998, at http://www.coc.nl/index.htm/ ?file=marriage (last visited August 18, 1999).

59. Waaldijk, Dutch Law Reform in Progress, note 41 above.

60. *See* Text of Dutch Bill, note 36 above.

and brought up in a lasting relationship of two women or two men, has a right to protection in that relationship, including legal protection. Both women or both men have taken on the responsibility for the care and upbringing of the child and readily want to have that responsibility. In the interest of the child this relationship with these adults deserves protection."[61] Finally, in December 2000, the Dutch parliament passed the bill opening up adoption to same-sex couples, a bill that was introduced in conjunction with the bill on same-sex marriage; both were signed into law December 21, 2000, and came into force on April 1, 2001. Accordingly, as of that date, two women or two men can jointly adopt a child in the Netherlands.[62] Under the terms of the new act, couples of the same sex wishing to adopt a child must meet the same criteria as heterosexual couples. Furthermore, adoption by same-sex partners is possible whether they are married or registered as partners. Foreign adoptions by same-sex couples are excluded from the act, and adoptions by homosexual couples are restricted to Dutch children.[63] Thus, intercountry adoption (i.e., adoption of a child whose ordinary place of residence is not in the Netherlands) is an option available only to different-sex married couples or to one individual.[64] The requirements of the act are similar to those of the prior law on adoption that applied only to opposite-sex partners: two partners who wish to adopt jointly, or a stepparent wishing to adopt (i.e., the same-sex partner of the child's parent), can do so only if the partners have been living together for at least three continuous years immediately prior to the submission of the adoption request and only if both partners have been caring together for the child for at least one year. An exception is made when a lesbian stepparent wishes to adopt her partner's child, in which case there is no minimum period of joint care before which such adoption can be

61. *Id.*

62. For a translation of the most important sections of the new act, see appendix A, sec. A.6.2.

63. *See* Waaldijk, Dutch Law Reform in Progress, note 41 above. In October 1998 the Hague Adoption Convention took effect in the Netherlands. According to the convention, only intercountry adoptions by two persons who are married or by one person—whether single or in a relationship—are allowed. *See id.* Notwithstanding the convention, Dutch officials fear, as do their neighbors in the Nordic countries, that allowing foreign adoptions by homosexuals would lead international adoption agencies to stop approving adoptions to all Dutch couples, heterosexuals included. *See* William J. Kole, *Dutch Cabinet Oks Gay Adoption,* Associated Press, November 14, 1998, at http://www.xs4all.nl/ ~nvihcoc/adoption.html.

64. *See* Kees Waaldijk, Latest News about Same-Sex Marriage in the Netherlands (and What It Implies for Foreigners), available at http://ruljis.leidenuniv.nl/user/cwaaldij/ www/NHR/news.htm (last updated March 30, 2001) [hereinafter Latest News about Same-Sex Marriage].

requested (yet the requirement for cohabitation during the past three years still applies).[65]

The act adds a new and stricter condition to all adoptions: irrespective of whether it is adoption by persons of the same sex or adoption by persons of different sexes, parties seeking adoption must prove to the satisfaction of the court that "the child has nothing more to expect from its original parent(s)."[66] This would be easy to prove in the case of adoption by the lesbian partner of a woman who conceives through artificial insemination but might be difficult under other circumstances.[67] As the Dutch Ministry of Justice explains, "this is about the question whether a parent can still mean something for the child as a parent. The answer to this question may be 'no' while there is still contact in the form of an arrangement concerning parental access, for example."[68]

4.4 The Dutch Act on Same-Sex Marriage

In April 2001 the Netherlands became the first country—and is still the only one—to have enacted legislation allowing marriage of same-sex couples. The process that led to the legislative reform was lengthy but was characterized by a steady movement toward redefining marriage, with very little backlash. As in the United States, no Dutch court has ever ruled in favor of couples asking to be admitted to the institution of marriage.[69] One such case had reached the Dutch Supreme Court in 1990, when a lesbian couple was refused the right to marry in Rotterdam.[70] The court ruled that the exclusion of same-sex couples from marriage was not unjustified and therefore not discriminatory, because one of the legal consequences of marriage was that a woman's husband was considered the legal father of any children; thus marriage was not applicable to same-sex couples.[71] The Dutch parliament, not the government

65. *Id.*

66. Adoption of a Child in the Netherlands, a fact sheet of the Dutch Ministry of Justice, available at http://www.minjust.nl:8080/a_BELEID/fact/fact.htm, April 2001.

67. *See* Text of Dutch Bill, note 36 above.

68. Adoption of a Child in the Netherlands, note 66 above.

69. Waaldijk, *Small Change,* note 3 above. In a case brought by two men who wanted to marry each other in 1989, after being rejected by the registrar's office, the court held that the legislature's intention to require marrying partners to be of different genders was evident. *See* Rechtbank Amsterdam, February 13 1990, NJCM 1990, at 456–560, reported by Kees Waaldijk, Tip of an Iceberg: Anti-Lesbian and Anti-Gay Discrimination in Europe 1980–1990, at 32 (1991).

70. *See* Tatchell, note 9 above, at 122.

71. Hoge Raad, October 19, 1990, RvdW 1990, nr. 176. *See* Waaldijk, Towards Full Equality, note 4 above. *See also* Waaldijk, Tip of an Iceberg, note 69 above, at 32–33. Nonetheless, the court, signaling toward the legislature, referred to the "possibility" that

or the courts, has paved the way for opening up the institution of marriage to same-sex couples. The Dutch government was initially against this step for two reasons: first, were the Netherlands to take this step, it would be the only country in the world to have done so; second, concern was expressed for gay couples who would find their marriage not recognized outside the Netherlands.[72] Many parliament members expressed the view that a registered partnership act would not be enough, since it would not provide full equality; in the words of one parliament member, registered partnership "is margarine. It's not real butter."[73]

As early as June 1995, the minister of justice and secretary of state for internal affairs announced that Dutch marriage law would be amended to include gay men and lesbians without any restriction.[74] In April 1996 the lower chamber of the Dutch parliament passed a resolution by a vote of 81 to 60, demanding the preparation of a bill to allow same-sex couples to marry.[75] The Justice Department responded by appointing the above-mentioned Kortmann Committee in June 1996, which examined the legal implications, as well as the advantages and disadvantages, of marriage for same-sex couples.[76] The committee was to look into the national and international consequences of including same-sex couples in the existing institution of civil marriage and to advise on possible legislation.[77] In October 1997 the parliamentary committee submitted its report, "Opening Civil Marriage to Same-Sex Couples," recommending, by a majority of 5 to 3, that marriage be made available to same-sex couples; the committee's majority was of the opinion that "same-sex couples can only be afforded equal treatment if they are allowed to enter into civil marriage" and that "the new type of marriage [is not] a break with tradition: after all, marriage has always been a flexible institution

---

there might be insufficient justification for making specific other consequences of marriage unavailable to same-sex couples in a lasting relationship. *See* Waaldijk, Towards Full Equality.

72. *See* Forder, note 31 above, at 360.

73. Deb Price, *Roads to Equality: Gay Rights in Europe: Danes Pave Way for Partnership: Copenhagen's Gay and Lesbian Couples Enjoy Rights That Remain a Distant Dream for American Same-Sex Couples*, Detroit News, October 29, 1997, at E1:4, quoting member of Parliament Mieke van der Burg, a member of the labor party.

74. Goransson, note 8 above, at 182.

75. *See* Waaldijk, Dutch Parliament Demands, note 15 above. For the text of the resolution, see appendix A, sec. A.6.3. At the time Parliament passed its resolution, the Dutch government strongly opposed same-sex marriage. *See* Reuters, *Committee Looks into Legalizing Same-Sex Marriages*, Amsterdam, May 28, 1996, at http://www.coc.nl/index.htm/?file=marriage (last visited August 18, 1999).

76. *See Dutch Commission on Civil Marriage*, ILGA-Europe Euroletter, note 12 above, no. 43, August 1996.

77. *See id. See also Committee Looks into Legalizing Same-Sex Marriages*, note 75 above.

which has kept pace with social change."[78] However, in February 1998 the Dutch government decided not to implement the majority's recommendation and instead proposed several amendments to the existing Registered Partnership Act. In accordance with the minority opinion of the Kortmann Committee, the Dutch government concluded that the Registered Partnership Act offered virtual equality of rights for same-sex couples; also, the government was not ready to open up marriage to same-sex couples since such marriage would not be recognized outside the Netherlands. Furthermore, the government did not want to consider allowing marriage to homosexual couples before the scheduled evaluation, in 2001, of the law on registered partnership.[79]

In April 1998 the lower chamber of the Dutch parliament reacted by repeating its call for same-sex marriage and again passed a resolution, by 81 to 56 votes, demanding legislation that would permit same-sex couples to marry.[80] In December 1998 the newly elected Dutch government, in response, approved a bill to allow same-sex couples to marry, the text of which was sent to the Council of State for advice.[81] On July 8, 1999, the government presented the bill before Parliament.[82] The passage of the bill became possible because of a variety of sociopolitical factors: since 1994 the government in the Netherlands, for the first time in more than eighty years, had a coalition that did not include the Christian Democrats, the leading opponents of allowing same-sex couples to marry and adopt,[83] and only 5 percent of Parliament's seats belonged to conservative Christian parties.[84] Numerous gay and lesbian members of Parliament had effectively pushed for fuller equality for same-sex partners and their children,[85] and there was a clear majority in the Dutch parliament for making marriage available to same-sex couples, whereas opposition was minimal. Moreover, the success of the Registered Partnership Act and the eagerness with which it had been welcomed by both

78. McBride, note 52 above.

79. *See* Waaldijk, Dutch Government Decides, note 16 above.

80. *See* Waaldijk, Dutch Parliament Repeats Calls, note 57 above.

81. Waaldijk, Dutch Law Reform in Progress, note 41 above.

82. *See* Text of Dutch Bill, note 36 above.

83. They claim that such laws defy biology, undermine the family, put adoptive children of homosexual couples in an awkward legal position, especially when they travel abroad, and could make the Netherlands a derided hub of "gay-wedding tourism." *See When My Old Dutch Is a Man,* note 28 above, at 52. The fact that no religious Christian parties are part of the government or the coalition has no doubt been a major factor in pushing ahead reforms for gay men and lesbians.

84. L. Hosek, *Special Report on Same-Sex Marriage,* Honolulu Star Bulletin, January 22, 1997, at 16–18.

85. *See* Waaldijk, *Small Change,* note 3 above.

same-sex couples and different-sex couples had also led to a strong demand for same-sex marriage.[86] Finally, most Dutch gays and lesbians were in favor of opening up marriage to same-sex couples, whereas only a marginal minority opposed it.[87] The active struggle to permit marriage to same-sex partners had included even those Dutch gays and lesbians who viewed marriage as an imposition of bourgeoisie and patriarchy and as a virtually medieval "straight" institution. The latter would simply not choose to marry, but they supported equal rights for homosexuals.[88] Moreover,

> [n]o other country in the world is as secular as the Netherlands; no country in the world has a less religious population. The Netherlands has a firm tradition of accommodating all kinds of minorities. And it has often been claimed that the interaction between the various minorities, especially through their political, social and academic elites, is faster and more productive than in most other countries. Furthermore, the Netherlands has a less direct, and therefore less populist, democratic system (no referendums, no district-based elections) than many other countries. And is there any other country where since the early 1980's the percentage of the population agreeing that homosexuals should be as free as possible to live their own life, has been 93% or more?[89]

As expected, in December 2000 the Dutch parliament passed the bill permitting same-sex couples to marry; the bill was signed into law December 21, 2000, and became effective April 1, 2001.[90] The explanatory memorandum to the bill states that "the principle of equal treatment of homosexual and heterosexual couples has been decisive in the debate

86. *See* Rex Wockner, *Dutch Gays Will Have Two Ways to Get Hitched,* ILGA-Europe Euroletter, note 12 above, no. 49, April 1997. *See also* Price, note 73 above. It is rare for a politician in the Netherlands (in contrast to U.S. politicians) to be vociferously antigay, and foes of same-sex marriage do not "rail about moral decay or the collapse of Western civilization. Instead, many would just prefer that their country not take the lead yet again on a controversial social issue," since the Dutch already have to defend their legalization of voluntary euthanasia and their lenient attitudes toward prostitution and "soft drugs." *Id.*

87. A survey conducted by the University of Utrecht found that 85% of Dutch gays and lesbians believed same-sex marriage should be legal, whereas only 7% did not want it legalized. *See* Rex Wockner, *Forty-Five Percent of Dutch Gays Will Marry,* ILGA Europe News, quoted in ILGA Bulletin of January 1998, at http://www.ilga.org/wwwlilga.org/information/europenews/htm.

88. *See* Price, note 73 above.

89. *See* Kees Waaldijk, The "Law of Small Change": How the Road to Same-Sex Marriage Got Paved in the Netherlands, June 19, 1999, paper presented at the conference Legal Recognition of Same-Sex Partnerships, Kings College, University of London, July 1–3, 1999; Price, note 73 above.

90. For an English translation of the most important sections of the new act, see appendix A, sec. A.6.4.

about the opening up of marriage for persons of the same sex."[91] Moreover, "for many people, marriage is a symbol that carries a special meaning. They see it as a way of confirming their commitment to each other. There is no reason why same-sex couples should be denied the opportunity to do so."[92] Hence, the act is based on the principle of gender neutrality, and it simply adds a new section to the existing law on marriage according to which "a marriage can be contracted by two persons of different sex *or of the same sex.*"[93] In the conditions for the contracting of marriage, its consequences, its dissolution, and the partners' obligations toward each other, there are no differences between marriage by heterosexuals and marriage by gays.[94] For example, only one of the persons wishing to marry needs either to have his or her domicile in the Netherlands or to possess Dutch citizenship. If neither partner is a Dutch national and both live abroad, they may not marry in the Netherlands. According to the act, a stepparent is obliged to provide financial support for her or his spouse's children who are under the age of twenty-one. There remain only two legal differences between same-sex marriage and different-sex marriage. The first has to do with parental rights: the spouse in a lesbian marriage whose partner gives birth to a child during the marriage is not considered to be the "father" (i.e., parent) of the child, whereas the male spouse of a married woman is deemed the father even in the absence of any biological link between him and the child. Thus, in a lesbian marriage only the biological mother is the legal parent of the child. However, two married women automatically acquire joint custody over each other's children with no need for a court order, which was previously required. Moreover, because adoption by same-sex couples is possible, the female spouse is able to adopt her partner's child and thus become its full legal parent.[95] In the matter of adoption, another difference exists: same-sex married couples (as well as same-sex registered partners) may not adopt a child from outside the Netherlands, whereas opposite-sex married couples have no such restriction. There

91. Text of Dutch Law on the Opening Up of Marriage for Same-Sex Partners, Summary-translation by Kees Waaldijk, January 11, 2001, available at http://ruljis.leidenuniv.nl/user/cwaaldij/www/.

92. *See* Same-Sex Marriages, a fact sheet of the Dutch Ministry of Justice on the new marriage act, available at http://www.minjust.nl:8080/a_BELEID/fact/fact.htm (April 2001).

93. Text of Dutch Bill, note 36 above, my emphasis.

94. *See* Same-Sex Marriages, note 92 above.

95. *See* Kees Waaldijk, The Latest about Lifting the Ban on Marriage for Same-Sex Couples in the Netherlands: Dutch Cabinet Introduces Bills Allowing Same-Sex Marriage and Same-Sex Adoption, June 27, 1999, at http://www.coc.nl/index.htm/?file=marriage (last visited August 18, 1999).

also are differences as far as international law is concerned: the rules of free movement of persons in relation to their spouses are not applicable to registered partners or married spouses of the same sex, because "marriage" in international-law instruments has yet to be interpreted as including same-sex marriage (i.e., an interpretation of treaties relating to marriage as a gender-neutral institution is improbable); new rules of private international law should be drawn.[96] Furthermore, recognition of marriage between persons of the same sex outside the Netherlands depends on the public policy of each country and on its private international-law rules; it is difficult to assess at this point how many countries will recognize Dutch same-sex marriage,[97] and spouses of the same sex may thus encounter various practical and legal problems outside the Netherlands.[98] However, the fact that a country does not recognize the marriage does not mean that it attaches no legal consequences to the marriage at all. It is possible, for instance, that the property law aspects of the relationship would be recognized.[99]

As to the relationship between marriage and registered partnership, the new act provides for the institution of registered partnership to exist alongside same- and opposite-sex marriage for at least five years, at which point it will be reevaluated, and for all couples who have registered their partnerships to be able to convert them into full marriage; the conversion does not affect paternity over children born before the conversion nor the consequences of the registered partnership.[100] As stated in the explanatory memorandum of the bill, "the relatively high number of different-sex couples that contracted a registered partnership in 1998 . . . make[s] it plausible that there is a need for a marriage-like institution devoid of the symbolism attached to marriage. . . . Therefore, the government wants to keep the institution of registered partnership in place, for the time being. After five years the development of same-sex marriage and of registered partnership will be evaluated. Then . . .

96. The conclusion that rules of free movement of persons in relation to their spouses will not be considered applicable to married spouses of the same sex is supported by the judgment of the European Court of Justice in Luxembourg in the matter of Grant v. South-West Trains, Case C-249/96 [1998] ECR I-621 (holding that European Union law did not prohibit employment discrimination on the basis of sexual orientation). *See* Waaldijk, Latest News about Same-Sex Marriage, note 64 above.

97. According to a survey conducted by the Kortmann Committee among member states of the Council of Europe, recognition can be expected only in a very few countries. *See* Waaldijk, Latest News about Same-Sex Marriage, note 64 above.

98. *See* Text of Dutch Bill, note 36 above.

99. *See* Same-Sex Marriages, note 92 above.

100. Waaldijk, Dutch Law Reform in Progress, note 41 above. *See also* Text of Dutch Bill, note 36 above.

it will be possible to assess whether registered partnership should be abolished."[101]

Similarly, two married persons may convert their marriage into a registered partnership, in which case paternity over children born before the conversion and the consequences of marriage will not be affected.[102] There remain very few differences between same-sex marriage and registered partnership in the Netherlands: for example, a marriage can be dissolved only by the court, whereas a registered partnership can be terminated by the partners themselves. Likewise, legal separation only applies to marriage, not to registered partnership.[103]

The first same-sex marriage ceremony took place on the night of March 31 to April 1, 2001. At midnight the registered partnerships of several same-sex couples were converted into full civil marriages.[104] During the first six months after gay marriage became available, almost two thousand same-sex couples had married, comprising more than 3 percent of all marriages in the Netherlands during that same period.[105]

101. Text of Dutch Bill, note 36 above.

102. *See id.*

103. *See* Same-Sex Marriages, note 92 above.

104. *See* Waaldijk, Latest News about Same-Sex Marriage, note 64 above.

105. Of these couples, 55% were same-sex male and 45% were same-sex female. *See Dutch Gay Marriage Stats Released*, Associated Press, December 12, 2001.

Chapter 5

Recognition of Same-Sex Partnerships in Other European Countries

5.1 Common Law Marriage in Hungary and Portugal

5.1.1 Hungary

Hungary is one of the few countries other than the northern European countries that provides recognition of same-sex partnerships at the national level. On March 8, 1995, the Hungarian Constitutional Court extended the application of common law marriage to gay and lesbian couples.[1] Thus, whereas in the northern European countries the reform process was a statutory one, the law in Hungary was changed through a judicial act and only afterward was implemented by legislation.

Until 1995 the statute regulating common law marriage in Hungary, which had been in effect since 1976,[2] applied only to "a man and a woman who are not married, share a household and live together in emotional and economic community."[3] In connection with its 1995 decision, the Hungarian Constitutional Court was petitioned to find not only that the law on common law marriage was unconstitutional since it did not apply to gay couples but also that it was unconstitutional to exclude same-sex couples from entering into regular marriage. The Court refused to open the institution of civil marriage to same-sex couples, stating that "the Constitution protects the institution of (civil) mar-

---

1. *See* Leslie Goransson, *International Trends in Same-Sex Marriage, in* On the Road to Same-Sex Marriage 165, 176 (Robert P. Cabaj & David W. Purcell eds., 1998).

2. *See* Lilla Farkas, *Nice on Paper: The Aborted Liberalization of Gay Rights in Hungary, in* Legal Recognition of Same-Sex Partnerships: A Study of National, European, and International Law 563 (Robert Wintemute & Mads Andenas eds., 2001).

3. Goransson, note 1 above, at 178.

riages, and defines it as a union between a man and a woman" and that "despite growing acceptance of homosexuality (and) changes in the traditional definition of a family, there is no reason to change the law on (civil) marriage." However, the Court held that the definition of common law marriage as limited to marriage between a man and a woman was unconstitutionally discriminatory. The Court wrote, "[I]t is arbitrary and contrary to human dignity . . . that the law (on common law marriages) withholds recognition from couples living in an economic and emotional union simply because they are same-sex." It held that common law marriage should be extended to same-sex couples and ordered Parliament to make the legislative changes necessary to implement its ruling within one year.[4] Consequently, on May 21, 1996, Parliament legalized common law marriage for gays and lesbians by a vote of 207 to 73[5] and enacted Hungary's Common Law Marriage Act.[6] The existence of common law marriage is a factual matter, which needs to be established retroactively in each individual case. The basic condition for its existence is that the couple have been living together in a common household in an emotional and economic communion; according to case law, there is no need for the partners to be involved in a sexual relationship.[7] Since no registration takes place, it is difficult to determine how many couples have actually taken advantage of the law thus far.[8] Under Hungarian law, common law marriage gives most of the rights conferred by marriage, including inheritance, pension and social security rights, common property rights, and immunity from spousal testimony.[9] How-

4. Blaise Szolgyemy, *Hungary High Court Gives Blessing to Gay Couples*, Reuters, March 8, 1995, *in* ILGA World Legal Survey: Hungary Recognizes Common-Law Gay Marriage, at http://www.ilga.org/Information/legal_survey/europe/hungary.htm (last updated March 29, 1999). Following the decision of the Constitutional Court, some religious groups and the leader of the strongest right-wing opposition party began a campaign against amending the law to include same-sex couples, claiming that "the Hungarian nation is in danger of extinction because the socialist-liberal government promotes gay marriages instead of aiding families." *See* Sandor Borsos, *Hungary Is Set to Legalize Same-Sex Partnerships*, ILGA-Europe Euroletter no. 41, April 1996 (Steffen Jensen et al. eds.) at http://www.qrd.org/qrd/www/orgs/ILGA/euroletter. At the same time, gay groups have started to lobby for the passage of the law. *Id.*

5. ILGA World Legal Survey: Hungary, note 4 above. Some gay activists claim that the legislation does not prove that most Parliament members are enlightened or liberal and that instead the law was basically imposed on Parliament by the Constitutional Court. *See id.*

6. Act of 1996: XLII Law 1–3 (May 21, 1996) (Stuard Schulte trans., 1996).

7. Farkas, note 2 above. *See also* Szolgyemy, note 4 above.

8. Goransson, note 1 above, at 178.

9. Szolgyemy, note 4 above. *See also* Scott Long, *Gay and Lesbian Movements in Eastern Europe: Romania, Hungary, and the Czech Republic, in* The Global Emergence of Gay and Lesbian Politics: National Imprints of a Worldwide Movement 242, 253 (Barry D. Adam et

ever, the new law in effect does not completely equate the status of common law marriage of homosexual couples with that of heterosexual couples, since it does not confer upon same-sex couples any parental rights: although the law does not expressly prohibit the adoption of children by single people and same-sex couples or prohibit artificial insemination, both adoption and artificial insemination services are in practice unavailable in Hungary for persons other than heterosexual couples.[10]

Hungary is in many respects one of the most socially liberal countries in the former Eastern bloc and is the first east European nation to extend traditional rights to gay couples. Still, it is quite surprising that it is one of the few countries in the world to have recognized same-sex partnerships. The aforementioned court ruling was completely unexpected and was not the result of any campaigning by gay groups.[11] The liberal ruling of the Constitutional Court is mainly due to Hungary's wish to become part of the "New Europe." Unlike the process in the northern European countries, recognition of same-sex partnerships in Hungary was not a "natural" step in the advancement of gay rights.[12] On the contrary, gays in Hungary were and still are discriminated against in many ways, such as by the unequal age of consent. Moreover, homosexuals in Hungary lack visibility and political power. The willingness to support common law marriage for gay men and lesbians was not rooted in a cultural history of social tolerance, as in the northern European countries and in France, but was based on a belief that it would be politically and economically advantageous to appear socially tolerant. The European Union has tied participation in economic success to compliance with an ideology that is supportive of human rights; this approach was what affected the developments in Hungary.[13] Thus, the single most important factor in forming the ruling of the Court was a report adopted by the European Union Parliament that provided a comprehensive endorsement of gay and lesbian civil equality. The European Union had made the elimination of sodomy laws a condition for admission. The

al. eds., 1999); Rex Wockner, *Hungary Recognizes Common-Law Gay Marriage,* ILGA-Europe Euroletter, note 4 above, no. 42, June 1996.

10. For adoption rights, see Farkas, note 2 above. The 1995 court decision did not address the issue of adoption by same-sex couples; the court expressed its view of same-sex partnerships as an entity without children. *See id.* For artificial insemination rights in Hungary, see Kate Griffin, *Lesbian Baby Boom—Motherhood within the Lesbian Community in Europe,* in ILGA World Legal Survey: Hungary, note 4 above.

11. Farkas, note 2 above.

12. For discussion of the typical or "necessary" process leading to comprehensive recognition of same-sex partnerships, see chap. 11.

13. *See* Goransson, note 1 above, at 186. For a more detailed account of the sociopolitical background that led to these developments, see id. at 176–77.

Hungarian judges apparently thought that their ruling might be a small and painless way for Hungary to look good before the European Union.[14] It is not surprising, then, that the Constitutional Court's decision and the subsequent legislation by Parliament implementing the ruling have been called only being "nice on paper" and characterized as an "aborted liberalization of gay rights in Hungary."[15] Moreover, despite the Court's ruling, official attitudes toward homosexuality have remained conservative, favoring the notion of heterosexuality and traditional family values over homosexuality.[16]

Another factor that may have contributed to the Court's liberal ruling was its composition at the time. The Hungarian Constitutional Court, which is the only Hungarian court with the power to review laws,[17] was created in the course of the political transition during the dissolution of the Soviet bloc from 1989 to 1990. Because the Court was new and its powers unclear, only a few older, "respectable" jurists wanted to be on it at the time, so its membership tended to be younger, more receptive to Western ideas, and generally imbued with an American-style concept of judicial activism.[18] Since its initiation, the Court has taken an activist

14. *Id.* at 178.

15. Farkas, note 2 above.

16. Such attitudes are exemplified by a 1996 Constitutional Court ruling that in effect denied gays the right of association (Hungarian Constitutional Court, Decision 21/1996: 17 May 1996). The court upheld a lower court's refusal to allow the registration of the new gay organization Rainbow Association for Gay Rights on the grounds that using in its name the term *meleg* (warm), which is the acceptable self-designation of gays and lesbians, was improper in Hungarian and that the group did not exclude minors under the age of eighteen as possible members, finding that the group disseminated a "threat to public morals"; the organization remains unregistered, and its small membership has drifted away. *See* Long, note 9 above, at 252. The ruling stemmed from the fear that advocating the rights of homosexuals would be detrimental to the Hungarian youth and would put them at risk of committing "unnatural sexual conduct" and being exposed to the negative social perception of homosexuality. *See* Farkas, note 2 above. Thus, the Constitutional Court itself appears to be biased against homosexuality, which further substantiates the argument that its decision regarding homosexual partnerships was not based on any kind of progay vision but rather on international political considerations. A challenge to the Constitutional Court's ruling was brought by the founders of the organization before the European Court of Human Rights. In its decision of May 12, 2000, the European Court declared the application manifestly ill founded and therefore inadmissible and thus did not debate the merits of the case. The reasoning of the Court is confined to the statement that the ban of persons under eighteen from membership in gay (rights) organizations was prescribed by law, that the ban pursued the legitimate aims of protection of morals and the rights and freedoms of others, and that the ban was proportionate to the aim pursued and could, therefore, reasonably be regarded as necessary in a democratic society. *See* Szivárvány, Juhász & Palfy v. Hungary (appl. 35419/97). *See also* Helmut Graupner, *European Court of Human Rights: Case Szivárvány et al. vs. Hungary—A Major Backlash for L/G/B Right, in* ILGA-Europe Euroletter, note 4 above, no. 84, November 2000.

17. *See* Long, note 9 above, at 252.

18. Goransson, note 1 above, at 176.

stance on social rights, overturning parts of the government's austerity program on grounds of social welfare.[19]

The developments in Hungary are therefore a clear exception to the general and "typical" process that took place in other countries and regions that have enacted legislation providing expansive recognition of same-sex partnerships, and I regard the case of Hungary as an anomaly rather than as part of the general progress of gay rights in the Western world. Therefore, in later discussions comparing same-sex partnerships in Europe and in the United States, I do not further address the Hungarian Common Law Marriage Act and the process that led to its adoption.

5.1.2 Portugal

In March 2001 Portugal joined other European countries that provide recognition of same-sex partnerships by enacting a new bill on de facto unions for both heterosexual and homosexual couples. Before the passage of the act, unmarried cohabitation was recognized in Portugal for some purposes by the Civil Code and in case law; however, this recognition did not extend to same-sex cohabiting couples,[20] except for the Housing Law, which applied to both homosexuals and heterosexuals, so that in the case of the death of a tenant, his or her partner had a preferential right to keep the lease.[21] Since the midnineties, the Portuguese gay movement has been making efforts to influence political parties to amend article 13 of the Portuguese Constitution by adding the term *sexual orientation* to the list of protected minorities, but these efforts have failed thus far.[22] In 1997 the Portuguese Socialist Party prepared a partnership bill that would include opposite-sex couples as well as same-sex couples who had been living together for at least two years.[23] The bill was rejected in June 1997, and it took four more years for it to become law. The bill was intended to equalize "the rights of members of a family living together with those of married couples, in civil, fiscal, social and labor matters, maintaining however the specificities of either situation." The rights provided by the bill were "transmission of lease

19. Long, note 9 above, at 252.

20. Homosexuality: A European Community Issue 94 (Kees Waaldijk & Andrew Clapham eds., 1993).

21. Gonçalo Diniz, *Report on Portugal, in* ILGA-Europe, Equality for Lesbians and Gay Men: A Relevant Issue in the Civil and Social Dialogue 86 (Brussels 1998).

22. *See* ILGA-Europe Euroletter no. 41, April 1996; ILGA-Europe Euroletter no. 45, November 1996, at 7 (see note 4 above).

23. *See* Diniz, note 21 above.

rights," "subsistence," and "right of residence."[24] The bill excluded homosexual couples from adoption rights and limited adoption to heterosexual couples.[25] Immigration and asylum were to be on the same basis as for married heterosexual couples.[26] Since publication of the bill, the Portuguese Socialist Party has revised it, and in January 1999 the party published another partnership bill, this time pertaining only to heterosexual couples.[27] The latter bill (termed "a bill on de facto unions") was passed by the Portuguese parliament in July 1999 and signed into law a month later, granting heterosexual couples living in a de facto union for more than two years marital rights in such areas as adoption, taxes, pensions, housing, contracts, and rental leases. Following the passage of the bill on de facto unions for heterosexual couples, and as a result of pressure by gay and lesbian organizations all over Portugal, the Portuguese Socialist Party announced its intention to extend that bill to same-sex couples. Consequently, a year afterward, on March 15, 2001, after having revised prior proposals, the Portuguese parliament passed a bill that replaces the act on de facto unions for heterosexual couples; the new bill recognizes de facto unions of both same- and opposite-sex couples.[28]

The law applies to couples living in a de facto union for more than two years regardless of the partners' gender. The Portuguese law can be regarded as recognition of same-sex common law marriage and is thus akin to the Hungarian act; however, compared to the Hungarian model, the Portuguese act offers a much less comprehensive list of rights and protections. First, it includes housing protections: if one of the partners dies, the other may continue living in their shared residence; in that case, and if the deceased partner was the owner of the house, the surviving partner has the right to live there for five years and to lease or buy the house if it is sold or leased during that period; if the house was leased by the deceased partner, the surviving partner may, under certain conditions, succeed him or her in the lease. Second, there are work-related benefits: the partners of both public- and private-sector employees are

24. Arts. 1, 3 of the proposed bill.

25. *See* art. 4 of the proposed bill. *Id.* In the only case to have reached the Portuguese Supreme Court regarding a custody dispute between a gay father and his ex-wife, the court refused to grant custody to the father, holding that "the child should be brought up in a traditional Portuguese family." *See* Diniz, note 21 above.

26. *See* art. 7 of the proposed bill. *Id.*

27. ILGA World Legal Survey: Portugal, at http://www.ilga.org/Information/legal_survey/europe/portugal/htm (last updated June 29, 1999).

28. Act no. 135/99. *See* Miguel Freitas, *The New Portuguese Law on Same-Sex Unions,* ILGA-Europe Euroletter, note 4 above, no. 88, May 2001.

accorded the spousal benefits previously available only to married couples (such as vacations, absences, and leaves). Third, the partners may enjoy the same property regime as married couples do, if they choose. Finally, the surviving partner in a de facto union has the right to receive a number of welfare pensions when the other dies. The bill allows opposite-sex couples to adopt as married couples can but does not confer parental rights (including adoption) on same-sex couples. A de facto union is dissolved by death of one of the partners, by the marriage of one partner, or by a court proceeding. Despite the significance of the new act, which came as a surprise both within and outside of Portugal and should be considered an achievement for gays in Portugal, it should be noted that the rights granted to same-sex couples are very limited and do not include most of the rights and benefits associated with marriage. It is far removed from the northern European registered partnership acts. However, as Miguel Freitas notes, "in a predominantly catholic country, where social, cultural and legal changes usually take their time to happen, the passage of these two bills is a clear proof of the growing visibility of the gay, lesbian, bisexual and transgender community (and of the problems that affect it) and may mark the beginning of a new era in the history of the gay rights movement in Portugal."[29]

5.2 Countries with a "Light" Version of Registered Partnership: France, Germany, and Belgium

5.2.1 The French PaCS
In 1995—five years before the enactment of the PaCS, which created a new status of cohabitation, regulating some aspects of opposite-sex as well as same-sex partnerships—more than three hundred French towns were already registering same-sex couples.[30] The registration was accomplished by issuing a cohabitation certificate (*certificat de concubinage*), but its significance was merely symbolic; it carried no legal rights or duties.[31]

In recent years the French legislature and the courts have gradually granted limited benefits to unmarried cohabiting couples. However, it was the French legislature that eventually provided some degree of equality to same-sex couples; the courts were more hesitant and reluctant to do so and limited themselves to expanding the rights of het-

29. Freitas, note 28 above.

30. René Lalement, *Report on France, in* ILGA-Europe, note 21 above, at 50 [hereinafter *Report on France*].

31. *Id.* at 47.

erosexual cohabitants. Thus, for example, the Cour de Cassation (the French Supreme Court), in a case brought before it by a lesbian asking to extend her social security insurance coverage to her unemployed partner—a right that by law is granted to persons living together in a marriage-like manner—held that rights derived from cohabitation should be limited to heterosexual couples, since a same-sex couple living together does not resemble a married couple.[32] Moreover, in 1997, in a case brought before it by a man who asked to retain the lease on the apartment of his deceased homosexual partner—a right derived from a 1989 law that applies to a tenant living in "concubinage" with another—the Cour de Cassation, this time more explicitly and as a general rule, refused to change its definition of concubinage as a heterosexual institution, reasoning that concubinage can result only from a stable, long-lasting relationship that resembles marriage, thus between a man and a woman, and stating that "there is no reason for society to allow homosexual couples to enjoy any more specific rights than the freedom to exist as they see fit."[33]

The first national registered partnership bill was introduced in 1990. Two years later, the term *registered partnership* was dropped and the bill was called Contract d'Union Civile (CUC); in 1997 the bill was rewritten and the arrangement called Contract d'Union Sociale (CUS).[34] None of these bills were brought to discussion in Parliament, and in 1998 the latter bill was redrafted and renamed the Pacte Civil de Solidarité (PaCS) (Civil covenant of solidarity) bill. It incorporated all the prior French bills on registered partnership.

The PaCS bill, which was sponsored by the Socialist government, was the first one of its kind to reach the French National Assembly.[35] The bill passed its first reading before the National Assembly in December 1998, with 316 votes in favor and 249 against.[36] Immediately following the passage of the bill, it met with heated political and public opposition. In January 1999 some one hundred thousand demonstrators from all over France

32. *See* Homosexuality, note 20 above. *See also* Blandine Grosjean, *Gay Couples beyond the Law—They Don't Even Come within the Definition of Concubinage, according to the Cour de Cassation, Liberation, March 6, 1998, in* France: Supreme Court Deems Same-Sex Partnership "Not Concubinage" (Alan Reekie trans.).

33. Grosjean, note 32 above.

34. Lalement, note 30 above, at 47.

35. *See* René Lalement, *France: A New Partnership Bill, in* ILGA-Europe Euroletter, note 4 above, no. 60, June 1998.

36. ILGA World Legal Survey: Report on France, at http://www.ilga.org/Information/legal_survey/europe/germany.htm (last modified June 15, 1999). After this first reading, there still had to be a reading in the Senate, another one in the National Assembly, and then another in the Senate.

gathered in Paris to oppose the PaCS bill.[37] The coalition fighting the bill included the two major right-wing political parties and leaders of the French Catholic, Protestant, Muslim, and Jewish communities.[38] In March 1999 the bill came before the Senate and was rejected by the right-wing majority by a vote of 216 to 99, mainly because they viewed the PaCS as a denial of the central role of marriage in French society. In a second reading in April 1999, the National Assembly reinstated the PaCS by a vote of 300 to 253, with a few changes, including a proposal to amend the Civil Code so that "concubinage" would also include same-sex couples. In May 1999 the right-wing majority of the Senate rejected the revised bill without debate.[39] However, on October 13, 1999, in its fourth and final reading, the National Assembly finally passed the PaCS without the consent of the Senate by a vote of 315 to 249.[40] Following the passage of the bill, the Constitutional Council ruled on November 9, 1999, that it conformed with the French Constitution, and the law was signed by President Chirac and took effect on November 15, 1999.[41] No law has been so much debated in Parliament since France revised its constitution in 1958.[42] It instigated heated debates among both politicians and the general public and was extremely controversial. Consequently, from its first introduction until its final adoption, the bill went through innumerable drafts and amendments, which have led to much confusion as to what the final legislation actually provides for.

The terms of the PaCS law as it was eventually adopted are as follows. The PaCS is a contract open to *any* two unrelated adults—either of the same sex or of different sexes—who are not already bound by a marriage or another PaCS, who cannot or do not want to get married "for the organization of their common life,"[43] and, as interpreted by the Consti-

37. This was the largest demonstration in the capital in fifteen years. *See* NewsPlanet Staff, *French Protest Legal DP,* February 1, 1999, at http://beta.planetout.com/newsplanet/article.html?1999/02/01/1.

38. *See* Ray Mosley, French Debating Legal Status of Unwed Couples; Coalition Opposes Government-Backed Bill to Extend Rights, Labeling It as Way to "Legalized Vice," Chicago Tribune, February 12, 1999, at 5N. *See also* Susannah Patton, *French Trigger Debate on Gay Unions,* Boston Globe, December 13, 1998, at A32.

39. ILGA World Legal Survey, note 36 above.

40. René Lalement, *The French PaCS, in* ILGA-Europe Euroletter, note 4 above, no. 74, October 1999 [hereinafter *The French PaCS*].

41. *See* Loi no. 99-994 du 15 Novembre 1999 Relative au Pacte Civil de Solidarité, which is an amendment to the Civil Code. The text of the law is available in French at http://www.casti.com/FQRD/texts/partnership/fr/pacs.html. For discussion of the final vote on the PaCS, see René Lalement, *France/PaCS: Law Effective November 17, in* ILGA-Europe Euroletter, note 4 above, no. 75, November 1999.

42. Suzanne Daley, *French Couples Take Plunge That Falls Short of Marriage,* New York Times, April 18, 2000, at A1.

43. Art. 1, sec. 1, of the PaCS (my translation). Loi no. 99-994, note 41 above.

tutional Council, who are living together as a couple.[44] Although the PaCS was originally intended to regulate solely gay unions in a manner similar to marriage,[45] in order to pass the legislation, in light of the vast opposition that the bill encountered and the homophobic reaction that it instigated, the supporters of the PaCS emphasized time and again that the law did not purport to imitate marriage and that it was also not a law for same-sex couples but a model for the regulation of cohabitation for any unmarried couple. And indeed, the law has very little in common with marriage. To initiate a PaCS, the couple is required to jointly sign and submit a written notification—a "common declaration"—to the clerk of the local court in the couple's common county of residence, rather than registering at the city hall.[46] The court clerk registers the couple in a local registry. French citizenship is not required in order to sign a pact.[47] But neither does the PaCS confer citizenship or residency on a foreign partner;[48] the fact that a non-French partner is bound by a PaCS to a French citizen is to be considered as a factor among others in assessing a partner's "personal tie" to France for the purpose of issuing a temporary residence permit.[49] The partners bound by a PaCS must provide each other with "mutual and material aid" as specified in the contract and are jointly liable to third parties for any debts incurred by either of them in the course of everyday life in relation to their common household, unless specified otherwise in the contract.[50]

The PaCS is terminated by the death of one of the partners, by the marriage of one of them (the signing of a pact does not alter one's status as single), or, in case of mutual consent, simply by a joint notification to the court clerk, which takes effect immediately upon its registration. A partner can also unilaterally terminate the PaCS by notifying the court and the other partner, in which case the termination takes effect three months after notification.[51] It is thus much easier to dissolve a PaCS than

---

44. Lalement, *The French PaCS,* note 40 above.

45. *See* Daley, note 42 above.

46. ILGA World Legal Survey, note 36 above. The bill initially provided registrations in town halls, but since hundreds of mayors in France made it clear that they would have nothing to do with blessing homosexual quasi-marriages, the registry venue was changed to courthouses. *See* Charles Trueheart, *Gay Couples in France Win Rights of Married,* International Herald Tribune, October 14, 1999, at 8.

47. Unless the pact is entered into outside of France at a French consulate, in which case one of the partners must be a French citizen. *See* art. 1, sec. 3, of the PaCS, note 41 above.

48. Lalement, *The French PaCS,* note 40 above.

49. *See* art. 12 of the PaCS, note 41 above.

50. *Id.,* art. 1, sec. 4.

51. *Id.,* art. 1, sec. 7. *See also* ILGA World Legal Survey, note 36 above.

a marriage, since divorce in France is a lengthy process, usually taking several years and involving several court appearances.[52]

According to section 5 of article 1, the default property regime is that of community property; that is, unless the couple specifically contracts otherwise and, in the case of real property, unless provided otherwise in the deed of purchase, the property acquired during the PaCS is regarded as joint property, to be divided equally upon termination.[53] In case of disagreement upon separation as to the division of property, the determination is made by the court.[54] Among the benefits granted by the PaCS are health insurance for a permanently dependent partner and the right to retain a lease on an apartment or house if one partner dies. Vast areas are not defined or regulated by the law. For example, the PaCS does not mention any rights pertaining to the relationship between parents and children, and it does not speak of inheritance rights. Although the PaCS does not provide inheritance rights, it provides for limited inheritance-tax deductions, but only if the couple was in a PaCS for at least two years before the death of the partner and only if the partners left each other property in their wills. Social security benefits under a partner's coverage and the option to submit a joint income tax return are both available only from the third year after a couple signs a pact.[55] Finally, if both partners are employed in the public service, each has the right to be transferred with the other partner or to be compensated in case one of the partners is required to move because of his or her job.[56]

The PaCS does not regulate the relationship between parents and children and does not accord homosexuals the right to adopt a child, to have joint custody over each other's children, or to obtain artificial insemination services.[57] Only married couples and single people are eligible to adopt children in France, and single people who have disclosed their homosexuality have been rejected on the basis of their sexual orientation. No same-sex or opposite-sex cohabiting couples, including those who have signed a PaCS, or single homosexuals are allowed to

52. Daley, note 42 above.

53. Art. 1, sec. 5, of the PaCS, note 41 above.

54. *Id.*, art. 1, sec. 7.

55. Lalement, *Report on France,* note 30 above. *See also* Eric Gutierrez, *French Connections,* Advocate, February 29, 2000, at 42–47.

56. Art. 13 of the PaCS, note 41 above.

57. Lalement, *Report on France,* note 30 above, at 47. However, it was reported that in January 2000 a French family court in Bressuire recognized a lesbian coparent as having the "status of a second mother" to the two children her former partner had borne by in vitro fertilization during their relationship, and it granted her visitation rights. *See* NewsPlanet Staff, *French Court OKs DP Visitation,* February 15, 2000, at http://beta. planetout.com/newsplanet/article.html?2000/02/15/2.

adopt.[58] After the enactment of the PaCS, a suit was filed by a lesbian couple asking that one partner be allowed to adopt the other's child, and the couple was eventually unsuccessful.[59] Similarly, artificial insemination is available by French law only to married couples or heterosexual cohabitants of more than two years. It is prohibited for single people and same-sex couples.[60]

PaCS came to stand both for the law itself and for the relationship contracted according to the law; it is also used as a verb to describe the entrance into this new institution. The law seems to have gained wide popularity since its enactment: in the first month and a half following its taking effect (November 15, 1999, through December 31, 1999), 6,211 couples had entered a PaCS,[61] and by September 2000 the government had recorded 23,000 PaCS, many of them—approximately 40 percent, according to some estimations—among heterosexual couples.[62] Apparently the law is used for different reasons by heterosexual couples than by homosexual ones. For gay couples, who have no other alternative to regulate their relationship, the PaCS is celebrated like a marriage, whereas heterosexual couples tend to regard the union as something like a trial run for marriage, a mere acknowledgment of a further step in the relationship before marriage.[63]

Besides its creation of the new institution PaCS, the act adds a definition of cohabitation to the Civil Code: "a de-facto stable and continuous relationship between two persons of the opposite or the same sex, who live together as a couple,"[64] so that "non-PaCS-ed" same-sex couples are now regarded as cohabitants for the purposes of French law (thus overturning the Cour de Cassation's cohabitation ruling discussed above and

58. Lalement, *Report on France,* note 30 above, at 47–48.

59. Although the lower tribunal in Besançon had ordered the adoption, an appeals court in Nancy on December 21, 2000, rejected the administrative tribunal's ruling. *See* PlanetOut News Staff, *French Court Denies Adoption,* December 21, 2000.

60. Lalement, *Report on France,* note 30 above, at 48.

61. *See France PACS Popular,* PlanetOut News & Politics, January 24, 2000, at http://www.planetout.com/news/article.html?2000/01/24/2.

62. Rex Wockner, *New French Partnership Numbers,* Wockner International News no. 338, October 16, 2000, at http://mother.qrd.org/qrd/world/wockner/news.briefs/274-07.26.99. In order to protect the privacy of the parties, it is illegal under French law to keep statistics on who has taken part in the ceremony. *See* Daley, note 42 above. It is estimated that 75% of the registered couples in Paris are same-sex couples and that only 40% of those reside in the Paris suburbs. *See France PACS Popular,* note 61 above. About a hundred new PaCSs are still being recorded every day. *See PaCS Figures Growing, despite "Flaws"* (Alan Reekie trans.), Liberation, April 12, 2000 (communication to the ILGA mailing list, at ilga-list@netmafia.org, April 12, 2000).

63. Daley, note 42 above.

64. Art. 3 of the PaCS, note 41 above.

the prior version of the Civil Code, both of which limited cohabitation to opposite-sex couples). In the months following the enactment of the PaCS, several courts in France extended the well-established case law on cohabitation to apply explicitly also to same-sex couples.[65] Since the PaCS itself is very limited, this latter trend is of great significance.

Now that the PaCS law is in place, there exist three models for the regulation of the legal status of couples in France: marriage, registration of a PaCS, and cohabitation, in descending order of comprehensiveness. A heterosexual couple may choose to cohabit, sign a pact, or marry, whereas only the former two are options open to a same-sex couple. The French reform is largely symbolic, since it confers very few rights, and even the execution of some of those rights is delayed for three years. It thus fails to address, except cosmetically, the equality gap between gays and heterosexuals. The major effects of the PaCS are social and political. For example, as a result of the heated debates and the large media coverage of the process of enacting the PaCS, unprecedented discussion of homosexuality has penetrated even small towns, lifting the taboo surrounding gays and lesbians in France.[66] The PaCS merely regulates some aspects of the cohabitation of unmarried couples, both homosexual and heterosexual. However, it is a step further than the limited French concept of cohabitation, which provides minimal rights, benefits, and obligations. Moreover, since it accords some rights that are traditionally associated with marriage, it should be categorized as something between marriage and cohabitation.[67] In enacting the PaCS, France became the largest country in Europe, and the first nominally Roman Catholic one, to regulate same-sex partnerships. Nonetheless, the PaCS is narrower and more restricted than the registered partnership acts of the Nordic countries and the Netherlands or the Hungarian common law marriage model.

5.2.2 Germany's Life Partnership
In November 2000 Germany enacted a version of a registered partnership act at the federal level. The new act has dramatically affected the status of gay men and lesbians in Germany, a country that until recently lacked any kind of federal recognition of same-sex partnerships. The former federal conservative coalition government of Germany, which

65. *PaCS Figures Growing,* note 62 above.

66. As Emmanuelle Cosse, president of the Paris chapter of Act Up wrote in *Le Monde,* "in practice, homosexuals don't gain very much." Quoted in Gutierrez, note 55 above.

67. *See* Daniel Borrillo, *The "Pacte Civil de Solidarité" in France: Midway between Marriage and Cohabitation, in* Legal Recognition of Same-Sex Partnerships: A Study of National, European, and International Law 475 (Robert Wintemute & Mads Andenas eds., 2001).

was in power for fifteen years, systematically ignored the interests and demands of gays and lesbians and refused to accord them any kind of legal rights or protections. Attempts by the opposition parties to improve the legal situation of gays and lesbians or to legally recognize gay and lesbian partnerships were thwarted by the conservative majority.[68] Before November 2000 the legal situation of lesbian and gay couples in Germany was much more uncertain and unprotected than it is today; but compared to homosexuals' status in some other European countries, their situation in Germany is still far behind.[69] Germany had recognized unmarried cohabitation for various legal purposes, most of which, such as social security, applied only to heterosexual cohabitation (*eheähnliche Gemeinschaft*); a few benefits, limited to the relationship between the partners themselves, were also applicable to same-sex couples (*nichteheliche Lebensgemeinschaft*).[70]

In October 1993 Germany's Federal Constitutional Court ruled against the opening up of marriage to same-sex couples.[71] The Court held that the refusal to allow same-sex marriage did not infringe upon the "freedom to marry"—guaranteed by the German Constitution—of same-sex partners, since the accepted legal interpretation of the term *marriage* in the constitution referred to a partnership between a man and a woman, the institution of marriage being dependent upon the reproductive capability of the partners. However, based on the constitutional right to equality before the law, the Court suggested that the legislature might be obliged to accord same-sex couples some legal protection, because it was questionable whether the existing disadvantages of gay couples as compared with married couples were constitutional.[72] In

68. *See* Klaus Jetz et al., *Report on Germany, in* ILGA-Europe World Legal Survey, at 51, http://www.ilga.org/Information/legal_survey/europe/germany.htm (last modified June 15, 1999).

69. *See* Judith Rauhofer, *The Possibility of a Registered Partnership under German Law, in* Legal Queeries: Lesbian, Gay, and Transgender Legal Studies 68, 73–75, 78 (Leslie J. Moran et al. eds., 1998).

70. Waaldijk & Clapham, note 20 above.

71. The appeal was brought by couples who were declined marriage licenses in the registry offices of several cities in 1992 and were turned down by the lower courts. *See* The Week in Germany, German Information Center, German Embassy, Washington, D.C., October 22, 1993. *See also German Court Leaves Ban on Gay Marriage Intact,* Reuters News Service (Western Europe), October 13, 1993.

72. *See* Rainer Hoffman et al., *Germany, in* Sociolegal Control of Homosexuality: A Multi-Nation Comparison 264 (Donald J. West & Richard Green eds., 1997). For an account of the deeply rooted notion of marriage as a union limited to a man and a woman under German constitutional law, see Rauhofer, note 69 above, at 69–73. For criticism of the court's interpretation of marriage as an institution deserving protection because it facilitates legal protection of the partners only when founding a family and having children together, see Hoffman et al., above, at 264–65. Following the court's decision,

1995 a bill proposed by Germany's Greens party to allow same-sex couples to marry was rejected by Parliament.[73] The German gay and lesbian movements are split as to the desirability of marriage for same-sex couples: whereas most organizations of gay men are in favor of both registered partnership and same-sex marriage, the Lesbenring, a nationwide lesbian organization, is against such measures, claiming that assimilation and adaptation to heterosexual values would necessarily lead to a loss of lesbian culture and thought.[74]

A progressive political reform has taken place in recent years at the regional level, in some of the German states, the Länder. Hamburg was the first state in Germany to approve a registered partnership law for same-sex couples; the law was passed in April 1999. It was introduced by the Social Democrat government in Hamburg, and reports indicate that by May 1999 only seven lesbian and gay couples had registered their partnerships.[75] After establishing a partnership contract before a notary public, a same-sex couple can also register the partnership at the Registry Office. The law is mainly of symbolic significance and carries no legal consequences—except for the right to hospital visitation—since these are not within the powers of Hamburg, and the state was unable to obtain the necessary approval from the federal government. In September 1999 the City Parliament of Berlin decided by a majority of votes to grant a residence permit to a foreigner who lived in a same-sex relationship with a German citizen.[76]

At the national level, a registered partnership bill for same-sex couples based on the Scandinavian model was first proposed in August 1998 before the federal upper house of Parliament, the Bundesrat.[77] How-

---

the Protestant Church voiced its opposition to same-sex marriage as well. *See* The Week in Germany, note 71 above.

73. The bill proposed to change the relevant article in the Civil Code as follows: "Marriage may be entered into by two persons [of] different [sexes] or [the] same-sex for a lifetime." *See* Hoffman et al., note 72 above, at 265; Rhea Wessel Zollo, *Gay Rights in Germany Lag behind Other EU Countries,* Deutsche Presse-Agentur, October 26, 1995; Dirk Siegfried, Same-Sex Couples under German Law: Litigation by Binational Couples and Proposed Partnership Legislation, oral presentation at the conference Legal Recognition of Same-Sex Partnerships, King's College, University of London, July 1–3, 1999.

74. *See* Rauhofer, note 69 above, at 73–75, 78; for additional arguments being made by German scholars for and against same-sex marriage, see Hoffman et al., note 72 above, at 265–66.

75. *City Registers Gay Couples,* Herald (Glasgow), May 7, 1999, at 7. *See also Germany: Same-Sex Couples Register as Partners,* Press Journal (Vero Beach, Fla.), May 7, 1999, at A15.

76. *See* Jetz et al., note 68 above, at 55; *see also* NewsPlanet Staff, *Germany DP Bill Published,* January 7, 2000, at http://beta.planetout.com/newsplanet/article.html?2000/01/07/3.

77. *See* Rex Wockner, *Partnership Measure Introduced in Germany, in* ILGA-Europe Euroletter, note 4 above, no. 62, August 1998.

ever, despite the election in September 1998 of a center-left government, which replaced the conservative coalition and initially showed support for such legislation,[78] the proposal has since been modified and drastically narrowed. Originally it was to provide nearly every privilege of matrimony, including the right to adopt. The limited later versions of the proposal were far less comprehensive than the Nordic model.[79] In January 2000 the Ministry of Justice published the first version of a bill on registered partnership (*Lebenspartnerschaftsgestetz* [life partnership], abbreviated LPart) that provided for the registration of a partnership at the registrar's office, as is the practice in the case of opposite-sex marriage. The bill included provisions regarding maintenance obligations; the proposed property regime was to be separate, unless the partners contracted otherwise (e.g., a community property regime, or an acquired property status, which is the default status for married couples); and divorce was to be similar to that of opposite-sex married couples. Absent from the bill were all other legal consequences associated with marriage, such as provisions regarding adoption and custody, joint taxation and inheritance tax, health insurance and pension rights, immigration rights for the non-German partner, and the like. Consequently, many gay organizations and activists in Germany expressed disappointment with the bill.[80] However, other government ministries in charge of some of the benefits not included in that version of the bill have filled in some of the gaps: for example, the Ministry of Finance recommended that registered partners be allowed to file joint tax returns as married couples are.[81] In June 2000 the ruling coalition of Social Democrats and Greens reached an agreement on a revised version of the LPart, and the bill, which included more rights and benefits than those in the original proposal, was redrafted.[82]

Later that year, the final version of the life partnership act was divided into two separate bills, one (which did not require the approval of the

78. *See Germany's New Government Said Planning Gay Marriage Bill,* Deutsche Presse-Agentur October 9, 1998. In the text of the coalition's contract, it was promised to initiate a registered partnership act for gays and lesbians. *See* Volker Beck, *First Break-through for Legal Recognition of Homosexuals in Germany* (Dorian Haseloff trans.), *in* ILGA-Europe Euroletter, note 4 above, no. 65, November 1998.

79. Siegfried, note 73 above, estimating that the chances of the bill's becoming law are quite slim.

80. *See* Gerald Pilz, *Germany: Registered Partnership Bill Published, in* ILGA-Europe Euroletter, note 4 above, no. 76, January 2000.

81. *See* NewsPlanet Staff, *German Government Moves on Taxation,* February 15, 2000, at http://beta.planetout.com/newsplanet/article.html?2000/02/15/2.

82. *See* PlanetOut News Staff, *Germany Plans Legal Partnerships,* June 23, 2000, at http://www.planetout.com/nes/article-print.html?2000/06/23/1.

upper house) recognizing same-sex couples as next of kin and according them a few enumerated rights and the other (which could be vetoed by the Bundesrat) providing gay couples various economic benefits, including taxation rights (income and inheritance taxes) and equal benefits for civil servants. On November 10, 2000, the lower house of the German parliament (the Bundestag) passed the two bills. Since, in terms of its subject matter, the first bill did not require the upper house's assent and could not be vetoed by the conservative Bundesrat, which is dominated by the Christian Democratic Union, the passage of this bill was final. The second bill, however, required the Bundesrat's approval and was defeated there in December 2000.[83] Thus, German registered life partners are excluded from most financial rights and benefits, especially in the field of taxation. The part of the bill that was approved by the lower house was signed into law January 2001 and took effect in August of the same year. After Parliament passed the life partnership act, and before the law took effect, the conservative southern German states of Bavaria and Saxony filed suit in Germany's Federal Constitutional Court for an injunction that would have postponed the law's start date pending a decision on their argument that the law violated the constitutional protections of marriage and the family. In July 2001 the Court dismissed the appeals, refusing to delay the law's effective date of August 1, 2001. Consequently, in October 2001, Bavaria and Saxony joined the rest of the German states by agreeing to apply the act in their territories beginning November 1, 2001, three months after the rest of the German states.[84]

According to the new German registered partnership act, the registration is performed by an official state authority. The law does not explicitly mention the responsible authority for registered partnerships; it recommends using the same authority as for straight couples, the registry office, but the state governments choose where to perform the registration and are required to pass an additional law to specify the details and requirements of the registration process. The act includes the following provisions: the partners are acknowledged as relatives and have mutual maintenance and alimony obligations; they are accorded spousal rights similar to those of married couples in the fields of tenancy (if one partner dies, the other partner is allowed to stay in the apartment and to take over the lease), inheritance (excluding inheritance taxes), health insur-

83. *See* PlanetOut News Staff, *German Parliament OKs DP*, November 10, 2000, at http://www.planetout.com/pno; and PlanetOut News Staff, *German Senate OKs DP Bill*, December 1, 2000, at http://www.planetout.com/pno.

84. Barbara Dozetos, *German High Court Keeps Partner Law on Track*, PlanetOut.com Network, July 18, 2001; Tom Musbach, *Bavaria Approves Same-Sex Partnerships*, Gay.com, October 26, 2001.

ance, and hospital visitation (including the right of one partner to make medical decisions for the other in the event of disability); the partners have the same right as married couples do to change their names to the same surname; the partners are accorded shared custody over each other's children and are eligible for social benefits for children; that is, if one partner is unemployed, she or he will receive higher unemployment payments if there are children in the registered partnership (however, the right to adopt children was excluded from the act); relatives of one partner are considered in-laws of the other partner; the partners are not required to testify against each other in criminal proceedings; dissolution of a life partnership requires a court proceeding, in which the court also determines matters of property division; and the law provides immigration and naturalization rights (e.g., a residence and a work permit) for the foreign partner as are provided for married couples.[85] Although the passage of the act is a remarkable achievement for gays and lesbians in Germany, they eventually received only a small part of the wedding cake, not all of it, as they originally demanded. Some claim that the division of the registered partnership proposal into two bills (only one having been adopted) created a situation whereby gay and lesbian couples ended up with the worst of both worlds, being saddled with certain financial responsibilities of marriage (such as support payments after dissolution) but missing important tax and other financial benefits.[86]

Notwithstanding its recognition of same-sex partnerships, Germany, like other European countries, grants gays and lesbians very few parental rights, and homosexuals remain excluded both from adoption and from the right to artificial insemination.[87]

5.2.3 Belgium's Statutory Cohabitation

Despite Belgium's statutory cohabitation law, which provides same-sex couples with a few enumerated rights, current Belgian law offers same-sex couples very little protection, and gay men and lesbians are discriminated against in many matters concerning their partnership, such as social security, taxes, pensions, and inheritance.[88] Moreover, although Belgian courts have gradually accorded cohabiting couples some limited recognition, holding, for example, that a cohabitant may sue the person

85. Gerald Pilz, *Law on Registered Partnership in Germany Accepted;* Gerald Pilz, *The Details of the Registered Partnership in Germany;* both in ILGA-Europe Euroletter, note 4 above, no. 84, November 2000.

86. PlanetOut News Staff, *German Parliament OK's DP,* November 11, 2001.

87. *See* Jetz et al., note 68 above.

88. Anke Hintjens, *Belgium, in* ILGA-Europe, note 21 above, at 86.

responsible for the loss of his or her partner, until recently such recognition has been denied to same-sex cohabitants.[89]

In November 1998 the Federal Parliament enacted a law creating a new institution, statutory cohabitation, intended to regulate the cohabitation of any two adults, either of opposite sexes or the same sex.[90] The law came into effect on January 1, 2000. According to the new law, any two adults, including siblings or other related or unrelated cohabitants, neither of whom is already married or bound by another Cohabitation Contract, may register with their local authorities as cohabitants, after signing the contract in the presence of a notary public. The cohabitants' limited rights and duties include a joint responsibility for contributing to the mutual household's living expenses, joint responsibility for reasonable debts contracted for the mutual household, and the right of the surviving partner to take over the lease of the common apartment following the death of the other. All heritable property and other assets acquired while the contract is in effect are deemed to be owned jointly in the absence of proof of individual title. However, the registration is basically symbolic and confers very few of the rights associated with marriage. For example, the couple is not accorded rights pertaining to taxation, social security and pension, immigration, or inheritance.[91] Moreover, such partnerships can be easily dissolved: by the death of one of the partners, by marriage of one of the cohabiting partners, or by a simple unilateral declaration of either party, which takes immediate effect without any legal proceedings and which leaves the abandoned party with no legal protection or support.[92] However, the local Magistrates Court is competent to rule in the event of any dispute regarding the practical aspects of the dissolution, for instance, occupation of accommodations, settlement of accounts, and division of jointly acquired property.[93]

Although artificial insemination is available for lesbians, adoption under Belgian law is possible only for married or unmarried heterosexual

89. *See* Olivier De Schutter & Anne Weyembergh, *"Statutory Cohabitation" under Belgian Law: A Step towards Same-Sex Marriage?* in Legal Recognition of Same-Sex Partnerships: A Study of National, European, and International Law 465 (Robert Wintemute & Mads Andenas eds., 2001).

90. Anke Hintjens, *The Present Situation of Partnership Regulations in Belgium* (Alan Reekie trans.), *in* ILGA-Europe Euroletter, note 4 above, no. 66, December 1998 [hereinafter *The Present Situation*].

91. Alan Reekie, *Statutory Cohabitation Contract in Belgium,* ILGA-Europe Euroletter, note 4 above, no. 75, November 1999.

92. De Schutter & Weyembergh, note 89 above.

93. Reekie, note 91 above.

couples and single persons;[94] in very few cases have adoption agencies provided services to gay and lesbian couples. There is one reported case in which a court granted visitation rights to the nonbiological "mother" after a lesbian couple broke up, but in most other cases, even visitation rights for biological parents have been revoked after the parent moved in with a same-sex partner. Moreover, Belgian courts have shown a clear tendency not to accord lesbian or gay biological parents custody of their children following a divorce, merely on the basis of their sexual orientation.[95] A court decision of July 2000 may represent a departure from the foregoing case law, however, since the court held that "a person's intimate orientation is no grounds for discrimination with regard to the exercise of parental rights," thus enabling a divorced mother of two who moved in with her same-sex partner to retain custody of her children.[96] In addition, the Belgian federal minister for family affairs announced in November 2000 that "homosexual couples living together will be able to adopt Belgian children" in the near future.[97] Nonetheless, the law on statutory cohabitation does not address these issues and thus maintains discrimination against gay men and lesbians in the field of parenthood.

For these reasons, and owing to the emphasis on securing the superiority of the institution of marriage, statutory cohabitation is far from being a substitute for marriage. The significance of the statutory cohabitation law is mainly symbolic, and it seems to be a failure as far as gay partnerships are concerned.[98] Only eight statutory cohabitation contracts were registered in the Borough of Brussels during the four months after the legislation took effect. Jean-Paul Leroy, the president of Infor-Homo in Belgium, stated that the law "is completely pointless, it offers nothing for anybody, whether heterosexual or homosexual."[99] However, at the end of the year 2000, Belgian parliament members showed inclination to expand the statutory cohabitation act to include more of the rights associated with marriage.[100]

94. On March 22, 2000, the Belgian Federal Cabinet approved a bill to amend the national Adoption Law that will allow unmarried couples, but not same-sex couples, to adopt for the first time. *See* PlanetOut News Staff, *International Briefs: Belgian Adoption Update Excludes Gays*, March 28, 2000.

95. *See* Hintjens, note 88 above.

96. Press Release from the Federation of Working Groups on Homosexuality (FWH), Ghent, Belgium, July 7, 2000 (English translation by Alan Reekie), available from the ILGA mailing list, ilga-list@netmafia.org.

97. PlanetOut News Staff, *More Advances in Europe: Belgium Moves towards Equality for Couples*, December 1, 2000 [hereinafter *More Advances in Europe*].

98. Hintjens, *The Present Situation*, note 90 above.

99. Alan Reekie, *Belgian "Symbolic" Statutory Cohabitation Law Flops*, communication to the ILGA mailing list, ilga-list@netmafia.org, May 7, 2000.

100. PlanetOut News Staff, *More Advances in Europe*, note 97 above.

Fifteen Belgian municipalities currently provide the option of symbolic registration for same-sex couples with the intention of pushing the federal government to adopt a registered partnership law at the national level. A registered partnership bill for same-sex couples was submitted to Parliament for discussion in 1998, the year that statutory cohabitation was established, but the bill has not yet been debated. Under the proposed legislation, same-sex couples would be guaranteed the same rights as married couples, except for rights relating to children, particularly in the field of intercountry adoptions.[101] In the last elections, the Christian Democrat Party, which was part of previous governments and whose strong opposition to the protection of gay couples was the main obstacle to any significant progress in the field, was strongly defeated. The new federal government coalition of Liberals, Social Democrats, and Greens promised a legal breakthrough; in the text of their Policy Agreement, the parties stated that they would secure a full-fledged legal partnership arrangement.[102] Accordingly, in June 2000 a working group of representatives from the political parties that form Belgium's government recommended that the scope of civil marriage be widened to include same-sex couples.[103] One year later, in June 2001, and shortly after the neighboring Netherlands became the first country to legalize same-sex marriage, the Belgian government approved a draft bill allowing marriage for same-sex couples; unlike the Dutch act, the Belgian draft bill excludes gays from the right to adopt children and allows same-sex marriage only if both partners are Belgian citizens or one is Dutch. The government stated that "as attitudes have evolved, there is no longer any reason for not opening marriage up to same-sex couples. The main argument in favor of this extension of the scope of marriage is, with the principle of nondiscrimination as a backcloth, that there is no longer an objective basis for restricting marriage to heterosexual couples . . . the Bill would eliminate a form of discrimination that features in our legislation purely because of its historic context."[104] If approval is forthcoming from Parliament as well, Belgium may become the second country, after the Netherlands, to recognize same-sex marriage.

101. Hintjens, note 88 above.

102. *See* Romko van Kol, *Belgium's New Government Coalition Promises Legal Breakthrough,* ILGA-Europe Euroletter, note 4 above, no. 73, September 1999.

103. *See* Alan Reekie, *FWH Happy with Agreement on Widening Scope of Marriage,* June 18, 2000, available from the ILGA mailing list, ilga-list@netmafia.org.

104. *See* the Belgian government's press release regarding its Council of Ministers' bill to open up marriage for same-sex couples, June 22, 2001 (Alan Reekie trans.), *in* ILGA-Europe Euroletter, note 4 above, no. 90, July 2001. *See also Belgium Considers Making Gay Marriage Legal,* Reuters, April 2, 2001; *Belgium Set to Legalize Same-Sex Marriages,* Reuters, June 25, 2001.

5.3 Countries Progressing toward the Recognition of Same-Sex Partnerships: Spain, Italy, Switzerland, and the Czech Republic

5.3.1 Spain

There is no recognition of same-sex partnerships in Spain at the national level. However, in addition to numerous Spanish cities and regions that offer symbolic registrations for same-sex couples, two out of Spain's seventeen regions, Catalonia in 1998[105] and Aragon in 1999,[106] have enacted progressive partnership legislation applicable to both heterosexual and homosexual couples, and a third region, Navarra, has provided same-sex couples with the right to adopt. These are the first and only Spanish statutes to regulate the status of unmarried cohabitation.

Although Spain is a strongly Catholic country, it is currently relatively less conservative than other European Catholic countries and is one of the more socially liberal European countries. The Spanish have been mainly concerned with regulating the status of unmarried couples in general, whether of the same sex or opposite sexes, and special regulations for homosexual partnerships at the national level have not been a matter of public or political debate.[107] It was clear to the leaders of the Spanish gay movement that lobbying for a partnership law for homosexuals would face severe opposition, both by the public and by politicians, and that the only way to secure some rights for homosexual couples would be to advocate for a general law regulating the cohabitation of both opposite-sex and same-sex couples. Thus, the issue became one of civil rights rather than gay rights, which made the progress toward partnership legislation socially acceptable and more feasible.[108]

In 1994 the Spanish Lower House voted for a proposal asking the federal government to produce legislation for unmarried couples, both heterosexual and homosexual. Since then, a few versions of a partnership bill have been drafted—most of which did not include the right to adopt—and have been debated and stalled in Parliament with no prospects of becoming law.[109] Four bills on domestic partnership for both

105. *See* Law 10/1998 of July 15 on the Stable Union of De-Facto Couples, at http://www.redestb.es/triangulo/leycatin.htm (in Spanish).

106. *See* The Unmarried Couples Law. For the English translation of the Aragon partnership law, see http://www.redestb.es/triangulo/leyarin.htm.

107. *See* Cézar Lestón, *Report on Spain, in* ILGA-Europe, note 21 above, at 86 [hereinafter *Report on Spain*].

108. *See* Cézar Lestón, *The Spanish Parliament Decides a Partnership Bill Will Have to Be Passed within This Legislature,* ILGA-Europe Euroletter, note 4 above, no. 51, July 1997.

109. *Id.* at 86. For an overview of the political structure and factors that contributed to the improbability of the passage of such law, see Pere Cruells, *Spanish Partnership Law Sold Out,* ILGA-Europe Euroletter no. 32, March 1995; Cézar Lestón, *News on the Partner-*

same- and opposite-sex couples at the national level that were introduced by opposition parties during the year 2000 were all defeated in Parliament in September of the same year.[110] Only one existing law explicitly covers same-sex couples at the national level, the Urban Lease Law of 1995. According to this law, if the lease for an apartment was signed by one partner and the partners have cohabited for at least two years, the other partner is entitled to the same rights as a legal spouse.[111] No provisions have been made, either at the national level or at the local level, regarding taxation, inheritance, or other matters that are regulated by marriage law. However, Spain's social security system grants medical care to any adult living with another adult who has coverage, so that an unemployed partner in a same-sex relationship has access to medical care through his or her partner's social security benefits. Moreover, artificial insemination for single women, including lesbians, is allowed, accessible, and covered by social security. Adoption is possible only for married couples or single individuals, either heterosexual or homosexual, but not for same-sex couples as such, although adoption by single persons serves as a "back door" for lesbian and gay couples to adopt. The nonadoptive partner has no rights as a foster parent or custody over the adopted child or, for that matter, over biological children of her or his partner.[112]

Despite the lack of progress at the national level, since 1993 many local governments have instituted partnership registration procedures for same-sex couples, and today virtually all major Spanish cities and regions have partnership registration offices. These registrations have very little significance, and their effect is mainly symbolic. They currently apply only to housing policies, so that same-sex couples are treated as one family unit for this specific purpose.[113]

The first regional Spanish law recognizing domestic partnerships and

---

ship Law in Spain, ILGA-Europe Euroletter no. 42, June 1996; Cézar Lestón, *Spanish Socialist Party Has Submitted a Partnership Law to Spanish Parliament,* ILGA-Europe Euroletter no. 46, December 1996; Cézar Lestón, *Spanish Parliamentary Debate on Partnership Bill Has Put the Government in a Difficult Position,* ILGA-Europe Euroletter no. 49, April 1997 (see note 4 above).

110. *See* Cézar Lestón, *Spanish Government Says "No" to Same-Sex Partners, in* ILGA Euroletter, note 4 above, no. 83, October 2000.

111. *See* Lestón, *Report on Spain,* note 107 above, at 86. A registration of the partnership, which is now available in most Spanish cities, serves as proof of the existence of a relationship.

112. *Id.* at 87, 86. However, when custody disputes arise, the courts tend to dismiss the suit of heterosexual parents for custody of a child when they sue on the grounds of the sexuality of a gay or lesbian former spouse now involved in a same-sex relationship. *Id.*

113. *See* Lestón, *Report on Spain,* note 107 above, at 86, 87.

regulating the rights and duties of, inter alia, same-sex couples was enacted by the parliament of Catalonia in June 1998, with 100 votes in favor and 12 against.[114] Less than a year afterward, in March 1999, the regional parliament in Aragon followed Catalonia by enacting the second domestic partnership law of its kind in Spain.[115] The partnership laws of Catalonia and Aragon are virtually the same, and each one is titled the Law on the Stable Union of Unmarried Couples. Like the Dutch Registered Partnership Act and the French PaCS, these laws are not aimed at regulating only homosexual partnerships; they define domestic partners as an opposite- or same-sex couple who have lived together "as spouses" for an uninterrupted period of at least two years.[116] The parties first enter into a notarized written contract expressing their willingness to be subject to the law, and then they register in the Administrative Registry of their region.[117] The partners have mutual obligations during the relationship: they are obliged to provide for one another and to contribute to the payment of common expenses, they are jointly responsible for the debts owed to a third party, and the individual's right to dispose of the common dwelling is restricted in favor of the couple's joint right.[118] Both laws offer employment benefits for partners who work for the regional government. In case of separation, the weaker party is entitled to maintenance for a limited period of time. The partnership can be dissolved without the involvement of the court, by mutual agreement, a unilateral decision, or a factual separation of more than one year.[119] If the partnership is dissolved owing to the death of one of the partners, the laws protect the tenancy rights of the surviving partner and deem the surviving spouse the owner of the household goods. As to same-sex couples, the surviving partner automatically receives 25 percent of the deceased's estate if no will was

114. *See* ILGA World Legal Survey, Country Reports: Spain, at http://www.ilga.org/Information/legal_survey/europe/spain.htm (last updated March 29, 1999). For the text of the partnership law in Spanish, see http://www.redestb.es/triangulo/leycatin.htm.

115. *See* Cézar Lestón, *Domestic Partnership Bill Passed in Aragon, in* ILGA World Legal Survey, note 114 above. For the English translation of the Aragon partnership law, see http://www.redestb.es/triangulo/leyarin.htm [hereinafter *Domestic Partnership Bill*].

116. *See* Catalonia and Aragon have Granted Domestic Partnership Rights, at http://www.redestb.es/triangulo/leycatin.htm (visited August 27, 1999). *See also* Francesc Jaurena Salas, *The Law on Stable Unions of Couples in the Catalonia Autonomous Community of Spain, in* Legal Recognition of Same-Sex Partnerships: A Study of National, European, and International Law 505 (Robert Wintemute & Mads Andenas eds., 2001).

117. ILGA World Legal Survey: Spain, note 114 above.

118. *See* Catalonia and Aragon Have Granted Domestic Partnership Rights, note 116 above. *See also* Salas, note 116 above.

119. *See* Catalonia and Aragon Have Granted Domestic Partnership Rights, note 116 above.

made.[120] If one member of the couple is declared legally incompetent to care for himself or herself, the other partner has first priority in the assignment of a guardian.[121]

The laws of both regions are limited in their scope and are limited to the region and to certain rights and duties between the partners themselves, with no application in regard to the state. The laws do not give same-sex couples the right to adopt. No rights in the fields of taxation, pensions, or social security are provided, as these matters, like adoption, are within the competency of the Spanish federal government.[122] However, at least the Catalan parliament considered the expansion of its act to provide for a residence permit for the non–European Union partner of a Spanish national if both were living in Catalonia and were in a domestic partnership according to the 1998 Catalan law.[123] This measure was later mandated by the Spanish Supreme Court, which held in October 2000 that domestic partnership and marriage should be equated for the purposes of residence permits for foreigners.[124]

A third region, Navarra, has provided same-sex couples with the right to adopt children, thus becoming the first Spanish region to do so; according to the new law, couples who enjoy "a free and public union in an affectionate relationship, independent of sexual orientation . . . can adopt children with the same rights and duties as those couples united in matrimony."[125] Finally, the Andalusian parliament in southern Spain is also considering legal recognition of domestic partnerships for both same- and opposite-sex couples.[126] It seems unlikely that the other fourteen regions will pass similar domestic partnership laws, since, unlike Catalonia, Aragon, and Andalusia, their statutes do not

120. The same does not apply to opposite-sex partners, since, according to the legislative text, they always have the option of getting married. *Id. See also* ILGA World Legal Survey: Spain, note 114 above; Salas, note 116 above.

121. *See* Catalonia and Aragon Have Granted Domestic Partnership Rights, note 116 above.

122. Both laws explicitly mandate that only heterosexual couples can jointly adopt. *See id.*

123. The new bill, which is titled Family Reunion for Domestic Partnerships, was submitted to the Catalan Parliament in May 2000. *See* Cézar Lestón, *Spain—A Bill on Family Regrouping for Same-Sex Couples in Catalan Parliament, in* ILGA-Europe Euroletter, note 4 above, no. 80, June 2000.

124. *See* Cézar Lestón, *Recent Spanish Supreme Court Ruling Has Equated DP's and Marriages for Residence Permits for Foreigners, in* ILGA-Europe Euroletter, note 4 above, no. 83, October 2000.

125. PlanetOut News Staff, *International Briefs: Spanish State Oks DP Adoption,* June 27, 2000. Note, however, that Navarra is the only region that has the jurisdiction to accord adoption rights to same-sex couples, given its self-ruling status.

126. *See* Cézar Lestón, *Southern Spain—Andalusian Parliament to Consider Legal Status for Domestic Partnerships, in* ILGA-Europe Euroletter, note 4 above, no. 80, June 2000.

allow them to legislate in such matters; it is up to the federal government to do so.[127]

5.3.2 Italy

The Constitutional Court of Italy ruled in 1989 that unmarried couples did not have the same rights as married couples, thus recognizing no form of cohabitation other than marriage. However, unmarried couples can register with a public notary or with a local authority as "living together." Such registration has very limited consequences—such as medical help and transfer of pension—and is not available to same-sex couples.[128] In May 1999 a bill was drafted to regulate the status of cohabiting couples. It would confer only the right of inheritance and would provide some protection for the economically weaker partner. It defines the de facto couple as two persons—without specifying their gender—who have lived together for at least four years.[129] No further steps have been taken to promote the bill.

Italian law does not recognize same-sex partners and does not accord them any rights or benefits. Thus, for example, only married couples can adopt; gay and lesbian couples, as well as single people, are automatically excluded.[130] Artificial insemination is not regulated by law, but in practice single women and lesbians are excluded from assisted artificial insemination, even in the private sector. The National Council of the Federation of Physicians approved in 1995 a regulation forbidding all physicians to inseminate anyone other than heterosexual couples, and clinics and doctors who do not comply are subject to expulsion from the federation and can no longer practice medicine in Italy.[131]

Beginning in 1993, some Parliament members have presented several bills on registered partnership based on the Scandinavian model, most of which apply to both heterosexual and homosexual couples, according them all the rights associated with the "traditional family."[132] The latest bill, which was put forward in March 1998—known as the

127. *See* Lestón, *Domestic Partnership Bill,* note 115 above.

128. The court, however, invited Parliament to legally recognize forms of cohabitation. *See* Homosexuality, note 20 above, at 94, 95.

129. *See* Gioia Scappucci, *Italy Walking a Tightrope between Stockholm and the Vatican: Will Legal Recognition of Same-Sex Partnerships Ever Occur? in* Legal Recognition of Same-Sex Partnerships: A Study of National, European, and International Law 519 (Robert Wintemute & Mads Andenas eds., 2001).

130. *See* Elena Biagini et al., Italy, *in* ILGA-Europe, note 21 above, at 71.

131. *See* ILGA World Legal Survey: Italy, at http://www.ilga.org/Information/legal_survey/europe/italy/htm (last updated June 15, 1999).

132. *Id.* at 70–71. The text of the proposals in Italian is available at http://www.gay.it/noi/indice.htm.

Soda bill on "Affective Unions"—proposes not only to recognize same-sex couples but also to include sexual orientation as a category for nondiscrimination legislation.[133] None of these bills have been scheduled for discussion in Parliament,[134] and they are unlikely to reach Parliament in the foreseeable future, mostly because of opposition by the Catholic Church, whose views carry a lot of weight, especially in policy matters concerning family law.[135] A few local authorities have tried to introduce symbolic civil union registers, but the CORECO (the Regional Supervision Committee) has always overruled these attempts, claiming that they conflict with national law, which does not recognize civil unions. Only Pisa and Bologna have enabled same-sex couples to register their unions as a "family" without being overruled by the CORECO.[136] These registrations have no legal consequences and are merely symbolic.[137]

5.3.3 Switzerland

Swiss law does not regulate unmarried cohabitation, and only general property rules and some of the provisions of the Code of Obligations apply to cohabiting couples upon the termination of their relationship.[138] According to case law of the Swiss Federal Supreme Court, same-sex partnerships are excluded from the definition of cohabitation; the few instances in which Swiss law regulates cohabitation are applicable only to different-sex couples.[139] In addition,

133. Scappucci, note 129 above.

134. Biagini et al., note 130 above, at 71.

135. For instance, before the May 1996 elections, the Vatican made gay rights an election issue when it urged Roman Catholic voters to shun candidates who backed proposed gay rights legislation, warning voters not to support candidates committed to gay rights and stating in its semiofficial newspaper that gay marriages "fundamentally undermined the family model on which human civilization was built." *See* Alan Balwin (Reuters), *Italian Gays Outraged by Church Advice to Voters,* ILGA-Europe Euroletter, note 4 above, no. 41, April 1996.

136. Biagini et al., note 130 above, at 71.

137. In July 1998 it was reported that the city of Pisa recognized the marriage of two lesbians and recorded it in the civil union registry. *See* ILGA World Legal Survey: Italy, note 131 above.

138. Barbara E. Graham-Siegenthaler, *Principles of Marriage Recognition Applied to Same-Sex Marriage Recognition in Switzerland and Europe,* 32 Creighton L. Rev. 121, 127 (1998).

139. For an interesting analysis as to whether same-sex registered partnerships that were formed in a jurisdiction where they are permitted would be recognized in Switzerland as well as in other European countries, see id. at 139–43. The Swiss Federal Court ruled in 1993 that recognizing as marriage a registered same-sex partnership entered into in Denmark would offend public policy, and it refused a couple's request to be registered in the Civil Registry. *See* Federal Court of March 3, 1993, BGE 119 II 266. Graham-Siegenthaler, note 138 above, at 139–40. Graham-Siegenthaler concludes that Austria, Italy, and the United Kingdom would also refuse to recognize "same-sex marriage" on

adoption and artificial insemination are available only to married couples.[140]

In January 1995 gay leaders presented the federal government with a petition called "Same Rights for Same-Sex Couples," which was signed by eighty-five thousand Swiss citizens.[141] To mark the one-year anniversary of their petition to Parliament, Swiss gay men and lesbians gathered in Parliament Square demanding that same-sex couples be granted the rights of marriage.[142] Consequently, in June 1996 the Swiss parliament enjoined the government to devise a plan to abolish all forms of legal discrimination against same-sex couples and to legalize gay and lesbian relationships. Parliament passed the measure by a vote of 68 to 61, with 1 abstention and 70 absentees.[143] The Swiss government took no action on the mandate. However, on September 27, 1999, the Swiss parliament voted 105 to 46 in favor of a private member's motion proposing to draft a registered partnership bill; Parliament instructed its Legal Affairs Committee to do so, recommending that the provisions applicable to heterosexual couples for mutual maintenance, joint responsibility for debts, and joint income tax returns be extended to same-sex partners, as well as immigration rights for a noncitizen in a partnership.[144] A year afterward, in November 2000, the Swiss federal Ministry of Justice began drafting a new registered partnership bill. However, the Federal Council opposes adoption rights for same-gender couples and fertility treatment for lesbians, so these rights will not be included in the bill.[145] The bill will not be as expansive as the Scandinavian registered partnership acts: it will be a light version of this model, as it would confer rights mainly in the fields of inheritance, taxation, government benefits, and immigration. Even if adopted, the new bill would probably not take effect before the year 2003. And even if the bill passes both legislative chambers, it could be blocked by a national referendum if one hundred thousand Swiss sign a petition to that effect.[146] According to several opinion polls,

---

grounds of public policy and based on these countries' conflict-of-laws rules. *See id.* at 142–43.

140. *See* François Baur, *At the End of the Fairy Tale, Will Heidi Stay Single? Same-Sex Partnerships in Switzerland, in* Legal Recognition of Same-Sex Partnerships: A Study of National, European, and International Law 531 (Robert Wintemute & Mads Andenas eds., 2001).

141. *See* Graham-Siegenthaler, note 138 above, at 132.

142. Goransson, note 1 above.

143. ILGA World Legal Survey: Switzerland, at http://www.ilga.org/Information/legal_survey/europe/switzerland/htm (last updated June 24, 1999).

144. *See Swiss Parliament Votes for Registered Partnership, in* ILGA-Europe Euroletter, note 4 above, no. 74, October 1999.

145. *See* PlanetOut News Staff, *Swiss Government Proposes DP,* October 25, 2000.

146. *See* ILGA-Europe Euroletter, note 4 above, no. 72, August 1999.

however, the official registration of homosexual partnerships is acceptable to a substantial majority of Swiss citizens, and it is thus likely that a referendum would favor the bill.[147]

5.3.4 The Czech Republic

In 1995 a registered partnership bill according same-sex couples every right of marriage except for the adoption of children was proposed by SOHO, the nation's leading gay rights group. The bill has gained the support of the head of the Czech Republic parliament, which forwarded the proposal to two parliamentary committees. In December 1995 the Czech government stated its opposition to the inclusion of the proposed registered partnership law in the new family law legislation, and in May 1998 a registered partnership bill was defeated in Parliament by only two votes.[148] Nonetheless, in March 1999 the cabinet reapproved a new draft of the bill, which was modeled after the Danish precedent, and the lower house agreed in principle, by a vote of 88 to 80, with 13 abstentions, to pass the bill. However, although the bill passed its first reading in April 1999, it was rejected by Parliament in its second reading on December 2, 1999, by a vote of 91 to 69. Even though two similar bills on registered partnership have been introduced and rejected by Parliament, the drafters of the bill stated that they would continue lobbying for its adoption and would propose the bill or a different version of it to Parliament again in the future.[149]

On May 4, 2000, the Czech Republic's human rights commissioner announced plans for a new registered partnership measure, and the ruling Social Democrats stated their support of the idea.[150] Consequently, in December 2000 a third bill on registered partnership for same-sex couples was drafted. Unlike the Scandinavian registered partnership acts, the Czech bill did not apply existing marriage law to same-sex couples but rather recognized their relationship for a number of specific purposes. Thus, for example, the bill did not require either party to a part-

147. *See* Swiss Parliament Votes for Registered Partnership, note 144 above.

148. ILGA World Legal Survey: Czech Republic, at http://www.ilga.org/Information/ legal_survey/europe/czech_republic/htm (last updated June 24, 1999). As in most countries, adoption in the Czech Republic is limited to married couples and single people and is not available for homosexuals. Artificial insemination is also limited to married couples. *Id.*

149. *See* Miluska Kotisova, *No to Registered Partnership in Czech Republic,* ILGA-Europe Euroletter, note 4 above, no. 76, January 2000.

150. *See* Rex Wockner, *Czech Republic Plans Partner Law,* International News Briefs, no. 317, May 22, 2000. Since the bill has to successfully pass three times by a majority in the lower house before it reaches the Senate, there is likely to be a long delay before a registered partnership bill is approved in the Czech Republic. *See* ILGA World Legal Survey: Czech Republic, note 148 above.

nership to be a Czech citizen; the bill allowed a homosexual partner to legally inherit from his or her partner and permitted a couple to collect social benefits together; the couple was also to be taxed and to have the right to share housing as legal partners, and to be regarded as spouses for purposes of health and citizenship laws; the right to adopt and the right to share a common surname were excluded from the proposal.[151] The government approved the bill in February 2001, and the Social Democratic Party has supported the bill. However, at the end of October 2001, the lower parliamentary chamber rejected this measure too, making it the third time a registered partnership bill has been defeated in the Czech Republic. Yet there is still hope for the adoption of a different and narrower version of the registered partnership bill, since Parliament did not completely reject the draft but decided to send it back to the government for revision.[152] The Roman Catholic Czech Bishops Conference's council for public affairs announced that it would stand aside from what it views as an entirely civil matter.[153] Since the Council of Europe Parliamentary Assembly has repeatedly called for Council of Europe member nations to recognize same-gender couples, and since the Czech Republic hopes to become a European Union member in the near future, and owing to the Czech church's stance on the matter, there remains a chance that a limited version of a registered partnership bill will pass in the future.

151. Michael Mainville, *Czech Republic: Couples Law Gains Steam, in* Euroletter no. 87, March 2001, at http://www.praguepost.cz/news030701c.html.

152. *See Czech Republic Rejects Partner Rights Law,* Gay.com UK, October 25, 2001.

153. *See* PlanetOut News Staff, *Czech Government Introduces DP Bill,* February 28, 2001.

Chapter 6

The Cohabitation Model

6.1 Canada

6.1.1 The Federal Level

Marriage and divorce in Canada come under federal jurisdiction; the Canadian provinces are in charge of the administration of justice and other family law matters, including separation, custody, and access arrangements. The federal government of Canada accords opposite-sex cohabitants most of the rights associated with marriage, whereas same-sex partners have been, until recently, excluded from these rights and benefits.[1] Since the 1996 Human Rights Tribunal decision in the matter of *Moore & Akerstrom v. Canada,*[2] however, same-sex cohabiting couples enjoy many public-sector employment benefits.[3]

Moreover, in July 1998 the Canadian Foundation for Equal Families launched a campaign against the federal government seeking changes

---

1. Kathleen A. Lahey, *Becoming "Persons" in Canadian Law: Genuine Equality or "Separate but Equal"?* in Legal Recognition of Same-Sex Partnerships: A Study of National, European, and International Law 237 (Robert Wintemute & Mads Andenas eds., 2001).

2. *See The State of the Play: A Summary of Lesbian and Gay Rights in Each Jurisdiction in Canada,* EGALE, at http://egale.ca/~egale/features.canada.htm (last updated December 27, 1998).

3. For example, the definition of common law spouse in collective agreements covering federal employees was amended by the government in 1997 to include same-sex couples. *See* ILGA World Legal Survey: Canada, at http://www.ilga.org/Information/legal_survey/americas/Canada/htm (last updated June 24, 1999). Likewise, a proposal is pending before the Canadian parliament to accord pension rights to the homosexual surviving partner of a federal employee. *See* John Urquhart, *Canada to Weigh Bill for Same-Sex Spousal Benefits,* Wall Street Journal, March 17, 1999, at A13.

in more than sixty federal statutes that discriminate against same-sex couples by according benefits on the basis of common law spousal status.[4] Finally, in February 2000, after a delay of a year and a half and largely owing to the Supreme Court's holding in the matter of *M. v. H.* in May 1999,[5] the Canadian government introduced an omnibus bill, The Modernization of Benefits and Obligations Bill (Bill C-23), to amend sixty-eight federal laws so that same-sex partners would enjoy the same rights and benefits as common law heterosexual couples. Included were the right to file joint tax returns, immigration rights, and other government benefits.[6] The omnibus bill passed its final reading in the House of Commons April 11, 2000, by a vote of 174 to 72,[7] and was approved unamended by the Senate on June 14, 2000.[8] The status of same-sex couples has thereby been equated with that of unmarried heterosexual common law partners in various fields, and most discrimination against same-sex couples by Canadian federal laws has been eliminated. Following the passage of the bill, the rights of marriage that Canada's gay and lesbian couples still do not now enjoy include, for example, hospital visitation, shared employee benefits in the private sector, spousal income tax deductions, adoption of children as a couple, parental tax deductions by a nonbiological coparent for a partner's biological child, transfer to a surviving partner of Registered Retirement Savings Plans, and sponsorship of a foreign partner for immigration.[9]

The possibility of a legislative action to open up marriage to same-sex couples in Canada seems quite remote. The Canadian minister of justice stated in June 1999 and again in February 2000—after introducing the omnibus bill—that the government has no intention of changing the definition of marriage or legislating same-sex marriage.[10] Following this statement, the House of Commons of the Canadian parliament adopted by a vote of 216 to 55 a resolution stating that "mar-

4. ILGA World Legal Survey: Canada, note 3 above.

5. The Court enjoined the province of Ontario to extend equal treatment to same-sex couples and unmarried heterosexual couples. *See* M. v. H., 62 C.R.R. (2d) (Supreme Court of Canada, May 1999). For more on the case, see the discussion regarding Ontario below.

6. *See* Reuters, *Canadian Government Considers Equal Status for Gay Couples,* New York Times, February 12, 2000, at 5A.

7. *See* Rex Wockner, *Canadian Partner Bill Passes House, in* ILGA-Europe Euroletter no. 79, April 2000 (Steffen Jensen et al. eds.) at http://www.qrd.org/qrd/www/orgs/ILGA/euroletter.

8. *See* PlanetOut News Staff, *Can Senate Oks Omnibus DP,* June 21, 2000.

9. *See* PlanetOut News Staff, *First Gay Banns Read in Toronto,* December 11, 2000.

10. *See The Love That Dare Not Be Legally Recognized: The Government's Archaic Definition of Marriage Is Out of Step with Most Canadians,* Globe & Mail (a Canadian national newspaper), June 10, 1999; *Canadian Government Considers,* note 6 above.

riage is and should remain the union of one man and one woman to the exclusion of all others" and that "Parliament will take all necessary steps to preserve this definition of marriage in Canada."[11] Although the resolution itself has no legal effect, it indicates the lack of willingness of the federal legislature to make the institution of marriage available to same-sex couples in the future. In addition, the omnibus bill discussed above was amended in March 2000, and its final version included a clause—equivalent to the American Defense of Marriage Act—that bans same-sex marriage by defining marriage as a heterosexual-only institution: "For greater certainty, the amendments made by this act do not affect the meaning of the word 'marriage,' that is, the lawful union of one man and one woman to the exclusion of all others."[12] However, the act's interpretive clause did not put an end to the debate in Canada over same-sex marriage. First, the clause now faces legal challenges from couples who claim that it violates the Canadian Charter of Human Rights. Moreover, in October 2000 and again in February 2001, Canada's first openly gay member of Parliament, Svend Robinson, introduced a private bill to extend marriage to same-gender couples.[13] The bill, which states that "a marriage between two persons is not invalid by reason only that they are of the same sex,"[14] was primarily a symbolic political statement, since it had no real chance of reaching a vote in Parliament, let alone passing. Marriage has already been defined by federal law (the omnibus act discussed above) as limited to a union of a man and a woman, and the Canadian provinces, which register marriages, have refused marriage certificates on the basis of that definition.[15] The Canadian government

11. Donald G. Casswell, *Any Two Persons in Canada's Lotusland, British Columbia, in* Legal Recognition of Same-Sex Partnerships: A Study of National, European, and International Law 215 (Robert Wintemute & Mads Andenas eds., 2001); *Love That Dare Not,* note 10 above.

12. Robert Wintemute, Lesbian/Gay Law Notes, April 2000, at 60 (Arthur S. Leonard ed.). Moreover, although marriage law is within the jurisdiction of the federal government, the province of Alberta took the symbolic step of passing legislation that bans same-sex marriage and the recognition thereof—the Marriage Amendment Act, which took effect March 23, 2000. *Id.*

13. *See* PlanetOut News Staff, *Robinson Intros Marriage Bill,* October 6, 2000; Reuters, *Canadian Government Opposes Gay Marriage Bill,* CNN, February 14, 2001, available at http://www.cnn.com/2001/WORLD/americas/02/14/canada.gays.reut/index.html.

14. *See* PlanetOut News Staff, *International Briefs on Couples Rights: Canadian MP Pushes for More,* February 14, 2001.

15. An interesting example is the case of two gay couples who claim they got married legally in January 2001 in the Metropolitan Community Church in Toronto. Following the ceremony, since the federal government does not allow same-sex marriage, the provincial government refused to register the marriages and claimed that as long as the marriage was not registered, it was not legally valid. A lawsuit was filed by the Metropolitan Community Church. For analysis of the case and its circumstances, see the section below regarding the status of same-sex couples in Ontario.

clearly expressed its opposition to Robinson's bill.[16] As we shall see, challenges to the exclusion of same-sex couples from marriage have also been brought in three Canadian provinces; two of these challenges are still pending.

6.1.2 Same-Sex Couples in Five Provinces

Out of Canada's twelve provincial governments, eight have extended benefits to their same-sex employees.[17] Six provinces—Ontario, British Columbia, Quebec, Nova Scotia, Alberta, and, more recently, Saskatchewan—have thus far accorded same-sex couples extensive family law rights and responsibilities.[18] In the provinces of Ontario, British Columbia, and Quebec, courts are now looking into the issue of whether same-sex couples should be granted the right to marry under Canadian human rights laws.

Ontario

Prior to the landmark decision of the Canadian Supreme Court in the matter of *M. v. H.*,[19] in which the Court held that the definition of *spouse* in Ontario's Family Law Act, which was limited to opposite-sex partners, was unconstitutional under the Canadian Charter of Rights, Ontario had amended many of its statutes pertaining to opposite-sex cohabitants to apply to same-sex couples. Consequently, same-sex couples were recognized for the purposes of, for example, health services, public-funded pensions, public-sector employment benefits, artificial insemination, child support, and custody for the nonbiological partner.[20] Further, according to Ontario law, a partner in a same-sex relationship can make medical decisions on behalf of his or her partner who is incapacitated.[21] In 1995 an Ontario trial court granted the partner of a parent in a same-

16. *Canadian Government Opposes Gay Marriage Bill,* note 13 above.

17. These provinces are British Columbia, Manitoba, New Brunswick, Nova Scotia, Northwest Territories, Ontario, Saskatchewan, and Yukon. *See* ILGA World Legal Survey: Canada, note 3 above.

18. In July 2001 the Canadian province of Saskatchewan became the sixth province to recognize same-sex couples as it passed two omnibus bills that amend twenty-four different existing provincial laws, including the right of gay and lesbian couples to adopt stepchildren and to qualify for public pensions. *See Canadian Province Recognizes Gay Couples,* PlanetOut News, July 9, 2001. Other provinces do not accord gay couples equal family law rights, i.e., they limit the definition of *spouse* or *common law partner* to heterosexuals and do not allow gays to have custody or adopt each other's or unrelated children. In Prince Edward Island, a statute limiting marriage to opposite-sex partners has been proposed. *See The State of the Play,* note 2 above.

19. 62 C.R.R. (2d) (Supreme Court of Canada, May 1999).

20. Lahey, note 1 above.

21. *See* ILGA World Legal Survey: Canada, note 3 above.

sex relationship the right to adopt her or his partner's biological child. The court also held that same-sex couples have the right to jointly adopt an unrelated child. The decision has not been appealed, and since the 1995 ruling, such adoptions have become available in Ontario.[22] Since the Court's decision in *M. v. H.*,[23] same-sex couples also have the right and the obligation to support each other following separation.

In order to comply with and implement the Supreme Court's ruling in *M. v. H.*[24] and place same-sex couples on an equal footing with opposite-sex common law couples, Ontario's parliament adopted a bill in October 1999 entitled Bill 5: The Amendments because of the Supreme Court of Canada Decision in *M. v. H.* Act, 1999.[25] The act did not change the definition of *spouse*, which includes married and unmarried opposite-sex partners. Instead, it amended sixty-seven statutes by inserting a new and separate category of "same-sex partnership" alongside the existing definition of *spouse*. The act provides same-sex couples most of the rights and obligations of unmarried opposite-sex partners, but it does not equate their status with opposite-sex married couples.[26] Moreover, the new law does not recognize same-sex couples as spouses under Ontario law.[27] It is thus questionable whether the legislature met the Supreme Court's mandate to include same-sex couples in the definition of *spouse*.

Finally, a same-sex marriage case is pending before an Ontario Divisional Court. The circumstances that led to the suit are unique and have spurred a national debate in Canada over same-sex marriage. In January 2001 two gay couples participated in a marriage ceremony in the Metropolitan Community Church in Toronto, and in accordance with the Ontario Marriage Act, the church announced the couples' "marriage banns" three Sundays in a row, an action that carries the same legal weight as obtaining a marriage license at city hall. The Ontario Marriage Act does

22. *In re* K., Ontario Court (Provisional Division) 1995, 23 Ontario Reports 3rd 679. *See* Douglas Sanders, Recent Canadian Developments on Equality, Family Law, and Same-Sex Couples, July 26, 1997, at http://www.ilga.org/Information/legal_survey/americas/canada.htm (last updated July 19, 1999).

23. 62 C.R.R. (2d) (Supreme Court of Canada, May 1999).

24. *Id.*

25. The text of the act is available at http://www.ontla.on.ca/Documents/documents index.htm.

26. *See* Robert Wintemute, *Ontario Adds Same-Sex Partners in 67 Laws,* Lesbian/Gay Law Notes, November 1999, at 173 (Arthur S. Leonard ed.).

27. The act also fails to address certain legal policies, including adoption rights and property tax issues, that result in discrimination against same-sex partners. *See* Arthur S. Leonard, *International Notes: Canada,* Lesbian/Gay Law Notes, December 1999, at 189; James McCarten, *Ontario Skirts Supreme Court Ruling with New Same-Sex Clause,* Canadian Press, October 25, 1999, available at http://ilga.org/Information/legal_survey/americas/ontario_skirts.supreme_court_rul.html.

not specify that the banns ceremony is limited to couples of the opposite sex. This is presumably a loophole in the laws governing marriage; by reading banns—that is, making a public announcement of intention to marry—three Sundays in a row, a minister can perform a legally binding marriage without first obtaining a marriage license from the province. The church's minister issued legal marriage certificates to the couples and sent the certificates to the Ontario registrar general. However, since the federal government does not allow same-sex marriage, the provincial government refused to register the marriages and claimed that as long as the marriage is not registered, it is not legally valid. The church claims that there is nothing in the marriage act that says the marriage is not valid unless it is registered by the registrar general.[28] Consequently, the Metropolitan Community Church filed suit against the Ontario government in Ontario Divisional Court over its refusal to recognize the marriages. The government is expected to argue that it has been established law in Canada for more than a quarter of a century that a couple that is legally ineligible to marry cannot become eligible by reading banns.[29]

British Columbia
The government of British Columbia has extended employment benefits to its employees' same-sex partners and their families. Moreover, various British Columbia laws have been amended so as to include same-sex couples within their definition of *spouse;* these include legislation pertaining to public-sector pension plans and medical services coverage.[30] In July 1997 British Columbia amended its Family Relations Act and Family Maintenance Enforcement Act so that the term *spouse* would include persons in a same-sex relationship. Thus, the provisions of the acts apply equally to same-sex partners, and they have the same rights and obligations as unmarried heterosexual couples, including maintenance, the duty to pay child support, and the right to have custody of each other's children.[31] In addition, British Columbia's 1996 Adoption Act provides that one or two *persons* may apply to adopt a child; this provision permits same-sex partners to jointly adopt a child and the nonbiological parent in a same-sex relationship to adopt his or her partner's

28. *See* Rex Wockner, *Toronto Gays Claim They Married Legally,* Wockner International News no. 351, January 15, 2001.

29. *See* Gloria Galloway, *Canadian Same-Sex Church Weddings,* Canadian Press News Service, December 6, 2000, available at http://www.canada.com/cgi-bin/cp.asp?f=/news/cp/stories/20001205/national-649024.html.

30. *See* ILGA World Legal Survey: Canada, note 3 above. *See also* Casswell, note 11 above.

31. *See* ILGA World Legal Survey: Canada, note 3 above. *See also The State of the Play,* note 2 above.

child.[32] Likewise, same-sex partners have access to artificial insemination.[33] According to British Columbia law, a partner in a same-sex relationship can also make medical decisions on behalf of her or his incapacitated partner.[34] Same-sex couples—as well as unmarried opposite-sex partners—may enter into and register a cohabitation agreement that regulates the division of property and is judicially enforceable; without such agreement, cohabiting partners do not have the right to judicial division of property upon separation.[35]

As a result of the ruling by the Canadian Supreme Court in the matter of *M. v. H.*,[36] the British Columbia government introduced in July 1999 legislation amending the definition of *spouse* in several laws to include "a person who has lived and cohabited with another person, for a period of at least 2 years immediately before the other person's death, in a marriage-like relationship, including a marriage-like relationship between persons of the same gender," and thus placed same-sex partners on an equal footing with unmarried opposite-sex partners in matters of wills, estates, and inheritance.[37]

In addition to the same-sex marriage cases pending in Ontario and Quebec, a similar challenge was brought before the British Columbia Supreme Court. The attorney general of British Columbia, who believed that denying marriage licenses to same-sex couples would be considered discrimination in violation of the federal Charter of Rights and Freedoms, petitioned the province's Supreme Court in July 2000 on behalf of two same-sex couples seeking a declarative judgment as to whether same-sex couples should be allowed marriage licenses under Canadian federal law, that is, whether the federal ban on same-sex marriage is constitutional. The attorney general's opinion was that such a move would be an extension of the equality legislation that British Columbia has been passing for several years. The need to turn to the courts instead of the provincial legislature stems from the rule that marriage is defined federally, even though licenses are distributed provincially. The suit challenged the current federal definition of marriage as limited to one man and one woman. This marked the first time a Canadian govern-

32. *See* Sanders, note 22 above.

33. Casswell, note 11 above.

34. *See* ILGA World Legal Survey: Canada, note 3 above.

35. However, according to British Columbia Supreme Court case law, in the absence of such an agreement, same-sex partners can nevertheless claim common law judicial remedy of constructive trust. *See* Casswell, note 11 above.

36. 62 C.R.R. (2d) (Supreme Court of Canada, May 1999).

37. *British Columbia Government to Expand Partnership Rights,* Wockner International News no. 274, at http://mother.qrd.org/qrd/world/wockner/news.briefs/274-07.26.99.

ment has ever expressed the view that same-sex couples should have an equal right to marry.[38] In January 2001 British Columbia's Supreme Court chief justice rejected the federal government's argument that the province's attorney general did not have standing to seek the declarative judgment.[39] However, in October 2001, the Supreme Court of British Columbia rejected the constitutional challenge and refused to strike down the definition of marriage, reasoning that it did not have jurisdiction to strike down the law.[40] Ultimately, the issue will go before the Supreme Court of Canada, which is expected to rule in favor of same-sex marriage.

Quebec

In June 1999 Quebec became the first province in Canada to treat same-sex couples equally with opposite-sex cohabitants and common law spouses after its National Assembly unanimously passed Bill 32, which recognizes same-sex relationships. The law amends the acts and regulations that contain a definition of *spouse* to expressly include same-sex couples; same-sex couples are thus regarded as common law spouses with no need to register their partnerships. In effect the law comes close to equating the status of same-sex partnerships with marriage, since opposite-sex cohabitants had already been accorded most of the rights associated with marriage. Same-sex couples in Quebec are now entitled to such marriage-related rights as health services, legal aid and welfare, social security, all tax benefits and exemptions, full public-employment benefits and pensions, family benefits, low-income support, and immigration rights.[41] Bill 32 does not address parental rights, including adoption rights.[42] Despite the lack of prohibition, the policy of sperm banks is not to allow lesbians or single women access to artificial conception; only heterosexual couples (either married or not) benefit from such services. Same-sex couples are also excluded from the right to jointly adopt an unrelated child or to adopt each other's children, since the law on adoption specifically states that it is applicable only to adoption by a man and a woman (including stepparent adoption) or by an individual;

38. *See* PlanetOut News Staff, *BC Asks Court for Gay Marriage*, July 21, 2000.

39. Reuters, *B.C. Allowed to Join Challenge to Gay Marriage Ban*, January 9, 2001.

40. *See* Rich Peters, *Canadian High Court Rejects Gay Marriage*, 365Gay.com, October 4, 2001.

41. *Quebec Changes the Definition of "Spouse" in 39 Laws & Regulations*, Egale Press Release, June 11, 1999, at http://www.ilga.org/Information/legal_survey/amendment/quebec_changes_the_definition_of.htm (last modified June 18, 1999). For a list of the laws and regulations amended by Bill 32, see id.

42. For legal regulation of adoption by same-sex couples, see Quebec Civil Code, art. 549.

although theoretically a single gay man or a lesbian can adopt, the policy of the social services is to inquire into the sexual orientation of the prospective adoptive parents and grant adoptions only to heterosexual individuals.[43]

As in Ontario and British Columbia, a same-sex marriage case is pending in Quebec. In August 2000 a Montreal gay couple filed an appeal with the Quebec Superior Court claiming that the provincial prohibition on same-sex marriage was unconstitutional. This case is also still pending.[44] Moreover, in October 2000 Quebec's provincial Liberal Party convention approved a resolution in support of equal civil marriage rights for gay and lesbian couples. This is more than the national party was willing to do when it met in March of the same year and voted down a similar proposal.[45]

Nova Scotia

The government of Nova Scotia, like some other provincial governments, decided to introduce new legislation in order to comply with two court decisions: the landmark Canadian Supreme Court ruling in the Ontario case *M v. H.*[46] and a Nova Scotia Court of Appeal ruling that found that the provincial Matrimonial Property Act discriminated against gay and lesbian couples.[47] Accordingly, on November 30, 2000, Nova Scotia passed Bill 75, titled An Act to Comply with Certain Court Decisions and to Modernize and Reform Laws in the Province, which gives statutory recognition to same-sex couples. The bill became effective June 4, 2001, except for the provisions relating to income taxation, which took effect January 1, 2001.[48] The act provides that a "common-law partner" of an individual means "another individual who has cohabited with the individual in a conjugal relationship for a period of at least two years" (in some instances, a period of one year is sufficient).[49] The legislation amends various acts, such as the Family Maintenance Act, the Fatal Injuries Act, the Health Act, the Pensions Benefits Act, the Succession Act, the Maintenance and Custody Act, the Matrimonial

43. Telephone conversation with Karol O'Brien of Gay Ecoute, a gay and lesbian organization in Quebec, February 22, 2000.

44. Rex Wockner, *Quebec Couple Demands Access to Marriage,* Wockner International News no. 331, August 28, 2000.

45. PlanetOut News Staff, *Quebec Liberals Support Marriage,* October 16, 2000.

46. 62 C.R.R. (2d) (Supreme Court of Canada, May 1999).

47. *See* PlanetOut News Staff, *Nova Scotia Introduces DP Bill,* November 10, 2000.

48. For the status of the bill and its text, see 2000 Statutes, chap. 27, at http://www.gov.ns.ca/legi/legc/.

49. *Id.*

Property Act, and the Income Tax and Insurance Acts. The act adds a domestic partner registry allowing the registration of two individuals who have been cohabiting in a conjugal relationship for more than two years; the new status accords the couple the same rights as spouses under the foregoing statutes. It thus extends to gay and lesbian common law partners the same legal status as unmarried heterosexual common law couples, in effect equating the status of same-sex couples with that of married couples under the province's law.[50] Nova Scotia has become, then, the first province in Canada to create a domestic partner registry. Finally, in July 2001 Nova Scotia's highest court struck down a law preventing gay and lesbian couples from adopting. Nova Scotia has thus joined several other Canadian provinces, including British Columbia, Ontario, and Alberta, that allow same-sex couples to adopt.[51]

Alberta

In May 1999 Alberta's legislature amended its Child Welfare Act to provide adoption rights to stepparents in same-sex relationships. The province thus allows second-parent adoption by gay men and lesbians.[52] Consequently, the Court of Queen's Bench in Alberta issued a precedent ruling in November 1999 according full adoption rights to a stepparent, namely, the nonbiological parent, in a same-sex relationship.[53]

Moreover, on April 2, 2001, after a gay man had filed a precedent-setting charter challenge to get a spousal share of the estate of his late same-sex partner, who died without a will, the Alberta Court of Queen's Bench ruled that according to the Canadian Charter of Rights and Freedoms, Alberta's inheritance laws discriminated against same-sex couples. Before the court's ruling, the law excluded gay and lesbian couples from the rights married couples had when a spouse died without a will.[54] The court suspended its ruling for nine months to allow the provincial government to rewrite its Intestate Succession Act to include same-sex couples. In light of this ruling, the province will probably be required to write into about a dozen different laws that mention the word *spouse* a new definition of common law relationships that includes same-sex couples.[55] As a consequence of the court's ruling, Alberta's government

50. *See* PlanetOut News Staff, *Nova Scotia Introduces DP Bill,* November 10, 2000.

51. *See* Ben Thompson, *Gay Adoption Victory in Canadian Province,* PlanetOut News, July 10, 2001.

52. *See* ILGA World Legal Survey: Canada, note 3 above.

53. *See* Arthur S. Leonard, *International Notes: Canada,* Legal Law Notes, December 1999, at 189.

54. Barbara Dozetos, *Inheritance Win for Canadian Gays,* PlanetOut News, April 4, 2001.

55. *See* Doug Beazley, *Charter Challenger Wins—Or Maybe Not,* Edmonton Sun, April 4, 2001.

has announced that it will amend provincial legislation to ensure that gays and lesbians are afforded equal protection under the law.[56] Such legislation, providing gay couples many of the rights associated with marriage, is not expected before mid-2002.

6.2 Australia

Except for a few domestic partner employment benefits, no rights are accorded to same-sex couples at the federal level.[57] The eight states that form the Commonwealth of Australia each enact their own laws in many fields, including various matters relating to family law, criminal law, and antidiscrimination legislation.[58] Two states, the Northern Territory and Western Australia, do not accord any recognition to same-sex couples. Legislative attempts to expand the definition of de facto relationships to cover same-sex couples and place them on an equal footing with opposite-sex de facto couples have been defeated in the parliaments of both Queensland and South Australia.[59] A bill offering the recognition of de facto relationships of same-sex couples is currently pending in Tasmania. The proposal, called the Significant Relationships Bill, was introduced before the Tasmanian parliament at the end of 1998. The bill accords legal status to a range of personal relationships, including same-sex relationships, and covers, inter alia, property division and inheritance.[60]

Only three states, the Capital Territory, New South Wales, and Victoria, have passed legislation recognizing de facto relationships of same-sex couples; for the most part, the legislation is limited to the division of property

56. *See* James Cudmore, *Alberta: Charter Case Prompts Alberta to Review Laws Affecting Gays,* National Post, April 3, 2001.

57. An Australian gay man has recently submitted a challenge before the U.N. Human Rights Committee regarding the federal government's refusal to recognize his same-sex relationship. He alleges violation of Australia's obligations under the antidiscrimination provisions of the International Covenant on Civil and Political Rights. *See The Law Report,* Radio National (Australia). A transcript of the program on same-sex marriage, April 9, 2001, is available from John Wilkinson (jwilk@eskimo.com).

58. ILGA World Legal Survey: Australia (Federal), at http://www.ilga.org/ Information/legal_survey/asia_pacific/australia_federal.htm (last updated June 24, 1999).

59. ILGA World Legal Survey: Australia (Queensland), at http://www.ilga.org/ Information/legal_survey/asia_pacific/australia_queensland.htm (last updated April 23, 1999); ILGA World Legal Survey: Australia (South Australia), at http://www.ilga.org/ Information/legal_survey/asia_pacific/australia_south_australia.htm (last updated April 23, 1999).

60. *See* ILGA World Legal Survey: Australia (Tasmania), at http://www.ilga.org/ Information/legal_survey/asia_pacific/australia_tasmania.htm (last updated April 23, 1999).

between the partners upon dissolution of the relationship. In June 2001 the parliament of Victoria passed a bill—The Statute Law Amendment (Relationships) Bill—that extends legislative definitions of de facto relationships to include same-sex couples and thus accords lesbian and gay couples the same rights that heterosexual de facto couples possess.[61] Victoria thus became the only Australian state with laws that completely equate same-sex couples with de facto heterosexual couples in the field of domestic relationships. The act changed the definition of *spouse* to the gender-neutral phrase "domestic partner" in some forty-four acts of the state of Victoria. The amendments deal with four key areas of law. Under the new act, a partner can make medical decisions regarding his or her disabled partner. Transfer of real property from one partner to the other involves the same tax exemptions as transfers between spouses. Partners share in pension benefits and have standing to inherit from each other in the absence of a will.[62] According to the act, in order to obtain rights similar to those of heterosexual de facto couples (i.e., in order to be regarded as domestic partners), same-sex couples have to prove to the court that they live together and are in a sexual and committed relationship.[63]

In 1994 the Capital Territory enacted the Domestic Relationships Act, which confers rights and imposes responsibilities—mainly with regard to the division of property and the payment of maintenance upon the breakup of the relationship—on members of same-sex de facto relationships comparable to the rights and duties pertaining to people in heterosexual de facto relationships.[64] In June 1999 the New South Wales Legislative Assembly passed the Property (Relationships) Legislation Amendment Bill 1999, which amends the De Facto Relationships Act of 1984.[65] The act amends numerous statutes to equalize the status of same-sex partners with that of opposite-sex couples. Furthermore, it provides

61. *See* ILGA World Legal Survey: Australia (Victoria), at http://www.ilga.org/Information/legal_survey/asia_pacific/australia_victoria.htm (last updated June 24, 1999); Sean Maher, *Victorian Reform Becomes Law,* Sydney Star-Observer, issue 563, June 2001.

62. PlanetOut News Staff, *Victoria Introduces Couples Bill,* November 28, 2000.

63. *See* Felicity Dargan, *Legal Proof for Gay Rights,* Melbourne Herald Sun, April 24, 2001.

64. *Domestic relationship* is defined as a personal relationship between two adults— other than marriage but including a de facto marriage—that has existed for at least two years, in which one provides personal or financial commitment and support of a domestic nature for the material benefit of the other; the couples need not cohabit. *See* ILGA World Legal Survey: Australia (Capital Territory), at http://www.ilga.org/Information/legal_survey/asia_pacific/australia_capital_territory.htm (last updated April 23, 1999).

65. ILGA World Legal Survey: Australia (New South Wales), at http://www.ilga.org/Information/legal_survey/asia_pacific/australia_new_south_wales.htm (last updated June 16, 1999).

a new definition of a de facto relationship to cover same-sex couples by defining it as the relationship between two unrelated adults who live together. The existence of a de facto relationship is determined by the court after taking into account various factors such as the duration of the relationship. The act affects mainly real and personal property rights, such as the division of property upon the breakup of the relationship, and rights relating to succession on intestacy; it also provides a few rights not related to property, such as guardianship and mental health decisions.[66]

As far as parenting rights are concerned, no state in Australia provides for joint adoption by same-sex couples, since the acts covering the adoption of children restrict adoption to married couples; in some cases of special need, they also provide for adoption by opposite-sex couples and individuals. Moreover, the Family Law Act allows the adoption of a partner's child only in a heterosexual relationship, so that same-sex couples are prohibited from adopting each other's children.[67] None of the eight states accord same-sex couples custody over each other's children. With regard to artificial insemination and in vitro fertilization (IVF) services, the laws and policies vary from one state to another. In Tasmania and New South Wales there are no legal restrictions concerning artificial insemination, and lesbians in fact have equal access to donor insemination services.[68] The Capital Territory's Domestic Relationships Act of 1994 offers services to single women but not to lesbian couples. Similarly, in 1997 the Queensland Supreme Court overturned a lower tribunal's ruling and denied lesbians access to insemination clinics.[69] Statutes regulating access to reproductive technology in Victoria and Western Australia expressly banned single women and lesbians from access to donor insemination and IVF services.[70] However, in July 2000 a federal court in Victoria struck down the state's statutory ban on reproductive treatment for single women and ruled that lesbians and single women had reproductive rights and should be given access to such services.[71] The court found that the section of the Victorian Infertility Treatment Act of 1995 restricting IVF and artificial insemination to married or de

66. Sec. 4 of the bill. For the full text of the bill, see http://www.parliament.nsw.gov.au/gi/billist9.html.

67. *See* Stevie Clayton, *Legal Recognition of Same-Sex Relationships: Where To from Here?* 3 Murdoch U. Electronic J.L. (September 1996) at http://www.murdoch.edu.au:80/elaw/issues/v3n3/clayton.html.

68. *See* ILGA World Legal Survey: Australia (Tasmania), note 60 above.

69. ILGA World Legal Survey: Australia (Queensland), note 59 above.

70. ILGA World Legal Survey: Australia (South Australia), note 59 above.

71. *See* PlanetOut News Staff, *Aus PM Moves to Limit Fertility,* August 1, 2000.

facto heterosexual couples was in conflict with the federal Sex Discrimination Act, which outlaws discrimination on the basis of sex or marital status.[72] The court's decision spurred a heated national debate regarding reproductive rights of lesbians, and various public figures have condemned the court, including the prime minister, John Howard, who announced that his government would attempt to override the court's ruling and introduce federal legislation to allow the states to reinstate such bans.[73] The prime minister stated, "This issue involves overwhelmingly . . . the right of children in our society to have the reasonable expectation, other things being equal, of the affection and care of both a mother and a father. And in those circumstances, we believe states have the right to legislate to that effect and as a result we propose an amendment to the Sex Discrimination Act to make it plain that legislation similar to the legislation enacted by the state of Victoria would not be struck down by the Sex Discrimination Act."[74]

6.3 New Zealand

Until recently, same-sex partnerships were not recognized in New Zealand.[75] However, a comprehensive bill—the De Facto Relationships Property Bill—that regulated the division of property upon dissolution of a de facto relationship, including that of same-sex couples, was drafted and later presented to Parliament. Another bill was introduced in March 1998 to amend the Matrimonial Property Act 1976 (for married couples) and to create a new De Facto Property Act to provide property rights for de facto different-sex couples. There was much debate about the inclusion of same-sex couples, and the National Party Government of the time delayed final consideration of both pieces of legislation to avoid responding to the call to include same-sex couples.[76]

In January 2000 New Zealand's new government, which supported the legal recognition of same-sex partnerships, announced its intention

72. McBain v. State of Victoria, FCA 1009 (July 28, 2000).

73. *See* PlanetOut News Staff, *Aus PM Moves to Limit Fertility,* August 1, 2000.

74. Rex Wockner, *Aussie Government Opposes Insemination Ruling,* Wockner International News no. 328, August 7, 2000.

75. For an evaluation of the social status of gays in New Zealand, see Thomas B. Stoddard, *Bleeding Heart: Reflections on Using the Law to Make Social Change,* 72 N.Y.U. L. Rev. 967 (1997) (the article also discusses the impact that legislation protecting homosexuals has on social attitudes toward them and argues that there is a wide gap between the progressive legislation regarding gays and lesbians in New Zealand and society's advancement and attitudes toward them).

76. Nigel Christie, *New Legislation in New Zealand for Same-Sex Couples,* a report to the Queer Law mailing list, March 30, 2001, at queerlaw@abacus.oxy.edu.

to move the two bills forward.[77] It divided the bills into several pieces of property legislation designed to provide for married couples, de facto different-sex partners, and same-sex partners. Consequently, on March 29, 2001, four new bills with significance for same-sex couples were passed by Parliament, each one with an effective date of February 1, 2002. The first act, the Property (Relationships) Amendment Act 2001, accords same-sex couples and de facto different-sex couples the same relationship property rights (and obligations) as married couples upon the dissolution of a relationship.[78] In effect the act provides for equal treatment in property division to all dissolving couples: married, unmarried heterosexual, and same-sex couples. All three kinds of couples must have been in a relationship at least three years prior to its dissolution in order for the new act to apply.[79] The second act, the Administration Amendment Act 2001, gives same-sex partners access to the same rights as married partners in relation to the estate of a deceased partner who has not left a will. The third act, the Family Protection Amendment Act 2001, provides same-sex partners with rights and legal standing to make a claim against the estate of a deceased partner when, for example, the deceased's will is out of date or the deceased has failed to make provision for the surviving partner. The fourth act, the Family Proceedings Act 2001, provides for "spousal maintenance" after relationship breakup, without regard for the division of property.[80] Although the four pieces of legislation deal only with property matters at the termination of the relationship, New Zealand has definitely made significant progress toward broad-based recognition of same-sex partnerships.

At the same time, the government is considering the extension of additional rights to same-sex couples, such as child adoption.[81] Currently, only married couples and single adults can adopt, and unmarried

77. *See NZ DP Bill to Proceed,* PlanetOut News & Politics, January 4, 2000, at http://www.planetout.com/news/article.html?2000/01/04/2.

78. Christie, note 76 above. Essentially, there is to be a presumption of fifty-fifty division of property for couples who have been together in a relationship "in the nature of marriage" for a period of three years or more. Division is based on contribution to the relationship (not just to the relationship property). There is a provision that allows for contracting out. *Id.* Patterned after the new law in the Australian state of New South Wales, the New Zealand act expands judicial discretion in determining property division and support payments to allow consideration of the circumstances of a relationship, including its duration, the nature and extent of common residence, whether or not a sexual relationship exists, the degree of financial dependence, the degree of mutual commitment to a shared life, and the care and support of children. *See* PlanetOut News Staff, *NZ Gay Couples Win Divorce Rights,* November 22, 2000.

79. *See Opponents Lose Row over De Facto Bill,* New Zealand Herald, March 14, 2001.

80. Christie, note 76 above.

81. *Id.*

men are barred from adopting girls.[82] Thus, although same-sex couples
in New Zealand can obtain custody over each other's children, they cannot jointly adopt a child or adopt each other's children.[83] Yet recognition of gays' and lesbians' ability to serve as good adoptive parents is
growing in New Zealand as placement agencies are encouraging same-
gender families to consider adoption and clearing the way for them to do
so.[84] Moreover, new rules from New Zealand's Health Funding Authority
permit lesbian couples and single women access to state-funded fertility
treatments.[85]

On the matter of same-sex marriage, in 1996 three lesbian couples
who had been denied marriage licenses brought a challenge to New
Zealand's Marriage Act of 1955, seeking a declaration that the registrar-
general of births, deaths, and marriages was acting in breach of New
Zealand's law by refusing to issue them marriage licenses. The High
Court of New Zealand refused to interpret the act to include same-sex
couples despite its gender-neutral language and despite the court's conclusion that the Marriage Act discriminated on the basis of sexual orientation contrary to the Bill of Rights Act, which prohibits such discrimination. Pointing out that case law since the eighteenth century had
limited marriage to one man and one woman, the court concluded that
only the legislature is authorized to redefine marriage and that a different interpretation would be contrary to the legislature's intention.[86] The
Court of Appeal reaffirmed the lower court's judgment in December
1997, holding unanimously that the Marriage Act applied only to the
union of a man and a woman and that same-sex partners were not to
be accorded equality with opposite-sex married couples.[87] Subsequently,

82. PlanetOut News Staff, *UK & NZ Expand Adoption Rights,* October 3, 2000.

83. *See* ILGA World Legal Survey: New Zealand, at http://www.ilga.org/Information/
legal_survey/asia_pacific/new_zealand.htm (last updated June 17, 1999).

84. PlanetOut News Staff, note 82 above.

85. *See* Rex Wockner, *N.Z. Lesbians Gain Fertility-Treatment Access,* Wockner International News no. 336, October 2, 2000.

86. Quilter et al. v. Attorney General [1996] NZFLR 481, 486, 505. For a thorough
analysis and critique of the High Court's ruling in *Quilter,* see Ruthann Robson, *The State
of Marriage,* 1 Y.B. N.Z. Jurisprudence 1 (1997) (arguing, among other things, that the
result of *Quilter* is that the Bill of Rights act's ban on discrimination on the basis of sexual
orientation is meaningless if it is contrary to judicial precedent or ancillary statutes), but
note that the New Zealand Bill of Rights is not a supreme law and cannot be invoked to
invalidate a statute. *See* Mary Bonauto et al., *Brief: The Freedom to Marry for Same-Sex Couples: The Reply Brief of Plaintiffs Stan Baker et al. in Baker et al. v. State of Vermont,* 6 Mich.
J. Gender & L. 1 n. 61 (1999).

87. Quilter et al. v. Attorney General [1998] NZLR 523. For an argument that the
present concept of marriage should be changed and that opposite- and same-sex marriage should be equally permissible under New Zealand marriage law—based on the gender neutrality of the law itself and on the New Zealand Bill of Rights Act of 1990—see

a communication was forwarded to the United Nations Human Rights Committee seeking a statement that by not amending the Marriage Act to include same-sex couples, the New Zealand government was in breach of its obligations under the International Covenant on Civil and Political Rights and the International Covenant on Economic, Social and Cultural Rights.[88] It remains to be seen whether the committee will require New Zealand's government to open up marriage to same-sex couples.

Robin Mackenzie, *Transsexuals' Legal Sexual Status and Same-Sex Marriage in New Zealand: M. v. M.*, 7 Otago L. Rev. 556, 569 (1993).

88. *See* Nigel C. Christie, *The New Zealand Same-Sex Marriage Case: From Aotearoa to the United Nations, in* Legal Recognition of Same-Sex Partnerships: A Study of National, European, and International Law 317 (Robert Wintemute & Mads Andenas eds., 2001).

Chapter 7

Same-Sex Partnerships
in the United States

During the past few decades, U.S. courts have been slowly expanding the definition of family. There is growing recognition of homosexuals as parents, because courts are increasingly granting visitation and custody rights not only to the gay or lesbian natural parent but also to stepparents in same-sex relationships. Courts are also approving adoption petitions of single gay men and lesbians and of same-sex coparents, as well as petitions of a same-sex couple to jointly adopt an unrelated child. The availability of artificial insemination for lesbians is another contributing factor to the expanding recognition of alternative families in the United States.

In recognizing new family structures and living arrangements alternative to marriage, the prevalent statutory solution to the status of unmarried cohabitants in the United States during the past decade has been domestic partner legislation and policies. Alongside the marketplace and statutory recognition of domestic partnership, a large number of state courts have taken into account the changes in society during the past few decades—the rise in nonmarital cohabitation of opposite-sex couples and the large number of same-sex cohabiting couples—and have provided some protections for these relatively new forms of cohabitation by way of according limited rights in various contexts to same-sex couples and recognizing certain kinds of cohabitation agreements. In addition to cohabitation contracts and domestic partnerships, adult adoption, whereby one partner in a same-sex relationship adopts the other partner, has been used as an alternative to marriage.

The latest and most controversial development in the United States in the field of same-sex partnerships is the fight of same-sex couples to enter the institution of marriage. In recent years, a few courts have come close to according gays the right to civil marriage; this in turn has led to a national backlash against gay rights and has prompted legislation whose aim is to prevent the opening up of marriage to gay and lesbian couples.

The different means of securing some of the rights associated with marriage as well as the possibility of same-sex couples' gaining access to marriage are the issues of this chapter.

7.1 Parental Rights of Same-Sex Couples in the United States

Traditional definitions of parenthood were exclusive and did not encompass the families of same-sex couples.[1] Yet definitions and conceptions of family and parenthood are quite flexible and are in constant fluctuation. American statutes and case law are unclear as to whether current definitions of parenthood preclude or include the families of same-sex couples: as I explain below, a large number of cases suggest the former, whereas others (some of the favorable decisions pertaining to second-parent adoptions [see below]) suggest the latter. It thus seems that, at least as far as some states are concerned, there is still a long way to go before we can say with some certainty that legal definitions of parenthood include the families of same-sex couples. The law requires a child to have only one parent of each sex, and natural parents have all of the rights and obligations of parenthood, whereas de facto parents have relatively few of the rights and obligations associated with parenthood.[2] However, despite the history of judicial hostility toward lesbian and gay families with children, and despite the negative stereotypes,[3] an increasing number of adoption petitions by gay and lesbian couples

1. *See* Katharine T. Bartlett, *Rethinking Parenthood as an Exclusive Status: The Need for Legal Alternatives When the Premise of the Nuclear Family has Failed,* 70 Va. L. Rev. 879 (1984).

2. *See* Kathryn E. Kovacs, *Recognizing Gay and Lesbian Families: Marriage and Parental Rights,* 5 L. & Sexuality 513, 515 (1995). With regard to the rights of de facto parents, in many states grandparents, stepparents, and a variety of other people have the right to maintain visiting relations with children, even over the objection of their parents. *See, e.g.,* Troxel v. Granville, 120 S.Ct. 2077 (2000).

3. *See* Sylvia A. Law, *Homosexuality and the Social Meaning of Gender,* 1988 Wis. L. Rev. 187, 188–92; Kath Weston, Families We Choose: Lesbians, Gays, Kinship 22–27 (1991).

have been filed in state courts around the country during the past two decades,[4] and courts have extended visitation and custody rights to non-biological parents. Artificial insemination has also become popular as a means for lesbian couples to create a two-parent family. Some attribute this increase to the growing visibility and political power of gay men and lesbians.[5] This section analyzes these developments, which are in sharp contrast to the almost complete prohibition on gay and lesbian parenthood in some of the European countries.[6]

7.1.1 Adoption

Same-sex couples have made a lot of progress regarding their adoption rights, and there is a growing number of judges who allow such adoptions; however, court decisions on adoption by gays and lesbians continue to be inconsistent and disconcerting.[7]

All forms of adoption are based on state law; in addition, every adoption in the United States, even if arranged privately, must be approved by the court.[8] The adoption statutes and procedures and the court decisions pertaining to these statutes are governed by each state individually—there is no national uniform set of laws.[9] Although the standard of review in cases of adoption, that is, the "best interest of the child" standard, is similar in all states, it is a very vague standard allowing wide

4. *See* Charlotte J. Patterson, *Adoption of Minor Children by Lesbian and Gay Adults: A Social Science Perspective,* 2 Duke J. Gender L. & Pol'y 191, 197 (1995); *see also* Karla J. Starr, Note, *Adoption by Homosexuals: A Look at Differing State Court Opinions,* 40 Ariz. L. Rev. 1497, 1499 (1998).

5. *See* William E. Adams Jr., *Whose Family Is It Anyway? The Continuing Struggle for Lesbian and Gay Men Seeking to Adopt Children,* 30 New Eng. L. Rev. 579, 580 (1996).

6. For a comparison between the parental rights of same-sex couples in the United States and the northern European countries, see chap. 8, sec. 8.3.2.

7. An examination of judicial decisions reveals that many courts are biased against lesbians and gay men and routinely discount empirical evidence and disregard the specific facts of the case; they deny adoptions to lesbians and gays as a result of prejudice and misconceptions. *See generally* Timothy E. Lin, Note, *Social Norms and Judicial Decisionmaking: Examining the Role of Narratives in Same-Sex Adoption Cases,* 99 Colum. L. Rev. 739 (1999). Such bias exists also among academic scholars. *See, e.g.,* Lynn D. Wardle, *The Potential Impact of Homosexual Parenting on Children,* 1997 U. Ill. L. Rev. 833 (arguing that gay and lesbian parents in ongoing homosexual relationships are harming their children because of their sexual orientation and that as a result there should be a codified rebuttable presumption that parenting by homosexuals who are in relationships is not in the best interests of children). *But see* Carlos A. Ball & Janice Farrell Pea, *Warring with Wardle: Morality, Social Science, and Gay and Lesbian Parents,* 1998 U. Ill. L. Rev. 253 (rebutting Wardle's assessment of the social science literature that has studied families headed by gays and lesbians and asserting the erroneousness of his proposed presumption based on tactical, normative, and constitutional arguments).

8. Lambda: Adoption by Lesbians and Gay Men: An Overview of the Law in the 50 States 5 (1996) [hereinafter Lambda Adoption Overview].

9. *See* Patterson, note 4 above, at 202; Lambda Adoption Overview, note 8 above, at 1.

discretion to the courts. It is thus being interpreted differently by each judge and has been used by various courts to prevent lesbians and gay men from adopting children.[10] Legislation asserting that lesbians and gay men per se were "unfit" to adopt and expressly prohibiting any form of adoption by any "homosexual" existed in New Hampshire until recently,[11] and as of May 2001 three states (Florida, Utah, and Mississippi) had bans on adoption by same-sex couples; only Florida explicitly bans adoptions by individual gay men and lesbians in addition to same-sex couples.[12] Furthermore, the state agency in charge of adoption and foster care in Arkansas decided in 1999 to ban homosexuals from becoming adoptive parents.[13]

In May 1999 New Hampshire lawmakers repealed that state's twelve-year-old ban on gay adoption and foster parenting.[14] In 1995 the supreme court of Florida upheld the constitutionality of the statutory ban against adoptions by gays.[15] The complete ban was upheld once again in August 2001 by the Federal Court for the Southern District of Florida.[16] Similar

10. *See* Julie Shapiro, *Custody and Conduct: How the Law Fails Lesbian and Gay Parents and Their Children,* 71 Ind. L.J. 623, 632 (1996); *see also* Lambda Adoption Overview, note 8 above, at 1–2; Lisa M. Pooley, *Heterosexism and Children's Best Interest: Conflicting Concepts in Nancy S. v. Michele G.,* 27 U.S.F. L. Rev. 477 (1993); Elizabeth Zuckerman, Comment, *Second-Parent Adoption for Lesbian-Parented Families: Legal Recognition of the Other Mother,* 19 U.C. Davis L. Rev. 729, 734–37 (1986).

11. *See* N.H. Rev. Stat. Ann. § 170-B:4 (1994).

12. *See* Fla. Stat. Ann. § 63.042(3) (West 1985). In accordance with Utah's new law (HB 103) on adoption and foster care that took effect May 1, 2000, and which applies to private as well as public adoptions, the state's Division of Child and Family Services voted in favor of a policy banning adoption and foster care by any unmarried cohabitants, including individual gay men and lesbians as well as same-sex couples. *See* Hillary Groutage, *State Board Adopts Policies on Adoption, Foster Care,* Salt Lake Tribune, April 1, 2000. The current policy replaces a similar one adopted by the division in 1999. For the 1999 policy, see William N. Eskridge Jr., Gaylaw: Challenging the Apartheid of the Closet 421 n. 6 (1999). On May 3, 2000, Mississippi's governor signed a new law on adoption, which took effect July 1, 2000, making it the third state to ban gay couples from adopting children. The act also makes Mississippi the first state to deny legal recognition of adoptions by same-sex couples performed in another state. *See* Gina Holland, *Mississippi Bans Homosexual Adoption,* Associated Press, May 3, 2000.

13. In Arkansas there is a presumption against adoptions by homosexuals as a matter of administrative practice. In order to reverse the Arkansas agency's decision, a bill was introduced that would have prohibited discrimination based on sexual orientation when an agency placed a child for adoption and when an adoption petition was presented to the court; however, the bill died in committee in March 1999, failing by one vote to obtain committee approval. *See* Nancy Maxwell et al., *Legal Protection for All the Children: Dutch-American Comparison of Lesbian and Gay Parent Adoptions,* 3.1 Electronic J. Comp. L. 13, 33 n. 11, 34 n. 116 (August 1999) at http://law.kub.nl/ejcl/31/art31-2.htm.

14. *See* H.B. no.90, 1999 Sess. (NH 1999). The law took effect on July 2, 1999.

15. *See* Cox v. Florida Dept. of Health & Rehabilitative Servs., 656 So.2d 902 (Fla. 1995).

16. *See* Lofton v. Kearney, 2001 WL 988038 (S.D. Fla.). The court held that Florida's statutory ban on adoptions by homosexuals does not violate the 14th Amendment's guar-

challenges to the new laws banning adoption in Utah and Mississippi are expected in the near future. Moreover, within the last two years, six states have had legislation introduced that would have restricted gay and lesbian adoptions. The bills introduced in Georgia, Missouri, and Oklahoma did not pass, and bills in Alabama, Indiana, and Texas are still pending.[17]

The term *second-parent adoption* or *coparent adoption* refers to adoption by a lesbian or a gay man of her or his partner's (biological or adoptive) children and the retention of legal parental rights on the part of the biological or adoptive parent.[18] In the case of second-parent adoption, the parties seek legal recognition for an already existing parental relationship.[19] Second-parent adoptions by gays and lesbians are a judicial creation derived by analogy from the recognition of stepparent adoption by married couples.[20] Most state adoption statutes provide that when a child is adopted, the existing parent loses all legal rights with respect to that child, unless the adopting party is the legal spouse and a stepparent to the child of the existing parent. In other words, an exception to the rule according to which the parental rights of the child's biological or otherwise legal parent are terminated and transferred to the new adoptive parent is limited to stepparents, who may adopt their spouse's children without altering the spouse's parental rights. That exception has until recently been reserved exclusively for marital relationships.[21] Since

---

antee of equal protection, reasoning that "plaintiffs have not asserted that they can demonstrate that homosexual families are equivalently stable, are able to provide proper gender identification or are no more socially stigmatizing than married heterosexual families." *See* Arthur S. Leonard, *Federal Court Rejects 14th Amendment Challenge to Florida Adoption Ban, in* Lesbian/Gay Legal News, September 2001, at 160.

17. *See ACLU Challenges Florida Ban,* note 16 above; *see also* Maxwell et al., note 13 above, at 33–34 nn. 111–13.

18. *See* Nancy D. Polikoff, *This Child Does Have Two Mothers: Redefining Parenthood to Meet the Needs of Children in Lesbian-Mother and Other Nontraditional Families,* 78 Geo. L.J. 459, 467 n. 27 (1990); *see also* Sunne Bryant, *Second Parent Adoption: A Model Brief,* 2 Duke J. Gender L. & Pol'y 233, 233–34 (1995). The concept of second-parent adoption was initially created to benefit heterosexual couples when the new stepparent wanted to adopt his or her partner's child and the noncustodial biological parent wanted to maintain visitation. In such cases, the child ended up with three parents. *See In re* Jacob, 660 N.E.2d 397 (N.Y. 1995).

19. *See* Theresa Glennon, *Binding the Family Ties: A Child Advocacy Perspective on Second-Parent Adoptions,* 7 Temple Pol. & Civ. Rts. L. Rev. 255, 256–57 (1998).

20. Starr, note 4 above, at 1506.

21. *See* Craig F. Christensen, *Legal Ordering of Family Values: The Case of Gay and Lesbian Families,* 18 Cardozo L. Rev. 1299, 1409 (1997); *see also* Julia Frost Davies, Note, *Two Moms and a Baby: Protecting the Nontraditional Family through Second-Parent Adoptions,* 29 New Eng. L. Rev. 1055 (1995) (discussing whether second-parent adoption necessitates termination of the biological parent's legal status as a parent).

same-sex marriage is not available in the United States, and since according to the above-mentioned "cut off" provision in most adoption laws, the existing parent in a same-sex relationship would lose all legal rights and responsibilities with respect to his or her child if the partner's petition was approved, and since the original parent would have no desire to give her or his consent to the termination of parental rights in second-parent adoption cases, such adoptions have usually been denied.[22] However, more recent court decisions in various jurisdictions have interpreted adoption statutes more liberally, and second-parent adoptions by same-sex couples have been accorded by various levels of courts in almost half the states. The highest state courts of Vermont, Massachusetts, and New York have expressly permitted lesbians and gay men to adopt the children of their partners without the legal parental rights of those parents being extinguished.[23] In 1995 three intermediate-level appellate courts—in New Jersey,[24] the District of Columbia,[25] and Illinois[26]—also permitted second-parent adoptions by same-sex couples.[27] Second-parent adoptions have been approved by lower courts in many other states.[28] Even though the letter of the law in each state prohibits biological parents from sharing parental rights and respon-

---

22. Lambda Adoption Overview, note 8 above, at 2.

23. Regarding Vermont, see *In re* Adoptions of B.L.V.B. and E.L.V.B., 628 A.2d 1271 (Vt. 1993) (allowing second-parent adoption under a statute that included a "cut off" provision with a stepparent exception); regarding Massachusetts, see Adoption of Tammy, 619 N.E.2d 315 (Mass. 1993) (allowing second-parent adoption without termination of the biological mother's parental relationship under the termination provision), and Adoption of Galen, 680 N.E.2d 70 (Ms. 1997); regarding New York, see *In re* Jacob, *In re* Dana, 660 N.E.2d 397 (N.Y. 1995). For a detailed analysis of the latter case, see Vincent C. Green, *Same-Sex Adoption: An Alternative Approach to Gay Marriage in New York*, 62 Brooklyn L. Rev. 399 (1996).

24. *See* Matter of Adoption of Two Children by H.N.R., 666 A.2d 535 (N.J. Super. Ct. App. Div. 1995).

25. *See In re* M.M.D. & B.H.M., 662 A.2d 837 (D.C. Ct. App. 1995).

26. *See In re* Petition of K.M. & D.M., 653 N.E.2d 888 (Ill. Ct. App. 1st Dist. 2d Div. 1995).

27. Lambda Adoption Overview, note 8 above, at 2–3.

28. *See, e.g.*, regarding Alaska, *In re* A.O.L. No. 1JU-85-25-P/A (Alaska 1st Jud. Dist. July 23, 1985); *In re* Adoption of a Minor (C), No. 1-JU-86-73 P/A (Alaska 1st Jud. Dist. Feb. 6, 1987); regarding California, *In re* Adoption of N.L.D., No. 18086 (Cal. Super. Ct. San Francisco County Sep. 4, 1987); *In re* Adoption Petition of Achtenberg, No. AD 18490 (Cal. Super. Ct. San Francisco County, 1989); *In re* Adoption of Carol, No. 18573 (Cal. Super. Ct. San Francisco County, 1989); *In re* Adoption of Nancy M., No. 18744 (Cal. Super. Ct. San Francisco County, 1990); regarding Indiana, *In re* Adoption of Hentgen-Moore, No. 91CO1-9405-AD-009 (Ind. Cir. Ct. White County Mar. 24, 1995); regarding Oregon, *In re* Adoption of M.M.S.A., No. D8503-61930 (Or. Cir. Ct. Multnomah County Sept. 4, 1985); regarding Pennsylvania, *In re* Adoption of E.O.G. & A.S.G., 14 Fiduc. Rep.2d 125 (Pa. C. P. York County Apr. 28, 1994); regarding Washington, Interest of E.B.G. No. 87-5-00137-5 (Wash. Super. Ct. Thurston County Mar. 29, 1989); *In re* Adoption of Child A and Child B, No. 88-5-00088-9 (Wash. Super Ct. 1988); *In re* Adoption of Child No. 1 and Child No. 2, No. 89-5-00067-7 (Wash. Super. Ct. Thurston County 1989). *See* Maxwell

sibilities with adoptive parents, and though second-parent adoption is not regulated by any adoption statute, each of these courts has looked beyond the language of the statute to its purpose—advancing the best interests of the child—in granting the adoptions and allowing the rights and responsibilities of the biological parent to continue.[29] The courts have applied the rules authorizing stepparent adoptions by analogy in order to grant second-parent adoption—a statutory interpretation approach known as the *functional equivalent analysis*—and have reasoned that such interpretation was in the best interests of the child involved; since the overriding purpose of all adoption statutes is to further the best interests of the children, such interpretation was justified by the courts.[30] Moreover, California's domestic partnership act, which took effect on January 1, 2002, specifically authorizes registered domestic partners to adopt each other's children using the second-parent adoption procedure.

Three states (in addition to Florida, Utah, and Mississippi, which have a complete ban on adoption by gays) expressly prohibit second-parent adoption by same-sex couples. The supreme court of Wisconsin,[31] an intermediate appellate court in Colorado,[32] and a Pennsylvania appeals court,[33] have interpreted these states' statutes to preclude second-parent adoption by lesbians and gay men. The supreme court of Connecticut instituted a similar ban in 1999,[34] but on May 3, 2000, the Connecticut legislature enacted a law that overturns the court's decision and

---

et al., note 13 above, at 26 n. 28. According to a 1996 report by Lambda Legal Defense and Education Fund, a number of trial courts in other states—including Alabama, Iowa, Maryland, Michigan, Minnesota, Nevada, New Mexico, Ohio, Rhode Island, and Texas— have also granted second-parent adoption to same-sex partners. *See* Lambda Adoption Overview, note 8 above, at 8–11.

29. *See* Elizabeth Rover Bailey, Note, *Three Men and a Baby: Second-Parent Adoptions and Their Implications,* 38 B.C. L. Rev. 569 (1997) (discussing and analyzing the above-mentioned three court decisions in Vermont, Massachusetts, and New York).

30. *See* Maxwell et al., note 13 above, at 5. This approach was also incorporated into the Uniform Adoption Act under the provision "Adoption of Minor Stepchild by Step-parent" to grant second-parent adoption to same-sex couples. *See* Unif. Adoption Act, Standing to Adopt Minor Stepchild, §4-102 (1994), 9 U.L.A. Comment, Electronic Pocket Part Update (1998).

31. *See In re* Angel Lace M., et al., 516 N.W.2d 678 (Wis. 1994) (holding that since the two women could not legally marry, a second-parent adoption could not take place without cutting off all legal rights and obligations of the biological mother, a condition to which the biological mother did not consent).

32. *See In re* Adoption of T.K.J. and K.A.K., 931 P.2d 488 (Colo. Ct. App. 1996), rehearing denied (1996), cert. denied (1997).

33. *In re* Adoption of CCG and *In re* Adoption of RBF (Penn. Appeals Court, November 2000). *See* PlanetOut News Staff, *Appeals Court Nixes Co-Adoption,* November 10, 2000.

34. *See In re* the Adoption of Baby Z, 724 A.2d 1035 (Conn. 1999) (the court was unwilling to interpret the adoption statute in a way that would allow the parental rights of the biological mother to be retained. The court held that the Connecticut adoption statutes do not allow for the granting of second-parent adoptions for gay couples).

allows gays and other unmarried couples to adopt their partner's children.[35]

When neither partner to a same-sex relationship has a child of his or her own, adoption by a gay man or a lesbian as an individual can be a first step to a subsequent petition for second-parent adoption—by the nonadoptive partner alone or as a joint petition including the adoptive parent. This used to be the only way for both partners in a same-sex relationship to pursue adoption of a child not related to either of them, since until recently, joint adoption by a same-sex couple (or by an opposite-sex unmarried couple) of an unrelated child who was not previously adopted by one of the partners as an individual was not permitted by any state. This was because all states' adoption statutes or administrative policies limited adoption to only one partner of unmarried cohabiting heterosexual couples or same-sex couples, thus restricting gay and lesbian couples from adopting jointly.[36]

Except for Florida, Utah, and Mississippi,[37] no state prohibits unmarried individual adults, including gay men and lesbians, from applying to become foster parents and from applying for adoption. In practice, however, states vary in their assessments of the fitness of lesbians and gay men, and although courts in more than twenty-two states have allowed adoption by individual lesbians and gay men,[38] in many cases such petitions are denied.[39] In December 1997 New Jersey became the first state to allow joint adoption by lesbian and gay couples, as well as unmarried heterosexual couples, on an equal footing with married

35. Gina Holland, *Mississippi Bans Homosexual Adoption*, Associated Press, May 3, 2000.

36. *See* Shapiro, note 10 above, at 625–26.

37. Single gay men and lesbians in Florida are prohibited from adopting, but they may become foster parents, since the legislation in Florida prohibits only *adoption* by homosexuals. *See* Matthews v. Weinberg, 645 So.2d 487 (Fla. Ct. App. 1994). Moreover, it has been reported that some judges throughout the state have granted adoption petitions brought by lesbians and gay men in the context of intrafamilial adoptions in spite of the legislation. *See* Lambda Adoption Overview, note 8 above, at 6.

38. *See ACLU Fact Sheet: Overview of Lesbian and Gay Parenting, Adoption, and Foster Care,* ACLU Freedom Network, April 6, 1999, at http://www.aclu.org/issues/gay/parent.html. States in which adoptions by individual gay men and lesbians were permitted include California, Connecticut, District of Columbia, Illinois, Massachusetts, New Jersey, New York, Rhode Island, Vermont, and Washington. Ohio's Supreme Court expressly permitted such adoptions. *See In re* Adoption of Charles B., 552 N.E.2d 884 (1990). For most other states, there is no definite answer, and the outcome of a petition for adoption may vary according to the judge and the county. *See* Lambda Adoption Overview, note 8 above, at 8–11.

39. Some states—such as Arizona, Arkansas, Georgia, Missouri, North Carolina, North Dakota, Tennessee, Utah, and Virginia—are known to be especially hostile to gay men and lesbians as parents; adoption in these states may be very difficult or even impossible. *See* Lambda Adoption Overview, note 8 above, at 8–11.

couples.[40] It has been reported that numerous joint adoptions by same-sex couples have also been granted in California,[41] and more recently in New York, where a County Surrogate issued an order granting joint adoption of a child to a same-sex male couple, neither of whom was previously the biological or adoptive parent of the child.[42]

Second-parent adoptions have apparently become a popular means of recognizing both parties to a same-sex relationship as parents, since in almost half of the states, courts have permitted such adoptions. Joint adoptions by same-sex couples of an unrelated child, though, are a recent development that is still limited to very few jurisdictions. Most decisions regarding second-parent adoptions have been made by trial courts, whose decisions are nonbinding, and there are very few definitive rulings of appellate courts. Thus, it remains to be seen whether higher courts will accord the same degree of recognition, which will bind the lower courts; if that occurs, petitions for second-parent adoptions will no longer be dismissed merely because of a judge's restricted interpretation of adoption laws as not providing for this option.

7.1.2 Custody

The growing approval of second-parent adoptions has generally not been accompanied by success in custody and visitation suits by gay and lesbian second parents (those who have not adopted the child in question).[43] Nonetheless, recent case law may suggest a move toward greater recognition of the rights of gay and lesbian stepparents.[44] As far as indi-

40. This was a result of the settlement of a lawsuit challenging the state's policy of not approving adoptions requested by unmarried couples. The state of New Jersey entered with the plaintiffs into a court-approved consent decree, allowing unmarried heterosexual and homosexual couples to adopt children together. The settlement affects only New Jersey's state adoption agencies, not its private ones. *See New Jersey Becomes First State to Allow Joint Adoption by Lesbian and Gay Couples,* ACLU Freedom Network News, December 17, 1997, at http://www.aclu.org/news/n121797a.html.

41. *See* Maxwell et al., note 13 above, at 9, 30 nn. 64–65. Furthermore, in a case of second-parent adoption in which one partner first adopted a child as an individual and later joined his partner's petition to adopt the child, the District of Columbia court of appeals conceptualized the case as a joint petition to adopt from an unmarried couple. *See In re* M.M.D. & B.H.M., 662 A.2d 837 (D.C. Ct. App. 1995). The court held that both same-sex couples and opposite-sex unmarried cohabiting couples should be eligible to file joint petitions for adoption of an unrelated child and that such petitions should be granted or rejected on a case-by-case basis. *Id.* at 848–49, 859.

42. *See* Matter of Baby Boy T, No. QDS 24228620 NYLJ 5/7/99 (N.Y. Surr. Ct., N.Y.Co., April 7, 1999).

43. *See* Kovacs, note 2 above, at 529.

44. For example, in May 2001 Tennessee's Supreme Court unanimously overturned an appeals court decision that barred a lesbian mother from having her partner in their home when her two daughters visited. The ruling increases protections for gay parents who live with their partners and have full or partial custody of their children. *See* Lambda Legal Defense and Education Fund News Release, May 2, 2001, at www.lambdalegal.org.

vidual gay men and lesbians are concerned, a few states have expressly pronounced sexual orientation by itself to be irrelevant to a custody decision,[45] and some other state courts have awarded custody to lesbian or gay parents on a case-by-case basis.[46] Although no state has adopted a rule that homosexuality per se should be a bar to granting custody, many courts' reasoning is masked by a "best interest" test while they virtually apply a per se rule, even when denying the existence of such a rule in their jurisdiction.[47] In many other jurisdictions, there are only a few reported decisions dealing with gay or lesbian custody or none at all.[48] Moreover, even when gays and lesbians have been permitted to maintain custody, the courts usually have imposed unreasonable restrictions upon the gay or lesbian parents' lifestyle.[49]

Custody and visitation rights have scarcely ever been accorded to the nonbiological parent upon the termination of a same-sex relationship. Although the determining standard applied by most courts is "the best interest of the child" (as in adoption),[50] as a general rule, custody and visitation rights are considered inherent rights only of biological parents, and courts are reluctant to accord such rights to nonbiological parents, even when there is a clear agreement as to the rights of coparents or a factual parental relationship between the nonbiological partner and her or his partner's children. An exception to the general tendency of courts not to accord visitation and custody rights upon the termination of a same-sex relationship is the groundbreaking decision of a unanimous New Jersey Supreme Court.[51] Basing its decision on precedents

45. For example, Iowa courts have expressly stated that sexual orientation is a "non issue" in custody cases. *In re* Marriage of Couples, 531 N.W.2d 656 (Iowa Ct. App. 1995). Similarly, an appeals court in Alaska granted custody to a lesbian mother without her sexual orientation's becoming a factor in the decision: S.N.E. v. R.L.B. 699 P.2d 875 (Alaska 1985). *See* Lambda: Lesbians and Gay Men Seeking Custody and Visitation: An Overview of the State of the Law 3 (1996) [hereinafter Lambda Custody Overview].

46. *See, e.g.,* California: *In re* Marriage of Birdah, 197 Cal. App. 3d 1024 (1988); New York: Paul C. v. Tracy C., 622 N.Y.S.2d 159 (App. Div. 4 Dept. 1994).

47. *See, e.g.,* White v. Thompson, 569 So2d. 1181 (Miss. 1990); Bottoms v. Bottoms, 457 S.E.2d 102 (Va. 1995); Lundin v. Lundin, 563 So.2d 1273 (La. Ct. App. 1st Cir. 1990); Glover v. Glover, 586 N.E.2d 159 (Ohio Ct. App. 19). In these cases, sexual orientation was a factor in finding the parent to be unfit. *See* Lambda Custody Overview, note 45 above, at 3–4.

48. *See* Lambda Custody Overview, note 45 above, at 8.

49. *See In re* Michael Lee Parson, No. 02A01-9403-JV-0037, 1995 WL 442587 (Tenn. Ct. App. July 27 1995) (holding that there should be no "inappropriate expression of sexual conduct between Ms. Carson and her roommate"). *Id.* at 5.

50. Mary Becker, *Strength in Diversity: Feminist Theoretical Approaches to Child Custody and Same-Sex Relationships,* 23 Stetson L. Rev. 701, 715 (1994).

51. V.C. v. M.J.B, 2000 WL 352404 (N.J. Sup. Ct., April 6, 2000).

from Wisconsin and Massachusetts,[52] that court held that according a lesbian coparent visitation and custody rights for her ex-partner's biological children whom she had not adopted but had served as their "psychological parent" could be considered.[53] In according the ex-partner legal standing akin to that of a biological-legal parent, the decision is one of the broadest and most far-reaching rulings on parental rights of same-sex couples in the nation to date.[54]

American courts generally refuse to enforce either custody and visitation agreements on behalf of nonbiological or nonadoptive coparents or agreements between unmarried biological parents, considering such enforcement to be contrary to public policy.[55] The agreements between unmarried biological parents may include agreements between the partners in a lesbian couple about custody over a child conceived by one of them through artificial insemination or a child adopted by one of them as an individual; or they may involve cases in which one of the partners to a lesbian relationship or a single woman has conceived via artificial insemination by a known donor with the agreement that he would waive some of his parental rights, such as custody, with respect to that child.[56] In these cases courts usually hold that rights to custody and

52. In 1995 a Wisconsin court ordered a lower court to reconsider its decision to turn down a woman's request for visits with the son of her former lesbian lover. *See* Custody of H.S.H.-K., 533 N.W.2d 419 (Wis. Sup. Ct., 1995). Similarly, in June 1999 a Massachusetts high court granted visitation rights to a lesbian who had participated in raising her ex-partner's son. *See* E.N.O. v. L.M.M., 711 N.E.2d 886 (Mass. Sup. Judicial Ct., 1999). The language of the courts in these decisions, unlike that in the New Jersey Supreme Court decision, did not amount to a strong and clear precedent, and both were limited to visitation rights with no mention of custody.

53. *See* V.C. v. M.J.B, 2000 WL 352404 (N.J. Sup. Ct., April 6, 2000). However, despite its holding that in such circumstances custody may also be accorded, the court granted only visitation rights to the ex-partner, since she had not been in contact with the children for the four years while the case was pending. According to the "psychological parent" test, an applicant has to meet four conditions in order to be regarded as a functional parent with legal rights: that her role as a parent has been permitted and fostered by the biological parent, that she has lived with the children, that she has performed parental functions "to a significant degree," and that a parent-child bond has been forged. Once the nonlegal "parent" qualifies as a psychological parent, the "best interests of the child" analysis takes hold. *See* Lesbian/Gay Law Notes, May 2000, at 72. *See also* Tom Avril, *Ex-Partner Is Parent, Not Nanny, Court Rules*, Philadelphia Inquirer, April 7, 2000.

54. In contrast, courts in California, New York, and Florida have ruled that lesbian ex-partners are not entitled to visitation rights with children they helped nurture, regardless of how deep the emotional bond was. *See* Ralph Siegel, *Lesbian 'Ex' Gets Visitation Rights*, Associated Press, April 6, 2000.

55. *See* Christensen, note 21 above, at 1352.

56. Most states have adopted legislation protecting married women against parental claims by sperm donors, but only a few have provided comparable protection for unmarried women. Moreover, in almost every reported case in which a donor has asserted parental claims against an unmarried woman, the donor has prevailed, notwithstanding any agreement that existed between the parties. Even when such agreements have been

visitation cannot be contracted away, since such contracts are contrary to public policy.[57] In only one major decision has an appellate court held that a coparenting agreement regarding the joint custody by a lesbian couple of a child conceived by one of them through artificial insemination was enforceable—subject to judicial modification in the best interest of the child—holding that a parent may contract with another person concerning the custody of a child.[58]

Moreover, notwithstanding the existence of any agreement between the parties, some courts refuse to accord custody and visitation rights to nonrelatives, specifically to nonbiological coparents in a same-sex relationship, even if they are the de facto parents of the child.[59] It is usually held that a nonparent in a same-sex relationship has no standing to seek custody or visitation upon the termination of the relationship; in so holding, courts refuse to protect nontraditional families or to expand the definition of *parent* to include a functional one; and usually they ignore the intention of the natural mother to create a parental relationship between her partner and her child and the reality of the de facto parenthood created between the nonbiological parent and her partner's children. Courts generally hold that the coparent who did not adopt the child does not have standing to bring an action for custody or visitation, without addressing the issue of whether custody or visitation by this partner would be in the best interests of the child.[60]

Very few courts have been willing to recognize the concept of de facto lesbian coparenthood; they have granted limited visitation rights to the nonbiological parent but have refused to accord her custody unless the biological parent was unfit to care for the child.[61] There are very

---

enforced by the courts, in nearly all of them the effect has been to favor the donor's claim. *See id.* at 1355–57.

57. *See, e.g.,* Sporleder v. Hermes (*In re* Z.J.H.) 471 N.W.2d 202, at 211 (Wis. 1991); Alison D. v. Virginia M., 572 N.2d 27, 28–29 (N.Y. 1991); *see also* Christensen, note 21 above, at 1352–53.

58. A.C. v. C.B. 829P.2d 660, 664 (N.M. Ct. App. 1992); see also Christensen, note 21 above, at 1354.

59. For the rights of de facto parents, see note 2 above.

60. *See, e.g.,* McGuffin v. Overton, 542 N.W.2d 288 (Mich. Ct. App. 1995) (per curium) (holding that a lesbian coparent lacked standing to challenge a biological father for custody of her deceased partner's children, although the biological father had not established any relationship with the children); *see also* Alison D. v. Virginia M., 572 N.E.2d 27 (N.Y. 1991); Curiale v. Reagan, 272 Cal. Rptr. 520 (Ct. App. 1990); Nancy S. v. Michele G., 279 Cal. Rptr. 212 (Ct. App. 1991); Sporleder v. Hermes (*In re* Z.J.H.), 471 N.W.2d 202 (Wis. 1991) (holding that a nonparent may bring an action to obtain custody of a minor child only if the natural or adoptive parent is unfit or unable to care for the child).

61. *See, e.g.,* Holtzman v. Knott (*In re* H.S.H.K.), 533 N.W.2d 419 (Wis.), cert. denied, 116 S. Ct. 475 (1995) (dismissing the custody action of the lesbian coparent since there was no showing of the biological mother's unfitness. The court also held that visitation

few cases in which partial custody and visitation rights have been granted to the nonbiological coparent in a same-sex relationship.[62] Most cases in which child custody has been granted to the lesbian de facto coparent have been cases in which the biological mother has died.[63] There is only one reported case where full joint custody, as opposed to mere visitation rights, has been granted to a nonbiological lesbian parent.[64]

7.1.3 Artificial Insemination

Every U.S. state has detailed laws and regulations dealing with adoption, but there is hardly any legislation relating to the new reproductive techniques, and access to sperm banks is not publicly regulated in the United States.[65]

Generally, artificial insemination by an anonymous donor is available for lesbians and single women in the United States. The availability is determined by private doctors and sperm banks. No state expressly prohibits sperm banks from providing services to unmarried women or to lesbians.[66] Three states have introduced legislation, eventually defeated, which would have required physicians to curtail or even completely forgo the artificial insemination of single women.[67] It appears that severe restrictions on reproductive processes that affect the right to procreate are suspect and that even if such legislation were passed, it

rights would be accorded to a petitioner in a same-sex relationship who has a parentlike relationship with the child, provided there existed a shared household, an assumption of parental obligation, and a bonded, dependent parental relationship).

62. *See, e.g.,* J.A.L. v. E.P.H., 682 A.2d 1314 (Pa. Super. Ct. 1996) (holding that a lesbian coparent had standing to seek partial custody and visitation rights for the child born to her former partner).

63. *See, e.g., In re* Pearlman, 15 Fam. L. Rep. (BNA) 1355 (Fl. Cir. Ct. 1989). *See also* Christensen, note 21 above, at 1397–98.

64. *See* Arthur S. Leonard, Lesbian/Gay Law Notes, December 1998, at 184–85, reporting that a superior court in Ocean County, New Jersey, granted joint legal custody to a nonbiological lesbian parent after she and the child's biological mother ended their seven-year relationship: REM v. SLV, Docket no. FD-15-748-98N (November 2, 1998). Despite the tendency in such cases to grant automatic standing only to the married partner of the biological parent and to require the petitioner in other cases to demonstrate that the natural parent is either unfit or has abandoned the child, the court in *REM* used its equitable power to consider custody without the requisite of finding parental unfitness/abandonment. The court has thus further legitimized a functional definition of *family* that ultimately favors lesbian and gay ex-couples and their children. *Id.*

65. Kathryn Venturatos Lorio, *The Process of Regulating Assisted Reproductive Technologies: What We Can Learn from Our Neighbors—What Translates and What Does Not,* 45 Loy. L. Rev. 247, 247 (1999).

66. 2 Alba Conte, Sexual Orientation and Legal Rights 45 (1998).

67. These states are Hawaii, Minnesota, and Oregon. *See* Holly J. Harlow, *Paternalism without Paternity: Discrimination against Single Women Seeking Artificial Insemination by Donor,* 6 S. Cal. Rev. L. & Women's Stud. 173, 175 (1996).

would likely be struck down as unconstitutional by the courts.[68] Although artificial insemination is legal in the United States and theoretically available to single women and lesbians, there are no rules stipulating that sperm banks must offer such services, and discrimination against single women and lesbians seeking artificial insemination exists. In practice, the feasibility of artificial insemination may be limited by the reluctance of sperm banks and private physicians to provide services for lesbians and other unmarried women.[69] Private physicians' refusal to inseminate single women and lesbians often stems from religious beliefs, prejudice toward lesbians as parents, or unfounded paternalistic views about the abilities of single women to raise children.[70] However, such limitation or discrimination in access to artificial insemination services is very rare in the United States; the greater percentage of women seeking such services obtain them with no difficulty.

7.2 Judicial Recognition of Opposite-Sex and Same-Sex Cohabitation in the United States

In the 1960s the typical American household consisted of a married couple with children under 18 at home.[71] Nonmarital cohabitation has increased in the United States since the beginning of the 1970s.[72] The number of unmarried opposite-sex cohabiting couples increased almost fivefold between 1970 and 1988, and between 1990 and 2000 that number rose by 72 percent from 3.19 million to 5.47 million.[73] Married-couple households dropped from 55 percent of all homes in 1990 to 52 percent in 2000.[74] Census data for 2000 reveal that nearly 500,000 couples are living together in same-sex relationships, rising from nearly 122,000 in 1990.[75] Unlike marriage, wherein marital property and

68. Lorio, note 65 above, at 266–67. *See also* John A. Robertson, *Assisted Reproductive Technology and the Family,* 47 Hastings L.J. 911, 913–14 (1996).

69. *See* Marc E. Elovitz, *Reforming the Law to Respect Families Created by Lesbian and Gay People,* 3 J.L. & Pol'y 431, 443–44 (1995).

70. *See* Harlow, note 67 above, at 219 (discussing the discrimination that single women face in seeking artificial insemination services and proposing that single women may be able to use state public-accommodations laws to challenge this discrimination).

71. Reuters, *Non-Traditional Households Increase,* May 16, 2001.

72. John De Witt Gregory et. al., Understanding Family Law 19 (1993).

73. U.S. Bureau of the Census, 1990 Vital Statistics, table 54, "Unmarried Couples, 1970 to 1988"; *see also* Reuters, note 71 above.

74. Reuters, note 71 above.

75. Andrew Quinn, *U.S. Census Finds Nearly 500,000 Gay Couples,* Reuters, August 8, 2001. The 2000 figures are the most comprehensive count of same-sex couples in U.S. history and reflect a change in polling questions that allowed gay and lesbian couples to identify themselves clearly to demographers. *Id.* As Closen and Maloney note, the 1990 figures did not reflect reality and the numbers were undoubtedly underreported. *See* Mi-

support rights are legally recognized and protected through state legislative and judicial authority, nonmarital relationships of opposite- and same-sex couples in most states lack any legal status.[76] Nonetheless, the shift from marriage as the almost universal living arrangement to unmarried cohabitation has instigated both statutory and judicial solutions of various kinds. As a California court stated as early as 1976, "[t]he mores of society have indeed changed so radically in regard to cohabitation that we cannot impose a standard based on alleged moral considerations that have apparently been so widely abandoned by so many."[77]

However, court recognition of cohabitation has been far from comprehensive; cohabiting couples have been recognized only for specific purposes and in specific contexts. A variety of mechanisms for recognizing unmarried cohabitants' relationships have been proposed and implemented in the United States, ranging from proposals to revive and extend the common law marriage doctrine[78] to different kinds of contractual arrangements.[79] No state is likely to recognize unconstrained freedom to contract in domestic relations.[80] Yet since the 1970s courts have accorded various rights to unmarried cohabitants of both the same and opposite sexes. Cohabiting couples can enter into an express cohabitation contract that regulates and limits mutual property rights; such contracts are generally enforced by the courts. Same-sex couples are thus

---

chael L. Closen & Joan E. Maloney, *The Health Care Surrogate Act in Illinois: Another Rejection of Domestic Partners' Rights*, 19 S. Ill. U. L.J. 479, 484 (1995) (citing and commenting on the Statistical Abstract of the United States 53, no. 71 [113th ed., 1993]).

76. Gregory et al., note 72 above, at 19–20.

77. Marvin v. Marvin, 557 P.2d 106, 122 (Cal. 1976).

78. Common law marriages are limited to opposite-sex couples and are recognized in the following twelve jurisdictions: Alabama, Colorado, Idaho, Iowa, Kansas, Montana, Pennsylvania, Rhode Island, South Carolina, Texas, Utah, and Washington, D.C. *See* A. Mechele Dickerson, *Family Values and the Bankruptcy Code: A Proposal to Eliminate Bankruptcy Benefits Awarded on the Basis of Marital Status*, 67 Fordham L. Rev. 69, 85 n. 82 (1998). *See also* Cynthia Grant Bowman, *A Feminist Proposal to Bring Back Common Law Marriage*, 75 Or. L. Rev. 709, 715 n. 24 (1996). States that recognize common law marriages generally define them as any informal marriage between heterosexuals that does not meet the formal statutory requirements for marriage. Dickerson, above; *see also* Gregory et al., note 72 above, at 27. States generally will find that a couple is in a common law marriage if the cohabiting couple agrees and has the present intent to enter into a matrimonial relationship and represents themselves to the community as husband and wife. *See* Dickerson, above; *see also* Ellen Kandoian, *Cohabitation, Common Law Marriage, and the Possibility of a Shared Moral Life*, 75 Geo. L.J. 1829, 1842, 1850 (1987). For commentary proposing to extend the doctrine of common law marriage to include long-term couples and same-sex couples, see David Chambers, *The Legalization of the Family: Toward a Policy of Supportive Neutrality*, 18 J.L. Reform 805 (1985).

79. *See* Craig A. Bowman & Blake M. Cornish, *A More Perfect Union: A Legal and Social Analysis of Domestic Partnership Ordinances*, 92 Colum. L. Rev. 1164, 1185 (1992).

80. *Id.* at 1186. The prohibition of contracts for sexual services is the most obvious limitation states place on such contracts. *Id.*

able to create some of the legal benefits of marriage by private contracts, as well as through wills, joint tenancies, bank accounts, powers of attorney, and the like.[81] But these instruments pertain only to very few of the rights that are traditionally associated with marriage.

Some courts have given their approval to express agreements between cohabiting couples, but that has been largely limited to heterosexual couples' agreements,[82] and only in a few cases have contracts between cohabiting same-sex couples been enforced.[83] Moreover, courts have approved cohabitation agreements only with respect to the couple's property rights. In the absence of an express contract of that sort, some courts have recognized implied contracts between cohabiting couples,[84] whereas others have refused to enforce cohabitation agreements made by unmarried couples because to do so would violate the state's public policy of promoting marriage.[85] Some courts have accorded recovery for the emotional distress suffered as the result of witnessing injury to an adult unmarried opposite-sex cohabitant because of the genuine familial

81. *See* William N. Eskridge Jr. & Nan D. Hunter, Sexuality, Gender, and the Law 785 (1997). *See also* Barbara J. Cox, *Alternative Families: Obtaining Traditional Family Benefits through Litigation, Legislation, and Collective Bargaining,* 2 Wis. Women's L.J. 1 (1986); Hayden Curry et al., A Legal Guide for Lesbian and Gay Couples (10th ed., 1999).

82. In cases of opposite-sex cohabitants, the courts have largely rejected arguments that implied or expressed contracts arising out of sexual relationships rest upon "meretricious" considerations, even though it was apparent that sexual companionship was part of the relationship. *See, e.g.,* Marvin v. Marvin, 557 P.2d 106 (Cal. 1976); Alderson v. Alderson, 225 Cal. App. 610 (Cal. App. 1986). These principles have been unequally applied to same-sex relationships. For example, in Jones v. Daly, 176 Cal. Rptr. 130 (Cal. App. 1981), the court refused to enforce an express cohabitation agreement between two men, reasoning that the contract rested upon meretricious consideration, although the agreement was identical to that in the case of *Marvin.* This case illustrates the traditional failure of courts to enforce cohabitation agreements between same-sex couples. *See* Eskridge & Hunter, note 81 above, at 784.

83. *See, e.g.,* Whorton v. Dillingham, 248 Cal. Rptr. 405 (Cal. App. 1988); Crook v. Gilden, 414 S.E.2d 645 (Ga. 1992).

84. *See* Closen & Maloney, note 75 above, at 511–12. For example, in Marvin v. Marvin, 557 P.2d 106 (Cal. 1976), the court held that it was not against public policy for courts to enforce cohabitation agreements made by unmarried couples pertaining to the distribution of their property when the relationship terminated, so long as sexual services were not the primary consideration for the agreement. The court also held that an implied cohabitation contract was possible, although no such contract was found to exist in the specific case. The courts in most states have followed *Marvin* to provide contractual or quasi-contractual remedies for cohabiting partners. *See* Eskridge & Hunter, note 81 above, at 783. *See, e.g.,* Alderson v. Alderson, 225 Cal. Rptr. 610 (Cal. App. 1986) (applying *Marvin* to create an implied contract for community property division of assets). *But see* Morone v. Morone, 413 N.E.2d 1154 (N.Y. Ct. App. 1980) (holding that New York courts will enforce cohabitation agreements made by unmarried couples so long as the agreement is either in writing or is an explicit verbal agreement between the parties).

85. See, for example, Hewitt v. Hewitt, 394 N.E.2d 1204 (Ill. 1979), in which the court flatly rejected *Marvin.*

relationship between them,[86] but others have refused to do so in the same circumstances;[87] and same-sex couples in particular have been denied recognition as being "closely related" in cases of emotional distress.[88] Only in a few cases, limited to the field of housing discrimination, have courts held that a law prohibiting marital status discrimination provided protection to unmarried couples.[89] Other courts have refused, because of the policy of promoting the institution of marriage, to protect unmarried cohabitants from housing discrimination, even where the law prohibited marital status discrimination.[90]

Courts have acknowledged unmarried cohabiting couples as families for other purposes as well, for example, by interpreting a state's domestic violence law to apply to same-sex cohabiting couples[91] or by allowing

86. Closen & Maloney, note 75 above, at 511–12. *See, e.g.,* Dunphy v. Gregor, 642 A.2d 372 (N.J. 1994) (holding that a person who witnesses the death of his or her unmarried partner may sue the wrongdoer for emotional distress so long as the couple was living together in a "familial relationship," even though they were not married to each other).

87. *See, e.g.,* Elden v. Sheldon, 758 P.2d 582 (Cal. 1988) (holding that an unmarried cohabitant who witnessed the death of her partner in an automobile accident may not sue the wrongdoer for emotional distress, although she could do so if she and her partner had been legally married).

88. *See* Coon v. Joseph, 192 Cal. App. 3d 1269 (Cal. Ct. App. 1987). Courts have restricted recovery to spouses, parents, and children of injury victims, and, as noted above, some have also authorized damages for opposite-sex cohabitants. *See* Arthur S. Leonard, *Legal Recognition of Same-Sex Partners under U.S. State or Local Law, in* Legal Recognition of Same-Sex Partnerships: A Study of National, European, and International Law 133 (Robert Wintemute & Mads Andenas eds., 2001).

89. *See, e.g.,* Swanner v. Anchorage Equal Rights Commission, 874 P.2d 274 (Alaska 1994) (holding that a housing statute that prohibits marital status discrimination provides protection to unmarried couples). Similarly, the supreme court of Michigan recently held that a statutory ban on marital status discrimination applies to the refusal of a landlord to rent a residence to unmarried cohabitants: McCready v. Hoffius, 586 N.W.2d 723 (Mich. Sup. Ct. 1998); in April 1999 the case was reconsidered as to whether the actions of the landlord were privileged under the first amendment and was remanded to the Circuit Court: McCready v. Hoffius, Nos. 108995/108996, rehearing 427 (April 16, 1999); however, it seems that the holding regarding violation of the state's ban on marital status discrimination in housing still stands.

90. *See* Cooper v. French, 460 N.W.2d 2 (Minn. Sup. Ct. 1990) (holding that unmarried couples are not protected from housing discrimination even though state law forbids "marital status" discrimination. The court reasoned that since another state law criminalizes unmarried cohabitation, the legislature could not have intended to protect unmarried couples from discrimination while at the same time criminalizing their cohabitation); County of Dane v. Norman, 497 N.W.2d 714 (Wis. 1993) (holding that a county ordinance that purported to protect unmarried couples from housing discrimination was invalid because it conflicted with the public policy of the state to promote marriage).

91. *See* State v. Hadinger, 573 N.E.2d 1191, 1193 (Ohio Ct. App. 1991) (the court held that a domestic violence statute that applies to "persons living as spouses" applied also to two persons of the same sex who are cohabiting or have cohabited within the past year). *See also* State v. Yaden, 1997 WL 106343 (Ohio App. 1st Dist. 1997) (holding that domestic violence within a cohabiting same-sex couple is covered by the state's domestic violence statute).

the payment of workers' compensation death benefits to the same-sex partner of a deceased employee[92] as well as to the surviving opposite-sex cohabiting partner of a deceased employee.[93] Unemployment benefits have also been accorded to an opposite-sex cohabiting partner.[94] In the case of the *Guardianship of Kowalski,* the Minnesota Appellate Court granted a lesbian woman guardianship status for her partner, who had been severely injured in an automobile accident, categorizing the couple's relationship as a "family of affinity."[95] Likewise, in the landmark *Braschi* decision, the New York Court of Appeals held that when the term *family* is used in a statute without definition, the term may include persons who are living together as a family unit even though they are not related by blood, marriage, or adoption. It thus held that a gay man could continue living in the apartment that was leased to his deceased gay lover, because the court interpreted the protection from eviction granted by New York law to a "family member" who had been living with the deceased tenant to include a same-sex partner.[96] The court concluded that

> the term family . . . should not be rigidly restricted to those people who have formalized their relationship by obtaining, for instance, a marriage certificate or an adoption order. The intended protection against sudden eviction should not rest on fictitious legal distinctions or genetic history, but instead should find its foundation in the reality of family life. In the context of eviction, a more realistic, and certainly equally valid, view of a family includes two adult lifetime partners whose relationship is long term and characterized by an emotional and financial commitment and interdependence. This view comports both with our society's traditional concept of "family" and with the expectations of individuals who live in such nuclear units.[97]

The *Braschi* decision was an important breakthrough for gays, lesbians, and other "nontraditional" families owing to its adoption of a func-

92. *See* Closen & Maloney, note 75 above, at 512 (referring to the case of Donovan v. Worker's Compensation Appeals Board, 187 Cal. Rptr. 869 [Cal. Ct. App. 1982]).

93. *See, e.g.,* Dept. of Industrial Rel. v. Worker's Comp. Bd., 156 Cal. Rptr. 183 (Cal. App. 1979) (the California court of appeal held that an unmarried cohabitant who lived with and was partially dependent on an employee may recover workers' compensation survivor benefits when the employee dies from a work-related injury).

94. *See* Reep v. Commissioner, 593 N.E.2d 1297 (Mass. Sup. Ct. 1992) (holding that an unmarried cohabitant is entitled to unemployment benefits when she quits her job in order to move to another area with an unmarried partner who is relocating his business).

95. *In re* Guardianship of Kowalski, 478 N.W.2d 790, at 797 (Minn. Ct. App. 1991).

96. Braschi v. Stahl Associates, 543 N.E.2d 49 (N.Y. 1989).

97. *Id.* at 53–54.

tional definition of *family*. Although the decision is restricted to eviction regulations regarding rent-control apartments, its reach has been expanding in New York and elsewhere.[98] However, the difficulty with *Braschi* is that it seems to require complicated case-by-case determinations of the nature of the relationship.[99]

As the above-mentioned court decisions suggest, despite the willingness of some courts to recognize the rights of cohabiting opposite- and same-sex couples, such recognition is very limited, and the couples have no assurance that these decisions will be followed in other jurisdictions or extended to other situations. Furthermore, these advances can be easily overturned by future court majorities or by rulings of higher courts. Moreover, in many cases and in many other jurisdictions, courts refuse to recognize or accord rights to cohabiting unmarried couples and are not willing to expand the traditional concept of family.[100] This is especially true regarding same-sex partners; in the majority of cases, such couples are denied recognition for specific purposes.[101]

To sum up, some rights traditionally associated with marriage have been recognized by the courts by way of expanding the definition of family, in terms of according a limited set of rights to opposite-sex cohabitants and an even more limited number of rights to same-sex cohab-

98. *See* Closen & Maloney, note 75 above, at 515. The New York State Division of Housing and Community Renewal has adopted regulations codifying *Braschi* and applying its test to rent-stabilized apartments as well: N.Y. Comp. Codes R. & Regs. tit. 9, § 2204.6(d)(3)(i) (Supp. 1992). *See* William B. Rubinstein, Sexual Orientation and the Law 779 (2d ed., 1997). This move was upheld against a challenge from landlords: Rent Stabilization Association of N.Y., Inc. v. Higgins, 562 N.Y.S.2d 962 (1990), aff'd 63N.E.2d 626 (1993).

99. *See* Cases and Materials on Family Law: Legal Concept and Changing Human Relationships 565 (Walter O. Weyrauch et al. eds., 1994).

100. *See* Closen & Maloney, note 75 above, at 516.

101. *See, e.g., In re* Estate of Cooper 564 N.Y.S.2d 684 (N.Y. Sup. Ct. 1990) (surviving same-sex partner is not entitled to claim spousal elective share against estate of deceased partner); Adams v. Howerton, 673 F.2d 1036 (9th Cir.), cert. denied, 458 U.S. 1111 (1982) (gay couples were not recognized as spouses for purposes of U.S. immigration law); Beaty v. Truck Insurance Exchange, 6 Cal. App.4th 1455 (Cal. Ct. App. 1992) (rejecting claim by gay couple for joint liability insurance policy for their jointly owned vehicle); Doe v. Roe, 475 S.E.2d 783 (S. Carolina Sup. Ct. 1996) (holding that neither a constructive trust nor an equitable lien exists in favor of partner in a dissolved long-term lesbian relationship); Gajovski v. Gajovski, 610 N.E.2d 431 (Oh. App. 1991) (holding that a same-sex relationship is not concubinage for purposes of disqualifying one partner from receiving alimony from a former spouse); Greenwald v. H & P 29th Street Association, 659 N.Y.S.2d 473 (N.Y. App. Div., 1st Dept. 1997) (rejecting a claim of evidentiary spousal privilege on behalf of a gay couple); Secord v. Fischetti, 653 N.Y.S.2d 551 (N.Y. App. Div., 1st Dept. 1997) (denying compensation to same-sex partner of crime victim); Seward v. Mentrup, 622 N.E.2d 756 (Ohio Ct. App. 1993) (same-sex couple not entitled to equitable distribution of property when long-term relationship ends); Van Dyck. v. Van Dyck, 425 S.E.2d 853 (Ga. Sup. Ct. 1993) (same-sex relationship is not a conjugal relationship for purposes of disqualifying one partner from receiving alimony from former spouse).

iting couples. As explained above, some other rights and obligations can be secured by way of contracts, wills, and the like. However, not only are contractual agreements limited in their scope, but they also do not provide same-sex couples with external validation of the part of their relationship that is beyond that of contracting parties; the law thus generally treats same-sex couples as unrelated for all purposes outside these legal instruments.[102]

The predominant legal relationship currently available to same-sex couples that provides some external validation as well as various rights and benefits is domestic partnership.[103] Another (less popular and more problematic) option that offers some external validation for same-sex couples is adult adoption.

7.3 Adult Adoption by Same-Sex Partners

Adult adoption as an alternative to the institution of marriage has not gained popularity and is being used by relatively few same-sex couples. In order to circumvent the impossibility of same-sex marriage,[104] some same-sex couples have used this quite unusual legal technique to create a legal family relationship that provides some of the rights associated with marriage. In these cases, since adult adoptions are permitted in the United States, one of the partners petitions to adopt his or her partner. In the most notable court decision pertaining to same-sex adult adoption, the New York Court of Appeals viewed a petition of a fifty-seven-year-old man to adopt his lifelong gay partner, fifty years old, as a quasi-marital vehicle and refused to permit adoptions between same-sex partners as a matter of public policy, reasoning that the purpose of adoption is the creation of a parent-child relationship and that under current adoption laws sexual lovers should not be permitted to adopt one another for the purpose of giving a nonmarital legal status to their relationship.[105] However, other courts in New York and elsewhere have granted

102. *See* Rubinstein, note 98 above, at 762.

103. *Id.*

104. For developments regarding the availability of marriage to same-sex couples in the United States, see sec. 7.6 below.

105. *See In re* the Adoption of Robert Paul P., 471 N.E.2d 424 (1984). For a detailed account of the advantages and disadvantages of adult adoption by same-sex couples as an alternative to marriage, see Gwendolyn L. Snodgrass, *Creating Family without Marriage: The Advantages and Disadvantages of Adult Adoption among Gay and Lesbian Partners,* 36 Brandeis J. Fam. L. 75 (1997–98), who argues that as long as same-sex marriage is not available to same-sex couples, adult adoption is "the only solution that creates a bona fide family relationship" and is to be regarded as a "useful legal maneuver" for gay and lesbian couples.

similar adoption petitions.[106] Most petitions for adult adoption of a gay or lesbian partner are filed in California and routinely granted.[107] The primary purposes behind adult adoption and the main legal effects that are relevant to same-sex couples through adoption of one partner by the other are estate planning and inheritance:[108] adoption automatically disinherits the parents and siblings of both the adopted and the adoptee, if either should die intestate; it also serves to deny parents and siblings standing to contest the will of the adoptive partner or the adoptee.[109] A drawback of adoption is that it, unlike marriage, is irrevocable: there can be no divorce. In addition, the adoptee loses the right to inherit from her or his natural parents if they die without wills or to contest their wills.[110] Moreover, in some states there is a possibility that same-sex couples who use adult adoption to create a familial relationship will be prosecuted, since some statutes provide that sexual relations between the parties to an adoption constitute incest.[111] In addition to being both legally and ethically problematic, this technique is undoubtedly far from a substitute for marriage for gay couples.

7.4 Domestic Partnerships

In the United States, benefits such as health insurance and retirement and disability coverage are tied to employment. In this way the United States is different from other developed countries. Employers are free to decide whether to offer such benefits and whether to extend them to partners and children. Marriage has usually been a prerequisite for obtaining benefits for an employee's partner. Various municipalities and private employers have attempted to remedy the overdependence on marriage as the precondition for benefits and privileges by passing

106. *See, e.g.,* 333 East 53rd Street Associates v. Mann, 503 N.Y.S.2d 752 (1986), aff'd, 518 N.Y.S.2d 958 (N.Y. 1987) (permitting adoption involving two adult women for purposes of succeeding in tenancy following the death of the cotenant under New York City Rent and Eviction Regulations, reasoning that economic concerns were the primary motivation of the adoption). Another case of adult adoption was reported in May 2001: a Maryland court allowed a gay man to adopt his same-sex partner in order to establish a legal family relationship. *See* Washington Post, May 26, 2001.

107. *See* Snodgrass, note 105 above.

108. *See* Thomas Adolph Pavano, *Gay and Lesbian Rights: Adults Adopting Adults,* 2 Conn. Prob. L.J. 251 (1987); Peter N. Fowler, Comment, *Adult Adoption: A "New" Legal Tool for Lesbians and Gay Men,* 14 Golden Gate U. L. Rev. 667 (1984).

109. *See* Rubinstein, note 98 above, at 772; *see also* Jeffrey Sherman, *Undue Influence and the Homosexual Testator,* 42 U. Pitt. L. Rev. 221, 253–56 (1981).

110. Rubinstein, note 98 above, at 772; Sherman, note 109 above, at 256–57.

111. *See* 2 Conte, note 66 above, at 82.

domestic partnership legislation or by adopting domestic partner benefit plans.[112] Since employment benefits, where provided, make up approximately 40 percent of a worker's total compensation,[113] employees who can obtain benefits for their spouses are in effect paid at a higher rate than employees in nonmarital relationships. Thus, the extension of such benefits to employees with a same-sex partner has a substantial economic value. It is rooted in the democratic notion of equal pay for equal work.[114]

Other than adult adoption, which cannot be regarded as public recognition of same-sex relationships as such, domestic partnership currently provides the only option in the United States for legal recognition of same-sex relationships.[115]

The broad concept of domestic partnership is a form of business or government recognition given to two unmarried adults of the same sex or opposite sexes seeking to share benefits normally conferred upon married couples because of conformity with a procedure established by the business or government; it is a civil partnership supported by private or public policy, or both.[116] Domestic partnership is one step beyond cohabitation[117] but a few steps behind marriage.[118] Recognition of domestic partnerships in the United States is usually limited in its scope to the workplace—state, municipal, or private—and in its implications to the allocation of various employment benefits to same-sex couples; such recognition purports to place them on an equal footing with opposite-sex married couples. There are a few hundred benefits in the public and private sector that are extended on the basis of marital status from which domestic partners are excluded.[119] Registration of a domestic partnership triggers very few benefits, if any, and is applicable only in the territory of the issuing jurisdic-

112. Lambda Legal Defense and Education Fund, Domestic Partnerships: Issues and Legislation 1 (1993) [hereinafter Lambda Domestic Partnerships].

113. *See Domestic Partnership Organizing Manual,* National Gay and Lesbian Task Force (NGLTF) Policy Institute (Washington D.C., May 1999), at 9 [hereinafter NGLTF Domestic Partnership].

114. *See* NGLTF Domestic Partnership, note 113 above, at 1.

115. *See* Bowman & Cornish, note 79 above, at 1187. For models of domestic partnership policies for businesses, see *Lesbian & Gay Rights: Model Domestic Partnerships,* American Civil Liberties Union Freedom Network, at http://www.aclu.org/issues/gay/dpmodel.html (last visited September 18, 1999).

116. *See* Raymond C. O'Brien, *Domestic Partnership: Recognition and Responsibility,* 32 San Diego L. Rev. 163, 164–65 (1995).

117. *Id.* at 164.

118. For a comparison of domestic partnership and marriage, see chap. 9, sec. 9.2.

119. *See* NGLTF Domestic Partnership, note 113 above, at 5.

tion.[120] Initially, domestic partner benefits were offered only to same-sex couples; many employers chose that option because heterosexual couples have the option of marriage; some view such policies as discriminatory against unmarried opposite-sex couples.[121] Today, however, the majority of plans and ordinances are available to both same-sex and opposite-sex cohabiting couples.[122] Some domestic partnership registrations are of only symbolic significance and provide no benefits or legal rights, and even in the limited field of workplace benefits, domestic partnership recognition accompanied by benefits usually does not place the same-sex couple on a completely equal footing with opposite-sex married couples. This is mainly because, unlike benefits for married couples, domestic partner registrations and benefit plans are not recognized by the Internal Revenue Service.[123] The IRS has determined that domestic partners do not qualify as spouses for purposes of the exclusion from gross income of employer-provided benefits. Thus, the benefits provided by the employer are part of the employee partner's gross income and subject to federal income tax, unless the other partner qualifies as a dependent.[124]

Domestic partnership usually requires registration and is commonly defined as an ongoing relationship between two unrelated adults of the same sex or opposite sexes who share a primary residence on a continuous basis in a nonmarital arrangement, who are financially and emotionally interdependent, and who have a long-term, close, and committed personal relationship with mutual caring.[125] Domestic partnership provisions

120. *See Domestic Partner Benefits: Philosophy and Provider List,* Partners Task Force for Gay & Lesbian Couples, at http://www.buddybudddy.com/d-p-1.html (last visited on October 1, 1999) [hereinafter *Philosophy and Provider List,* Partners].

121. *See* NGLTF Domestic Partnership, note 113 above, at 2.

122. *See Philosophy and Provider List,* Partners, note 120 above. Among the cities that limit registration to same-sex couples are Tucson, Ariz.; Chicago, Ill.; New Orleans, La.; and Baltimore, Md. Cities that offer registration to both opposite- and same-sex couples include Berkeley, Calif.; Boulder, Colo.; and Seattle, Wash. *See States and Municipalities Offering Domestic Partner Benefits and Registries,* Lambda Legal Defense and Education Fund, August 10, 1999, at http://www.lambdalegal.org/cgi-bin/pages/documents/record?record=403.

123. *See* Conte, note 66 above, at 78.

124. *See* Nancy J. Knauer, *Domestic Partnership and Same-Sex Relationships: A Marketplace Innovation and a Less Than Perfect Institutional Choice,* 7 Temple Pol. & Civ. Rts. L. Rev. 337, 342–43 (1998). Under I.R.C. 152(9), an individual other than the taxpayer's spouse who is a member of the taxpayer's household can qualify as a dependent provided the taxpayer is responsible for more than one-half of the individual's support. However, according to I.R.C. 152 (b) (5), if the relationship between the taxpayer and the individual is in violation of local law, the latter is not regarded as a member of the taxpayer's household. Thus, gay couples residing in a state that still criminalizes sodomy can be "in violation of local law." *Id.*

125. *See, e.g.,* New York City: Executive Order no.48 (Jan. 7, 1993); San Francisco, Calif.: Code ch. 62 (1990). Beyond this basic framework, each company, university, and

impose various eligibility requirements similar to those for marriage, such as the requirement that the parties be at least eighteen years old and mentally competent, that the parties not be related by blood ties that would bar marriage in the state, and that neither of the parties has an existing marriage or domestic partnership.[126] Furthermore, in order to be eligible to receive domestic partner benefits, the parties must prove that the relationship has existed for a certain period of time prior to the application. Some registration provisions may stipulate that any prior domestic partnership must have been terminated for a minimum interim period of time before another partnership can be registered.[127] No corresponding conditions exist for marriage or for remarriage. In some cities, such as San Francisco, a couple may register as domestic partners only if at least one partner lives or works in the city; other cities, such as Berkeley and West Hollywood, allow nonresidents to register; Santa Barbara and West Hollywood are the only cities that recognize domestic partnerships registered in other cities.[128] A domestic partnership is terminated by the death of one of the partners or by the unilateral act of one of the partners with notification of the other partner and, where applicable, of the registration office.

Broadly speaking, there are two kinds of domestic partnerships and two avenues of obtaining recognized status and benefits as same-sex domestic partners. One is through individual private-sector employers and benefit plans. The other is state or municipal recognition of domestic partnership provided for by law, by an ordinance, or by an executive order. Each venue has a different procedure and produces different results. As of May 1999, domestic partner benefits are offered by 10 percent of all U.S. employers and are available to employees at more than 570 companies, 141 colleges and universities,[129] and more than 87 city, county, and state governments. Among companies with more than five thousand employees, almost one-quarter offer these benefits.[130] More than two-thirds of employers that have implemented this coverage are

---

state or local government chooses how to define the concept of domestic partnership in its benefit plans. For additional definitions of domestic partnership, see Closen & Maloney, note 75 above, at 481 nn. 19–20.

126. *See* Conte, note 66 above, at 98.

127. For example, Ann Arbor requires a three-month interim period, whereas San Francisco and New York City require six months. *See id.*

128. Conte, note 66 above, at 99; *States and Municipalities Offering Domestic Partner Benefits and Registries,* note 122 above.

129. *See* Knauer, note 124 above, at 340. Numerous colleges and universities offer domestic partner benefits to faculty, administrators, and staff. Some educational organizations also extend benefits to students, for instance, allowing same-sex partners to qualify for housing on the same basis as married students. *Id.* at 340 n. 15.

130. *See* NGLTF Domestic Partnership, note 113 above, at 7, 10.

also providing it to unmarried opposite-sex couples.[131] Most of the private employers that offer domestic partner benefits are in California, New York, and Massachusetts, and Pennsylvania, Illinois, and the District of Columbia are in close pursuit.[132]

In the private sector, employers who recognize domestic partnerships extend health-care and other employment-related benefits to the domestic partners of their employees. Although more than one thousand companies have equal opportunity statements that bar discrimination based on sexual orientation, many companies that grant additional benefits to married heterosexual employees do not accord those benefits to same-sex couples.[133] Federal, state, and local laws do not expressly require an employer to provide domestic partner benefits; and although some municipalities—such as Los Angeles, New York City, and Seattle—provide for the extension of benefits to the domestic partners of municipal employees, none of the registration ordinances require that all private employers provide such benefits.[134] Most state and local governments that offer domestic partner benefits to their employees and prohibit sexual orientation discrimination in employment have not attempted to enforce these laws against private-sector employee benefit plans because it is widely assumed that the federal Employee Retirement Income Security Act of 1974 (ERISA)[135] would preempt such an application of the law.[136] The Village Voice Newspaper was the first private business to offer health insurance benefits to the domestic partners of its gay and lesbian employees, in 1982.[137] By 1990 fewer than two dozen U.S. employers offered domestic partner benefits, but during the following decade, the number grew at an increasing rate.[138]

In June 1997 the domestic partnership legislation of the city and

131. *See* Kim I. Mills & Daryl Herrschaft, The State of the Workplace for Lesbian, Gay, Bisexual, and Transgendered Americans, The Human Rights Campaign 6 (Washington D.C., September 1999).

132. *Id*. at 20.

133. *See* NGLTF Domestic Partnership, note 113 above, at 1.

134. *See* Conte, note 66 above, at 97.

135. Employee Retirement Income Security Act of 1974, 29 U.S.C. §§ 1001–461 (1988).

136. *See* Catherine L. Fisk, *ERISA Preemption of State and Local Laws on Domestic Partnership and Sexual Orientation Discrimination in Employment*, 8 UCLA Women's L.J. 267, 269–70 (1998) (arguing that ERISA does not preempt state and local laws requiring employers to provide domestic partner benefits on the same term as spousal benefits, since it impairs another federal law—the Defense of Marriage Act—according to which federal law provides the states freedom to decide what legal benefits to grant to same-sex relationship; the author's use of antigay federal legislation to promote domestic partnership for gays and lesbians seems paradoxical but is nevertheless convincing).

137. NGLTF Domestic Partnership, note 113 above, at 17.

138. *See* Mills & Herrschaft, note 131 above, at 9.

county of San Francisco—the Equal Benefits Ordinance—went into effect.[139] It was the first domestic partnership ordinance that required some private sector companies (all companies contracting with the city or county of San Francisco) to offer the same benefits to the domestic partners of their employees as they offer to employees' legal spouses. The ordinance prohibits the city from contracting with firms whose benefit plans discriminate based on the marital status or sexual orientation of employees.[140] A few other jurisdictions, including Berkeley; Los Angeles; Seattle; Tumwater, Washington; and San Mateo County, California, have followed San Francisco's lead and expanded their ordinances to require all contractors with the governmental unit to provide full benefits to their employees' domestic partners;[141] other cities are considering such expansions to their ordinances.[142] The San Francisco ordinance was upheld after a challenge against it was brought by air carriers using the city's airport; though it struck down parts of the ordinance, the court ordered those carriers to comply with the amended city ordinance.[143] The San Francisco ordinance instigated the adoption of domestic partner benefit plans by many private companies and businesses.[144] In its 1999 report entitled "The State of the Workplace for Lesbian, Gay, Bisexual and Transgendered Americans," the Human Rights Campaign argues that much of the rapid spread of domestic partner benefits in the last two years can be attributed to San Francisco's Equal Benefits Ordi-

139. *See* San Francisco, Cal., Ordinance 97-66-33.1 (June 1, 1997).

140. *See Landmark San Francisco Benefits Requirement for City Contractors Upheld,* Lambda Legal Defense and Education Fund Press Release, May 27, 1999, at http://www.lambdalegal.org/cgi-bin/pages/documents/record?record=421.

141. *See* PlanetOut News Staff, *Berkeley Moves for Equal Benefits,* February 23, 2001; PlanetOut News Staff, *Partners Ahead in 3 States,* February 7, 2001.

142. *See* Knauer, note 124 above, at 350 n. 57. These include West Hollywood and New York City. The Philadelphia proposed domestic partnership ordinance would include the same requirement. *Id.*

143. *See* Air Transport Association of America v. San Francisco, No. C 97-01763 CW, The District Court for the Northern District of California, May 27, 1999. On September 11, 2001, the case was upheld on appeal by the Ninth Circuit. *See* 266 F.3d 1064 (2001). Moreover, on June 14, 2001, in another case challenging San Francisco's Equal Benefits Ordinance (raising different federal issues), the Ninth Circuit Court of Appeals unanimously upheld key parts of the city's landmark ordinance (S.D. Myers v. San Francisco, No. 97-04463 CW). *See* Will O'Brayan, *Court Upholds San Francisco Equal Benefits Law,* Washington Blade, June 22, 2001. The Ninth Circuit rejected the arguments of a contractor that wanted to do business with San Francisco yet refused to offer domestic partnership benefits to its unmarried employees. The court stated that cities have a legitimate interest in enacting these laws and refusing to contract with businesses that discriminate against unmarried families, gay and nongay alike. Additionally, the court found that there is no undue economic burden placed upon contractors by requiring that they provide domestic partnership benefits. *See Court Upholds San Francisco's Landmark Domestic Partnership Law,* Lambda Legal Defense and Education Fund News Release, June 14, 2001, at www.lambdalegal.org.

144. *See Philosophy and Provider List,* Partners, note 120 above.

nance.[145] However, this domino effect seems to be limited to companies conducting business with San Francisco; and contrary to past predictions, registration of domestic partnerships offered by other cities and counties has proved not to motivate and encourage private businesses to offer benefits.[146]

In the second kind of domestic partnership recognition, by local governments, there are two ways in which states or municipalities recognize same-sex relationships as domestic partnerships.[147] Some municipalities allow a couple who live together in a committed relationship and who meet certain qualifications to publicly register as domestic partners. This process allows same- and opposite-sex couples to have a symbolic recognition of their union with no legal effects;[148] in other words, the existence of a registry can be and often is merely symbolic and independent of any grant of domestic partner benefits. Other states or municipalities extend to the domestic partner of the state or municipal employee the health-care and other work-related benefits that would have been extended to the spouse of the employee. Depending on the ordinance, this is being done either with or without registration as domestic partners. estic partnership legislation is being enacted on a case-by-case, municipality-by-municipality basis.[149] In addition to employment benefits to domestic partners of state, county, or local government employees, such as health insurance coverage, bereavement leave, family sick leave, and relocation expenses, most registrations of domestic partnerships offer a limited set of rights such as student housing and access to a same-sex partner in prison or in the hospital.[150] The most valuable and crucial benefit seems to be access to medical care by the unemployed or uncovered domestic partner of an employee who enrolls in a domestic partnership plan. Few domestic partnership laws go beyond the workplace or minor public accommodations.[151]

Berkeley, California, was the first municipality to enact a domestic partnership ordinance; that ordinance was enacted in 1985.[152] As of

145. *See* Mills & Herrschaft, note 131 above, at 5.

146. *See Philosophy and Provider List,* Partners, note 120 above.

147. *See* Conte, note 66 above, at 98.

148. For example, registrations with no benefits are being offered by a number of cities, including Albany, N.Y.; Boulder, Colo.; Hartford, Conn.; and Milwaukee, Wis. *See Registration for Domestic Partnership,* Partners Task Force for Gay & Lesbian Couples, at http://www.buddybuddy.com/d-p-reg.html (last visited September 20, 1999).

149. Lambda Domestic Partnerships, note 112 above, at 1.

150. *See Philosophy and Provider List,* Partners, note 120 above.

151. For example, New York State partnership law covers domestic partners under family rent control law. *See Philosophy and Provider List,* Partners, note 120 above.

152. *Id.*

May 2001, only seven states—Connecticut, Hawaii, New York, Vermont, Massachusetts, California, and Oregon—provide domestic partner benefits to their public employees. Otherwise, domestic partnership legislation has been enacted only at the municipal level; more than eighty city and county governments nationwide have thus far offered various domestic partner benefits.[153]

In September 1992 the governors of New York and Massachusetts issued executive orders to allow state workers to register as domestic partners for purposes of bereavement leave and visitation rights in state prisons and hospitals.[154] The state of Vermont adopted its domestic partnership law in 1994, and in 1998 Oregon's Court of Appeals upheld a circuit court's ruling that ordered the state to extend insurance benefits to the partners of gay and lesbian state employees.[155] Colorado may be the eighth state to enact a statewide domestic partner ordinance.[156] On July 8, 1997, Hawaii became the first state to offer comprehensive benefits to same-sex couples, after passing its Reciprocal Beneficiaries Act.[157] According to the act, any two single adults who cannot get married—including same-sex partners, blood relatives, or just friends—have access to a range of rights and benefits on the state level, including inheritance rights, workers' compensation, the right to sue for wrongful death, health and pension benefits for state employees, hospital visitation, health-care decision making, and the like.[158] However, no private

153. Municipalities that have passed measures allowing unmarried couples to register as domestic partners include Ann Arbor, Mich.: Code §§ 9:85–9:95 (1991); Atlanta, Ga.: Ordinance 93-0-0776 (1993); Berkeley, Calif.: Admin. Proc. no.2-37 (1988); Ithaca, N.Y.: Ordinance no.91-5 (January 28, 1991); Madison, Wis.: Code §§ 7.1–7.8 (1991); New York City: Executive Order no.48 (January 7, 1993); San Francisco, Calif.: Code ch. 62 (1990); West Hollywood, Calif.: Code §§ 4220–28 (1985). For a full list of cities and counties with domestic partner benefits, see Mills & Herrschaft, note 131 above, at 16.

154. *See States and Municipalities Offering Domestic Partner Benefits and Registries,* note 122 above. In 1995 the Civil Service Employees Association, representing most New York public employees, reached an agreement to include domestic partner benefits in its new contract. *Id.*

155. *See* Tanner v. Oregon Health Sciences University, 971 P.2d 435 (Or. Ct. App. 1998).

156. The Colorado state Senate Judiciary Committee on February 5, 2001, approved a bill to give gay and lesbian partners standing to inherit from each other as spouses do, even if there is no will, and also to make medical decisions for each other should one be too incapacitated to do so. To qualify, the couple would have to file an affidavit declaring themselves "committed partners." The measure will next move to the Senate floor. *See* PlanetOut News Staff, *Partners Ahead in 3 States,* February 7, 2001.

157. Haw. Rev. Stat. 572C (Supp. 1997).

158. *See Registered Partnership, Domestic Partnership, and Marriage: A Worldwide Summary,* IGLHRC Fact Sheet, November 3, 1998, at http://www.iglhrc.org/news/faqs/marriage_981103.html. The act allows access to fewer than 60 spousal rights on the state level, whereas full legal marriage in Hawaii carries more than 160 rights and responsibilities on the state level, not to mention more than 1,000 federal-level rights. *See Reciprocal Beneficiaries: The Hawaiian Approach,* Partners Task Force for Gay & Lesbian Couples, at http://www.buddybuddy.com/d-p-rec.html (last visited September 20, 1999).

business in Hawaii is required to offer domestic partner benefits; moreover, the Hawaii attorney general rendered invalid workplace medical insurance benefits, thus withdrawing the most important benefit of the statewide partnership law and reducing its significance and success.[159]

In October 1999 the state of California adopted its domestic partnership law, which went into effect January 1, 2000. The law extends health insurance benefits to both same- and opposite-sex unmarried partners of state employees on an equal footing with married couples; it provides local governments and municipalities the option of providing the same benefits to their employees.[160] The law also creates a registry of domestic partnerships, which is open to any same-sex couple in California as well as to heterosexual couples who are over the age of sixty-two—on the grounds that same-sex couples cannot legally marry and that marriage often threatens the benefits received by those over sixty-two.[161] Registered domestic partners were accorded only the right to hospital visitation of their partners. However, in October 2001, California greatly expanded its original domestic partnership act by according more rights to same-sex couples. The new law took effect January 1, 2002.[162] California's act defines domestic partners as two unrelated people who are com-

159. But see Brian W. Burnette, *Hawaii's Reciprocal Beneficiaries Act: An Effective Step in Resolving the Controversy Surrounding Same-Sex Marriage,* 37 Brandeis L.J. U. Louisville 81, 82, 94 (1998–99), arguing that the act "effectively gives same-sex couples a level of equal protection, as mandated by the Hawaii Supreme Court, while protecting the sanctity of traditional heterosexual marriage" and is an effective compromise that accomplishes a level of equality that is similar to the level of equality marriage provides. However, it should be noted that the article was written before the repeal of the most important provision of the act, the requirement that private employers supply health-care benefits to reciprocal beneficiaries.

160. *See* Carl Ingram, *Davis Signs 3 Bills Supporting Domestic Partners, Gay Rights; Legislation: Controversial Package Gives Protection to Students and Extends Health Benefits to Live-In Couples,* Los Angeles Times, October 3, 1999, at A24; Matthew Yi & Robert Salladay, *Governor Signs Trio of Gay Rights Bills; Benefits for Same-Sex Partners of State Workers, Student Protection,* San Francisco Examiner, October 3, 1999, at A1.

161. *See* PlanetOut News Staff, *First Couples Register in California,* PlanetOut News and Politics, January 4, 2000, available at http://www.planetout.com/news/article/html?2000/01/04/1. Unmarried heterosexual couples who are at least sixty-two years old are allowed to sign up with the state registry so that widowers living with new partners will be able to register and still keep certain social security and pension benefits that would be eliminated if they remarried. *See* Yi & Salladay, note 160 above.

162. According to the new law, registered couples now enjoy some significant additional rights and benefits, such as the ability to adopt each other's children through the "second-parent adoption" procedure; relocate with a domestic partner without losing unemployment benefits; make medical decisions for each other if either is incapacitated; use sick leave to care for an ill partner or the child of a domestic partner; file disability benefits on behalf of an incapacitated partner; sue for wrongful death as well as sick damages for negligent infliction of emotional distress; administer a partner's estate; bequeath property to a domestic partner using the statutory will; and continue health benefits for surviving partners of government employees and retirees. *See California Governor Gray Davis Signs AB 25, Boosting Rights of Gay, Lesbian and Senior Couples Significantly,* Cape Press Release, October 14, 2001.

mitted to mutual caring, have reached the age of eighteen (heterosexuals: over sixty-two), share a common residence, and are responsible for each other's living expenses; neither partner can be married or in another domestic partnership.[163] As a consequence of a contract arbitration ruling between a coalition of unions representing state employees and the state, Connecticut began offering the partners of its gay and lesbian state employees health insurance and pension benefits on March 9, 2000. To qualify for the benefits, employees must sign an affidavit declaring that they are in a long-term relationship that they expect to last into the indefinite future, and they must demonstrate evidence of mutual dependence such as joint financial obligations or proof of a common household.[164]

Other than Vermont's broad supreme court decision (see below), only one court has ruled thus far that a state has an obligation to extend benefits to the domestic partners of all public employees in the state on an equal footing with spouses of such employees.[165] Several courts have struck down domestic partner benefit laws, holding that the municipality had exceeded its legislative authority,[166] and other courts have upheld

---

163. *See* Ingram, note 160 above; Yi & Salladay, note 160 above.

164. Nicole Itano, *State's Gay Employees Gain in Benefits Ruling,* New York Times, March 19, 2000.

165. In the matter of Tanner v. Oregon Health Sciences University, 971 P.2d 435 (Or. Ct. App. 1998), the court of appeals held that the state was obliged to extend health and life insurance benefits to the same-sex domestic partners of all public employees in Oregon—not just state employees—on the same basis as that on which benefits were made available to spouses of such employees. The court of appeals premised its decision on art. 1, sec. 20, of the Oregon Constitution, the Equal Privileges and Immunities Clause, which provides that "no law shall be passed granting to any citizen or class of citizens privileges, or immunities, which, upon the same terms, shall not equally belong to all citizens," and concluded that homosexuals are to be regarded as a suspect class under the Oregon Constitution and that the denial of benefits to same-sex couples was a sex-based discrimination in violation of the Oregon Constitution. *Id.* at 444–46.

166. In the matter of City of Atlanta v. McKinney, 454 S.E.2d 517 (Ga. 1995), the Georgia Supreme Court upheld the city of Atlanta's right to establish a domestic partnership registry providing for jail visitation. However, it struck down the city's ordinance that accorded domestic partners employment benefits, reasoning that by enacting the ordinance, the city exceeded its legislative authority, since it was limited to the extension of benefits to persons who were dependent under state law. Similarly, in Lilly v. City of Minneapolis, 527 N.W.2d 107 (Minn. Ct. App. 1995), the court found that the city of Minneapolis lacked authority under state law to extend domestic partner insurance benefits to its municipal same-sex employees, reasoning that the city did not have the power to expand the list of people who would be considered "dependents," a term that was defined by state law as limited to children and legal spouses. More recently, on April 21, 2000, in Arlington County v. White, 2000 WL 429453, a unanimous Virginia Supreme Court struck down an Arlington County law that conferred health insurance benefits on the unmarried domestic partners of local government employees, reasoning that the General Assembly had never expressly granted such authority to local governments. *See* R. H. Melton & Ann O'Hanlon, *Virginia Justices Strike Down Benefits for Partners,* Washington Post, April 22, 2000.

the denial of domestic partner benefits.[167] Similarly, although many states include marital status among the categories upon which an employer may not discriminate,[168] challenges to the denial of domestic partner benefits based on marital status discrimination have met with little success, and courts generally have not held that these state and local laws require employers to offer benefits to unmarried partners.[169] Domestic partner benefits have also been blocked by referenda.[170]

Even though domestic partnership policies have met with considerable backlash,[171] employers all over the nation have continued to extend

167. *See, e.g.,* Rovira v. AT&T, 817 F.Supp. 1062 (S.D. N.Y. 1993) (holding that a private employer's refusal to provide death benefits to the surviving same-sex partner of an employee does not violate any federal law and that state antidiscrimination laws may not attempt to regulate benefits governed by federal ERISA law); Ross v. Denver Dept. of Health, 883 P.2d 516 (Colo. App. 1994) (holding that the refusal of the city to provide sick leave benefits to an employee who wanted to care for her same-sex domestic partner did not constitute sexual-orientation discrimination, nor did it violate the equal-protection clause of the constitution).

168. Legislation to this effect exists in various states, such as Alaska, California, Connecticut, Florida, Illinois, Nebraska, New York, Washington, and Wisconsin. *See* Conte, note 66 above, at 105–6 n. 29.

169. *See, e.g.,* Phillips v. Wisconsin Personnel Commission, 482 N.W.2d 121 (Wis. App. 1992) (holding that the state's denial of health insurance coverage to the domestic partner of a state employee did not constitute illegal discrimination on the basis of, inter alia, marital status); Rutgers Council of AAUP Chapters v. Rutgers, The State University, 689 A.2d 828 (App. Div. 1997) (holding that the denial of health benefits to same-sex domestic partners of university employees did not constitute illegal discrimination on the basis of marital status). Similarly, in Hinman v. Department of Personnel Administration, 213 Cal.Rptr. 410 (1985), the California Court of Appeals held that the state's refusal to provide dental benefits to the family partner of a state employee was not illegal discrimination on the basis of marital status, nor did it violate the equal-protection clause of the constitution. *See also* Conte, note 66 above, at 105–6. However, there are a few cases in which courts have held that a law prohibiting marital status discrimination provides protection to unmarried couples. *See, e.g.,* Swanner v. Anchorage Equal Rights Commission, 874 P.2d 274 (Alaska 1994); Smith v. Fair Employment and Housing Commission, 913 P.2d 909 (Cal. 1996). In both of these cases, the courts held that a housing statute that prohibited marital status discrimination provided protection to unmarried couples and that the landlords had no right to discriminate merely because they believed unmarried cohabitation was a sin. In the case of University of Alaska v. Tumeo, 933 P.2d 1147 (Alaska, 1997), the court ruled that the refusal of the University of Alaska to accord domestic partner health insurance benefits to its employees' same-sex partners on an equal footing with married couples violated the state law barring marital status discrimination in employment. However, the Alaska state legislature subsequently passed a law that created an exception to the marital status discrimination provisions in the state's Human Rights Act; the exception allows public employers to provide greater benefits to married employees and thus renders the case of Tumeo moot.

170. For example, a referendum was used to repeal domestic partnership measures in Austin, Tex., and in Columbus, Ohio. *See* Steve Bryant & Demian, *Marrying Apartheid: The Failure of Domestic Partnership Status,* Partners Task Force for Gay & Lesbian Couples, May 1999, at http://www.buddybuddy.com/mar-apar.html.

171. For example, when the Walt Disney Company adopted a domestic partnership policy, the gay community was attacked by conservative organizations, and nearly 16 million members of the Southern Baptist Convention boycotted the company. *See* Knauer, note 124 above, at 346 n. 43.

benefits to same-sex couples. Domestic partner policies have symbolic significance, and they can provide substantial financial advantages and benefits, such as employer-provided health insurance for covered employees, which is a particularly valuable benefit as long as health insurance remains linked to employment in the United States. However, domestic partnership ordinances are extremely limited in their scope, availability, and applicability; they do not override state marriage laws, and since marriage itself is not within any particular city's jurisdiction, municipalities have a very limited role in assuring full rights for domestic partners.[172] Furthermore, domestic partnership may provide couples with greater liabilities than benefits: municipalities typically charge couples between thirty-five and sixty-five dollars to register, yet deliver few or no benefits. For example, a registered domestic partner could unexpectedly be held financially responsible for a former partner's ongoing welfare and debts, whether or not they were jointly incurred—a responsibility that the partners had not agreed to and had not been aware of since it was not documented in the original benefit document. Thus, registration may be more harmful should a court later interpret it as creating joint financial liabilities, thereby imposing responsibilities similar to those of marriage with very few benefits.[173]

In the private sector, many companies require unmarried employees to sign an affidavit before receiving benefits; the form often contains statements (not required of married couples) that, for example, the couple shares financial obligations and has lived together for six months to a year.[174] Partners Task Force for Gay and Lesbian Couples, which has been tracking domestic partner benefits since 1987, views these policies as "a crude bandage for an exclusionary benefits system" and concludes that "the reality for most couples is that the benefits are limited and could have negative tax consequences."[175] Furthermore, decisions by private employers or trade unions to grant benefits to same-sex couples, though often important both materially and symbolically, do not constitute or carry the same weight as government recognition of those relationships.[176]

Finally, it should be noted that the arguments by opponents of domestic partnership—namely, that the ordinances serve as evidence of a moral decline and diminish the institution of marriage—are also

172. Lambda Domestic Partnerships, note 112 above, at 1.

173. *See* Bryant & Demian, note 170 above.

174. *See Philosophy and Provider List,* Partners, note 120 above.

175. *Id.*

176. *See Registered Partnership, Domestic Partnership, and Marriage,* note 158 above.

asserted in opposition to calls for legalization of same-sex marriage, and vice versa.[177] However, a distinction must be made: although opponents of same-sex marriage view domestic partnership legislation as a backdoor way to create gay marriage, domestic partnership in fact does not create a new and distinct family relationship.[178] Furthermore, domestic partnership legislation and policies could not alter the rights, benefits, and obligations of married people conferred by state or federal law; domestic partnerships are much more limited than the institution of marriage, so that the two are far from being comparable.

7.5 Vermont's Civil Union Act

On December 20, 1999, in the matter of *Baker v. State of Vermont*[179] (discussed in sec. 7.6.1 below), the Vermont Supreme Court enjoined the state legislature to extend to same-sex couples the benefits and protections associated with marriage. The court did not direct the legislature as to how it should effectuate the ruling, however; it suggested that the legislature might look to the registered partnership acts of the Scandinavian countries or to the original, broadly conceived domestic partnership proposal in Hawaii as a model for compliance. Consequently, on February 9, 2000, the Vermont House of Representatives Judiciary Committee, after weeks of hearing testimony, opted to move forward with an alternative to civil marriage for same-sex couples, and on February 29, 2000, the committee approved a bill (House Bill 847) that would create a new status for gay couples, civil unions.[180] The Vermont House of Representatives on March 16, 2000, passed the civil union bill by a

177. *See* Closen & Maloney, note 75 above, at 518. The arguments for and against same-sex marriage as compared to domestic partnership are discussed in chap. 9, sec. 9.2.

178. *See* Shoshana Bricklin, *Legislative Approaches to Support Family Diversity,* 7 Temple Pol. & Civ. Rts. L. Rev. 379, 383 (1998). Some claim that the solution to the inequality of same-sex couples is the enactment of comprehensive domestic partnership laws rather than the pursuit of same-sex marriage. *See* Nancy K. Kubasek et al., *Fashioning a Tolerable Domestic Partners Statute in an Environment Hostile to Same-Sex Marriage,* 7 L. & Sexuality 55 (1997) (offering a model statute of domestic partnership and arguing that the best way to secure justice and equality for same-sex couples "without providing a direct assault on the popular concept of acceptable marriages" is through the enactment of state domestic partnership statutes). Furthermore, according to a survey conducted among lesbians and gay men, whereas 69% of the respondents thought that marriage should be a priority, 90% stated that they thought domestic partnership laws should be a priority for lesbian and gay organizations. *See* Gretchen A. Stiers, From This Day Forward: Commitment, Marriage, and Family in Lesbian and Gay Relationships 177, 183 (1999).

179. 744 A.2d 864 (Vt. Sup. Ct. 1999).

180. *See* Mary Bonauto, *Vermont Update #4,* March 8, 2000. Available from Gay & Lesbian Advocates & Defenders (GLAD) at http://www.glad.org/update4.htm. The text of the bill as it was first presented to the House (before the Senate amendments) is available at http://www.leg.state.vt.us/dosc/2000/bills/intro/h-847.htm.

vote of 76 to 69.[181] The bill was forwarded to the state Senate, which, following some modifications to the original text of the bill, approved the bill on April 19, 2000, by a vote of 19-11.[182] Brought back to the House for final approval on April 25, the bill passed by a vote of 79 to 68 and was signed into law by Governor Howard Dean on the following day.[183] The act took effect July 1, 2000, except for the provisions relating to insurance and taxation, which were effective January 1, 2001.[184] From July 1, 2000, through the end of June 2001, a total of 2,258 civil unions were conducted; that is almost one-half of the number of marriages contracted in Vermont in the same period. Only about one-fifth of the unions were between Vermonters—the rest were entered into by couples who came from other states within the United States and from foreign countries.[185] The act could thus be regarded as a success. A year after the passage of the act, two bills that would have completely repealed the civil union act were defeated in the state House of Representatives; moreover, on December 26, 2001, the Vermont Supreme Court rejected a challenge to the civil union law brought by a few legislators and town clerks who refused to issue civil union licenses.[186]

181. *See* Carey Goldberg, *Vermont House Passes Bill on Rights for Gay Couples,* New York Times, March 17, 2000.

182. Mary Bonauto, *Vermont Senate Approves Civil Unions: Focus Shifts to the House,* Press Release of the Gay & Lesbian Advocates & Defenders (GLAD), April 19, 2000.

183. *Vermont Governor Signs Landmark Same-Sex "Civil Union" Bill,* Press Release of the Human Rights Campaign, April 26, 2000.

184. *See* An Act Relating to Civil Unions, 2000 Vt. Acts & Resolves 91 (codified at Vt. Stat. Ann. tit. 15, §§ 1201–7 [Supp. 2000]).

185. *See* Fred Bayles, *Civil Unions Blur at Vt.'s State Line,* USA Today, July 11, 2001. During the first few months in which civil unions were made available, unions between women outnumbered those between men by nearly two to one. *See* PlanetOut News Staff, *VT Civil Unions: So Far, So Good,* October 6, 2000.

186. On the supreme court's December 26 order, see Ross Sneyd, *Vermont Rejects Civil Unions Challenge,* Associated Press, January 3, 2002. On the two bills to repeal the act, see Barbara Dozetos, *Vt. Civil Union Repeal Defeated,* PlanetOut.com Network, May 23, 2001. One measure was entitled "The Marriage Restoration Act." It not only proposed to repeal the law but also included language declaring same-sex sexual relationships "contrary to public policy and in violation of the Vermont Constitution." The second measure made no specific pronouncements about the morality of same-sex relationships, but it proposed to add another specific prohibition of same-sex marriage to the Vermont statutes. *Id.* Additionally, in March 2001 Vermont's House Judiciary Committee drafted a bill that would have repealed the civil union law and replaced it with "reciprocal partnerships," which, unlike civil unions, would have been far removed from marriage. The object of the bill was to open the legal status to any couple barred by law from marrying. The bill required couples wishing to become reciprocal partners to simply file a form with the state Health Department to achieve legal status and required only a mutual agreement between the parties and a notarized form to dissolve the partnership, provided there were no children involved. *See* Barbara Dozetos, *Vermont Rejects Marriage Ban,* PlanetOut.com Network, March 30, 2001; Ross Sneyd, *House Judiciary Committee Pushes Ahead on Repeal of Civil Unions,* Associated Press, April 24, 2001. This latter bill passed by a single vote in the House, but the Democratic-controlled Senate refused to consider the measure. *See* Bayles, note 185 above. A complete repeal of the civil union act or its replacement with a less

Vermont's civil union act is an exceptionally significant breakthrough and is one of the most important recent developments in the status of same-sex partnerships worldwide. The Vermont legislature has done all that it could do apart from using the term *marriage* (i.e., apart from revising the state's definition of marriage to include same-sex couples). The act extends to same-sex couples all the benefits and responsibilities of marriage that are within the state's power but none of the rights and benefits at the federal level, since the Vermont legislature is legally unable to require equal treatment of same-sex couples for federal purposes. Thus, parties to a civil union do not qualify for any of the benefits and protections contained in the 1,049 federal laws affecting the spousal relationship, such as assumption of the spouse's pension, bereavement leave, immigration, Social Security survivor benefits, and federal tax breaks for married couples. The act provides a definition of marriage as the legally recognized union of one man and one woman both in the marriage chapter and in the civil union chapter under the domestic relations title (secs. 1, 2[4]),[187] and the new status it creates—civil union—is open *only to same-sex couples.* According to section 2, which makes specific reference to the Vermont Supreme Court decision in *Baker,* the purpose of the act is "to respond to the constitutional violation found by the Vermont Supreme Court in *Baker v. State,* and to provide eligible same-sex couples the opportunity to 'obtain the same benefits and protections afforded by Vermont law to *married opposite-sex couples*' as required by Chapter I, Article 7th of the Vermont Constitution."[188]

The requirements for entering a civil union are virtually identical to those for marriage. Civil union status is available to two persons of the same sex who are not related to each other. Parties to the civil union must be at least eighteen years old and competent to enter a contract. To enter a civil union, a person may not already be a party to another

---

expansive model would seem to be contradictory to Vermont's Supreme Court's ruling in the matter of Baker v. State of Vermont, 744 A.2d 864 (Vt. Sup. Ct. 1999), and might open the door for the plaintiffs to return to court and challenge the repeal.

187. This is in accordance with the court's ruling in *Baker,* which explicitly states that "there is no doubt that the plain and ordinary meaning of 'marriage' is the union of one man and one woman as husband and wife" and that "this understanding of the term is well rooted in Vermont common law." Accordingly, the court rejected the plaintiffs' claim that they were entitled to a marriage license under Vermont's marriage laws. *See* Baker v. State of Vermont, 744 A.2d 864 (Vt. Sup. Ct. 1999).

Despite the clear definition of marriage in the civil union act, in March 2001 the state's House approved a bill that would outlaw marriage for gays and lesbians. The bill now moves to Vermont's Senate, which is unlikely to consider the bill. *See* Dozetos, note 186 above. This "clarification" is clearly unnecessary, since the one-man, one-woman definition already exists in the state's laws.

188. An Act Relating to Civil Unions, note 184 above, my emphasis.

civil union or a marriage. The licensing scheme and the certification process for a civil union closely parallel those of marriage. A person makes an application to his or her town clerk and receives a civil union license in the same way as a person who applies for a marriage license. Within sixty days of issuance of the license, a couple must have the civil union certified by an authorized person. The same people who are authorized to solemnize a marriage are authorized to certify a civil union: judges, justices of the peace, and (willing) members of the clergy. The latter are not required to certify a civil union and may choose whether or not to do so according to the rules, customs, or traditions of their religion, just as they currently choose whether to perform civil marriage. Nonresidents may obtain a civil union license from any town clerk in the state rather than having to obtain the license from a town clerk in the county in which the civil union is going to be certified (note that Vermont currently requires a six-month residency period before one files for divorce, and this requirement applies equally to civil unions). Once certified, a person receives a civil union certificate instead of a marriage certificate.

The dissolution of civil unions follows the same procedures and is subject to the same substantive rights and obligations as those involved in the dissolution of a marriage, including any residency requirements. In other words, divorce laws and procedures apply to civil unions just as they do to marriages, and the family court has exclusive jurisdiction over all matters and proceedings relating to the dissolution of civil unions. The entire law of domestic relations, including annulment, separation and divorce, child custody and support, and property division and maintenance, applies to parties to a civil union.

The rights extended are comprehensive and parallel marriage: "Parties to a civil union shall have all the same benefits, protections and responsibilities under law, whether they derive from statute, administrative or court rule, policy, common law or any other source of civil law, *as are granted to spouses in marriage*" (sec. 3). Moreover, "[a] party to a civil union shall be included in any definition or use of the terms 'spouse,' 'family,' 'immediate family,' 'dependent,' 'next of kin,' and other terms that denote the spousal relationship, as those terms are used throughout the law" (sec. 3).[189] For example, parties to a civil union have mutual support obligations, as married couples do; the parties are considered legal next-of-kin for purposes of inheritance, workers' compensation, hospital visitation and notification, and medical decision making and are eligible for family leave benefits. Gay and lesbian couples are entitled to joint title, are able to transfer property to one another

189. *Id.,* my emphasis.

without paying property transfer taxes, and can own property in a way that is secure from the individual debts of either partner; state taxes on married couples and parties to a civil union are the same. Civil union partners are also entitled to all the protections available when adopting a child (same-sex couples are already allowed under Vermont state law to adopt, but the act makes clear that those couples are to be treated as spouses). Moreover, a party to a civil union can sue for the wrongful death of a partner, the emotional distress caused by a partner's death or injury, and the loss of consortium caused by death or injury. All probate law and procedures related to spouses are applicable to civil union parties. As with spouses, parties in a civil union cannot be compelled to testify against one another, and laws relating to the marital communication privilege apply.

Discrimination or different treatment of parties to a civil union is considered discrimination based on both sexual orientation and marital status. There are broad nondiscrimination provisions with respect to insurance that endeavor to ensure the equal treatment of spouses and parties to a civil union. Insurers must make available dependent coverage to parties to a civil union that is equivalent to that provided to married persons; an individual or group health insurance policy that provides coverage for a spouse or family member of the insured shall also provide the equivalent coverage for a party to a civil union. Although insurers are required to offer equivalent coverage, private employers are not required to provide coverage to parties to a civil union and may decide which employees are eligible for the insurance (because of the federal employment benefits law preemption,[190] the state cannot order private employers to treat civilly united couples as spouses for purposes of employment benefit plans). The act also attempts to equalize the tax treatment of spouses and parties to a civil union. For the purpose of state income taxes, parties to a civil union are taxed in the same manner as married persons.

The act established a Civil Union Review Commission for two years, whose purpose is to prepare and implement a plan to inform members of the public, state agencies, and private- and public-sector businesses and organizations about the act; to collect information about the implementation, operation, and effect of the act; and to report to the general assembly and the governor its findings, conclusions, and recommendations.[191]

190. *See* Federal Employee Retirement Income Security Act of 1974, 29 U.S.C. §§ 1001–461 (1988).

191. *See* An Act Relating to Civil Unions, note 184 above.

In addition to the civil union status created by the law, it created an institution called "reciprocal beneficiaries," which provides several new protections for eligible blood relatives and relatives related by adoption. Such relatives can sign a notarized declaration to become "reciprocal beneficiaries" so that they may receive certain benefits and protections and be subject to certain responsibilities that are granted to spouses. A reciprocal beneficiary may not be a party to another reciprocal beneficiaries relationship, a civil union, or a marriage.[192]

The act does not purport to apply outside the state of Vermont, since Vermont's legislature cannot bind other states, and other states are not likely to recognize Vermont's civil unions. Although the act makes it possible for nonresidents to enter a civil union in Vermont, there is no clear indication of whether the new status would be recognized by any other state. Most states are unlikely to recognize civil unions entered into in Vermont. First of all, there are no comparable civil union laws on the books anywhere else. Second, some of the more than thirty states' defense of marriage acts, such as Kentucky's DOMA of 1998, not only bar the recognition of out-of-state same-sex marriages but also require that state courts give no legal effect to any obligation arising from such marriages.[193] Furthermore, states may still refuse to recognize another state's laws, public acts, and records if they violate the public policy of the state in which recognition is sought.[194] Thus, even a state's defense of marriage act that only bars recognition of same-sex marriage may be invoked as a public-policy reason not to recognize civil unions, because the difference between marriage and civil unions could be regarded as merely a matter of nomenclature. An interesting option of indirect recognition of civil unions entered into in Vermont by other states is their conceptualization as *contractual* rather than as a new civil status. That is, same-sex Vermont couples are considered to have acquired state-conferred contractual rights and obligations vis-à-vis each other that

192. Reciprocal Beneficiaries are people such as brothers and sisters or parents and children, who are prohibited from establishing a marriage or a civil union with one another because they are related by blood or adoption. Such relatives already have many legal protections, such as inheritance rights, because they are already legally recognized family members. The act supplements rights they already have in a few enumerated limited areas of law, such as hospital visitation and medical decision making, death, and disability. Unlike a civil union, which must be dissolved by the divorce laws, a Reciprocal Beneficiaries relationship may be dissolved unilaterally by the filing of a notice of dissolution or upon entry by one Reciprocal Beneficiary into a civil union or a marriage.

193. Personal communication by Samuel A. Marcosson, posted on the Queer Law List at queerlaw@abacus.oxy.edu, May 18, 2000.

194. For a full discussion of the federal and state defense of marriage acts as well as the Full Faith and Credit Clause and general principles of conflict laws that apply to the status of same-sex couples, see the next section.

would be enforceable in other states.[195] However, a few states have already expressed their intent not to recognize civil unions entered into in Vermont. Thus, for example, relying on the state's "legitimate public policy," Illinois's attorney general stated that "Illinois is not required to recognize civil unions entered into under the laws of Vermont or extended to persons who have entered into a civil union the benefits which may be extended to married persons."[196] A case that marked the first time any state court was asked to interpret Vermont's civil union act was brought before the Georgia Court of Appeals in May 2001: a woman who entered a civil union with her same-sex partner in Vermont asked the court to recognize the union as a marriage.[197] On January 23, 2002, in a brief decision, the court stated that "a civil union is not marriage" and ruled that the civil union did not make her legally related to her partner and *could not substitute for legal marriage.* The court added that even had Vermont opened up marriage to same-sex couples—or, alternatively, even if Georgia viewed civil unions as equivalent to marriage—owing to the defense of marriage act, as well as general public-policy principles, such a union would probably not be recognized in the state of Georgia.[198]

Vermont's act is the most extensive and far-reaching statutory recognition of same-sex partnerships in the United States; all other statewide as well as local domestic partner schemes pale in comparison to the Vermont act. The (formerly) broadest statewide domestic partner scheme, Hawaii's Reciprocal Beneficiaries Act, provides a number of benefits that are usually reserved for marriage; however, the benefits provided to reciprocal beneficiaries constitute just a small fraction of those provided to spouses and thus also only a fragment of the benefits provided to parties to a civil union. For example, termination of the Hawaii reciprocal beneficiaries relationship is by unilateral notification, whereas Vermont's civil unions are dissolved by the regular laws and procedures of divorce; in addition, hundreds of rights that are missing from Hawaii's act are present in civil unions. Nevertheless, even the Vermont act cannot and does not grant the more than one thousand rights and benefits that the federal government provides.

195. For the possibility of contractual recognition of civil unions, see scholarly writings pertaining to recognition of same-sex marriages not under marriage law but under *contract law,* for example, F. H. Buckley & Larry E. Ribstein, *Calling a Truce in the Marriage Wars,* 2001 U. Ill. L. Rev. 561.

196. PlanetOut News Staff, *Queer Families' Ups and Downs: Illinois Won't Recognize Vt. Civil Unions,* February 2, 2001.

197. *See* Penny Weaver, *GA Appeals Court to Hear Civil Unions Test Case,* Southern Voice, May 3, 2001.

198. *See* Burns v. Burns, 2002 Ga. App. Lexis 85.

In Vermont there are now three categories: marriage for heterosexual couples, civil unions for gay and lesbian couples, and reciprocal benefi- ciary status for people related by blood or adoption. The civil union, albeit a new legal institution and a new status parallel to marriage, is not to be confused with marriage for same-sex couples: as the act states, the system of civil unions "does not bestow the status of civil mar- riage," and the granting of "benefits and protections to same-sex couples through a system of civil unions will provide due respect for tradition and long-standing social institutions" (sec. 1 [10]);[199] that is, the civil union system is not intended to undermine the primacy of the institu- tion of marriage. Moreover, as stated above, a same-sex couple's civil union is not recognized under federal law, and no federal statute is appli- cable to the couple, meaning that they are not eligible to receive the rights available to married couples, such as those pertaining to immigra- tion, social security, and federal taxes. Not only are civil unions different and separate from marriage per se, but they are also largely limited to the state of Vermont and to the rights, benefits, and protections accorded to opposite-sex married couples within Vermont. Therefore, civil unions should not be categorized as "Vermont gay marriages" or as a new na- tional status for same-sex couples. However, since the act creating civil unions is extremely broad in comparison to existing U.S. domestic part- ner ordinances and acts, it should be regarded as an exception within the United States and classified as an institution that, because of its broad scope, is more akin to the European registered partnership model than to any U.S. domestic partner scheme.[200]

A few other states may follow Vermont's lead by enacting a civil union act or similar legislation (or even opening up the institution of marriage to same-sex couples [see the next section]). The most advanced campaigns have been mounted in Connecticut and Rhode Island; these two states were the first to hold legislative hearings on civil union bills— voluntarily, without a court order.[201] In a few additional states, such as

199. An Act Relating to Civil Unions, note 184 above.

200. However, because the act is limited in its *application* to the state of Vermont and does not (and cannot) regulate the status of same-sex partnerships at the national level (unlike the registered partnerships acts), and as a pure matter of classification, the civil union act could also be categorized as a broad version of domestic partnership. See my definition of domestic partnership in chap. 2. For an extensive assessment of the civil union act and a comparison between the act and other domestic partner schemes in the United States, as well as a comparison with the northern European Registered Partner- ships, see chap. 8, secs. 8.2 and 8.3.

201. E. J. Graff, *Civil Unions Are Homemaking Here for a Reason*, Boston Globe, at E3, February 11, 2001. As Graff points out, "[h]istory suggests that Rhode Island and Connect- icut are predisposed to the philosophy behind civil unions. During the past decade, one or both states have banned discrimination based on sexual orientation, enacted hate

California[202] and Washington,[203] civil union bills have been introduced and are currently pending. It seems, however, that it will take quite some time for such developments to take place,[204] especially in light of the political turmoil in Vermont in the aftermath of the enactment of civil unions: some Vermont politicians who supported the civil union bill were replaced by conservatives in the elections of fall 2000.[205] Lawmakers in other states are now hesitant to engage their states in what looks to be inevitable political turmoil. A civil union proposal has already been defeated in Hawaii,[206] but it will probably be reintroduced in future legislative sessions.

7.6 Opening Up Marriage to Same-Sex Couples

7.6.1 Developments toward Judicial Recognition of Same-Sex Marriage
According to U.S. law, domestic relations in general and marriage law in particular are within the jurisdiction of the states; marital relationships have always been controlled and regulated by the individual states, not by the federal government.[207] Therefore, the attempts to open up civil marriage to same-sex couples have taken place in various states and through scattered challenges brought before state courts.

For many years American courts have rejected petitions of same-sex couples who wished to get married, despite the recognition of a constitu-

---

crimes laws, repealed sodomy laws, and enabled hospital visitation and funeral planning for same-sex pairs." *Id.*

202. On March 1, 2001, California State Assemblyman Paul Koretz introduced a bill he calls the Family Protection Act, which echoes Vermont's civil union law. *See* Barbara Dozetos, *California Lawmaker Backs Civil Unions,* Gay.com Network, March 5, 2001.

203. The proposal in Washington has very slim chances in the Republican-dominated state legislature. *See* PlanetOut News Staff, *Civil Unions Action in VT, WA,* February 5, 2001.

204. For example, in April 2001 it was decided in Connecticut not to go ahead with a legislative vote on civil unions, since there was not enough support in either party to go forward with a full civil union bill that year. *See* Lisa Prevost, *Conn. Backs Away from Gay Unions,* Boston Globe, April 5, 2001; Christopher Hoffman, *State Bills Would Bring New Rights to Gays, Lesbians,* New Haven Register, March 24, 2001.

205. More than twenty legislators who supported the law were voted out of office in November 2000, and the governor barely held his seat. Prevost, note 204 above.

206. Hawaii House Bill (HB) 1468, which would have allowed for civil unions, was not heard by the House Committee on Judiciary and Hawaiian Affairs by the deadline necessary to keep the bill alive. In addition to civil unions, the bill also would have allowed for state recognition of substantially similar legal arrangements from other jurisdictions. *See* Martin Rice, *CU 3434: Hawaii Civil Union Bill Dies,* personal communication to E-mail list, lambda@aloha.net, March 5, 2001.

207. Gregory et al., note 72 above, at 2, 12. Although the individual state legislatures regulate family law relationships, Congress has also entered the field of family law regulation, especially in the areas of child-custody and child-support enforcement remedies. *Id.* at 2.

tionally protected fundamental right to marry.[208] The reason for the exclusion by the courts has been a definitional one: the common meaning and usage of the word *marriage* has been viewed as excluding any definition other than a union between a man and a woman. Moreover, courts have emphasized again and again the link between procreation, child raising, and marriage as a reason to exclude same-sex couples from the institution of marriage.

In 1972 the National Coalition of Gay Organizations drew up a list of demands for law reform including a call for "repeal of all legislative provisions that restrict the sex or number of persons entering into a marriage unit and extension of legal benefits of marriage to all persons who cohabit regardless of sex or numbers."[209] At the same time, same-sex couples who were denied marriage licenses by their town officials began challenging these denials in state courts. They asserted that because marriage statutes were construed to require different-sex partners— although most state laws did not explicitly prohibit same-sex marriages or define marriage to be a union between a man and a woman—these laws constituted unconstitutional discrimination on the basis of sex or sexual orientation. The first cases to challenge the denial of marriage to same-sex couples were filed in 1971—*Baker v. Nelson*[210] and *Singer v. Hara*.[211] Two years later, a similar challenge was brought in the case of *Jones v. Hallahan*.[212] In these cases the courts upheld the government's refusal to issue marriage licenses to same-sex couples, relying upon the definition of marriage as inherently involving opposite-sex partners and reasoning that same-sex persons, *by definition,* cannot marry each other. The courts ruled that the institution of marriage is limited to a union between one man and one woman that exists as a protected legal institution primarily because it is the appropriate and desirable forum for the procreation and the rearing of children.[213] Another challenge that met

208. *See* Loving v. Virginia, 388 U.S. 1 (1967).

209. Eskridge, note 12 above, at 134.

210. 191 N.W.2d 185 (Minn. 1971) (holding that Minnesota marriage law precluded same-sex couples owing to the historic definition of marriage as between a man and a woman, thus finding that same-sex marriage falls outside the spirit, although not the letter, of the state's marriage laws), appeal dismissed 409 U.S. 810 (1972).

211. 522 P.2d 1187 (Wash. Ct. App. 1974) (rejecting equal-protection, due process, and equal-rights-amendment challenges to the denial of a marriage license to a same-sex couple), review denied, 84 Wn.2d 1008 (1974).

212. 501 S.W.2d 588 (Ky 1973) (summarily rejecting constitutional challenges based on the right to marry, the right of association, and the right to free exercise of religion).

213. *See* Singer v. Hara, 522 P.2d 1187 (Wash. Ct. App. 1974), review denied, 84 Wn.2d 1008 (1974); Baker v. Nelson, 191 N.W.2d 185 (Minn. 1971), appeal dismissed 409 U.S. 810 (1972); Jones v. Hallahan, 501 S.W.2d 588 (K1973).

with no success was the 1984 decision in *DeSanto v. Barnsley*.[214] Unlike the other cases, *DeSanto* did not challenge a refusal to provide a marriage license. Instead, the plaintiff filed for divorce claiming that a common law marriage existed between him and his lover. The court dismissed the case, refusing to recognize common law marriages between persons of the same sex.[215] The case of *Dean v. District of Columbia* was filed in 1990 and was eventually lost on appeal in 1995.[216] In that case, despite the District of Columbia broad Human Rights Act requirement that lesbians and gay men be accorded "equal opportunity to participate in all aspects of life," the court found that it would be contrary to the legislature's intent in enacting the Human Rights Act to change the definition of marriage.[217]

In May 1993, in the landmark decision in the case of *Baehr v. Lewin*,[218] the supreme court of Hawaii became the first U.S. court to accept the argument that the denial of marriage licenses to same-sex couples is prima facie sex discrimination requiring justification. The court ruled that the state's refusal to issue civil marriage licenses to same-sex couples under the Hawaii marriage law was discrimination based on sex and presumptively violated the state constitutional guarantee in its Equal Rights Amendment (ERA), which bars discrimination on the basis of sex, since the law was construed by the state to allow men to marry women but not men and to allow women to marry men but not women. The court held that sex is a "suspect category" for purposes of equal-protection analysis under article 1, section 5 of the Hawaii Constitution and therefore applied "strict scrutiny" analysis.[219] The court thus held that the "different-sex restriction" on marital choice constitutes prima facie unconstitutional sex discrimination.[220] In so doing, the Hawaii court found

214. 476 A.2d 952 (Pa. 1984).

215. DeSanto v. Barnsley, 476 A.2d 952 (Pa. 1984). *See also In re* Succession of Bascot, 502 So.2d 1118, 1127–30 (L 1987) (holding that two men cannot establish the status of "concubinage").

216. 653 A.2d 307 (D.C. App. 1995).

217. Dean v. District of Columbia, 653 A.2d 307, 320 (D.C. App. 1995). The position that marriage is limited to opposite-sex partners and that same-sex couples should be barred from entering the institution was expressed in several other court decisions: *See In re* Estate of Cooper, 564 N.Y.S.2d 684, 687 (Sup. Ct. 1990) aff'd, 592 N.S.2d 797 (1993); Anonymous v. Anonymous, 325 N.Y.S.2d 499, 500 (Sup. Ct. 1971); Slayton v. State, 633 S.W.2d 934, 93 (Tex. 1982); Jennings v. Jennings, 315 A.2d 816, 820 n. 7 (Md. 1974).

218. 852 P.2d 44, 67 (Haw. 1993).

219. Baehr v. Lewin, 852 P.2d 44, 67 (Haw. 1993).

220. *Id.* at 60, 74. The sex discrimination theory upon which the *Baehr* court relied to impose a strict scrutiny standard of review was proposed by commentators before the court's decision. *See, e.g.,* Law, note 3 above, at 218–21, 230–33 (arguing that any effort by the state to hard-wire sex differences into the concept of marriage perpetuates traditional sex-based stereotypes). For further commentary on the argument that exclusion

the argument made thirty years earlier in the case of *Loving v. Virginia* regarding interracial marriages as racial discrimination[221] to be equally specious when applied to sex in the context of same-sex marriages.[222] Unlike prior cases dealing with access of same-sex couples to the institution of marriage, the Hawaii Supreme Court found illegitimate the definition of the "nature" of marriage as restricted to opposite-sex couples based on the rationale of promotion of an asserted link between procreation, child raising, and marriage—justifications that had been used and accepted in other jurisdictions to claim state interests in restricting marriage to opposite-sex partners.[223] However, the court rejected the argument that substantive due process issues were also implicated, reasoning that there is no fundamental right of persons of the same sex to marry because same-sex marriage was not "so rooted in the traditions and collective conscience of Hawaii's people that failure to recognize it would violate the fundamental principles of liberty and justice."[224] In sending the case back to the lower court, the supreme court mandated that the state prove it had a compelling reason to limit civil marriage to opposite-sex partners.[225] Absent such proof, the court stated, the ban would violate the protections against sex discrimination contained in the state's constitution.

In 1996, on remand, the state circuit court found that no such compelling state interest existed and that the state had failed to meet its burden to show that excluding same-sex couples from the institution of marriage was necessary and narrowly tailored to achieve a compelling state interest.[226] The state's main argument was that it was preferable that children be raised by opposite-sex couples and that if raised by same-sex couples, the children would lose intimate contact with a parent of one gender and never observe at close hand the modeling of male-female relationships. All the evidence introduced at trial, by both sides, addressed the impact on children of lesbian and gay family settings.[227] Not

---

of same-sex couples from civil marriage is to be regarded as sex discrimination, see Andrew Koppelman, *Why Discrimination against Lesbians and Gay Men Is Sex Discrimination,* 69 N.Y.U. L. Rev. 197 (1994).

221. Loving v. Virginia, 388 U.S. 1 (1967).

222. *See* Patricia Novotny & Gwynne L. Skinner, Same-Sex Marriage: The State of the Law (1998), at http://www.buddybuddy.com/novotny1.html.

223. *See* text above accompanying notes 212–15.

224. Baehr v. Lewin, 852 P.2d 44, 57 (Haw. 1993). For a critique of the court's failure to recognize a fundamental right of same-sex couples to marry based on the *Loving* precedent, see Mark Strasser, *Domestic Relations Jurisprudence and the Great, Slumbering Baehr: On Definitional Preclusion, Equal Protection, and Fundamental Interests,* 64 Fordham L. Rev. 921 (1995).

225. Baehr v. Lewin, 852 P.2d 44, 68 (Haw. 1993).

226. Baehr v. Miike, CIV. No. 91-1394, 1996 WL 694235 (Haw. Cir. Ct. Dec. 3, 1996).

227. *See* Eskridge & Hunter, note 81 above, at 815.

only did the court hold that the state failed to prove its assertions; it also stated that if same-sex marriage were allowed, the children being raised by gay or lesbian parents and same-sex couples might benefit because they might obtain certain protections and benefits that come with or become available as a result of marriage.[228] The court thus concluded that the exclusion of same-sex couples from civil marriage violated Hawaii's constitution. The decision has been appealed back to the state supreme court, delaying the enforcement of the circuit court's decision.

Meanwhile, the Hawaii legislature responded by adopting the Reciprocal Beneficiaries Act in July 1997 for couples who were unable to marry as a matter of law (see above, sec. 7.4). The enactment did not stem from a real interest in expanding domestic partner benefits and providing same-sex couples with equal rights. The legislature of Hawaii initiated the act only because it hoped that doing so would avert the supreme court's ruling allowing legal marriage for same-sex couples.[229] The act was thus an effort by the Hawaii legislators to circumvent providing full legal marriage for all citizens. The legislature hoped that the act would persuade the court that Hawaii no longer discriminated against same-sex couples, thereby eliminating the need to order the state to offer legal marriage.[230]

Another attempt to circumvent the supreme court's decision, which eventually met with success, took place on November 3, 1998. Following a state referendum, the voters in Hawaii ratified a constitutional amendment authorizing, but not requiring, the legislature to restrict marriage to opposite-sex couples.[231] The constitutional amendment, providing that the legislature "shall have the power to reserve marriage to a man

228. For an assessment of the validity of the state's child-protection rationale, see Samuel A. Marcosson, *The Lesson of the Same-Sex Marriage Trial [Baehr v. Lewin, 852 P.2d 44 (Haw. 1993)]: The Importance of Pushing Opponents of Lesbian and Gay Rights to Their "Second Line of Defense,"* 35 U. Louisville J. Fam. L. 721 (1996–97) (arguing that the trial court correctly found that Hawaii proffered an insufficient basis for refusing to recognize same-sex marriages and that the child-protection claim was actually a "second line" of defense and a mere pretext for the state's deeper reason—moral judgment against homosexual couples as unworthy of recognition). For the effects on children of being raised by same-sex couples, see Patterson, note 4 above, at 197, 199–200 (arguing not only that studies have failed to produce conclusive evidence that the children of lesbian mothers or gay fathers have significant difficulties in development relative to children of heterosexual parents but also that the studies have produced no evidence at all in support of this proposition).

229. *See* Bryant & Demian, note 170 above.

230. *See Reciprocal Beneficiaries: The Hawaiian Approach,* Partners Task Force for Gay & Lesbian Couples, at http://www.buddybuddy.com/d-p-rec.html (last visited September 20, 1999).

231. *See* Lambda Legal Defense and Education Fund, at http://www.lambdalegal.org/cgi-bin/pages/cases/record?record=17 (last updated June 8, 1999).

and a woman," passed by an overwhelming majority of 69 percent to 29 percent, with 2 percent of the ballots blank or spoiled.[232] Although the legislature had taken no action to that effect and had never passed a new statute banning marriage licenses for same-sex couples, on December 9, 1999, almost nine years after the suit was filed, the Hawaii Supreme Court rendered its final decision in the matter and declared the case moot.[233] The court issued a brief order holding that the constitutional amendment took the issue out of the hands of the courts and gave the legislature the power to reserve marriage to opposite-sex couples. It required the lower court to reverse its decision and enter judgment in favor of the state.

The court did not overrule its 1993 decision that the denial of the freedom to marry is sex discrimination; it limited its decision to stating that the 1998 constitutional amendment removed access to marriage licenses from the reach of the state constitution's equal-protection clause. In effect, the decision terminated the move to recognize same-sex marriage in Hawaii. However, future claims for the protections, benefits, and responsibilities that are associated with marriage might be considered as a separate issue.[234] In an important footnote to the decision, the court stated that even had the case been decided on the basis of sexual orientation discrimination, rather than discrimination based on sex, strict scrutiny was still required. The court interpreted the Hawaii constitution as implicitly prohibiting sexual orientation discrimination in the ambit of its prohibition of sex discrimination, both being regarded as a "suspect class." Thus, and although the state would not be required to issue marriage licenses to same-sex couples, denial of benefits that flow from marriage might be deemed unconstitutional. Moreover, the case "spawned a revolution in the law as it stimulated state and federal legislation, prompted numerous prominent people and organizations to endorse same-sex marriage, persuaded the lesbian and gay legal movement to take up the quest for same-sex marriage as an important goal, and made the idea of same-sex marriage seem inevitable to a growing majority of the population."[235]

232. David M. Smith, *Blue Hawaii: Lessons Learned from the Same-Gender Marriage Battle*, Hum. Rts. Campaign Q., spring 1999, at 4; *Freedom to Marry Update: Marriage Project Fact Sheet*, Lambda Legal Defense and Education Fund, June 16, 1999, at http://www.lambdalegal.org/cgi-bin/pages/documents/record?record=50.

233. Baehr v. Miike, No. 20371, 26 Fam. L. Rep. (BNA) 1075 (December 9, 1999).

234. *See Preliminary Notes on the Hawaii Supreme Court's 12/9/99 Decision*, Lambda Legal Defense and Education Fund, December 10, 1999, available at http://www.lambdalegal.org/cgi-bin/pages/documents/record?record=54.

235. *See* Lesbian/Gay Law Notes, January 2000, at 4.

Alaska was the second state to rule in favor of a same-sex couple, and it came close to recognizing same-sex marriage. In February 1998, after an Alaskan male couple sued for civil marriage, the Superior Court of Alaska ruled in the matter of *Brause v. Bureau of Vital Statistics*[236] that because the right to choose one's life partner is fundamental, a ban on same-sex marriage must be justified by a compelling state interest in order to pass constitutional muster under the state constitution. The court did not legalize same-sex marriage in Alaska but mandated the state to demonstrate a compelling reason why such unions should be excluded from marriage.[237] However, in November 1998 a referendum was conducted in Alaska, and the voters decided to directly alter their state constitution to define marriage as limited to a union between a man and a woman, thus barring any possibility that the state's courts could expand the definition to include same-sex couples.[238] Consequently, the litigants decided to stop pursuing legal marriage and continue their fight for equal rights and benefits associated with marriage,[239] but in September 1999 their lawsuit was dismissed.[240]

In another case, not directly related to the right of same-sex couples to marry, the attorney general of Georgia terminated the employment of a newly hired attorney, Robin Shahar, because she planned to have a religious marriage ceremony with her lesbian partner. The Eleventh Circuit upheld the decision of the attorney general, holding that the public interest in the efficient operation of the Law Department outweighed any personal associational interests that Shahar may have had.[241] Although the case was confined to the field of employment discrimination law and the ruling was based on considerations of government efficiency, the court implicitly approved of a policy opposing the recognition of same-sex couples' right to marry.

As mentioned in the previous section, the most successful challenge

236. No. 3AN-95-6562 CI., 1998 WL 88743 (Alaska Super. Ct. February 27, 1998).

237. The court in Alaska, unlike the courts in Hawaii and Vermont, had to deal with a statute that explicitly defined marriage as a civil contract entered into by one man and one woman. *See* Novotny & Skinner, note 222 above.

238. *See Judge Dismisses Same-Sex Lawsuit,* Anchorage Daily News, September 24, 1999, at 2B.

239. *See Legal Marriage Court Cases—A Timeline,* Partners Task Force for Gay & Lesbian Couples, at http://www.buddybuddy.com/t-line-1.html (last visited September 20, 1999) [hereinafter Partners Timeline].

240. *See Judge Dismisses Same-Sex Lawsuit,* note 238 above.

241. Shahar v. Bowers, 114 F.3d 1097 (11th Cir. 1997), cert. denied, 118 S. Ct. 69 (1998). The Eleventh Circuit denied a request for rehearing after Bowers admitted adultery and resigned from his job. *See* Shahar v. Bowers, 120 F. 211 (11th Cir. 1997). For an analysis of the case and its ramifications, see Noel K. Wolfe, *Shahar v. Bowers: The Balance between Constitutional Rights and Governmental Efficiency,* 8 L. & Sexuality 713 (1998).

to the exclusion of same-sex couples from marriage thus far occurred in Vermont.[242] In July 1997 three same-sex couples brought a challenge, similar to the challenge brought in Hawaii, to the state of Vermont's denial of their application for marriage licenses. The plaintiffs argued that the state's refusal to issue marriage licenses to same-sex couples violated the right to equal protection and the "Common Benefit Clause" of the Vermont constitution, which provides in part that the "government is, or ought to be, instituted for the common benefit, protection and security of the people, nation, or community, and not for the particular emolument or advantage of any single person, family, or set of persons, who are part of that community."[243] The case, *Baker v. State of Vermont*, reached the Vermont Supreme Court, which rendered its groundbreaking decision on December 20, 1999.[244] The supreme court did not base its decision on federal law (i.e., the Equal Protection Clause of the Fourteenth Amendment to the U.S. Constitution); it held that the state's statutes that excluded same-sex couples from the benefits and protections incident to marriage under Vermont law violated the "Common Benefits Clause" of Vermont's constitution (chap. 1, art. 7) and that the state could not exclude same-sex couples from the benefits and protections that its laws provide to opposite-sex married couples. Chief Justice Jeffrey L. Amestoy departed from the (federal) three-tiered approach in construing the state's constitution and held that all equal-protection challenges under the Vermont constitution should be evaluated by a flexible, fact-based analysis—a "balancing approach"—that takes into account the weight of the interests affected on both sides of the issue, thus not following the example of the Hawaii Supreme Court, that is, not requiring strict scrutiny and not basing the decision on a determination that sex or sexual orientation discrimination is a suspect classification.[245]

242. *See* Mary Bonauto et al., *The Freedom to Marry for Same-Sex Couples: The Opening Appellate Brief of Plaintiffs Stan Baker et al. in Baker et al. v. State of Vermont*, 5 Mich. J. Gender & L. 409 (1999); Mary Bonauto et al., *The Freedom to Marry for Same-Sex Couples: The Reply Brief of Plaintiffs Stan Baker et al. in Baker et al. v. State of Vermont*, 6 Mich. J. Gender & Law 1 (1999). In addition to the text of the briefs, the authors provide a full background of the case, as well as an account of how the state of Vermont has long been at the forefront in the pursuit of equality in the United States.

243. Vt. Const. Ch. I. Art. 7. *See* Novotny & Skinner, note 222 above.

244. Baker v. State of Vermont, 744 A.2d 864 (Vt. Sup. Ct. 1999).

245. In rejecting the sex-based discrimination argument on which the Hawaii court based its decision in *Baehr*, Justice Amestoy reasoned that "the marriage laws are facially neutral; they do not single-out men or women as a class for disparate treatment, but rather prohibit men and women equally from marrying a person of the same sex . . . each sex is equally prohibited from precisely the same conduct." *Id.* In her dissent, Justice Johnson stressed that the court should have adhered to the three-tier approach, categorized the discrimination as based on sex, and classified it as suspect.

The principal purpose proffered by the state in justifying its exclusion of same-sex couples from the legal benefits of marriage was the state's interest in "furthering the link between procreation and child rearing." The court flatly rejected this rationale as significantly underinclusive, stating that "many opposite-sex couples marry for reasons unrelated to procreation . . . some of these couples never intend to have children, [and] others are incapable of having children." It further stated that a significant number of children today are actually being raised by same-sex partners and that increasing numbers of children are being conceived by such parents through a variety of assisted reproductive techniques. It noted that the Vermont legislature "has not only recognized this reality, but has acted affirmatively to remove legal barriers so that same-sex couples may legally adopt and rear the children conceived through such efforts." The court thus concluded that "if anything, the exclusion of same-sex couples from the legal protections incident to marriage exposes their children to the precise risks that the State argues the marriage laws are designed to secure against. In short, the marital exclusion treats persons who are similarly situated for purposes of the law, differently."[246] The court ordered the state legislature to extend to same-sex couples the same rights, benefits, and protections that are offered only to married heterosexual couples in Vermont. It did not require the legislature to open up marriage to same-sex couples. In her partial dissent, Justice Denise Johnson stated that the majority should have enjoined the state from denying marriage licenses to same-sex couples (based on sex discrimination)[247] since the only acceptable remedy for the discrimination would be the opening up of marriage to same-sex couples: "[A]llowing plaintiffs to obtain a license would further the overall goals of marriage, as defined by the majority—to provide stability to individuals, their families, and the broader community by clarifying and protecting the rights of married persons."[248]

However, as discussed above, the legislature opted for a broad domestic partner scheme in lieu of same-sex marriage. The option of same-sex marriage was rejected by a vote of 8 to 3 in the House Judiciary Committee and by a vote of 125 to 22 of the full House of Representatives. The

---

246. Baker v. State of Vermont, 744 A.2d 864 (Vt. Sup. Ct. 1999).

247. Using reasoning similar to that of the supreme court of Hawaii in the matter of *Baehr*, Justice Johnson asserted that the marriage statutes established a classification based on sex, which was "simply a vestige of the common-law unequal marriage relationship," and thus that the exclusion of same-sex couples from marriage was "a straightforward case of sex discrimination." Moreover, none of the state's justifications meets the rational-basis test under the Common Benefits Clause. *Id.*

248. Baker v. State of Vermont, 744 A.2d 864 (Vt. Sup. Ct. 1999).

Senate Judiciary Committee voted unanimously to reject same-sex marriage in favor of the civil union bill, and the issue of same-sex marriage was never debated on the floor of the Senate. Instead, the legislature enacted the civil union law. Owing to the defense of marriage acts in more than thirty states and at the federal level, as well as general principles of conflict law—both of which are discussed in the sections that follow—an argument may be made that only by conferring the right to marry, which, at least potentially (i.e., if the defense of marriage acts were found to be unconstitutional), would have had federal and extra-territorial consequences, and not by enacting the civil union scheme, broad as it may be, would the Vermont legislature have fully met the equality mandate set down by the court.[249] The *Baker* court left its doors open for the plaintiffs to return to court if the Vermont legislature did not place same-sex couples on an equal footing with opposite-sex married couples.[250] The supreme court implicitly ruled that a broad domestic partner scheme conferring upon same-sex couples all the rights, benefits, and protections of marriage would suffice,[251] and by enacting the civil union act, the legislature indeed provided same-sex couples all the rights and protections of opposite-sex marriage in the state of Vermont. The fact that the legislature chose a separate scheme for gay couples was in accordance with the court's recommendations as to how the legislature might effectuate its ruling.[252] Thus, the civil union act seems to satisfy the requirements of the court in *Baker*. Moreover, once the civil union act took effect in July 2000, the three plaintiff couples terminated

249. *See* Lesbian/Gay Law Notes, January 2000, at 2.

250. "In the event that the benefits and protections in question are not statutorily granted, plaintiffs may petition this Court to order the remedy they originally sought." Baker v. State, 744 A.2d 864, at 887 (1999).

251. The majority held that although the plaintiffs initially sought a marriage license, their focus was on the benefits associated with marriage, and thus the majority concluded that "[w]hile some future case may attempt to establish [that] the denial of a marriage license operates per se to deny constitutionally-protected rights, that is *not* the claim we address today." Baker v. State, 744 A.2d 864, at 886 (1999). Later on in the decision, the court explicitly held that the plaintiffs were not necessarily entitled to a marriage license and that marriage was only *one* acceptable remedy among others ("That the State could do so through a marriage license is obvious. But *it is not* required to do so." *Id.* at 887, my emphasis).

252. The court stated that statutory schemes such as the Danish Registered Partnership Act or a broad version of domestic partnership are "potentially constitutional" and would suffice to fulfill its mandate, as long as they provided the same rights and benefits that flow from marriage in the state of Vermont. *See* Baker v. State, 744 A.2d 864, at 887–88 (1999) ("We do not intend specifically to endorse any one or all of the referenced acts, particularly in view of the significant *benefits omitted from several of the laws,*" my emphasis). For a critique of the civil union act as an objectionable separate but equal regime for same-sex couples, see chap. 10.

their lawsuit against the state, and in January 2001 the Vermont Supreme Court officially closed the case; the court's termination of jurisdiction indicates its satisfaction that civil unions meet the standards of the state constitution's equal-benefits clause and indicates that the court will not act to force inclusion of gays and lesbians under the existing marriage law.[253]

On April 11, 2001, a court challenge to the exclusion of same-sex couples from marriage was brought in Suffolk Superior Court in Massachusetts by seven gay and lesbian couples who had been denied marriage licenses at their city or town halls (*Goodridge v. Department of Public Health*).[254] If the *Goodridge* case follows exactly the same path as its Vermont counterpart, a decision from the high court could come as early as March 2003.[255] The lawsuit could be regarded as the first of the second wave of legal challenges seeking the right to marry (the first wave having ended with the supreme court decision in Vermont).[256] The couples are asking for actual marriage, not for an alternative scheme such as civil union. Mary Bonauto, the civil rights director of Gay and Lesbian Advocates and Defenders and cocounsel in the landmark Vermont marriage case, expressed her view that there was a good chance Massachusetts would recognize gay marriage, since

> Massachusetts has a long track record of leadership on civil-rights issues. In the lesbian and gay context, Massachusetts was the second state to pass a lesbian and gay civil-rights law [in 1989], amended the student nondiscrimination law to include sexual orientation [in 1993], and has a comprehensive hate-crimes law [as of 1996]. The Massachusetts Supreme Judicial Court was the second appellate court in the country to approve of second-parent adoption [three months behind Vermont in 1993], allows unmarried couples to create enforceable financial contracts [1998], and created rights for de facto parents who are not related to their children through birth, marriage or adoption [1999]. The state Constitution contains broad guarantees of freedom and equality which should apply forcefully in this case.[257]

253. *See* PlanetOut News Staff, *Vermont's Court Ends Civil Union Battle,* January 22, 2001.

254. The suit was filed by seven couples taking part in Gay and Lesbian Advocates & Defenders (GLAD). *See* Lawrence Ferber, *The Marrying Kind: Massachusetts Couples Hopeful As They Go to Court to Fight for the Right to Wed,* Frontiers Newsmagazine, April 27, 2001.

255. Barbara Dozetos, *Mass. Couples File Suit to Marry,* Gay.com/PlanetOut.com Network, April 11, 2001.

256. Deb Price, *Couples Deserve Equal Government Help,* Detroit News, April 23, 2001.

257. *See* Lawrence Ferber, note 254 above.

7.6.2 The Legislative Reaction—Federal and State
"Defense of Marriage" Laws

Despite the advances made toward legal recognition of same-sex part-nerships in general and same-sex marriage in particular, both in local governments and in the courts, a backlash has occurred in the federal and state legislatures.[258] As a reaction to the Hawaii Supreme Court deci-sion in the matter of *Baehr*,[259] many states and the federal government have passed laws to prevent the possibility of recognizing marriages be-tween same-sex couples, in case such marriages become possible in one or more states.

In 1996, although no state recognized same-sex marriage, Congress passed and the president signed the Defense of Marriage Act (DOMA),[260] which consists of two parts. The first one relieves states of any obligation under the Full Faith and Credit Clause by declaring that states need not recognize same-sex marriages registered in other jurisdictions.[261] The sec-ond part of the act provides that the federal government will recognize only opposite-sex marriages—defining marriage to be between a man and a woman for all purposes of federal law.[262] Accordingly, all federal statutes and regulations referring to either married persons or spouses are to be read as applying only to opposite-sex couples. In December 1996 the Administrative Office of the U.S. Courts issued a memorandum construing DOMA, according to which same-sex marriages could not be recognized for benefit entitlements under the Federal Employee Retire-ment System, the Civil Service Retirement System, the Federal Employ-ees Health Benefits Program, the Federal Employees Group Life Insur-ance, or the Family and Medical Leave Act.[263] Although a provision in

258. *See* Gilbert Zicklin, *Legal Trials and Tribulations on the Road to Same-Sex Marriage, in* On the Road to Same-Sex Marriage 129, 137–38 (Robert P. Cabaj & David W. Purcell eds., 1998).

259. Baehr v. Lewin, 852 P.2d 44 (Haw. 1993).

260. Pub. L. no.104-199, 110 Stat. 2419 (1996) (codified as 28 U.S.C. § 1738C [1996]) [hereinafter DOMA].

261. According to the act, "[n]o state, territory, or possession of the United States, or Indian tribe, shall be required to give effect to any public act, record, or judicial proceed-ing of any other State, territory, possession, or tribe respecting a relationship between persons of the same sex that is treated as a marriage under the laws of such other State, territory, possession, or tribe, or a right or claim arising from such relationship." 28 U.S.C.A. 1738C (West 1997).

262. DOMA adds the following definition of *marriage* and *spouse* to the U.S. Code: "In determining the meaning of any Act of Congress, or of any ruling, regulation or interpre-tation of the various administrative bureaus and agencies of the United States, the word 'marriage' means only a legal union between one man and one woman as husband and wife, and the word 'spouse' refers only to a person of the opposite sex who is a husband or a wife." 1 U.S.C.A. 7 (West 1997).

263. *See* 1 Conte, note 66 above, at 615.

DOMA allows states not to recognize same-sex marriages performed in another state, the act does not mandate that states disregard such marriages; each state needs to determine individually whether to take advantage of the act's exception to the Full Faith and Credit Clause of the U.S. Constitution.[264]

Accordingly, between 1996 and mid-2001 (also as a reaction to the Hawaii Supreme Court decision), thirty-five states passed laws that restrict marriage to opposite-sex couples by specifically defining marriage as a union between persons of the opposite-sex, specifically prohibiting marriage between persons of the same sex in the state, and avoiding recognition of same-sex marriages lawfully performed in other states.[265] The most controversial and publicized measure to prevent recognition of same-sex marriages has been California's "Knight Initiative" ("Proposition 22"), officially entitled the Limit on Marriage Initiative, an anti-same-sex-marriage ballot measure that was overwhelmingly passed by the voters on March 7, 2000.[266] The initiative added the following provision to the California Family Code: "Only a marriage between a man and a woman shall be valid or recognized."[267] Accordingly, California

264. *See* Beth A. Allen, *Same-Sex Marriage: A Conflict-of-Laws Analysis for Oregon,* 32 Willamette L. Rev. 619, 623 (1996).

265. As of August 2001 the thirty-five states with laws banning same-sex marriage were Alaska (in 1998, Alaska voters ratified an anti-same-sex-marriage amendment to their state constitution), Alabama (1998), Arkansas (1997), Arizona (1996), California (2000), Colorado (2000), Delaware (1996), Florida (1997), Georgia (1996), Hawaii (1996, 1998), Iowa (1998), Idaho (1996), Illinois (1996), Indiana (1997), Kansas (1996), Kentucky (1998), Louisiana (1999), Maine (1997), Michigan (1996), Minnesota (1997), Mississippi (1997), Missouri (2001), Montana (1997), North Carolina (1996), North Dakota (1997), Nebraska (2000), Oklahoma (1996), Pennsylvania (1996), South Carolina (1996), South Dakota (1996, 2000), Tennessee (1996), Utah (1995), Virginia (1997), Washington (1998), and West Virginia (2000). *See State Legislative Reactions to Suits for Same-Sex Marriage: Anti-Marriage Laws in the U.S.,* Partners Task Force for Gay and Lesbian Couples, at http://www.buddybuddy.com/toc.html (last updated June 2001); Pamela Ferdinand, *Vermont Legislature Clears Bill Allowing Civil Unions: Gay Couples Given Rights like Those of Married Couples,* Washington Post, April 25, 2000. For an analysis of the specific language of the statutes enacted prior to 1998, see David Orgon Coolidge & William C. Duncan, *Definition or Discrimination? State Marriage Recognition Statutes in the "Same-Sex Marriage" Debate,* 32 Creighton L. Rev. 3, 11–13 (1998). It should be noted that decisions to restrict marriage to opposite-sex couples date as early as 1975, and presumably the early ones were a reaction to the first same-sex marriage cases discussed above. Thus, the attorneys general of seven states have issued opinions that same-sex marriage is prohibited in their states: Colorado (1975), South Carolina (1976), Kansas (1977), Mississippi (1978), Alabama (1983), Maine (1984), and Tennessee (1988). *See* Rubinstein, note 98 above, at 749.

266. Sixty-one percent supported the gay marriage ban. *See* Bob Egelko, *Effects of Gay Marriage Ban Unknown,* Associated Press, March 8, 2000. For further discussion of the initiative, see Ingram, note 160 above; *Freedom to Marry Update,* note 232 above.

267. Michael S. Wald, Same-Sex Couples: Marriage, Families, and Children: An Analysis of Proposition 22—the Knight Initiative, at v (1999). For an extensive analysis of the initiative and its implications, see id.

would not recognize same-sex marriages entered into in other states. The passage of the initiative in California, the most populous state in the union, was viewed by many as the most contentious and crucial measure of its kind in the country and the most detrimental to the rights of same-sex couples. Moreover, the debate regarding the measure was framed in terms of a referendum on same-sex marriage itself, rather than the recognition thereof.[268] Three more states are considering legislation that would prohibit recognition of same-sex marriages in their states.[269] The "defense of marriage" laws have been termed by different scholars "anti-recognition statutes," "anti-marriage laws," or "anti-gay initiatives,"[270] whereas proponents of these laws prefer to use more positive terms, such as "marriage recognition statutes."[271] I will employ the term *anti-same-sex-marriage laws,* which seems to be an accurate description of the nature and intent of these statutes. The anti-same-sex-marriage laws invoke a public-policy exception for out-of-state same-sex marriages, so that such marriages would be void in the states that have passed these statutes.[272]

It should be noted that while states have been adopting anti-same-sex-marriage laws, bills to legalize same-sex marriage have also been introduced in a number of states. However, these bills, except for the two that are still pending in Rhode Island and New York, have all failed.[273] During the period January 2000 through December 2001, bills banning same-sex marriage have been introduced in fourteen states; four have passed, two are still pending, and such measures have been blocked in eight other states.[274]

268. *Id. See also Fact Sheet: Update on the National Fight to Win the Freedom to Marry,* Lambda Legal Defense and Education Fund, June 29, 1999, available from Lambda's National Headquarters in New York.

269. Those states are Colorado, Nevada, and Ohio. *See State Legislative Reactions,* note 265 above.

270. *See, e.g.,* Germaine Winnick Willett, *Equality under the Law or Annihilation of Marriage and Morals? The Same Sex Marriage Debate,* 73 Ind. L.J. 355 (1997); Jennifer Gerarda Brown, *Extraterritorial Recognition of Same-Sex Marriage: When Theory Confronts Praxis,* 16 Quinnipiac L. Rev. 1 (1996); Barbara Cox, *Are Same-Sex Marriage Statutes the New Anti-Gay Initiatives?* 2 Nat'l J. Sexual Orientation L. 194 (1996); Knauer, note 124 above; Barbara A. Robb, Note, *The Constitutionality of the Defense of Marriage Act in the Wake of Romer v. Evans,* 32 New Eng. L. Rev. 263 (1997); Lisa M. Farabee, Note, *Marriage, Equal Protection, and the New Judicial Federalism: A View from the States,* 14 Yale L. & Pol'y Rev. 237 (1996).

271. *See, e.g.,* Coolidge & Duncan, note 265 above, at 14.

272. For an overview of legislative process as well as the nature and content of anti-same-sex-marriage bills in various states, see Coolidge & Duncan, note 265 above, at 5–13.

273. Such bills were proposed in Nebraska, Maryland, Oregon, New York, Washington, Wisconsin, and Rhode Island. *See State Legislative Reactions,* note 265 above.

274. The anti-same-sex-marriage bills were adopted in California, Missouri, Nebraska, and West Virginia; such bills are still pending in Nevada and Colorado; similar measures

Anti-same-sex-marriage laws may have detrimental implications regarding the equal rights of lesbians and gay men in other areas of life, beyond the exclusion from civil marriage. Lambda Legal Defense and Education Fund forewarns that such laws could be regarded as "a public policy license to discriminate against lesbian and gay couples" and could be used to prohibit domestic partnership registries and plans and to deny adoptions and custody to gay men and lesbians, as well as to allow sexual orientation discrimination.[275] Although such concerns may be somewhat overwrought from a legal perspective, no doubt arguments of this sort will be used by opponents of gay rights.

7.6.3 Choice of Law and the Prospects of Full Recognition of Same-Sex Marriage in the United States

Even if same-sex couples gain access to the institution of marriage in one state or another, the federal Defense of Marriage Act and similar state laws may perpetuate discrimination against their marriages across state lines. Moreover, the complexity of conflict laws, the abundance of choice-of-law theories, and the court's wide discretion in these matters suggest that it is far from clear whether even states that have not enacted versions of DOMA will recognize out-of-state same-sex marriages. I analyze these questions first with regard to general choice-of-law considerations and later in light of the federal and state defense of marriage acts.

Article 4, section 1, of the U.S. Constitution states that "Full Faith and Credit shall be given in each State to the public Acts, Records, and judicial proceedings of every other State." If same-sex marriage is legalized in one or more states, the question will arise whether marriages performed there are to be recognized in other jurisdictions. It is debatable whether the U.S. Constitution will compel such recognition, because the Full Faith and Credit Clause has not commonly been relied upon by courts in determining whether they should recognize out-of-state marriages (e.g., common law marriages) that could not have been performed within the jurisdiction.[276] Such considerations therefore will be made not only in light of the Full Faith and Credit Clause but also based on other conflict-law rules. Notwithstanding the Full Faith and Credit Clause, in situations involving marriage validity, and according

---

have been blocked in New York, New Jersey, Massachusetts, New Hampshire, Maryland, Wyoming, New Mexico, and Texas. The only states in which anti-same-sex-marriage bills have thus far not been proposed are Oregon, Wisconsin, Connecticut, and Rhode Island. *See id.*

275. *Freedom to Marry Update,* note 232 above.

276. *See* 1 Conte, note 66 above, at 632, citing Andrew Sullivan *in* New Republic, December 30, 1996, at 15–16.

to traditional choice-of-law rules, courts have generally followed the rule of *lex celebrationis,* which states that a marriage valid where entered into should be recognized as valid everywhere, and the tendency in American conflicts cases is to validate marriages entered into in other jurisdictions, unless the legislature has rejected the rule of validity or the marriage is so abominable that validating it would offend the public sense of morality. Although each state has its own conflicts doctrine, many states look to the *Restatement (Second) of Conflicts of Laws* (1996) for direction,[277] which states in its pertinent section that a marriage valid in the state where it was contracted will be recognized as valid by other states unless it violates a strong public policy.[278]

An argument that is likely to be made as soon as one state recognizes the right of same-sex couples to marry is that other states can avoid recognition since same-sex marriages violate public policy, especially in states that still criminalize consensual sodomy.[279] Larry Kramer argues that the public-policy exception is unconstitutional and that states should uphold the validity of same-sex marriages, concluding that if same-sex marriage is allowed in one state, it should be generally recognized by other states unless other choice-of-law rules dictate otherwise.[280] Other commentators have argued, based on the public-policy exception, that states are free to lawfully refuse to recognize such marriages and that one state cannot and should not "bind the world."[281]

277. 1 Conte, note 66 above, at 631–32.

278. *See* Restatement (Second) of Conflicts of Laws (1971), § 283.

279. For the public-policy exception and states' recognition of same-sex marriages, see Lynn Hogue, *State Common-Law Choice-of-Law Doctrine and Same-Sex "Marriage": How Will States Enforce the Public Policy Exception?* 32 Creighton L. Rev. 29 (1998); Richard S. Myers, *Same-Sex "Marriage" and the Public Policy Doctrine,* 32 Creighton L. Rev. 45 (1998); Michael E. Solimine, *Competitive Federalism and Interstate Recognition of Marriage,* 32 Creighton L. Rev. 83 (1998).

280. *See* Larry Kramer, *Same-Sex Marriage, Conflict of Laws, and the Unconstitutional Public Policy Exception,* 106 Yale L.J. 1965 (1997) [hereinafter *Same-Sex Marriage*] (arguing that states do not have the ability to assert policy interests for only certain kinds of marriages, such as same-sex marriages, and that they may not distinguish between the choice-of-law rules they apply to different impediments to marriage). Kramer further argues that states should adhere to the traditional rule of upholding the validity of a marriage that is valid where it was celebrated and that the "public policy exception," which could be used to refuse recognition of same-sex marriages, is unconstitutional; he reasons that the public-policy exception violates the Full Faith and Credit Clause and that "the Full Faith and Credit Clause prohibits states from selectively discriminating in choice of law based on judgments about the desirability or obnoxiousness of other states' policies." Thus, states should not refuse recognition of same-sex marriages celebrated lawfully elsewhere, based on public policy. *See also* Larry Kramer, *The Public Policy Exception and the Problem of Extra-Territorial Recognition of Same-Sex Marriage,* 16 Quinnipiac L. Rev. 153 (1996).

281. *See* Linda J. Silberman, *Can the Island of Hawaii Bind the World? A Comment on Same-Sex Marriage and Federalism Values,* 16 Quinnipiac L. Rev. 191 (1996).

Notwithstanding arguments about its constitutionality, there is an overwhelming tendency not to invoke the public-policy exception and to recognize out-of-state marriages,[282] with the exception of those states that have marriage-evasion statutes that declare void marriages of persons who travel elsewhere in order to avoid their home state's marriage restrictions.[283] Therefore, it is likely that at least some of the states would recognize "Vermont marriages." Some strong arguments have been made that states are obliged to do so by virtue of conflict-law principles, the Full Faith and Credit Clause, the right to interstate travel, and the fundamental interest in marriage.[284]

The federal DOMA and state-enacted anti-same-sex-marriage laws that purport to prevent such recognition further complicate choice-of-law questions. These statutes indicate that those states have decided that there exists a strong public-policy exception to the recognition of same-sex marriages entered into in other states. It thus seems as though by virtue of these statutes, the question of recognition of same-sex marriages has been fully answered: no recognition for federal purposes and

282. *See* Barbara J. Cox, *Same-Sex Marriage and the Public Policy Exception in Choice-of-Law: Does It Really Exist?* 16 Quinnipiac L. Rev. 61 (1996). Based on an evaluation of countless court decisions pertaining to the public-policy exception and recognition of out-of-state marriages in thirty-two states, Cox concludes that except for states with marriage-evasion statutes, although courts recognize the existence of a public-policy exception, they do not use it to refuse to validate an out-of-state marriage, even when the domicile has an explicit statutory prohibition against the marriage in question.

283. *See* Andrew Koppelman, *Same-Sex Marriage, Choice of Law, and Public Policy,* 76 Tex. L. Rev. 921, 923 (1998). Thirteen states and the District of Columbia currently have marriage-evasion statutes. *Id.* In contrast, in a number of other states, there are statutes validating all foreign marriages that are valid where celebrated, with no public-policy exception. *Id.*

284. *See* Thomas M. Keane, Note, *Aloha, Marriage? Constitutional and Choice of Law Arguments for Recognition of Same-Sex Marriages,* 47 Stan. L. Rev. 499 (1995). *See also* Mark Strasser, *Judicial Good Faith and the Baehr Essentials: On Giving Credit Where It's Due,* 28 Rutgers L.J. 313 (1997) (arguing that courts cannot in good faith refuse to recognize a same-sex marriage legally celebrated in another state unless the legislature of the domicile has declared that such marriages will not be recognized); Habib A. Balian, Note, *Till Death Do Us Part: Granting Full Faith and Credit to Marital Status,* 68 S. Car. L. Rev. 397 (1995) (arguing that other states should grant full faith and credit to Hawaiian same-sex marital decrees because other states' interests for not doing so pale in comparison to the interests at stake for married couples and Hawaii); Barbara J. Cox, *Same-Sex Marriage and Choice of Law: If We Marry in Hawaii, Are We Still Married When We Return Home?* 1994 Wis. L. Rev. 1033 (surveys the major choice-of-law theories and concludes that courts, when faced with the question whether to recognize out-of-state same-sex marriages, should rule in the affirmative based on an analogy to choice-of-law decisions pertaining to antimiscegenation statutes, advocating the adoption of "the better rule of law" to resolve these conflicts by way of recognition of out-of-state same-sex marriages); Joseph W. Hovermill, *A Conflict of Laws and Morals: The Choice of Law Implications of Hawaii's Recognition of Same-Sex Marriages,* 53 Md. L. Rev. 450 (1994) (arguing that a court should not refuse to recognize a same-sex marriage legally performed in another state unless the state legislature has clearly stated a public policy to the contrary).

no recognition in the large number of states that have enacted versions of DOMA.

However, it is highly questionable whether the federal DOMA is constitutional. First, it seems that the federal DOMA could be challenged as a violation of the constitutional principle of full faith and credit. This would be based on the argument that Congress overstepped its grant of legislative authority, since it has power to give force to full faith and credit but not to remove the requirements of the clause. An argument can also be made that Congress intruded on a constitutional power reserved to the states, since matters relating to domestic relations have traditionally been within the sovereignty of the states. Second, the act can be challenged based on arguments grounded in substantive guarantees, such as the equal-protection component of the due process clause and respect for lawful marriages based on the fundamental right to marriage.[285] With regard to the equal-protection argument, it has been suggested that the courts should invalidate DOMA based on the precedent set by the Supreme Court in *Romer v. Evans*,[286] in which the Court held that a law that stemmed from mere animus toward gays and lesbians would not pass equal-protection scrutiny because it would be based on

---

285. *See* Mark Strasser, *Baker and Some Recipes for Disaster: On DOMA, Covenant Marriages, and Full Faith and Credit Jurisprudence*, 64 Brooklyn L. Rev. 307 (1998) (arguing that the Full Faith and Credit and the Due Process Clauses prohibit Congress from passing DOMA and prevent states from refusing to recognize marriages valid in the states of celebration and domicile at the time of the marriage); Kramer, *Same-Sex Marriage*, note 280 above (arguing that DOMA is unconstitutional: Congress's power to create choice-of-law rules is limited under the Effects Clause of art. 4 since Congress cannot authorize states to selectively discriminate against each other's laws); Evan Wolfson & Michael F. Melcher, *Constitutional and Legal Defects in the "Defense of Marriage" Act*, 16 Quinnipiac L. Rev. 221 (1996) (arguing that DOMA is unconstitutional since Congress has no power to limit Full Faith and Credit nor to regulate domestic relations law, particularly: defining and regulating civil marriage is within the jurisdictions of the states and not the federal government. DOMA is also unconstitutional as an abridgment of the right to marry and the right to travel and is a violation of the constitutional guarantee of equal protection). *See also* Heather Hamilton, Comment, *The Defense of Marriage Act: A Critical Analysis of Its Constitutionality under the Full Faith and Credit Clause*, 47 DePaul L. Rev. 943 (1998); Scott Ruskay-Kidd, Note, *The Defense of Marriage Act and the Overextension of Congressional Authority*, 97 Colum. L. Rev. 1435 (1997); Stanley E. Cox, *DOMA and Conflicts Law: Congressional Rules and Domestic Relations Conflicts Law*, 32 Creighton L. Rev. 1063 (1999); and Kristian D. Whitten, *Section Three of the Defense of Marriage Act: Is Marriage Reserved to the States?* 26 Hastings Const. L.Q. 419 (1999). The Establishment Clause has also been used to question the constitutionality of DOMA: *see* James M. Donovan, *DOMA: An Unconstitutional Establishment of Fundamentalist Christianity*, 4 Mich. J. Gender & L. 335 (1997). Only a few commentators hold the view that DOMA is not in violation of the Constitution: *see, e.g.,* Daniel A. Crane, *The Original Understanding of the "Effects Clause" of Article IV, Section 1 and Implications for the Defense of Marriage Act*, 6 Geo. Mason L. Rev. 307 (1998); Ralph U. Whitten, *The Original Understanding of the Full Faith and Credit Clause and the Defense of Marriage Act*, 32 Creighton L. Rev. 255 (1998).

286. 517 U.S. 620 (1996).

irrational prejudice and motivated by unconstitutional bias toward gays and lesbians without any legitimate governmental interest.[287] Similar arguments support the assertion that state-enacted versions of DOMA are unconstitutional as well.[288]

Furthermore, even if state and federal DOMAs pass constitutional muster, there are scholars who claim that states would still be obliged to recognize out-of-state same-sex marriages, building on precedents pertaining to recognition of interracial marriages, according to which it would be wrong to invoke a public-policy exception for same-sex marriages.[289]

287. *See* Robb, note 270 above (arguing that DOMA is unconstitutional under the equal-protection component of the Fifth Amendment's Due Process Clause in light of the similarities between the amendment, which was scrutinized in the case of *Romer v. Evans,* and DOMA, since both are motivated by animus and single out gays and lesbians by broadly denying them protection); Andrew Koppelman, *Dumb and DOMA: Why the Defense of Marriage Act Is Unconstitutional,* 83 Iowa L. Rev. 1 (1997) (arguing that DOMA is unconstitutional based on an equal-protection analysis that relies on *Romer v. Evans,* owing to the similarities between that case and the provisions of DOMA; Koppelman further argues that Congress was limited by the Due Process Clause, rather than the Full Faith Clause); Cass R. Sunstein, *The Supreme Court 1995 Term Forward: Leaving Things Undecided,* 110 Harv. L. Rev. 4 (1996), 97 n. 492 (suggesting that DOMA is a violation of the equal-protection component of the Fifth Amendment's Due Process Clause, because it transgresses the "impermissible selectivity" principle of *Romer v. Evans*); Evan Wolfson & Michael F. Melcher, *The Supreme Court's Decision in Romer v. Evans and Its Implications for the Defense of Marriage Act,* 16 Quinnipiac L. Rev. 217 (1996) (arguing that the federal DOMA is unconstitutional on equal-protection grounds based on the Supreme Court's decision in the matter of *Romer v. Evans*). *See also* Kevin H. Lewis, Note, *Equal Protection after Romer v. Evans: Implications for the Defense of Marriage Act and Other Laws,* 49 Hastings L.J. 175 (1997).

288. *See, e.g.,* Nancy J. Feather, *Emerging Issues in State Constitutional Law: Article: Defense of Marriage Acts: An Analysis under State Constitutional Law,* 70 Temple L. Rev. 1017 (1997) (arguing that state DOMAs may be regarded as unconstitutional because state constitutions often provide for greater individual rights in terms of privacy, equal rights, and equal protection than does the federal Constitution; further, federal and state DOMAs are unnecessary, since even without them states could use traditional means for avoiding the recognition of same-sex marriages performed legally in other states; the underlying justification for the enactment of DOMA provides the basis for refusing to recognize the marriage because it is considered an affront to existing state public policy); Cox, note 270 above (applying *Romer v. Evans* and arguing that states' anti-same-sex-marriage laws are unconstitutional because their purpose is to discriminate against same-sex couples). *See also* Jennifer Wriggins, *Maine's "Act to Protect Traditional Marriage and Prohibit Same-Sex Marriages": Questions of Constitutionality under State and Federal Law,* 50 Me. L. Rev. 345 (1998); Bradley J. Betlach, *The Unconstitutionality of the Minnesota Defense of Marriage Act: Ignoring Judgments, Restricting Travel, and Purposeful Discrimination,* 24 Wm. Mitchell L. Rev. 407 (1998); Michael J. Kanotz, Comment, *For Better or for Worse: A Critical Analysis of Florida's Defense of Marriage Act,* 25 Fla. St. U. L. Rev. 439 (1998). For an argument that states' versions of DOMA are constitutional, see Coolidge & Duncan, note 265 above.

289. *See* Koppelman, note 283 above (arguing that in states that did not enact a DOMA statute, as well as in states that have adopted a version of DOMA, there is no public-policy exception against same-sex marriages that would be sufficient to invalidate them if they were recognized by other states. State DOMA laws do not foreclose choice-of-law reasoning, and none of them support a blanket rule of nonrecognition, which is also objection-

Only after one of the states makes marriage accessible to same-sex couples could challenges to these laws be brought before the courts. If one or more American states recognize same-sex marriages, most other states and the federal government will probably refuse to recognize such unions based on their defense of marriage acts or on the argument that such unions violate their public policies. Full recognition of same-sex marriages in the United States will be possible only if and when the U.S. Supreme Court decides that both state and federal DOMAs are unconstitutional and that states cannot constitutionally invoke a public-policy exception to refuse recognition of out-of-state same-sex marriages, as it did in the case of antimiscegenation laws more than thirty years ago.[290] Until then, same-sex marriages in the United States will probably not be recognized beyond the borders of the individual state that decides in favor of opening up marriage to same-sex couples, and such recognition will likely be limited in its scope, that is, only for intrastate purposes. This would be so unless states recognize a same-sex marriage validly performed elsewhere in spite of their power not to do so (i.e., if the federal DOMA is upheld). Absent statute or case law making it clear which way the state will go, there will be no guarantee that a sister state will recognize such a marriage. The states that have enacted their own version of DOMA would not recognize a same-sex marriage lawfully entered into in another state, and if such mini-DOMAs are upheld, then recognition would be denied in the majority of sister states. Hence, it seems that full marital equality for gays and lesbians with opposite-sex married couples is not to be expected anytime soon. In the words of one commentator: "A married gay couple traveling on this country's interstate roadways would, without much fiction, present its marriage license at each border crossing. And the legend would read, 'void where prohibited by law.' "[291]

---

able as a radical departure from preexisting choice-of-law principles). As to the obligation of states to recognize out-of-state same-sex marriages, see also Mark Strasser, *For Whom Bell Tolls: On Subsequent Domiciles' Refusing to Recognize Same-Sex Marriage,* 66 U. Cin. L. Rev. 339 (1998).

290. *See* Loving v. Virginia, 388 U.S. 1 (1967).

291. *See* Rodney Patton, *A Focus Edition: Domestic Issues and Crimes of Intimacy: Student Work: Queerly Unconstitutional? South Carolina Bans Same-Sex Marriage,* 48 S.C. L. Rev. 685, 704 (1997).

Chapter 8

Contrasts between the Models of Recognition and the Status of Same-Sex Partnerships in the United States and Northern Europe

The preceding chapters provide separate analyses of the status of same-sex partnerships in various countries and regions, emphasizing the individual country's unique form of recognition and the scope of protections, rights, and benefits it confers upon same-sex couples. In this chapter we return to the two main models of recognition that serve as alternatives to marriage for same-sex couples—registered partnership and domestic partnership.[1]

8.1 The European Registered Partnership Acts

Previous chapters provide a detailed overview of the registered partnership acts of the Nordic countries—Denmark, Norway, Sweden, Iceland, Finland—and the Netherlands. Also discussed are the French PaCS and the German life partnership, which resemble in some pertinent aspects the northern European registered partnership acts and are to be regarded as variations of this model. As illustrated in table 1, whereas the Nordic states and Germany limit the applicability of their registered partnership acts to same-sex couples, the Netherlands and France offer the same

1. For a detailed examination and discussion of the cohabitation model, see chap. 6. This model is applicable only in Canada, Australia, and New Zealand, since, as explained in chap. 2, it is limited to countries that have extensive regulation of unmarried cohabitation for opposite-sex couples.

Table 1 Registered Partnerships in Europe

Country	Residence & Citizenship Requirements	Recognition of Foreign Registered Partnership in Domestic Law?	Immigration Rights for Foreign Registered Partner?	Parental Provisions	Availability of Assisted Procreation (Insemination & IVF)	Church Ceremony	Registration & Dissolution	Open to Opposite-Sex Partners?	Regulation of Cohabitation Other than Registered Partnership?
Denmark 1989	One partner must be citizen/resident of Denmark, Norway, Sweden, or Iceland, or both residents of Denmark for 2 years	From Norway, Sweden, Iceland; minister of justice has discretion to recognize from other countries	Yes, if one is Danish national (like marriage); if no registered partnership, like cohabitation	No joint custody; can adopt only partner's child/ren (unless originally adopted from foreign country); cannot jointly adopt unrelated children	Not for lesbians or single women	No state-sanctioned church wedding for registered partners; individual priests allowed	Like marriage; act refers to legislation regarding marriage and divorce	No	No
Norway 1993	One partner must be citizen and resident	From Denmark, Iceland, Sweden	Yes, if one is a Norwegian national (like marriage)	No joint custody; cannot adopt partner's child/ren or jointly adopt unrelated children; individual adoption allowed	Not for lesbians or single women	Same as Denmark	Same as Denmark	No	Joint Household Act applicable to heterosexual couples only
Sweden 1995	One partner must be citizen and resident or both residents of Sweden for 2 years	From any country with a registered partnership act	Yes, if one is Swedish national (like marriage)	No joint custody; cannot adopt partner's child/ren or jointly adopt unrelated children	Not for lesbians or single women	Same as Denmark	Same as Denmark	No	Cohabitees (Joint Home) Act extended to homosexuals in 1987
Iceland 1996	Same as Denmark	From Denmark, Sweden, Norway	Yes, if one is Icelandic national (like marriage)	Automatic joint custody; can adopt only partner's children;	Not for lesbians or single women	Same as Denmark	Same as Denmark	No	No

Netherlands 1998	One partner must be either citizen or lawful resident	No (except for Dutch citizens who registered in Nordic countries)	Yes, if one is Dutch national (like marriage)	cannot jointly adopt unrelated children Joint custody available—1998 law on custody, court order required; as of 2001, can adopt partner's children and jointly adopt unrelated children from within Netherlands	Yes: no restrictions; protection from discrimination if service not provided	No; state recognizes only civil ceremony of both same- and opposite-sex couples	Like marriage; optional dissolution agreement out of court	Yes	Yes; regulation in various fields for both same- and opposite-sex couples
France PaCS 1999	Both partners must be legal residents in France	No	No automatic right; PaCS to be considered among other factors as a personal tie to France	No joint custody; cannot adopt partner's children or jointly adopt unrelated children	Not for lesbians or single women	No; same as Netherlands	Notification to court; no application of divorce laws	Yes	Regulation of cohabitation extended by PaCS to same-sex cohabitants
Germany 2000	No citizenship/residency requirements	No	Yes	Joint custody allowed; cannot adopt partner's children or jointly adopt unrelated children	Not for lesbians or single women	No	Court proceeding	No	Yes, only for heterosexual couples
Finland 2002	Same as Denmark	Yes, from any country with a registered partnership act	Yes (like common law couples)	Joint custody allowed; cannot adopt partner's child/ren or jointly adopt unrelated children	Not regulated; available in practice	No	Same as Denmark	No	No

framework of regulation to both same- and opposite-sex couples.[2] Thus, opposite-sex couples in the Nordic states and Germany can choose between marriage and cohabitation. Opposite-sex couples in the Netherlands and France can choose cohabitation, registered partnership (PaCS in France), or marriage. Same-sex couples in all states but the Netherlands have two options: either cohabiting or registering a partnership. What same-sex couples have in common in these jurisdictions is that they are excluded from the institution of marriage (except, of course, for same-sex marriage in the Netherlands). *Opposite*-sex couples in the Netherlands and France can choose among three forms of legally regulated cohabitation, since these countries have created a third gender-neutral category for the recognition of partnerships. Thus, in the Netherlands and France, same-sex couples and opposite-sex couples have the same regulatory options (except that in France, marriage is not open to same-sex couples). Should we therefore conclude that the status of same-sex couples is more equal to that of opposite-sex couples in France than in the Nordic states and Germany? I think not. It is only that *opposite*-sex couples in France enjoy an additional form for regulating their partnerships. If any disparity between these jurisdictions exists, it is between the status of opposite-sex couples in Germany and the Nordic states on the one hand and in France on the other, and we may consider them discriminated against in Germany and the Nordic states, since they are excluded from the registered partnership acts.

Moreover, if we look to the rationale for the exclusion or inclusion of opposite-sex couples in the registered partnership acts of the different countries, we find that in all seven countries, whether or not their acts eventually included heterosexual couples, the motivation for introducing an additional form of cohabitation was the same: a desire to regulate the status of same-sex partnerships and accord the partners rights traditionally associated with marriage. The inclusion of heterosexual couples (in the Netherlands and France), merely reflected a desire to please the heterosexual majority or to expand the available options.

The underlying rationale for the exclusion of opposite-sex couples from registered partnership in Denmark and Norway was apparently the wish to preserve the predominance of the institution of marriage and to discourage heterosexual couples from choosing other forms of part-

2. Table 1 addresses only countries with a registered partnership act; thus, Hungary and Portugal, whose recognition of same-sex couples is more akin to the cohabitation model than to the registered partnership acts, are excluded from the table. The Belgian act on same-sex partnerships is extremely limited and is mainly symbolic; therefore, it is also not included in table 1 and is not addressed in the comparative discussion that follows.

nership regulation.[3] Sweden and Germany did not see any reason to include opposite-sex couples in their registered partnership acts, simply because these couples have the option of marriage. France had initially considered an act similar to the Nordic one, which would have been reserved for same-sex couples, and it was due to vast public and political opposition that later versions of the PaCS extended its application to opposite-sex couples.[4] It is for similar political reasons that the scope of the rights and benefits provided by the PaCS were narrowed in each and every draft until it reached its current version, which lacks most rights associated with marriage. The public in France was less threatened by an institution that would regulate the status of heterosexual couples as well as of homosexual couples. Inclusion of opposite-sex partners made the PaCS less controversial and more publicly acceptable and consequently led to its adoption. Had it not included opposite-sex couples in its bill, the French parliament would not have been able to portray the PaCS as merely another option for recognizing the partnerships of straight couples, which is *also,* but not primarily, applicable to gay men and lesbians. Finally, the Netherlands, rather like Sweden, encourages all forms of cohabitation equally, with no preference given to one model over the other; it wishes to provide its citizens with multitudinous and diverse options for regulating their status. It is for this reason that the Dutch legislature decided not to limit the registered partnership act to same-sex couples, although the impetus for introducing a registered partnership act was similar to that in the Nordic countries—to place same-sex couples on an equal footing with opposite-sex married couples. At the same time, the inclusion of heterosexual couples in the Dutch act was not meant to further the equality of same-sex couples as compared to opposite-sex couples. The gender-neutral language of the act was simply intended to provide opposite-sex couples with an additional

3. *See* Norway Ministry of Children and Family Affairs, The Norwegian Act on Registered Partnerships for Homosexual Couples 27–30 (1993) [hereinafter The Norwegian Bill]. For the same reason—preservation of marriage as the predominant institution—all Nordic countries with the exception of Sweden largely refrain from regulating the status of unmarried cohabitants, so as not to discourage opposite-sex couples from getting married. *See id.*

4. The first version of the French PaCS arose from a 1992 bill and was called Contract d'Union Civile (CUC); it was limited to the regulation of *gay* partnerships. In 1997 the CUC bill was rewritten, and the partnership it established was named Contract d'Union Sociale (CUS); it also was limited to same-sex couples. Not until 1998, after the latter bill was redrafted and the partnership renamed Pacte Civil de Solidarité (PaCS), did the Socialist party expand the bill to apply to any two people living together in concubinage (this was later limited to couples, either same- or different-sex couples). The inclusion of opposite-sex couples in later versions of the PaCS (in summer 1998) was politically motivated, since support was to be enlisted both from the public and from certain members of right-wing and Christian parties.

form of cohabitation. I thus conclude that the question of whether registered partnerships are limited to same-sex couples or not has no bearing on the degree of equality provided to same-sex couples. It is an irrelevant distinction between the various countries in the assessment of the relative degree of equality provided to same-sex couples.

The acts in the seven countries also differ in terms of their citizenship and residency requirements (see table 1). According to the Norwegian act, one partner must be a citizen and a resident in order for the couple to be eligible for registration. In Denmark, Sweden, and Iceland, it is sufficient for one of the partners to be a citizen of the country or that *both* partners have been lawful residents for two years prior to registration. According to the Dutch act, one partner must be either a citizen or a lawful resident of the Netherlands. According to the French PaCS, it is enough for both partners to be legal residents in France when entering a pact. Finally, the German act has the most relaxed requirements in this respect, as it has no citizenship or residency requirements.

In terms of parental rights or the lack thereof, the legislation and policies in these countries are similar except for a few minor distinctions (see table 1). Denmark, the Netherlands, and Iceland allow registered partners to adopt each other's children, but, unlike the Netherlands, Denmark and Iceland still prohibit the partners from jointly adopting unrelated children. Norway, Sweden, France, and Germany all prohibit same-sex registered partners from adopting each other's children or jointly adopting an unrelated child. Moreover, joint custody of partners over each other's children is available automatically only in Iceland and Germany, and only if the parent-partner had sole custody over the child at the time the partnership was entered into. Joint custody is also available in the Netherlands but requires a court order. Denmark, Norway, Sweden, and France do not grant custody rights to same-sex couples. Access to artificial insemination and in vitro fertilization services is available only in the Netherlands; the rest of the registered partnership countries prohibit lesbians and single women from using artificial procreation, limiting such services to cohabiting or married opposite-sex couples.

When it comes to rights, benefits, and obligations, it should be noted that the French PaCS and the German life partnership act are much more limited than the registered partnership acts of the northern European countries. Unlike the registered partnership acts, the life partnership and the PaCS do not incorporate and apply existing marriage law to same-sex couples, with a few exceptions; rather, they provide for a limited set of rights enumerated in their acts. Registration of a partnership in the northern European countries takes place in city hall with a ceremony akin to marriage, but a PaCS is entered into by the couple's common notification of a court clerk. Moreover, also unlike registered partnership and life partnership, a pact does not alter one's status as single and is not a bar for a subsequent marriage, which would simply terminate the pact. Whereas regular divorce proceedings are applicable to the dissolution of a registered partnership in the northern European countries (in cases of mutual consent, the Dutch act provides for dissolution by agreement out of court with notification of the registrar in addition to regular divorce proceedings), a PaCS is terminated by joint or unilateral notification given to the court clerk. In this respect, the German act is closer to the northern European acts, since it provides for court proceedings for the dissolution of a life partnership and the division of property. Furthermore, whereas all northern European countries and Germany provide immigration rights to the foreign registered partner, a PaCS does not confer immigration rights on the foreign partner and is only one of the factors to be considered in assessing a foreign partner's personal ties to France.

The Nordic countries recognize each other's registered partnerships (with Sweden also recognizing partnerships entered into in the Netherlands), but France and Germany do not recognize foreign registered partnerships, and the Netherlands recognizes partnerships entered into in the Nordic countries only if the partners are Dutch citizens.

There is also a disparity among the different countries in the relative number of partnerships that have been registered; statistics show that the institution is more popular in the Netherlands than in the Nordic countries (France and Germany are excluded from this comparison because there is not enough information yet on the numbers of partnerships in those countries to make any conclusions for a statistical comparison). In Denmark, with a population of approximately 5.5 million, during the first full year registration was available, 450 couples registered their partnership, and throughout the period October 1989 through December 1999, a total of 2,908 couples registered (1,077 female couples and 1,831 male couples). The number of registrations in Norway, with a population of approximately 4.5 million, was 133 during the first full year and a total of 892 between August 1993 and December 1999 (319 female couples and 573 male couples). In Sweden, with a population of approximately 8.9 million, 333 couples registered during the first full year, and between 1995 and the end of 2000, 1,072 registrations took place (378 female couples and 694 male couples); Iceland, with a population of approximately .3 million, recorded 12 registrations during the first full year and 57 from July 1996 through December 1999 (27 between men and 30 between women); the Netherlands, with an approximate population of 16 million, recorded 4,626 registrations during the first year (3,010 same-sex couples—with the number of female couples close to that of male couples [27% more male couples]; and 1,616 between opposite-sex couples). We find that the interest of same-sex couples in registering their partnership in the Netherlands (without taking into account the number of opposite-sex registrations, which are possible only in the Netherlands)—adjusted for population size during the same time period—is about six times higher than in Norway, five times higher than in Sweden, and about two and a half times higher than in Denmark, making the total of Dutch registration rates 3.8 times higher than those of the Scandinavian states as a whole. Moreover, the number of same-sex male partnerships in comparison to the number of female partnerships is more equal in the Netherlands, whereas at least two times as many same-sex male partnerships as female partnerships are entered into on average in the Nordic countries, making female registered partnerships more popular in the Netherlands than in any other country.[5]

8.2 Domestic Partnerships in the United States

As explained in chapter 7, section 7.4, there are two kinds of domestic partner schemes in the United States. One form is domestic partnership acts and ordinances of states and municipalities. The other is private-sector employers' benefit plans. Since my concern is with domestic partnership as a model for the recognition of same-sex partnerships *by the state,* only the kind of domestic partnership pertaining to statutory state-sanctioned recognition is relevant to the discussion here.[6]

State and municipal domestic partnerships in the United States differ from one another much more than the European registered partnership acts do. Each local or state domestic partner scheme in the United States is unique and different from others, since the domestic partnerships are enacted on a case-by-case, municipality-by-municipality basis. It is thus difficult to categorize all domestic partnerships as one model of recognition; in fact, each domestic partner scheme can be regarded as an independent model for the recognition of same- and opposite-sex partnerships.

Domestic partner ordinances and acts differ not only in their definition of domestic partnership but, as table 2 demonstrates, also in their

---

5. The numbers of registrations are based on Kees Waaldijk, *Small Change: How the Road to Same-Sex Marriage Got Paved in the Netherlands, in* Legal Recognition of Same-Sex Partnerships: A Study of National, European, and International Law 437, 463 (Robert Wintemute & Mads Andenas eds., 2001).

6. For a detailed discussion of private-employment domestic partner plans and benefits, see chap. 7, sec. 7.4.

scope, applicability, and availability. Whereas some acts or ordinances are applicable only to same-sex couples, other domestic partnerships recognize both opposite- and same-sex partners.[7] Some require or provide for registration, whereas others do not, and some cities, such as San Francisco, limit their registration to their residents; others, such as Berkeley and West Hollywood, allow nonresidents to register. Some domestic partner registries have no legal consequences, provide no benefits, and are only of symbolic significance, whereas others provide for various rights and benefits. Those that do offer rights and benefits also differ from one another in the scope of rights they provide: some offer benefits to the partners of state or local employees, such as health insurance benefits and bereavement leave; some offer hospital and prison visitation rights; and some offer a combination of the foregoing. Thus, for example, there are wide disparities among the seven states—Connecticut, Hawaii, California, Vermont, New York, Massachusetts, and Oregon—that have thus far adopted domestic partner legislation. For instance, Hawaii's Reciprocal Beneficiaries Act, which for a time was the most comprehensive act of its kind in the United States (until Vermont enacted its civil union act [see below]), does not offer statewide registration, is open to any two single adults who cannot marry (including relatives and friends) and who are state employees, and provides for a relatively large number of rights—such as inheritance and workers' compensation, to name a few. In comparison, California's domestic partnership scheme—though it is the only statewide registry open to any same-sex or opposite-sex couple (but not to family and friends) and is not contingent upon employment—offers very few rights, such as hospital visitation and health insurance coverage for the partners of state employees, and is viewed as largely symbolic. Similarly, Connecticut's statewide domestic partner scheme provides only health and pension benefits to the partners of gay and lesbian state employees. Vermont's civil union act is the most extensive and comprehensive statewide recognition of same-sex partnerships available in the United States. Unlike all other U.S. domestic partnership acts and ordinances, the Vermont act equates the status of same-sex couples with that of opposite-sex married couples in the state.[8] But however broad, civil unions are still limited in the sense that they do not (and cannot) confer any federal rights, and they will probably not be recognized by most other states.

7. The rationale for same-sex restrictions in the United States, as in the Nordic countries, is that unmarried opposite-sex couples could choose to marry. *See* Nancy J. Knauer, *Domestic Partnership and Same-Sex Relationships: A Marketplace Innovation and a Less Than Perfect Institutional Choice,* 7 Temple Pol. & Civ. Rts. L. Rev. 337, 346 (1998).

8. For discussion of the act, its scope, and its limitations, see chap. 7, sec. 7.5.

Table 2 States and Municipalities Offering Domestic Partnership Benefits and Registries

State	Municipality	Registry Effective Dates & Features (for State/Municipal Residents)	Benefit Effective Dates & Features (for State/Municipal Employees)
Arizona	Pima County		March 1998
	Tucson		April 28, 1997; same-sex partners only
Arkansas	Fayetteville	May 6, 1998	
California	State of California	October 2, 1999	
	Alameda County		Date unavailable; nonhealth benefits
	Berkeley	October 1991; open to all	April 1982; first in U.S.
	Davis	Date unavailable	
	Laguna Beach	June 1990	June 1990
	Long Beach	May 6, 1997	
	Los Angeles	Date unavailable	October 1988
	Los Angeles County	March 23, 1999	December 19, 1995
	Marin County	Date unavailable	Date unavailable
	Oakland	June 1996	June 1996; same-sex partners only
	Palo Alto	December 1995	
	Petaluma	April 19, 1999	Nonhealth benefits
	Sacramento	October 1992	Date unavailable
	San Diego		June 1994
	San Francisco	November 1990	July 1991; city contractors required to offer equal benefits
	San Francisco County		July 1991
	San Mateo County		Date unavailable
	Santa Barbara	Date unavailable; recognizes domestic registered partnerships from other cities	1998
	Santa Cruz		May 1996
	Santa Cruz Company		May 1986
	West Hollywood (L.A.)	1985; recognizes domestic registered partnerships from other cities	February 1985
Colorado	Boulder	Date unavailable; open to all	Date unavailable
	Denver		September 1996
Connecticut	State of Connecticut		March 9, 2000; same-sex partners only
District of Columbia	Washington, D.C.	April 1992; congress bars city from using federal and D.C. funds for implementation	April 1992 (See note to left)

State	Locality		
Florida	Broward County		January 1, 2000
	Miami Beach		July 1998; nonhealth benefits
	Key West		February 12, 1998
	Monroe County		February 11, 1998
	West Palm Beach		February 1992
Georgia	Atlanta	1993; *Atlanta v. McKinney*	August 1996
Hawaii	State of Hawaii	July 1, 1997	July 1, 1997
Illinois	Chicago		1997; same-sex couples only
	Cook County		Date unavailable
	Oak Park	September 1997; same-sex partners only	April 1994
Indiana	Bloomington		March 1997
Iowa	Iowa City	November 1994	August 1994
Louisiana	New Orleans	July 16, 1993	Date unavailable; same-sex partners only
Maine	Portland		Date unavailable
Maryland	Baltimore		January 1995; same-sex partners only
	Takoma Park		November 1988
Massachusetts	State of Massachusetts	1992; executive order; state workers can register for bereavement leave and visitation in state prisons and hospitals	Date unavailable
	Boston	December 1993	August 4, 1998; executive order
	Brewster		Date unavailable
	Brookline	June 1993; same-sex only	Date unavailable; nonhealth benefits
	Cambridge	September 1992	September 1992
	Nantucket	Date unavailable	Date unavailable
	Provincetown	1993; not limited to city residents	Date unavailable
	Springfield		April 1997
Michigan	Ann Arbor	November 1991	August 1992
	Detroit		Date unavailable
	East Lansing	March 1991	June 1993
	Wayne County		Date unavailable
Missouri	St. Louis	March 1997; executive order; hospitals and prison visitation	
New Jersey	Delaware		Date unavailable; nonhealth benefits
	Gloucester County		Date unavailable; nonhealth benefits

(continued)

Table 2 (continued)

State	Municipality	Registry Effective Dates & Features (for State/Municipal Residents)	Benefit Effective Dates & Features (for State/Municipal Employees)
New York	State of New York	September 1992; executive order; state workers may register for bereavement leave, visitation rights in state prisons and hospitals	1995 Civil Service Employees Association reached agreement to include domestic partnerships benefits in its new contract
	Albany	Date unavailable	Date unavailable
	Ithaca	August 1990	January 1991; nonhealth benefits
	New York City	January 1993	October 1993
	Rochester	April 1994	April 1994
North Carolina	Carrboro	October 11, 1994	Date unavailable
	Chapel Hill	April 24, 1995	April 24, 1995
Oregon	State of Oregon	October 5, 1999	1998 Court order: *Tanner v. Oregon*
	Ashland		Date unavailable
	Corvallis		July 1, 1998
	Eugene		Date unavailable
	Multnomah County		June 1994
	Portland		
Pennsylvania	Philadelphia	Date unavailable	June 7, 1998; same-sex partners only
	Pittsburgh	Date unavailable	nonhealth benefits
	Travis County		
Vermont	State of Vermont	April 2000: civil union act	August 1994
	Burlington		January 1993
	Middlebury		September 1995
Washington	King County		January 1993
	Olympia		November 1994
	Seattle	Sept 1994; open to all	March 1990
	Tumwater		May 1997
Wisconsin	Dane County		Date unavailable; nonhealth benefits
	Madison	August 1988	October 1999
	Milwaukee (Milwaukee County)		September 1, 1999
	Shorewood Hills (Dane County)		Date unavailable; nonhealth benefits

SOURCE: Adapted from Lambda Legal Defense and Education Fund, October 25, 1999 (http://lambdalegal.org).

Domestic partnerships usually carry no legal significance in any other jurisdiction but are limited to the residents of the specific jurisdiction that offers them.[9] Thus, the seven states that have enacted versions of domestic partnership do not recognize each other's domestic partnerships. The Vermont act also does not purport to recognize out-of-state domestic partnerships or to be recognized by other states. Out of the approximately eighty municipalities that have adopted domestic partner ordinances, only Santa Barbara and West Hollywood recognize registered partnerships from other cities.

Finally, only a few domestic partnership schemes, such as San Francisco's Equal Benefits Ordinance,[10] require private employers who contract with the city to extend benefits to the partners of their employees; other domestic partnership acts and ordinances are limited to local or state public employees (see table 2).

8.3 Same-Sex Partnerships in the United States and Northern Europe Contrasted

Both domestic partnerships and the registered partnership acts addressed in this section, that is, the acts of the Nordic countries and the Netherlands (excluding "light" versions of registered partnership, such as the French PaCS and the German life partnership) emphasize the regulation of the economic aspects of the partners' relationship with each other rather than their parental rights, such as custody, joint adoption, and artificial insemination. Yet, unlike registered partnership acts, which do address to a certain extent the parental rights of same-sex couples—even if by exclusion of same-sex couples from such rights—U.S. domestic partnership acts and ordinances make no reference to parental rights of same-sex couples; as we saw in chapter 7, section 7.1, these regulations are to be found elsewhere, mainly in state domestic relations statutes and state court decisions. Thus, when comparing the status of same-sex partners in northern Europe and the United States, in addition to contrasting the two models of recognition (sec. 8.3.1 below), I address the differences between the regions in terms of parental rights of same-sex couples (sec. 8.3.2 below). In the course of those discussions, I also explore some potential rationales for those differences, especially in the field of parent-child relationships.

---

9. *See Marriage and Domestic Partnership: A Fact Sheet,* Lambda Legal Defense and Education Fund, June 17, 1999, at http://www.lambdalegal.org/cgi-bin/pages/documents/record?record=437.

10. *See* San Francisco, Cal., Ordinance 97-66-33.1 (June 1, 1997).

8.3.1 Rights, Benefits, and Obligations of the Partners

The northern European model of registered partnership, to say nothing of same-sex marriage in the Netherlands, is very different from the American domestic partnership model. This is, of course, with the exception of Vermont's civil union act, which, for the purposes of the following comparison, is not classified as part of the U.S. domestic partnership model. Registered partnership refers to recognition of same-sex partnerships at the national level; it is based on the marriage model and requires some form of preliminary affirmation of the relationship before a government authority. Domestic partnership, in contrast, refers to recognition of same-sex partnerships by local and provincial jurisdictions or by nonstate entities, including private businesses and corporations, and usually requires a minimum duration of the relationship, proof of cohabitation, and proof of economic and emotional interdependence, none of which are required for registration of a partnership in Europe.[11] The Nordic countries recognize each other's registered partnerships,[12] but no state or municipality in the United States—except for two cities—recognizes domestic partnerships from other jurisdictions. Unlike the acts of the Nordic countries and similar to those of the Netherlands and France, most domestic partner ordinances in the United States are open to both opposite- and same-sex couples.

Since registered partnership acts are applied at the national level, they offer same-sex couples many of the rights that are, by federal law, provided only to married couples in the United States, for example, immigration rights. Such rights are not and cannot be provided by state or local domestic partner schemes. Moreover, registered partnerships entail most of the rights associated with marriage, with a few exceptions, whereas domestic partnerships as currently construed make no reference to marriage law and provide only a few limited rights—mostly work-related benefits. Thus, for example, whereas the rules of divorce apply for the dissolution of a registered partnership, a unilateral declaration is sufficient for the termination of a domestic partnership. Whereas domestic partnerships are largely contingent upon employment and are usually available only to employees, registered partnerships are open to any same-sex couple who wishes to regulate their relationship. Whereas domestic partnerships confer upon the couple no *obligations* vis-à-vis

---

11. *See Registered Partnership, Domestic Partnership, and Marriage: A Worldwide Summary*, IGLHRC Fact Sheet, November 3, 1998, at http://www.iglhrc.org/news/faqs/marriage_981103.html.

12. *See* ILGA-Europe Euroletter no. 35, September 1995 (Steffen Jensen et al. eds.) at http://www.qrd.org/qrd/www/orgs/ILGA/euroletter; Kees Waaldijk, *Free Movement of Same-Sex Partners*, 3 Maastricht J. Eur. & Comp. L. 271, 277 (1996).

each other and third parties, registered partnerships provide for the full range of obligations that flow from marriage, obligations of the partners both toward each other and toward third parties. Moreover, at the state level, domestic partnership schemes in the United States have been adopted thus far by only *seven states* out of fifty, and even in those states, with the exception of Vermont, the benefits of the acts are usually available to a limited number of same-sex couples. Most U.S. states and municipalities have not adopted any form of domestic partnership, whereas registered partnerships are available to any same-sex couple living in any part of the northern European countries. Thus, even if existing domestic partnerships were more comprehensive in their scope, their availability and applicability would still be diminutive as compared to the registered partnership acts of northern Europe.

Domestic partnerships do not even begin to address the scope of rights, benefits, and obligations associated with marriage, whereas the five northern European countries' registered partnership acts, being much broader, are much closer to providing same-sex couples equality with married couples. Most of the rights that the registered partnership acts provide for automatically, such as divorce protections, social security, property arrangements, inheritance rights, and immunity from testifying against a partner, are not provided by any domestic partner scheme. Thus, the registered partnership model is an alternative much more comparable to marriage than domestic partnership is.

We can conclude, then, that registered partnership is a broader and much more comprehensive model of legal recognition of same-sex partnerships than any existing American domestic partner scheme. In this context, we should note the exception within the United States, the extraordinary achievement in Vermont. No other U.S. statute dealing with the rights of same-sex couples comes even close to what Vermont has done. In terms of its scope, Vermont's civil union act is akin to the European registered partnership model more than to any existing domestic partner scheme in the United States. Indeed, short of opening up marriage to same-sex couples, Vermont's legislature has done all that it can do in order to place same-sex couples on an equal footing with opposite-sex married couples in the state of Vermont. Like the registered partnership acts of the Nordic countries and Germany, and unlike those of the Netherlands and France, the Vermont act is applicable only to same-sex couples, according them most of the rights associated with opposite-sex marriage. However, civil unions are more restricted than registered partnerships, since the Vermont act, unlike the northern European acts, is limited to the state of Vermont, will probably not be recognized by other states within the United States, provides only rights that flow from marriage in the state of Vermont, and does not attach any of the rights at the federal level. It should be noted that even had Vermont recognized same-sex marriage, its law would still not guarantee federal benefits or recognition by other states.[13] However, had Vermont opened up marriage to same-sex couples, federal and state defense of marriage acts could be challenged constitutionally, and a successful challenge would have made possible recognition at both the federal and state levels.

One may argue that an analogy can be drawn between Vermont's act within the United States and the Nordic-Netherlands model within Europe, claiming that the latter countries are rather small in population, as Vermont is, and are now embedded in a quasi-federal European Union, in which their same-sex registration systems do not have effect. However, the analogy between the United States and Vermont on the one hand, and the European Union and the Nordic-Netherlands countries on the other hand—which would have led us to regard the developments in Vermont as more consequential than we have regarded them thus far—is flawed, for numerous reasons. First, as explained above, unlike the northern European acts, Vermont's act lacks more than one thousand rights that flow from marriage at the federal level in the United States, rights that *are fully* provided to same-sex couples who register their partnerships in the northern European states, since their acts are *national* in nature. Vermont's act is thus substantively less comprehensive than European registered partnerships. Second, whereas the population of Vermont is about six hundred thousand (less than .25 percent of the entire U.S. population), the northern European countries' population is approximately 35 million, which is a much greater percentage of the European population. Moreover, despite the movement toward a "united Europe," analogizing the U.S. federal system with the European Union is incoherent, since the European states are completely sovereign and the European Union would be reluctant to enforce its policy on member states, especially in matters concerning family law recognition.[14] In addition, the European Union is notorious for its democratic

13. Vermont should not be faulted for not doing what it simply cannot do (i.e., bind other states or the federal government). However, the fact that recognition in European countries has occurred at the *national* level, whereas in the United States such recognition has thus far been demonstrated only at the state level (and a scheme analogous to the European registered partnership acts has been adopted thus far by only one state), is a significant difference, which should be given due weight when assessing U.S. schemes as compared to the northern European registered partnership acts.

14. The European Court of Justice in Luxembourg has significant enforcement mechanisms: member states that do not enforce E.U. law properly can be brought before the Court of Justice of the European Union and fined. However, its main goal is to implement equal standards in granting jurisdiction and enforcing foreign judgments throughout Europe. Moreover, the Court of Justice deals mainly with environmental law, labor law,

deficit. More importantly, there is no political movement within the European Union comparable to the movements that propound antigay policies and legislation in the United States at the federal level (e.g., DOMA); on the contrary, the European Union has been quite influential in pushing for gay rights legislation (see chap. 11, sec. 11.2).[15]

It can thus be concluded that the civil union status, which is an exception within the United States, is less expansive than the Nordic-Netherlands registered partnership model. All other American domestic partnerships as currently construed may be regarded as one step beyond mere cohabitation but a few steps short of registered partnerships, let alone marriage.

8.3.2 Parental Rights of Same-Sex Couples

Many U.S. states protect gay and lesbian parenting without recognizing gay and lesbian couples, but we find an opposite trend in Europe, where some countries extensively regulate same-sex partnerships but provide very little recognition of gay and lesbian parenting.[16]

Initially, most European countries largely excluded same-sex couples from basic parental rights: gay and lesbian couples were not allowed to adopt children or have joint custody over each other's children; except for the Netherlands, lesbians are still excluded from artificial conception services in all the countries with registered partnership acts.[17] However, during the past couple of years, the northern European countries have amended their acts to confer quite a few parental rights on same-sex couples. The disparity in the field of parental rights between northern Europe and the United States, which was a strong difference until

---

competition law, and other issues of civil and commercial law (unlike the U.S. Supreme Court, which adjudicates in all fields of law). Theoretically, it has the power to adjudicate in matters relating to discrimination and equality, but in fact it is the European Court of Human Rights (which lacks enforcement mechanisms similar to those of the Court of Justice) that deals, almost exclusively, with matters pertaining to discrimination on the basis of sexual orientation and other matters of human rights. Thus, despite the existence of enforcement mechanisms in Europe, both European courts combined do not even begin to resemble the degree of enforcement and the range of subject matters that come under the jurisdiction of the U.S. federal judiciary.

15. It should also be noted that the Vermont-rights-versus-federal-rights disparity does not exist to the same extent in E.U.-E.C. countries because the European Union–European Community has a smaller role in immigration and no role in direct taxation or in social security (except for sex and race discrimination).

16. Nancy D. Polikoff has pointed to this general distinction. *See* Nancy D. Polikoff, *Lesbian and Gay Couples Raising Children: The Law in the United States, in* Legal Recognition of Same-Sex Partnerships: A Study of National, European, and International Law 153 (Robert Wintemute & Mads Andenas eds., 2001).

17. For specific distinctions among the northern European countries in terms of parental rights, see sec. 8.1 above and table 1, which provides a comparison of registered partnerships in Europe.

recently, has begun to erode and is on its way to disappearing. This trend is not seen in other European countries. Until recently, parental rights in the northern European countries were limited to the availability of joint custody in Iceland and the Netherlands and the right to adopt each other's children under the Danish and Icelandic laws. With the exception of the new Dutch act, same-sex couples in Europe are prohibited from jointly adopting unrelated children. The Netherlands now accords same-sex couples the right to adopt each other's children and to jointly adopt unrelated children from within the Netherlands. Denmark, Norway, and Sweden still do not allow joint custody, and in the latter two countries, same-sex couples cannot adopt each other's children. Other European countries, including France and Germany, also exclude same-sex couples from most parental rights.

In the United States, however, same-sex couples enjoy many rights concerning parenthood: various levels of courts in almost half the states have recognized second-parent adoptions, some jurisdictions allow same-sex couples to jointly adopt unrelated children, and nowhere in the United States are artificial conception services for lesbians prohibited.

Moreover, whereas adoption by single gay men and lesbians is legal in the United States in all states but three,[18] most European countries ban adoptions by individual gay men and lesbians. Whereas alternative reproduction services, albeit unregulated, are legal and available to lesbians in all U.S. states, all European countries except the Netherlands explicitly prohibit lesbians (and single women) from obtaining such services.

There are three main reasons why European countries with registered partnership laws prohibit joint adoptions and limit other parental rights of gay men and lesbians, such as assisted procreation for lesbians. The first is a conviction that a child must have both a mother and a father[19]— both heterosexual—and the perception of gay men and lesbians per se as unfit parents, a concept that, as stated above, has dramatically changed in some of the northern European countries. The second reason has to do with European conventions on intercountry adoptions, which limit the availability of adoptions to heterosexual couples or individuals. The third reason is a practical one, related to the low number of children

18. In addition to the complete prohibition on any form of adoption by gay men and lesbians in Florida, the state agencies in charge of adoption and foster care in both Arkansas and Utah decided in 1999 to ban homosexuals from becoming adoptive parents. *See* chap. 7, sec. 7.1.

19. *See* Linda Nielsen, *Family Rights and the "Registered Partnership" in Denmark,* 4 Int'l J.L. & Fam. 297, 305 (1990).

available for adoption in the European countries as compared to the large number of unwanted children who are put up for adoption in the United States. The latter is the reason most commonly given by European countries as the justification for their ban on adoption by same-sex couples.

With regard to the first reason, some politicians and advocates in the European countries have based their rationale for the prohibition on the notion that it was not clear whether the best interests of the child would be served by being raised by a homosexual couple; they feared that children would suffer discrimination if they live with same-sex parents. This fear seems unsubstantiated, because it contradicts the reality that thousands of children are being raised by lesbian and gay couples, children who are disadvantaged not because of social discrimination but rather because they do not have two legal parents. Furthermore, there are many studies according to which there is no proof that it is not in the best interest of the child to be brought up by same-sex parents.[20] There is clearly no reason for Norway, Sweden, France, and Germany to prohibit same-sex couples from at least adopting each other's children, and it is to be hoped that these countries will follow Denmark's lead in this matter. Another argument that has been made in some northern European countries was that the limitations are not based on prejudice toward homosexuals but rather stem from the clear dichotomy in their statutes between the regulation of the relationships between parents and children on the one hand and the relationship of the partners vis-à-vis each other on the other. For example, the Norwegian Ministry of Children and Family Affairs stated that "[t]he basis for a Partnership Act is the desire of homosexual couples for legislation concerning the economic and legal aspects of a relationship" and that the ministry "fails to see that the provision of adoption should be an automatic consequence of the right to legislated cohabitation."[21] This argument seems to serve as a mere pretext for the bias toward homosexuals as parents and is unpersuasive as a rationale for the exclusion of gays from parental rights. The dichotomy between legal regulations governing the relationship of parents and children and rules regulating the couple's own relationship is a technical one and is a poor excuse for excluding gays from the right to adopt. It was never argued that because acts on adoption are separate from marriage legislation, they should not be applicable to married couples, and I find no

20. For an overview of recent studies conducted in the United States, see E. J. Graff, *What Is Marriage For?* 117–141 (1999).

21. The Norwegian Bill, note 3 above, at 53.

compelling argument for the decision not to apply these rules to same-sex partners as well.[22]

In addition to the preference given to heterosexual couples who wish to adopt in most European countries, some European conventions on intercountry adoptions limit the availability of adoptions to heterosexual couples. For example, according to the Hague Adoption Convention, only intercountry adoptions by a married couple or an individual are allowed.[23] Such treaties serve in effect to limit the adoption rights of same-sex couples as far as the adoption of a foreign child is concerned.

With regard to the practical reason given by some European countries, it is true that there are hardly any children available for adoption within these countries and that most adoptions by opposite-sex married couples are foreign adoptions. In 1995, for example, 91 percent of Danish adoptions and 69 percent of Dutch adoptions were foreign. In comparison, only 15 percent of U.S. adoptions were foreign that year. For this reason, European countries state as their main reason for the prohibition on adoption by homosexuals the fear that Third World countries prejudiced against gay men and lesbians would refuse to give up their unwanted babies to a country that allows adoption by gay couples.[24] Even the progressive Dutch act allowing same-sex couples to adopt is restricted to the adoption of children from within the Netherlands. It seems likely that this reasoning will hold for quite a long time and that even in European countries that are considering same-sex adoptions, there will be a limitation on intercountry adoptions. For instance, based on the same fears, the 1999 Danish amendment that allows same-sex partners to adopt each other's children still does not allow joint adoption of unrelated children. Limiting same-sex couples to intracountry adoptions in northern Europe would make it almost impossible for homosexual couples to obtain a child together, since most adoptions in

22. It should be noted that a distinction between adoption rules and those governing marriage also exists in the United States and, theoretically, could also account for the difference between the advanced status of same-sex couples in matters pertaining to parenthood and their status as a couple. However, the distinction was not used in this country as an argument to refrain from regulating the status of same-sex couples, and for the reasons mentioned above, such an argument in the United States would also be objectionable and unjustifiable.

23. *See* Kees Waaldijk, Dutch Law Reform in Progress (Adoption & Marriage, Foreign Partners), January 1, 1999, at http://www.coc.nl/index.htm/?file=marriage (last visited August 18, 1999).

24. *See* Deb Price, *Roads to Equality: Gay Rights in Europe: Danes Pave Way for Partnership: Copenhagen's Gay and Lesbian Couples Enjoy Rights That Remain a Distant Dream for American Same-Sex Couples,* Detroit News, October 29, 1997, at E1:4. *See also* Andy Quan, *Dutch Gay Marriage: A Moral Victory but Battles Still Ahead,* ILGA-Europe Euroletter, note 12 above, no. 41, April 1996, at 1.

the Nordic countries and the Netherlands are foreign. Moreover, the reasoning for denying joint adoptions to same-sex couples, that is, the fear that Third World counties might be reluctant to send children for adoption in countries where homosexual adoption is allowed, does not seem substantial enough to justify the denial, especially if, as in the United States, "the primary concern in the adoption law is to promote the welfare of children."[25] It also serves to perpetuate gender stereotyping in general and prejudice against gay men and lesbians in particular.

The second and the third rationales may account for the ban on joint adoption of an unrelated child *from a foreign country* by same-sex couples, but they do not explain why same-sex couples are excluded from other parental rights, such as joint custody over children brought into the relationship, artificial insemination, and adoption of each other's children or joint adoption of children from within the country. Only prejudice against homosexuals as parents may account for both the ban on adoption *and* the other restrictions on gay and lesbian parenthood in European countries. Therefore, the three proposed "rationales" are not to be viewed as alternative explanations of the European countries' refusal to protect gay and lesbian parenting. Rather, it is the combination of the three factors that serves to explicate the European restrictions on parental rights.

It should be emphasized, however, that the new Dutch act allowing adoption by same-sex couples and the Danish and Icelandic laws allowing for second-parent adoptions are evidence of an ongoing move in the northern European countries toward recognition of parental rights of same-sex couples—similar to the practice in the United States. As the legislative process in the Nordic countries has proved in the past, other Nordic countries will probably follow suit. It is to be expected that in the near future same-sex couples in northern Europe will be accorded most parental rights. At the same time, some U.S. states have introduced bills to prohibit joint adoption or second-parent adoption by same-sex couples in an attempt to halt American state court decisions granting such adoptions.[26] It thus may well be that the differences between the United States and Europe in terms of parental rights will completely erode in the years to come, at least as far as northern Europe is concerned.

25. Craig A. Sloane, *A Rose by Any Other Name: Marriage and the Danish Registered Partnership Act,* 5 Cardozo J. Int'l & Comp. L. 189, 209–10 (1997), referring to Arthur S. Leonard, *Lesbian and Gay Families and the Law: A Progress Report,* 21 Fordham Urb. L.J. 927, 964 (1994). For further criticism of the exclusion, see Sloane, above, at 210–11.

26. See Nancy Maxwell et al., *Legal Protection for All the Children: Dutch-American Comparison of Lesbian and Gay Parent Adoptions,* 3.1 Electronic J. Comp. L. 14 (August 1999) at http://law.kub.nl/ejcl/31/art31-2.htm.

In addition to the aforementioned rationales for the discrimination against same-sex couples as parents in Europe, we need to explore what may account for the current disparity between Europe and the United States and examine why the status of same-sex couples as parents is currently more advanced in the United States. One of the most apparent differences between the United States and Europe is that the pursuit of parental rights in the United States has taken place at the judicial level, whereas the process of recognition of same-sex partnerships in both Europe and the United States has been largely a legislative one. In the United States, a common law country, courts are allowed to "create" law where there is a lacuna in the statute. Moreover, courts in the United States are characterized by their activist judicial review in controversial matters of human rights, a practice that has been both criticized and defended.[27] In contrast, courts in civil law countries—including the Nordic countries, the Netherlands, France, and Germany—are largely prohibited from "creating" law when none exists; they are restricted to the application of existing legislation.[28] Does the difference between the legislative and the judicial processes in both the United States and in northern Europe account for the differences between Europe and the United States in terms of parental rights of same-sex couples? Some scholars claim that courts are not the countermajoritarian force they are believed to be and that there is some judicial reluctance to create social change, especially when it has to do with changes in the concept of the family and the protection of sexual minorities, and that legislation is a better tool for the advancement of minority rights in general.[29] They argue that only legislation serves to provide security for gay and lesbian families, since it is more stable, reliable, and reflective of public opinion than judicial decisions.[30] These sweeping statements seem to be inaccurate. The abundance of court decisions providing protection to sexual minorities, on the one hand, such as the judicial construction of second-parent adoption and the decision of the Vermont Supreme Court in the case of *Baker*, and the legislation that sharply limits the rights of gays and

27. On this point, see generally David A. J. Richards, Conscience and the Constitution: History, Theory, and Law of the Reconstruction Amendments (1993); David A. J. Richards, Foundations of American Constitutionalism (1989); David A. J. Richards, Toleration and the Constitution (1986).

28. *See* Maxwell et al., note 26 above, at 14.

29. *See, e.g.,* Martha M. Ertman, *Contractual Purgatory for Sexual Marginorities: Not Heaven, but Not Hell Either,* 73 Denv. U. L. Rev. 1107, 1115 (1997).

30. *See, e.g.,* Barbara J. Cox, *Love Makes a Family—Nothing More, Nothing Less: How the Judicial System Has Refused to Protect Nonlegal Parents in Alternative Families,* 8 J.L. & Pol. 5, 9–10 (1991); Kathryn E. Kovacs, *Recognizing Gay and Lesbian Families: Marriage and Parental Rights,* 5 L. & Sexuality 513, at 532 (1995).

lesbians, on the other hand, such as state and federal defense of marriage acts and the European exclusion of same-sex couples from various parental rights, prove that it is inaccurate to assert that legislation is usually a better instrument for social change and a better solution for the inequality of sexual minorities. Moreover, some court decisions force public acceptance in the face of legislative inaction.[31] Nonetheless, there are plenty of court decisions in the United States that limit the rights of same-sex couples, since "in the end judges . . . share all the biases and limitations of the public itself,"[32] as well as progressive legislation in Europe that provides same-sex couples with extensive economic rights. Thus, we cannot attribute the European limitations and the U.S. "liberalism" in the field of parental rights on the one hand, and the advanced status of same-sex partnerships in northern Europe as compared to the limited regulation of such partnerships in the United States on the other, to the nature of the legislative process as compared to the judicial process. We must look for additional or alternative factors to account for the differences between the United States and northern Europe in the rights of same-sex couples.

In the matter of adoption, whereas the majority of adoptions in northern Europe are foreign, most U.S. adoptions are from within the United States; the number of foreign adoptions is relatively small. The difference between the large number of unwanted children in the United States and the unavailability of children for adoption from within the European countries stems mainly from the European practice of mandatory sex education, legal state-sponsored abortion, greater availability of contraception, and the social acceptability of unwed motherhood in northern Europe,[33] in contrast with the more conservative social concepts and poor education in the areas of contraception and abortion in the United States. The differences in adoption rules of the United States and of northern Europe may be the consequence of a difference in social conceptions regarding adoptions and not only due to the difference in the availability of children for adoption. Adoption is generally not a favored institution in Europe; it is less acceptable in the Nordic countries and the Netherlands, and generally much less popular in Europe, than in the United States. For example, whereas adoption legislation was not enacted in the Netherlands until 1956, most

31. Kovacs, note 30 above, at 532, referring to Brown v. Board of Education, 347 U.S. 483 (1954).

32. William B. Rubinstein, *We Are Family: A Reflection on the Search for Legal Recognition of Lesbian and Gay Relationships,* 8 J.L. & Pol. 89, at 105 (1991), quoted in Kovacs, note 30 above, at 532.

33. *See* Price, note 24 above.

adoption legislation in the American states was enacted during the second half of the nineteenth century.[34]

Furthermore, a distinction between two ideologies may account for the existing differences in parental rights of same-sex couples between Europe and the United States. Some nations approach parental rights from a "child-oriented" perspective, and others approach such rights from a "parent-oriented" perspective.[35] The child-oriented approach is generally more conservative, viewing access to artificial reproductive technologies and other parental rights, such as adoption, within the context of the traditional creation of the family and thus limiting their availability to *heterosexual* married or cohabiting couples.[36] The parent-oriented perspective is more liberal, focusing on the rights of individuals

34. In the United States, the percentage of adoptions per capita is far higher than in the Netherlands. For example, in Kansas, with a population of 2.5 million people, 2,000 adoptions were granted by the state courts in 1998. In the Netherlands, with a population of over six times that of Kansas, only 1,989 adoptions were granted in 1998. *See* Maxwell et al., note 26 above, at 16. Maxwell and coauthors provide an interesting historical explanation for the contrasting views on adoption in Europe and the United States:

> One of the historical reasons is the European tradition of placing children in apprenticeships at a very young age in order for the child to learn a trade. It did not matter if the child had biological parents or was an orphan. The majority of children were placed outside their natural parents' care and the thought of the master or mistress "adopting" the apprentice as his or her own child would never have been a consideration. This system of "putting out" children never developed to the same extent in the United States, however. At a time when Europe was coping with overpopulation, famine, and intense competition for land and natural resources, America had abundant resources, except for a shortage of cheap labor. Immigrant populations began to pour into the urban centers on the East Coast. During the mid-1880s, child-protection societies developed in urban areas with high immigrant populations, with the goal of caring for vagrant immigrant children. Many of these children were sent on "orphan" trains to the western regions of the country, where labor was in short supply. In addition, disease claimed the lives of many adults, leaving children without natural parents. Their children were placed with older siblings, aunts, uncles, and other relatives or friends, who cared for them. Because adoption was not recognized in the common law, the adults who wanted to adopt these children began to file private bills in the state and territorial legislatures, requesting private legislation granting the adoptions. Eventually, the legislatures enacted adoption legislation because the requests for private legislation evidenced a need for a statutory remedy. *Id.* at 16–17.

For additional potential reasons for specific distinctions between the United States and the Netherlands, such as the unique foster care system in the Netherlands, see id. at 17–19.

35. *See* Demetrio Neri, *Child or Parent Oriented Controls of Reproductive Technologies? in* Creating the Child 145, 145–46 (Donald Evans & Neil Pickering eds., 1996); Kathryn Venturatos Lorio, *The Process of Regulating Assisted Reproductive Technologies: What We Can Learn from Our Neighbors—What Translates and What Does Not,* 45 Loy. L. Rev. 247, 254–55 (1999). The distinction Neri makes is in relation to eligibility for the use of artificial reproductive technologies, but in my view it is applicable to the full set of parental rights of same-sex couples.

36. Neri, note 35 above.

who are in need of these services. This is not to say that the best interest of the child is not a major factor in parent-oriented countries; the emphasis in these countries on the rights of the parents is an additional rather than an alternative factor. The Nordic states and France, which have adopted a more child-oriented perspective, tend to restrict the parental rights of same-sex couples. The United States, which is more inclined toward the latter ideology, emphasizing the rights of individuals to have children, legally recognizes a broader spectrum of parental rights, such as artificial procreation and adoption. Unlike the Nordic countries and France, the United States emphasizes the individual's right of autonomy in relation to having children; a natural consequence of such emphasis is also the insistence on the rights of gay men and lesbians to have children and raise them. I would categorize the Dutch ideology as an exceptional approach within Europe, since it allows lesbians access to artificial procreation services and also recognizes the right of same-sex couples to adopt.

The differences between Europe and the United States regarding parental rights of same-sex couples may also be attributed to different concepts of what a family is. Despite the general shift toward delinking procreation and marriage in the West, the United States is still very much a child-centered society.[37] In Europe there is less emphasis on children as the center of society; that view, as exemplified by most registered partnership schemes, leaves room for conceptualizing same-sex partners without children as a family unit in and of itself.

In conclusion, current models of recognition prove that it is easier for "public and legal actors to grant economic rights [than] familial or personal rights and benefits."[38] It seems that other than scattered U.S. court decisions providing same-sex couples with some parental rights,

37. Thus, although reluctant to recognize the relationships of gay couples per se, the United States has a greater tendency to view the homosexual couple as a family when and if they have children. One may argue that the matter of *Braschi,* in which the court held that the surviving gay partner of a deceased tenant was to be regarded as part of the family of the decedent and thus entitled to protection under New York City rent and eviction regulations, may serve as a counterexample, standing for the proposition that the court recognized same-sex couples as a family unit even without children. *See* Braschi v. Stahl Associates, 543 N.E.2d 49 (N.Y. 1989). However, such a broad reading of *Braschi* should probably be avoided. Although its reach has been somewhat expanding in New York and elsewhere, the decision is restricted to eviction regulations regarding rent-control apartments and should not be interpreted as implying that the United States as a whole views gays without children as family units. Moreover, my theory regarding the status of children in different societies is not necessarily based on (or reflected in) statutes or case law; it is a sociocultural observation, not a legal conclusion.

38. Martin D. Dupuis, *The Impact of Culture, Society, and History on the Legal Process: An Analysis of the Legal Status of Same-Sex Relationships in the United States and Denmark,* 9 Int'l J.L. & Fam. 86, 108–9 (1995).

both domestic partnerships in the United States and registered partnerships in northern Europe show a trend toward granting same-sex couples more economic rights than rights that may conflict with common notions of religion and morality, which are grounded in tradition and culture.[39]

39. *Id.*

Chapter 9

Domestic Partnership, Registered Partnership, and Marriage

The comparative analysis in the previous chapter shows us that whereas most U.S. states provide same-sex couples with extensive parental rights and hardly regulate the relationship between the partners, some European countries provide comprehensive recognition of the couple's relationship but offer relatively few parental rights. This chapter compares the American and European models on the one hand and opposite-sex marriage on the other hand, in terms of the rights, benefits, and obligations each of the institutions provides.

9.1 Registered Partnership and Marriage Compared

There is a clear distinction between registered partnership and marriage. As the explanatory part of the Norwegian registered partnership bill states:

> [t]he Act will not give homosexual partnerships equal status with marriage. Marriage is the most fundamental social unit and the natural framework for bringing up children. Marriage has a unique status, and no provision is proposed for marriage between homosexuals. The Bill employs the expressions "registration" and "partnership." The terms "wedlock" and "marriage" are reserved for the heterosexual marriage, with its ideological and religious status. . . . Marriage is the fundamental social institution, [it is] a relationship between a man and a

woman. Lifelong monogamy is the ideal that most people hope to achieve. Divorce and the prevalence of unmarried cohabitation have reduced the importance of marriage as the dominant family institution. But this applies to relations between men and women. . . . A homosexual relationship can however never be the same as marriage, neither socially nor from a religious point of view. It does not replace or compete with heterosexual marriage.[1]

Nevertheless, registered partnership in the Nordic countries and the Netherlands is the model closest to marriage, incorporating most existing marriage law. The registered partnership acts closely resemble marriage in many significant ways, because large parts of the marriage and divorce statutes; the succession laws; and the pension, tax, and social security laws apply to registration as well. The two institutions could be regarded as analogous for the following reasons: (1) In order to establish the registered partnership, the gay couple must register and proclaim a desire to provide mutual support. That, according to some, mimics the marriage vows and the concomitant support obligation inherent in the marital union. (2) The registration, like marriage, upholds monogamy by prohibiting a person from registering if she or he is already married or registered as the partner of another. (3) The registration reinforces the incest taboo by disallowing registrants who are ascendants and descendants or siblings of each other. (4) Various support obligations between the partners during the partnership and after its dissolution are similar to obligations of marriage.[2] However, owing to its exceptions— for example, in the field of parental rights—and its limitations in terms of private international law, the registered partnership model does not place same-sex couples on an equal footing with opposite-sex married couples.[3]

There are four principal differences between registered partnership and marriage. First, unlike opposite-sex couples in the Nordic countries, who may choose between a civil wedding ceremony and a church wedding, same-sex couples who wish to register their partnership do not

1. *See* Norway Ministry of Children and Family Affairs, The Norwegian Act on Registered Partnerships for Homosexual Couples 5, 12 (1993) [hereinafter The Norwegian Bill].

2. *See* Deborah Henson, *A Comparative Analysis of Same Sex Partnership Protections: Recommendations for American Reform*, 7 Int'l J.L. & Fam. 282, 295 (1993).

3. The French PaCS and the German life partnership, although they are variations of the registered partnership model, are not part of the current comparative discussion, since they are much less comprehensive than the registered partnership acts of the northern European countries. For an overview of the limitations of the PaCS and the German act and a comparison between them and the northern European registered partnership acts, see chap. 5 and chap. 8, sec. 8.1.

have the option of a state-sanctioned official church wedding. Second, unlike marriage, some registered partnership acts require that at least one of the partners be a citizen or a resident or that both partners be residents of the country in which the partnership is registered.[4] The citizenship/residency requirement is unique to registered partnerships. The registered partnership acts were specifically intended not to apply to outsiders. Thus, foreign same-sex couples, unlike their heterosexual counterparts, are excluded in most cases from the option of entering into a partnership in the countries that recognize such unions. The acts are largely limited to the citizens/residents of the northern European countries.[5]

The third difference between marriage and registered partnership, which currently applies also to same-sex marriage, has to do with private international-law rules that are beyond the power and jurisdiction of the Nordic countries and the Netherlands. Although an individual juris-diction has no control over the private international consequences of same-sex registered partnership or marriage, we should still note that the legal effects of registered partnerships are limited to the countries where they were entered into, and a registered partnership entered into in one of the Nordic countries is recognized only by the other Nordic countries that have similar registered partnership acts. Thus, unlike mar-riage, which is usually recognized by other countries except for the rare case in which there is a strong public policy against such recognition, registered partnerships are not recognized by other countries; if a same-sex couple travels or moves from the country in which they registered their partnership, they are regarded as complete legal strangers. As Waal-dijk notes, "[t]he status of 'registered partner' does not have any conse-quences in the domestic law of other countries, nor in European Union law, nor in human rights law."[6] In addition to the inequality as com-pared to married couples, this limitation may lead to various specific

4. For the distinctions among the six countries in which registered partnership is avail-able, see chap. 8, sec. 8.1.

5. Sloane rightfully critiques this requirement by stating: "This exception is pure dis-crimination against gays and lesbians. It should be of no concern to the [parliaments of the Nordic countries] whether another country will give recognition to [their] laws on this matter. If two foreigners register in Denmark, and their native country does not ap-prove, then they will not receive recognition of their relationship at home. However, this would not change the fact that their 'marriage' is legally recognized in Denmark." Craig A. Sloane, *A Rose by Any Other Name: Marriage and the Danish Registered Partnership Act,* 5 Cardozo J. Int'l & Comp. L. 189, 205 (1997).

6. Kees Waaldijk, *Free Movement of Same-Sex Partners,* 3 Maastricht J. Eur. & Comp. L. 271, 273 (1996). Waaldijk claims that even if same-sex marriage were allowed, such mar-riage would also not be recognized abroad, according to principles of public and private international law. *See id.*

problems of private international law. For instance, registered partnership would not represent a bar to marriage by one or both of the partners in other countries: it would not be possible to prevent a person who is party to a registered partnership from being legally and validly able to marry abroad without first having dissolved the registered partnership. If a registered homosexual partner married abroad without first having dissolved the registered partnership and was also domiciled abroad, the authorities of the country in which the partnership was entered into would not be able to demand extradition. Likewise, if one or both partners had property in a foreign country, there would be problems of enforcement of the inheritance rights of the partners vis-à-vis each other and with the administration of the foreign estate. Conflicts could arise between the surviving partner and heirs of the deceased domiciled abroad. If the bequeather of the property lived in a country that did not recognize a registered partnership, the heirs of the bequeather would be given priority over the homosexual partner.[7] Furthermore, the registered partnership acts explicitly declare that provisions of international treaties and rules of private international or European law that apply to marriage are inapplicable to registered partnerships.[8] By exempting the application of international treaties concerning marriage to registered partnerships, the acts further make it clear that they do not purport to place same-sex couples on an equal footing with opposite-sex married couples.[9]

The fourth and maybe the most significant difference is the exclusion of registered partners from various parental rights. As explained in previous chapters, this exclusion manifests itself in the lack of access to artificial conception services (with the exception of the Netherlands), the prohibition in all countries except the Netherlands on joint adoption of an unrelated child, and the prohibition on second-parent adoption (with the exception of Denmark, Iceland, and the Netherlands), in addition to limitations that same-sex couples are subject to in terms of joint

7. *See* The Norwegian Bill, note 1 above, at 50.

8. Moreover, even if same-sex couples are allowed to marry, "marriage" in international-law instruments would not be interpreted as including same-sex marriage; new rules of private international law should be drawn.

9. It should be noted, however, that this third difference—the one pertaining to private international law, applies also to Dutch same-sex marriage as well as to acts of countries that may open up marriage to gay couples in the future. Since, unlike registered partnership, the institution of marriage exists all over the world, same-sex marriage has better chances of being recognized than registered partnerships do, but recognition may still be quite unlikely in many countries (a public-policy exception might be used to refuse recognition of same-sex marriage; for example, the U.S. defense of marriage acts, as long as they are not constitutionally challenged and struck down, will probably be used to justify nonrecognition of a same-sex marriage entered into in the Netherlands).

custody over each other's children.[10] In an opposite-sex marriage, the birth of a child automatically creates all the relationships regulated under family law between the two spouses and the child. Both spouses are parents in the eyes of the law. In a registered partnership, the birth of the child creates a relationship under family law only between the mother and the child. Only the biological mother is a legal parent; the partner is not considered a parent and has very few rights or duties toward the child. A registered partnership, unlike marriage, thus creates no relationship between a child and a nonparent who (jointly) brings up the child.[11] Thus, though willing to regulate same-sex relationships as far as all financial matters between the partners are concerned, most of the northern European countries, in their registered partnership acts, accord such couples relatively few parental rights. Because registered partnership acts regulate a relationship that is largely distinct from parenthood, as exemplified by the Nordic countries' division between the relationship of parents and children and the one between the partners themselves, it appears that these countries view opposite-sex marriage as the most suitable institution for the rearing of children and believe that only in marriage should both kinds of relationships be fully recognized.

Some scholars argue that the basic provisions of the registered partnership acts should be regarded as legislation establishing same-sex marriage, since in many ways the acts are similar to and analogues to opposite-sex marriage. I do not agree that "registered partnership is same-sex marriage."[12] The two institutions are eminently different, and the existence of *some* or even *many* similarities to marriage should not in itself lead to the conclusion that the registered partnership acts could be regarded as marriage.

Because of the foregoing exceptions and limitations, I conclude that registered partnerships do not place same-sex couples on an equal footing with opposite-sex married couples. Some of these distinctions are

10. For a detailed discussion of the distinctions among the northern European countries themselves in terms of parental rights, see chap. 8, sec. 8.1. For explanation of the rationale for these exclusions and its critique, as well as a comparison with the status of same-sex couples as parents in the United States, see chap. 8, sec. 8.3.2.

11. *See* Yvonne Scherf, Registered Partnership in the Netherlands: A Quick Scan 8 (1999) [hereinafter Quick Scan].

12. *See, e.g.,* Sloane, note 5 above, at 202–3 (claiming that registered partners in Denmark have almost all the legal duties and benefits of marriage and that the two institutions are analogous, since same-sex partners who choose not to register are treated the same as different-sex couples who choose not to marry: neither group is granted any marriage-like rights). The analogy to marriage is further reinforced, according to Sloane, by the ability of both same-sex couples and opposite-sex couples to obtain legal recognition through "registration" and "marriage," respectively. *Id.* at 203.

slowly eroding, as exemplified by the adoption act in the Netherlands, which equates the status of same-sex registered partners with that of heterosexual married couples, and the move in the Nordic countries to allow second-parent adoptions. In the near future, most distinctions between registered partners and heterosexual married couples are likely to evaporate, except for problems relating to private international law, which will be solved only as other countries enact similar legislation or begin recognizing registered partnerships from the European countries. The differences between marriage and registered partnership will eventually be largely limited to the name and to the existence of two separate institutions—one primarily for same-sex couples and the other for opposite-sex partners.

9.2 Domestic Partnership and Marriage Compared

It should first be noted that in this discussion I do not classify civil unions as part of the American domestic partnership model; my comparison concerns itself with the other forty-nine states, which comprise over 99.5 percent of the U.S. population. As explained in earlier chapters, the civil union act of Vermont is more like the European registered partnership acts than it is like the U.S. domestic partnership model; in some aspects, however, it is still less comprehensive than these acts.[13] This is so because, for example, the status of parties to a civil union will probably not be recognized outside Vermont, and as with U.S. domestic partner schemes, there is no access to the 1,049 protections for married couples under federal law.[14] Since the Vermont act is unique and exceptional as compared to domestic partner schemes in the United States, the focus of this comparison between domestic partnerships and marriage pertains to the common U.S. domestic partner scheme and mentions particular instances in which the Vermont act differs from these other schemes.

As is evident from the discussion comparing registered partnership with domestic partnership, the latter is clearly inferior to the former: we have already established that domestic partnerships provide fewer rights

---

13. Regarding the scope of Vermont's act and a comparison between its provisions and those of the European registered partnership acts, see chap. 7, sec. 7.5, and chap. 8, sec. 8.3.

14. The U.S. General Accounting Office identified a total of 1,049 federal protections, benefits, and responsibilities available only to married couples, in addition to those available to couples under state laws and from private entities. *See* the U.S. General Accounting Office's list of the 1,049 rights afforded by marriage and denied to gay couples, available at http://www.marriageequality.com.

and are more restrictive than registered partnerships (see chap. 8, sec. 8.3.1). These facts, coupled with our determination in the previous section that the registered partnership model in Europe is less comprehensive than marriage, naturally enables us to infer that domestic partnerships are also inferior to marriage. We could end our current discussion comparing domestic partnerships and marriage with this conclusion. However, the unique characteristics of U.S. domestic partnerships and the ways in which they are subordinate to marriage, as well as the unique regulation of marriage in the United States by both federal and state laws—unlike the one set of national rules in the northern European countries—warrant a separate discussion comparing domestic partnership to marriage.

Unlike marriage, domestic partnership is not a fundamental right.[15] As demonstrated in table 3, unlike marriage, which carries standard protections, domestic partnerships differ from one another in terms of the number and scope of benefits they provide and are usually limited to employees in the public and private sector; they are not open to the general public. As explained in chapter 7, section 7.4, recognition of domestic partnerships in the United States is usually limited in its scope to the workplace—state, municipal, and private—and in its implications to the allocation of various employment benefits to same-sex couples and opposite-sex unmarried couples, purporting to place them on an equal footing with opposite-sex married couples. Making the benefits contingent on employment precludes wide participation by those who need the benefits and who would otherwise qualify for them—the unemployed and the underemployed. Thus, domestic partner benefits are limited both with regard to the types of benefits conferred and with regard to those eligible to participate in such benefits.[16] Even in the limited field of the workplace, domestic partnership recognition accompanied by benefits usually does not place the same-sex couple on an equal footing with opposite-sex married couples. For example, unlike benefits for married couples, domestic partner registrations and benefit plans are not recognized by the Internal Revenue Service, with the result that the benefits provided by the employer are part of the employee partner's gross income subject to federal income tax, unless the other partner qualifies as a dependent.[17] In addition, there are more than four hundred

15. Compare Loving v. Virginia, 338 U.S. 1 (1967).

16. *See* Nancy J. Knauer, *Domestic Partnership and Same-Sex Relationships: A Marketplace Innovation and a Less Than Perfect Institutional Choice,* 7 Temple Pol. & Civ. Rts. L. Rev. 337, 338, 338 n. 4, 358 (1998).

17. *See* chap. 7, sec. 7.4. *See also* Knauer, note 16 above, at 342–43; 2 Alba Conte, Sexual Orientation and Legal Rights 78 (1998).

work-related benefits in the public and private sectors that are extended on the basis of marital status from which domestic partners are excluded.[18] Furthermore, domestic partnership policies focus only on benefits and, unlike marriage, do not treat issues of mutual responsibility and obligation.[19]

The American domestic partnership model is thus very confined and—except for a few work-related benefits—does not confer the rights, benefits, obligations, and protections associated with either the institution of marriage or the European institution of registered partnership. Since domestic partner schemes vary from one jurisdiction to another, some domestic partner schemes are indeed more comprehensive than others, and not all are limited to work-related benefits. For instance, Hawaii's Reciprocal Beneficiaries Act is broader than the domestic partnership act in the state of California. Except for a few domestic partnership ordinances and acts that are broader than most others, domestic partner legislation in the United States is not public-regarding; it is akin to a private arrangement that does not vest the domestic partners with rights vis-à-vis third parties and does not require third parties to recognize the partnership.[20]

Domestic partnership measures and provisions as currently construed do not begin to approach the scope and scale of marriage protections and benefits or to address the many other aspects of inequality between same-sex partners and married couples in terms of both state and federal law. The institution of marriage determines which workers and which citizens are accorded what privileges and benefits; to a great extent laws and benefit systems in the United States center around one's marital status.[21] Most of the benefits that one automatically assumes come with marriage are not accorded to domestic partners. Domestic partners are excluded from all benefits and rights that arise automatically at the moment of marriage at the *federal level,* including those stemming from the

18. *See* National Gay and Lesbian Task Force Policy Institute, Domestic Partnership Organizing Manual 5 (1999).

19. *See* Raymond C. O'Brien, *Domestic Partnership: Recognition and Responsibility,* 32 San Diego L. Rev. 163, 171 (1995) (arguing for need to expand responsibility as well as benefits to domestic partners). Similarly, Eskridge claims that the main problem with domestic partner laws is not their "ridiculously skimpy" array of benefits but their failure to insist on partnership obligations. Dissolving a domestic partnership is very easy, and therefore such arrangements do little to cement the interpersonal commitment of the domestic partners. He thus concludes that without some attention to reciprocal obligations, the domestic partner movement is an empty liberalism. *See* William N. Eskridge Jr., Gaylaw: Challenging the Apartheid of the Closet 289 (1999).

20. *See* Knauer, note 16 above, at 338 n. 5, 340.

21. Lambda Legal Defense and Education Fund, Domestic Partnerships: Issues and Legislation 1 (1993).

Table 3 Marriage and Domestic Partnership

	Marriage	Domestic Partnership
Standard protections and responsibilities	Yes. The U.S. General Accounting Office identified a total of 1,049 federal protections, benefits, and responsibilities available only to married couples. This is in addition to those available to married couples under state laws and from private entities.	No. Each domestic partner benefit program is unique. Some recognize only nongay couples, others recognize only lesbian and gay couples, but many recognize both. Available benefits differ according to the resources and choices of the entity providing them.
Range of benefits	Comprehensive. Marriage grants the power to make medical decisions for the spouse, inheritance rights, access to divorce, custody and visitation rights, the ability to take out loans together, tax deductions, credits and exemptions, and hundreds of other legal privileges in the workplace and at all levels of government.	Limited. Benefits are determined by employers and may include medical and life insurance coverage, family leave, and retirement benefits. Additional legal rights and protections are extended to domestic partners registered in certain cities. New York City local law, for example, treats spouses and domestic partners as equals.
Availability	Restricted to different-sex couples. Only heterosexual couples can apply for marriage licenses. No state currently grants same-sex couples the freedom to marry.	Limited. Domestic partner benefits are available to the employees of nearly 100 public employers and more than 1,000 private employers. More than 30 cities have domestic partner registries.
Recognized by other jurisdictions	Yes. Different-sex marriages performed in other jurisdictions are automatically recognized by other cities, states, and countries. Should same-sex couples gain the freedom to marry, however, the federal Defense of Marriage Act and similar state laws may perpetuate discrimination against their marriages across state lines, requiring further legal challenges.	No. Domestic partnership is recognized only by the employer and by cities with registries, and because it is not the legal equivalent of marriage, it generally carries no legal significance in any other jurisdiction. Most cities with domestic partner registries do not recognize domestic partnerships registered in other jurisdictions.
Intangibles	Considerable. The act of getting married is invested with public, historical, and spiritual significance and is often emotionally charged for the individuals involved, as well as society.	Considerable. Domestic partnerships offer couples a way to celebrate their relationships and obtain access to some of the benefits historically available only to married couples.

SOURCE: *Marriage and Domestic Partnership: Marriage Project Fact Sheet*, Lambda Legal Defense and Education Fund, June 17, 1999 (http://lambdalegal.org/cgi-bin/pages/documents/record?record=436).

Employees Retirement Individual Security Act (ERISA) annuity and pension plans, wherein a spouse is included as a beneficiary; immigration rights for a foreign partner, which are attainable only through marriage; the right to file joint federal tax returns; the unlimited marital deduction for transfer tax purposes; social security benefits; and veterans' benefits, including educational and medical services.

Domestic partners are also excluded from most rights accorded automatically by marriage at the *state level*. First of all, domestic partner ordinances and acts provide no rights pertaining to parenthood and do not regulate relationships between parents and children. They thus do not provide for basic rights such as joint adoption and foster care. Although joint adoption is available to same-sex couples in a few states, and second-parent adoption is available to same-sex couples in almost half the states, these rights are not accorded through domestic partnership legislation; they are the result of scattered court decisions at various levels, most of which are nonbinding. They are not comparable to the right of adoption provided to married couples in every state. Domestic partnerships also do not provide automatic custody and visitation rights for nonbiological parents. Other marital rights and protections conferred automatically by the state that same-sex domestic partners are excluded from include spousal support; divorce protections, including property rights and child support; inheritance benefits, including spousal right of election, taxes, and transferal of property in cases of intestacy; guardianship and proxy powers; the right to assume a spouse's pension; the ability to take out loans together; insurance benefits; judicial protection, including evidentiary privileges and crime victims' recovery benefits; the ability to file tort cases, particularly for damages for emotional distress, loss of consortium, and wrongful death; the power to make medical decisions on behalf of the partner; and hundreds of other legal privileges at the workplace and at all levels of government.[22]

Moreover, whereas opposite-sex marriage is automatically recognized by other states and countries, domestic partnerships are recognized only by various cities and a few states.[23] Thus, if domestic partners move from one city to another or from one state to another, they cease to receive their domestic partnership benefits unless such benefits are offered in their new locality.

Marriage statutes impose very few requirements on the individuals

22. *See Marriage and Domestic Partnership: A Fact Sheet,* Lambda Legal Defense and Education Fund, June 17, 1999, at http://www.lambdalegal.org/cgi-bin/pages/documents/record?record=437 [hereinafter Lambda Fact Sheet]. *See also* Domestic Partnerships: Issues and Legislation, note 21 above, at 3–5.

23. *See* Lambda Fact Sheet, note 22 above.

applying for a marriage license, and opposite-sex married couples need only show a marriage certificate to prove their status. Domestic partners, however, cannot rely on a certificate or an affidavit of domestic partnership; a same-sex couple must prove their status as a couple in other ways; the relationship is tested on a case-by-case basis, and the partners usually have to provide proof that they actually "share the common necessities of life."[24] Another important requirement that exists for the formation of a domestic partnership in many cities but not for marriage is a cohabitation requirement.[25] In addition, unlike marriage, domestic partnership legislation is easily subject to change and repeal, either by courts, the localities themselves, or the state.[26] The state, as creator of local governments, has plenary power to alter or even abolish the local governments and their ordinances at will, unless restricted by the state constitution or a state statute providing for municipal home rule. The majority of current activity in the area of domestic partnership is taking place at the local level, and since municipal authority to regulate domestic relations is limited by state law, the courts may strike down local legislation if they conclude that an ordinance conflicts with state law or policy. In fact courts have struck down domestic partnership ordinances.[27] Furthermore, the ability of local governments to equalize the provision of spousal benefits between married employees and employees in domestic partnerships is greatly limited by the federal Employee Retirement Income Security Act (ERISA),[28] which preempts any law that relates to any employee benefit plan described in that act, unless specifically exempted.[29]

To be comparable to legal marriage, a domestic partnership policy would need to provide for a few hundred rights and responsibilities at the state level, depending on the couple's state of residence, as well as activating at least 1,049 federally regulated rights and responsibilities that are triggered by legal marriage.[30] No domestic partner scheme in

24. Knauer, note 16 above, at 341 n. 19, 346.

25. *See* Craig A. Bowman & Blake M. Cornish, *A More Perfect Union: A Legal and Social Analysis of Domestic Partnership Ordinances,* 92 Colum. L. Rev. 1164, 1192–93 (1992). This requirement exists for evidentiary reasons, to show that the parties do in fact form a committed, mutually supportive relationship. *Id.*

26. The attorney general of Hawaii's modification and restriction of Hawaii's Reciprocal Beneficiaries Act serves as an example of how easily a domestic partner scheme can be changed, as compared to marriage law. *See* chap. 7, sec. 7.4.

27. *See* Bowman & Cornish, note 25 above, at 1198, 1201. For court decisions abolishing domestic partnership ordinances, see chap. 7, note 166 above.

28. Employee Retirement Income Security Act of 1974, 29 U.S.C. §§ 1001–461 (1988).

29. *See* Bowman & Cornish, note 25 above, at 1202. *See also* Shaw v. Delta Airlines, 463 U.S. 85 (1983).

30. *See* U.S. General Accounting Office, note 14 above.

the United States provides or could come even close to providing that range of benefits and obligations. Even recognition of same-sex marriage by one or more states would not trigger federal rights that attach to opposite-sex marriage, but such recognition would pave the way for challenging the federal DOMA, and a successful challenge would enable recognition at the federal level.

Some claim that, compared to the struggles for same-sex marriage and parental rights of gays and lesbians, which have met with mixed results,[31] domestic partner benefits in the private and public workplace represent relatively high success, seen especially in changes in corporate policies that cover thousands of employees as well as legislation by municipalities in their capacity as employers.[32] Moreover, domestic partnerships accord same-sex couples some valuable financial benefits and provide gays and lesbians moral support and recognition of their relationships.[33] Indeed, domestic partner benefits represent a positive step toward the recognition and protection of same-sex couples. However, if domestic partnership is viewed as a means for same-sex couples to obtain broad recognition and protection as well as equality with opposite-sex partners, the limitations of those ordinances and policies—in terms of their scope, availability, and applicability—appear to outweigh the aforementioned advantages. Thus, domestic partnership policies have "considerable limitations that make them a less than desirable means of attaining broad-based recognition and protection of same-sex relationships,"[34] and they should be regarded only as a small and interim step in the struggle of same-sex couples for equality, rather than as establishing a valuable and distinct family relationship in and of itself.[35]

9.3 Existing Models of Recognition as "Second-Class Marriage"

One indication that registered partnerships and domestic partnerships are regarded as "second-class marriage" is their unpopularity, the rela-

31. For same-sex marriage, see chap. 7, sec. 7.6; for parental rights of same-sex couples in the United States, see chap. 7, sec. 7.1.

32. *See* Urvashi Vaid, Virtual Equality: The Mainstreaming of Gay and Lesbian Liberation 10 (1995).

33. *See* Knauer, note 16 above, at 342, 350 (noting that the establishment of a domestic partnership scheme also signifies that an employer values its gay employees and their partners and claiming that the existence of domestic partnerships may make homosexual employees more comfortable with their orientation and thus more loyal and productive. Furthermore, the policies allow gay and lesbian employees to be out in their jobs, instead of being closeted and trying to conceal their sexual orientation on a daily basis).

34. *Id.* at 348, 360, quotation at 360.

35. *See* Shoshana Bricklin, *Legislative Approaches to Support Family Diversity*, 7 Temple Pol. & Civ. Rts. L. Rev. 379, 383 (1998).

tively low number of registrations in comparison to the number of marriages of opposite-sex couples. In northern Europe, only a small percentage of gay couples make use of the registered partnership. Evidence suggests that many same-sex couples are not registering their partnerships because they prefer to wait for full marriage rights.[36] Even in the Netherlands, where the number of registration is higher than in any other country, the registered partnership is not popular. A Dutch survey found that over 80 percent of the same-sex couples who registered their partnerships before the Netherlands opened up marriage to same-sex couples would have chosen marriage had that option been available at the time, and a large majority (more than 60%) said they would like to convert their registered partnership into marriage when it became available (many have done so since gay marriage became available), stating that the main reason for their desire to convert to marriage was "full equality" or that "marriage has more significance." Marriage is thus perceived as an institution with more weight than a registered partnership, and marriage for same-sex couples is seen as a symbol of full equality.[37] Moreover, since opposite-sex registration is also relatively low as compared to the number of couples who get married in the Netherlands, there is at least socially a significant difference between marriage and registered partnership.[38] Opposite-sex couples who chose registration over marriage have indicated that their reason for doing so was the notion that "registered partnership is less binding than marriage."[39]

Registration of domestic partnerships in the United States has also been very low. Less than 1 percent of gay and lesbian employees elect domestic partner benefits, presumably because they do not find the domestic partner status to be of practical use.[40] Therefore, unless domestic partnerships are greatly expanded, they should be viewed not as an equivalent or a substitute for same-sex marriage but as a means of according rights and benefits to cohabiting partners and obtaining

36. *See* Kees Waaldijk, *Small Change: How the Road to Same-Sex Marriage Got Paved in the Netherlands, in* Legal Recognition of Same-Sex Partnerships: A Study of National, European, and International Law 437 (Robert Wintemute & Mads Andenas eds., 2001).

37. Scherf, Quick Scan, note 11 above, at 22, 28, quotation at 22.

38. *See* Waaldijk, note 36 above.

39. Scherf, Quick Scan, note 11 above, at 21.

40. *See Domestic Partner Benefits: Philosophy and Provider List,* Partners Task Force for Gay & Lesbian Couples, at http://www.buddybuddy.com/d-p-1.html (last visited on October 1, 1999). For instance, in the state of Hawaii, only 435 couples signed up in one year, and not all were same-sex partners. *See Reciprocal Beneficiaries: The Hawaiian Approach,* Partners Task Force for Gay & Lesbian Couples, at http://www.buddybuddy.com/d-p-rec.html (last visited September 20, 1999). Nancy Knauer attributes the low level of participation in domestic partner benefits to "the perceived views of the employee's supervisor or co-workers, or internalized homophobia." *See* note 16 above, at 358–59.

economic parity in the workplace with married couples. The same is applicable to registered partnerships: until the exceptions to marriage are removed, this model also cannot be regarded as an equal substitute for marriage. This seems to have been the concept or rationale that led to the reform in the Dutch marriage law: although its Registered Partnership Act, according same-sex couples most of the rights associated with marriage, had been in effect since 1998, the Dutch legislature did not consider this alternative sufficient and insisted on opening up the existing institution of marriage to same-sex couples. The Dutch legislature hence clearly expressed its position that full equality for same-sex couples could be achieved only by their inclusion in the institution of marriage. The Netherlands is thus the only country in the world to have accorded full equality to gays and lesbians.

Assessing the alternative models in light of the goals of marriage further exemplifies the second-class status of such institutions. As discussed in chapter 2 above, the state has three main reasons for regulating and supporting marriage, which are also the three major goals of marriage.[41] The first goal is to further the couple's affective and emotional bonds, as exemplified by the right of a person to take family care and medical leave from work in order to care for his or her spouse and children, hospital and prison visitation rights, and the like. The second goal of marriage is to facilitate economic sharing so as to enable the couple to organize their lives in ways that maximize their joint well-being. This is exemplified by, inter alia, community property regime and mutual support obligations during the marriage, the right to receive additional social security benefits based upon the spouse's contribution, and the right to file joint tax returns. The third goal of marriage is to support parents in the raising of children by, for instance, the right to automatic joint custody, adoption of children by stepparents, and the right to jointly adopt unrelated children.

The registered partnership acts of the northern European countries and Vermont's civil union act do indeed bring lesbian and gay relationships into the closest proximity to marriage that currently exists anywhere in the world. However, legislation in the European countries is largely limited to the first two goals of marriage discussed above—the furtherance of affective relations and the economic rights of same-sex couples—with very little recognition of same-sex couples as parents. In contrast, legislation and case law in the United States are largely limited to providing same-sex couples with parental rights; except for Vermont's

41. For an elaborate discussion of the goals of marriage, including a more exhaustive list of examples for the achievement of each goal, see chap. 2.

civil union act, they provide very few rights in connection with the first two goals of marriage regulation.[42] However, in terms of the aforementioned *goals of marriage,* the civil union act, in addition to case law and legislation in Vermont conferring various parental rights on same-sex couples—is the closest alternative to marriage available in the world. As explained earlier, the act's limitations have to do with its inability to attach rights at the U.S. federal level. In that sense only, it is more limited than the registered partnership acts.[43]

In light of the foregoing, and as is evident from the comparison of both the American domestic partnership and the European registered partnership with marriage,[44] it is clear that, with the exception of Dutch same-sex marriage, no existing model places same-sex couples on an equal footing with opposite-sex married couples. Full equality for same-sex couples has not been achieved even by the most comprehensive alternatives to marriage, such as Vermont's civil union act or the European registered partnership acts. Both models of recognition are inferior to marriage because each of them, in its own way, is less comprehensive and more restrictive than marriage. No alternative model fully encompasses all three main goals of marriage regulation, and both models are less extensive than opening up marriage to same-sex couples. Thus, existing alternative models to marriage cannot be regarded as equivalent to opposite-sex marriage or as a substitute for same-sex marriage. Excluding same-sex couples from various parental rights in Europe and from most other rights associated with marriage in the United States perpetuates the most common prejudice against same-sex couples and cannot be justified on any other ground than bigotry. Therefore, I regard existing models that are alternative to marriage not only as a "restricted form of marriage"[45] but also as "second-class marriage" for people who are evidently still considered second-class citizens. As chapter 10 shows, society's acceptance of *some* degree of legal equality for gays is not equivalent to recognition of the *equal value* of their relationships.[46]

---

42. For an explanation of the reasons and rationales for the different emphases in the United States and northern Europe, see chap. 8, sec. 8.3.

43. Moreover, it is not insignificant that the Vermont legislature, trying hard to mimic its marriage legislation, enacted the civil union law specifically in order to avoid the inclusion of same-sex couples in its definition of (regular) marriage. Similar intentions could be discerned in the registered partnership countries. *See* chap. 10.

44. *See* secs. 9.1 and 9.2 above.

45. Henning Bech, *Report from a Rotten State: Marriage and Homosexuality in Denmark, in* Modern Homosexualities: Fragments of Lesbian and Gay Experience 134, 141 (Ken Plummer ed., 1992).

46. *See also id.* at 142.

Chapter 10

Alternatives to Marriage and the Doctrine of "Separate but Equal"

This chapter addresses an issue that is currently at the heart of the debate over the rights of same-sex couples—the question whether the status of same-sex couples should be recognized outside and separately from the institution of marriage or as part of it. As explained in chapter 9, models alternative to marriage for the recognition of same-sex partnerships— registered partnership and domestic partnership—are, to varying degrees, unequal to marriage and thus constitute discrimination against same-sex couples. Until such schemes accord same-sex couples *all* the rights, benefits, obligations, and protections associated with opposite-sex marriage, as has been done in the Netherlands, they will remain unsatisfactory. Indeed, as pointed out earlier, some of the distinctions between registered partnership and marriage are already beginning to fade as the northern European countries amend their acts to equate the status of same-sex couples with that of opposite-sex married couples; note, for example, the Danish second-parent adoption amendment and the relaxation of requirements in the field of citizenship and residency. Similarly, if additional states follow Vermont's lead and adopt civil union acts, a development that will quite likely take place in the next few years, then regulation of same-sex partnerships in the United States may also begin to resemble marriage.

However, even if the existing models were amended and expanded so as to include *all* the rights that flow from marriage, which most probably will occur, and even if all the distinctions between registered or domestic partnership and marriage disappeared but for the name, full equality would still not have been achieved, because these models would still be separate institutions for same-sex couples, distinct from the institution of marriage. Most scholars who compare registered and domestic partnerships with marriage take into account only the differences in terms of rights, obligations, and benefits. Their assumption is that if the rights and benefits are similar, then the alternatives are equal to marriage. This assumption fails to consider the impact of segregation that the exclusion from marriage, a highly esteemed institution that has social and cultural meanings that transcend the "bundle of rights," has on gay men and lesbians. Both registered partnership and domestic partnership single out gays as an unprivileged group that is in need of special treatment. Substantive equality is to be achieved *only* by the inclusion of same-sex couples in existing marriage legislation.

In chapter 2 of this book I provide an overview of the ways in which race, gender, and sexual orientation are analogous as grounds for discrimination. My concern here is with the application of the analogy between homophobia and racism in the specific context of the debate as to whether marriage substitutes serve to disadvantage same-sex couples. In this connection, the segregation of African Americans is extremely instructive as an analogy to the harm of excluding gays from marriage and providing them with separate models of regulation. The fact that the models are self-consciously separate from marriage renders them inherently unequal to opposite-sex marriage; "separate but equal" in this context instantiates the same constitutional evil that led the U.S. Supreme Court to condemn this doctrine in the racial domain. This is yet another reason why marriage substitutes constitute second-class marriage. The only remedy for the existing discrimination against same-sex couples would be their inclusion in the institution of marriage.

10.1 Racial Segregation in the United States

The doctrine of "separate but equal" originated in the context of racial discrimination in the United States in 1896, when the U.S. Supreme Court held in the case of *Plessy v. Ferguson* that a Louisiana statute requiring all railway companies within the state to provide separate but equal accommodations for white and black persons did not violate the Thirteenth Amendment.[1] The court found that discrimination based on race was an inherent part of society that should not and could not be remedied by the judiciary, and new doctrine of "separate but equal" was

1. 163 U.S. 537 (1896).

created.[2] Plessy did not argue in his brief that the accommodations were not equal. Rather, he argued that the statute that required blacks and whites to ride in separate railroad cars when traveling intrastate was unconstitutional; he explicitly demanded the right to racially integrated train accommodations, not just "equal" ones.[3] The only question at issue was thus whether the statute requiring separate but equal train accommodations violated the equal protection clause of the Fourteenth Amendment. Justice Henry Brown rejected the proposition "that equal rights cannot be secured to the negro except by the enforced commingling of the two races" and contended that laws requiring racial segregation did not "necessarily imply the inferiority of one race to the other" and "that the enforced separation of the two races" did not stamp "the colored race with a badge of inferiority."[4] The court explained that the standard of reasonableness is determined "with reference to the established usages, customs, and traditions of the people."[5] In fact, the court in *Plessy* justified legislation that was based on prejudice in the American South, which had been threatened by the abolition of slavery, reasoning that racial segregation was rooted in tradition and that a law based on such tradition was reasonable. The court thus constitutionalized the enactment of race prejudice and justified white supremacy.[6] In his dissent, Justice John Harlan declared that the obvious rationale for segregation was that blacks "are so inferior and degraded that they cannot be allowed to sit" with whites; he expressed the view that separate racial accommodations, even if perfectly equal, are essentially unequal.[7]

Plessy was not directly challenged for more than half a century. It was in 1954 that the Supreme Court abolished the "separate but equal" doctrine in the landmark decision *Brown v. Board of Education*,[8] adopting

---

2. *Id.* at 552.

3. *See* Stephen J. Riegel, *The Persistent Career of Jim Crow: Lower Federal Courts and the "Separate but Equal" Doctrine 1865–1896, in* 12 Black Southerners and the Law 1865–1900, at 349, 369–70 (Donald G. Nieman ed., 1994).

4. Plessy v. Ferguson, 163 U.S. 537, at 551 (1896).

5. *Id.* at 550 (1896). *See also* Barton J. Bernstein, *Plessy v. Ferguson: Conservative Sociological Jurisprudence, in* 12 Black Southerners and the Law 1865–1900, at 4–5 (Donald G. Nieman ed., 1994).

6. *See* Bernstein, note 5 above, at 6–8.

7. Plessy v. Ferguson, 163 U.S. 537, at 560 (1896).

8. 347 U.S. 483 (1954). Although the Court had decided six cases involving the "separate but equal" doctrine in public education prior to *Brown*, the legitimacy of the doctrine itself had not been challenged directly before *Brown*. *See* Brown v. Board of Education, 347 U.S. 483, 491–92 (1954). *See, e.g.*, Sweatt v. Painter, 339 U.S. 629 (1950) (holding that a segregated African American law school could not provide equal educational opportuni-

Justice Harlan's dissent in *Plessy* and holding that "separate educational facilities are *inherently unequal*."[9] *Brown* arose when African American children from four different states—Kansas, South Carolina, Virginia, and Delaware—brought a class action suit after they were refused admission to schools established under state laws that allowed local districts to mandate racial segregation.[10] The *Brown* Court held that legally mandated racial segregation in public primary and secondary schools cannot result in equal education under the law because such a situation stigmatizes students belonging to the minority racial group.[11] It explicitly overruled the "separate but equal" doctrine, holding separate educational facilities in public schools unequal and therefore invalid under the Equal Protection Clause of the Fourteenth Amendment. The Court looked to the effect of segregation on public education and found segregated schools unequal because they generated a feeling of racial inferiority in African American children.[12] The Supreme Court's unanimous decision in *Brown* was the starting point for a major change in American race relations and is consequently considered one of the most important events in recent U.S. history.[13] *Brown* attempted to remedy two centuries of legalized racism,[14] and despite criticism over the decision,[15] it clearly opened many doors, providing educational opportunities previously inaccessible to African Americans and advancing the

---

ties); McLaurin v. Oklahoma State Regents for Higher Educ., 339 U.S. 637 (1950) (requiring that an African American admitted to a white graduate school be treated like all other students).

9. Brown, 347 U.S. 483, 495 (1954).

10. *Id.* at 486–88. For example, Topeka, Kans., maintained a segregated public school system in accordance with Chapter 72-1724 of the General Statutes of Kansas, 1949. *See* Brown v. Board of Educ., 98 F. Supp. 797, 797 (D. Kan. 1951), rev'd, 347 U.S. 483 (1954). This statute authorized "cities of the first class" to establish and maintain separate schools for white and African American children in grades below high school. *Id.*

11. *See* Brown, 347 U.S. 483, 494–95 (1954).

12. *Id.* at 495, 494–95. According to later case law, for a segregation challenge to be successful, a plaintiff must establish that there was purpose or intent to segregate; the existence of segregation by itself does not render it unconstitutional. *See* Keyes v. School District #1, 413 U.S. 189 (1973); Washington v. Davis, 426 U.S. 229 (1976).

13. Maria A. Perugini, Note, *Board of Education of Oklahoma City v. Dowell: Protection of Local Authority or Disregard for the Purpose of Brown v. Board of Education,* 41 Cath. U. L. Rev. 779, 784 (1992).

14. Richard Cummings, *All-Male Black Schools: Equal Protection, the New Separatism, and Brown v. Board of Education,* 20 Hastings Const. L.Q. 725, 747 (1993).

15. *See, e.g.,* Robert H. Bork, The Tempting of America: The Political Seduction of the Law 75–77 (1990) (criticizing *Brown*'s holding as "disingenuous" because the Court relied on the stigmatic injury of African American children to prove the unconstitutionality of segregation. Bork claims that *Brown* is not about racial inferiority, that it had nothing to do with the context of education or the infliction of stigma, and attributes the *Brown* decision to the Warren Court's ability to make political decisions because it had the support of a political constituency).

integration of African Americans into mainstream society through the classroom.[16]

Although the Supreme Court decided *Brown* in 1954, for the next thirteen years it avoided applying the logic of its holding to another aspect of racial segregation and discrimination, the antimiscegenation laws.[17] These statutes and their repeal are of special significance to our current discussion since they dealt with discrimination and segregation within the specific context of marriage.

Antimiscegenation laws that prohibited interracial marriages were in force in the United States as early as the 1660s, but only later did they begin "to function as a central sanction in the system of white supremacy."[18] At one time or another, forty-one American colonies and states enacted such laws.[19] In 1967 the case of an interracial married couple, *Loving v. Virginia,* reached the U.S. Supreme Court.[20] The 1924 statute under which the couple were prosecuted, entitled An Act to Preserve Racial Integrity, decreed that in Virginia no white person could marry anyone other than another white person. Not only did this law criminalize interracial marriage within the state; it also criminalized entering into an interracial marriage outside the state with the intent of evading Virginia's prohibition.[21] The Court struck the law down and declared that "the clear and central purpose of the Fourteenth Amendment was to eliminate all official state sources of invidious racial discrimination in the States," that the Virginia statute was "designed to maintain White Supremacy," and that there existed "no legitimate overriding purpose [for the statute] independent of invidious racial discrimination." Moreover, the Court found that the prohibition solely on interracial marriage with whites could serve to protect only the white community's interest in racial integrity and racial pride, and the inconsistencies along racial group lines in the government's pursuit of its claimed interest allowed the Court to conclude that an unconstitutional motivating animus toward people of color was at work in the law.[22]

16. Drew Days III, *Brown Blues: Rethinking the Integrative Ideal,* 34 Wm. & Mary L. Rev. 53, 74 (1992).

17. *See* Andrew Koppelman, *The Miscegenation Analogy: Sodomy Law as Sex Discrimination,* 98 Yale L.J. 145, 163 (1988).

18. Andrew Koppelman, *Same-Sex Marriage and Public Policy: The Miscegenation Precedents,* 16 Quinnipiac L. Rev. 105, 114 (1996).

19. *Id.,* citing Peggy Pascoe, *Miscegenation Law, Court Cases, and Ideologies of "Race" in Twentieth-Century America,* 83 J. Am. Hist. 44, 49 (1996).

20. 388 U.S. 1 (1967).

21. *See* Randall Kennedy, How Are We Doing with Loving? Race, Law, and Intermarriage 77 B.U. L. Rev. 815, at 819 (1997).

22. Loving v. Virginia, 388 U.S. 1, 10–11 (1967). In the process of doing so, the Court also implicitly invalidated similar laws then in existence in fifteen other states. *See* Kennedy, note 21 above, at 819.

10.2 Segregation Based on Gender and Sexual Orientation

The Supreme Court applied the logic of *Brown* also in the context of gender discrimination in the matter of *United States v. Virginia*. The Court held that the Commonwealth of Virginia violated the Equal Protection Clause by prohibiting women from attending the state-supported Virginia Military Institute (VMI) because the state failed to show an exceedingly persuasive justification for denying women the right to attend VMI and because the remedial plan for women established at Mary Baldwin College (VWIL) did not provide women with a *substantially equal* alternative.[23] The Court compared Virginia's VWIL solution to the remedy proposed in the matter of *Sweatt*, in which the state of Texas, reluctant to admit African Americans to its flagship University of Texas Law School, set up a separate school for Heman Sweatt and other black law students.[24] Analogizing to the segregation of African Americans in higher education during the 1940s, the Court in VMI held that maintaining a separate but equal military educational institution for women was in violation of the Constitution because, again, it was inherently unequal, since VMI reserved unique educational opportunities for men not afforded to women.[25] The Court stated that

23. 116 S. Ct. 2264, 2276 (1996). *See also* Jason M. Bernheimer, Note, *Single-Sex Public Education: Separate but Equal Is Not Equal at the Young Women's Leadership School in New York City*, 14 N.Y.L. Sch. J. Hum. Rts. 339, 354 (1997).

24. *See* Sweatt v. Painter, 339 U.S. 629 (1950).

25. For cases in which distinctions between men and women were upheld as justifying separate treatment of women or their exclusion from participation in "male institutions," see, for example, Bradwell v. Illinois, 83 U.S. (16 Wall.) 130 (1872) (holding that the Fourteenth Amendment did not preclude Illinois from barring women from the practice of law); Muller v. Oregon, 208 U.S. 412 (1908) (holding that states had the authority to regulate the working hours of women based upon their police powers and right to protect the health of their citizens); Goesaert v. Cleary, 335 U.S. 464 (1948) (holding that a rule against women's being allowed to tend bar was justified as a protection of their virtue); Rostker v. Goldberg, 453 U.S. 57 (1981) (holding that Congress acted within its constitutional authority when it authorized registration of men, not women, under the Military Selective Service Act); Michael M. v. Superior Court, 450 U.S. 464 (1981) (holding that age and gender discrimination in statutory rape laws is not unconstitutional); Mississippi University for Women v. Hogan, 102 S. Ct. 3331 (1982) (holding that exclusion from a publicly funded school based on sex is unconstitutional unless the exclusion served important governmental objectives and the means employed substantially relate to the achievement of these objectives). For cases striking down statutes based on such distinctions, see, for example, Reed v. Reed, 404 U.S. 71 (1971) (holding that mandatory preference of one gender over the other in appointment of administrators of intestate decedents' estates violated the Equal Protection Clause); Frontiero v. Richardson, 411 U.S. 677 (1973) (holding that a federal law that automatically allowed a male uniformed services member to claim his spouse as a dependent but required a female uniformed services member to show that her spouse was dependent on her for more than half his support violated the equal-protection component of the Fifth Amendment).

"[i]nherent differences" between men and women, we have come to appreciate, remain cause for celebration, but not for denigration of the members of either sex or for artificial constraints on an individual's opportunity. Sex classifications may be used to compensate women "for particular economic disabilities [they have] suffered," . . . to "promote equal employment opportunity," to advance full development of the talent and capacities of our Nation's people. *But such classifications may not be used, as they once were . . . to create or perpetuate the legal, social, and economic inferiority of women. . . .*

. . . Holding that the remedy proffered by Virginia—maintain VMI as a male-only college and create VWIL as a separate program for women—does not cure the constitutional violation.[26]

Yet other parts of the Court's reasoning may suggest that its holding was mainly based on the fact that the two institutions were simply unequal, suggesting that unlike *Brown, VMI* dealt with separate but *un*equal institutions and that had the two schools offered the same courses, and so forth, the exclusion of women from VMI would not have violated equal protection principles:

In myriad respects other than military training, *VWIL does not qualify as VMI's equal*. VWIL's student body, faculty, course offerings, and facilities hardly match VMI's. Nor can the VWIL graduate anticipate the benefits associated with VMI's 157-year history, the school's prestige, and its influential alumni network. . . .

. . . Virginia, in sum, while maintaining VMI for men only, has failed to provide any "comparable single-gender women's institution." . . . Instead, the Commonwealth has created a VWIL program fairly appraised as *a "pale shadow" of VMI* in terms of the range of curricular choices and faculty stature, funding, prestige, alumni support and influence.[27]

The Court's stance on "separate but equal" in *VMI* cannot be definitively discerned.[28] Yet I would argue that even if the Court had explicitly

26. United States v. Virginia, 518 U.S. 515, 533–34 (1996), my emphasis.

27. *Id.* at 551, 553, my emphasis.

28. *VMI* seems to have left open the question of whether a separate but equal regime for women would be constitutional. It is only Chief Justice Rehnquist's concurring opinion that explicitly declares that VMI could have avoided a constitutional attack if Virginia had created a separate school for women of equal caliber to VMI. *See id.* at 558–66. Note that the Supreme Court has consistently avoided addressing this issue in cases involving gender classifications. Moreover, the Court avowed that since VMI is unique, it was not faced with a question of the legality of separate but equal institutions (116 S. Ct. at 2276). Therefore, the question that remains open after *VMI* is whether a separate, but truly equal, VMI counterpart would have been constitutional.

upheld a "separate but equal" regime in the case of gender, the basic logic of *Brown* would nevertheless have been sustained: as long as it was not to further the special needs of women and redress past discrimination based on gender, "separate but equal" would have been held unconstitutional by the *VMI* Court for the same reasons *Brown* held separate but equal education facilities for blacks and whites unconstitutional.[29] As Justice Ruth Bader Ginsburg explains, "inherent differences" between men and women may justify separate institutions in order to *further* the equality of women: "[i]t is the mission of some single-sex schools to dissipate, rather than perpetuate, traditional gender classifications."[30] As I explain below, it is my opinion that, much as segregation based on race is objectionable, and despite differences that may exist between homosexual and heterosexual couples, there are *no relevant* differences between same- and opposite-sex couples for the purposes of the legal regulation of a couple's cohabitation (in particular, marriage). Thus, unlike some instances of justifiable segregation based on gender that are designed to redress past discrimination and thus further the equality of women, a separate scheme for same-sex couples is inherently unequal and thus constitutionally objectionable.[31] In the matter of excluding gays from marriage, it is highly unlikely that an argument according to which separate institutions further the equality between gays and heterosexuals would be accepted as constitutional. Therefore, If *VMI* is read as standing for the proposition that segregation may be upheld only when there are relevant inherent differences and *not* when the differences are irrelevant, then the analogy between *VMI* and the exclusion of gays from marriage is a valid one. On this reading, VMI would be the equivalent of opposite-sex marriage, and VWIL would stand for alternatives to marriage designed for same-sex couples, except that the latter case may be categorized as discrimination based on sexual orientation rather than, or in addition to, sex discrimination. This difference,

29. The *VMI* Court implied that the reasoning of *Brown* supported the interpretation that its holding applied to sex classifications when it quoted scholars who equated all-male institutions with all-white institutions, implying that just as the latter reinforces ideas of white supremacy, the former contributes to the perpetuation of a patriarchal society. *See* VMI, 116 S. Ct. at 2277 n. 8 (quoting Christopher Jencks & David Riesman, The Academic Revolution 297–98 [1968]). Thus, the possibility exists that in cases in which the separation serves to perpetuate the inferiority of women, the Court would find separate but equal schooling for men and women to be inherently defective, as it did in the racial context.

30. 116 S. Ct. at 2277 n. 7, 2276.

31. Same-sex-marriage opponents maintain that there are relevant differences between homosexuals and heterosexuals that do justify the exclusion of gays from (opposite-sex) marriage or the creation of a separate but equal institution for same-sex couples. For discussion of this argument, see below.

however, should not lead to a different conclusion in the case of separate institutions for gays.

In the specific context of sexual-orientation discrimination, the U.S. Supreme Court, in *Romer v. Evans*,[32] struck down what has become known as Amendment 2, a 1992 amendment to the Colorado Constitution that would have repealed all legislation prohibiting discrimination on the basis of sexual orientation and prevented any future such enactments.[33] The Supreme Court invalidated Amendment 2 on the ground that it defied rational basis analysis under the Equal Protection Clause. The Court held that Amendment 2 went far beyond repealing past legislation benefiting gays, lesbians, and bisexuals. It also prevented any future legislation with a similar effect short of a constitutional amendment. The Court emphasized that a state had no legitimate purpose in completely removing a select group of citizens from the general protection of discrimination laws. By removing homosexuals from the general protection of antidiscrimination laws, Amendment 2 essentially separated homosexuals from the rest of the population, creating two classes of unequal citizens. Quoting Justice Harlan's famous dissent in *Plessy v. Ferguson,* the Court reasoned that the law "neither knows nor tolerates classes among citizens." It argued that Amendment 2 was so broad in scope that it could be read as nothing more than an attempt to single out a politically and socially unpopular group of citizens and deny that group equal protection under the laws. A bare desire to harm a politically unpopular group was not a legitimate purpose and could not withstand even minimal constitutional scrutiny.[34]

A case in which segregation on the basis of sexual orientation was held constitutional by the U.S. Supreme Court, albeit in the context of the First Amendment, is the *Boy Scouts* case.[35] In his dissent, Justice Stevens said the following, which I view as applicable to the current exclusion of gays from marriage: "The only apparent explanation for the majority's holding, then, is that homosexuals are simply so different from

32. 517 U.S. 620 (1996).

33. Amendment 2 provides: "No Protected Status Based on Homosexual, Lesbian, or Bisexual Orientation. Neither the State of Colorado, through any of its branches or departments, nor any of its agencies, political subdivisions, municipalities or school districts, shall enact, adopt or enforce any statute, regulation, ordinance or policy whereby homosexual, lesbian or bisexual orientation, conduct, practices or relationships shall constitute or otherwise be the basis of or entitle any person or class of persons to have or claim any minority status, quota preferences, protected status or claim of discrimination. This Section of the Constitution shall be in all respects self-executing." Colo. Const., art. 2, at 30b.

34. Romer v. Evans, 517 U.S. 620, 631, 626–27, 621–30, 633–34 (1996), quotation at 622.

35. Boy Scouts of America v. Dale, 530 U.S. 640 (2000).

the rest of society that their presence alone—unlike any other individu-al's—should be singled out for special First Amendment treatment. Un-der the majority's reasoning, an openly gay male is irreversibly affixed with the label 'homosexual.' That label, even though unseen, communi-cates a message that permits exclusion wherever he goes. His openness is the sole and sufficient justification for his ostracism. Though unin-tended, *reliance on such a justification is tantamount to a constitutionally prescribed symbol of inferiority.*"[36]

Based on the cases discussed above, Supreme Court jurisprudence seems to suggest that there are parallels between decisions pertaining to segregation of blacks and those pertaining to other disadvantaged groups, including women and gays. It should be noted, however, that in the matter of *Bowers v. Hardwick*,[37] which was decided before *Romer*, the Supreme Court held "homosexual sodomy" laws constitutional, and an argument can be made that unless *Hardwick* is explicitly overturned, separate and discriminatory treatment of homosexuals in a context that is not as broad as *Romer*'s Amendment 2 may be upheld as constitu-tional. Nevertheless, some have suggested that *Romer* is to be regarded as a rhetorical overturning of *Hardwick*.[38]

Notwithstanding *Hardwick*'s authority in light of *Romer*, and as Mar-tha Ertman asserts, "Evans stands most clearly for the simultaneously modest and radical proposition that gay people may not be relegated to second class citizenship as a matter of law. Future cases will determine whether *Evans* is to sexual orientation discrimination what *Brown v. Board of Education* was to racial discrimination."[39] The cases of *Loving*, *VMI*, and *Romer* are largely based on the same general rationale, philoso-phy, and logic as *Brown*. Moreover, these cases are analogous and

36. *Id.* at 696, my emphasis.

37. 478 U.S. 186 (1986).

38. *See* David A. J. Richards, Women, Gays, and the Constitution: The Grounds for Feminism and Gay Rights in Culture and Law 444 (1998) (arguing that *Bowers* was wrongly decided and should be overruled and that a reasonable interpretation of *Romer* suggests implicitly that it has been). For similar arguments, see also Andrew M. Jacobs, *Romer Wasn't Built in a Day: The Subtle Transformation in Judicial Argument over Gay Rights*, 1996 Wis. L. Rev. 893; Akhil Reed Amar, *Attainder and Amendment 2: Romer's Rightness*, 94 Mich. L. Rev. 203 (1996); Kevin G. Walsh, Comment, *Throwing Stones: Rational Basis Review Triumphs over Homophobia*, 27 Seton Hall L. Rev. 1064 (1997); Katherine M. Hamill, Comment, *Romer v. Evans: Dulling the Equal Protection Gloss on Bowers v. Hardwick*, 77 B.U. L. Rev. 655 (1997); Courtney G. Joslin, *Recent Development, Equal Protection, and Anti-Gay Legislation: Dismantling the Legacy of Bowers v. Hardwick—Romer v. Evans*, 116 S. Ct. 1620, 32 Harv. C.R.-C.L. L. Rev. 225 (1996). *See also* Robert D. Dodson, *Homosexual Discrimina-tion and Gender: Was Romer v. Evans Really a Victory for Gay Rights?* 35 Cal. W.L. Rev. 271, 272 (1999). For further discussion of the case and its implications, see chap. 11.

39. Martha M. Ertman, *Sexuality: Contractual Purgatory for Sexual Marginorities: Not Heaven, but Not Hell Either*, 73 Denv. U. L. Rev. 1107, 1150 (1997).

instructive to the issue at hand, the enactment of separate but equal alternatives to marriage for same-sex couples.

10.3 The *Loving* Analogy

The *Loving* analogy is certainly not a new one. It argues that in much the same way as interracial marriages were unconstitutional based on racism and the ideology of white supremacy, so is the exclusion of same-sex couples from marriage unconstitutional, based on comparable bases of discrimination (sex, gender, sexual orientation) and on comparable ideologies: homophobia, gender binarism, and compulsory heterosexuality. For almost thirty years, there has been a debate going on about the implications of *Loving* for the status and rights of same-sex couples in the United States.[40] The meaning of *Loving* has been debated by litigants in most cases pertaining to same-sex marriage, from *Baker v. Nelson*[41] through *Baker v. Vermont*.[42] In *Singer v. Hara* the analogy was rejected,[43] whereas in *Baehr v. Miike* it was accepted.[44] Cogent application of the *Loving* analogy to the exclusion of same-sex couples from marriage is found in the scholarly writings of Andrew Koppelman,[45] William Eskridge,[46] and Mark Strasser,[47] as well as the accounts of many other scholars who have examined the applicability and accuracy of the analogy.[48]

40. *See* David Orgon Coolidge, *Playing the Loving Card: Same-Sex Marriage and the Politics of Analogy*, 12 BYU J. Pub. L. 201, 202 (1998), referring to Robert J. Sickles, Race, Marriage, and the Law, 148 (1972), who argued in 1972 that *Loving* might eventually be used to challenge laws that define marriage as the union of a man and a woman.

41. 191 N.W.2d 185 (Minn. 1971).

42. Baker v. State of Vermont, 744 A.2d 864 (Vt. Sup. Ct. 1999).

43. 522 P.2d 1187 (Wash. Ct. App. 1974).

44. 910 P.2d 112 (Haw. 1996).

45. *See* Koppelman, note 17 above, at 145; Andrew Koppelman, *Why Discrimination against Lesbians and Gay Men Is Sex Discrimination*, 69 N.Y.U. L. Rev. 197 (1994); Koppelman, note 18 above; Andrew Koppelman, *Survey of Books Relating to the Law: Sex, Law, and Equality: Three Arguments for Gay Rights*, 95 Mich. L. Rev. 1636, 1661 (1997).

46. *See* William N. Eskridge Jr., The Case for Same-Sex Marriage 153–63 (1996) [hereinafter Case for Same-Sex Marriage]; William N. Eskridge Jr., *A History of Same-Sex Marriage*, 79 Va. L. Rev. 1419, 1504–10 (1993).

47. *See* Mark Strasser, Legally Wed: Same-Sex Marriage and the Constitution 66–69 (1997); Mark Strasser, *Family, Definitions, and the Constitution: On the Miscegenation Analogy*, 25 Suffolk U. L. Rev. 981, 1001 (1991); Mark Strasser, *Domestic Relations Jurisprudence and the Great, Slumbering Baehr: On Definitional Preclusion, Equal Protection, and Fundamental Interests*, 64 Fordham L. Rev. 921, 927 (1995); Mark Strasser, *Constitutional Limitations and Baehr Possibilities: On Retroactive Legislation, Reasonable Expectations, and Manifest Injustice*, 29 Rutgers L.J. 271, 275–76 (1998).

48. *See, e.g.*, Robert Wintemute, *Recognizing New Kinds of Direct Sex Discrimination: Transsexualism, Sexual Orientation, and Dress Codes*, 60 Mod. L. Rev. 334 (1997); Robert Wintemute, *Sexual Orientation and Human Rights*, chap. 8 (Clarendon Press, 1995).

Commentators employing the *Loving* analogy have not addressed the problem of a separate but equal institution for same-sex couples and have largely overlooked the fact that courts striking down antimiscegenation laws did not suspend their judgment to allow the legislature an opportunity to enact a separate licensing scheme for interracial marriages.[49] Moreover, unlike same-sex couples, black couples were not excluded from marriage per se but rather from equal participation in marriage. Blacks could still often marry the object of their love, whereas same-sex couples are totally excluded from doing so. Statistics from 1990 regarding the low rate of interracial marriages, more than two decades after the abolition of all antimiscegenation laws, are further proof that although stigmatizing blacks as a group and severely discriminating against them on racist grounds, the miscegenation laws had an actual effect on very few couples.[50]

There is no doubt that the *Loving* analogy is still an important and a useful one in arguing for the right of same-sex couples to enter the institution of marriage. Moreover, based on its facts (i.e., dealing directly with the right to marriage), *Loving seems, at first,* to be more relevant to the exclusion of same-sex couples from marriage than *Brown.* Yet there are several reasons why I chose to employ *Brown* as the *principal* analogy rather than *Loving.* First, the *Loving* analogy as applied to the current exclusion of same-sex couples would have been more accurate if, instead of antimiscegenation laws, the legislature had created a separate institution of marriage for blacks or for mixed-race couples and had preserved the institution of "regular" marriage for whites only. Thus, although *Loving* involved marriage, the situation there was different from the current exclusion of gays from marriage, since there had been no (separate but equal) marriage scheme for interracial couples. Most American scholars employed the *Loving* analogy when the options were largely limited to either inclusion of gays in marriage or no recognition *at all,* and they did so long before options such as the civil union act were considered; in addition, they did not consider the analogy's application to foreign jurisdictions and solutions, such as the registered partnership acts and other European alternatives to marriage.

Today, however, with domestic partnerships, Vermont's civil unions,

---

49. *See* Baker v. State of Vermont, 744 A.2d 864 (Vt. Sup. Ct. 1999; Justice Johnson, dissenting).

50. According to the calculations of Douglas Besharov and Timothy Sullivan, in 1990 about 5.9% of married blacks had a white spouse. *See* Douglas J. Besharov & Timothy S. Sullivan, *One Flesh,* New Democrat, July–Aug. 1996, at 21, cited in Kennedy, note 21 above, at 818. On antimiscegenation in the United States, see generally Martha Elizabeth Hodes, White Women, Black Men: Illicit Sex in the Nineteenth-Century South (1997).

and the European registered partnership acts, we are facing a somewhat different situation: inclusion in marriage or an alternative to marriage. In addition to the many existing and developing alternatives to marriage worldwide, a version of Vermont's act will probably be implemented by other U.S. states rather than opening up marriage to same-sex couples, which is not to be expected in the foreseeable future in the United States. *Loving* did not address the problem of a separate but equal institution with which we are faced today. Thus, and contrary to other scholarly accounts that regard the *Loving* analogy as the most comparable to the exclusion of gays from marriage, it is my view that the *Brown* analogy is the most useful in assessing marriage alternatives for gays and in analyzing the current exclusion of same-sex couples from marriage. Although I emphasize *Brown*, I wish to make it clear that I view *both* analogies combined as making a strong case for rejecting marriage alternatives and as mandating the inclusion of gay couples in marriage.

10.4 The *Brown* Analogy

Unlike *Loving*, which dealt with antimiscegenation laws, *Brown* is not limited to cases of separate educational facilities and is more far reaching in its application. *Brown* should be interpreted broadly as standing for the tenet that segregation based on an intent to discriminate against an unprivileged group out of prejudice or animus is not only unconstitutional but is also socially and morally objectionable. For the purposes of marriage, there is no relevant distinction between same- and opposite-sex couples; both are similarly situated, just as blacks and whites were similarly situated for purposes of education. Why, then, should segregation in marriage be less objectionable when it comes to the treatment of same-sex couples?[51]

It should be noted at the outset that I do not view the *Brown* analogy as limited to the United States or to U.S. (federal) constitutional law. As explained below, I find it applicable also to foreign jurisdictions that have created a separate scheme for same-sex couples. In terms of current U.S. constitutional standards, and unlike distinctions based on race, as long as classifications based on sex (currently, intermediate scrutiny) or

51. Since the *Loving* analogy is still important and useful, it seems that, based on its rationale, it would also lead us to the conclusion that civil unions (and registered partnership acts)—even if affording exactly the same benefits and rights—are objectionable for similar reasons. I.e., the rationale of *Loving* would not permit civil unions and would have mandated the opening up of marriage to same-sex couples, since the civil union legislation is as stigmatizing as antimiscegenation laws and its enactment stems from similar biases.

sexual orientation (currently, rational basis scrutiny) are not regarded as "suspect" and are not subject to "heightened scrutiny," there is no guarantee that a separate but equal regime for same-sex couples would be held unconstitutional (at least, not by the U.S. Supreme Court); that is, there is no guarantee that *Brown* would be applied in cases of segregation based on sexual orientation. However, as held by various state courts,[52] and in light of the many persuasive accounts of U.S. scholars,[53] sexual orientation should be regarded as "suspect" and subject to strict scrutiny. Moreover, if viewed as discrimination based on sex, then even under current American Supreme Court case law, a separate but equal regime for same-sex couples might be held unconstitutional.

An argument may be made that models for the recognition of same-sex partnerships that are also open to opposite-sex couples—such as many U.S. domestic partnerships and the Dutch and French registered partnership laws—treat gay and straight couples in the same manner and should therefore not be viewed as illegitimate segregation between heterosexuals and homosexuals. This argument is clearly false. The original claim of the gay communities in every country, including the plaintiffs in *Baker,* was that marriage should be available to same-sex couples—with only a minority opposing the inclusion of gays in the institution of marriage—and *not* that the status of same-sex couples should be regulated separately from marriage. For various political, social, religious, and cultural reasons, no country in the world except the Netherlands has been able or willing to open up marriage to same-sex couples. This is why alternative models to marriage, which are less comprehensive than marriage but yet imitative of the institution, were proposed, developed, and adopted. Although this compromise reflects an effort to provide extensive recognition to same-sex couples, which in fact it does, it should nevertheless be regarded as unconstitutional discrimination.

Models for the recognition of same-sex partnerships, whether or not applied to opposite-sex couples as well, were a compromise intended to regulate the status of *same-sex* couples *separately* from (opposite-sex) marriage. Thus, models open to opposite-sex couples as well as models that are restricted to same-sex couples—such as the Nordic countries' registered partnership acts—similarly discriminate against gays and lesbians, since all were enacted with the intention to exclude same-sex couples from marriage and preserve and maintain heterosexual superiority

52. *See, e.g.,* Tanner v. Oregon Health Sciences University, 971 P.2d 435 (Or. Ct. App. 1998).

53. *See, e.g.,* David A. J. Richards, Identity and the Case for Gay Rights: Race, Gender, Religion as Analogies, chap. 2 (1999).

and compulsory heterosexuality, much as school segregation was intended to maintain and further white supremacy. Moreover, in all countries except for the Netherlands, same-sex couples, unlike opposite-sex couples, who can always choose to marry, are excluded from marriage and are confined to the marriage alternatives. No argument can be made that the law disadvantages heterosexuals and gays in a similar manner, since it is only same-sex couples who are excluded from marriage. The question is thus not whether some domestic partner schemes or registered partnership acts are also open to heterosexuals but rather whether these models are separate institutions for same-sex couples, and the answer is clearly in the affirmative. So long as gays are excluded from marriage, the use of facially gender-neutral alternatives invidiously discriminates against them. Hence, recognition of same-sex partnerships in the United States as well as legislation in the Nordic countries, France, and Germany, should all be viewed as separate schemes for gay men and lesbians. These countries could have simply amended their marriage acts to include same-sex couples, in which case the moral evil of segregation would not have taken place. It is my argument that those legislatures should have indeed amended their marriage laws to be gender neutral and thus apply also to same-sex couples, as has been done in the Netherlands. This would have eliminated the distinction that is the root of the inequality.[54]

The majority in *Baker v. State of Vermont* took a different view.[55] The concurring justices invoked the U.S. Supreme Court's desegregation decision in *Watson v. City of Memphis*[56] as comparable to the exclusion of same-sex couples from marriage and criticized the majority for refusing to order the state to open up marriage to same-sex couples. In response, Justice Jeffrey L. Amestoy, writing for the plurality, asserted: "The analogy is flawed. We do not confront in this case the evil that was institutionalized racism, an evil that was widely recognized well before the Court's decision in Watson and its more famous predecessor, Brown v. Board of Education [citation omitted]. Plaintiffs have not demonstrated that the exclusion of same-sex couples from the definition of marriage was intended to discriminate against women or lesbians and gay men, as racial segregation was designed to maintain the pernicious doctrine of white supremacy."[57] Based on the foregoing, and on the court's choice

54. *See also* Craig A. Sloane, *A Rose by Any Other Name: Marriage and the Danish Registered Partnership Act,* 5 Cardozo J. Int'l & Comp. L. 189, 205 (1997).

55. *See* Baker v. State of Vermont, 744 A.2d 864 (Vt. Sup. Ct. 1999). For discussion and analysis of the case, see chap. 7.

56. 373 U.S. 526 (1963).

57. Baker v. State of Vermont, 744 A.2d 864 (Vt. Sup. Ct. 1999).

of remedy—not requiring the state to issue marriage licenses to same-sex couples and directing it toward a comprehensive domestic partnership scheme or the adoption of the registered partnership model[58]—the court implicitly rejected the *Brown* analogy, and the decision's outcome reflects the concept that "separate but equal" is inherently equal in the context of the demand for same-sex marriage.[59]

It is my opinion that Justice Amestoy erred and that discriminatory impact as well as intent could have been established based on the analogy to *Brown,* which he rejected. The analogy is a valid and instructive one for a few reasons. First, as racial segregation was premised on the morally objectionable philosophy of white supremacy, the exclusion of same-sex couples is premised on comparable bases of discrimination, homophobia and sexism, and on an intent to maintain a philosophy that is equally objectionable—compulsory heterosexuality and compulsory gender binarism. Exclusion of gays from marriage and segregation of blacks in education discriminate against both groups for a similar reason: the purpose of both is to "support a regime of caste that locks some people into inferior social positions."[60]

Language that was used by courts in defending segregation and antimiscegenation laws is quite similar to the rationales brought today for the exclusion of gays from marriage and for the creation of separate institutions for the recognition of their partnerships: "The purity of public morals, the moral and physical development of both races, and the highest advancement of our cherished southern civilization, under which two distinct races are to work out and accomplish the destiny to which the Almighty has assigned them on this continent—all require that they should be kept *distinct and separate,* and that connections and alliances so unnatural that God and nature seem to forbid them, should be prohibited by positive law."[61] *Brown* is a flat rejection of this ideology and for similar reasons should be applied to the freedom of same-sex couples to marry.

---

58. The court explicitly held that the plaintiffs were not necessarily entitled to a marriage license and that marriage is only *one* acceptable remedy among others: "That the State could do so through a marriage license is obvious. But *it is not* required to do so." Baker v. State of Vermont, 744 A.2d 864, at 887 (1999), my emphasis.

59. Had the plaintiffs been given the opportunity to prove bias as the basis for denying them marriage licenses, the court might have accepted the analogy. Thus, the question was not whether the remedy was separate but equal (which was not disputed) but whether intent to discriminate had been proven.

60. This argument is borrowed from Koppelman's analogy between antimiscegenation laws and sodomy laws as sex discrimination. I apply the argument made there regarding the unconstitutionality of sodomy laws to the unconstitutionality of current models for the recognition of same-sex partnerships. *See* Koppelman, note 17 above, at 147.

61. Kinney v. Commonwealth, 71 Va. (30 Gratt.) 858, 869 (1878), my emphasis.

The decision in *Brown* rested on one or more of the following conceptions of discrimination: stigma, subordination, second-class citizenship, and the encouragement of private prejudice[62]—all of which apply equally in the case of homophobia. The violent disparate impact that affects lesbians and gay men is similar to the structural violence affecting African Americans, which was enough to motivate the Court in *Brown* to dispel the "separate but equal" doctrine of *Plessy v. Ferguson*.[63] As Kendall Thomas argued, albeit in a different context, "[t]here is a resonant resemblance between the condition of gay men and lesbians under the current legal regime and the condition of African Americans in the era of racial segregation."[64] If homophobia were held to be a moral evil equal to racism, as, based on Richards's account, I suggest it should,[65] then there would be no acceptable reason, under *Brown,* to allow separate but equal marriage-like institutions for gay men and lesbians. Under *Brown,* official racial segregation per se would be a constitutional violation even if a defendant were to introduce evidence showing that the schools serving Caucasian children and the schools serving African American children were provided with equal "buildings, curricula, qualifications and salaries of teachers, and other 'tangible' factors."[66] Likewise, even if the state accords same-sex couples benefits, rights, protections, and obligations equal to those associated with marriage, official marriage-like institutions that are separate from marriage should also be regarded as per se unconstitutional.

In a similar manner, and based on the logic of *Brown,* a Canadian federal court explicitly held in the matter of *Moore* that a separate *definition* of *same-sex partner* was discriminatory and unconstitutional.[67] Prior

62. David A. Strauss, *Discriminatory Intent and the Taming of Brown,* 56 U. Chi. L. Rev. 935, 950 (1989).

63. Christopher J. Keller, *Divining the Priest: A Case Comment on Baehr v. Lewin,* 12 Law & Ineq. J. 483, 522 (1994).

64. Kendall Thomas, *Beyond the Privacy Principle,* 92 Colum. L. Rev. 1431, 1491 n. 203 (1992). Thomas further argues that as the court in *Brown* concluded that "the social meaning of segregation was racist domination of the Negro," so a similar case can be made in regard to the gay community. *Id.* Thomas arrives at this conclusion based on an analogy to Black's account. For instance, Thomas argues that sodomy laws subjugate and confine an entire group "within a system which is set up and continued for the very purpose of keeping it in an inferior station" and that the combined force of homosexual sodomy law and homophobic violence is to impose invisibility on gays and lesbians, to make it as difficult as possible for gays and lesbians to enter "the common political life of the community," and to restrict as much as possible their access to political power. *Id.,* citing and quoting Charles L. Black Jr., *The Lawfulness of the Segregation Decisions,* 69 Yale L.J. 421, 424–25 (1960).

65. *See* Richards, note 53 above, at 6–38. *See also* chap. 2 of this volume.

66. Brown v. Board of Education, 347 U.S. 483, 492 (1954).

67. Canada (Attorney General) v. Moore, 55 C.R.R. (2d) 254 (Federal Court Trial Division, August 14, 1998).

to *Moore,* the Supreme Court of Canada had rejected the "separate but equal" doctrine in *Andrews v. Law Society of British Columbia,*[68] stating that

> Mere equality of application to similarly situated groups or individuals does not afford a realistic test for a violation of equality rights. For, as has been said, a bad law will not be saved merely because it operates equally upon those to whom it has application . . . s. 15(1) read as a whole constitutes a compendious expression of a positive right to equality in both the substance and the administration of the law. . . .
> . . . discrimination may be described as a distinction, whether intentional or not but based on grounds relating to personal characteristics of the individual or group . . . which withholds or limits access to opportunities, benefits, and advantages available to other members of society. Distinctions based on personal characteristics attributed to an individual solely on the basis of association with a group will rarely escape the charge of discrimination.[69]

In the matter of *Moore,* an employer had provided same-sex couples with all the benefits it accorded opposite-sex spouses and seemingly had met the standard of equality. However, the fact that the employer introduced a new and separate definition of same-sex common law relationships for the purposes of extending benefits to same-sex couples, instead of changing the definition of *spouse* to a gender-neutral one—that is, deleting the words "of the opposite-sex" from the definition of spouse—was held by the court as discrimination based on sexual orientation in violation of the Canadian Human Rights Act.[70] Thus, although same-sex couples had been receiving all spousal benefits, the creation of a separate provision to deal with same-sex couples was viewed by itself as illegitimate discrimination, based on *Brown*'s rejection of the "separate but equal" doctrine. In oral arguments, Moore stated before the court:

> Although, on the merits of the case, this is about benefits for the person behind that, the person being talked about today, it goes well beyond benefits to me. The manner in which I am treated, the manner in which I am made to feel is really what's at issue here and *I do not feel equal.* . . .

68. 1 Canada S.C.R. 143, 166 (1989) (holding that the Canadian citizenship requirement for admission to the British Columbia bar was in violation of sec. 15(1) of the Canadian Charter of Rights and Freedoms).

69. Andrews v. Law Society of British Columbia, 1 Canada S.C.R. 143, at 167, 171, 174 (1989).

70. Canada (Attorney General) v. Moore, 55 C.R.R. (2d) 254 (Federal Court Trial Division, August 14, 1998).

> ... It is not about special rights, it's not about special treatment, it's not about special mention in any document or any collective agreement any more than any other person would be mentioned in those documents by virtue of their age, of their religion, of their sex or of their color. Rather, what the gay agenda is about is about belonging, about being included about having a place around the table not because I am gay, but because, in the true meaning of family, it doesn't matter.[71]

Another applicant argued—and, based on its interpretation of the Canadian Supreme Court's holding in the matter of *Egan*,[72] the court accepted—that "the separate regime introduced by the Treasury Board perpetuates a distinction drawn on the lines of sexual orientation and while there may be no discrimination in terms of access to benefits, this manner of providing these benefits does not recognize the innate dignity of human beings, and carries with it a stigmatization that the same-sex relationship is not deserving of the status of 'spouse.'"[73] The introduction of two definitions, one for same-sex couples and one for common law spouses, albeit accompanied by the same benefits, was in and of itself discriminatory since it created a separate class of persons entitled to employment benefits, but on the basis of their sexual orientation rather than their spousal relationship: "the scheme proposed by the employer establishes a regime of *'separate but equal,'* one that distinguishes between relationships on the basis of the sexual orientation of the participants. Thus, this scheme remains discriminatory. Further, though the two classes receive the same benefits, in my view, such a distinction continues to differentiate adversely between persons, within the meaning of the Act."[74]

I view the following analysis of the court as similarly applicable to the discriminatory impact of state-enacted separate (but equal) schemes for the regulation of same-sex partnerships, that is, domestic and registered partnerships:

> Legislative distinctions between persons on the basis of sexual orientation, even though in practical terms they may not give rise to substantive inequality, e.g., discriminatory, access to benefits, may reaffirm preexisting discriminatory notions and, on this basis, be

71. *Id.* at 278, my emphasis.

72. Egan v. Canada, 29 C.R.R. (2d) 79 (1995).

73. Canada (Attorney General) v. Moore, 55 C.R.R. (2d) 254, at 274–75 (Federal Court Trial Division, August 14, 1998).

74. *Id.* at 277, my emphasis.

themselves discriminatory. In my view, on the facts of the case at bar, the employer's separate definition of same-sex partners, made without explanation, reinforces a distinction drawn between same-sex and heterosexual couples, one made typically on discriminatory grounds. Such a distinction, relying on classifications reflecting pre-existing biases without a plausible non-discriminatory rationale, in my view, constitutes adverse differentiation within the meaning of s. 7 of the Canadian Human Rights Act. . . . it is no more appropriate for the employer in this case to have established a separate definition for persons in same-sex relationships than it would have been for the employer to create separate definitions for relationships of persons based on their race, color or ethnicity, or any other prohibited ground enumerated in the Act.[75]

Finally, the court cited with approval Justice Allen Martin Linden's dissent in the Federal Court of Appeals in *Egan v. Canada,* which is extremely instructive to our analysis of marriage substitutes:

[T]he fact that similar benefits may be available to gay and lesbian partners under a different scheme . . . cannot remedy the discriminatory impact of denying benefits to gay and lesbian partners on the same footing as heterosexual partners. . . .
. . . Restricting a group's eligibility for equal benefits (merely on the basis of a personal characteristic related to a ground of discrimination) so that those benefits are available only under a separate or different scheme places a limitation of separateness or difference on the promise of equality. Such a compromise is reminiscent of the now-discredited "separate but equal doctrine," developed by the United States Supreme Court in Plessy v. Ferguson, 163 U.S. 537 (1896). . . .
One cannot avoid the conclusion that offering benefits to gay and lesbian partners under a different scheme from heterosexual partners is a version of the separate but equal doctrine. That appalling doctrine must not be resuscitated in Canada 40 years after its much-heralded death in the United States.[76]

Although *Brown* was decided in the context of American racism, its application as a constitutional standard and its philosophy could be implemented not only in similar situations in the United States but also

75. *Id.* at 280–81.
76. 15 C.R.R. (2d) 310, at 361 (1993), my emphasis. Cited in Canada (Attorney General) v. Moore, 55 C.R.R. (2d) 254, at 278–79 (Federal Court Trial Division, August 14, 1998).

in foreign jurisdictions. The Canadian case of *Moore* and the opening up of marriage to same-sex couples in the Netherlands, which explicitly reject a separate but equal scheme for same-sex couples, reaffirm the extraterritorial validity and applicability of the principles of *Brown*.[77] Therefore, the harm that lies in the inherently unequal institutions for same-sex couples in the United States is similar in the northern European countries. I see no reason why "separate but equal" should be more acceptable in Europe than in the United States, since the rationales for opposing the application of this doctrine hold similarly in both regions. For instance, it has been suggested that the only reason the Danish parliament enacted separate legislation, rather than including same-sex unions in the Danish Marriage Acts, is due to prejudice against gays and lesbians.[78] Commenting on the Norwegian registered partnership act, Halvorsen makes the following observation, which is applicable to other European registered partnership acts as well as domestic partner schemes in the United States:

> It is not stated directly and bluntly that couples of the same and "opposite" sex are of different value, or that heterosexuality should be privileged, or that lesbians and gays and heterosexuals are ascribed an unequal quality. Instead, the judgment is expressed through euphemisms whereby one avoids explicitly expressing the view that heterosexuality is better. The euphemisms work as a neutralization of the political relation between heterosexuality and homosexuality: By using euphemisms the actors in the discussion were able to present their political choice as less controversial by neutralizing either the claims of sameness or difference of heterosexuals and lesbians and gays.
>
> The changing views of the division of the population into two sexual categories is visible in the very naming of the institution as "Registered Partnership" in public, in official schemes, and in the liturgy. The use of the words demarcates gay and lesbian partnerships from marriage.[79]

77. It should be noted that *Moore* is only a Federal Court Trial Division decision, which was ignored by the federal Parliament in the Modernization of Benefits and Obligations Act in 2000. However, I do not use *Moore* in order to state positive Canadian case law; rather, I employ the decision as an example to stress the detrimental implications of a separate but equal regime for gay men and lesbians. Moreover, notwithstanding its rejection in Canada, I view the decision as a correct and cogent application of the separate but equal doctrine.

78. *See* Sloane, note 54 above, at 192.

79. Rune Halvorsen, *The Ambiguity of Lesbian and Gay Marriages, Change and Continuity in the Symbolic Order*, 34 J. Homosexuality 214–15 (1998).

Similarly, "the members of a same-sex couple who register are called registered partners, not spouses, and their legal bond is recorded in a 'partnership certificate,' as opposed to a marriage license. This may seem like semantics, but to the parties involved it is a denial by the state to recognize same-sex permanent unions on equal terms as heterosexual permanent unions."[80]

10.5 Intracommunity Perceptions of a Separate Regime for Same-Sex Couples

Today, some segments of the African American community fight to maintain segregated schools, supporting the "separate but equal" doctrine that *Brown* sought to overturn. Some other members of the African American community view this new political stance as a blasphemous disregard for the civil rights movement.[81] This very much resembles the disagreement within the gay community, whereby those who oppose same-sex marriage are usually in favor of domestic or registered partnership, and others demand nothing less than inclusion in marriage.

Indeed, some feminist theorists have argued that "separate" can be regarded as substantially equal or at least not objectionable. Some even insist that traditions of gender inequality owing to gender differences should be sustained and that in many circumstances, being treated differently and "separately" from men does not necessitate inequality and should be encouraged or celebrated.[82]

The views of these African Americans and feminists are similar to a perspective that may be found among gays. Some scholars from the gay community argue that models alternative to and separate from marriage, even if they remain unequal to marriage, are not only acceptable but are even preferable to same-sex marriage.[83] This argument is based on a

---

80. Sloane, note 54 above, at 204.

81. Note, *Using Discourse Ethics to Provide Equality in Education for African-American Children Forty Years after Brown v. Board of Education,* 5 B.U. Pub. Int. L.J. 99, at 101 (1995).

82. *See, e.g.,* Carol Gilligan, In a Different Voice: Psychological Theory and Women's Development (1993); Robin West, *Jurisprudence and Gender,* 55 U. Chi. L. Rev. 1 (1988). For a critique of these accounts, see Catharine MacKinnon, *Feminist Discourse, Moral Values, and the Law—A Conversation,* 34 Buff. L. Rev. 11 (1985).

83. *See, e.g.,* Charles R. P. Pouncy, *Marriage and Domestic Partnership: Rationality and Inequality,* 7 Temple Pol. & Civ. Rts. L. Rev. 363 (1998). It should be noted that some gay critics of marriage base their view on their strict opposition to (or fear of) monogamy. Thus, for example, Edmund White contends that marriage is "hopelessly dreary" and a "monogamous air lock" that is in utter opposition to his definition of gay life, since, he writes, "being gay seemed at first like another way of being a bohemian," freed from "the most narrow, creepy, selfish sort of conformism." *See* Edmund White, *What Century Is This Anyway?* Advocate, June 23, 1998, quoted in E. J. Graff, What Is Marriage For? at 188 (1999). *See also* Michael Warner, The Trouble with Normal: Sex, Politics, and the Ethics

fear that gays will conform and assimilate within the heterosexual majority, and it is usually, but not necessarily, accompanied by opposition to the institution of marriage. Thus, for example, Paula Ettelbrick provides a feminist critique of marriage and argues that same-sex marriage would obliterate domestic partnership legislation, which is preferable to marriage in terms of regulating gay relationships.[84] Nancy Polikoff, who strongly opposes same-sex marriage and instead supports domestic partnership, argues that "the desire to marry in the lesbian and gay community is an attempt to mimic the worst of mainstream society, an effort to fit into an inherently problematic institution that betrays the promise of both lesbian and gay liberation and radical feminism."[85] Charles Pouncy, among others, shares the feminist critique of marriage; he asserts that same-sex marriage is objectionable since it would suggest that gays accept heterosexuality as the superior norm and take part in a religious-related, heterosexist, patriarchal institution: "As whiteness remained the standard by which all other racial and ethnic minorities are measured, heterosexuality will remain the guiding paradigm for marriage, and its norms will continue to circumscribe the parameters of the institution." Furthermore, queer culture, community, integrity, and identity, which now serve to challenge convention and tradition, would all be marginalized and ultimately abandoned. Pouncy thus argues that domestic partnership as currently construed is the only means by which the gay community would be able to maintain its identity and culture, which are in and of themselves much more significant than the pursuit of equality in terms of rights and benefits. Domestic partnership is preferable to same-sex marriage because it "will promote the cultural integrity, autonomy, and self-determination of queer cultures and communities," which same-sex marriage would not.[86]

Such arguments for the segregation of same-sex couples are unpersua-

---

of Queer Life (1999) (arguing that same-sex marriage would "mainstream" and "normalize" the gay community, which would consequently lose its sexual autonomy and identity). These latter criticisms are less relevant to our current discussion, since they do not offer any solution or alternative to the inequality that same-sex couples are faced with. Those who hold such views oppose any kind of state-sanctioned regulation of their relationships and thus do not address questions of equality and separateness in terms of the regulation of same-sex partnerships, which are the subject of this chapter.

84. *See* Paula L. Ettelbrick, *Since When Is Marriage a Path to Liberation?* in Lesbian and Gay Marriage: Private Commitments, Public Ceremonies 20 (Suzanne Sherman ed., 1992). For a different view, see Thomas B. Stoddard, *Why Gay People Should Seek the Right to Marry, in* Lesbian and Gay Marriage, above, at 13.

85. Nancy Polikoff, *We Will Get What We Ask For: Why Legalizing Gay and Lesbian Marriage Will Not "Dismantle the Legal Structure of Gender in Every Marriage,"* 79 Va. L. Rev. 1535, 1536 (1993).

86. Pouncy, note 83 above, at 369, 374, 365, quotations at 369, 365.

sive, flawed, and incoherent. They ignore the fact that domestic partnership is a product of political compromise envisioned and created by the heterosexual majority for the purpose of maintaining the segregation of homosexuals and warding off an ultimate ruling by a court in favor of equal marriage rights. This was the sole reason for the enactment of domestic partnership in Hawaii,[87] as well as the reason for the efforts made by the Vermont legislature to enact anything but marriage, which led to the adoption of the civil union act. Moreover, the main characteristic of domestic partnership is its imitation, poor as it may be, of the institution of marriage. The fact that most domestic partnerships are open to heterosexuals does not support their conceptualization as uniquely gay or any possibility of their future transformation into a "queer institution." Even domestic or registered partnership schemes that are restricted to same-sex couples, which have been in force for more than a decade, such as the Danish act, simply mirror marriage. They have not become unique queer institutions that attempt to accommodate some sort of "special needs" or the "unique relationships" of gay couples. Thus, for example, the Danish gay community, though fully aware that registered partnership is different from and "less than" marriage, has been trying to mimic marriage by, inter alia, referring to the institution of registered partnership as marriage and to gay registered partners as married, in an attempt to ignore or expunge any distinctions between registered partnership and marriage. It thus seems that Danish gay couples wish to gain full equality with opposite-sex married couples rather than challenge the institution of marriage or create a "gay alternative" to marriage. This also suggests no need for a different and separate institution for same-sex couples.

The statements of Ettelbrick, Pouncy, and Polikoff ignore the fact that marriage is a changing institution whose religious, sexist, and patriarchal characteristics are fading more and more as time passes (see chap. 2 above). In this connection, Graff rightly responds to the critics of the institution of marriage, including those from within the gay community, when she says that "antimarriage rhetoric wrongly groups lesbian and gay liberationists with other lesbians and gay men—when really they belong with other sexual utopians in history, or with the heterosexual cultural-leftists of their era who have also been trying to invent new, alternative kinds of families."[88] Moreover, I reject the view that rights and benefits as such are insignificant factors in the debate. To

87. *See* Evan Wolfson, *Crossing the Threshold: Equal Marriage Rights for Lesbians and Gay Men and the Intra-Community Critique,* 21 N.Y.U. Rev. L. & Soc. Change 567, 605 (1994).
88. Graff, note 83 above, at 187.

most people, the right to visit their partner in the hospital or the right to be appointed guardian of that partner are more important than the preservation of some notion of a queer culture. There is no reason that as a community, and not only as individuals, we should cease the pursuit of such rights in the form of marriage.

Finally, the fear of "normalcy" or assimilation seems equally unsubstantiated and unconvincing: What is unique about being second-class citizens? What are those unique characteristics of the gay culture that same-sex marriage would eradicate? Is it not the case that most same-sex couples, in a world of no state recognition, are treating their partnerships in a manner similar to that of heterosexuals? How, by being outside the institution of marriage, do we "challenge tradition" in a way that is both constructive and advantageous to our community or to society at large? Indeed, some of our relationships may be different from those of opposite-sex couples—differences that are, in my view, irrelevant as far as the freedom to marry is concerned—but does it follow that we should remain legally inferior just for the sake of challenging the norms of the majority or, as Pouncy seems to suggest, just for the sake of being different? If the entrance into a legal institution that would provide same-sex couples equality is so threatening to our "unique identity," as some commentators suggest, then it is the uniqueness of the identity that should be questioned, not the pursuit of same-sex marriage. That which makes us different or unique would not be lost if same-sex couples were allowed to marry. The segments in the gay community who oppose same-sex marriage would not be forced to join the institution; they would have a choice. Moreover, demands for same-sex marriage should not necessarily be viewed as assimilatory: "[I]s assimilating yourself conforming at all? Are not gay men and lesbians conforming to the expectations and demands of heterosexual society exactly when they relinquish the right to marriage?"[89] Why should those of us within the gay community who are in favor of same-sex marriage be forced by intracommunity opponents not to have this choice? Is it the proper course for the movement to force domestic or registered partnership on those who would prefer a choice regarding marriage? Therefore,

> Insisting that lesbians and gay men enter into domestic partnerships, while reserving marriage for different-sex couples, perpetuates without justification (let alone a compelling state interest) the discrimination challenged in *Baehr*. Like most non-gay people, most gay men

89. Rainer Hoffman et al., *Germany, in* Sociolegal Control of Homosexuality: A Multi-Nation Comparison 255, 265 (Donald J. West & Richard Green eds., 1997).

and lesbians want the equal right to *marry*, not merely access to some other domestic status. If *all* were free to *choose* either domestic partnership or marriage, then it might be appropriate for the state to proffer such an additional status. However, when the state arbitrarily restricts people's choice, whether based on gender or any other invidiously discriminatory factor, it does not eliminate inequality, but rather reinforces second-class citizenship.[90]

Other, less radical thinkers, who are not necessarily against same-sex marriage, argue that a separate but equal institution for same-sex couples, as long as it is indeed formally equal, would be an acceptable solution for the current inequality of same-sex couples. That view is much like the contention of Justice Amestoy in the case of *Baker*. For example, both William Eskridge and Nan Hunter are willing to settle for a registered partnership scheme that would provide rights similar to those of marriage.[91] Although Eskridge is a great proponent of same-sex marriage, he views the registered partnership model of the northern European countries as an acceptable and satisfactory solution because "these laws provide all the obligations as well as almost all the benefits of marriage but not the name." He suggests that a version of a registered partnership law could be useful for the United States, so long as it included obligations as well as benefits, since "[s]ame-sex couples would be able to marry in the eyes of religious and social communities that recognize their union as marriage, and the state could back up their interpersonal commitments with tangible obligations making the unions harder to dissolve. Whatever the legal name of the institution thus created, it could stand as a less gendered counterexample to patriarchal marriage. Indeed, I would urge that such partnerships be open to transgendered people and different-sex couples as well as to gay and lesbian couples."[92]

This contention seems to be based on the belief that a political compromise is inevitable, not on a normative view according to which registered partnership is of equal worth with same-sex marriage. In fact, Eskridge has elsewhere dismissed alternatives to marriage, arguing that "the main thing that a Danish-style compromise would sacrifice is formal equality."[93] There may be cases wherein separate institutions would be preferable to integrated ones and would also not compromise substan-

90. *See* Wolfson, note 87 above, at 606.

91. *See* William N. Eskridge Jr., Gaylaw: Challenging the Apartheid of the Closet 289 (1999).

92. *Id.* This view is not in line with Eskridge's "apartheid of the closet" thesis, according to which the segregation of gays is objectionable. *See id.* at 7, 59.

93. Eskridge, Case for Same-Sex Marriage, note 46 above, at 122.

tive equality.[94] This may hold true when the different characteristic of the group is relevant to the distinction made. However, providing equality to same-sex couples by way of separation is objectionable and, for the reasons stated above, could never be regarded as inherently equal. Separate "marriage-like" institutions only serve to perpetuate homophobia, heterosexual superiority, and gender binarism. The ways in which gay couples may be different from heterosexual ones do not necessitate differentiation between them and are simply irrelevant in terms of access to marriage.

An illuminating example in this connection is the military exclusion. Gay men and lesbians in the United States have been fighting not to be discriminated against in access to military service. Whether we personally wish to join the military or not, or whether we think it is a good or a bad institution—these are separate questions; but most liberals within and outside the gay community agree that we deserve full equality when it comes to access to military service. No one is suggesting that gays should be allowed to serve in the military in *separate units* as a solution for the current exclusion. If that were proposed, it would justifiably generate much greater opposition than the current discriminatory exclusion does. During the hearings in the House as to whether the ban on gays in the military should be lifted, even the most radical opponents of lifting the ban have not suggested that gays should be allowed access to military service but in special and separate "gay units," although this would have in fact alleviated the major concern of the ban's proponents—the asserted harm to unit cohesion.[95] Such a scheme was utilized in the case of African Americans in the U.S. military; they were officially segregated and served in separate units until the end of World War II, except for a few experimental desegregated units that were established close to the end of the war.[96] This racist regime of separation was abol-

94. For examples, see Gilligan, note 82 above; West, note 82 above.

95. *See* Hearings before the Senate Committee on Armed Services, 103d Congress, 2d sess., 595–97, 599–602, 606–9, 618–19 (May 11, 1993). "The introduction of an open homosexual into a small unit immediately polarizes that unit and destroys the very bonding that is so important for the unit's survival in time of war . . . whenever it became known in a unit that someone was openly homosexual, polarization occurred, violence sometimes followed, morale broke down and unit effectiveness suffered." *See id.* at 595–97 (General Schwarzkopf).

96. *See* Kenneth L. Karst, *The Pursuit of Manhood and the Desegregation of the Armed Forces*, 38 UCLA L. Rev. 499 (1991); William N. Eskridge Jr. & Nan D. Hunter, Sexuality, Gender, and the Law 331 (1997); Richard M. Dalfiume, Desegregation of the US Armed Forces (1969). Women were similarly excluded from the armed forces until the end of World War II; thereafter, women were allowed to serve only in segregated noncombat units, and even when integration took place, women were (and still are) excluded from certain infantry combat roles. Eskridge & Hunter, above, at 342–65. In Rostker v. Goldberg, 453 U.S. 57 (1981), the U.S. Supreme Court upheld a law that required the draft of

ished soon thereafter. Since then, it has not been suggested that military units should be divided based on one's race or other irrelevant characteristics, such as sexual orientation. The debate whether the ban on gays in the military should be lifted was thus an issue of either full inclusion or full exclusion. The legislature's "compromise" known as the "don't ask, don't tell" policy was not a creation of a separate military institution for gays but rather allowed them participation on condition that they do not disclose their sexual identity. Nevertheless, this solution, which stems from bias and prejudice, has had an extremely discriminatory impact on gay men and lesbians in the military. For that reason, gays continue to fight for full equality in access to the military. Similarly, I find no reason why we should settle for anything less than full inclusion when it comes to the institution of marriage.

Today we tend to think about the transition from slavery to segregation as a clear case of invidious racial discrimination, whereas "white Americans in the nineteenth century viewed the changes in racial status law of their day in very different terms: as elevating African-Americans from subordination in slavery to *equality* at law."[97] Many, including the Vermont Supreme Court, tend to think today that through the enactment of models alternative to and separate from marriage, gay men and lesbians have been elevated from subordination to full equality, whereas in fact such regulations should be viewed for what they really are: marriage-like institutions that provide far less than substantive equality, the enactment of which stems from an intent to discriminate based on homophobia and sexism.

There is thus no question that domestic and registered partnerships are "an inferior solution to the marriage problem, a 'separate but equal' status for yet another group of people disenfranchised by the majority."[98] As one journalist has written, "domestic partnership proposals are

men and not women into the armed forces, stating that women and men were not similarly situated for the purposes of military draft based on the policy, which the Court did not dispute, according to which women were restricted from most combat positions. For arguments for and against the inclusion of women in combat positions, see Mady Wechsler Segal, *The Argument for Female Combatants, in* Female Soldiers: Combatants or Noncombatants? 267 (Nancy Loring Goldman ed., 1982).

97. Reva Siegel, *The Critical Use of History: Why Equal Protection No Longer Protects: The Evolving Forms of Status-Enforcing State Action,* 46 Stan. L. Rev. 1111, 1119 (1997).

98. David Link, *The Tie That Binds: Recognizing Privacy and the Family Commitments of Same-Sex Couples,* 23 Loy. L.A. L. Rev. 1055, 1149 (1990). *See also* Christine Jax, *Same-Sex Marriage—Why Not?* 4 Widener J. Pub. L. 461, 490 (1995) (arguing that domestic partnership "is not a suitable remedy to the prohibition of same-sex marriage . . . this is a public policy creation that discriminates in the same manner as the concept of separate but equal" and that "a domestic partnership is for better or worse, second-class citizenship"); Sherri L. Toussaint, *Defense of Marriage Act: Isn't It Ironic . . . Don't You Think? A Little Too Ironic?* 76 Neb. L. Rev. 924, 946–47 (1997) ("just as the Plessy decision perpetuated the

no more than a political dodge, an unconscionable sop to bigots who will tolerate homosexuality only if it can be segregated in some parallel universe. But gay and lesbian people do not live in a parallel universe. They live in this one."[99] Registered partnership and domestic partnership are not a commitment to recognize gay and lesbian couples as equals in all spheres of civil and social life; they signal mere toleration of these relationships, rather than acceptance, and convey the message that such partnerships, even if tolerated, are morally wrong. Creating alternatives that are separate from marriage can be regarded as even a worse case of discrimination than not according same-sex couples rights at all: "To grant homosexuals all the substance of marriage while denying them the institution is, in some ways, a purer form of bigotry than denying them any rights at all. It is to devise a pseudo-institution to both erase inequality and at the same time perpetuate it."[100] This is reminiscent of Freud's "narcissism of small differences."[101] Applying his concept to our discussion, it seems that despite the existence of many commonalties between same-sex couples and opposite-sex couples and between homosexuals and heterosexuals, when it comes to the freedom to marry, some tend to emphasize the small, irrelevant differences, using them to justify discrimination against gays and lesbians, whereas in fact the relationships of both merit equal participation in marriage. As Richards contends, the dehumanization of the homosexual, from which the condemnation of same-sex marriage stems, "enables a culture with a long history of uncritical moral slavery of women and homosexuals to disregard the growing convergences of heterosexual and homosexual human love in the modern world."[102]

Thus, and because domestic and registered partnership legislation is a compromise that codifies a second-class status, because it in fact treats

---

disguised harm facilitated by the separate but equal doctrine, practical arguments also camouflage the impact discrimination has on the lives of gays and lesbians").

99. Eileen McNamara, *Marriage Lite Just Won't Cut It,* Boston Globe, December 22, 1999.

100. Editors of the New Republic, *Separate but Equal?* New Republic, January 10, 2000.

101. Sigmund Freud, *Civilization and Its Discontents, in* Civilization, Society, and Religion: Group Psychology, Civilization and Its Discontents, and Other Works 251, 305 (1985). Freud developed the idea in the context of explaining the ferocious force of European anti-Semitism: namely, as Jews in fact assimilated so brilliantly (like Freud) into German culture, political anti-Semitism ferociously focused on very small cultural differences and, in fact, forged mythological differences that did not exist. This could be regarded as a theory of political prejudice, which is applicable to our current discussion, because anti-Semitism and homophobia share common themes in stigmatizing forms of public identity that challenge dominant stereotypes of dehumanized religious or sexual identity. *See* David A. J. Richards, note 38 above, at 438.

102. Richards, note 38 above, at 438, 447.

one group of citizens in a separate and inferior manner despite their identical circumstances, continuing the pressure for the fully equal civil right of marriage seems to be preferable in terms of both strategy and principle to the pursuit of domestic partnerships or registered partnerships, which some view as a more attainable objective.[103]

103. *See* Steve Bryant & Demian, *Marrying Apartheid: The Failure of Domestic Partnership Status,* Partners Task Force for Gay & Lesbian Couples, May 1999, at http://www.buddybuddy.com/mar-apar.html.

Chapter 11

The Feasibility of
Opening Up Marriage
to Same-Sex Couples

11.1 The Necessary Process

In many countries, including most U.S. states, gays do not enjoy the protection of antidiscrimination laws. Moreover, homosexuals are often regarded as criminals simply by expressing their love, since some states and countries still regard consensual sodomy a crime. Only a minority of nations around the world have thus far enacted legislation to protect sexual minorities from discrimination in employment (both private and public, including the military), housing, access to services, and other areas of public and private life. Reducing such discrimination in relation to marriage—that is, according most or some of the rights and benefits associated with marriage to same-sex couples—has taken place even in fewer countries, and only in those countries that have decriminalized sodomy and have abolished most other forms of discrimination against gay men and lesbians.

Not only are gay men and lesbians not legally protected from discrimination, but, to varying degrees and depending on the country, the vast majority of the legal systems of the Western world still covertly discriminate against them. In that respect, and unlike racial minorities and women, homosexuals still suffer inhumane degradation and do not enjoy full citizenship. Thus, the fight of gays for inclusion in the institution of marriage should not be examined as an independent claim; rather, it should be assessed in light of the status of gay men and lesbians in Western societies in general and in fields of law other than marriage. The recognition of same-sex couples, I argue, is dependent upon and connected to the status of gays in fields other than family law. Developments such as the repeal of sodomy laws and the enactment of antidiscrimination statutes are required for the later recognition of same-sex couples in family law.

We find in different regions and countries a common process for the recognition of gay partnerships that comprises three levels, each successive level reflecting greater tolerance. The first and basic level is to remove from the criminal code (if they exist) sanctions against homosexual and lesbian conduct; the second level is to prohibit discrimination against gay men and lesbians on the basis of their sexual orientation; the third level, which is also the most comprehensive and advanced one, is to affirmatively recognize same-sex partnerships as equal to opposite-sex unions for various purposes, beginning with "soft" rights such as various economic benefits and following that step with comprehensive recognition of same-sex partnerships.[1] I call this the *necessary process* for expansive recognition of same-sex partnerships, since the repeal of sodomy laws and the enactment of antidiscrimination legislation are prerequisites for such recognition.

I argue that this process is both descriptive and normative. That is to say, it reflects the process by which countries in fact have moved toward recognition of same-sex partnerships, and it is also the necessary process that needs to take place in countries that have not yet reached comprehensive recognition of same-sex partnerships. My comparative examination shows that only the necessary process will place gays on an equal footing with opposite-sex married couples. The case for gay rights has a certain normative structure, involving both the illegitimacy of criminalization of gay/lesbian sexuality (as a violation of the right to intimate life, based on inadequate sectarian grounds) and the right to be treated with equal concern and respect (which requires equal respect for gay/ lesbian intimate life, including legal recognition of same-sex partnerships); it is only when the criminalization predicate is removed that the question of equal respect becomes possible. There is also, obviously, an important linkage between the causal and the normative argument: it is because the case for gay rights has a certain normative structure that the implications of the argument are seen and acted on in a certain natural explanatory order, which reflects gradual political recognition of the force of the underlying normative argument. The analysis from this perspective also accounts for the differences between the status of same-sex partnerships in different countries within Europe and in different states

---

1. *See* Amnon Rubinstein & Barak Medina, 2 The Constitutional Law of the State of Israel 326 (5th ed., 1996) (Hebrew).

within the United States, as well as between the United States as a whole and the northern European countries.

11.2 Repeal of Sodomy Laws and Protection from Discrimination in Europe

11.2.1 Repeal of Sodomy Laws

Many major industrial countries in Europe—such as the Netherlands, France, and Italy—decriminalized sodomy during the nineteenth century and simply left consensual sodomy unregulated. It was exactly at that period of time that such laws were adopted in the United States: by 1881 thirty-six out of the thirty-nine states had criminalized sodomy.[2] As for the European countries that still criminalized consensual sodomy in the 1950s and 1960s—such as Norway, Hungary, Germany, and Finland—it was European regional instruments and treaties that were the most effective and influential in causing those countries to repeal their sodomy laws.

The European Court of Human Rights, the European Parliament, and the Council of Europe have long been urging member states to provide complete equality for gay men and lesbians in all fields of legislation. The decisions, resolutions, and declarations of these bodies have led to greater uniformity among the European states in their treatment of homosexuals and to the lessening of discrimination against gays and lesbians.[3] For example, in February 1993 the Parliamentary Assembly of the Council of Europe adopted Written Declaration No. 227, which stressed the need to end discrimination against homosexuals in former Communist countries.[4] Although the European Convention for the Protection of Human Rights and Fundamental Freedoms[5] does not refer explicitly

2. *See* William N. Eskridge Jr., Gaylaw: Challenging the Apartheid of the Closet 25–26, 157–59 (1999).

3. *See* Alan Reekie, *European International Control, in* Sociolegal Control of Homosexuality: A Multi-Nation Comparison 179, 179, 185 (Donald J. West & Richard Green eds., 1997).

4. *Id.* at 185–86.

5. European Convention for the Protection of Human Rights and Fundamental Freedoms, November 4, 1950, 213 U.N.T.S. 221. It was signed in Rome on November 4, 1950, and took effect on September 3, 1953, after ratification by eight nations: Denmark, the Federal Republic of Germany, Iceland, Ireland, Luxembourg, Norway, Sweden, and the United Kingdom. The Convention has been ratified by all member states of the Council of Europe (for a list of member states of the European Council, see note 16 below). A few other countries have signed the Convention but have not ratified it: Andorra, Croatia, Latvia, Lithuania, Macedonia, Moldova, Russian Federation, and Ukraine. *See* Kathleen Marie Whitney, *Does the European Convention on Human Rights Protect Refugees from "Safe" Countries?* 26 Ga. J. Int'l & Comp. L. 375 n. 5 (1997).

to sexual orientation, the European Court of Human Rights has interpreted its provisions as applicable to homosexuals.[6] Accordingly, the Court has held numerous times that states' sodomy laws are in violation of article 8 of the Convention as a breach of the right to private life.

The landmark case in this respect was the 1981 decision in the matter of *Dudgeon v. UK,* in which the Court ruled that Northern Ireland's ban on homosexuality contravened the European Convention by violating the right to privacy set forth in article 8.[7] The Court has reaffirmed *Dudgeon* in two subsequent cases, *Norris v. Ireland* (1988)[8] and *Modinos v. Cyprus* (1993),[9] holding in both cases that criminalization of private homosexual relationships between consenting adults was in breach of the Convention. The Court's holding in *Dudgeon, Norris,* and *Modinos* made it plain that the contracting states to the Convention can no longer criminalize consensual adult homosexual sodomy, even where the

6. *See* Reekie, note 3 above, at 180.

7. 45 Eur. Ct. H. R. (ser. A), 4 EHRR at 149 (1981). Although no prosecutions were brought between 1972 and 1980, the Court ruled that a total prohibition on acts of sodomy and of gross indecency between adult males under the law of Northern Ireland was a breach of art. 8 of the Convention, because it failed to recognize the right to respect for private life. According to the Court, the very existence of the legislation continuously and directly affected Dudgeon's private life. Once it had accepted the argument that homosexual relationships could be a matter of private life, the only issue of the *Dudgeon* Court was whether proscription of those relationships was, in the language of art. 8 of the Convention, necessary in a democratic society in the interest of public order or morals. The Court interpreted "necessary" as implying "a pressing social need" that must exist to justify the interference. The existence of competing, liberalized attitudes throughout Europe toward homosexuality led the Court to narrow the discretion it accorded the government. The Court noted that there was now a better understanding and an increased tolerance of homosexual behavior to the extent that, in the great majority of the member states of the Council of Europe, it was no longer considered to be necessary or appropriate to treat homosexual practices as a matter to which the sanctions of the criminal law should be applied. The Court stated that it could not overlook the marked changes that had occurred in this regard in the domestic law of the member states. Therefore, the Court held that no pressing need existed for the statute and that it should be invalidated. *See id.*

8. 142 Eur. Ct. H.R. (ser. A), at 186 (1988). Although Norris was not charged with any criminal offense, the Court decided that he was still legally at risk of being prosecuted and was thus directly affected by the law, since a "law which remains on the statute book, even though it is not enforced in a particular class of cases for a considerable time may be applied again in such cases at any time." The Court renewed its commitment to protecting consensual adult homosexual relationships from the criminal sanctions of European governments.

9. 259 Eur. Ct. H.R. (ser. A), at 485 (1993). In this case the applicant challenged a Cypriot statute that criminalized all male homosexual activity. The applicant successfully argued that the statute violated his right to privacy guaranteed under art. 8 of the Convention and art. 15 of the Constitution of the Republic of Cyprus. Although there were no recent prosecutions under the sodomy law, like Norris, Modinos could still claim to be a victim of the law because the commission found that the challenged provisions had not yet been abolished and that Modinos could be affected by the Cypriot prohibition of homosexual acts.

relevant statutes have fallen into desuetude. Its holding has led other countries to reform their criminal law by decriminalizing consensual sodomy. It should be noted, however, that until quite recently, the scope of protection accorded by the Court was limited to breaches of the right of privacy in terms of sexual behavior and that the Court has not provided comprehensive rulings based on more fundamental issues of discrimination, such as equal protection under the law. Homosexuals have thus received little support for their rights beyond the *Dudgeon, Norris,* and *Modinos* decisions. These decisions, though establishing the repeal of sodomy laws as a minimum standard in Europe, have failed to provide a suitable framework on which equal rights for same-sex couples can be built.[10] The European Commission on Human Rights has repeatedly determined that the notion of family life under article 8 does not include lesbian and gay families,[11] since *family* has been defined as a man and a woman with all their possible offspring.[12] Recent decisions of the European Court of Human Rights indicate a tendency toward expanding the scope of protection it is willing to accord gay men and lesbians, but these decisions too have no direct bearing on the rights of same-sex couples.[13]

10. *See also* Clarice B. Rabinowitz, *Proposals for Progression: Sodomy Laws and the European Convention on Human Rights,* 21 Brooklyn J. Int'l L. 425, 447 (1995). In particular, the Court and the commission have consistently rejected challenges to laws that establish a higher age of consent for male homosexuals than for heterosexuals or lesbians. *See* Laurence R. Helfer, *Finding a Consensus on Equality: The Homosexuality Age of Consent and the European Convention on Human Rights,* 65 N.Y.U. L. Rev. 1044, 1044 (1990).

11. Andrew Clapham & J. H. H Weiler, *Lesbians and Gay Men in the European Community Legal Order, in* Homosexuality: A European Community Issue: Essays on Lesbian and Gay Rights in European Law and Policy 7, 43 (Kees Waaldijk & Andrew Clapham eds., 1993).

12. Evert Van der Veen et al., *Lesbian and Gay Rights in Europe: Homosexuality and the Law, in* The Third Pink Book: A Global View of Lesbian and Gay Liberation and Oppression 225, 230–32 (Aart Hendriks et al. eds., 1993).

13. *See, e.g.,* Lustig-Prean & Beckett v. United Kingdom (Applications nos. 31417/96 and 32377/96); and Smith & Grady v. United Kingdom (Applications nos. 33985/96 and 33986/96): both were handed down in September 1999. The Court found that the United Kingdom's policy of banning lesbians and gays from the armed forces violated art. 8 of the Convention. The U.K. government's main argument for the ban rested on "the negative attitudes of heterosexual personnel towards those of homosexual orientation." The Court found that "[t]o the extent that they represent a predisposed bias on the part of a heterosexual majority against a homosexual minority, these negative attitudes cannot, of themselves, be considered by the Court to amount to sufficient justification for the interferences . . . any more than similar negative attitudes towards those of a different race, origin or color." On January 12, 2000, the U.K. government lifted the ban. *See Discrimination against Lesbian, Gay, and Bisexual Persons in Europe—A Report Submitted by ILGA-Europe to the Legal Affairs and Human Rights Committee of the Parliamentary Assembly of the Council of Europe as a Contribution to the Preparation of Its Report and Recommendations on the Situation of Lesbians and Gays in the Member States of the Council of Europe* (Motion for a Resolution—Doc. 8319), ILGA-Europe, February 16, 2000, at 11.2.3, available at http://www.steff.suite.dk/final_report.rtf [hereinafter: ILGA-Europe Discrimination Report]. Furthermore, in the recent case of Salgueiro Da Silva Mouta v. Portugal (Application no

Nevertheless, decisions of the U.N. Human Rights Committee affect European countries that have ratified the U.N. International Covenant on Civil and Political Rights (ICCPR).[14] Therefore, the U.N. Human Rights Committee's decision in the matter of *Toonen* provides broader protection for gay men and lesbians than the European Court's case law, because its recommendation to strike down Tasmania's sodomy law was based not only on the right to privacy (art. 17 of ICCPR) but also on the nondiscrimination clauses of the Covenant (arts. 2 and 26 of the ICCPR), categorizing the law as discrimination based on sex.[15]

Moreover, states applying for membership in the Council of Europe[16] have been investigated by the council in regard to the human rights situation of their homosexual citizens; they have been expected to first provide protection to gays and lesbians in their national laws in accordance with the standards of the Convention, primarily in the field of criminal law. The repeal of sodomy laws thus became a prerequisite for joining the council.

33290/96) (Dec. 21, 1999), in which a gay father was denied parental authority by the Lisbon Court of Appeal on the grounds of his sexual orientation, the European Court of Human Rights ruled that the fact that the applicant's homosexuality had been decisive in the decision to deny him parental rights amounted to a distinction that it was not permissible to draw under the Convention. The Court therefore held that there had been a violation of art. 8 taken together with art. 14 and recognized that sexual-orientation discrimination is a prohibited ground of discrimination under art. 14. *Id.* at 12.5, 14.1.

14. For discussion of the committee and its composition and an overview of the relevant articles of the ICCPR, see Laurence R. Helfer & Alice M. Miller, *Sexual Orientation and Human Rights: Toward a United States and Transnational Jurisprudence,* 9 Harv. Hum. Rts. J. 61, 63 (1996).

15. Toonen v. Australia, Comm. No. 488/1992, U.N. GAOR Hum. Rts. Comm., 49th Sess., Supp. No. 40, vol. II, at 226, U.N. Doc. A/49/40 (1994). *See also* Reekie, note 3 above, at 188–89. The decision in Toonen is extremely significant, since 130 states have ratified the Covenant, and in all these states there is now potential for gay plaintiffs to invoke the Covenant as interpreted in Toonen and argue before national courts and legislatures (in countries that ratified the Optional Protocol) or before the U.N. Human Rights Committee that sexual-orientation discrimination of particular kinds is contrary to international human-rights law. Furthermore, the committee's observation that "sex" in arts. 2(1) and 26 includes "sexual orientation" seems to mean that the Covenant prima facie prohibits discrimination based on sexual orientation, both in relation to rights specified in the Covenant (art. 2[1]), and in relation to other rights, interests, or opportunities not protected by the Covenant (art. 26). This is potentially a very broad principle, which could provide comprehensive protection against sexual-orientation discrimination, going well beyond that offered by the European Court to date. *See* Robert Wintemute, Sexual Orientation and Human Rights 5–6, 148 (1995).

16. The Council of Europe is currently composed of the following forty-one states: Albania, Andorra, Austria, Belgium, Bulgaria, Croatia, Cyprus, Czech Republic, Denmark, Estonia, Finland, France, Georgia, Germany, Greece, Hungary, Iceland, Ireland, Italy, Latvia, Liechtenstein, Lithuania, Luxembourg, Malta, Moldova, Netherlands, Norway, Poland, Portugal, Romania, Russian Federation, San Marino, Slovakia, Slovenia, Spain, Sweden, Switzerland, the "former Yugoslav Republic of Macedonia," Turkey, Ukraine, and United Kingdom. *See* The 41 Member States of the Council of Europe, at http://www.coe.fr/eng/std/states.htm (visited April 21, 2000).

Similarly, the European Parliament has encouraged member states that still maintained discriminatory legislation in their criminal codes to follow the example of those who have already adopted gender-neutral criminal laws on sexual behavior.[17] In 1981, the year in which *Dudgeon* was decided, Recommendation 924 of the Parliamentary Assembly, "On Discrimination against Homosexuals," urged, inter alia, the decriminalization of homosexual acts between consenting adults in private and the application of the same minimum age of consent for homosexual and heterosexual acts.[18] Moreover, the Parliament's resolution on "Sexual Discrimination in the Workplace" of 1984 urged member states to abolish sodomy laws and to equalize the age of consent for heterosexual and homosexual sex.[19] Since then, all existing and new E.U. member states have abolished their sodomy laws, and the vast majority of states have repealed all other penal laws discriminating against homosexual sex, for example, those establishing unequal ages of consent.

Owing to the European bodies' resolutions and the European Court's jurisprudence, as of May 2001 only three European countries and regions still criminalized consensual sodomy: Republika Srpska (in Bosnia and Herzegovina), the Chechen Republic, and Armenia.[20] However, in some countries that have long decriminalized consensual sodomy, such as Italy and Spain, laws on "public indecency" and "obscenity" are used in discriminatory ways against gay men and lesbians who display affection by hugging and kissing in public places.[21]

11.2.2 Antidiscrimination Legislation
Both the European Union[22] and the Council of Europe have adopted resolutions and recommendations to combat discrimination against gay men and lesbians in general and against same-sex couples in particular.

17. Reekie, note 3 above, at 182.

18. *See* ILGA-Europe Discrimination Report, note 13 above.

19. Reekie, note 3 above, at 183.

20. *See* http://www.ilga.org/Information/legal_survey/Summary%20information/countries_where_same_sex_acts%20Illegal.htm (visited April 21, 2000). *See also* ILGA-Europe Discrimination Report, note 13 above, at 2.2. Azerbaijan was the latest European country to repeal its sodomy law; its new Criminal Code, effective September 2000, no longer criminalizes sodomy. The law reform was attributed to the nation's aspiration to join the Council of Europe and followed the Council of Europe Parliamentary Assembly's vote of July 2000 to support the membership application of Azerbaijan on the condition that it decriminalize sex between men. *See* PlanetOut News Staff, *International Briefs: Azerbaijan Repeals Sodomy Law,* June 27, 2000.

21. *See* Reekie, note 3 above, at 184.

22. The fifteen member states of the European Union are Austria, Belgium, Denmark, Finland, France, Germany, Greece, Ireland, Italy, Luxembourg, the Netherlands, Portugal, Spain, Sweden, and the United Kingdom. *See* http://www.europarl.eu.int/members/en/default.htm (visited April 21, 2000).

On February 8, 1994, the European Parliament passed another significant resolution, "Equal Rights for Homosexuals and Lesbians in the European Union," calling for member states of the European Union to end
all legal and administrative discrimination on the grounds of sexual orientation, to pass legislation providing homosexuals access to "marriage
or an equivalent legal framework," and to allow "the adoption and fostering of children."[23] The European Parliament has reaffirmed its 1994
resolution, and on March 16, 2000, adopted the nonbinding "Resolution on the Respect for Human Rights in the European Union for 1998–
1999."[24] This resolution goes further than the 1994 one by calling E.U.
member states and the thirteen nations currently seeking E.U. membership to "guarantee one-parent families, unmarried couples and same-sex
couples rights equal to those enjoyed by traditional couples and families,
particularly as regards to tax law, pecuniary rights and social rights."[25]
The European Parliament thus recommends that gay and lesbian couples
be accorded the same legal recognition as heterosexual couples, that
member states recognize registered partnerships of same-sex couples and
grant equal rights of marriage to unmarried couples, including same-sex
couples. Member states are thus required to provide greater equality
than the mere repeal of sodomy laws. The most important step in the
recognition of lesbian, gay, and bisexual rights by the European Union
has been the adoption of the Treaty of Amsterdam, which was signed
in October 1997 by the E.U. member states but did not take effect until May 1, 1999. It includes the first explicit mention of sexual orientation in any international treaty, specifying sexual orientation as one of
the prohibited grounds of discrimination (part 1, art. 13, of the treaty).[26]

23. Resolution on Equal Rights for Homosexuals and Lesbians in the EC, paragraph 14, p. 40, of the 1994 *Official Journal of the European Communities* (February 28,
1994).

24. EP Document A5-0050/2000.

25. *Id.* arts. 56–60 of the resolution.

26. *See* European Union: Consolidated Version of the Treaty on European Union and
Consolidated Version of the Treaty Establishing the European Community, Oct. 2, 1997,
37 I.L.M. 56 [hereinafter Amsterdam Treaty]. The article provides as follows: "Without
prejudice to the other provisions of this Treaty and within the limits of the powers conferred by it upon the Community, the Council, acting unanimously on a proposal from
the Commission and after consulting the European Parliament, may take appropriate
action to combat discrimination based on sex, racial or ethnic origin, religion or belief,
disability, age or *sexual orientation.*" Amsterdam Treaty, above, part 1, art. 13, my emphasis. For a detailed discussion of art. 13 and its limitations, see Sejal Parmar, *The Treaty of
Amsterdam, in* After Amsterdam: Sexual Orientation and the European Union: A Guide
15–25 (ILGA Europe, September 1999). Prior to the ratification of the treaty, the European
Court of Justice held that E.U. law did not prohibit employment discrimination on the
basis of sexual orientation. *See* Grant v. South West Trains, Case C-249/96 [1998] ECR 1-
621. Under the treaty, the court may arrive at a different result in the future. *See* Parmar,
above, at 16.

Significant resolutions and recommendations adopted by both European bodies also took place in September and October of 2000.[27]

However, the resolutions of regional European instruments urging member states to enact antidiscrimination legislation, which are quite recent, have thus far met with less success than the call to repeal sodomy laws, and it will take quite a few years for member states to adopt legislation implementing these recommendations. The repeal of sodomy laws in various European countries during the past two decades can be largely attributed to adjudication and resolutions of international instruments; in contrast, providing gay men and lesbians protection from discrimination, including the equalization of the age of consent between homosexuals and heterosexuals and access to rights associated with marriage, has largely taken place at the national level of various European countries, and not necessarily as a result of regional instruments' conditions for granting membership. For example, recognition of same-sex partnerships in none of the European countries that are the subject of this study, except for Hungary and Portugal, stemmed from regional or international political pressure or from aspirations to join such instruments.

We thus find less uniformity among the European countries in the general field of protection from discrimination than in the particular case of repealing sodomy laws. It should be emphasized that since the 1960s, no European country (except for the United Kingdom) has introduced new antihomosexual legislation and that all have made some legislative progress in the legal recognition of homosexuality.[28] Among the European countries that are the subject of this study, discrimination in terms of access to military service and discriminatory ages of consent

27. In October 2000 the governments of the fifteen E.U. member states approved a program to combat discrimination based on, inter alia, sexual orientation in all aspects of employment and occupation, including recruitment and vocational training. The program is one of three implementation instruments of art. 13 of the Amsterdam Treaty. It is the first piece of E.U. legislation with relevance for all member states that explicitly covers sexual orientation. The full text of the decision can be found at http://europa.eu.int/eur-lex/en/dat/2000/l_303/l_30320001202en00230028.pdf. A similar recommendation in support of lesbian and gay rights was adopted by the Council of Europe in September 2000. The Assembly called upon the governments of Europe to, among other things, adopt legislation that provides for registered partnership. The Assembly also repeated its call for sexual orientation to be added to the grounds for discrimination prohibited by the European Convention on Human Rights. The recommendation is available at the Parliamentary Assembly Web site, http://stars.coe.int/asp/DocByDate.asp. *See* ILGA-Europe Euroletter no. 83, October 2000 (Steffen Jensen et al. eds.) at http://www.qrd.org/qrd/www/orgs/ILGA/euroletter.

28. *See* Kees Waaldijk, *Towards the Recognition of Same-Sex Partnerships in European Union Law: Expectations Based on Trends in National Law, in* Legal Recognition of Same-Sex Partnerships: A Study of National, European, and International Law 635 (Robert Wintemute & Mads Andenas eds., 2001).

still exist only in Hungary and Portugal. Affirmative protection from discrimination is provided by all European countries that I deal with in this book except for Germany, Portugal, Italy, Belgium, and the Czech Republic. Both hate speech legislation (banning insults or other statement that could incite discrimination, harassment, or violence based on sexual orientation) *and* immigration rights for same-sex couples exist only in the five European countries that have thus far adopted comprehensive registered partnership legislation (Denmark, Norway, Sweden, Iceland, and the Netherlands [see table 4 below]).

Only nine countries out of the forty-one member states of the Council of Europe provide gays and lesbians specific protection from discrimination. Only Denmark, Norway, Sweden, Finland, France, and the Netherlands provide protection from discrimination in employment on the ground of sexual orientation.[29] In 1987 Denmark amended article 289 of its criminal code so as to protect homosexuals from discrimination in the provision of goods and services and to guarantee equal access to public facilities.[30] Also in 1987, Denmark added article 266a to its criminal code, which protects from incitement to hatred on the basis of sexual orientation.[31] However, it was not until 1996 that Denmark passed legislation providing protection against discrimination based on sexual orientation in the private sector as well.[32] In 1981 Norway became the first country in the world to institute a ban on discrimination in the provision of goods and services and on incitement to hatred against lesbians and gay men.[33] Likewise, since 1987 Sweden has forbidden public officials and private businesses to discriminate in the provision of goods and services on the basis of sexual orientation;[34] in the same year Sweden

29. ILGA-Europe Discrimination Report, note 13 above, at 11.2.4.

30. Peter Tatchell, Europe in the Pink: Lesbian and Gay Equality in the New Europe 107 (1992); Kees Waaldijk, Tip of an Iceberg: Anti-Lesbian and Anti-Gay Discrimination in Europe 1980–1990, at 94 (1991).

31. Art. 266a reads as follows: "Any person who publicly or with the intention of wider dissemination, makes a statement or imparts other information by which a group of people are threatened, insulted or degraded on account of their race, color, national or ethnic origin, religion or sexual orientation, shall be liable to a fine or to simple detention or to imprisonment for any term not exceeding two years." *See* Tatchell, note 30 above, at 107; Waaldijk, note 30 above, at 65.

32. ILGA World Legal Survey: Denmark, at http://www.ilga.org/Information/legal_survey/europe/denmark.htm (last updated November 29, 1999).

33. Tatchell, note 30 above, at 123–24; *See also* Rob Tielman & Hans Hammelburg, *World Survey on the Social and Legal Position of Gays and Lesbians, in* The Third Pink Book: A Global View of Lesbian and Gay Liberation and Oppression 249, 312–13 (Aart Hendriks et al. eds., 1993); Norway Ministry of Children and Family Affairs, The Norwegian Act on Registered Partnerships for Homosexual Couples 18 (1993) [hereinafter The Norwegian Bill].

34. Tatchell, note 30 above, at 132.

made incitement to hatred for gay individuals and derogatory remarks about a person's homosexuality criminal offenses. As of May 1, 1999, new and specific legislation providing protection against discrimination in employment took effect in Sweden.[35] In the Netherlands, article 1 of the constitution, which provides that "discrimination on the grounds of religion, belief, political opinion, race or sex, or *any grounds* whatsoever shall not be permitted," was interpreted by the courts and Parliament as prohibiting discrimination on the basis of sexual orientation.[36] In 1992 provisions covering discrimination on the basis of sexual orientation were added to the Dutch Penal Code, including antigay libel and incitement.[37] In 1994 the Netherlands adopted the General Equal Treatment Act, which outlaws discrimination on the basis of sexual orientation in the fields of labor (including private-sector labor), housing, medical care, and access to goods and services.[38] In a similar manner, French legislation from 1985 that provides protection from discrimination in private employment and in the access to goods and services[39] was interpreted as also covering discrimination based on sexual orientation.[40] Furthermore, in 1986 and 1990, the French Code of Labor Law was amended to prohibit discrimination based on sexual orientation in public employment.[41]

As to the rest of the European countries that are the subject of this book, only Iceland, Finland, Spain, Hungary, and Switzerland provide protection for gay men and lesbians against discrimination; Germany, Portugal, Italy, Belgium, and the Czech Republic provide no such protection. We should also bear in mind that in most European countries, lesbians and gay men face extensive discrimination related to parenting: they may be denied custody or access rights, refused the possibility to adopt, or, in the case of lesbians, denied access to medically assisted reproduction services.[42]

35. Tielman & Hammelburg, note 33 above, at 329; ILGA World Legal Survey: Sweden, at http://www.ilga.org/Information/legal_survey/europe/sweden.htm (last updated October 11, 1999). Moreover, as of May 1999 Sweden became the first country in the world to appoint a special ombudsman for discrimination against gay men and lesbians in the workplace and at other levels of society. *Id.*

36. Tatchell, note 30 above, at 121–22, my emphasis.

37. Tielman & Hammelburg, note 33 above, at 308.

38. *See* ILGA World Legal Survey: The Netherlands, at http://www.ilga.org/Information/legal_survey/europe/netherlands.htm (last updated July 11, 1999). It does not, however, cover religious schools, which may bar gay teachers if necessary for the fulfillment of their function. *Id.*

39. Arts. 187-1, 187-2, 416, and 416-1 of the French Penal Code. *See* Tielman & Hammelburg, note 33 above, at 279–80.

40. Tatchell, note 30 above, at 110; Waaldijk, note 30 above, at 37.

41. Arts. 122-35 and 122-45. *See* Tielman & Hammelburg, note 33 above, at 280.

42. ILGA-Europe Discrimination Report, note 13 above, at 12.2.

11.3 Repeal of Sodomy Laws and Protection from Discrimination in the United States

11.3.1 Repeal of Sodomy Laws

During the period 1946 to 1961, when all states in the United States criminalized consensual and private oral or anal sex between adults, and most European countries no longer had such laws on their books, the states imposed criminal punishments on as many as 1 million lesbians and gay men who engaged in consensual adult intercourse, danced, kissed, or held hands. Sodomy-law arrests reached historic highs in that period, and at least 40 percent of the arrests were for consensual same-sex adult intimacy.[43] As recently as the beginning of the 1970s, all states but one had sodomy laws.[44] In 1961 Illinois adopted the Model Penal Code, which included the decriminalization of consensual sodomy. Between 1969 and 1977, nineteen other states repealed their consensual sodomy laws as part of a general recodification of their criminal codes along the lines of the Model Penal Code; most legislatures were not aware that the recodification included repeal of homosexual sodomy, and none had the specific intention to take that step. When the legislatures realized that the reform included decriminalization of homosexual sodomy, two of these states reinstated their sodomy laws and six other states decided to decriminalize only different-sex sodomy, leaving same-sex sodomy a crime. An exception was California, which was the first state that focused on reforming sodomy law, not as part of a general law reform; its decriminalization took effect in 1976. During the following two years, a few other states repealed sodomy laws as part of general criminal code revision; after 1978 sodomy repeal stood on its own, and decriminalization was mainly through judicial decision rather than legislative acts. Not until 1986 had half the states repealed their sodomy laws or nullified the application of the laws to consenting adults.[45]

As of December 2001 thirteen states still criminalized adult consensual sodomy.[46] Three states criminalize only same-sex sexual relations,

43. Eskridge, note 2 above, at 60–62.

44. Only one state repealed its sodomy law in the 1960s (Illinois); twenty states repealed their laws in the 1970s, four states during the 1980s, and the other nine in the 1990s. *See Status of US Sodomy Laws*, American Civil Liberties Union Freedom Network: Lesbian & Gay Rights, available at http://www.aclu.org/issues/gay/sodomy.html (visited March 20, 2000).

45. Eskridge, note 2 above, at 84, 106, 107, 160. Decriminalization by judicial decree took place in New York (1980), Pennsylvania (1980), Kentucky (1992), Tennessee (1996), Montana (1997), and Georgia (1998). Repeal of sodomy laws in four additional states was effected by legislative action. *Id.*

46. States currently criminalizing sodomy are Alabama (Ala. Code 13A-6-65[a][3] [1994]); Florida (Fla. Stat. Ann. 800.02 [West 1992 Supp. 1995]); Idaho (Idaho Code 18-6605 [1987]); Kansas (Kan. Stat. Ann. 21-3505 [1988 Supp. 1993]); Louisiana (La. Rev. Stat.

their courts or legislatures having decriminalized different-sex sodomy;[47] sodomy laws in the other ten apply to both same- and opposite-
sex couples (see table 4 below). Even the latter—sodomy laws that apply
equally to same-sex partners and opposite-sex partners—have been used
disproportionately to justify discrimination against lesbians and gay
men.[48] Therefore, although only a minority of existing sodomy laws in
the United States explicitly discriminate against same-sex partners, all
sodomy laws in fact have a distinct discriminatory impact on gay men
and lesbians rather than on heterosexual couples.[49] Today, sodomy laws,
even if they encompass opposite-sex sexual behavior, are targeted at and
are being used to perpetuate discrimination mainly against same-sex
partners. Thus, whatever the reasons for the repeal of sodomy laws may
have been until the end of the 1970s, it is clear that since the beginning
of the 1980s, especially following *Bowers v. Hardwick,*[50] sodomy laws
have become a gay rights issue, even if they were facially gender neutral.

When a challenge to Georgia's sodomy law was brought before the

---

Ann. 14:89 [West 1986]); Massachusetts (Mass. Gen. L. ch. 272, 34–35 [1992]); Mississippi
(Miss. Code Ann. 97-29-59 [1973]); North Carolina (N.C. Gen. Stat. 14-177 [1994]); Oklahoma (Okla. Stat. tit. 21, 886–88 [1983 Supp. 1995]); South Carolina (S.C. Code Ann. 16-
15-120 [Law. Co-op. 1985]); Texas (Tex. Penal Code Ann. 21.06 [West 1997]); Utah (Utah
Code Ann. 76-5-403 [1978]); and Virginia (Va. Code Ann. 18.2–361 [Michie 1988]). *See
State-by-State Map of Sodomy Laws,* Lambda Legal Defense and Education Fund, at http://
www.lambdalegal.org (updated May 25, 2001). Michigan, Minnesota, and Missouri are
to be regarded as states that are "free" of sodomy laws: In Michigan Organization for
Human Rights v. Kelly, no. 88-815820 CZ (Mich. Cir. Ct. July 9, 1990), a trial court held
that Michigan's sodomy law was unconstitutional under the state constitution, and since
then the decision has not been appealed. In State v. Cogshell, a Missouri appeals court
has construed the state sodomy law not to apply to consensual sexual relations. *See State-
by-State Map of Sodomy Laws,* above. On May 18, 2001, a district court judge in Minnesota
struck down the state's sodomy law. *See* Barbara Dozetos, *Minnesota Sodomy Law Struck
Down,* PlanetOut.com Networks, May 21, 2001. In July 2001, the district court certified
its ruling as a class action so there would be no doubt that it applied throughout the
state; in September, the Minnesota Attorney General's office announced that it would
not appeal the district court's decision, thereby reaffirming the repeal of the state's sodomy law. *See Attorney General Will Not Appeal Sodomy Ruling Statewide,* Minneapolis Star
Tribune, September 1, 2001.

47. Kansas, Oklahoma, and Texas. In seven other states, similar discrimination has
been directed solely at same-sex couples: Nevada repealed its same-sex sodomy law in
1993, and six other states have judicially invalidated such statutes (Kentucky, 1992; Tennessee, 1996; Maryland, 1999; Montana, 1997; Minnesota, 2001; and Arkansas, 2001).
See Eskridge, note 2 above, at 328–37 (app. A1, State Consensual Sodomy Laws, 1610–
1998); Matt Alsdorf, *Arkansas Sodomy Law Struck Down,* Gay.com/PlanetOut.com Network, March 26, 2001; *State-by-State Map of Sodomy Laws,* note 46 above.

48. There is no doubt that sodomy laws impact gays and lesbians more than heterosexual couples. See, for example, the interpretation of the Georgia law in the matter of Bowers
v. Hardwick, 478 U.S. 186 (1986) as pertaining solely to "homosexual sodomy." In most
cases, sodomy laws are not being enforced, but they are used to justify other kinds of
discrimination against gay men and lesbians.

49. *See State-by-State Sodomy Law Update,* Lambda Legal Defense and Education Fund,
August 3, 1999, at http://lambdalegal.org/cgi-bin/pages/documents/record?record=275.

50. 478 U.S. 186 (1986).

U.S. Supreme Court in the matter of *Bowers v. Hardwick*,[51] the Court held that the law was constitutional and did not infringe upon the right of privacy of gay men and lesbians.[52] The statute was of general application, since it applied to all persons, whether single or married, heterosexual or homosexual. Indeed, the case began as a challenge by both Hardwick and a married couple, but the married couple's challenge was dismissed in the lower court. Accordingly, the state of Georgia defended the statute only insofar as it criminalized homosexual sodomy,[53] and the majority opinion of the Supreme Court regarded the sodomy act as applicable only to gays ("homosexual sodomy"), although it was gender neutral. The case thus clearly turned on the fact that Hardwick was a homosexual: it was a case about homosexual sodomy, not heterosexual sodomy, and it is quite likely that had the plaintiff been a straight man, the Court would not have reached the same conclusion; the heterosexual couple's dismissal from the case supports this conclusion.[54]

According to the Court's analysis, a judgment by the state that sodomy is immoral provided a sufficiently rational basis for sodomy laws to satisfy the requirements of substantive due process. The Supreme Court held that the U.S. Constitution did not confer a fundamental right upon homosexuals to engage in sodomy, and as such, the Georgia state law criminalizing sodomy did not violate the U.S. Constitution.[55] Under *Bowers*, the thirteen laws that still criminalize sodomy are purportedly constitutional, at least insofar as they prohibit the sexual activities of homosexual males. *Hardwick* left open the possibility that heterosexual sodomy is constitutionally protected. Thus, an equal-protection attack would be available in those jurisdictions that ban homosexual but not

51. *Id.* The Georgia statute that criminalized the act of sodomy, Ga. Code Ann. at 16-6-2 (1984 & Supp. 1987), provided that (a) A person commits the offense of sodomy when he performs or submits to any sexual act involving the sex organs of one person and the mouth or anus of another; (b) A person convicted of the offense of sodomy shall be punished by imprisonment for not less than one nor more than 20 years.

52. Since then the state's highest court has overturned that law. State appellate courts in Montana, Kentucky, and Tennessee have also interpreted their state constitutions to prohibit the criminalization of sodomy. In 1999 two separate courts in Louisiana found that the state sodomy law violated the state constitution's privacy guarantee; both cases are now on appeal to the Louisiana Supreme Court. *See State-by-State Sodomy Law Update*, Lambda Legal Defense and Education Fund, August 3, 1999, at http://lambdalegal.org/cgi-bin/pages/documents/record?record=275.

53. *See* Brief for Petitioner at 3–4, Bowers v. Hardwick, 478 U.S. 186 (1986) (stating intent to limit enforcement of statute to homosexual conduct).

54. The majority noted that "the only claim properly before the Court . . . is Hardwick's challenge to the Georgia statute as applied to consensual homosexual sodomy. We express no opinion on the constitutionality of the Georgia statute as applied to other acts of sodomy." *See* Bowers v. Hardwick, 478 U.S. 186, 188 n. 2 (1986).

55. *Id.* at 196.

heterosexual sodomy.[56] In *Romer v. Evans*,[57] the Supreme Court did not explicitly overturn *Hardwick*. Nevertheless, its holding further opens the door to an equal-protection challenge to sodomy laws, at least the ones that are limited to same-sex partners. However, such a challenge has not come before the U.S. Supreme Court since *Hardwick*, and sodomy laws in the United States remain constitutional. Moreover, sodomy laws of general application that are gender neutral probably cannot be challenged on an equal-protection basis.

11.3.2 Antidiscrimination Legislation

Discrimination against gay men and lesbians in the United States has touched virtually every aspect of life. Gay men and lesbians have been excluded from employment in the private, public, governmental, and military sectors. Denial of business or professional licenses has deprived homosexual individuals of opportunities to earn a living in chosen professions. In addition, homosexuals have been prevented from immigrating to the United States and have experienced discrimination in seeking public accommodations, housing, insurance, credit, and corporate status. Underlying the plight of homosexual persons in America is the criminalization through state sodomy statutes of private consensual sexual behavior among consenting adults and its constitutional legitimation by the Supreme Court.[58]

In *Romer v. Evans*,[59] the U.S. Supreme Court struck down one of the most discriminatory measures against the rights of gay men and lesbians—Amendment 2 to the Colorado Constitution, which provided

> No Protected Status Based on Homosexual, Lesbian, or Bisexual Orientation. Neither the State of Colorado, through any of its branches or departments, nor any of its agencies, political subdivisions, municipalities or school districts, shall enact, adopt or enforce any statute, regulation, ordinance or policy whereby homosexual, lesbian or bisexual orientation, conduct, practices or relationships shall constitute or otherwise be the basis of or entitle any person or class of persons to have or claim any minority status, quota preferences, protected status or claim of discrimination. This Section of the Constitution shall be in all respects self-executing.[60]

---

56. *See* Cass R. Sunstein, *Sexual Orientation and the Constitution: A Note on the Relationship between Due Process and Equal Protection*, 55 U. Chi. L. Rev. 1161, 1187 n. 84 (1988).

57. 517 U.S. 620 (1996). For discussion of the case, see below; see also chap. 10.

58. *See* Yvonne L. Tharpes, Comment, *Bowers v. Hardwick and the Legitimization of Homophobia in America*, 30 How. L.J. 537, 538–40 (1987).

59. 517 U.S. 620 (1996).

60. Colo. Const., Art. 2, at 30b.

The Court held that the state had no legitimate purpose in completely removing a select group of citizens from the general protection of discrimination laws.[61] Although the Supreme Court declared invalid a provision of the Colorado Constitution that would have prohibited protection of gay men and lesbians from discrimination based on sexual orientation, it seems that the Court's decision in *Romer* does not in itself *provide* protection to gay men and lesbians from discrimination in the United States. It merely protects them from the repeal of antidiscrimination legislation; it does not require that gays be *provided* protection from discrimination. In other words, Amendment 2 was extremely broad, applying to every aspect of homosexual life (housing, education, insurance, health, employment, and the like), both in the private and the public spheres, and was specifically targeted at gays out of sheer animus. Had the statute in question not been extremely broad, imposing a special disability on homosexuals as a group out of animus, it might have been upheld. *Romer* can thus be easily distinguished from other cases of discrimination against gay men and lesbians. Moreover, we find that in subsequent cases with similar circumstances, some lower courts tend to wrongfully disregard *Romer*. Thus, for example, in the matter of *Equality Foundation of Greater Cincinnati v. City of Cincinnati*,[62] in spite of *Romer*, the Sixth Circuit upheld a city charter amendment[63] that was *substantially similar* to the Colorado initiative—prohibiting the passage of any legislation in Cincinnati to protect people from discrimination based on sexual orientation—and the Supreme Court declined to review the case.[64] Cincinnati thus became the first city in the country to outlaw specific protection of homosexuals, and its measure stood a constitutional challenge and remains in force.[65] The significance of the Cincin-

61. Romer v. Evans, 517 U.S. 620, 626–27 (1996).

62. 128 F.3d 289 (6th Cir. 1997).

63. The amendment reads: "The City of Cincinnati and its various Boards and Commissions may not enact, adopt, enforce or administer any ordinance, regulation, rule or policy which provides that homosexual, lesbian, or bisexual orientation, status, conduct, or relationship constitutes, entitles, or otherwise provides a person with the basis to have any claim of minority or protected status, quota preference or other preferential treatment. This provision of the City Charter shall in all respects be self-executing. Any ordinance, regulation, rule or policy enacted before this amendment is adopted that violates the foregoing prohibition shall be null and void and of no force or effect." Equality Foundation of Greater Cincinnati v. City of Cincinnati 128 F.3d 289, at 291 (6th Cir. 1997).

64. *See* Equality Found. of Greater Cincinnati, Inc. v. City of Cincinnati, 119 S. Ct. 365 (1998).

65. *See* Julie Irwin, *Cincinnati Amendment Now in Effect*, Cincinnati Enquirer, October 14, 1998, at A8; James E. Barnett, Comment, *Updating Romer v. Evans: The Implications of the Supreme Court's Denial of Certiorari in Equality Foundation of Greater Cincinnati v. City of Cincinnati*, 49 Case W. Res. 645, 646 (1999); *see also* Jill Dinneen, Comment, *Equality Foundation of Greater Cincinnati, Inc. v. City of Cincinnati: The Sixth Circuit Narrowly Construes Romer V. Evans*, 73 St. John's L. Rev. 951 (1999).

nati case is the court's refusal to apply *Romer* (and the erroneous distinction it makes between the Cincinnati measure and Amendment 2) *despite* the similar facts. As a result there is much uncertainty about the degree of protection against discrimination that *Romer* seemingly provides. Moreover, the *Romer* Court did not address the question of whether homosexuals had a fundamental right to engage in the political process and to be treated as equal citizens and thus refrained from finding that gay men and lesbians had such right.

Unlike the northern European countries, therefore, the federal Constitution, federal statutes, and U.S. Supreme Court case law do not provide gay men and lesbians *any* protection from discrimination. There is no federal civil rights law that prohibits discrimination on the basis of sexual orientation in public or private employment, except for an executive order issued by President Clinton in 1998 that bars discrimination on the basis of sexual orientation in the civil sector of the federal government.[66] Not only does the protection in the form of an executive order carry less weight and permanence than a statute does, but it is also limited to civilian public employees of the federal government. Moreover, the order is mostly symbolic, since it has no enforcement mechanism. Only federal legislation such as the proposed Employment Non-Discrimination Act (ENDA), which has been defeated in Congress time and again,[67] or a similar statute could guarantee full and comprehensive protection from discrimination for gays and lesbians in the workplace.

At the state and local level, the scope and the availability of such protections are quite limited. Only eleven states provide protection from discrimination in both public and private employment.[68] Executive or-

66. *See* Further Amendment to the Executive Order 11478, Equal Employment Opportunity in the Federal Government (as amended on May 28, 1998, adding sexual orientation to the list of categories for which discrimination is prohibited), signed by President Clinton August 17, 1998. *See Clinton's Executive Order on Discrimination,* 5 Fed. Hum. Resources Wk., no. 17, August 17, 1998 (available on Lexis at the news library).

67. The Employment Non-Discrimination Act (ENDA) was first introduced in Congress on June 23, 1994. On September 10, 1996, ENDA came within one vote of passing in the U.S. Senate. ENDA was reintroduced June 24, 1999, and was defeated once again. *See* Kim I. Mills & Daryl Herrschaft, The State of the Workplace for Lesbian, Gay, Bisexual, and Transgendered Americans, The Human Rights Campaign 11 (Washington D.C., September 1999).

68. *See* California Labor Code §§ 1101, 1102, 1102.1 (1992); Connecticut Public Act 91-58 (1991); Hawaii Rev. Stats., §§ 368-1, 378-2 (1991); Massachusetts Gen. L., Ch. 151B, §§ 3–4 (1995); Minnesota Ch. 22, H.F. No. 585 (1993); Nevada NRS 610.010 et seq. (1999); New Hampshire RSA 21 (as amended by H.B. 421, 3/19/97); New Jersey Ch. 519, L.N.J. 1991; Hum Rts. Law [C.10:5-3] (1/92); Rhode Island 95-H 6678 Sub.A (1995); Vermont Hum. Rts. Law (1992); Wisconsin Laws of 1981, Ch. 112. Some of these states also provide protection in public accommodations and education (such as California, Connecticut, and Vermont) or housing (e.g., Massachusetts, New Hampshire, and New Jersey). *See Summary of States Which Prohibit Discrimination Based on Sexual Orientation,* Lambda Legal Defense and Education Fund, October 25, 1999, available at http://lambdalegal.org/cgi-bin/pages/documents/record?record=185. *See also* table 4, below.

ders in a few other states protect public employees from discrimination based on sexual orientation.[69] Furthermore, the civil rights ordinances, policies, or proclamations of more than one hundred cities and eighteen counties prohibit discrimination based on sexual orientation in public and private employment.[70] In terms of protection from discrimination, the status of gay men and lesbians has improved dramatically during the past decade. The National Gay and Lesbian Task Force reports that, whereas in 1990, 18 million Americans lived in towns, cities, or counties with laws banning sexual orientation discrimination, that number has dramatically increased so that today 37 million people live in *localities* that provide such protections, and 24 percent of the U.S. population is provided protection from discrimination on the basis of sexual orientation by *state* law in both public and private employment.[71] These figures also demonstrate a gap between the status of gays in various towns and cities and their status at the state and federal level, the latter having provided much less protection to gay men and lesbians on the basis of their sexual orientation.

In conclusion, in addition to the exclusion from marriage itself, supported by the federal and state defense of marriage acts, gays in the United States are discriminated against by the criminal laws of thirteen states, which prohibit sodomy, and by Supreme Court jurisprudence upholding the criminalization of homosexual sodomy; they are excluded from openly serving in the military; and, among other things, they lack immigration rights for their partners. Moreover, no federal legislation provides gays and lesbians protection from discrimination in the workplace on the basis of their sexual orientation.

69. Colorado Executive Order 90-13-98 (1990); Iowa Executive Order no.7 (1999); Maryland Executive Order 01.01.1995.19 (1995); New Mexico Executive Order 85-15 (1985); New York Executive Order no.28 (11/18/83), no. 33 (4/9/96); Pennsylvania Executive Order no.1988-1 (1985). *See Summary of States Which Prohibit Discrimination Based on Sexual Orientation,* note 68 above.

70. Wayne van der Meide, Legislating Equality: A Review of Laws Affecting Gay, Lesbian, Bisexual, and Transgendered People in the United States (2000). For examples of specific ordinances, see, e.g., Berkeley, Calif. (Berkeley Municipal Code, Ch. 13.28 et seq., 11/9/78: public and private employment, education, and housing); New York City (Administrative Code, Title 8 [civil rights] amended 1993: public and private employment, education, and housing); Austin, Tex. (City Code, Ch. 7-3; Ordinance 75-710-A, 7/75: public and private employment and housing). *See Summary of States, Cities, and Counties Which Prohibit Discrimination Based on Sexual Orientation,* Lambda Legal Defense and Education Fund, October 25, 1999, available at http://lambdalegal.org/cgi-bin/pages/documents/record?record=217. *See also* James Button, The Politics of Gay Rights in American Communities (1994). Given the lack of federal protection and the uncertainty or nonexistence of state and local laws, private and public employers have taken the lead in implementing nondiscrimination policies for their gay and lesbian workers. For a detailed account of antidiscrimination policies in the private sector, see Mills & Herrschaft, note 67 above.

71. Van der Meide, note 70 above.

11.4 Sodomy Laws, Antidiscrimination, and Recognition of Same-Sex Partnerships

Legislation recognizing same-sex partnerships in the northern European countries has followed decriminalization of consensual sodomy and the enactment of extensive antidiscrimination protections. In the United States, which has yet to adopt a comprehensive model for the recognition of same-sex partnerships at the federal or the state level (with the exception of the state of Vermont), not only do thirteen states still criminalize consensual sodomy and are under no constitutional requirement to repeal these laws,[72] but also most states (as well as the federal government) do not provide gay men and lesbians basic protections from discrimination based on sexual orientation (see the sections above, and see table 4).

There is thus a standard pattern or process, which comprises three stages of progression, or "standard sequences,"[73] toward a high level of recognition of same-sex partnerships, each stage being a prerequisite for the next one. Although a few countries have deviated from this general process, the model is applicable to most countries in the world, including the northern European countries and the United States; most of them seem to progress in the same order. The first step is the decriminalization of homosexual acts and the equalization of sexual offenses, along with equalization of the age of consent. After that, protection from discrimination is introduced.

Only then do we reach the third level, which is the most comprehensive one: affirmative recognition of same-sex partnerships in family law through legislation recognizing same-sex partnerships and/or parental rights of gays and lesbians, depending on the country and region.[74] In

---

72. As explained in previous sections, some scholars question whether Bowers v. Hardwick, 478 U.S. 186 (1986), is still good law after the Supreme Court's ruling in Romer v. Evans, 517 U.S. 620 (1996). Nevertheless, U.S. states are still constitutionally allowed to criminalize sodomy.

73. *See* Kees Waaldijk, *Standard Sequences in the Legal Recognition of Homosexuality— Europe's Past, Present, and Future,* 4 Australian Gay & Lesbian L.J. 50 (1994); *see also* Robert Wintemute, *Sexual Orientation Discrimination, in* Individual Rights and the Law in Britain (Christopher McCrudden & Gerald Chambers eds., 1994), at 530.

74. Waaldijk has termed this process "the law of standard sequences." *See* Waaldijk, note 28 above. See also Eric Heinze, Sexual Orientation: A Human Right 105–15 (1995), identifying four "models" for the recognition of homosexuals: (1) "Expansive Recognition": this model comprises three "rungs." The "first rung" is decriminalization; the second is general antidiscrimination protections and hate crime legislation; and the third is embodied in "affirmative assimilation," i.e., recognition of same-sex partnerships falling short of full equality; (2) "Intermediate Recognition": encompasses the first and second rungs of the expansive recognition model; (3) "Minimum Recognition": comprises only decriminalization: "[T]he minimum recognition model represents a bottom line. Beyond that limit, a regime cannot in any way be said to respect the rights of sexual

other words, in terms of its sociopolitical and legal climate, a country is ready to provide broad recognition only after it has completed the necessary process in the order described above. For example, it is highly unlikely that a state or a country would prohibit discrimination on the basis of sexual orientation in employment while preserving its sodomy law. It is even less likely that in such an environment gay couples would be recognized in family law and their status would be equalized with that of opposite-sex married couples. As we have seen in chapter 8, section 8.3, although the United States lags behind the northern European countries in terms of same-sex partnership recognition, many U.S. states provide wider protections for gay men and lesbians as parents than the European countries do. Thus, whereas parental rights for same-sex couples in Europe may be classified as a fourth step, *following* recognition of gay partnerships, the recognition of homosexual parenthood in the United States, for reasons explained in chapter 8, section 8.3.2, may be regarded as the third step in the process,[75] following decriminalization and antidiscrimination and preceding a fourth step, *comprehensive* partnership recognition.[76] The *necessary process* hypothesis is both descriptive and normative: it reflects how countries have actually moved toward the recognition of same-sex partnerships, and it prescribes what has to take place in countries and states that have yet to provide comprehensive recognition to same-sex couples, such as the United States. The causal connection between the prerequisites was emphasized, for example, in the explanatory part of the Norwegian bill on registered partnership, which explicitly stipulated that decriminalization of homosexual acts in Norway and the subsequent enactment of antidiscrimination measures had considerably altered social attitudes toward homosexual-

---

minorities" (*id.* at 112); (4) "Mixed Recognition" or the federalist model: this is the U.S. model, according to which the states have different levels of recognition or different combinations of "rungs." Heinze concludes that this model is actually no model at all. *See id.* at 113.

75. It should be noted, however, that parental rights in the United States do not necessarily fit the *necessary process* model, since they are mainly a creation of the judiciary, not the legislature, and are intended to benefit the child, rather than the child's lesbian or gay parent(s). However, the main concern of the *necessary process* model is the movement toward recognition of same-sex partnerships (i.e., the relationship between the partners themselves) and not parental rights of same-sex couples.

76. We thus find that the three states that have a complete ban on adoption by gay men and lesbians—Florida, Utah, and Arkansas—have all had sodomy laws (Arkansas's sodomy law has recently been struck down), and none of them provide homosexuals protection against discrimination. In contrast, all the states that have accorded gays and lesbians parental rights, such as second-parent adoption, had previously decriminalized sodomy (with the exception of Massachusetts), and most of them had also enacted antidiscrimination legislation, for example, Vermont, Massachusetts, New York, New Jersey, California, Oregon, and Pennsylvania. See chap. 7, sec. 7.1, and compare with the notes to table 4.

Table 4 Sodomy Laws and Antidiscrimination Legislation

Country	Repeal of Sodomy Law	Age of Consent	Protection from Discrimination	Hate-Speech Legislation	Access to Military	Immigration Rights for Partner?
Denmark RP Act 1989	1930	Equal since 1976	Provided since 1987	Since 1987	Since 1970	Yes (prior to RP Act)
Norway RP Act 1993	1972	Equal since 1972	Provided since 1981	Since 1981	No exclusion	Yes (prior to RP Act)
Sweden RP Act 1995	1944	Equal since 1978	Provided since 1987	Since 1987	No exclusion	Yes (since 1972)
Iceland RP Act 1996	1940	Equal since 1992	Protection provided	Protection provided	No exclusion	Yes (based on RP Act)
Finland RP Act 2002	1970	Equal since 1998	Provided since 1995	Since 1995	No exclusion	Yes
Netherlands RP Act 1998	1810	Equal since 1971	Constitutionally provided since 1983	Since 1992	Since 1974	Yes (prior to RP Act)
France PaCS 1999	1810	Equal since 1982	Provided since 1985	None provided	No exclusion	Partial, PaCS considered
Hungary	1961	Discriminatory: 18, 14	1989 constitution potentially protects	None provided	"Recommended" not to join	No
Germany	1968 (East); 1969 (West)	Equal since 1989 (East); 1994 (West)	None provided (except for a few local governments)	None provided	No exclusion	Yes (based on RP Act)
Spain	1932	Equal since 1978	Provided since 1995	Since 1995	Since 1984	No
Portugal	1945	Discriminatory: 16, 14	None provided	Non provided	Full exclusion	No
Italy	1889	Equal since 1996	Proposal pending	None provided	No exclusion	No
Belgium	1867	Equal since 1985	Proposal pending	None provided	No exclusion	Yes
Switzerland	1937–1942	Equal since 1992	Provided since 1999	None provided	No exclusion	No
Czech Republic	1961	Equal since 1990	None provided	Non provided	No exclusion	No
Canada	1969	Equal except same/opposite anal sex 14, 18	Protection at federal level and in 12 of 13 provinces	Hate-crime legislation provided	Since 1992	Yes

Australia	All states repealed 1972–1997	Discriminatory in 4 states	Protection in 7 of 8 states and territories	Protection in 2 of 8 states and territories	Since 1992	Yes
New Zealand	1986	Equal since 1986	Protection provided	None provided	Since 1993	Yes
United States	Unrepealed in all states until 1961; 13 still criminalize sodomy: 3, same-sex;[a] 10, opposite- and same-sex[b]	In states free of sodomy laws: discriminatory in 4 states, equal in 14 states[c]	11 states provide protection in public and private employment[d]	Hate-crime protection provided in 22 states and D.C.[e]	Full exclusion ("don't ask, don't tell")	No

SOURCES: Legal Age of Consent Table, available at http://www./ageofconsent.com/ageofconsent.htm (visited March 20, 2000); Anti-Defamation League: 1999 Hate Crime Laws, http://www./adl.org/99hatecrime/provisions.html (visited 3/15/2000); Lambda Legal Defense and Education Fund, http://www.lambda.org; ILGA World Legal Survey: Country Reports, http://www.ilga.org; Rob Tielman & Hans Hammelburg, *World Survey on the Social and Legal Position of Gays and Lesbians*, in The Third Pink Book: A Global View of Lesbian and Gay Liberation and Oppression 249 (Aart Hendriks et al. eds., 1993); Peter Tatchell, *Europe in the Pink: Lesbian and Gay Equality in the New Europe* (1992); *Sociolegal Control of Homosexuality: A Multi-Nation Comparison* (Donald J. West & Richard Green eds., 1997); Walter Barnett, *Sexual Freedom and the Constitution: An Inquiry into the Constitutionality of Repressive Sex Laws* 293 (1973); *Discrimination against Lesbian, Gay, and Bisexual Persons in Europe—A Report Submitted by ILGA-Europe to the Legal Affairs and Human Rights Committee of the Parliamentary Assembly of the Council of Europe as a Contribution to the Preparation of Its Report and Recommendations on the Situation of Lesbians and Gays in the Member States of the Council of Europe* (Motion for a Resolution—Doc. 8319), ILGA-Europe, February 16, 2000, available at http://www.steff.suite.dk/final_report.rtf.

[a] Kansas, Oklahoma, and Texas.

[b] Alabama, Florida, Idaho, Louisiana, Massachusetts, Mississippi, North Carolina, South Carolina, Utah, and Virginia.

[c] Discriminatory ages of consent exist in Connecticut (16, 18), Nevada (16, 18), New Hampshire (16, 18), and West Virginia (16, 18). Ages of consent are equal in Alaska, California, Colorado, Georgia, Illinois, Indiana, Maine, Montana, New Jersey, New York, Oregon, Pennsylvania, Washington, and Wisconsin. No data available regarding the other 19 states.

[d] Of the 11, 10 states began providing protection after 1990: California, 1992: employment, public accommodations, and education; Connecticut, 1991: employment, public accommodations, housing, and education; Hawaii, 1991: only employment; Massachusetts, 1995: employment, public accommodations, housing, and education; Minnesota, 1993: employment, public accommodations, housing, and education; Nevada, 1999: only employment; New Hampshire, 1997: employment, public accommodations, and housing; New Jersey, 1991: employment, public accommodations, housing, and education; Rhode Island, 1995: employment, public accommodations, and housing; Vermont, 1992: employment, public accommodations, housing, and education; Wisconsin, 1981: employment, public accommodations, housing, and education. An Oregon appellate court ruled that the prohibition on sex discrimination in the workplace included sexual orientation. Executive orders in six states and the federal government also ruled that public employees from discrimination based on sexual orientation: federal government, 1998; Colorado, 1990; Iowa, 1999; Maryland, 1995; New Mexico, 1985; New York 1983; Pennsylvania, 1985.

[e] Arizona, California, Connecticut, District of Columbia, Delaware, Hawaii, Florida, Illinois, Iowa, Louisiana, Maine, Massachusetts, Minnesota, Nebraska, Nevada, New Hampshire, New Jersey, New York, Oregon, Rhode Island, Vermont, Washington, and Wisconsin.

ity and that these tolerant attitudes had in turn paved the way for the ultimate broad recognition of same-sex partnerships.[77]

Waaldijk has found that although the social and legal recognition of homosexuality varies from one European country to another, the process of legal recognition in those countries shows an almost universal pattern: almost all jurisdictions seem to move through the same "standard sequence" of legislative steps, namely, decriminalization, equalization of age limits, antidiscrimination legislation, and partnership legislation. We can thus make a distinction between countries based on the number of typical steps that they have taken in the legal recognition of homosexuality.[78] Indeed, we can identify a similar process in all European countries that currently provide broad recognition of same-sex partnerships. First, all countries with national registered partnership acts, including France (the PaCS) and Germany, decriminalized sodomy at least two decades before their recognition of same-sex partnerships. This also applies to Hungary and Portugal, which decriminalized sodomy almost half a century ago. All those countries—with the exception of Hungary and Portugal, which, as explained above, should be regarded as exceptions to the rule and not as examples of the typical process toward broad recognition of same-sex partnerships[79]—equalized the age of consent; provided immigration rights to same-sex partners (with the exception of France); repealed any exclusion from the military that they may have had; and most importantly, enacted broad protections against discrimination, including hate crime or hate speech legislation, *before* they recognized same-sex partnerships (with the exception of Germany; see table 4).

It is not surprising that three of the countries that have yet to enact national protection from discrimination for gays and lesbians or to enact hate-speech legislation—France, Germany, and Portugal—have also provided the least expansive recognition of same-sex partnerships. These countries accord same-sex couples only a few enumerated rights, very far from the Nordic-Netherlands model, which is akin to marriage. In this respect, Finland—the last Nordic country to have adopted a registered partnership act—serves as another example of the necessary process. Finland was the last Nordic country to enact antidiscrimination legislation. Moreover, until quite recently (1998) Finland maintained

77. *See* The Norwegian Bill, note 33 above, at 10.

78. Waaldijk, note 73 above.

79. *See* chap. 5. Both Portugal and Hungary surprised the world when they decided to provide recognition to same-sex couples; unlike the rest of the countries surveyed in this study, they did so in order to access regional European instruments. Their acts are thus not a result of national developments in the rights of gay men and lesbians.

discriminatory ages of consent and had a criminal-law provision that prohibited "promoting" or "encouraging" homosexuality.[80] These factors account for the fact that Finland adopted a registered partnership act only in late 2001. Another Nordic exception is the Faroe Islands, which, like Greenland, are part of Denmark but, unlike Greenland, have not adopted the Danish Registered Partnership Act. Although the Faroe Islands decriminalized sodomy as early as 1930, its criminal code still contains discriminatory provisions regarding age of consent, prostitution, and "seduction."[81] In contrast, we find that Spain (in which two regions—Catalonia in 1998, and Aragon in 1999—have enacted registered partnership legislation) and Switzerland (which is seriously considering the adoption of a national registered partnership act) not only decriminalized sodomy and equated the age of consent, but both also provided protection from discrimination *before* registered partnership was even considered.

Countries that are not likely to recognize same-sex couples any time soon, such as Italy and the Czech Republic, do not provide protection from discrimination or hate speech. Belgium, which provides some recognition to same-sex partnerships, albeit to a lesser extent than the northern European countries, has also repealed its sodomy law and equated the age of consent, and though it has yet to adopt national anti-discrimination legislation, it provides immigration rights to the partners of its gay citizens. As table 4 shows, the aforementioned process and prerequisites are exemplified also by those countries outside Europe and the United States that have been discussed in this book: Canada, Australia, and New Zealand have all decriminalized sodomy. None of these countries exclude gays from the military, and all provide some degree of protection from discrimination on the basis of sexual orientation as well as immigration rights to same-sex couples. Therefore, these countries, and especially Canada, are ready to provide broad-based recognition to same-sex partnerships. There is thus a clear correlation between the repeal of sodomy laws and that of other discriminatory provisions in

80. *See* Reekie, note 3 above, at 184. Until its repeal in 1998, art. 9 (as amended in 1971) of Chapter 20 of the Penal Code stipulated as follows: "If someone publicly engages in an act violating sexual morality, thereby giving offense, he shall be sentenced for publicly violating sexual morality to imprisonment for at most six months or to a fine. If someone publicly encourages unchastity between persons of the same sex, he/she shall be sentenced for incitement of unchastity between members of the same sex as mentioned in Subsection 1 for at least six months and at the most four years." *See* Tielman & Hammelburg, note 33 above, at 279. *See also* ILGA World Legal Survey: Finland, at http://www.ilga.org/Information/legal_survey/europe/finland.htm (last updated July 11, 1999).

81. ILGA-Europe Discrimination Report, note 13 above, at 2.3.3.

the criminal code, the enactment of antidiscrimination laws (including repeal of discriminatory military policies), and the recognition of same-sex couples in family law in a manner close or similar to opposite-sex marriage. It is interesting to note, for example, that Germany abolished the few remaining discriminatory practices in its military *prior to* the enactment of its life partnership.[82]

The necessary process discussed here is evident not only from an international comparative examination but also when comparing states within the United States in terms of the degree of recognition they accord same-sex couples. Six of the seven states that have thus far enacted statewide domestic partner legislation—California, Connecticut, Hawaii, New York, Oregon, and Vermont—had previously repealed their sodomy laws (and in February 2002 the Massachusetts Supreme Judicial Court ruled unanimously that the state's sodomy law, which prohibits consensual sex between *both* different-sex and same-sex couples, was inapplicable to private consensual conduct),[83] and all seven provide statewide protection from discrimination based on sexual orientation. Moreover, the two states that have thus far come the closest to opening up marriage to same-sex couples—Hawaii and Vermont—have also long ago decriminalized sodomy and enacted statewide protections against discrimination. In particular, Vermont, whose Supreme Court has issued the most favorable decision to same-sex couples in the United States and whose legislature has enacted the most comprehensive model of recognition of same-sex partnerships in the United States, repealed its sodomy law in 1977; was one of the first states to enact statewide legislation prohibiting discrimination in employment, housing, and other services based on sexual orientation (1992); and has the most comprehensive antidiscrimination law in the country.[84] Moreover, sexual

82. Germany abolished its last discriminatory practice in the military two months before it enacted its registered partnership act, i.e., in August 2000. *See* Rex Wockner, *German Military Equalizes Gays,* Wockner International News no. 332, September 4, 2000. This is an interesting fact, although it is not clear whether there was a causal connection between the two.

83. *See* Gay & Lesbian Advocates & Defenders v. Attorney General, 2002 Mass. Lexis 84 (February 21, 2002). The court did not rule on the constitutionality of the act, since none of the plaintiffs who filed the suit were subject to prosecution, but made it clear that the criminal law provisions do not apply to private, consensual conduct. Thus, while previously it might have been argued that Massachusetts provides an exception to the necessary process thesis, it has now joined those states that are ripe for broad-based recognition of same-sex partnerships (by adopting, for example, a civil union law or by opening up the institution of marriage to same-sex couples). I.e., in light of the aforementioned decision, Massachusetts has practically repealed its sodomy law (as far as consenting adults are concerned) and has done so *before* it considered the recognition of same-sex marriage.

84. *See* 21 V.S.A. § 495 (employment); 9 V.S.A. § 403 (housing); 8 V.S.A. § 4724 (insurance); 9 V.S.A. § 4502 (public accommodations).

orientation is among the categories specifically protected against hate-motivated crimes in Vermont;[85] it was one of the first states to accord second-parent adoption and to enact legislation removing all barriers to adoption by same-sex couples, and it had a statewide domestic partnership act prior to its Supreme Court's decision in *Baker* and the passage of the civil union act.[86] In *Baker*, Justice Johnson clearly articulated the concept of a necessary process and the causal connection between the prerequisites and comprehensive recognition of same-sex partnerships: "Allowing same-sex couples to obtain the benefits and protections of marriage is a *logical extension* of Vermont's legislatively enacted public policy prohibiting discrimination on the basis of sex and sexual orientation . . . decriminalizing consensual homosexual conduct between adults . . . and permitting same-sex partners to adopt children."[87] However, at the federal level and in most other states, the United States is far from being ready to accord same-sex couples any kind of comprehensive recognition.

11.5 Same-Sex Marriage

Before same-sex marriage becomes possible, the final step of the necessary process must be completed, namely, broad recognition in the form of registered partnership or civil union—*not* merely a version of U.S. domestic partner schemes as currently construed. For example, it became a viable possibility to open up marriage to same-sex couples in the Netherlands only after (and as a consequence of) the passage and success of the Dutch Registered Partnership Act. The process and experience of the northern European countries have shed a new and instructive light on the legal and social processes that need to take place in order for U.S. states to open up marriage to same-sex couples. Thus, for example, Vermont was not ready to open up marriage to gay couples in 1999, but future recognition of same-sex marriage in Vermont became more plausible when Vermont completed the third step of providing broad recognition to same-sex couples through the passage of its civil union act in April 2000.

Therefore, the *necessary process* theory can also be used as a tool to predict possible future recognition of same-sex partnerships. In light of the process that has led to comprehensive recognition in Europe, it

85. *See* 13 V.S.A. § 1455.

86. *See* 15A V.S.A. §§ 1-102, 1-112. For an overview of the background that enabled the Court to mandate broad-based protections for same-sex couples, see also Baker v. State of Vermont, 744 A.2d 864 (Vt. Sup. Ct. 1999).

87. Baker v. State of Vermont, 744 A.2d 864 (Vt. Sup. Ct. 1999, Justice Johnson), my emphasis.

should now become clearer why the United States is far behind the northern European countries and some of the other countries surveyed in this study. Unlike the northern European countries, the United States at the federal level and most of the states have adopted defense of marriage acts; they do not provide protection from discrimination on the basis of sexual orientation, nor do they have hate-crime legislation, not to mention comprehensive recognition of same-sex partnerships. Moreover, the United States does not accord immigration rights to gay couples, and it maintains a discriminatory policy toward gays in the military. Some states still criminalize sodomy, whereas a few others maintain an unequal age of consent (see table 4). For these reasons, the battle to recognize same-sex marriage has thus far failed at both the federal and the state level: at neither level has the necessary process been carried out, which, as I have argued, is a prerequisite to comprehensive recognition of same-sex partnerships. Since the prerequisites for expansive recognition of same-sex partnerships were not met in the United States, it is not surprising that the federal government has been and still is zealously unwilling to extend *any* kind of recognition to gay partnerships. On the contrary, the federal government and thirty-five states have enacted legislation that explicitly prohibits either the opening up of marriage to same-sex couples or—as soon as this option becomes available—the recognition of such marriages entered into in other states or countries, and no constitutional challenge to those defense of marriage acts is expected in the foreseeable future.

We should draw a distinction between the possibility of opening up marriage at the federal level, on the one hand, and at the state level, on the other. The legislature in states with no DOMA and with no sodomy laws (and, theoretically at least, even those with sodomy laws)—are certainly free to introduce same-sex marriage, and state supreme courts can interpret their own states' constitutions as requiring same-sex marriage. Although opening up marriage to same-sex couples is not expected in the foreseeable future in any of the states, the eleven states with antidiscrimination laws should be ripe for legislative introduction of a version of civil unions. At the federal level, the United States still maintains the constitutionality of sodomy laws (*Hardwick*). Although the decision in *Hardwick* said nothing about homosexuals' rights in other areas, many courts have used *Hardwick* and the mere existence of sodomy laws, even if not enforced, to justify discrimination against homosexuals[88] or to

88. *E.g.*, Appeal in Pima County Juvenile Action B-10489, 151 Ariz. 335, 340, 727 P.2d 830, 835 (1986) (citing *Hardwick* in upholding an administrative decision declaring a bisexual unacceptable to adopt children); Opinion of the Justices, 129 N.H. 290, 530 A.2d

support the notion that homosexuals are not a suspect or quasi-suspect class for equal protection purposes.[89] Sodomy laws, or the mere constitutionality of such acts, are thus commonly used as a rationale for denying lesbians and gay men basic civil rights and equal treatment, and they have been used as a rationale for not enacting civil rights laws to bar discrimination based on sexual orientation.[90] Therefore, despite the assertion that *Romer* can be regarded as a rhetorical overturning of *Hardwick*, the fact remains that *Hardwick* is still unresolved; until it is overturned, and until DOMA is struck down as unconstitutional, the U.S. federal government will not be ready to recognize marriage for same-sex couples (unlike DOMA, *Hardwick* is not a *legal* barrier for the recognition of same-sex marriage, but its overturning would represent a greater acceptance of gays and lesbians). This conclusion is based not only on the Court's explicit holding in *Hardwick* that homosexuals have no fundamental right to engage in consensual sodomy (the repeal of sodomy laws being a sociopolitical prerequisite to further recognition of the rights of gays and same-sex couples) but also on the Court's refusal to recognize same-sex couples as a family. The Court interpreted precedents pertaining to the right of privacy—*Pierce, Meyer, Skinner, Loving, Griswold, Eisenstadt, and Roe*[91]—so that the right of privacy in these cases was protected only when and because it had to do with family decision making.[92] The Court refused to apply these precedents to "homosexual sodomy" and to provide homosexuals with the right of privacy because, inter alia, it was reluctant to even consider gays and lesbians as family units and viewed them as outside any definition of *family*. Since we have established that current sodomy laws, even if they are of general application, are being used to discriminate disproportionately against gay men

---

21 (1987) (noting *Hardwick*, finding that a statute prohibiting homosexuals from adopting or fostering children would be constitutional).

89. *E.g.*, Padula v. Webster, 822 F.2d 97 (D.C. Cir. 1987) (allowing the FBI to deny employment to a homosexual); Gay and Lesbian Students Ass'n v. Gohn, 656 F. Supp. 1045, 1057 (W.D. Ark. 1987) (*Hardwick* "lends support to the idea that homosexuality is not a suspect class"); State v. Walsh, 713 S.W.2d 508, 510–11 (Mo. 1986) (upholding a homosexual's conviction for sexual misconduct).

90. *See State-by-State Sodomy Law Update*, Lambda Legal Defense and Education Fund, August 3, 1999, at http://lambdalegal.org/cgi-bin/pages/documents/record?record=275. Thus, for example, in both Florida and Texas, these statutes have been used to deny employment to homosexual applicants. In North Carolina and Virginia, such laws have provided a basis for denying child custody and visitation rights to lesbian mothers or gay fathers. *See id.*

91. Pierce v. Society of Sisters, 268 U.S. 510 (1925); Meyer v. Nebraska, 262 U.S. 390 (1923); Skinner v. Oklahoma ex rel. Williamson, 316 U.S. 535 (1942); Loving v. Virginia, 388 U.S. 1 (1967); Griswold v. Connecticut, 381 U.S. 479 (1965); Eisenstadt v. Baird, 405 U.S. 438 (1972); Roe v. Wade, 410 U.S. 113 (1973).

92. *See* Bowers v. Hardwick, 478 U.S. 186, 190 (1986).

and lesbians, and if same-sex couples do not have the basic right to engage in sexual relations, let alone the right to be protected from discrimination, how could they be regarded socially as deserving the right to marriage? Even if all sodomy laws were abolished and *Hardwick* were overturned, most U.S. states would still have to provide gays protection from discrimination before they would be ready to consider same-sex marriage.

Many activists, legal scholars, and proponents of same-sex marriage in the United States tend to neglect these factors—the prerequisites and the necessary process—and view same-sex marriage as independent of the unequal status of gays in other fields.[93] Pushing for equality in marriage before the repeal of sodomy laws and the enactment of antidiscrimination laws, or giving priority to the fight for same-sex marriage over these other aspects of discrimination, is not only tactically and politically incongruous, but it is also illogical and erroneous from a *sociopolitical* point of view (although, as mentioned before, from a *legal* perspective it may not be a logical error, since sodomy laws are, theoretically, not a bar for same-sex marriage recognition). Admittedly, in a federal country like the United States, where some states have enacted antidiscrimination laws protecting gay men and lesbians and other states still criminalize homosexuality, there is no legal reason why the former states might not accord same-sex couples the right to marry or a status equivalent to marriage. Moreover, from a technical legal point of view, there is nothing to bar states, and even the federal government, from making marriage available to same-sex couples, even where they are officially discriminated against in other fields or considered criminals by the penal code. This is so even if *Hardwick* is not overturned, since *Hard-*

93. Eskridge, for one, argues that there is simply no connection between the repeal of sodomy laws and the freedom of gays and lesbians to marry in the United States (since, among other things, other kinds of "criminals" are also not barred from marriage) and that pushing for same-sex marriage has nothing to do with the existence of sodomy laws and the authority of *Hardwick*. *See* William N. Eskridge Jr., The Case for Same-Sex Marriage 133–37 (1996). Eskridge also reads *Hardwick* narrowly, as not connected to the right to marriage, and maintains that "only if *Bowers* is read as an openly homophobic opinion . . . can it override *Turner* and *Zablocki*." *Id*. at 136. Since I regard *Hardwick* as "an openly homophobic opinion," I cannot agree with Eskridge's "narrow" interpretation of the case. His view may hold true in states that criminalize both heterosexual and homosexual sodomy, but not in the states that criminalize only "homosexual sodomy." Moreover, as explained above, it is quite naive not to regard sodomy laws today (whether of general application or not), at least socially, as strictly an issue of gay rights and thus as a barrier to the provision of rights, including marriage, to same-sex couples. And the fact remains that such laws have indeed been used to block claims of gays for equal rights; in my opinion, the existence of these laws, combined with *Hardwick*, is one of the underlying social rationales for opposing same-sex marriage. As suggested above, the European processes and experience support these conclusions.

wick does not *legally* bar the recognition of same-sex marriage by individual states; however, its holding and the fact that it has not yet been overturned suggest that such recognition is not *plausible* in the United States in the foreseeable future (at least not at the federal level). Such a development is highly unlikely and in fact has not taken place anywhere in the world without prior decriminalization of homosexual acts and the enactment of antidiscrimination statutes.

Thus, until *Hardwick* is resolved, sodomy laws are abolished, antidiscrimination legislation is adopted, and broad recognition of gay partnerships is provided, same-sex marriage is not feasible in the United States, either at the federal level or in most states—the states that have not yet met the prerequisites for broad-based recognition of same-sex partnerships. Moreover, even if one or more states opens up marriage to same-sex couples, unless the federal and state defense of marriage acts are repealed, such marriages would remain unequal to opposite-sex marriage, since they would not be recognized federally or by most other states.

In contrast, recognition of same-sex marriage in the Netherlands should be attributed, among other things, to its completion of *all* steps of the necessary process, including the adoption of a registered partnership act prior to opening up marriage to same-sex couples, an act which proved quite successful. For this reason, I consider the five Nordic countries with comprehensive registered partnership acts to be also ripe for the opening up of marriage to same-sex couples, and it is to be expected that they will be the first to follow the lead of the Netherlands.

Chapter 12

Conclusion

As we have seen all through this book, many factors play a part in the degree of advancement of same-sex couples toward broad-based recognition of their partnerships, and many factors account for the differences in the status of same-sex couples that are found when countries and regions are compared. The social and legal processes that implicate the progression of gays toward full equality are diverse and complex.

We began by addressing one set of factors, which is not directly connected to the *legal* status of gay men and lesbians but has implications for the degree of equality provided to same-sex couples. These factors include current conceptions and characteristics of the institution of marriage, namely, its transformation from a procreative, child-oriented, patriarchal institution into a unitive institution that serves to regulate the relationship between two people who love each other on equal terms. Moreover, general changes in family law, such as the movement toward unmarried cohabitation as a common, accepted, and in some instances legally regulated way of life; the introduction of no-fault divorce; and the opening up of marriage to other minorities and to women on equal terms, further influence conceptions of the living arrangement of gay and lesbian couples and their legal status.

Finally, broader social, political, and legal phenomena also affect the attitudes toward gays and lesbians and account for the degree of their social acceptance and legal recognition. These include the move toward secularization in the Western world (and in particular the secular concept of marriage), the degree of society's openness toward issues concerning sexuality in general and alternative lifestyles in particular, rigid or flexible conceptions of gender roles, and the degree of pluralism in each country, including the degree of equality provided to other minorities and women.

I have argued that both gender equality and the legal status of other minorities are relevant to the status of same-sex couples. The more "compulsory heterosexuality" erodes in a particular society, as conceptions of gender roles become flexible and both formal and substantive equality between men and women is achieved, the more advanced is the status of gays in general and of same-sex couples in particular.

Chapter 11 introduces another set of factors that have implications for the status of same-sex couples, factors that have to do with the legal status of gay men and lesbians and their equality in fields other than family law. These include the decriminalization of homosexual acts between consenting adults and the provision of protection from discrimination based on sexual orientation.

As I have shown, there is a direct link between the repeal of sodomy laws and the enactment of antidiscrimination measures, on the one hand, and the status of same-sex couples, on the other. In order to arrive at a high level of recognition of same-sex relationships, a state has to go through a necessary social and legal process: it must first repeal its sodomy laws, equate the age of consent, and enact antidiscrimination statutes to protect gay men and lesbians. Only then will the public and the legislature be ready to accord expansive rights to same-sex couples.

The countries with the most expansive recognition of same-sex partnerships—the Nordic countries and the Netherlands—have gone through the process, first repealing sodomy laws and enacting various protections against discrimination before recognizing same-sex couples for the purposes of family law. Furthermore, gays in those countries, as compared with gays in the United States, had more legal protections to begin with, before the issue of same-sex marriage or its alternatives arose.

The combination of those two sets of factors serves not only to explain the degree of progression of same-sex couples toward equality in each individual country but also to account for the idiosyncrasies in the status of same-sex couples in the different regions and countries discussed herein. As we have seen, with regard to the relationship between the partners, the status of same-sex couples is currently more advanced in the northern European countries than anywhere else in the world.

Although the United States provides partial recognition to same-sex couples—with the exception of the state of Vermont, which comes close to equating the status of gay couples with that of married couples—the

Nordic countries and the Netherlands have adopted a model that is the closest alternative to marriage currently available, the registered partnership acts. With few exceptions, these acts place same-sex couples on an equal footing with opposite-sex married couples, and as soon as the exceptions that currently distinguish registered partnership from marriage are abolished, complete formal equality will have been achieved. By providing gays the freedom to marry, the Netherlands has taken the next step and has fully placed gays and lesbians on an equal footing with opposite-sex married couples.

However, as I have argued, even the most comprehensive acts of the Nordic countries, as well as Vermont's civil unions, maintain a "separate but equal" status of same-sex couples and are thus not only unsatisfactory but also inherently unequal and therefore objectionable.

It has been my contention that the most comprehensive model of recognition that gays and lesbians should aspire to is their inclusion in the institution of marriage. Furthermore, as I have explained, there is no rational public-policy reason to exclude gay couples from the modern institution of marriage. In the words of David A. J. Richards, "One may be personally moved, as I am, by some of the postmodernist arguments . . . not to want to define one's long-term passionately loving homosexual attachments . . . in terms of the frigid stereotypes of ascribed roles implicit in conventional marriage, and yet find [these] arguments quite inadequate as compelling public reasons that justify limiting the right to marriage to heterosexual intimate life."[1] Other alternatives are poor imitations of the institution; they purport to accord gays and lesbians some degree of recognition and equality but in fact serve to discriminate against gays and lesbians by keeping them segregated in their own "second-class marriage-like" institutions.

The social and legal changes that have taken place in the Netherlands, that is, the achievement of a high level of both formal and substantive equality between the sexes, the openness toward sexuality and varied sexual practices, the abandonment of gender binarism, the equation of the rights of cohabitants with those of married couples, the complete secularization of the institution of marriage, the repeal of sodomy laws, and the constitutional protection from discrimination against lesbians and gay men, have all made possible and led to the opening up of marriage to same-sex couples.

Most of these changes have not taken place in the United States as a

1. David A.J. Richards, *Introduction: Theoretical Perspectives, in* Legal Recognition of Same-Sex Partnerships: A Study of National, European, and International Law 25, 29 (Robert Wintemute & Mads Andenas eds., 2001).

whole, at least not to the same extent as in the Netherlands. Conceptions of gender roles are more rigid in the United States than in the Netherlands; the general attitude toward sexuality in this country is more conservative; religion still plays a major part in the lives of many Americans; unmarried cohabitation is not widely encouraged and is unregulated; most states, as well as the federal government, do not provide gays and lesbians protection from discrimination (there is even overt legal discrimination, e.g., the defense of marriage acts); and some states still retain the criminalization of homosexual acts and unequal ages of consent. Thus, from a socio-legal and political point of view, the situation in the United States is not ripe for allowing marriage to same-sex couples, and the fact that recent efforts to achieve this goal have failed supports this conclusion.

In the United States, the state of Vermont has always been at the forefront of civil rights. As Vermont became the first state to outlaw slavery in 1777, so it became the first state to "free," to a certain extent, same-sex couples from their second-class citizenship status in 2000, by passing the civil union act. However, as the abolition of slavery was only the beginning of the fight of African Americans for equality, so the new act regarding same-sex couples is only the beginning for gays. The civil union legislation and the registered partnership acts of the Nordic countries symbolize toleration of same-sex partnerships, but they are only the first step. In this regard, civil unions for gay couples are what *Plessy v. Ferguson*[2] was for African Americans: a philosophy that equality is achieved once two groups are accorded the same rights, notwithstanding issues of segregation and the inherent inequality of separate but equal institutions.

Same-sex couples in the United States and around the world are thus still awaiting our *Brown v. Board of Education,*[3] which will place us on an equal footing with opposite-sex married couples by abolishing marriage-like alternatives for homosexuals and completely opening up the institution of marriage to gay men and lesbians. The Netherlands, more than any other country in the world, had already provided full substantive equality for gay men and lesbians in all fields of life, and it was thus only natural that it has been the first country to recognize same-sex marriage. It is to be hoped that other countries will follow that lead.

2. 163 U.S. 537 (1896).
3. 347 U.S. 483 (1954).

Appendix A

European Same-Sex Legislation in Translation

A.1 Denmark

A.1.1 The Danish Registered Partnership Act
We Margrethe The Second, by the Grace of God Queen of Denmark, do make known that:—
The Danish Folketing has passed the following Act which has received the Royal Assent:
1.—Two persons of the same sex may have their partnership registered.

Registration
2.—(1) Part I, sections 12 and 13(1) and clause 1 of section 13(2) of the Danish Marriage (Formation and Dissolution) Act shall apply similarly to the registration of partnerships, cf. subsection 2 of this section.
(2) A partnership may only be registered provided both or one of the parties has his permanent residence in Denmark and is of Danish nationality.
(3) The rules governing the procedure of registration of a partnership, including the examination of the conditions for registration, shall be laid down by the Minister of Justice.

Legal Effects
3.—(1) Subject to the exceptions of section 4, the registration of a partnership shall have the same legal effects as the contracting of marriage.
(2) The provisions of Danish law pertaining to marriage and spouses shall apply similarly to registered partnership and registered partners.
4.—(1) The provisions of the Danish Adoption Act regarding spouses shall not apply to registered partners.

(2) Clause 3 of section 13 section 15(3) of the Danish Legal Incapacity and Guardianship Act regarding spouses shall not apply to registered partners.

(3) Provisions of Danish law containing special rules pertaining to one of the parties to a marriage determined by the sex of that person shall not apply to registered partners.

(4) Provisions of international treaties shall not apply to registered partnership unless the other contracting parties agree to such application.

Dissolution

5.—(1) Parts 3, 4 and 5 of the Danish Marriage (Formation and Dissolution) Act and Part 42 of the Danish Administration of Justice Act shall apply similarly to the dissolution of a registered partnership, cf. subsections 2 and 3 of this section.

(2) Section 46 of the Danish Marriage (Formation and Dissolution) Act shall not apply to the dissolution of a registered partnership.

(3) Irrespective of section 448c of the Danish Administration of Justice Act, a registered partnership may always be dissolved in this country.

Commencement etc.

6.—This Act shall come into force on October 1, 1989.

7.—This Act shall not apply to the Faroe Islands nor to Greenland but may be made applicable by Royal order to these parts of the country with such modifications as are required by the special Faroese and Greenlandic conditions.

Given at Christiansborg Castle, this seventh day of June, 1989.
Under Our Royal Hand and Seal
MARGARETHE R[1]

A.1.2 Act to Amend the Conditions of Partnership Registration and Stepchild Adoption

I. The Registered Partnership Act No. 372 of June 7, 1989, shall be amended as follows:

1. Section 2(2) shall be repealed and worded as follows:

A Partnership may only be registered if:

1) One of the parties has his permanent residence in Denmark or a Danish nationality or

2) Both parties have had permanent residence in Denmark for the preceding two years before registration.

3) Norwegian, Swedish and Icelandic nationality will be treated as equivalent to Danish nationality according to 2(1). The Minister of Justice may designate that nationality in another country with a Registered Partner-

---

1. Act no. 372 of June 7, 1989 (Den.), translation in Jorge Martin, Note, *English Polygamy Law and the Danish Registered Partnership Act: A Case for the Consistent Treatment of Foreign Polygamous Marriages and Danish Same-Sex Marriages in England,* 27 Cornell Int'l L.J. 419, 432 n. 79 (1994).

ship Act corresponding to the Danish Act will be treated as equivalent to Danish Nationality.

2. Section 4(1) shall be amended as follows:

A Registered Partner may, however, adopt the other partner's child, unless the child is adopted from another country.

II. This Act shall come into force on July 1, 1999.

III. (1) This Act shall not apply to the Faroe Islands nor to Greenland.

(2) This Act may be applicable by Royal Order to Faroe Islands or Greenland with such modifications as are required by the special Faroese and Greenlandic conditions.[2]

A.2 Norway

The Norwegian Act on Registered Partnership for Homosexual Couples

Section 1

Two homosexual persons of the same sex may register their partnership, with the legal consequences which follow from this Act.

Section 2

Chapter 1 of the Marriage Act, concerning the legal conditions for contracting a marriage, shall apply correspondingly to the registration of partnerships. No person may enter into a registered partnership if a previously registered partnership or marriage exists.

Chapter 2 of the Marriage Act, on verification of compliance with legal conditions for marriage, and Chapter 3 of the Marriage Act, on contracting and solemnization of a marriage, do not apply to the registration of a partnership.

A partnership may only be registered if one or both of the parties is domiciled in Norway and at least one of them has Norwegian nationality.

Verification of compliance with the legal conditions and the procedure for the registration of partnerships shall take place according to rules laid down by the Ministry.

Section 3

Registration of partnership has the same legal consequences as contraction of a marriage, with the exceptions mentioned in Section 4.

The provisions in Norwegian legislation dealing with marriage and spouses shall apply correspondingly to registered partnerships and registered partners.

Section 4

The provisions of the Adoption Act concerning spouses shall not apply to registered partnerships.

2. Act no. 360 of June 2, 1999 (Den.), translation in Ingrid Lund-Andersen, The Danish Registered Partnership Act, 1989—Has the Act Meant a Change in Attitudes? A paper presented at the conference Legal Recognition of Same-Sex Partnerships, King's College, University of London, July 1–3, 1999.

Section 5

Irrespective of the provision in Section 419a of the Civil Procedure Act, actions concerning the dissolution of registered partnerships that have been entered into in this country may always be brought before a Norwegian court.

Section 6

The Act shall enter into force on a date to be decided by the King.

Section 7

From the date on which the Act enters into force, the following amendments to other Acts shall come into force: . . .[3]

A.3 Sweden

The Registered Partnership [Family Law] Act
Issued on 23 June 1994
In accordance with the decision of the Parliament the following is enacted:

Chapter 1. Registration of partnership

Section 1

Two persons of the same sex may request the registration of their partnership.

Section 2

Registration may only take place if at least one of the partners is a Swedish citizen, domiciled in Sweden.

Section 3

Registration may not take place in the case of a person who is under the age of 18 years or of persons who are related to one another in the direct ascending or descending line or who are sisters or brothers of the whole blood.

Neither may registration take place in the case of sisters or brothers of the half blood without the permission of the Government or such authority as is stipulated by the Government.

Registration may not take place in the case of a person who is married or already registered as a partner.

The right to register a partnership shall be determined according to Swedish law.

Section 4

Before registration takes place, inquiry shall be made as to whether there is any impediment to registration.

Section 5

The provisions of Chapter 3 and Chapter 15 of the Marriage Code applicable to the procedure for inquiries into impediments to marriage shall apply correspondingly to this inquiry.

---

3. Act no. 40 of April 30, 1993, translation by the Norwegian Ministry of Children and Family Affairs.

Section 6
Registration shall take place in the presence of witnesses.

Section 7
At the registration both partners shall be present at the same time. Each of them separately shall, in response to a question put to them by the person conducting the registration, make it known that they consent to the registration. The person conducting the registration shall thereafter declare that they are registered partners.

A registration is invalid if it has not taken place as indicated in the first paragraph or if the person conducting the registration was not authorized to perform the registration.

A registration which is invalid under the second paragraph may be approved by the Government if there are extraordinary reasons for such approval. The matter may only be considered on the application of one of the partners or, if either of them has died, of the heirs of the deceased.

Section 8
Registration may be conducted by a legally qualified judge of a district court or a person appointed by a county administrative board.

Section 9
In other respects the provisions of Chapter 4, Sections 5, 7 and 8, of the Marriage Code and regulations issued by the Government apply to registration.

Decisions concerning registration may be appealed against in accordance with the provisions of Chapter 15, Sections 3 and 4, of the Marriage Code.

Chapter 1, Sections 4–9, of the Act concerning certain International Legal Relationships relating to Marriage and Guardianship (1904:26 p. 1) apply to international circumstances relating to registration.

Chapter 2. Dissolution of registered partnership

Section 1
A registered partnership is dissolved by the death of one of the partners or by a court decision.

Section 2
The provisions of Chapter 5 of the Marriage Code apply correspondingly to issues concerning the dissolution of a registered partnership.

Section 3
Cases concerning the dissolution of registered partnerships and cases involving proceedings to determine whether or not a registered partnership subsists are partnership cases. Provisions stipulated by statute or other legislation relating to matrimonial cases also apply to issues concerning partnership cases.

Section 4
Partnership cases may always be considered by a Swedish court if registration has taken place under this Act.

Chapter 3. Legal effects of registered partnership

Section 1

Registered partnership has the same legal effects as marriage, except as provided by Sections 2–4.

Provisions of a statute or other legislation related to marriage and spouses shall be applied in a corresponding manner to registered partnerships and registered partners unless otherwise provided by the rules concerning exceptions contained in Sections 2–4.

Section 2

Registered partners may neither jointly nor individually adopt children under Chapter 4 of the Code on Parents, Children and Guardians. Nor may registered partners be appointed to jointly exercise custody of a minor in the capacity of specially appointed guardians under Chapter 13, Section 8 of the Code on Parents, Children and Guardians.

The Insemination Act (1984:1140) and the Fertilization outside the Body Act (1988:711) do not apply to registered partners.

Section 3

Provisions applicable to spouses, the application of which involves special treatment of one spouse solely by reason of that spouse's sex, do not apply to registered partners.

Section 4

The provisions of the Ordinance concerning Certain International Legal Relationships relating to Marriage, Adoption and Guardianship (1931: 429) do not apply to registered partnerships.

This Act enters into force on 1 January 1995.[4]

A.4 Iceland

Recognized Partnership Act

1. Two persons of the same sex can contract a recognized partnership.
2. What is provided in the Part II of the Marriage Act on the legal prerequisites of marriage shall apply to this Act, as well. However, *see* subsection 2. A recognized partnership can only be contracted if at least one of the parties is a citizen of Iceland and is domiciled in Iceland.
3. Before a partnership is officially recognized, both parties are to certify that the prerequisites of such a partnership are fulfilled. Part III of the Marriage Act regulates the certification. The Minister of Justice shall issue more precise instructions on the certification.
4. The contracting of such partnerships is to be carried out by heads of a police district or their representatives with a juridical education. Paragraphs 21–26 of the Marriage Act regulate how certificates are to be issued.
5. Persons living in a recognized partnership are to enjoy the same rights as those in a marriage with the exception of what is said in subsection 6. What

4. Act no. 1117 of June 23, 1994, translation by Carl Bildt and Gun Hellsvik of the Swedish Ministry of Justice. *See* http://www.casti.com/FQRD/texts/partnership/se/sweden-act.html (last modified April 24, 1998).

is said on marriage and legally married spouses in the legislation in force applies to the parties of a partnership, too.

6. What is said on adoption and artificial conception does not apply to recognized partnerships. What is provided in the international agreements, signed by the Republic of Iceland, shall not apply to the recognized partnership unless all parties to the agreement approve of it.

7. A recognized partnership is deemed having ended at the death of one of the partners, in the case of cancellation or divorce.

8. The regulations on cancellation, divorce and division of property in the Marriage Act shall apply to the recognized partnership, however, with regard to subsections 2–4. Otherwise, what is regulated upon the end of a marriage and its legal entailments shall apply to the partnership, too. The head of the police district or a judge will arbitrate according to subsection 42 of the Marriage Act. Despite what is said in subsection 1 of Section 114, it is always possible to proceed with a charge in an Icelandic court on the basis of Section 113, if the partnership has been recognized in Iceland. Despite what is said in Subsection 1 of Section 123 of the Marriage Act, an Icelandic court is always entitled to solve issues pertaining to partnerships recognized in this country.

9. These Acts are enacted on 27 June 1996.[5]

A.5 Finland

Approved Finnish Legislation of Same-Sex Partnerships

Chapter 1 Partnership registration (paragraphs 1–6)
Partnership registration is open to two persons of the same sex, both of whom have to be 18 years old. There is no requirement for specific sexual orientation.

The legal objections to marriage such as being related by blood also apply to partnership registration.

The partnership shall be serviced by an authority entitled to perform civil marriages.

Chapter 2 Dissolution of a registered partnership (paragraph 7)
Dissolution of a registered partnership is to happen according to the provisions in the Marriage Act.

Chapter 3 Legal effects of partnership registration (paragraphs 8–9)
The legal consequences of the registered partnership are the same as with marriage unless otherwise stated (8§).

All provisions concerning married couples or spouses apply to registered partners unless otherwise stated (8§).

---

5. Translation from Finnish to English is made by Mika Vepsalainen. This translation is made from the Finnish text, translated from Icelandic by Steinunn Gudmundsdottir. The original wording of the act uses the expression "confirmed living together" where "recognized partnership" appears in this translation. Act number 87 of June 4, 1996. *See* http://www.casti.com/FQRD/texts/partnership/is/iceland-bill.html; and http://www.casti.com/FQRD/texts/partnership/is/iceland-chng.html.

The Act on Fatherhood and other provisions based only on the fact that spouses are of the specific sex do not apply to registered partners (9§).

The provisions enabling spouses to adopt in the Adoption Act do not apply to registered partners (9§), neither do the provisions of Names Act which enables married couples to take a joint family name.

Chapter 4 Paragraphs referring to international private law (paragraphs 10–15)

Conditions of registration of partnership: at least one of the partners is a Finnish citizen and resident in Finland or both parties have resided in Finland during the preceding two years.

Other nationality of a country where registered partnership is provided can be designated as a qualifying nationality for the purposes of registering a partnership in Finland.

Registered partnership between members of the same sex is valid in Finland if it is valid in the country where the registration took place.

Chapter 5 Other provisions (paragraph 16)

Coming into force provisions.[6]

Current State of Parenthood Legislation in Finland

The Act on Child Custody allows the custody of a child to be given to person(s) other than parents. This can be done by court order if it is in the best interest of the child. Finnish courts have given joint custody of a child to same-sex couples even though one of the cohabitants is not a parent of the child. There is no legislation regulating access to assisted reproduction. Clinics give treatment to lesbian couples or single women who have no partner.

A.6 Netherlands

A.6.1 Resolution on Adoption by Same-Sex Couples

The Chamber, having heard the debate, noting that there is a social need for adequate legal protection of children who are being brought up by two people of the same sex; considering that it is in the evident interest of the child that these couples have the possibility of adoption, provided that they meet the other conditions laid down for adoption; resolves, that in the Civil Code adoption by two persons of the same sex and by two persons of different sexes as well as adoption by one person be permitted, and requests the government to prepare a bill to this effect; and resumes the work of the day.[7]

A.6.2 Dutch Act on Adoption by Persons of the Same Sex

We Beatrix [. . .]; [*preamble:*] considering that it is desirable to amend the rules

---

6. Registered Partnership Act, as accepted in Finnish parliament on September 28, 2001. The law took effect in March 2002. Unofficial summary and translation by Mr. Rainer Hiltunen, Master of Laws, secretary general, SETA-Finland, at http://www.seta.fi/fi/setafi6424.htm (last visited January 18, 2002).

7. Dutch Parliament (Lower Chamber), Parliamentary Papers 1995/96, nr. 22700/14; proposed by Mr. Dittrich (Democrats) and Ms. Van der Burg (Labor); adopted on April 16, 1996 (83 votes in favor, 58 against; see Parliamentary Debates 1995/96, 4884). Kees Waaldijk, Dutch Parliament Demands Legislation to Open Up Marriage and Adoption for Same-Sex Couples, April 17, 1996, at http://www.coc.nl/index.htm/?file=marriage (last visited August 18, 1999).

on adoption and related provisions in Book 1 of the Civil Code as regards the introduction of the possibility of adoption by persons of the same sex;

Article I
Book 1 of the Civil Code shall be amended as follows:
A, B and C: [consequential amendments to articles 5, 204 and 207]
D: Article 227 shall be amended as follows:
The first paragraph shall read as follows:
Adoption is effected by a decision of the district court at the joint request of two persons or at the request of one person alone. Two persons cannot make a joint adoption request if according to article 41 they are not allowed to marry each other.
[i.e., the words "of different sex" after "two persons" are deleted]
b. A second sentence shall be added to the second paragraph
["2. The joint request by two persons can only be done, if they have been living together during at least three continuous years immediately before the submission of the request."]
reading as follows: The request by an adopter who is the spouse, registered partner or other life partner of the parent, can only be done, if he has been living together with that parent during at least three continuous years immediately before the submission of the request.
c. The third paragraph shall read as follows:
3. The request can only be granted if:
the adoption is in the evident interest of the child,
at the time of the adoption request it is established, and for the future it is reasonably foreseeable, that the child has nothing to expect anymore from its parent or parents in his/her/their capacity of parent(s), and
the conditions specified in article 228 are fulfilled as well.
E: Article 228, first paragraph, shall be amended as follows:
Sub-paragraph (f) shall read as follows:
[the condition] that for at least three continuous years the adopter has been caring for the child and bringing it up, or, in the case of joint adoption by two persons, that for at least one year they have been caring for the child and bringing it up; if the spouse, registered partner or other life partner of the parent of the child is adopting, the condition is that the adopter and that parent have been caring for the child and bringing it up for at least one year, unless the child is born of the relationship of the mother with a life partner of the same sex;
b. [consequential amendments to sub-paragraph (g)]
F, G and H: [consequential amendments to articles 229, 253b and 327]

Article II
1. [transitional provision]
2. [amendment to article 5, paragraph 3, which will now read:
3. If through adoption a child becomes a descendant of two married adopters of different sexes, the child shall have the family name of the father, unless the adopters jointly declare that it shall have the family name of the mother. If the adopters are unmarried or married and of the same sex, the child shall keep its original family name, unless the

adopters jointly declare that it shall have the family name of one of its adopters. (. . .)]

[. . .] Given in The Hague, 21 December 2000: *Beatrix*

The State-Secretary for Justice: *M. J. Cohen*

Published on 11 January 2001 (The Minister for Justice: *A. H. Korthals*)[8]

A.6.3 Resolution on Same-Sex Marriage

The Chamber, having heard the debate, noting that often in our society two people of different sexes and of the same sex want to enter into a lasting and committed relationship; noting furthermore that according to the Civil Code the concluding of a civil marriage is permitted to two people of different sexes; being of the opinion that in line with the General Equal Treatment Act there is no objective justification for the marriage prohibition for same-sex couples; resolves, that the legal marriage prohibition for two people of the same sex be lifted; requests the government to embark as soon as possible on the preparation of legislation to this effect, taking into account the international aspects, especially in a European context; and also requests the government, because of the width of substance of the aforementioned preparation, to appoint a non-departmental commission in which different relevant disciplines will be represented, and to instruct it to complete a pre-draft of a bill on this matter before 1 August 1997; and resumes the work of the day.[9]

A.6.4 Act of 21 December 2000 Amending Book 1 of the Civil Code, concerning the Opening Up of Marriage for Persons of the Same Sex (Act on the Opening up of Marriage)

We Beatrix [. . .]; [*preamble:*] considering that it is desirable to open up marriage for persons of the same sex and to amend Book 1 of the Civil Code accordingly;

Article I

A, B and C: [amendments to articles 16a, 20 and 20a, concerning administrative duties of the registrar]

D: [amendment of article 28, concerning the change of sex in the birth certificates of transsexuals: Being not-married shall no longer be a condition for such change.]

E: Article 30 shall read as follows:

Article 30

A marriage can be contracted by two persons of different sex or of the same sex.

The law only considers marriage in its civil relations.

[Until now, article 30 only consists of the text of the second paragraph.]

F: Article 33 shall read as follows:

---

8. *See* Text of Dutch Law on Adoption by Persons of the Same Sex. Summary-translation by Kees Waaldijk (January 11, 2001), available at http://ruljis.leidenuniv.nl/user/cwaaldij/www/.

9. Dutch Parliament (Lower Chamber), Parliamentary Papers 1995/96, nr. 22700/18 (replacing 22700/9); proposed by Ms. Van der Burg (Labor) and Mr. Dittrich (Democrats); adopted on April 16, 1996 (81 votes in favor, 60 against; see Parliamentary Debates 1995/96, 4883–84). Waaldijk, note 7 above.

Article 33
A person can at the same time only be linked through marriage with one person.
[Until now, the text of article 33 only outlaws heterosexual polygamy.]
G: [Insertion of the words "brothers" and "sisters" in article 41, which will now read as follows:
Article 41
A marriage cannot be contracted between those who are, by nature or by law, descendant and ascendant, brothers, sisters or brother and sister.
Our Minister of Justice can, for weighty reasons, grant exemption from this prohibition to those who are brothers, sisters or brother and sister through adoption.]
H: A new article 77a shall be inserted:
Article 77a
When two persons indicate to the registrar that they would like their marriage to be converted into a registered partnership, the registrar of the domicile of one of them can make a record of conversion to that effect. If the spouses are domiciled outside the Netherlands and want to convert their marriage into a registered partnership in the Netherlands, and at least one of them has Dutch nationality, conversion will take place with the registrar in The Hague.
Articles 65 and 66 apply correspondingly.
A conversion terminates the marriage and starts the registered partnership on the moment the record of conversion is registered in the register of registered partnerships. The conversion does not affect the paternity over children born before the conversion.
I: [consequential amendment to article 78, concerning proof of marriage]
J: [amendments to article 80a, concerning registered partnership. The minimum age for marriage and registered partnership is 18, but for marriage it is reduced to 16, if the woman is pregnant or has given birth; this exception shall now also apply to registered partnership. Furthermore, annulment of an underage marriage is not possible after the female spouse has become pregnant; the same shall now apply to an underage registered partnership.]
K: [consequential amendment to article 80c]
L: A new article 80f shall be inserted:
Article 80f
When two persons indicate to the registrar that they would like their registered partnership to be converted into a marriage, the registrar of the domicile of one of them can make a record of conversion to that effect. If the registered partners are domiciled outside the Netherlands and want to convert their registered partnership into a marriage in the Netherlands, and at least one of them has Dutch nationality, conversion will take place with the registrar in The Hague.
The articles 65 and 66 apply correspondingly.
A conversion terminates the registered partnership and starts the marriage on the moment the record of conversion is registered in the register of marriages. The conversion does not affect the paternity over children born before the conversion.
M: [consequential amendment to article 149]

N: Article 395 shall read as follows:

Article 395

Without prejudice to article 395a, a stepparent is obliged to provide the costs of living for the minor children of his spouse or registered partner, but only during his marriage or registered partnership and only if they belong to his nuclear family.

O: Article 395a, second paragraph, shall read as follows:

2. A stepparent is obliged to provide [the costs of living and of studying] for the adult children of his spouse or registered partner, but only during his marriage or registered partnership and only if they belong to his nuclear family and are under the age of 21.

Article II

[technical amendments concerning registered partnership]

Article III

Within five years after the entering into force of this Act, Our Minister of Justice shall send Parliament a report on the effects of this Act in practice, with special reference to the relation to registered partnership.

Article IV

This Act shall enter into force on a date to be determined by royal decree.

Article V

This Act shall be cited as: Act on the Opening up of Marriage.

[. . .] Given in The Hague, 21 December 2000: *Beatrix*

The State-Secretary for Justice: *M. J. Cohen*

Published on 11 January 2001 (The Minister for Justice: *A. H. Korthals*)[10]

10. *See* Text of Dutch law on the Opening up of Marriage for Same-sex Partners. Summary-translation by Kees Waaldijk (January 11, 2001), available at http://ruljis. leidenuniv.nl/user/cwaaldij/www/.

Appendix B

Developments in the United Kingdom, Israel, South Africa, and Brazil

B.1 The United Kingdom

In October 1997 the U.K. government announced a fundamental change in immigration policy, which gave some formal recognition, for the first time, to same-sex partners. Under the new policy, the same-sex partner of a British citizen, a European Union national, or a permanent resident of the United Kingdom can, subject to certain conditions, be granted permission to remain in the United Kingdom. The policy, which applies equally to heterosexual partners who are unable to marry, stipulates a two-year relationship requirement.[1] Britain's House of Lords also ruled in October 1999 that a homosexual man was entitled to the same tenancy rights as a heterosexual spouse.[2]

More recent developments in the United Kingdom include the Adults with Incapacity (Scotland) Act 2000, which was passed by the Scottish parliament in March and received the Royal Assent on May 9, 2000. Section 87(2) recognizes a same-sex partner as the "nearest relative" for purposes of the act. This is the first time same-sex partnerships have been expressly recognized in an act of a legislative body in the United Kingdom.[3] In June 2001 London became the first governmental body in England to officially recognize same-sex couples, as it created a "Partnerships Register," which enables both gay and straight unmarried couples to register their relationship with the city, provided that one of the partners lives in London. Although the registration carries no formal legal status, it is hoped that it will be accepted as proof of a relationship in legal

---

1. *See* http://www.ilga.org/Information/legal_survey/europe/united_kingdom.htm#* Partnership (last updated August 19, 2000).

2. *See* Fitzpatrick v. Sterling Housing Association Ltd (2001) AC 27.

3. *See* Robert Wintemute, Lesbian/Gay Law Notes (Arthur S. Leonard ed.), June 2000, at 105–6.

proceedings on such issues as pensions, immigration, and tenancy.[4] Finally, in October 2001, a member of the British Parliament, Jane Griffiths, declared her intention to introduce a bill called "the Relationships (Civil Registration) Bill," which will allow any couple living together in the United Kingdom to register their partnership. The bill includes provisions that equate the status of same-sex partners with that of married couples in a few fields including inheritance tax, housing succession, pensions, compensation in fatal accidents, and social security benefits.[5]

B.2 Israel

In 1994 the Israeli Supreme Court ruled that not extending work-related benefits to the same-sex partner of an employee of Israel's national airline was unconstitutional and contrary to the Equal Employment Opportunity Act, which was amended in 1992 to protect gays and lesbians from discrimination in the workplace.[6] Consequently, many public- and private-sector employers in Israel began according benefits to the same-sex partners of their employees. In the same year, following lengthy court proceedings, the military and the Ministry of Defense agreed to accord to a same-sex partner of a colonel who had died during his military service the benefits normally granted to opposite-sex partners, by virtue of two acts that provide benefits to partners of soldiers who die during their military service. This out-of-court settlement was the first instance in which the Israeli military recognized the rights of same-sex couples. In 1997 a family court in Haifa issued a restraining order prohibiting a woman from entering the apartment where her "life partner" lived, holding that the word "spouse" in the Prevention of Violence in the Family Law included same-sex spouses.[7] In May 2000 and then again in July 2001, the Israeli Supreme Court mandated the registration of a lesbian coparent in accordance with a second-parent adoption decree obtained in California.[8] In addition, an appeal brought by two lesbians who wish to adopt each other's biological children is now pending before the Israeli Supreme Court. They challenge the Israeli Adoption Law, arguing that it should be interpreted as allowing for second-parent adoption. Furthermore, Israel's Interior Ministry announced in July 2001 that it allowed same-sex partners to receive immigration benefits on equal terms with

4. *See* Barbara Dozetos, *London, Taiwan, Australia Advance Gay Rights*, PlanetOut.com Network, June 28, 2001. For an overview of the status of gay partnerships in the United Kingdom, see also Rebecca Bailey-Harris, *Same-Sex Partnerships in English Family Law*, *in* Legal Recognition of Same-Sex Partnerships: A Study of National, European, and International Law 605 (Robert Wintemute & Mads Andenas eds., 2001).

5. *See* Stonewall, *Bill to Introduce Civil Partnership Registers in England and Wales*, ILGA-Europe Euroletter no. 92, October 2001.

6. *See* El-Al v. Danilowitz, 48(5) Piskei Din (P.D.) 749 (1994).

7. *See* Family File 32520/97, Roe v. Doe (unpublished) (1997).

8. *See* File 1779/99, Roe v. Minister of the Interior (2000). For an overview of all these developments, see Alon Harel, *The Rise and Fall of the Israeli Gay Legal Revolution*, 31 Colum. Hum. Rts. L. Rev. 443, 443–45 (2000). *See also* Aeyal M. Gross, *Challenges to Compulsory Heterosexuality: Recognition and Non-Recognition of Same-Sex Couples in Israeli Law*, *in* Legal Recognition of Same-Sex Partnerships: A Study of National, European, and International Law 391 (Robert Wintemute & Mads Andenas eds., 2001).

heterosexual common law spouses; under the ministry's policy, the noncitizen partner is granted a renewable one-year tourist permit with employment authorization and may request temporary resident status after four years; eventually, the partner may seek permanent residence and then citizenship.[9]

B.3 South Africa

South Africa was the first country in the world to enshrine lesbian and gay rights in its constitution, prohibiting discrimination on the basis of, inter alia, sexual orientation. In addition, South Africa has recognized same-sex couples for the purposes of immigration. In 1998 a challenge to the constitutionality of South Africa's immigration law (the Aliens Control Act), which denies immigration rights to binational same-sex couples, was brought before the South African High Court. In February 1999 the High Court ruled that the act unfairly discriminated against same-sex couples.[10] On December 2, 1999, the Constitutional Court of South Africa affirmed the High Court's decision and ruled that the Aliens Control Act had to be changed in order to recognize same-sex partners as having essentially the same immigration rights as legal spouses.[11] The amendment of the law took effect immediately, since the Court's remedy was to read into the law after the word "spouse" the words "or partner, in a permanent same-sex life partnership."[12] Moreover, in November 2000 South Africa's parliament took a significant step toward recognizing gay and lesbian couples by giving them a spousal exemption from inheritance taxes. Under the Revenue Laws Amendment Bill, the Estate Duties Act redefines *spouse* to include "a permanent same-sex life relationship."[13]

B.4 Brazil

In addition to a "civil partnership" bill, which was introduced before the Brazilian parliament in 1995 and has since been languishing, in February 1998 the Brazilian High Court ruled unanimously that a gay man was entitled to half the estate of his partner of seven years, who died in 1989. Furthermore, citing article 5 of the National Constitution, which prohibits all forms of discrimination, a federal court rendered a groundbreaking decision in April 2000 according to which Brazilian gay and lesbian couples in a "stable union" have

9. *See* Human Rights Watch: World Report 2001—Lesbian and Gay Rights, at http://www.hrw.org/wr2k1/special/gay.html.

10. *See* ILGA World Legal Survey: South Africa, at http://www.ilga.org/Information/legal_survey/africa/southafrica.htm (last updated April 23, 1999).

11. *See* National Coalition for Gay and Lesbian Equality v. Minister of Home Affairs, 1999 (3) BCLR 280 (C) (High Court, Cape of Good Hope Provincial Division, December 2, 1999).

12. *Id.*

13. *See* PlanetOut News Staff, *Tax Break for South African Gays,* November 20, 2000. For an overview of the status of gay partnerships in South Africa, see also Craig Lind, *Politics, Partnership Rights, and the Constitution in South Africa . . . (and the Problem of Sexual Identity), in* Legal Recognition of Same-Sex Partnerships: A Study of National, European, and International Law 279 (Robert Wintemute & Mads Andenas eds., 2001).

the same status as heterosexual couples for purposes of social security benefits and public pensions.[14]

14. *See* ILGA World Legal Survey: Brazil, at http://www.ilga.org/Information/ legal_survey/americas/brazil.htm (last updated July 19, 1999); PlanetOut News Staff, *International Partners Briefs: Brazilian Social Security DP Benefits,* April 18, 2000, at http:// www.planetout.com/news/article-print.html?2000/04/18/2; Larry Rother, *Brazil Grants Some Legal Recognition to Same-Sex Couples,* New York Times, June 10, 2000, at A3. For an overview of the status of same-sex partnerships in Brazil, see also Marcelo Dealtry Turra, *Brazil's Proposed "Civil Unions between Persons of the Same Sex": Legislative Inaction and Judicial Reactions, in* Legal Recognition of Same-Sex Partnerships: A Study of National, European, and International Law 337 (Robert Wintemute & Mads Andenas eds., 2001).

Bibliography

Adam, Barry D. *The Rise of a Gay and Lesbian Movement*. Rev. ed. New York: Twayne, 1995.

Adam, Barry D., et al., eds. *The Global Emergence of Gay and Lesbian Politics: National Imprints of a Worldwide Movement*. Philadelphia: Temple University Press, 1999.

Adamik, Maria. Feminism and Hungary. In *Gender Politics and Post-Communism*, ed. N. Funk and M. Mueller. New York: Routledge, 1993.

Adams, Wendy A. Same-Sex Relationship and Anglo-Canadian Choice of Law: An Argument for Universal Validity. *Canadian Y.B. Int'l L.* 34 (1996): 103.

Adams, William E., Jr. Whose Family Is It Anyway? The Continuing Struggle for Lesbians and Gay Men Seeking to Adopt Children. *New Eng. L. Rev.* 30 (1996): 579.

Allen, Beth A. Same-Sex Marriage: A Conflict-of-Laws Analysis for Oregon. *Willamette L. Rev.* 32 (1996): 619.

Amar, Akhil Reed. Attainder and Amendment 2: Romer's Rightness. *Mich. L. Rev.* 94 (1996): 203.

Amnesty International USA. *Breaking the Silence: Human Rights Violations Based on Sexual Orientation*. New York: Amnesty International Publications, 1994.

Andersen, Eric G. Children, Parents, and Nonparents: Protected Interests and Legal Standards. *BYU L. Rev.* (1998): 935.

Andreassen, Jens Edvin. State and Church in Norway. *Scandinavian Stud. in L.* 36 (1992): 11.

Appiah, K. Anthony. The Marrying Kind. *New York Review of Books*, June 20, 1996, at 48.

Archer, Clive, and Stephen Maxwell, eds. *The Nordic Model: Studies in Public Policy Innovation*. Westmead, U.K.: Gower, 1980.

Arkes, Hadley. Questions of Principle, Not Predictions: A Reply to Macedo. *Geo. L.J.* 84 (1995): 321.

Arriola, Elvia R. "What's the Big Deal?" Women in the New York City Construction Industry and Sexual Harassment Law, 1970–1985. *Colum. Hum. Rts. L. Rev.* 22 (1990): 21.

———. Law and the Family of Choice and Need. *U. of Louisville J. Fam. L.* 35 (1996–97): 691.

Arter, David. *The Nordic Parliaments: A Comparative Analysis*. New York: St. Martin's Press, 1984.

Babcock, Barbara Allen, et al., eds. *Sex Discrimination and the Law: History, Practice, and Theory.* 2d ed. Boston: Little, Brown, 1996.

Bailey, Martha. How Will Canada Respond to Same-Sex Marriages? *Creighton L. Rev.* 32 (1998): 105.

Baird, Robert M., and M. Katherine Baird, eds. *Homosexuality: Debating the Issues.* Amherst, N.Y.: Prometheus Books, 1995.

Baird, Robert M., and Stuart E. Rosenbaum, eds. *Same-Sex Marriage: The Moral and Legal Debate.* Amherst, N.Y.: Prometheus Books, 1997.

Baker, Lynn A. Promulgating the Marriage Contract. *U. Mich. L.J. Reform* 23 (1990): 217.

Balian, Habib A. Note, Till Death Do Us Part: Granting Full Faith and Credit to Marital Status. *S. Car. L. Rev.* 68 (1995): 397.

Ball, Carlos A., and Janice Farrell Pea. Warring with Wardle: Morality, Social Science, and Gay and Lesbian Parents. *U. Ill. L. Rev.* (1998): 253.

Barnett, James E. Comment, Updating Romer v. Evans: The Implications of the Supreme Court's Denial of Certiorari in Equality Foundation of Greater Cincinnati v. City of Cincinnati. *Case W. Res.* 49 (1999): 645.

Barnett, Walter. *Sexual Freedom and the Constitution: An Inquiry into the Constitutionality of Repressive Sex Laws.* Albuquerque: University of New Mexico Press, 1973.

Bartlett, Katharine T. Rethinking Parenthood as an Exclusive Status: The Need for Legal Alternatives When the Premise of the Nuclear Family Has Failed. *Va. L. Rev.* 70 (1984): 879.

————. Gender Law. *Duke J. Gender L. & Pol'y* 1 (1994): 1.

Bech, Henning. Report from a Rotten State: Marriage and Homosexuality in Denmark. In *Modern Homosexualities: Fragments of Lesbian and Gay Experience,* ed. K. Plummer. London: Routledge, 1992.

————. *When Men Meet: Homosexuality and Modernity.* Trans. T. Mesquit and T. Davies. Chicago: University of Chicago Press, 1997.

Beck, Phyllis W. The Metamorphosis of the Family. *Temple Pol. & Civ. Rts L. Rev.* 7 (1998): 251.

Becker, Mary. Strength in Diversity: Feminist Theoretical Approaches to Child Custody and Same-Sex Partnerships. *Stetson L. Rev.* 23 (1994): 701.

Benardete, Seth. *On Plato's Symposium.* Munich: Carl Friedrich von Siemens Stiftung, 1994.

Bernheimer, Jason M. Note, Single-Sex Public Education: Separate but Equal Is Not Equal at the Young Women's Leadership School in New York City. *N.Y.L. Sch. J. Hum. Rts.* 14 (1997): 339.

Bernstein, Barton J. Plessy v. Ferguson: Conservative Sociological Jurisprudence. In *12 Black Southerners and the Law 1865–1900,* ed. D. G. Nieman. New York: Garland, 1994.

Betlach, Bradley J. The Unconstitutionality of the Minnesota Defense of Marriage Act: Ignoring Judgments, Restricting Travel, and Purposeful Discrimination. *Wm. Mitchell L. Rev.* 24 (1998): 407.

Björgvinsson, David Thór. Iceland: General Principles and Recent Developments in Icelandic Family Law. In *The International Survey of Family Law 1995,* ed. A. Bainham. The Hague: Martinus Nijhoff, 1997.

Blackstone, William. *Commentaries on the Laws of England.* Vol. 1. New York: Collins and Hannay, 1832.

Blair, Anita K. Constitutional Equal Protection, Strict Scrutiny, and the Politics of Marriage Law. *Cath. U. L. Rev.* 47 (1998): 1231.

Boer, Madzy Rood-de. The Netherlands: New Legal Facts. *J. Fam. L.* 31 (1992–93): 389.

Bogdan, Michael, and Eva Ryrstedt. Marriage in Swedish Family Law and Swedish Conflicts of Law. *Fam. L.Q.* 29 (1995): 675.

Boje, Thomas P., and Sven E. Olsson Hort, eds. *Scandinavia in a New Europe.* Oslo: Scandinavian University Press, 1993.

Bollobás, Enikö. "Totalitarian Lib": The Legacy of Communism for Hungarian Women. In *Gender Politics and Post-Communism,* ed. N. Funk and M. Mueller. New York: Routledge, 1993.

Bonauto, Mary, Susan M. Murray, and Beth Robinson. The Freedom to Marry for Same-Sex Couples: The Opening Appellate Brief of Plaintiffs Stan Baker et al. in Baker et al. v. State of Vermont. *Mich. J. Gender & L.* 5 (1999): 409.

———. The Freedom to Marry for Same-Sex Couples: The Reply Brief of Plaintiffs Stan Baker et al. in Baker et al. v. State of Vermont. *Mich. J. Gender & L.* 6 (1999): 1.

Borchers, Patrick J. Baker v. General Motors: Implications for Inter-Jurisdictional Recognition of Non-Traditional Marriages. *Creighton L. Rev.* 32 (1998): 147.

Boswell, John. *Same-Sex Unions in Premodern Europe.* New York: Vintage Books, 1995.

Bowman, Craig A., and Blake M. Cornish. A More Perfect Union: A Legal and Social Analysis of Domestic Partnership Ordinances. *Colum. L. Rev.* 92 (1992): 1164.

Bowman, Cynthia Grant. A Feminist Proposal to Bring Back Common Law Marriage. *Or. L. Rev.* 75 (1996): 709.

Boyd, Susan B. Case Comment: Commentaire: Best Friends or Spouses? Privatization and the Recognition of Lesbian Relationships in M. v. H. *Can. J. Fam. L.* 13 (1996): 321.

Boyle, Stacey Lynne. Marital Status Classifications: Protecting Homosexuals and Heterosexual Cohabitors. *Hastings Const. L.Q.* 14 (1986): 111.

Bozett, Frederick W., and Marvin B. Sussman. Homosexuality and Family Relations: Views and Research Issues. In *Homosexuality and Family Relations,* ed. F. W. Bozett and M. B. Sussman. New York: Haworth Press, 1990.

Bradley, David. The Development of a Legal Status for Unmarried Cohabitation in Sweden. *Anglo-American L. Rev.* 18 (1989): 322.

———. Sexual Equality and Maintenance Allowances in Sweden. *Oxford J. Legal Stud.* 9 (1989): 403.

———. Children, Family, and the State in Sweden. *J.L. & Soc'y* 17 (1990): 427.

———. Marriage, Family, Property, and Inheritance in Swedish Law. *Int'l & Comp. L.Q.* 39 (2) (1990): 370.

———. Perspectives on Sexual Equality in Sweden. *Mod. L. Rev.* 53 (1990): 283.

———. Radical Principles and the Legal Institution of Marriage. *Int'l J.L. & Fam.* 4 (1990): 154.

———. Unmarried Cohabitation in Sweden: A Renewed Social Institution? *J. Legal Hist.* 11 (1990): 300.

———. *Family Law and Political Culture: Scandinavian Laws in Comparative Perspectives.* London: Sweet and Maxwell, 1996.

———. The Antecedents of Finnish Family Laws: Legal Tradition, Political Culture, and Social Institutions. *J. Legal Hist.* 19 (1998): 93.

———. Politics, Culture, and Family Law in Finland: Comparative Approaches to the Institution of Marriage. *Int'l J.L., Pol'y & Fam.* 12 (1998): 288.

Bricklin, Shoshana. Legislative Approaches to Support Family Diversity. *Temple Pol. & Civ. Rts. L. Rev.* 7 (1998): 379.

Brill, Alida, ed. *A Rising Public Voice: Women in Politics Worldwide.* New York: Feminist Press, 1995.

Brown, Anne B. The Evolving Definition of Marriage. *Suffolk U. L. Rev.* 31 (1998): 917.

Brown, Berit I., ed. *Nordic Experiences: Exploration of Scandinavian Cultures.* Westport, Conn.: Greenwood Press, 1997.

Brown, Jennifer Gerarda. Extraterritorial Recognition of Same-Sex Marriage: When Theory Confronts Praxis. *Quinnipiac L. Rev.* 16 (1996): 1.

Bryant, Steve, and Demian. *An Indispensable Guide for Gay & Lesbian Couples: What Every Same-Sex Couple Should Know.* Seattle: Partners Task Force (Sweet Corn Productions), 1993.

Bryant, Sunne. Second Parent Adoption: A Model Brief. *Duke J. Gender L. & Pol'y* 2 (1995): 233.

Bull, Kirsti Strøm. Non-Marital Cohabitation in Norway. *Scandinavian Stud. in L.* 30 (1986): 29.

Burght, Gregor Van Der. Registered Partnership in the Netherlands. 1999. Copy on file with Merin.

Burguière, André, et al., eds. *A History of the Family.* Trans. Sarah Hanbury Tenison et al. Cambridge: Polity Press, 1996.

Burnette, Brian W. Hawaii's Reciprocal Beneficiaries Act: An Effective Step in Resolving the Controversy Surrounding Same-Sex Marriage. *Brandeis L.J. U. Louisville* 37 (1998–99): 81.

Burns, Karen, and Vallance Kannelly. The Legal Definition of Marriage. *Responsa Meridiana* (1995): 487.

Burris, Scott. Gay Marriage and Public Health. *Temple Pol. & Civ. Rts. L. Rev.* 7 (1998): 417.

Burton, Anne M. Gay Marriage—A Modern Proposal: Applying Baehr v. Lewin to the International Covenant on Civil and Political Rights. *Indep. J. Global Legal Stud.* 3 (1995): 177.

Butler, Charles J. Note, The Defense of Marriage Act: Congress's Use of Narrative in the Debate over Same-Sex Marriage. *N.Y.U. L. Rev.* 73 (1998): 841.

Button, James W., et al. *Private Lives, Public Conflicts: Battles over Gay Rights in American Communities.* Washington, D.C.: Congressional Quarterly Press, 1997.

Cabaj, Robert P., and David W. Purcell, eds. *On the Road to Same-Sex Marriage.* San Francisco: Jossey-Bass, 1998.

Cain, Particia A. Imagine There's No Marriage. *Quinnipiac L. Rev.* 16 (1996): 27.

Calhoun, Cheshire. The Case for Same-Sex Marriage: From Sexual Liberty to Civilized Commitment. *J. Homosexuality* 35 (2) (1998): 102.

Cantarella, Eva. *Bisexuality in the Ancient World.* Trans. C. Ó. Cuilleanáin. New Haven, Conn.: Yale University Press, 1992.

Caplan-Cotenoff, Scott A. Parental Leave: The Need for a National Policy to Foster Sexual Equality. *Am. J.L. & Med.* 13 (1987): 71.

Cappellanus, Andreas. *The Art of Courtly Love.* Trans. J. J. Parry. New York: W. W. Norton, 1969.

Case, Mary Anne. Couples and Coupling in the Public Sphere: A Comment on the Legal History of Litigating for Lesbians and Gay Rights. *Va. L. Rev.* 79 (1993): 1643.

———. Disaggregating Gender from Sex and Sexual Orientation: The Effeminate Man in the Law and Feminist Jurisprudence. *Yale L.J.* 105 (1995): 1.

Chabora, Paige E. Congress' Power under the Full Faith and Credit Clause and the Defense of Marriage Act of 1996. *Neb. L. Rev.* 76 (1997): 604.

Chambers, David L. The Legalization of the Family: Toward a Policy of Supportive Neutrality. *J.L. Reform* 18 (1985): 805.

———. What If: The Legal Consequences of Marriage and the Legal Needs of Lesbian and Gay Male Couples. *Mich. L. Rev.* 95 (1996): 447.

Christensen, Craig F. Legal Ordering of Family Values: The Case of Gay and Lesbian Families. *Cardozo L. Rev.* 18 (1997): 1299.

Christensen, Craig W. If Not Marriage? On Securing Gay and Lesbian Family Values by a "Simulacrum of Marriage." *Fordham L. Rev.* 66 (1998): 1699.

Chusid, Jodie Leith. Tanner v. Oregon Health Sciences University: Justifying the Mandate for Domestic Partner Benefits. *Col. J. Gender & L.* 8 (1999): 261.

Clapham, Andrew. *Human Rights in the Private Sphere.* Oxford: Clarendon Press, 1996.

Clapham, Andrew, and J. H. H. Weiler. Lesbians and Gay Men in the European Community Legal Order. In *Homosexuality: A European Community Issue: Essays on Lesbian and Gay Rights in European Law and Policy,* ed. K. Waaldijk and A. Clapham. Dordrecht, Netherlands: Martinus Nijhoff, 1993.

Clark, J. Michael, Joanne Carlson Brown, and Lorna M. Hochstein. Institutional Religion and Gay/Lesbian Oppression. In *Homosexuality and Family Relations,* ed. F. W. Bozett and M. B. Sussman. New York: Haworth Press, 1990.

Clayton, Stevie. Legal Recognition of Same-Sex Relationships: Where To from Here? *Murdoch U. Electronic J.L.* 3 (3) (1996).

Closen, Michael L., and Carol R. Heise. HIV-AIDS and the Non-Traditional Family: The Argument for State and Federal Judicial Recognition of Danish Same-Sex Marriages. *Nova L. Rev.* 16 (1992): 809.

Closen, Michael L., and Joan E. Maloney. The Health Care Surrogate Act in Illinois: Another Rejection of Domestic Partners' Rights. *S. Ill. U. L.J.* 19 (1995): 479.

Clulow, Christopher, ed. *Women, Men, and Marriage.* N.J.: Jason Aronson, 1996.

Colker, Ruth. 1991. Marriage. *Yale J.L. & Feminism* 3 (1996): 321.

———. Marriage. In *Feminist Legal Theory,* ed. F. E. Olsen. New York: New York University Press, 1995.

Conte, Alba. *Sexual Orientation and Legal Rights.* New York: Wiley Law Publications, 1998.

Coolidge, David Orgon. Playing the Loving Card: Same-Sex Marriage and the Politics of Analogy. *BYU J. Pub. L.* 12 (1998): 201.

Coolidge, David Orgon, and William C. Duncan. Definition or Discrimination? State Marriage Recognition Statutes in the "Same-Sex Marriage" Debate. *Creighton L. Rev.* 32 (1998): 3.

Coombs, Mary. Emerging Issues in Sexual Orientation Law: Sexual Dis-Orientation: Transgendered People and Same-Sex Marriage. *UCLA Women's L.J.* 8 (1998): 219.

Cornell, Drucilla. *At the Heart of Freedom: Feminism, Sex, and Equality*. Princeton, N.J.: Princeton University Press, 1998.

Corvino, John, ed. *Same Sex: Debating the Ethics, Science, and Culture of Homosexuality*. New York: Rowman and Littlefield, 1997.

Cox, Barbara J. Alternative Families: Obtaining Traditional Family Benefits through Litigation, Legislation, and Collective Bargaining. *Wis. Women's L.J.* 2 (1986): 1.

———. Love Makes a Family—Nothing More, Nothing Less: How the Judicial System Has Refused to Protect Nonlegal Parents in Alternative Families. *J.L. & Pol.* 8 (1991): 5.

———. Same-Sex Marriage and Choice of Law: If We Marry in Hawaii, Are We Still Married When We Return Home? *Wis. L. Rev.* (1994): 1033.

———. A (Personal) Essay on Same-Sex Marriage. *Nat'l J. Sexual Orientation L.* 1 (1995): 87.

———. Are Same-Sex Marriage Statutes the New Anti-Gay Initiatives? *Nat'l J. Sexual Orientation L.* 2 (1996): 194.

———. Same-Sex Marriage and the Public Policy Exception in Choice-of-Law: Does It Really Exist? *Quinnipiac L. Rev.* 16 (1996): 61.

———. Towards a Radical and Plural Democracy: The Lesbian Wife: Same-Sex Marriage as an Expression of Radical and Plural Democracy. *Cal. W.L. Rev.* 33 (1997): 155.

Cox, Stanley E. DOMA and Conflicts Law: Congressional Rules and Domestic Relations Conflicts Law. *Creighton L. Rev.* 32 (1999): 1063.

Crane, Daniel A. The Original Understanding of the "Effects Clause" of Article IV, Section 1 and Implications for the Defense of Marriage Act. *Geo. Mason L. Rev.* 6 (1998): 307.

Croce, Benedetto. *Etica e politica, aggiuntovi il "Contributo alla critica di me stesso."* Bari, Italy: Laterza, 1931.

Crotty, Patricia McGee. *Women and Family Law: Connecting the Public and the Private*. New York: Peter Lang, 1997.

Culhane, John G. Uprooting the Arguments against Same-Sex Marriage. *Cardozo L. Rev.* 20 (1999): 1119.

Cummings, Richard. All-Male Black Schools: Equal Protection, the New Separatism, and Brown v. Board of Education. *Hastings Const. L.Q.* 20 (1993): 725.

Curry, Hayden, et al. *A Legal Guide for Lesbian and Gay Couples*. 10th ed. Berkeley, Calif.: Nolo Press, 1999.

Dahl, Børge, et al., eds. *Danish Law in a European Perspective*. Copenhagen: Cadjura, 1996.

Dahl, Tove Stang. *Women's Law: An Introduction to Feminist Jurisprudence*. Trans. R. L. Craig. Oslo: Norwegian University Press, 1987.

Dahlberg, Anita, and Nadine Taub. Notions of the Family in Recent Swedish Law. In *Family Law and Gender Bias: Comparative Perspectives*, ed. B. Stark. Greenwich, Conn.: JAI Press, 1992.

Dahlerup, Drude. Is the New Women's Movement Dead? Decline or Change of the Danish Movement. In *The New Women's Movement: Feminism and Political Power in Europe and the USA*, ed. D. Dahlerup. London: Sage, 1986.

Dahlsgård, Inga. *Women in Denmark Yesterday and Today*. Trans. G. French. Copenhagen: Det Danske Selskab, 1980.

Dalton, Harlon L. Reflections on the Lesbian and Gay Marriage Debate. *L. & Sexuality* 1 (1991): 1.

D'Amato, Anthony Dominic. Conflict of Laws Rules and the Interstate Recognition of Same-Sex Marriages. *U. Ill. L. Rev.* (1995): 911.

Danielsen, Svend. Unmarried Partners: Scandinavian Law in the Making. *Oxford J. Legal Stud.* 3 (1983): 59.

Davies, Julia Frost. Note, Two Moms and a Baby: Protecting the Nontraditional Family through Second Parent Adoptions. *New Eng. L. Rev.* 29 (1995): 1055.

Davis, Victoria. Domestic Relations: Marriage Generally: Prohibit Same-Sex Marriage. *Ga. St. U. L. Rev.* 13 (1996): 137.

Days, Drew, III. Brown Blues: Rethinking the Integrative Ideal. *Wm. & Mary L. Rev.* 34 (1992): 53.

Dean, Craig R. Gay Marriage: A Civil Right. *J. Homosexuality* 27 (3–4) (1994): 111.

Department for Economic and Social Information and Policy Analysis, United Nations. *Abortion Policies: A Global Review.* Vol. 1. New York: United Nations, 1992.

———. *Abortion Policies: A Global Review.* Vol. 2. New York: United Nations, 1993.

De Rougemont, Denis. *Love in the Western World.* Trans. M. Belgion. Rev. ed. Princeton, N.J.: Princeton University Press, 1983.

Derry, T. K. *A History of Scandinavia.* Minneapolis: University of Minnesota Press, 1979.

Developments in the Law: Sexual Orientation and the Law: Part 5. Same-Sex Couples and the Law. *Harv. L. Rev.* 102 (1989): 1583.

de Vos, Pierre. Same-Sex Marriage: The Right to Equality and the South-African Constitution. *South African Pub. L.* 11 (1996): 355.

Dickerson, A. Mechele. Family Values and the Bankruptcy Code: A Proposal to Eliminate Bankruptcy Benefits Awarded on the Basis of Marital Status. *Fordham L. Rev.* 67 (1998): 69.

Dinneen, Jill. Comment, Equality Foundation of Greater Cincinnati, Inc. v. City of Cincinnati: The Sixth Circuit Narrowly Construes Romer v. Evans. *St. John's L. Rev.* 73 (1999): 951.

Dodson, Robert D. Homosexual Discrimination and Gender: Was Romer v. Evans Really a Victory for Gay Rights? *Cal. W.L. Rev.* 35 (1999): 271.

Donovan, James M. DOMA: An Unconstitutional Establishment of Fundamentalist Christianity. *Mich. J. Gender & L.* 4 (1997): 335.

Duclos, Nitya. Some Complicating Thoughts on Same-Sex Marriage. *L. & Sexuality* 1 (1991): 31.

Duncan, Richard F. "They Call Me 'Eight Eyes'": Hardwick's Respectability, Romer's Narrowness, and Same-Sex Marriage. *Creighton L. Rev.* 32 (1998): 241.

Dunlap, Mary C. The Lesbian and Gay Marriage Debate: A Microcosm of Our Hopes and Troubles in the Nineties. *L. & Sexuality* 1 (1991): 63.

Dupuis, Martin D. The Impact of Culture, Society, and History on the Legal Process: An Analysis of the Legal Status of Same-Sex Relationships in the United States and Denmark. *Int'l J.L. & Fam.* 9 (1995): 86.

Duyvendak, Jan Willem. From Revolution to Involution: The Disappearance of the Gay Movement in France. *J. Homosexuality* 29 (4) (1995): 369.

Eckols, Linda S. The Marriage Mirage: The Personal and Social Identity Implications of Same-Gender Matrimony. *Mich. J. Gender & L.* 5 (1999): 353.

Editors of the Harvard Law Review. *Sexual Orientation and the Law.* Cambridge, Mass.: Harvard University Press, 1989.

Edwards, John N., ed. *Sex and Society.* Chicago: Markham, 1972.

Eekelaar, John M., and Sanford N. Katz, eds. *Marriage and Cohabitation in Contemporary Societies: Areas of Legal, Social, and Ethical Change: An International and Interdisciplinary Study.* Toronto: Butterworths, 1980.

Eekelaar, John M., and Thandabantu Nhlapo, eds. *The Changing Family: International Perspectives on the Family and Family Law.* Oxford: Hart, 1998.

Ellingsæter, Anne Lise. *Gender, Work, and Social Change: Beyond Dualistic Thinking.* Oslo: Institute for Social Research, 1995.

Ellingsæter, Anne Lise, and Mary-Ann Hedlung. *Employment and Gender Equality in Norway.* Oslo: Institute for Social Research, 1998.

Elmer, Michael, and Marianne Lund Larsen. Explanatory Article on the Legal Consequences etc., of the Danish Law on Registered Partnership. *Juristen,* no. 3 (1990). The English translation of this article is available from Landsforeningen for Bosser Og Lesbiske (National Danish Organization for Gays and Lesbians), Copenhagen.

Elovitz, Marc E. Reforming the Law to Respect Families Created by Lesbian and Gay People. *J.L. & Pol'y* 3 (1995): 431.

Ertman, Martha M. Contractual Purgatory for Sexual Marginorities: Not Heaven, but Not Hell Either. *Denv. U. L. Rev.* 73 (1997): 1107.

Eskridge, William, N., Jr. A History of Same-Sex Marriage. *Va. L. Rev.* 79 (1993): 1419.

———. *The Case for Same-Sex Marriage: From Sexual Liberty to Civilized Commitment.* New York: Free Press, 1996.

———. Three Cultural Anxieties Undermining the Case for Same-Sex Marriage. *Temple Pol. & Civ. Rts. L. Rev.* 7 (1998): 307.

———. *Gaylaw: Challenging the Apartheid of the Closet.* Cambridge, Mass.: Harvard University Press, 1999.

Eskridge, William, N., Jr., and Sheila Rose Foster. Discussion of Same-Sex Marriage. *Temple Pol. & Civ. Rts. L. Rev.* 7 (1998): 329.

Eskridge, William, N., Jr., and Nan D. Hunter. *Sexuality, Gender, and the Law.* Westbury, N.Y.: Foundation Press, 1997.

Ettelbrick, Paula L. Since When Is Marriage a Path to Liberation? In *Lesbian and Gay Marriage: Private Commitments, Public Ceremonies,* ed. S. Sherman. Philadelphia: Temple University Press, 1992.

———. Wedlock Alert: A Comment on Lesbian and Gay Family Recognition. *J.L. & Pol'y* 5 (1996): 107.

Fajer, Marc A. Can Two Real Men Eat Quiche Together? Storytelling, Gender-Role Stereotypes, and Legal Protection for Lesbians and Gay Men. *U. Miami L. Rev.* 46 (1992): 511.

Farabee, Lisa M. Note, Marriage, Equal Protection, and the New Judicial Federalism: A View from the States. *Yale L. & Pol'y Rev.* 14 (1996): 237.

Fawcett, Matthew. Taking the Middle Path: Recent Swedish Legislation Grants Minimal Property Rights to Unmarried Cohabitants. *Fam. L.Q.* 24 (1990): 179.

Feather, Nancy J. Emerging Issues in State Constitutional Law: Article: Defense of Marriage Acts: An Analysis under State Constitutional Law. *Temple L. Rev.* 70 (1997): 1017.

Feldblum, Chai R. The Pursuit of Social and Political Equality: Sexual Orientation, Morality, and the Law: Devlin Revisited. *U. Pitt. L. Rev.* 57 (1996): 237.

———. A Progressive Moral Case for Same-Sex Marriage. *Temple Pol. & Civ. Rts. L. Rev.* 7 (1998): 485.

Findlay, Barbara. All in the Family Values. *Canadian J. Fam. L.* 14 (1997): 129.

Fineman, Martha Albertson. The Concept of the Natural Family and the Limits of American Family Law. In *Family Law and Gender Bias: Comparative Perspectives,* ed. B. Stark. Greenwich, Conn.: JAI Press, 1992.

———. Our Sacred Institution: The Ideal of the Family in American Law and Society. *Utah L. Rev.* (1993): 387.

Fisk, Catherine L. ERISA Preemption of State and Local Laws on Domestic Partnership and Sexual Orientation Discrimination in Employment. *UCLA Women's L.J.* 8 (1998): 267.

Fletcher, Anthony. *Gender, Sex, and Subordination in England 1500–1800.* New Haven, Conn.: Yale University Press, 1995.

Fogo, Credence. Cabining Freedom: A Comparative Study of Lesbian and Gay Rights in the United States and Canada. *Cardozo J. Int'l & Comp. L.* 16 (1998): 425.

Forder, Caroline. The Netherlands: Re-Thinking Marriage, Parenthood, and Adoption. In *The International Survey of Family Law 1995,* ed. A. Bainham. The Hague: Martinus Nijhoff, 1997.

Foster, Sheila Rose. The Symbolism of Rights and the Costs of Symbolism: Some Thoughts on the Campaign for Same-Sex Marriage. *Temple Pol. & Civ. Rts. L. Rev.* 7 (1998): 319.

Fowler, Peter N. Comment, Adult Adoption: A "New" Legal Tool for Lesbians and Gay Men. *Golden Gate U. L. Rev.* 14 (1984): 667.

Franke, Katharine M. The Central Mistake of Sex Discrimination Law: The Disaggregation of Sex from Gender. *U. Pa. L. Rev.* 144 (1995): 1.

———. Becoming a Citizen: Reconstruction Era Regulation of African American Marriages. *Yale J.L. & Human.* 11 (1999): 251.

French, Maggie. Loves, Sexualities, and Marriages: Strategies and Adjustments. In *Modern Homosexualities: Fragments of Lesbian and Gay Experience,* ed. K. Plummer. London: Routledge, 1992.

Friedman, Andrew H. Same-Sex Marriage and the Right to Privacy: Abandoning Scriptural, Canonical, and Natural Law Based Definitions of Marriage. *How. L.J.* 35 (1992): 173.

Fullerton, Brian, and Richard Knowles. *Scandinavia.* London: P. Chapman, 1991.

Gardner, Jane F. *Women in Roman Law and Society.* Bloomington: Indiana University Press, 1995.

Geest, Hans van der. Homosexuality and Marriage. *J. Homosexuality* 24 (3–4) (1993): 115.

George, Robert P., and Gerald V. Bradley. Marriage and the Liberal Imagination. *Geo. L.J.* 84 (1995): 301.

Gerard, Kent, and Gert Hekma, eds. *The Pursuit of Sodomy: Male Homosexuality in Renaissance and Enlightenment Europe.* New York: Harrington Park Press, 1989.

Giddens, Anthony. *The Transformation of Intimacy: Sexuality, Love, and Eroticism in Modern Societies*. Stanford, Calif.: Stanford University Press, 1992.

Gilson, Etienne. *Heloïse and Abélard*. Ann Arbor: University of Michigan Press, 1960.

Glavinovich, Mikel A. International Suggestions for Improving Parental Leave Legislation in the United States. *Ariz. J. Int'l & Comp. L.* 13 (1996): 147.

Glendon, Mary Ann. Family Law Reform in the 1980's. *La. L. Rev.* 44 (1984): 1553.

———. *Abortion and Divorce in Western Law*. Cambridge, Mass.: Harvard University Press, 1987.

———. *The Transformation of Family Law: State, Law, and Family in the United States and Western Europe*. Chicago: University of Chicago Press, 1989.

Glennon, Theresa. Binding the Family Ties: A Child Advocacy Perspective on Second-Parent Adoptions. *Temple Pol. & Civ. Rts. L. Rev.* 7 (1998): 255.

Goldberg, Jonathan. Sodomy in the New World: Anthropologies Old and New. In *Fear of a Queer Planet*, ed. M. Warner. Minneapolis: University of Minnesota Press, 1997.

Goldfarb, Sally F. Family Law, Marriage, and Heterosexuality: Questioning the Assumptions. *Temple Pol. & Civ. Rts. L. Rev.* 7 (1998): 285.

Goldschmidt, Jane. *Gay, Lesbian, Bisexual & Transgender Civil Rights Laws in the U.S.* Washington, D.C.: Policy Institute of the National Gay and Lesbian Task Force, 1998.

Goransson, Leslie. International Trends in Same-Sex Marriage. In *On the Road to Same-Sex Marriage*, ed. R. P. Cabaj and D. W. Purcell. San Francisco: Jossey-Bass, 1998.

Goven, Joanna. Gender Politics in Hungary: Autonomy and Anti-Feminism. In *Gender Politics and Post-Communism*, ed. N. Funk and M. Mueller. New York: Routledge, 1993.

Graff, E. J. *What Is Marriage For?* Boston: Beacon Press, 1999.

Graham-Siegenthaler, Barbara E. Principles of Marriage Recognition Applied to Same-Sex Marriage Recognition in Switzerland and Europe. *Creighton L. Rev.* 32 (1998): 121.

Grant, Brenda. Comments and Cases on Same-Sex Marriage: Homosexual Marriage and the Constitution. *South African J. Hum. Rts.* 12 (1996): 568.

Graubard, Stephen R., ed. *Norden—The Passion for Equality*. Oslo: Norwegian University Press, 1986.

Graversen, Jørgen. Family Law as a Reflection of Family Ideology. *Scandinavian Stud. in L.* 34 (1990): 67.

Green, Vincent C. Same-Sex Adoption: An Alternative Approach to Gay Marriage in New York. *Brooklyn L. Rev.* 62 (1996): 399.

Greenberg, David F. *The Construction of Homosexuality*. Chicago: University of Chicago Press, 1988.

Gregory, John De Witt, et al. *Understanding Family Law*. New York: Matthew Bender, 1993.

Grosz, Maya. To Have and to Hold: Property and State Regulation of Sexuality and Marriage. *NYU Rev. L. & Soc. Change* 24 (1998): 235.

Guillerman, Diane M. Comment, The Defense of Marriage Act: The Latest Maneuver in the Continuing Battle to Legalize Same-Sex Marriage. *Hous. L. Rev.* 34 (1997): 425.

Haavio-Mnnila, Elina, et al. *Unfinished Democracy: Women in Nordic Politics.* Trans. C. Badcock. Oxford: Pergamon Press, 1985.

Hakansson, P. A. Longing and Lifestyle: Lesbians' and Gay Men's Situation in a Heterosexual Society. Department of Sociology, University of Lund, Sweden, 1987.

Halkett, John. *Milton and the Idea of Matrimony: A Study of the Divorce Tracts and Paradise Lost.* New Haven, Conn.: Yale University Press, 1970.

Halperin, David M. *One Hundred Years of Homosexuality and Other Essays on Greek Love.* New York: Routledge, 1990.

Halsall, Paul. *Lesbian and Gay Marriage through History and Culture.* 1996. Available at http://www.bway.net /halsall/lgbh /lgbh-marriage.html.

Halvorsen, Rune. The Ambiguity of Lesbian and Gay Marriages: Change and Continuity in the Symbolic Order. In *Scandinavian Homosexualities: Essays on Gay and Lesbian Studies,* ed. J. Löfström. New York: Haworth Press, 1998.

Hamill, Katherine M. Comment, Romer v. Evans: Dulling the Equal Protection Gloss on Bowers v. Hardwick. *B.U. L. Rev.* 77 (1997): 655.

Hamilton, C., K. Standley, and D. Hodson, eds. *Family Law in Europe.* London: Butterworths, 1995.

Hamilton, Heather. Comment, The Defense of Marriage Act: A Critical Analysis of Its Constitutionality under the Full Faith and Credit Clause. *DePaul L. Rev.* 47 (1998): 943.

Hansen, Bent, and Henning Jørgensen. The Danish Partnership Law: Political Decision Making in Denmark and the National Danish Organization for Gays and Lesbians. In *The Third Pink Book: A Global View of Lesbian and Gay Liberation and Oppression,* ed. A. Hendriks, R. Tielman, and E. v. d. Veen. Buffalo: Prometheus Books, 1993.

Hansen, Erik Jørgen, Stein Ringen, Hannu Uusitalo, and Robert Erikson, eds. *Welfare Trends in the Scandinavian Countries.* New York: M. E. Sharpe, 1993.

Hansen, Marianne Nordli. *Sex Segregation and the Welfare State.* Oslo: Institute for Social Research, 1995.

Hansen, Preben, Bent Rying, Thorkild Borre, eds. *Women in Denmark in the 1980s.* Trans. Barbara Robin Steenstrup. Copenhagen: Royal Danish Ministry of Foreign Affairs, 1985.

Harlow, Holly J. Paternalism without Paternity: Discrimination against Single Women Seeking Artificial Insemination by Donor. *S. Cal. Rev. L. & Women's Stud.* 6 (1996): 173.

Heinze, Eric. *Sexual Orientation: A Human Right.* Dordrecht, Netherlands: Martinus Nijhoff, 1995.

Helfer, Laurence R. Finding a Consensus on Equality: The Homosexual Age of Consent and the European Convention on Human Rights. *N.Y.U. L. Rev.* 65 (1990): 1044.

———. Lesbian and Gay Rights as Human Rights: Strategies for a United Europe. *Virginia J. Int'l L.* 32 (1991): 157.

Helfer, Laurence R., and Alice M. Miller. Sexual Orientation and Human Rights: Toward a United States and Transnational Jurisprudence. *Harv. Hum. Rts. J.* 9 (1996): 61.

Helminiak, Daniel A. *What the Bible Really Says about Homosexuality.* San Francisco: Alamo Square Press, 1994.

Hendriks, Aart, Rob Tielman, and Evert van der Veen, eds. *The Third Pink Book: A Global View of Lesbian and Gay Liberation and Oppression.* Buffalo, N.Y.: Prometheus Books, 1993.

Henson, Deborah M. A Comparative Analysis of Same Sex Partnership Protections: Recommendations for American Reform. *Int'l J.L. & Fam.* 7 (1993): 282.

Herdt, Gilbert. *Same-Sex Different Cultures: Exploring Gay and Lesbian Lives.* Boulder, Colo.: Westview Press, 1997.

Herman, Jordan. The Fusion of Gay Rights and Feminism: Gender Identity and Marriage after Baeh v. Lewin. *Ohio St. L.J.* 56 (1995): 985.

Hernes, Helga Maria. *Welfare State and Women Power: Essays in State Feminism.* Oslo: Norwegian University Press, 1987.

Hogue, Lynn. State Common-Law Choice-of-Law Doctrine and Same-Sex "Marriage": How Will States Enforce the Public Policy Exception? *Creighton L. Rev.* 32 (1998): 29.

Hohengarten, William M. Note, Same-Sex Marriage and the Right of Privacy. *Yale L.J.* 103 (1994): 1495.

Holland, Maurice. The Modest Usefulness of DOMA Section 2. *Creighton L. Rev.* 32 (1998): 395.

Homer, Steven K. Against Marriage. *Harv. C.R.-C.L. L. Rev.* 29 (1993): 505.

Horne, Philip S. Challenging Public- and Private-Sector Benefit Schemes Which Discriminate against Unmarried Opposite-Sex and Same-Sex Partners. *L. & Sexuality* 4 (1994): 35.

Hosek, Linda. Denmark: Special Report on Same-Sex Marriage. *Honolulu Star Bulletin,* January 22, 1997, 16–18.

Hovermill, Joseph W. A Conflict of Laws and Morals: The Choice of Law Implications of Hawaii's Recognition of Same-Sex Marriages. *Md. L. Rev.* 53 (1994): 450.

Hunter, Nan D. Banned in the U.S.A.: What the Hardwick Ruling Will Mean. In *Sex Wars: Sexual Dissent and Political Culture,* ed. L. Duggan and N. D. Hunter. New York: Routledge, 1995.

———. Identity, Speech, and Equality. In *Sex Wars: Sexual Dissent and Political Culture,* ed. L. Duggan and N. D. Hunter. New York: Routledge, 1995.

———. Life after Hardwick. In *Sex Wars: Sexual Dissent and Political Culture,* ed. L. Duggan and N. D. Hunter. New York: Routledge, 1995.

———. Marriage, Law, and Gender: A Feminist Inquiry. In *Sex Wars: Sexual Dissent and Political Culture,* ed. L. Duggan and N. D. Hunter. New York: Routledge, 1995.

———. Sexual Dissent and the Family: The Sharon Kowalski Case. In *Sex Wars: Sexual Dissent and Political Culture,* ed. L. Duggan and N. D. Hunter. New York: Routledge, 1995.

ILGA-Europe. Equality for Lesbians and Gay Men: A Relevant Issue in the Civil and Social Dialogue. Brussels: ILGA-Europe, 1998.

———. Discrimination against Lesbian, Gay, and Bisexual Persons in Europe: The Legal Affairs and Human Rights Committee of the Parliamentary Assembly of the Council of Europe, February 16, 2000. ILGA-Europe, Brussels.

Ingebristen, Christine. *The Nordic States and European Unity.* Ithaca, N.Y.: Cornell University Press, 1998.

In Sickness and in Health, in Hawaii and Where Else? Conflict of Laws and Recognition of Same-Sex Marriages. *Harv. L. Rev.* 109 (1996): 2038.

Jacobs, Andrew M. Romer Wasn't Built in a Day: The Subtle Transformation in Judicial Argument over Gay Rights. *Wis. L. Rev.* (1996): 893.

Jallinoja, Riitta. Independence or Integration: The Women's Movement and Political Parties in Finland. In *The New Women's Movement: Feminism and Political Power in Europe and the USA,* ed. D. Dahlerup. London: Sage, 1986.

Jax, Christine. Same-Sex Marriage—Why Not? *Widener J. Pub. L.* 4 (1995): 461.

Jensen, Steffen. Recognition of Sexual Orientation: The Scandinavian Model. 1997. The English translation of this article is available from Landsforeningen for Bosser Og Lesbiske (National Danish Organization for Gays and Lesbians), Copenhagen.

Johnson, Julie L. B. Comment, The Meaning of "General Laws": The Extent of Congress's Power under the Full Faith and Credit Clause and the Constitutionality of the Defense of Marriage Act. *U. Pa. L. Rev.* 145 (1997): 1611.

Jones, Marian M. Lessons from Gay Marriages. *Psychology Today,* May–June 1997, at 22.

Joslin, Courtney G. Recent Development, Equal Protection, and Anti-Gay Legislation: Dismantling the Legacy of Bowers v. Hardwick—Romer v. Evans, 116 S. Ct. 1620. *Harv. C.R.-C.L. L. Rev.* 32 (1996): 225.

Kandoian, Ellen. Cohabitation, Common Law Marriage, and the Possibility of a Shared Moral Life. *Geo. L.J.* 75 (1987): 829.

Kanotz, Michael J. Comment, For Better or for Worse: A Critical Analysis of Florida's Defense of Marriage Act. *Fla. St. U. L. Rev.* 25 (1998): 439.

Kaplan, Gisela. *Contemporary Western European Feminism.* New York: New York University Press, 1992.

Karst, Kenneth L. The Pursuit of Manhood and the Desegregation of the Armed Forces. *UCLA L. Rev.* 38 (1991): 499.

Karvonen, Lauri, and Per Selle, eds. *Women in Nordic Politics: Closing the Gap.* Aldershot, Eng.: Dartmouth, 1995.

Katzenstein, Mary Fainsod, and Carol McClurg Mueller, eds. *The Women's Movements of the United States and Western Europe: Consciousness, Political Opportunity, and Public Policy.* Philadelphia: Temple University Press, 1987.

Katzenstein, Mary Fainsod, and Hege Skjeie, eds. *Going Public: National Histories of Women's Enfranchisement and Women's Participation within State Institutions.* Oslo: Institute for Social Research, 1990.

Keane, Thomas M. Aloha, Marriage? Constitutional and Choice of Law Arguments for Recognition of Same-Sex Marriage. *Stan. L. Rev.* 47 (1995): 499.

Keefer, Timothy Joseph. Note, DOMA as a Defensible Exercise of Congressional Power under the Full-Faith-and-Credit Clause. *Wash & Lee L. Rev.* 54 (1997): 1635.

Keller, Christopher J. Divining the Priest: A Case Comment on Baehr v. Lewin. *Law & Ineq. J.* 12 (1994): 483.

Kelly, Jon-Peter. Act of Infidelity: Why the Defense of Marriage Act Is Unfaithful to the Constitution. *Cornell J.L. & Pub. Pol'y* 7 (1997): 203.

Kendell, Kathryn Dean. Principles and Prejudice: Lesbian and Gay Civil Marriage and the Realization of Equality. *J. Contemp. L.* 22 (1996): 81.

Kennedy, Randall. How Are We Doing with Loving? Race, Law, and Intermarriage. *B.U. L. Rev.* 77 (1997): 815.

Knauer, Nancy J. Domestic Partnership and Same-Sex Relationships: A Marketplace Innovation and a Less Than Perfect Institutional Choice. *Temple Pol. & Civ. Rts. L. Rev.* 7 (1998): 337.

————. Foreword to Symposium: Constructing Family, Constructing Change: Shifting Legal Perspectives on Same-Sex Relationships. *Temple Pol. & Civ. Rts. L. Rev.* 7 (1998): 245.

Kohm, Lynne Marie. The Homosexual "Union": Should Gay and Lesbian Partnerships Be Granted the Same Status as Marriage? *J. Contemp. L.* 22 (1996): 51.

Koppelman, Andrew. The Miscegenation Analogy: Sodomy Law as Sex Discrimination. *Yale L.J.* 98 (1988): 145.

————. Why Discrimination against Lesbians and Gay Men Is Sex Discrimination. *N.Y.U. L. Rev.* 69 (1994): 197.

————. *Antidiscrimination Law & Social Equality.* New Haven, Conn.: Yale University Press, 1996.

————. Same-Sex Marriage and Public Policy: The Miscegenation Precedents. *Quinnipiac L. Rev.* 16 (1996): 105.

————. 1997 Survey of Books Relating to the Law: Sex, Law, and Equality: Three Arguments for Gay Rights. *Mich. L. Rev.* 95 (1997): 1636.

————. Dumb and DOMA: Why the Defense of Marriage Act Is Unconstitutional. *Iowa L. Rev.* 83 (1997): 1.

————. Same-Sex Marriage, Choice of Law, and Public Policy. *Tex. L. Rev.* 76 (1998): 921.

Kovacs, Kathryn E. Recognizing Gay and Lesbian Families: Marriage and Parental Rights. *L. & Sexuality* 5 (1995): 513.

Kramer, Larry. The Public Policy Exception and the Problem of Extra-Territorial Recognition of Same-Sex Marriage. *Quinnipiac L. Rev.* 16 (1996): 153.

————. Same-Sex Marriage, Conflict of Laws, and the Unconstitutional Public Policy Exception. *Yale L.J.* 106 (1997): 1965.

Kreimer, Seth F. Territoriality and Moral Dissensus: Thoughts on Abortion, Slavery, Gay Marriage, and Family Values. *Quinnipiac L. Rev.* 16 (1997): 161.

Kubasek, Nancy K., et al. Fashioning a Tolerable Domestic Partners Statute in an Environment Hostile to Same-Sex Marriage. *L. & Sexuality* 7 (1997): 55.

Kuykendall, Mae. On Defined Terms and Cultural Consensus. *J.L. & Pol.* 13 (1997): 199.

La Fayette, Madame de. *The Princess of Clèves.* Trans. W. J. Cobb. New York: Signet, 1961.

Landau, Eve C. *The Rights of Working Women in the European Community.* Luxembourg: Commission of the European Communities, 1985.

Laslett, Peter, ed. *John Locke: Two Treatises on Government.* Cambridge: Cambridge University Press, 1960.

Law, Sylvia A. Women, Work, Welfare, and the Preservation of Patriarchy. *U. Pa. L. Rev.* 131 (1983): 1249.

————. Rethinking Sex and the Constitution. *U. Pa. L. Rev.* 132 (1984): 955.

————. Homosexuality and the Social Meaning of Gender. *Wis. L. Rev.* (1988): 187.

———. Is the Law Male? The Case for Family Law. *Chicago-Kent L. Rev.* 69 (1993): 345.

Leonard, Arthur S. Lesbian and Gay Families and the Law: A Progress Report. *Fordham Urb. L.J.* 21 (1994): 927.

———. Review of *Going for the Brass Ring: The Case for Same-Sex Marriage,* by Arthur S. Leonard. *Cornell L. Rev.* 82 (1997): 572.

Lewin, Ellen. *Recognizing Ourselves: Ceremonies of Lesbian and Gay Commitment.* New York: Columbia University Press, 1998.

Lewis, Claudia. From This Day Forward: A Feminine Moral Discourse on Homosexual Marriage. *Yale L.J.* 97 (1988): 1783.

Lewis, Kevin H. Note, Equal Protection after Romer v. Evans: Implications for the Defense of Marriage Act and Other Laws. *Hastings L.J.* 49 (1997): 175.

Liliequist, Joanes. State Policy, Popular Discourse, and the Silence on Homosexual Acts in Early Modern Sweden. *J. Homosexuality* 34 (3–4) (1998): 15.

Lin, Timothy E. Note, Social Norms and Judicial Decisionmaking: Examining the Role of Narratives in Same-Sex Adoption Cases. *Colum. L. Rev.* 99 (1999): 739.

Link, David. The Tie That Binds: Recognizing Privacy and the Family Commitments of Same-Sex Couples. *Loy. L.A. L. Rev.* 23 (1990): 1055.

Lødrup, Peter. Norway: The New Marriage Act. *J. Fam. L.* 31 (1992–93): 411.

———. Registered Partnership in Norway. In *The International Survey of Family Law,* ed. A. Bainham. The Hague: Martinus Nijhoff, 1994.

Löfström, Jan, ed. *Scandinavian Homosexualities: Essays on Gay and Lesbian Studies.* New York: Haworth Press, 1998.

Lopez, Alma G. Homosexual Marriage, the Changing American Family, and the Heterosexual Right to Privacy. *Seton Hall L. Rev.* 24 (1993): 347.

Lorio, Kathryn Venturatos. The Process of Regulating Assisted Reproductive Technologies: What We Can Learn from Our Neighbors—What Translates and What Does Not. *Loy. L. Rev.* 45 (1999): 247.

Lützen, Karin. Gay and Lesbian Politics: Assimilation or Survivorship: A Danish Perspective. *J. Homosexuality* 34 (3–4) (1998): 233.

Macedo, Stephen. Homosexuality and the Conservative Mind. *Geo. L.J.* 84 (1995): 261.

———. Reply to Critics. *Geo. L.J.* 84 (1995): 329.

Mackenzie, Robin. Transsexuals' Legal Sexual Status and Same-Sex Marriage in New Zealand: M. v. M. *Otago L. Rev.* 7 (1993): 556.

Madar, Donald. Exclusion, Toleration, Acceptance, Integration: The Experience of Dutch Reformed Churches with Homosexuality and Homosexuals in the Church. *J. Homosexuality* 25 (4) (1993): 101.

Mahkonen, Sami. From Control of the Family to Its Autonomy. *Scandinavian Stud. in L.* 32 (1988): 117.

Malin, Martin H. Fathers and Parental Leave. *Tex. L. Rev.* 17 (1994): 1047.

Marcin, Raymond B. Natural Law, Homosexual Conduct, and the Public Policy Exception. *Creighton L. Rev.* 32 (1998): 67.

Marcosson, Samuel A. The Lesson of the Same-Sex Marriage Trial: The Importance of Pushing Opponents of Lesbian and Gay Rights to Their "Second Line of Defense." *U. Louisville J. Fam. L.* 35 (1996–97): 721.

Marcus, Eric. *Together Forever: Gay and Lesbian Marriage.* New York: Anchor Books, 1998.

Martin, Jorge. English Polygamy Law and the Danish Registered Partnership Act: A Case for the Consistent Treatment of Foreign Polygamous Marriages and Danish Same-Sex Marriages in England. *Cornell Int'l L.J.* 27 (1994): 419.

Martinac, Paula. *The Gay and Lesbian Book of Love and Marriage.* New York: Broadway Books, 1998.

Mattigssen, Astrid A. M., and Charlene L. Smith. Dutch Treats: The Lessons the U.S. Can Learn from How the Netherlands Protects Lesbians and Gays. *American U. J. Gender & L.* 4 (1996): 303.

Maxwell, Nancy, Astrid Mattigssen, and Charlene Smith. Legal Protection for All the Children: Dutch-American Comparison of Lesbian and Gay Parent Adoptions. *Electronic J. Comp. L.* 3.1 (1999), http://law.kub.nl/ejcl/31/art31-2.htm.

McCarthy, Martha A., and Joanna L. Radbord. Family Law for Same-Sex Couples: Chart(er)ing the Course. *Canadian J. Fam. L.* 15 (1998): 101.

McGee Crotty, Patricia. *Women and Family Law: Connecting the Public and the Private.* New York: Peter Lung, 1997.

McGowan, Sharon M. Recent Development: The Fate of ENDA in the Wake of Maine: A Wake-Up Call to Moderate Republicans. *Harv. J. on Legis.* 35 (1998): 623.

Meier, Catharine G. Protecting Parental Leave: A Fundamental Rights Model. *Willamette L. Rev.* 33 (1997): 177.

Meyer, Donald. *Sex and Power: The Rise of Women in America, Russia, Sweden, and Italy.* Middletown, Conn.: Wesleyan University Press, 1987.

Meyer, Jan. Guess Who's Coming to Dinner This Time? A Study of Gay Intimate Relationships and the Support for Those Relationships. In *Homosexuality and Family Relations,* ed. F. W. Bozett and M. B. Sussman. New York: Haworth Press, 1990.

Michigan Legislative Service Bureau. Same-Sex Marriage. In *Research Brief No. 15.* Michigan Legislative Service Bureau, Legislative Research Division, 1996.

Mills, Kim I., and Daryl Herrschaft. The State of the Workplace for Lesbian, Gay, Bisexual, and Transgendered Americans. Washington, D.C.: Human Rights Campaign, 1999.

Ministry of Children and Family Affairs. Translation of the Norwegian Bill on Registered Partnerships for Gays and Lesbians. Oslo, Norway, 1998.

Minow, Martha. The Free Exercise of Families. *U. Ill. L. Rev.* (1991): 925.

Mohr, Richard D. *A More Perfect Union: Why Straight America Must Stand Up for Gay Rights.* Boston: Beacon Press, 1994.

Moran, Leslie J., Daniel Monk, and Sarah Beresford, eds. *Legal Queeries: Lesbian, Gay, and Transgender Legal Studies.* London: Cassell, 1998.

Morris, Robert J. Symposium: Intersections: Sexuality, Cultural Tradition, and the Law: Configuring the Bo(u)nds of Marriage: The Implications of Hawaiian Culture & Values for the Debate about Homogamy. *Yale J.L. & Human.* 8 (1996): 105.

———. "What Though Our Rights Have Been Assailed?" Mormons, Politics, Same-Sex Marriage, and Cultural Abuse in the Sandwich Islands (Hawaii). *Women's Rts. L. Rep.* 18 (1997): 129.

Mosikatsana, T. L. Comment on the Adoption by K and B, RE (1995) 31 CRR (2d) 151. *South African J. Hum. Rts.* 12 (1996): 582.

——. The Definitional Exclusion of Gays & Lesbians from Family Status. *South African J. Hum. Rts.* 12 (1996): 549.

Myers, Richard S. Same-Sex "Marriage" and the Public Policy Doctrine. *Creighton L. Rev.* 32 (1998): 45.

Neal, Odeana R. Writing Rules Does Not Right Wrongs. *Temple Pol. & Civ. Rts. L. Rev.* 7 (1998): 303.

Neri, Demetrio. Child or Parent Oriented Controls of Reproductive Technologies? In *Creating the Child*, ed. D. Evans and N. Pickering. Boston: Martinus Nijhoff, 1996.

Nicolson, Marjorie Hope. *John Milton: A Reader's Guide to His Poetry.* New York: Octagon Books, 1990.

Nielsen, Linda. Family Rights and the "Registered Partnership" in Denmark. *Int'l J.L. & Fam.* 4 (1990): 297.

——. Denmark: New Rules Regarding Marriage Contracts and Reform Considerations concerning Children. *U. Louisville J. Fam. L.* 31 (1992–93): 309.

——. Denmark: Harmonizing Family and Work and Protecting the Vulnerable. *U. Louisville J. Fam. L.* 33 (1995): 317.

——. Denmark: The Family Principle and the Individual Principle and Recent Legislative News. In *The International Survey of Family Law 1995*, ed. A. Bainham. The Hague: Martinus Nijhoff, 1997.

Nielsen, Ruth. *Equality in Law between Men and Women in the European Community: Denmark.* Ed. M. Verwilghen and F. V. Prondzynski. The Hague: Martinus Nijhoff, 1995.

Nijeholt, Greertje Lycklama à, Virginia Vargas, and Saskia Wieringa, eds. *Women's Movements and Public Policy in Europe, Latin America, and the Caribbean.* Ed. C. T. Mohanty. Vol. 2, *Gender, Culture, and Global Politics.* New York: Garland, 1998.

Nilsson, Gert. Intercession or Blessing? Theological Reflections on a Swedish Liturgy for Homosexual Couples. *Ecumenical Rev.* 50 (1998): 64.

Noble, Simone. Same-Sex Marriage under the Final Constitution. *Responsa Meridiana* (1997): 91.

Nordic Council of Ministers. *Women and Men in the Nordic Countries: Facts and Figures 1994.* Copenhagen: Nordic Council of Ministers, 1994.

Norrie, Kenneth. Reproductive Technology, Transsexualism, and Homosexuality: New Problems for International Private Law. *Int'l & Comp. L.Q.* 43 (1994): 757.

Norwegian Ministry of Children and Family Affairs. *Gender Equality in Norway: The National Report to the Fourth UN Conference on Women in Beijing 1995.* 1994.

Note, Patriarchy Is Such a Drag: The Strategic Possibilities of a Postmodern Account of Gender. *Harv. L. Rev.* 108 (1995): 1973.

Nozari, Fariborz. The 1987 Swedish Family Law Reform. *Int'l J. Legal Info.* 17 (3) (1989): 219.

——. *The 1987 Swedish Marriage Code.* Washington, D.C.: Law Library of Congress, 1989.

Nussbaum, Martha C. *Sex and Social Justice.* New York: Oxford University Press, 1999.

Nygh, Peter. Homosexual Partnerships in Sweden. *Australian J. Fam. L.* 11 (1997): 11.

O'Brien, Raymond C. Domestic Partnership: Recognition and Responsibility. *San Diego L. Rev.* 32 (1995): 163.

———. Single-Gender Marriage: A Religious Perspective. *Temple Pol. & Civ. Rts. L. Rev.* 7 (1998): 429.

O'Connor, Eugene. Introduction to *On Homosexuality: Lysis, Phaedrus, and Symposium,* trans. B. Jowett. Great Books in Philosophy. Buffalo, N.Y.: Prometheus Books, 1991.

Olyan, Saul M., and Martha C. Nussbaum, eds. *Sexual Orientation and Human Rights in American Religious Discourse.* New York: Oxford University Press, 1998.

Outshoorn, Joyce. The Feminist Movement and Abortion Policy in the Netherlands. In *The New Women's Movement: Feminism and Political Power in Europe and the USA,* ed. D. Dahlerup. London: Sage, 1986.

Pantazis, A. An Argument for the Legal Recognition of Gay and Lesbian Marriage. *South African L.J.* 114 (1997): 556.

Parmar, Sejal. The Treaty of Amsterdam. In After Amsterdam: Sexual Orientation and the European Union: A Guide. ILGA Europe, Brussels, September 1999. Available at http://www.steff.suite.dk/ilgaeur.htm.

Parry, Martin L. *The Law Relating to Cohabitation.* 3d ed. London: Sweet and Maxwell, 1993.

Pascoe, Peggy. Miscegenation Law, Court Cases, and Ideologies of "Race" in Twentieth-Century America. *J. Am. Hist.* 83 (1996): 44.

Pateman, Carole. *The Sexual Contract.* Stanford, Calif.: Stanford University Press, 1988.

———. *The Disorder of Women: Democracy, Feminism, and Political Theory.* Stanford, Calif.: Stanford University Press, 1989.

Patten, James M. Comment, The Defense of Marriage Act: How Congress Said "No" to Full Faith and Credit and the Constitution. *Santa Clara L. Rev.* 38 (1998): 939.

Patterson, Charlotte J. Adoption of Minor Children by Lesbian and Gay Adults: A Social Science Perspective. *Duke J. Gender L. & Pol'y* 2 (1995): 191.

Patton, Rodney. A Focus Edition: Domestic Issues and Crimes of Intimacy: Student Work: Queerly Unconstitutional? South Carolina Bans Same-Sex Marriage. *S.C. L. Rev.* 48 (1997): 685.

Pavano, Thomas Adolph. Gay and Lesbian Rights: Adults Adopting Adults. *Conn. Prob. L.J.* 2 (1987): 251.

Pedersen, Inger Margrete. Features of Danish Law concerning Property Rights and Obligations of Unmarried Cohabitants. *Scandinavian Stud. in L.* 25 (1981): 131.

Pedersen, Marianne H. Denmark: Homosexual Marriages and New Rules Regarding Separation and Divorce. *J. Fam. L.* 30 (1992): 289.

Perugini, Maria A. Note, Board of Education of Oklahoma City v. Dowell: Protection of Local Authority or Disregard for the Purpose of Brown v. Board of Education. *Cath. U. L. Rev.* 41 (1992): 779.

Plato. *The Symposium and The Phaedrus: Plato's Erotic Dialogues.* Trans. W. S. Cobb. Albany: State University of New York Press, 1993.

Pocar, Valerio, and Paola Ronfani, eds. *Family, Law, and Social Policy.* Onati, Spain: Onati International Institute for the Sociology of Law, 1991.

Polikoff, Nancy D. This Child Does Have Two Mothers: Redefining Parenthood to Meet the Needs of Children in Lesbian-Mother and Other Nontraditional Families. *Geo. L.J.* 78 (1990): 459.

————. We Will Get What We Ask For: Why Legalizing Gay & Lesbian Marriage Will Not "Dismantle the Legal Structure of Gender in Every Marriage." *Va. L. Rev.* 79 (1993): 1535.

Pooley, Lisa M. Heterosexism and Children's Best Interest: Conflicting Concepts in Nancy S. v. Michele G. *U.S.F. L. Rev.* 27 (1993): 477.

Popenoe, David. *Disturbing the Nest: Family Change and Decline in Modern Societies.* New York: Aldine de Gruyter, 1988.

Posner, Richard A. *Sex and Reason.* Cambridge, Mass.: Harvard University Press, 1992.

Pouncy, Charles R. P. Marriage and Domestic Partnership: Rationality and Inequality. *Temple Pol. & Civ. Rts. L. Rev.* 7 (1998): 363.

Price, Deb. Roads to Equality: Gay Rights in Europe: Danes Pave the Way for Partnerships: Copenhagen's Gay and Lesbian Couples Enjoy Rights That Remain a Distant Dream for American Same-Sex Couples. *Detroit News,* October 29, 1997, E1:4.

Prinz, Christopher. *Cohabiting, Married, or Single? Portraying, Analyzing, and Modeling New Living Arrangements in the Changing Societies of Europe.* Aldershot, Eng.: Avebury, 1995.

Provost, Melissa A. Comment, Disregarding the Constitution in the Name of Defending Marriage: The Unconstitutionality of the Defense of Marriage Act. *Seton Hall Const. L.J.* 8 (1997): 157.

Rabinowitz, Clarice B. Proposals for Progress: Sodomy Laws and the European Convention on Human Rights. *Brooklyn J. Int'l L.* 21 (1995): 425.

Rahdert, Mark C. Same-Sex Relationships: A Constitutional Commentary. *Temple Pol. & Civ. Rts. L. Rev.* 7 (1998): 495.

Ramsøy, Natalie Rogoff. Non-Marital Cohabitation and Change in Norms: The Case of Norway. *Acta Sociologica* 37 (1994): 23.

Regan, Milton C., Jr. *Alone Together: Law and the Meanings of Marriage.* New York: Oxford University Press, 1999.

Rensberger, Jeffrey L. Same-Sex Marriages and the Defense of Marriage Act: A Deviant View of an Experiment in Full Faith and Credit. *Creighton L. Rev.* 32 (1998): 409.

Rhode, Deborah L. *Justice and Gender: Sex Discrimination and the Law.* Cambridge, Mass.: Harvard University Press, 1989.

————. *Speaking of Sex: The Denial of Gender Inequality.* Cambridge, Mass.: Harvard University Press, 1997.

Richards, David A. J. *Toleration and the Constitution.* New York: Oxford University Press, 1986.

————. *Foundations of American Constitutionalism.* New York: Oxford University Press, 1989.

————. *Conscience and the Constitution: History, Theory, and Law of the Reconstruction Amendments.* Princeton, N.J.: Princeton University Press, 1993.

————. *Women, Gays, and the Constitution: The Grounds for Feminism and Gay Rights in Culture and Law.* Chicago: University of Chicago Press, 1998.

————. *Identity and the Case for Gay Rights: Race, Gender, Religion as Analogies.* Chicago: University of Chicago Press, 1999.

Riegel, Stephen J. The Persistent Career of Jim Crow: Lower Federal Courts and the "Separate but Equal" Doctrine 1865–1896. In *12 Black Southerners and the Law 1865–1900,* ed. D. G. Nieman. New York: Garland, 1994.

Robb, Barbara A. Note, The Constitutionality of the Defense of Marriage Act in the Wake of Romer v. Evans. *New Eng. L. Rev.* 32 (1997): 263.

Robertson, John A. Assisted Reproductive Technology and the Family. *Hastings L.J.* 47 (1996): 911.

Robson, John M., ed. *Collected Works of John Stuart Mill.* Toronto: University of Toronto Press, 1984.

Robson, Ruthann. The State of Marriage. *Y.B. New Zealand Jurisprudence* 1 (1997): 1.

Roleff, Tamara L., ed. *Gay Marriage.* San Diego: Greenhaven Press, 1998.

Roleff, Tamara L., and Mary E. Williams, eds. *Marriage and Divorce.* San Diego: Greenhaven Press, 1997.

Rolston, Bill, and Anna Eggert, eds. *Abortion in the New Europe: A Comparative Handbook.* Westport, Conn.: Greenwood Press, 1994.

Ross, Michael W. Married Homosexual Men: Prevalence and Background. In *Homosexuality and Family Relations,* ed. F. W. Bozett and M. B. Sussman. New York: Haworth Press, 1990.

Roth, Marianne. The Norwegian Act on Registered Partnership for Homosexual Couples. *U. Louisville J. Fam. L.* 35 (1996–97): 467.

Rotondi, M., ed. *The Marriage.* Ed. M. Rotondi. Vol. 11, *Inchieste di diritto comparato.* Milan: Dott A. Giuffrè, 1998.

Rover Bailey, Elizabeth. Note, Three Men and a Baby: Second-Parent Adoptions and their Implications. *B.C. L. Rev.* 38 (1997): 569.

Rubinstein, William B. We Are Family: A Reflection on the Search for Legal Recognition of Lesbian and Gay Relationships. *J.L. & Pol.* 8 (1991): 89.

———. *Sexual Orientation and the Law.* 2d ed. St. Paul: West, 1997.

Rule, Sheila. Rights for Gay Couples in Denmark. *New York Times,* October 2, 1989, A8.

Ruskay-Kidd, Scott. Note, The Defense of Marriage Act and the Overextension of Congressional Authority. *Colum. L. Rev.* 97 (1997): 1435.

Sachdev, Paul, ed. *International Handbook on Abortion.* New York: Greenwood Press, 1988.

Saldeen, Ake. Sweden: Reforms of Marriage, Inheritance, and Cohabitation Proposed. *J. Fam. L.* 26 (1987–88): 197.

———. Sweden: More Rights for Children and Homosexuals. *J. Fam. L.* 27 (1988–89): 295.

———. Sweden: Changes in the Code on Marriage and Plans for Reform in the Areas of Adoption, Child Custody, and Fetal Diagnostics. *J. Fam. L.* 29 (1990–91): 431.

———. Sweden: Family Counseling, The Tortious Liability of Parents and Homosexual Partnership. *U. of Louisville J. Fam. L.* 33 (1995): 513.

Samar, Vincent J. *The Right to Privacy: Gays, Lesbians, and the Constitution.* Philadelphia: Temple University Press, 1991.

Sanders, A. J. G. M. Homosexuality and the Law: A Gay Revolution in South Africa? *J. African L.* 41 (1997): 100.

Schadbach, Kai. The Benefits of Comparative Law: A Continental European View. *B.U. Int'l L.J.* 16 (1998): 331.

Scherf, Yvonne. Registered Partnership in the Netherlands: A Quick Scan. Amsterdam: Dutch Ministry of Justice, Scientific Research, and Documentation Center, 1999.

Schneider, Carl E. Moral Discourse and the Transformation of American Family Law. *Mich. L. Rev.* 83 (1985): 1803.

———. The Channeling Function in Family Law. *Hofstra L. Rev.* 20 (1992): 495.

————. Marriage, Morals, and the Law: No-Fault Divorce and Moral Discourse. *Utah L. Rev.* (1994): 503.

Schreiber, Anna P. The Status of Women in the United States and the Scandinavian Countries. In *Comparative Human Rights,* ed. R. P. Claude. Baltimore: Johns Hopkins University Press, 1976.

Scott, Elizabeth S. Rehabilitating Liberalism in Modern Divorce Law. *Utah L. Rev.* (1994): 687.

Scott, John. *Same-Sex Partnerships? A Christian Perspective.* Michigan: Fleming H. Revell, 1998.

Scott-Moncrieff, C. K., trans. *The Letters of Abélard and Heloïse.* London: Guy Chapman, 1925.

Seager, Joni. *The State of Women in the World Atlas.* New rev. 2d ed. London: Penguin Reference, 1997.

Shanley, Mary Lyndon, and Carole Pateman, eds. *Feminist Interpretations and Political Theory.* University Park: Pennsylvania State University Press, 1991.

Shapiro, Julie. Custody and Conduct: How the Law Fails Lesbian and Gay Parents and Their Children. *Ind. L.J.* 71 (1996): 623.

Sherman, Jeffrey. Undue Influence and the Homosexual Testator. *U. Pitt. L. Rev.* 42 (1981): 221.

Sherman, Suzanne, ed. *Lesbian and Gay Marriage: Private Commitments, Public Ceremonies.* Philadelphia: Temple University Press, 1992.

Shuki-Kunze, Jennie R. Note, The "Defenseless" Marriage Act: The Constitutionality of the Defense of Marriage Act as an Extension of Congressional Power under the Full Faith and Credit Clause. *Case W. Res.* 48 (1998): 351.

Siegel, Reva. The Critical Use of History: Why Equal Protection No Longer Protects: The Evolving Forms of Status-Enforcing State Action. *Stan. L. Rev.* 46 (1997): 1111.

Silberman, Linda J. Can the Island of Hawaii Bind the World? A Comment on Same-Sex Marriage and Federalism Values. *Quinnipiac L. Rev.* 16 (1996): 161.

Silén, Birgitta. Women and Power. *Scandinavian Rev.* 76 (1987–88): 91.

Silver, Bradley. 'Til Deportation Do Us Part: The Extension of Spousal Recognition to Same-Sex Partnerships. *South African J. Hum. Rts.* 12 (1996): 575.

Singer, Irving. *The Nature of Love.* 3 vols. Vol. I, *Plato to Luther* (2d ed.); vol. 2, *Courtly and Romantic;* vol. 3, *The Modern World.* Chicago: University of Chicago Press, 1984.

Singer, Jana B. The Privatization of Family Law. *Wis. L. Rev.* (1992): 1443.

Sirluck, Ernest, ed. *Complete Prose Works of John Milton.* Vol. 2. New Haven, Conn.: Yale University Press, 1959.

Skocpol, Theda. *Gender and the Origin of Modern Social Policies (Vilhelm Aubert Memorial Lecture 1992).* Oslo: Institute for Social Research, 1993.

Sloane, Craig A. A Rose by Any Other Name: Marriage and the Danish Registered Partnership Act. *Cardozo J. Int'l & Comp. L.* 5 (1997): 189.

Smith, George P., II. *Family Values and the New Society: Dilemmas of the 21st Century.* Westport, Conn.: Praeger, 1998.

Smith, Henry. Preparative to Marriage. In *The Sermons of Maister Henre Smith.* London: T. Tabb, 1657.

Snodgrass, Gwendolyn L. Creating Family without Marriage: The Advantages and Disadvantages of Adult Adoption among Gay and Lesbian Partners. *Brandeis J. Fam. L.* 36 (1997–98): 75.

Solimine, Michael E. Competitive Federalism and Interstate Recognition of Marriage. *Creighton L. Rev.* 32 (1998): 83.

Spackman, Paul L. Grant v. South West Trains: Equality for Same-Sex Partners in the European Community. *Am. U. J. Int'l L. & Pol'y* 12 (1997): 1063.

Stark, Barbara. Foreword, Rappaccini's Daughters? In *Family Law and Gender Bias: Comparative Perspectives,* ed. B. Stark. Greenwich, Conn.: JAI Press, 1992.

———. Guys and Dolls: Remedial Nurturing Skills in Post-Divorce Practice, Feminist Theory, and Family Law Doctrine. *Hofstra L. Rev.* 26 (1997): 293.

Starr, Karla J. Note, Adoption by Homosexuals: A Look at Differing State Court Opinions. *Ariz. L. Rev.* 40 (1998): 1497.

Stiers, Gretchen A. *From This Day Forward: Commitment, Marriage, and Family in Lesbian and Gay Relationships.* New York: St. Martin's Press, 1999.

Stoddard, Thomas B. Why Gay People Should Seek the Right to Marry. In *Lesbian and Gay Marriage: Private Commitments, Public Ceremonies,* ed. S. Sherman. Philadelphia: Temple University Press, 1992.

———. Bleeding Heart: Reflections on Using the Law to Make Social Change. *N.Y.U. L. Rev.* 72 (1997): 967.

Stone, Lawrence. *The Family, Sex, and Marriage in England 1500–1800.* New York: Harper and Row, 1977.

Stone, Lawrence, and Jeanne C. Flawtier Stone. *An Open Elite? England 1540–1880.* Oxford: Clarendon Press, 1984.

Strassberg, Maura I. Distinctions of Form or Substance: Monogamy, Polygamy, and Same-Sex Marriage. *N.C. L. Rev.* 75 (1997): 1501.

Strasser, Mark. Domestic Relations Jurisprudence and the Great, Slumbering Baehr: On Definitional Preclusion, Equal Protection, and Fundamental Interests. *Fordham L. Rev.* 64 (1995): 921.

———. Judicial Good Faith and the Baehr Essentials: On Giving Credit Where It's Due. *Rutgers L.J.* 28 (1997): 313.

———. *Legally Wed: Same-Sex Marriage and the Constitution.* Ithaca, N.Y.: Cornell University Press, 1997.

———. Baker and Some Recipes for Disaster: On DOMA, Covenant Marriages, and Full Faith and Credit Jurisprudence. *Brooklyn L. Rev.* 64 (1998): 307.

———. DOMA and the Two Faces of Federalism. *Creighton L. Rev.* 32 (1998): 457.

———. Ex Post Facto Laws, Bills of Attainder, and the Definition of Punishment: On DOMA, the Hawaii Amendment, and Federal Constitutional Constraints. *Syracuse L. Rev.* 48 (1998): 227.

———. For Whom Bell Tolls: On Subsequent Domiciles' Refusing to Recognize Same-Sex Marriage. *U. Cin. L. Rev.* 66 (1998): 339.

———. Queer Matters: Emerging Issues in Sexual Orientation Law: Sodomy, Adultery, and Same-Sex Marriage: On Legal Analysis and Fundamental Interests. *UCLA Women's L.J.* 8 (1998): 313.

———. *The Challenge of Same-Sex Marriage: Federalist Principles and Constitutional Protections.* Westport, Conn.: Praeger, 1999.

Strauss, David A. Discriminatory Intent and the Taming of Brown. *U. Chi. L. Rev.* 56 (1989): 935.

Strommen, Erik F. Hidden Branches and Growing Pains: Homosexuality and the Family Tree. In *Homosexuality and Family Relations,* ed. F. W. Bozett and M. B. Sussman. New York: Haworth Press, 1990.

Styrkársdóttir, Audur. From Social Movement to Political Party: The New Women's Movement in Iceland. In *The New Women's Movement: Feminism and Political Power in Europe and the USA,* ed. D. Dahlerup. London: Sage, 1986.

Sullivan, Andrew. Recognition of Same-Sex Marriage. *Quinnipiac L. Rev.* 16 (1996): 13.

———. *Virtually Normal: An Argument about Homosexuality.* New York: Vintage Books, 1996.

———. *Same-Sex Marriage: Pro and Con.* New York: Vintage Books, 1997.

Sunstein, Cass R. The Supreme Court 1995 Term Forward: Leaving Things Undecided. *Harv. L. Rev.* 110 (1996): 4.

———. Sexual Orientation and the Constitution: A Note on the Relationship between Due Process and Equal Protection. *U. Chi. L. Rev.* 55 (1988): 1161.

Tannenbaum, Steven M. *Adoption by Lesbians and Gay Men: An Overview of the Law in the 50 States.* New York: Lambda Legal Defense and Education Fund, 1996.

Tatchell, Peter. *Europe in the Pink: Lesbian and Gay Equality in the New Europe.* London: Gay Men's Press, 1992.

Tharpes, Yvonne L. Comment, Bowers v. Hardwick and the Legitimization of Homophobia in America. *How. L.J.* 30 (1987): 537.

Thomas, Kendall. Beyond the Privacy Principle. *Colum. L. Rev.* 92 (1992): 1431.

Thompson-Schneider, Donna. The Arc of History: Or, the Resurrection of Feminism's Sameness/Difference Dichotomy in the Gay and Lesbian Marriage Debate. *L. & Sexuality* 7 (1997): 1.

Tielman, Rob, and Hans Hammelburg. World Survey on the Social and Legal Position of Gays and Lesbians. In *The Third Pink Book: A Global View of Lesbian and Gay Liberation and Oppression,* ed. A. Hendriks, R. Tielman, and E. v. d. Veen. Buffalo, N.Y.: Prometheus Books, 1993.

Tillyard, E. M. W. *Milton.* New York: Barnes and Noble, 1967.

Tosswill, Kate. *Lesbian and Gay Men Seeking Custody and Visitation: An Overview of the State of the Law.* New York: Lambda Legal Defense and Education Fund, 1996.

Tóth, Olga. No Envy, No Pity. In *Gender Politics and Post-Communism,* ed. N. Funk and M. Mueller. New York: Routledge, 1993.

Toussaint, Sherri L. Defense of Marriage Act: Isn't It Ironic . . . Don't You Think? A Little Too Ironic? *Neb. L. Rev.* 76 (1997): 924.

Vaid, Urvashi. *Virtual Equality: The Mainstreaming of Gay and Lesbian Liberation.* New York: Anchor Books Doubleday, 1995.

Valdes, Francisco. Queers, Sissies, Dykes, and Tomboys: Deconstructing the Conflation of "Sex," "Gender," and "Sexual Orientation" in Euro-American Law and Society. *Calif. L. Rev.* 83 (1995): 3.

———. Sexuality, Cultural Tradition, and the Law: Unpacking Hetero-Patriarchy: Tracing the Conflation of Sex, Gender & Sexual Orientation to Its Origins. *Yale J.L. & Human.* 8 (1996): 161.

Van der Meer, Theo. Sodom's Seed in the Netherlands: The Emergence of Homosexuality in the Early Modern Period. *J. Homosexuality* 34 (1) (1997): 1.

Van der Meide, Wayne. Legislating Equality: A Review of Laws Affecting Gay, Lesbian, Bisexual, and Transgendered People in the United States. Washington, D.C.: Policy Institute of the National Gay and Lesbian Task Force, 2000.

Van Naerssen, A. X., ed. *Gay Life in Dutch Society*. New York: Harrington Park Press, 1987.

Vlaardingerbroek, Paul. Marriage, Divorce, and Living Arrangements in the Netherlands. *Fam. L.Q.* 29 (1995): 635.

Waaldijk, Kees. *Tip of an Iceberg: Anti-Lesbian and Anti-Gay Discrimination in Europe 1980–1990*. Utrecht, Netherlands: International Lesbian and Gay Association, 1991.

———. Standard Sequences in the Legal Recognition of Homosexuality: Europe's Past, Present, and Future. *Australian Gay & Lesbian L.J.* 4 (1994): 50.

———. Free Movement of Same-Sex Partners. *Maastricht J. Eur. & Comp. L.* 3 (1996): 271.

Waaldijk, Kees, and Andrew Clapham, eds. *Homosexuality: A European Community Issue*. Dordrecht, Netherlands: Martinus Nijhoff, 1993.

Wald, Michael S. *Same-Sex Couples: Marriage, Families, and Children: An Analysis of Proposition 22—the Knight Initiative*. Stanford, Calif.: Stanford Institute for Research on Women and Gender, 1999.

Walen, Alec. The "Defense of Marriage Act" and Authoritarian Morality. *Wm. & Mary Bill of Rts. J.* 5 (1997): 619.

Walsh, Kevin G. Comment, Throwing Stones: Rational Basis Review Triumphs over Homophobia. *Seton Hall L. Rev.* 27 (1997): 1064.

Wardle, Lynn D. Williams v. North Carolina, Divorce Recognition, and Same-Sex Marriage Recognition. *Creighton L. Rev.* 32 (1988): 187.

———. A Critical Analysis of Constitutional Claims for Same-Sex Marriage. *Brigham Young U. L. Rev.* (1996): 1.

———. The Potential Impact of Homosexual Parenting on Children. *U. Ill. L. Rev.* (1997): 833.

———. Legal Claims for Same-Sex Marriage: Efforts to Legitimate a Retreat from Marriage by Redefining Marriage. *S. Tex. L. Rev.* 39 (1998): 735.

Warner, Michael. *The Trouble with Normal: Sex, Politics, and the Ethics of Queer Life*. New York: Free Press, 1999.

Weisberg, D. Kelly, and Susan Frelich Appleton, eds. *Modern Family Law: Cases and Matarials*. 2d ed. New York: Aspen, 1998.

West, Donald J., and Richard Green, eds. *Sociolegal Control of Homosexuality: A Multi-Nation Comparison*. New York: Plenum Press, 1997.

West, Robin. Universalism, Liberal Theory, and the Problem of Gay Marriage. *Fla. St. U. L. Rev.* 25 (1998): 705.

Weston, Kath. *Families We Choose: Lesbians, Gays, Kinship*. New York: Columbia University Press, 1991.

Weyrauch, Walter O., et al. *Cases and Materials on Family Law: Legal Concept and Changing Human Relationships*. St. Paul: West, 1994.

Whitney, Kathleen Marie. Does the European Convention on Human Rights Protect Refugees from "Safe" Countries? *Ga. J. Int'l & Comp. L.* 26 (1997): 375.

Whitten, Kristian D. Section Three of the Defense of Marriage Act: Is Marriage Reserved to the States? *Hastings Const. L.Q.* 26 (1999): 419.

Whitten, Ralph U. The Original Understanding of the Full Faith and Credit Clause and the Defense of Marriage Act. *Creighton L. Rev.* 32 (1998): 255.

Wilets, James D. International Human Rights Law and Sexual Orientation. *Hastings Int'l & Comp. L. Rev.* 18 (1994): 1.

Wilkowski, E. Todd. Comment, The Defense of Marriage Act: Will It Be the Final Word in the Debate over Legal Recognition of Same-Sex Unions? *Regent U. L. Rev.* 8 (1997): 195.

Willett, Germaine Winnick. Equality under Law or Annihilation of Marriage and Morals? The Same-Sex Marriage Debate. *Ind. L.J.* 73 (1997): 355.

Willis, Gladys J. *The Penalty of Eve: John Milton and Divorce.* New York: Peter Lang, 1984.

Wintemute, Robert. *Sexual Orientation and Human Rights.* Oxford: Clarendon Press, 1995.

Witte, John. *From Sacrament to Contract: Marriage, Religion, and Law in the Western Tradition.* Louisville: Westminster John Knox Press, 1997.

Wockner, Rex. *Danes Make History: Gays Legally Marry.* Available at http://users.cybercity.dk/dko12530/internet.htm, cited January 14, 1999.

Wolfe, Noel K. Shahar v. Bowers: The Balance between Constitutional Rights and Governmental Efficiency. *L. & Sexuality* 8 (1998): 713.

Wolfson, Evan. Crossing the Threshold: Equal Marriage Rights for Lesbians and Gay Men and the Intra-Community Critique. *N.Y.U. Rev. L. & Soc. Change* 21 (1994): 567.

———. Fighting to Win and Keep the Freedom to Marry: The Legal, Political, and Cultural Challenges Ahead. *Nat'l J. Sexual Orientation L.* 1 (1995): 258.

———. The Freedom to Marry: Our Struggle for the Map of the Country. *Quinnipiac L. Rev.* 16 (1996): 209.

Wolfson, Evan, and Michael F. Melcher. Constitutional and Legal Defects in the "Defense of Marriage" Act. *Quinnipiac L. Rev.* 16 (1996): 221.

———. The Supreme Court's Decision in Romer v. Evans and Its Implications for the Defense of Marriage Act. *Quinnipiac L. Rev.* 16 (1996): 217.

Wriggins, Jennifer. Maine's "Act to Protect Traditional Marriage and Prohibit Same-Sex Marriages": Questions of Constitutionality under State and Federal Law. *Me. L. Rev.* 50 (1998): 345.

Zalesne, Deborah. When Men Harass Men: Is It Sexual Harassment? *Temple Pol. & Civ. Rts. L. Rev.* 7 (1998): 395.

Zambrowicz, Kevin Aloysius. "To Love and Honor All the Days of Your Life": A Constitutional Right to Same-Sex Marriage? *Cath. U. L. Rev.* 43 (1994): 907.

Zicklin, Gilbert. Legal Trials and Tribulations on the Road to Same-Sex Marriage. In *On the Road to Same-Sex Marriage,* ed. R. P. Cabaj and D. W. Purcell. San Francisco: Jossey-Bass, 1998.

Zuckerman, Elizabeth. Comment, Second-Parent Adoption for Lesbian-Parented Families: Legal Recognition of the Other Mother. *U.C. Davis L. Rev.* 19 (1986): 729.

Zweigert, Konrad, and Hein Kötz. *Introduction to Comparative Law.* 3d rev. ed. Oxford: Clarendon Press, 1998.

Index

Germany
  discrimination protection, lack of, 317
  necessary process status, 330
  registered partnerships (*see* life partner-
    ship, Germany)
  sodomy laws and antidiscrimination
    legislation, 328t
Ginsburg, Ruth Bader, 285
Goethe, Johann Wolfgang von, 9
Goodridge v. Department of Public Health,
  227
Graff, E. J., 301
Greenland, 67n28
Guardianship of Kowalski, 194

Halvorsen, Rune, 83, 93, 298–99
Harlan, John, 280
Hawaii, U.S.
  domestic partner benefits and regis-
    tries, 247t
  domestic partnership law, 204–5
  political motivation for partnership
    legislation, 301
  Reciprocal Beneficiaries Act, 215
  sex discrimination rulings, 219–22
Hegel, Georg, 27
Holand, Lesbeth, 94
homophobia and sexism, 44–45. *See also*
  homosexuality
Homosexual Cohabitants Act, Sweden
  (1987). *See* cohabitation laws,
  Sweden
homosexuality
  attitudes toward, 49–50
  homophobia and sexism, 44–45
  impact of decriminalization and anti-
    discrimination measures on social
    attitudes, 327, 330, 338–39
  intracommunity views on marriage,
    144
  negative social perception of, 133n16
  Plato's philosophies on homosexual
    love, 12–14
  social perceptions of registered part-
    nerships, 142, 267–68
homosexuals' perceptions of separate regime
  acceptability of alternative models,
    303–4
  antimarriage rhetoric, rebuttal of,
    301–2
  arguments against segregation, 301,
    305–7
  arguments for segregation, 299–301
  fundamental right of choice, 302–3
  military exclusion view, 304–5
  related views of African Americans
    and feminists, 299

Howard, John, 173
Hungary
  common law marriages (*see* common
    law marriages, Hungary)
  discrimination protection, 318
  necessary process status, 330
  sodomy laws and antidiscrimination
    legislation, 328t
Hunter, Nan, 303
Hygen Committee, Norway, 84

ICCPR (U.N. International Covenant on
  Civil and Political Rights), 313
Iceland
  discrimination protection, 318
  registered partnerships (*see* registered
    partnerships, Iceland)
  sodomy laws and antidiscrimination
    legislation, 328t
Identity and the Case for Gay Rights (Richards), 43
Illinois, U.S.
  domestic partner benefits and regis-
    tries, 247t
  sodomy laws, 319
Indiana, U.S., 247t
interracial marriages, 30n112, 41, 51,
  220, 282. See also *Loving v. Virginia*
Iowa, U.S., 247t
Israel, 356–57
Italy
  cohabitation laws, 155–56
  discrimination protection, lack of, 317
  necessary process status, 331
  sodomy laws and antidiscrimination
    legislation, 328t

Johnson, Denise, 225, 333
Joint Council of Gay and Lesbian Organizations, Norway, 82–83
Joint Household Act, Norway (1991),
  81–82
Jones v. Hallahan, 218
judicial recognition of same-sex marriages, U.S.
  challenges to denial of marriage, 218–
    19
  constitutionality of, state-level, 222,
    223, 224
  judicial rulings, 219–20, 222
  legislative responses, 221, 225–26
  potential for action by states, 227
  public opinion, 222
  satisfaction of Vermont court man-
    date, 225–27
  sex discrimination rulings, 219–20,
    222
  state jurisdiction, 217